SENSATION AND PERCEPTION

SENSATION AND PERCEPTION

AN INTEGRATED APPROACH
Third Edition

HARVEY RICHARD SCHIFFMAN
Rutgers, The State University

JOHN WILEY & SONS

WILEY NEW YORK CHICHESTER BRISBANE TORONTO SINGAPORE

Library of Congress Cataloging in Publication Data:

Schiffman, Harvey Richard, 1934–
    Sensation and perception : an integrated approach / Harvey Richard
Schiffman. — 3rd ed.
        p.   cm.
    Includes bibliographical references.
    ISBN 0-471-61048-8
    1. Senses and sensation.   2. Perception.   I. Title.
BF233.S44   1990
152.1—dc20   89-37666
                                                        CIP

Printed in the United States of America

10 9 8 7 6 5 4

To Jan and Noah, again

PREFACE TO THE THIRD EDITION

As with the previous editions, this book strives for an integrated treatment of the main principles of sensation and perception within a bio-behavioral context, stressing specialized anatomy, physiological mechanisms, and functional behavior with adaptive consequences. For the most part, the emphasis, the topical structure, the overall organization, and the scope and theme of this edition remain unchanged from the earlier editions. In addition, the same central objective is retained: to provide an introductory textbook for use in undergraduate courses in sensation and perception. To meet this goal I have tried for a broad and balanced treatment of the theories, principles, and basic findings of the area, and I have assumed no specialized background beyond, perhaps a basic course in psychology.

However, a comparison of the earlier editions with the present one will reveal numerous and substantial changes. Many sections have been reorganized, expanded, and updated to reflect and accommodate recent advances and to enhance clarity. Each chapter has undergone some change in content and sometimes an extensive change from the last edition.

PEDAGOGICAL AIDS

A number of pedagogical features have been added: The reader will find a detailed preview or outline at the beginning of each chapter, a set of general survey-study questions for assignment, "self-testing," or for class discussion at the end of each chapter, and a listing of the chapter's important or "key" terms. The study questions require the student to examine the critical topics and principles in the chapter. The key terms are printed in boldface when they first appear in the text, this will help the reader to identify the important terms. In addition, a unified and updated glossary is placed at the end of the book to make it easier for the reader to look up terms that reappear from chapter to chapter.

DEMONSTRATIONS

The reader will also confront a series of demonstrations dispersed throughout the text and identified by two vertical lines in the margin. Whereas some demonstrations were integrated within the text of earlier editions, they are now more numerous and are highlighted in this edition. However, they continue to be integrated within the text. These demonstrations are quite easily performed and in many instances help clarify and illuminate specific concepts. Moreover, by engaging the reader, the demonstrations make possible a first hand experience with some of the phenomena described and thus provide direct evidence for some of the generalizations that are discussed within the text. In this sense, the demonstrations help close the gap between the richness of our sensory-perceptual experiences and their traditional laboratory treatment. In some cases, they may also serve as a focal point in class discussions and lectures.

The reader will also find that ample use is made of reference citations, particularly for the major statements of results or conclusions. This is done, of course, to give investigators their due credit, but it is done also to provide sufficient reference sources to enable the curious or interested reader to find specific papers on a given topic.

ACKNOWLEDGMENTS

This is my opportunity to acknowledge the contributions of the individuals who helped in various capacities in the preparation of this edition. The project required a tremendous amount of support, and I am grateful to a large number of individuals. Many of the chapters have been read at various stages by a number of knowledgeable and expert psychologists and I am indebted to them. Indeed, in some cases portions of the revision have been guided by the thoughtful and useful comments and suggestions of these experts. It is clear to me that the manuscript has improved considerably as a result of their contributions. I hereby acknowledge my debt to

Morton Heller
Winston-Salem State University

Michael Seigel
SUNY-Oneonta

Janet Proctor
Purdue University

Larry Berger
University of Montana

Sol Schwartz
Kean College

Dean Owens
Ohio State University

Robert Allan
Fairleigh Dickinson University

Frank Bagrash
California State-Fullerton

Seth Kalichman
University of South Carolina

Thomas Alley
Clemson University

Thomas Ayres
Colgate University

John Pittenger
University of Arkansas-Little Rock

I wish to take this occasion to cite the very special, indeed invaluable contributions made by my friend and colleague, Suzanne Greist-Bousquet. She read and reread all versions of this revision in manuscript and page form; she commented, she criticized, and she contributed creatively. She suggested, devised, and constructed many illustrations. She helped extensively in rewriting and performed the major revision of Chapter 17 on illusions. Overall Sue helped make the final manuscript a better organized, more coherent and attractive product, and her effort and enthusiasm in all phases of the project is evident throughout.

Many individuals at John Wiley earn my sincere gratitude for their thorough, conscientious, and competent efforts in producing this edition and bringing a very "rough" manuscript to completion. In particular, I wish to thank Deborah Herbert and her excellent staff, especially Gilda Stahl and Sally Ann Bailey, for the careful reading and editing of the manuscript. Marcia Samuels, the senior production supervisor for this project, has my gratitude; she supervised the final production process with extreme patience and competence throughout an especially difficult stage. My thanks also go to Savoula Amanatidis for continuing this effort in the final production stage. In addition, I placed an enormous burden of preparing and revising art work on the Illustration Department of John Wiley and I am in their debt. It goes without saying that the responsibility of any remaining flaws or inaccuracies in fact or interpretation in this edition is mine alone.

A special thanks is due Deborah Moore, my editor at Wiley, who showed patience with me but also was determined that I make this a more useful, student-oriented book. She helped me focus on the intended audience on this revision—the students. Many of the changes in this edition, especially those of a pedagogical nature, are due to her insistence that I consider the needs of the students. It is to her credit that she did this without requiring any compromise in comprehension and scholarship.

Special credit is due to a number of persons who either directly or subtly contributed to this project.

Maria Watson read several chapters with great care and scrutiny, I never thanked her properly. As always, Harold Schiffman was there to help me and to explain and analyze. From time to time Jan and Noah listened to my complaints in silence, and they helped in the construction of many illustrations, although only several of these are directly cited. I wish to formally acknowledge their overall contribution here, I hope they know how I feel about them.

Finally I hope that the readers of this book will share some of the excitement and enthusiasm that I and many psychologists have for the topics of sensation and perception. They are truly fascinating areas of science.

CONTENTS

INTRODUCTION

STIMULATION
SENSORY RECEPTORS
SENSATION, PERCEPTION, AND
    RELATED DISCIPLINES

PLAN OF THE BOOK
CLASSIFICATION OF MODALITIES
WHY STUDY SENSATION AND
    PERCEPTION

This text contains a presentation of the methods, principles, and findings concerning sensation and perception. Many meanings and distinctions have been attached to the terms "sensation" and "perception," but it must be stressed at the outset that the distinction between the two is of greater historical relevance than of contemporary utility. Traditionally, **sensations** refer to certain immediate and direct qualitative experiences—qualities or attributes such as "hard," "warm," "red," and so on—produced by simple isolated physical stimuli. Moreover, the study of sensations is primarily associated with structure, physiology, and general sense-receptor activity. The study of **perception,** on the other hand, generally refers to psychological processes whereby meaning, past experience, or memory and judgment are involved. Perceptions are associated with the organization and integration of sensory attributes, that is, the awareness of "things" and "events" rather than mere attributes or qualities. Moreover, there is a growing trend to view many of the "perceptual" processes as part of a third, closely allied area—*cognition* or cognitive psychology.

The emphasis of our exposition will reflect the vast body of research literature on both structural and functional features of the receptor mechanisms as well as those "higher" processes that are perceptual in nature. Hence, although these terms will be part of our vocabulary, we will generally avoid a clear sensation–perception distinction and where possible, maintain an integrated approach.

Stated quite generally, sensation and perception

1

refer to the study of a train of biological activity: stimulation from the external environment, impinging on sense receptors, which in turn produce neural activity, terminating in experience or behavior.

STIMULATION

The information necessary for effective stimulation of the sentient (or sensing) organism lies within the energy that emanates from the environment. A variety of forms of energy with particular biological utility can be identified: mechanical (including pressure and vibratory force), thermal, chemical, and electromagnetic (including photic or light energy). Each of these forms of energy acts on specialized sense organs and **receptors** uniquely suited to their reception.

But this only hints at the complexity of the issues involved: certainly, an understanding of the processes of sensing and perceiving requires a level of analysis far exceeding the examination of the environmental energy. In addition there are important distinctions to be made between the stimulation from the objective physical environment, its immediate impact as stimuli on the sentient organism, and its eventual perception. For example, while we may perceive or "see" solid objects lying within three-dimensional space, the mechanism for achieving this begins with a fluctuating mosaic pattern of light falling upon an essentially flat surface within the eye. Actually, because of the normal functioning of the lens that is contained within the eye, the pattern of light will produce an image, generally termed the *retinal image* (the *retina* is a light-sensitive region at the back of the eye, about which we will have much to say in Chapter 11). However, an analysis of the information in the retinal image by itself is still insufficient to account for what is seen. Consider the perception of a single object located in space: a retinal image of the object will be produced, but it will differ significantly from the physical object. In fact, based upon principles of physical optics, the

image will be inverted, it will be considerably smaller, it will change constantly as the eyes move, and because we have two eyes, it will be given in two slightly different versions. Yet the fact remains that, to a surprising degree, we see the object accurately. In other words, we do not see the retinal image; we see instead the "real" environment of objects and events. That is, our internal representation—our *perception*—of the object is generally accurate in spite of the fact that our retinal image differs markedly from the physical object. Clearly, the retinal image is not looked at, but *processed* (at least to some extent); accordingly we must consider the role played by structures and mechanisms that occur after initial impact by environmental stimulation. Indeed one of our major tasks in the chapters to follow will be to trace the course of environmental stimulation from its initial organismic contact to those processes that eventuate in its perception; accordingly, the next topic considers the specialized organs and receptors that react to physical energies.

SENSORY RECEPTORS

Although our primary focus will be on human sensation and perception, our presentation will be organized around a functional, evolutionary theme. The assumption is made here, for example, that the sense–receptor structures and mechanisms of a given species are shaped by natural selection to meet the informational needs required for survival. That is, random variations lead to the evolution of adaptive sensory structures and functions that provide the form and level of sensory input adequate for the survival of each species of animal. Accordingly, we will encounter many instances of specialized anatomy, physiology, and behavior with adaptive consequences.

All forms of life must interact with their external surroundings to extract information and to perform some form of energy exchange. For a one-celled animal such as the amoeba, the simplest of protozoa, environmental information is received without specialized receptors. Most of the amoeba's external surface is responsive to gravity, light, heat, and pressure. However, for most multicellular animals the demands of interacting with their habitat have led to the evolution of specialized receptor cells and units. All such receptor cells share in common the function of generating neural activity in response to stimulation, that is, the **transduction** or conversion of the energy of the incident stimulus from the environment into neural form.

Aggregations of such receptor units form sense organs of diverse structures and functions that are differentially sensitive to various forms of energy changes in the environment of the organism. Thus, receptive portions of the eyes are specialized to receive and react neurally to electromagnetic or radiant energy, the taste buds to react to chemical molecules in the mouth, the inner regions of the ear to receive airborne vibrations, the skin surface to respond to thermal changes and to mechanical deformations, and so on. However, mechanical energy properly applied as pressure can produce effects on hearing and vision; similarly, because of the bioelectric basis of living tissue, electrical energy has the unusual property of actuating all sensory units.

In general, specialized sense receptors have evolved to perform the survival tasks of a species through selective response to particular forms of energy—energy that provides the species with information about its habitat. Indeed, sense-receptor structures and mechanisms can be studied in terms of their function in the behavior of the species, that is, by examining the relationship of a species' behavioral requirements for survival in its unique habitat to its sensory equipment. For example, the highly developed and specialized acoustic anatomy of the bat can be understood when this species is viewed in an ecological context. Bats are most active at night and often live in environments so dark that photoreceptor or light-sensitive mechanisms would be nearly useless. As an adaptive consequence, they have evolved sensory structures and behavioral capacities uniquely suited to locomotion in a lightless environ-

ment. Thus, their peculiar auditory structures and their extended range of sound emissions and receptions can be studied in terms of the bat's remarkable ability to locate and catch prey on the wing, and to navigate and avoid obstacles in the complete absence of light.

Another instance of a specialized sensory structure accommodating behavioral specialization is provided by the extreme tactual sensitivity of the hands of the raccoon. Raccoons use their hands to forage for food, particularly in places where vision and smell are of limited value, for example, in shallow water. Moreover, in captivity raccoons are often observed handling their food underwater before eating it. Although this behavior has been labeled "washing," its function most likely is to soften the skin of the hands thereby increasing their sensitivity (Radinsky, 1976). Presumably, the sensitivity of the raccoon's hands evolved in response to a selective pressure—the need in a carnivore to compensate for a reduced capacity to utilize vision and smell. Of some interest is the report that the area of the raccoon's brain that receives touch information from the hands is unusually enlarged compared to other cortical sensory areas (Welker & Campos, 1963).

Sensory structures may also adapt to a decrease in the functional demands of the environment, as indicated by this unusual example:

> The tunicate sea squirt in its larval form swims freely about, guided by its eyes and ears, finding food and avoiding predators. Reaching adulthood, it loses its tail and attaches itself to a rock. For about two years, it sits on the rock, vegetating. Its eyes, its ears, and then its brain—all degenerate and become useless. (Alpern, Lawrence, & Wolsk, 1967, p. 1)

But in general, the outcome of the specialization of sensory structures is an increase in the potential information that can be extracted from the environment. As the range of functional demands increases, there is a need for greater sensitivity to energy and the capacity to make finer sensory discriminations.

This is provided by the development of more specialized sensory mechanisms.

SENSATION, PERCEPTION, AND RELATED DISCIPLINES

Although we consider the topics of sensation and perception as comprising a distinct and unified subarea of psychology proper, it is clear that they are strongly interdisciplinary, in that they draw extensively upon and are complemented by the concepts, techniques, and facts of many fields of science, especially the biological and physical ones. Thus a study of the subject matter of sensation and perception requires some knowledge of the nature of light for vision, the physics of sound waves for hearing, the chemistry of compounds for taste and smell, the physics of pressure and heat transfer for touch, and gravitational and inertial force for an understanding of bodily orientation and position in space.

Just as sensation and perception each draw freely from other disciplines, we also observe that they often overlap with and contribute in important ways to these disciplines. As examples, the familiar unit of sound intensity, the decibel, is based upon presumed minimal limits of human audibility, and the familiar and ubiquitous "color" television screen is in some measure a practical product of the application of certain physiological and psychological phenomena that promote color vision. In particular, modern color television technology takes advantage of the early discovery in vision that most of the colors that the human eye can see can be duplicated in appearance by an appropriate mixture of only three so-called primary colors (we will return to this matter in Chapter 13).

In addition, the *history* of other sciences has been significantly affected by the phenomena that are central to sensation and perception. In particular, the study of light is intimately associated with visual perception. Indeed until the beginning of the nineteenth century, optics and vision were intermixed, with light treated as subsidiary to visual perception

(Le Grand, 1975). As Boring (1942) observed on this issue,

> light *is a concept invented to explain vision, since it was perception that set the first problems for physics. In fact, three of the classical chapters of physics—light, heat and sound—were fixed by the nature of perception; it was only much later that imperceptibles like electricity, magnetism, invisible light, radiant energy and wave-motion became equally important. For this reason, then, the first important knowledge of color and its stimulus was contributed by Newton, of visual space perception by Kepler, of the tonal stimulus by Galileo. (p. 97)*

E. G. Boring (1950) describes a provocative example of a role played by the senses in the history of astronomy. In 1796, the royal astronomer at Greenwich Observatory, Maskelyne, dismissed his assistant, Kinnebrook, because Kinnebrook observed the time at which the trajectory of stars crossed at a certain point in the sky eight-tenths of a second later than he, Maskelyne, did. It was Maskelyne's conclusion that the difference in their observation times was due to his assistant's error.

At the time this was no small matter, for such astronomical observations were used to calibrate many of the world's clocks. The method used for such tasks at that time required the observer to make a complex comparison of information using both vision and hearing: the observer focused upon the star through a telescope while at the same time listened to the beat of a clock. Boring's (1950) words capture the difficulty of performing the task:

> The observational problem consisted in noting, to one tenth of a second, the time at which a given star crossed a given wire. The observer looked at the clock, noted the time to a second, began counting seconds with the heard beats of the clock, watched the star cross the field of the telescope, noted and "fixed in mind" its position at the beat of the clock just before it came to the critical wire, noted its position at the next beat

after it had crossed the wire, estimated the place of the wire between the two position in tenths of the total distance between the positions, and added these tenths of a second to the time in seconds that he had counted for the beat before the wire was reached. It is obviously a complex judgment. (p. 135)

The report of Kinnebrook's observational error and subsequent dismissal was reported in the journal of the Greenwich Observatory. Years later, in 1816, it was noted by Bessel, the chief astronomer at the Königsberg observatory (then part of Germany), who had a special interest in instrumental and procedural errors of measurement. It was to Bessel's credit that he did not conclude that Kinnebrook's observation necessarily represented an error, or as Maskelyne concluded, that Kinnebrook had fallen "into some irregular and confused method of his own" (Boring, 1950, p. 135). Instead Bessel interpreted the difference in stellar observations between the two astronomers as the result of a "personal difference" in their measurements; that is, an individual difference in measuring events using the eyes and ears. Clearly, Bessel's analysis indicated that supposedly objective judgments of the external world were measurably affected by variations in the functioning of the sense organs. While Bessel's contribution had far-ranging effects upon the history of physical measurement, his insight for psychology was that the mental processes involved in making complex judgments based on the senses takes time, and that the time required varies among individuals. This recognition eventually led to a quest for more objective methods of measurement using procedures and instruments less subject to the inherent variability introduced by the direct use of the senses.

PLAN OF THE BOOK

Most meaningful sensory interactions between an organism and its environment are not restricted to a single sensory input. Indeed there is physiological evidence that the input from different sensory modalities interact and are processed by common cortical pathways (e.g., Pons et al., 1987). Hence, a study of the relationship of the total organism to its environment must generally take into account the biology and the ongoing activity of more than an isolated sense modality. However, there are vast differences in the nature of the effective physical energies, in the physiologies and functionings, and in the experimental methodologies required for studying the different sensory modalities. To make clear the detailed activity of the various sense modalities, for the most part we will deal with each sense modality separately. Because more research has been performed on the visual modality, it will be dealt with more extensively than the others.

In addition in many instances we will further isolate and individually discuss topics within modalities. For example, "touching" using the skin enables the pickup of information about contact and pressure, temperature, pain, and shape, and each of these sources of environmental information will be treated in separate sections. Similarly, we will deal individually with distinct attributes of visual stimulation; thus visual properties such as color, form, movement and depth are treated in separate chapters. This division is not only done on pedagogical grounds, but parallels the idea that the visual system is subdivided into separate structural components whose functions are quite distinct from one another (Livingstone & Hubel, 1988).

It should be noted in this context that, whereas perception is based upon the environmental stimulation reaching the sense organs, the manner in which one conceptualizes the role of the stimulation for perception has important consequences on the kind of phenomena and research one advances. Two main approaches to this issue currently flourish. There is the view that the perception of the physical world of objects and events is a constructive achievement, perhaps even an inference, based on the interpretation of the stimulation. Central to this view is that there is some internal constructive process that is held to occur on the part of the observer that mediates between the environmental stimulation and its perception (see Rock, 1984, 1986, for a thorough analysis of this view).

In contrast James J. Gibson (1904–1979) proposed that inner mental processes play little or no role in perception: the stimuli themselves (e.g., the optic array) contain and specify the necessary and sufficient information for the perception of the physical world *directly*, without recourse to additional stages of processing or mediation on the part of the organism. According to this Gibsonian view, we see objects in the third dimension owing to the "pickup" of their surface characteristics, such as variations and discontinuities in textures, as well as the manner in which imagery flows across the retina as the objects or the observer shifts or moves in position. That is, we pick up relevant information directly from the spatial and temporal pattern of environmental information contained within the retinal image.

CLASSIFICATION OF MODALITIES

The basis of organizing and classifying the sense modalities is not a simple matter, and, as is the case for most matters of definition, it is not universally agreed on. Some attempts at a taxonomy are made on the basis of specific morphological differences or distinct sensory qualities (e.g., Geldard, 1972) or are based on the nature of the energy to which receptors selectively respond (e.g., Scharf, 1975).

In contrast, J. J. Gibson (1966, 1979, 1983) has argued for a more functional, ecological organization and has proposed that animals guide their behavior by perceiving directly what environmental objects or encounters offer or *afford* for action. In this ecological approach the needs and capabilities of the animal and its environment are viewed as intimately interlinked. Indeed, Gibson has even coined a term to specify the adaptive value of objects or events relative to an organism, which he calls **affordances** and defines these as follows: "The affordance of anything is a specific combination of the properties of its substance and its surfaces taken with reference to an animal" (Gibson, 1977, p. 67; see also Bruce & Green, 1985). Thus the affordances of the environment are the possibilities for action that it offers or provides the organism. Affordances imply the functional complementarity of the animal and the environment (Gibson, 1983; see also Ben-Zeev, 1984). Thus a discontinuity or an edge on an otherwise continuous surface—that is, a cliff or a falling-off place—affords the possibility of avoiding a fall. The optical information specifying a rapid rate of magnification in a surface's optical texture as it is approached affords an impending collision with the surface. As Warren (1984) points out, the affordances of many natural and architectural environments and their structures provide sufficient information for activities such as "reaching, grasping, lifting, sitting, passing through apertures, stepping down ledges, jumping gaps, locomotion over surfaces with varying properties, foraging and food selection, predation, and so on" (p. 700).

In addition Gibson has also questioned the traditional study of a sense organ as a passive receiver of imposed stimulation; rather, he has stressed the information-gathering aspects of the senses. To this end he proposes a classification based on "modes of activity" and on the kinds of information picked up by the active organism. Accordingly, his inventory is organized with respect to the organism's behavior—"smelling," "looking," and so on —accomplished by *perceptual systems* and the sorts of external information so obtained, rather than with respect to specialized receptor structures. His classification, shown in Table 1.1, corresponds to an extent with the usual sensory categories of vision, audition, touch, taste, and smell, but there are important differences. For example, his notion of a *haptic* system conceptually includes inputs from the skin, joints, and muscles. Another difference from the usual categorization is that taste (gustation) and smell (olfaction), usually treated as distinct sense modalities, are grouped into a unitary chemical-receiving system. Functionally, Gibson's classification is a useful one, and we will encompass aspects of it in the pages to follow.

Table 1.1
The Perceptual Systems

SYSTEM	GENERAL MODE OF ACTIVITY	GENERAL RECEPTOR UNITS	SENSE STRUCTURE	TYPICAL ACTIVITY OF THE ORGAN	EFFECTIVE STIMULI	EXTERNAL INFORMATION OBTAINED
Basic orienting	Posturing, general orientation	Mechano-receptors and gravity-receptors	Vestibular organs	Bodily equilibrium, balance	Forces of gravity, and acceleration	Direction of gravity, being pushed and pulled
Auditory	Listening	Mechano-receptors	Ear	Orienting to sounds	Vibrations in the air	Nature and location of vibratory sources and events
Haptic	Touching	Mechano-receptors, thermo-receptors	Skin, joints, muscles, tendons, ligaments, kinesthetic receptors	General exploration by appendages, skin, tongue	Deformations of tissues, configurations of joints, stretching of muscle fibers, thermal and painful stimuli	Contact with surfaces, object shapes; Material states: solidity or viscosity; Heat and cold
Taste—smell: Smelling	Smelling	Chemo-receptors	Nose	Sniffing	Chemical composition of inspired vapors	Nature of odors
Tasting	Tasting	Chemo- and mechano-receptors	Mouth	Savoring	Chemical composition of ingested substances	Nutritive and noxious values
Visual	Looking	Photo-receptors	Eyes, ocular muscles	Accommodation, pupillary adjustment, fixation, convergence, scanning	Light	Size, shape, distance, location, color, texture, movement information

Source: Revised from A. H. Buss, *Psychology: Man in Perspective*, 2nd ed. (New York: John Wiley, 1973), after J. J. Gibson, *The Ecological Approach to Visual Perception* (Boston: Houghton Mifflin, 1979).

WHY STUDY SENSATION AND PERCEPTION

Finally this question arises: Why study sensation and perception? There are numerous reasons, but three warrant noting here. First, the topics and major themes of sensation and perception occupy an essential and fundamental place in the history of science, in general, and in psychology, specifically. Indeed, basic philosophical queries on the manner in which knowledge of the external world is obtained centered on the role played by the senses, and in fact, experimental psychology began with a concern for problems central to sensation and perception.

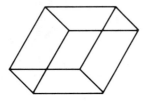

FIGURE 1.1   Necker's rhomboid. It is generally the case that we are not cognizant of the problem of perception unless we are confronted with unusual examples. As you view Figure 1.1, you are not aware of the reception of light energy, or the formation of a retinal image, or the propagation of information along neural paths to the brain, or the processing that gives rise to its perception: all of this occurs without effort. However, we easily perceive a depiction of a three-dimensional figure. This immediate experience—the perception of a form of a three-dimensional figure from a two-dimensional surface—in itself is both profound and extraordinary. However, consider further that with continued viewing of the figure and without any change in photic energy, or the retinal image, or additional neural information, the simple transparent figure reverses in depth: what was once a front surface becomes a surface in the back of the figure. Indeed, a change in perception occurs without any change in the stimulus that gives rise to it. Although this example of a problem of perception is unusual, we must stress that our "normal" perceptions are equally extraordinary events. (Based on a description by the Swiss naturalist L. A. Necker in 1832.)

Another reason is that our facile perception of the external world in fact poses an important scientific problem that must be examined. As Howard (1982) cogently observes, "Many people do not realize that perception is a problem; they perceive the world so effortlessly and continuously that they take the mechanism for granted. Perception is the most neglected of all the major problems of science, and this may be because it is the most difficult problem of them all" (p. 1). For an example of perception as a "problem," see Figure 1.1.

A third reason to study sensation and perception is that it is intrinsically interesting and seeks to answer basic questions concerning our moment-to-moment existence: how we see, hear, taste, and so on. However, before discussing the relevant processes, mechanisms, and issues of these topics, we must introduce some of the methods for studying sensation and perception.

KEY TERMS

Affordance

Perception

Receptors

Sensation

Transduction

STUDY QUESTIONS

1. What are the traditional definitions of sensation and perception? Consider how they can be distinguished from each other and how their respective issues and concerns overlap one another.

2. Enumerate the variety of stimulus information necessary for the sensory–perceptual system.

3. What are sensory receptors and transducers? Trace the course of environmental energy to the sensory receptors and transducers.

4. What is a retinal image? In what ways is an analysis of only the retinal image insufficient to account for perception?

5. Consider some historical landmarks that help to define sensation and perception as a distinct, unified subarea of experimental psychology.

6. Distinguish between the two main approaches to the treatment of stimulation for perception; that is, is it interpreted and processed, or is it immediately informative, not requiring processing or interpretation?

7. What is J. J. Gibson's view of stimulation and *direct* perception? How does Gibson treat the role of cognitive processes in perception?

8. What is an affordance? What do affordances specify about the relation of an animal to its environment?

9. What does Gibson mean by "modes of activity" and perceptual systems? How are they useful in classifying the information picked up by an animal? As an example, consider why the inputs from the skin, joints, and muscles are usefully treated as a unitary perceptual system.

10. Why should one study sensation and perception? In your answer, consider the issues and problems that concern sensation and perception.

2

PSYCHOPHYSICS

Virtually every living species has evolved some means of extracting information from its habitat for its survival—information such as the location and identification of food, water, prey, predators, and mates. Many facts on this characteristic have been gathered by ethologists, who observe behavior directly in natural, nonlaboratory situations. However, it is also necessary to resort to the experimental controls imposed by laboratory conditions of testing to investigate the dimensions and bounds of stimulus reception, that is, of sensation and perception.

   Accordingly, it is the purpose of this chapter to introduce some of the general issues and quantitative methods employed for this task of measurement. The area of inquiry in which psychologists study the link between variation in specified characteristics of en-vironmental stimulation (physical dimension) and the attributes and magnitude of subjective experience (psychological dimension) is called **psychophysics,** and the methodologies used to describe a lawful relationship between the physical and psychological dimensions are termed *psychophysical methods*. The problems of psychophysics are among the oldest of psychology, and historically they have often been tied to such philosophical issues as the nature and meaning of subjective experience and the mind-body relationship. (For an historical perspective see Boring, 1942). In an important sense what psychophysics attempts to do is to relate our inner mental experience—our sensations—to external stimulation.

   As we noted in the preceding chapter, the

physical dimensions of stimulation have been reasonably well identified and measured. As well as varying along an intensity dimension stimulation takes a variety of forms: photic, electrical, vibratory and mechanical, thermal and chemical. It is the determination of how these dimensions relate to subjective experience that accounts for an extensive experimental approach to quantification in psychology. It must be stated that the issues of psychophysics define a distinct area of psychological inquiry with its unique set of problems and theoretical issues. However, our major objective will be well served by limiting the scope of this chapter to a general introduction to some of the main issues of psychophysics. We focus on two of the most important: threshold measurement and the determination of the function relating the amount of physical energy to the perceived (or judged) magnitude of the resulting sensation.

DETECTION AND THE ABSOLUTE THRESHOLD

In the course of studying the relation of certain features of the stimulus to attributes of experience, an important and specific experimental question arises. What is the minimal amount of stimulus energy required for the detection of a stimulus? That is, how intense must the stimulus be for an observer to reliably distinguish its presence from its absence? Clearly, no organism is responsive to *all* portions of the possible range of physical energies. Instead, the potential stimulus must be of sufficient or minimal intensity (and duration) to cause a certain degree of neural activation for it to be sensed.

The minimum magnitude values of the stimulus necessary for detection are generally known as **absolute threshold** values or **absolute limen** (Latin for threshold) values. Traditionally, these values define an approximation of the lower limit of the organism's absolute sensitivity. If the magnitude of the stimulus is too weak, not producing a reliable response, the stimulus magnitude is said to be **subthreshold** or **subliminal;** in contrast, above-threshold values of the stimulus are termed **suprathreshold** or **supraliminal.** Some threshold values, not to be taken too seriously in their present form, are shown in Table 2.1. More detailed and precise values for most sensory modalities will be given in subsequent chapters. Quite obviously, the minimal detectable stimulus varies with the modality investigated, with conditions of testing, and with a number of observer factors.

The concept of an absolute threshold assumes that there is a precise stimulus point on the intensity or energy dimension that when administered, be-

Table 2.1
Some Approximate Detection Threshold Values

Sense Modality	Detection Threshold
Light	A candle flame seen at 30 miles on a dark clear night (ca. 10 quanta).
Sound	The tick of a watch under quiet conditions at 20 ft (ca. 0.0002 dynes/cm²).
Taste	One teaspoon of sugar in 2 gal of water.
Smell	One drop of perfume diffused into the entire volume of a three-room apartment.
Touch	The wing of a bee falling on your back from a distance of 1 cm.

Source: E. Galanter, "Contemporary psychophysics," in R. Brown, E. Galanter, E. H. Hess, & G. Mandler (Eds.), *New Directions in Psychology* (New York: Holt, Rinehart and Winston, 1962), p. 97.

comes just perceptible. Accordingly, a stimulus one single unit weaker will not be detected. If this were the case, then some form of the hypothetical curve such as that shown in Figure 2.1*a* would result. That is, the observer would not detect the stimulus until a certain energy level was reached (e.g., four energy units, in the figure) at which point and beyond the stimulus is detected 100% of the time. In the case of tones, for example, there would either be a sound heard or complete silence would result. However, this rarely if ever happens. Rather, laboratory investigation typically yields *ogival* or *S-shaped* curves like that shown in Figure 2.1*b*. This indicates that as the energy level is increased there is also an increase in the probability that a stimulus will be detected.

Thus, we must conclude that there is no single immutable or absolute value that represents the minimum stimulus energy necessary for a detection response, that is, no fixed point separating the energy levels that *never* yield a detection response from those that *always* do. As one approximation of the threshold value, psychologists have adopted a statistical concept. By convention the absolute threshold value is assumed to correspond to that stimulus magnitude

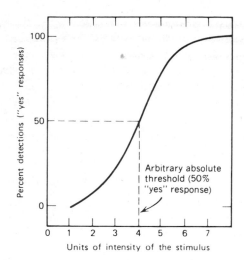

FIGURE 2.1*b*.   An empirical threshold function. By convention the absolute threshold is defined as the intensity at which the stimulus is detected on 50% of the trials.

eliciting a detection response on half of its test trials, that is, 50% of the time. This arbitrarily defined value is indicated by the dotted line in Figure 2.1*b*.

There is a traditional set of procedures used to determine the threshold (originated by Gustav Fechner). One of the simplest procedures is called the **method of limits** or **the method of minimal change.** For example, to determine the absolute threshold for the detection of light we might start with a light sufficiently intense to be perceived by an observer and then systematically reduce its intensity in small graded steps with a light dimmer until the observer reports that the light is no longer detectable. We then record that intensity level and then show the light at a still dimmer setting but now gradually increasing its intensity level until the observer reports that it is just perceptible. After a number of *descending* and *ascending* series of trials, we compute an average based on the energy levels at which the stimulus just crosses the boundary between being undetectable and just becoming perceptible. That is, we compute a numerical estimate of the absolute threshold by taking the average of the stimulus

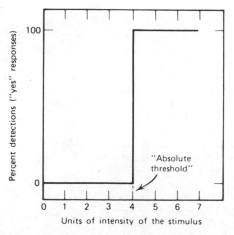

FIGURE 2.1*a*.   A hypothetical curve linking the stimulus intensity to the absolute threshold. Theoretically, below four units of stimulus intensity no stimulus is detected, whereas above four units the stimulus is detected 100% of the time.

intensity reached when the observer attains a limit or makes a response shift for the ascending and for the descending series of stimuli. This average serves as the statistical measure of the threshold for that observer under the general experimental conditions of testing. See Table 2.2 for an example of the method of limits.

In comparison, the **method of adjustment** has the intensity of the stimulus under the *observer's control*, who is required to maintain it at a just detectable level. The experimenter can arrive at an estimate of the observer's threshold by calculating the intensity that the observer attempts to maintain.

Another often employed technique of determin-

Table 2.2

Use of Method of Limits to Determine the Detection Threshold for a Visual Stimulus

Light Intensity (Arbitrary Units)	Observer's Response Series					
	1	2	3	4	5	6
10	YES					
9	YES		YES			
8	YES	YES	YES		YES	
7	YES	NO	YES	YES	YES	YES
6	NO	NO	YES	NO	YES	NO
5		NO	NO	NO	NO	NO
4				NO		NO
3						NO
2						
1						
Limit Value	6.5	7.5	5.5	6.5	5.5	6.5

In the results of the three descending series of trials alternated with the three ascending series illustrated, the "YES" responses mean that on a given trial the stimulus is detected, and the "NO" responses mean that it is not detected. The horizontal bar in each series column represents the stimulus value of the "limit" in which a transition from detection to no detection, or vice versa, occurs. Typical of this method is some variation in the limit obtained for each series, which in this example ranges between 5.5 and 7.5. The threshold value is computed as the average of the limits obtained for each series, or $(6.5 + 7.5 + 5.5 + 6.5 + 5.5 + 6.5)/6 = 6.333$. That is, the threshold value for the detection of the light is 6.333 intensity units.

One of the drawbacks of this simple form of the method of limits is that the change in stimulus magnitudes is regular and, accordingly, may be somewhat predictable on the part of the observer. That is, the observer's expectation that the stimulus values are increasing or decreasing may bias the response. To counteract this possible source of bias, modifications of the method are commonly used. In one form, called the *staircase* method (Cornsweet, 1962), the experiment begins with an intensity level below the assumed threshold value, yielding a "NO" response, and increases it until the observer reports it as visible, that is, reports, "YES." As soon as the report changes from "NO" to "YES" the direction of the magnitude of the stimulus is reversed. Now stimulus values decrease until the response changes again; that is, the observer reports "NO," following which the intensity increases again. In a typical staircase method the threshold is thus calculated as the average of all stimulus values at which the observer's response changes. Variations upon this simple form of the staircase method are also generally employed.

ing the absolute threshold, called **the method of constant stimuli,** requires a series of forced choice trials. In this case a fixed number of stimuli of different intensities are singly presented many times in random order. Upon each presentation the observer makes a detection response— either "yes" he or she detects it or "no" he or she does not. For each stimulus intensity, we can compute the percentage of trials in which the stimulus was detected. The intensity of the stimulus that was detected on 50% of the trials is often used as a measure of the absolute threshold.

THEORY OF SIGNAL DETECTION

The observation that the value of the stimulus required for a threshold or detection response shows some variation, especially for weak, marginal conditions of stimulation, suggests that factors additional to the observer's discriminative capacity or the magnitude of the stimulus may play some role in the observer's response. For example, in the forced choice method of constant stimuli (i.e., saying either "yes, the stimulus is perceived," or "no, it is not") the observer may say he or she detects the stimulus when, actually, he or she is relatively uncertain. In fact, for the variety of techniques that are used to make a threshold determination that were just described, there is no objective way to assess the observer's uncertainty. However, by slightly modifying the task so that on some trials, stimuli appear and on other trials there is no stimulus, we can determine how many times the observer will say "yes" even when no stimulus is present (i.e., a false positive or a **false alarm;** an opposite error, that of not reporting the stimulus when it is, in fact, present—a **miss**—is also possible). A number of methods has been developed about how to use such information about the observer's uncertainty, and we will outline one of the methods here.

Based on certain theoretical considerations as well as a good deal of empirical research, it is held that the proportion of correct detections of a stimulus

(especially a weak one) depends on not only the observer's discriminative capacity but on certain nonsensory factors (called response bias), that is, by the **criterion** set for deciding whether a stimulus was present or not. Thresholds estimated by the classical methods are subject to a number of response bias variables, such as the observer's interpretation of the task instructions, level of attention to the stimulus (or the **signal,** as it is typically called in such contexts), or the motivation for the task, and other *nonsensory* factors that might affect the observer's decision as to whether a signal is present or absent. Hence, during a detection task, when the observer sometimes responds "yes" and at other times responds "no" for a constant stimulus intensity, we do not know for sure whether this is a result of changes in discriminative capacity or whether this merely represents changes in the observer's decision criteria upon which the responses are based.

An approach to this problem, called the **Theory of Signal Detection** or **TSD,** rejects the traditional notion of a precise, fixed threshold completely (Green & Swets, 1966; Swets, 1973). In its specific details, TSD requires a discussion of statistical concepts and topics that cannot be treated here. Moreover there are a number of different models of TSD. However, it is our objective to outline one general scheme and to indicate the significance of TSD for the concept of the threshold and stimulus detection.

A basic assumption of TSD is that every stimulus presentation induces some constant change in the observer. However, there is ever present a constellation of interfering background or **noise** factors (noise as used here is in no way restricted to the auditory modality), factors whose presence may vary from trial to trial. Noise factors may consist of actual sensory stimuli such as "white noise" (a form of acoustic energy that contains a great number of different frequencies with intensities that take on random values and sounds like a background "hiss"). Noise may also include random effects of fatigue and attention or merely spontaneous or random neural activity. It is further assumed that over many trials the effects of background noise (or N) on the observer's sensation can be represented as a normal probability distribution. In essence, this means that sometimes the noise may be minimal, and sometimes the noise may be extreme; however, most frequently the background noise is of some moderate, average intensity. It is further assumed that the effects of the signal plus the noise (or *SN*) on the observer's sensation, over many trials, can also be represented as a normal probability distribution. Specifically, if a signal is added to all possible levels of the randomly varying background noise, over many trials the effects of the signal plus background noise can be represented as a normal probability distribution. The normal distributions of *N* and *SN* means that on a

series of *N* trials (in which case no signal is present) or *SN* trials, the stimuli do not give rise to constant or stable sensory effects. Instead, the sensory effects from the same signal and noise or from noise alone stimulation vary from presentation to presentation giving rise to the usual bell-shaped curves. The effects of *N* and *SN* can be graphically depicted on the same coordinates as shown in Figure 2.2. The abscissa represents the magnitude of the sensory effects—the sensation continuum.

The observer's task in the typical TSD experiment is to decide on each trial whether the trial contains the signal or is a trial with noise alone. That is, the observer must decide whether the sensation

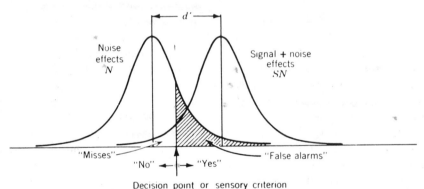

FIGURE 2.2. Distribution of *N* and *SN* effects in TSD. The *N* and *SN* effects are normally distributed. The height of each curve represents the relative frequency with which a sensory effect of a given magnitude will occur, and the abscissa represents the magnitude of the sensory effect. The vertical lines through the center of each curve indicate the average effects of *N* and *SN*. The average sensory effect of *SN* is slightly greater than the average effect of the *N*, due to the addition of the signal to the noise; hence in marking the average of the *SN* effects, the line is displaced to the right of the one for *N*. The two curves for *N* and *SN* overlap, so that on some trials, the sensory effects from the *SN* distribution are less than those from the *N* distribution. The decision point indicated on the abscissa represents the cut-off on the sensory continuum at which the observer decides

whether he or she will report "yes" or "no" as to the presence of the signal on a given trial. Any number of criterion points could be adopted. In the hypothetical one employed here, all signals that produce effects that are below the criterion sensory level (i.e., that lie to the left of the criterion) are responded to by a "no" response; all signals whose effects are above the criterion sensory level (i.e., that lie to the right) are responded to by "yes." Clearly, the observer cannot always be correct. That is, there is no perfect criterion because some sensory effects can be caused by either the *N* or *SN* (shown where the *N* and *SN* curves overlap), and errors of "misses" and "false alarms" are possible. The meaning of *d'* is described later on in the text. (Based on E. Galanter, *Textbook of Elementary Psychology*, Holden-Day, San Francisco, 1966.)

produced by the trial is more likely to come from a signal having been presented or from noise alone. Indicated on Figure 2.2 is the decision point or sensory criterion adopted by the observer, which determines whether he or she says "yes" or "no" as to the presence of the signal on a given trial. The criterion, thus, is the sensation level set by the observer for deciding whether a signal was administered or not. In short the probability of saying "yes, the signal is present," or "no, the signal is not," is influenced by the decision-making strategy adopted by the observer. According to the criterion point plotted in Figure 2.2 the observer will say "yes" when the magnitude of the sensory effect, shown on the abscissa, exceeds that point and "no" when the sensory effect is less. In both instances the observer may be in error. This follows because usually the SN and N distributions have some overlap, making it impossible for an observer to set a sensory criterion or cut-off point that permits a correct response on every presentation of the signal. In fact, the form of the overlap represents the possibility that on some SN trials the sensory effects may be less than those resulting from noise alone.

As noted, on a given detection trial the observer's task is to decide whether his or her sensory impression is due to the actual presence of the signal within a noise background or from noise alone, that is, whether the stimulus presented comes from the SN or N distribution. The observer's decision is determined by the criterion level adopted at the moment. In the situation where the observer reports either "yes" or "no" there are four possible outcomes, shown in Table 2.3. The observer can be correct by responding "yes" when the signal is present (called a **hit**) or by responding "no" when the signal is not present (called a **correct rejection**). Incorrect responses—false alarms and misses—are also indicated in Table 2.3. The probability associated with each class of outcomes is due to two independent measures of the observer's performance—the observer's *decision criterion* or *response bias* and his or her ability to differentiate between the effects of SN from those of N alone, or the observer's *sensitivity*, as it is usually called. One of the important bias factors affecting the setting of the criterion is the observer's *expectation* as to the presence of a signal. This may be created during the course of the experiment: if the signal occurs on almost every trial, then the observer will come to expect a signal almost always and the probability of false alarms will be higher than if no such expectation was created. In contrast, if the signal is rarely present, the result might be many more "no" responses when, in fact, the signal was

Table 2.3

The Stimulus–Response Outcome Matrix for the Observer Responding Either "Yes" or "No" on Each Trial of a Detection Experiment

		RESPONSE ALTERNATIVES	
		"Yes, signal is present."	*"No, signal is absent."*
STIMULUS ALTERNATIVES	*SIGNAL + NOISE*	Probability of a positive response when the signal is present HIT	Probability of a negative response when the signal is present MISS
	NOISE	Probability of a positive response when *no* signal is present FALSE ALARM	Probability of a negative response when *no* signal is present CORRECT REJECTION

present. Table 2.4*a* presents some reported response probabilities for the case when the signal is presented on 90% of the trials and no signal on 10% (Galanter, 1962). Table 2.4*b* shows the outcome probability for the case when no signal is presented on 90% of the trials and a signal is presented on 10%. It thus appears that variation in the proportion of signal presentations markedly affects the expectations of the observer; consequently he or she produces systematic changes in the proportions of hits and false alarms. Significantly, the changes in the *apparent* value of the detection "threshold" occur without change in the stimulus energy.

Another factor that affects the criterion level is the observer's *motivation* toward detecting a specific outcome, that is, his or her concern with the consequences of the response. For instance, if the observer is motivated toward always detecting the signal, never missing it, he or she will likely lower the criterion level for reporting its presence and thereby increase the number of "yes" responses. This, of course, also raises the number of false alarms. The adoption of a more conservative criterion might yield fewer false alarms, but there would be fewer hits. Thus, there appears to be no simply observed absolute threshold; rather, the observer adjusts his or her response criterion to both the signal strength and to certain variables such as his or her motivation and expectation concerning the signal's occurrence.

The detectability of the signal and the observer's sensitivity are generally analyzed in terms of the relationship between the proportion of hits and the proportion of false alarms—a relationship that shifts as the criterion the observer employs is varied. Typically, the proportion of hits is plotted on the ordinate and false alarms on the abscissa. The resultant curves, called **receiver operating characteristic** or **ROC curves,** show the relationship between the proportions of hits to false alarms (see Figure 2.3*a*). The term "receiver operating characteristic" or "ROC" refers to the idea that the curve measures and describes the *operating* or *sensitivity* characteristics of the receiver (observer) for detecting signals.

As shown by Figure 2.3*b*, the form of these curves for any observer depends on two factors: the observer's sensitivity and his or her response bias. All points on a given ROC curve represent performance in detecting the *same* signal relative to the constant background noise. That is, the entire curve

Table 2.4a

Response Probabilities for a Signal Presented on 90% of the Trials and No Signal on 10%

		RESPONSE	
		Yes	No
S			
I			
G	Present	0.97	0.03
N			
A			
L	Absent	0.62	0.38

Source: Based on E. Galanter, "Contemporary psychophysics," in R. Brown, E. Galanter, E. H. Hess, & G. Mandler (Eds.), *New Directions in Psychology* (New York: Holt, Rinehart and Winston, 1962), p. 102.

Table 2.4b

Response Probabilities for a Signal Presented on 10% of the Trials and No Signal is Presented on 90%

		RESPONSE	
		Yes	No
S			
I			
G	Present	0.28	0.72
N			
A			
L	Absent	0.04	0.96

Source: Based on E. Galanter, "Contemporary psychophysics," in R. Brown, E. Galanter, E. H. Hess, & G. Mandler (Eds.), *New Directions in Psychology* (New York: Holt, Rinehart and Winston, 1962), p. 102.

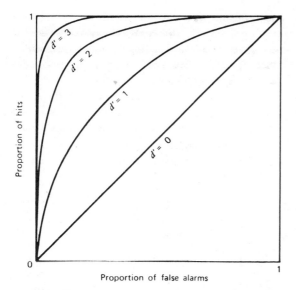

FIGURE 2.3*a*.   ROC curves for three signals that are detectable to different degrees. Proportion of hits is plotted against false alarms. The value of d' is a measure of the observer's sensitivity or of the signal's detectability.

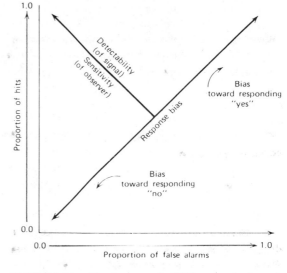

FIGURE 2.3*b*.   The features of a ROC curve. Indicated are the two components of a detection task: the observer's sensitivity and response bias.

is generated without any change in the physical characteristics of the situation: the N and SN levels are the same for all points. The different points result from a shifting decision criterion exercised by the observer—an effect of the observer's response bias. Every point plotted on a given ROC curve represents the same measure of detectability. That is, for a fixed signal, manipulating certain variables, such as the proportion of trials that contain the signal, may affect the hit rate and false alarm rate, but these proportions will fall on a ROC curve corresponding to the same value of sensitivity. For example, the data from Tables 2.4*a* and *b* can be plotted in Figure 2.3*a*—from each table, the value of the probability of a hit is plotted against the value of the probability of a false alarm—and the points fall on the same ROC curve (at approximately $d' = 1$). The measure of the sensitivity of the observer to a given signal strength is estimated by the linear distance of the ROC curve to the 45° diagonal "chance" line (a line representing chance performance where $d' = 0$ as shown in Figure

2.3*a*). This distance is given by a single statistic known as d', which represents the observer's sensitivity, and is independent of the observer's response bias. The procedure for computing d' goes beyond our present interests. Suffice it to note that it is derived from the proportion of hits to false alarms which estimates the linear distance between the distribution of the N and SN distributions. In practice, a large d' value results when an observer has a high hit rate and a low false alarm rate. A d' representation was shown in Figure 2.2 as the distance between the two vertical lines, representing the means of the N and SN distributions.

Figure 2.3*a* shows the ROC curves for signals that are detectable to differing degrees. These differences in detectability can be brought about by varying the intensity of the signal. For instance, for $d' = 1$, the distributions of N and SN lie relatively close together; the signal is relatively weak and therefore is difficult to detect. In contrast, for $d' = 3$, the signal is relatively strong and is quite easy to detect. These distributions of SN and N are suggested by the representation in Figure 2.4. Thus with increasing signal intensity the distribution of SN is displaced further from the distribution of N, resulting in a larger value of d'. When the signal strength is fixed, d' varies with the observer's sensitivity. Hence, d' is a measure dependent only on the signal intensity and the observer's sensitivity. That is, a high d' value means that the signal is intense or the observer is sensitive; note again that a high d' is a direct function of a high hit rate and low false alarm rate. For an impression of a signal detection task, see Figure 2.5.

Perhaps the most significant feature of TSD is that it makes possible the isolation and evaluation of the separate effects of the observer's sensory capacity and response bias on his or her performance. Clearly, there is no single and absolute minimal magnitude value of a stimulus for its detection. However, this is not to say that there is no sensory threshold, but rather that it encompasses and describes a range of values whose expression is influenced by a variety of nonsensory environmental and observer effects. In fact, a threshold notion, as a statistical average, is a very useful concept that has a widespread application, and in terms of energy values, it provides an important approximation of the range and limits of

the sensory system. The directive made here is that we must interpret threshold statements cautiously: they serve as statistical approximations suggesting an average magnitude and/or a range of magnitudes rather than a single energy value.

Before leaving the notion of an absolute sensory threshold or limen, we must consider the controversial notion that a stimulus magnitude below a level of apparent detection, that is, subthreshold or *subliminal* stimuli, may have a measurable effect on the observer's behavior.

SUBLIMINAL PERCEPTION

There are some marginal input conditions—for example, when stimuli are shown at very weak intensity levels or at extremely fast exposure times—where the stimuli apparently do not yield a detection response. Nonetheless, the "imperceptible" subliminal stimuli may produce somewhat indirect but measurable effects on the individual's behavior. We are here addressing the role played in perception by *subliminal* input that is incapable of yielding a detection response yet exerts an observable influence on vari-

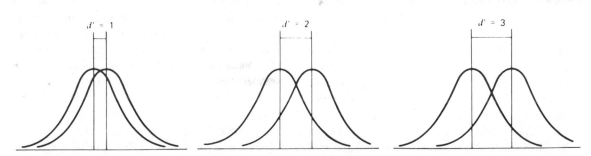

FIGURE 2.4. A schematic graphic representation of the distributions of N and SN for the three ROC curves ($d' = 1$, 2, and 3, respectively) of Figure 2.3a. Here the value of d' is shown to vary with signal intensity relative to noise intensity as indicated by the distance between the average of the distributions of N and SN. Thus, for $d' = 1$ the N and SN distributions lie close together, and

the signal is difficult to detect relative to the case of $d' = 2$ or 3. For $d' = 3$, the means of the distributions for SN and N lie comparatively far apart and the signal is more easily detected. The relative detectability for $d' = 2$ lies between $d' = 1$ and $d' = 3$. The value of d', then, represents a measure of signal strength and the observer's sensitivity to the signal, independent of response bias.

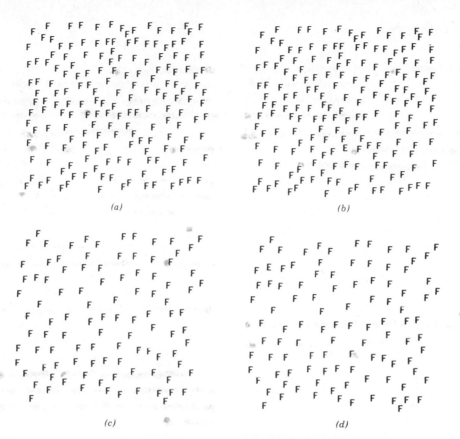

(a)

(b)

(c)

(d)

FIGURE 2.5. A signal detection task. In the example, the observer is instructed to detect the presence of a signal—the letter E. Background noise is represented by the letter F; noise alone is shown in (a). The signal E is added to the background noise in (b). The presence of noise makes the detection of the signal in (b) difficult. As is typical in a signal detection task, a brief presentation of either noise alone or signal plus noise (for example, either a or b) makes consistent, correct decisions about the presence or absence of the signal difficult. Over the course of many trials in this example of a signal detection task, the observer is presented with displays containing a field in which the placement and density of F's varies (thus, noise varies) and each display may or may not contain a randomly located E (signal). The display in (c) may help clarify how noise can fluctuate from trial to trial in a signal detection task. In (c), the background noise is less than the noise contained in (a). The signal is added to this lower level of background noise in (d). Notice that the presence of the signal in both (b) and (d) represents a *constant* addition of sensory information to the noise in (a) and (c), respectively. Hence, it

should be apparent that over many trials, the signal plus noise distribution (SN) is identical to but is displaced to the right of the noise only (N) distribution on a sensation continuum as shown in Figure 2.2. This is due to the addition of a constant amount of sensory information contained in the signal.

Response bias here would be affected by the likelihood that the display contains the signal E. Also response bias is influenced by the observer's motivation. If the E represented a belligerent enemy aircraft on a radar scope in a wartime situation, the consequence of missing the signal could result in a serious loss of life. (It is interesting to note here that signal detection theory was originally used to measure the capability of radar equipment for detecting aircraft, and then extended to human capabilities in detecting light signals.) The detectability of the signal (and hence d') depends upon signal strength: for example, the E could be made more clearly defined than the F's. Of course, the observer's sensitivity would also have an effect on d'. (Demonstration devised by S. Greist-Bousquet; based on Levy, Fischler, and Griggs, 1979.)

21

ous response parameters. This raises the obvious but controversial question: Can material, in some way, be picked up or "detected" at a level below conscious awareness? In other words, can stimulation of which the observer is unaware exert a measurable influence upon certain response outcomes?

Concern with **subliminal perception** has led to an extensive conceptual and empirical literature, but at the same time its validity has been a source of much controversy (e.g., Dixon, 1971; Erdelyi, 1974; Cheesman & Merikle, 1984; Duncan, 1985; Vokey & Read, 1985). The evidence offered in support of subliminal perception comes from a variety of experimental sources, but our purpose will be served by several representative examples.

Fowler et al. (1981) performed a study that suggested that the meaning of subliminal stimuli may be available to the observer even when the stimuli themselves are not detectable. In this experiment words (such as "cook") were flashed on a screen so rapidly that observers were not aware of what was presented. However when this was followed by the presentation of two recognizable words (e.g., "bake" and "view"), and the observers were instructed to make a forced choice response—that is, to choose or even guess which word was most like the subliminally flashed word—the observers' choices were significantly better than chance. This finding suggests that the semantic properties of weak sensory information, below a stimulus magnitude necessary for detection, is received and processed by the observer.

Another demonstration of subliminal perception is given by a technique called **semantic priming.** Basically, semantic priming involves a condition in which there is a presentation of two successive words, and the meaning of the first word biases or "primes" a response to the subsequent word. Thus, presenting the word "nurse" may serve as a prime for the target word "doctor," and accordingly, an observer's response (such as naming the word) to "doctor" when preceded by the priming word "nurse" is faster than when it is preceded by an unrelated word like "yard." In one experiment by Balota (1983), one group of observers was presented with word primes at a subliminal level (i.e., presented so briefly that observers did not report seeing the primes), whereas another group of observers received the word primes at a suprathreshold level. For a given target word (e.g., "yard"), the primes were related (e.g., "inch"), unrelated (e.g., "frog"), or neutral ("xxxx"). The major result of the priming task was that observers responded more quickly to a given target word when it was preceded by a related prime (e.g., "inch-yard") than when it was preceded by an unrelated prime (e.g., "frog-yard"). The facilitative effect of semantic priming was observed in both the suprathreshold and subliminal priming condition. These results on subliminal semantic priming thus provide evidence that material of which the viewer is not aware can influence ongoing perceptual judgment (see also Marcel, 1983; note, however, that there is some dispute concerning the status of subliminal semantic priming, see Bernstein et al., 1989).

It thus appears that weak—subliminal—stimuli can be picked up and registered by the sensory system and encoded at a level beneath conscious awareness. However it is important to stress that there is no empirical support that subliminal sensory input and its accompanying neural encoding have any substantial impact on one's thoughts or that it can, in any way, modify or influence behavior. That is, the evidence for subliminal perception per se does not imply that humans can be "controlled" or persuaded by subliminal messages. Thus the suggestion made from time to time that advertisers, by way of various forms of media, can influence behavior has little scientific merit. This controversial issue does, however, draw attention to the distinction between simple response processes such as the detection and recognition of stimuli in the laboratory and more complex responses such as purchasing or preference behavior.

As a final point on subliminal perception we may examine Dixon's (1971) provocative speculation concerning its origin and function.

It can be argued that this (subliminal perception) is no evolutionary accident. With the evolving of brains that provided the potential for conscious experience, there had to evolve control mechanisms whereby this new, limited-capacity, system could be used to maximal advantage. In theory, this control could be exercised in two ways, either by a drastic restriction on peripheral sensory inflow, or by a variable restriction on entry into consciousness. From an evolutionary point of view, the first of these two alternatives would obviously have low survival value. (p. 321)

THE DIFFERENTIAL THRESHOLD

The **differential threshold** (or **difference limen**) is a measure of the smallest difference between two stimuli that can be detected. Basically, it answers the psychophysical question: How different must two stimuli, say, two colors, or two sounds or two textures, be from each other in order for us to detect the difference? It is traditionally defined as the difference in the magnitude between two stimuli, usually a standard and a comparison stimulus, that is detected 50% of the time. For instance, if two tones of the same intensity or nearly the same intensity are presented, one immediately following the other, the listener will generally report that they are identical in loudness. However, as we gradually increase the intensity difference between the two tones, a difference in intensities will be reached at which a "different" judgment on half the trials will be reported. The magnitude of this difference specifies the differential threshold. Put in other words, the differential threshold is the amount of change in a physical stimulus necessary to produce a **just noticeable difference** (or **jnd**) in sensation. As an example, if the magnitude of a physical stimulus, say, a sound, is 100 units, and the sound has to be increased to 110 units to produce a just noticeable change in the sound, the differential threshold of 10 units (i.e., 110 − 100) corresponds to one jnd. Thus the differential threshold is a measure of the ability to discriminate two stimulus magnitudes from each other, and as such it is measured in physical units,

whereas the jnd refers to the resultant psychological unit, that is, the unit of sensory magnitude. The differential threshold, like the absolute threshold, is a derived statistical measure, that is, a difference in magnitude that is detected 50% of the time. Also like the absolute threshold, the differential threshold is a statistical concept of some questionable validity, but nonetheless it is a useful measure.

A psychophysical measure related to the differential threshold is a measure of the estimate that the magnitude of two stimuli are perceptually equal: it is called the **point of subjective equality (PSE).** PSE's have a wide range of applicability. For example, in the case of illusions, two lines may appear equal when, in fact, there is a significant physical difference in their magnitude. The PSE is defined as that magnitude of a comparison stimulus that is equally likely to be judged greater or less than the magnitude of a standard stimulus. In practice the PSE lies halfway between the stimulus just noticeably smaller than the standard and the one just noticeably larger. Many variations in design, experimental methodology, and statistical procedures exist for the determination of the differential threshold and related measures such as the PSE.

Some of the background on this issue is quite significant in the history of the measurement of sensation. In 1834 E. H. Weber, a German physiologist, investigated the ability of subjects to perform discrimination tasks. What he noted was that discrimination is a *relative* rather than an absolute judgment matter. That is, the amount of change, increase or decrease, in a stimulus necessary to detect it as different is proportional to the magnitude of the stimulus. For example, whereas the addition of 1 candle to 60 lit ones results in a perception of a difference in brightness, 1 candle added to 120 does not. For a just noticeable difference in the brightness of 120 candles, at least 2 candles are required. Extending this, then, the differential threshold for the brightness of 300 candles requires 5 or more lit candles and for 600 candles, 10 additional ones are required, and so forth. There is a fundamental principle of relative sensitivity involved referred to as **Weber's fraction** (or **ratio**) symbolized as follows:

$$\frac{\Delta I}{I} = k$$

where I is the magnitude of the stimulus intensity at which the threshold is obtained, ΔI is the differential threshold value or the increment of intensity that, when added to the stimulus intensity I, produces a just noticeable difference, and k is the resultant constant of proportionality, which differs for different modalities. The equation states that the smallest detectable increment (ΔI) in the intensity continuum of a stimulus is a constant proportion (k) of the intensity of the original stimulus (I). Thus, in the example of the brightness of candles, the Weber fractions for 60, 120, 300, and 600 lit candles would be 1/60, 2/120, 5/300, and 10/600, respectively, or $k = 1/60$. In general, k is solved by computing the proportion of a stimulus that must be changed in order to yield a just noticeable difference. The smaller the fraction, the greater is the discriminative capacity of the observer for that task. In other words, the smaller the value of the fraction, the smaller the change in intensity necessary to produce a just noticeable difference. Some representative Weber fractions for different modalities are given in Table 2.5.

Table 2.5
Representative (Middle-Range) Values of the Weber Fraction for the Different Senses

	Weber Fraction ($\Delta I/I$)
Vision (brightness, white light)	1/60
Kinesthesis (lifted weights)	1/50
Pain (thermally aroused on skin)	1/30
Audition (tone of middle pitch and moderate loudness)	1/10
Pressure (cutaneous pressure "spot")	1/7
Smell (odor of India rubber)	1/4
Taste (table salt)	1/3

Source: F. A. Geldard, *Fundamentals of Psychology*, (New York: John Wiley, 1962), p. 93. Reprinted by permission of the publisher.

Weber and others who followed him thought that the fraction remained constant across the intensity continuum for a given modality. However, in the course of much research, this view on the constancy of the fraction has been corrected, and it does not have the broad validity claimed by Weber and others. In general, the constancy of the ratio has not been found to hold at all levels of intensities for any sensory modality. It holds reasonably well in the middle ranges, which include most of our every day experiences, but the constancy of the fraction breaks down at weak and strong intensity levels for all modalities (Boring, 1942). This is not to say that Weber's fraction should be discarded. Under certain conditions in the middle range of intensities the fraction provides a useful measure of discriminability, and we will encounter it in subsequent chapters. Without a doubt it has played an important role in the measurement of sensation, and it stands as one of the broadest empirical generalizations in the history of psychology.

FECHNER'S LAW

In 1860 the physicist-physician-philosopher Gustave Fechner published *The Elements of Psychophysics*, a treatise that has had a profound effect on the measurement of sensation and perception. His basic premise was that inner mental experience—sensation—is lawfully related to the physical stimulus, and he attempted to derive an expression between the two. More specifically, he proposed that the differential threshold or the jnd as described by Weber could be used as a standard unit to measure the subjective magnitude of sensation. His inquiry led to a formalization and extension of Weber's ratio into an important equation relating the magnitude of sensation to the magnitude of the stimulus. He began with the assumption that for a given sensory modality all jnd's represent subjectively equal units of sensation. According to Weber's constant fraction, a given jnd corresponds to a constant proportional increase in the stimulus. If the basic intensity is low, the increment for the jnd is small; if the initial intensity is high, the stimulus increment necessary for the jnd will be large. Under the assumption that all jnd's are psychologically equal, it follows that as the number of jnd's grows arithmetically, stimulus intensity increases geometrically (see Figure 2.6). In other words, relatively larger and larger outputs in stimulus energy are required to obtain corresponding sensory effects. "The sensation plods along step by step while the stimulus leaps ahead by ratios" (Woodworth, 1938, p. 437). This arithmetic to geometric progression reduces mathematically to a logarithmic relation,

that is, the magnitude of a sensation is a logarithmic function of the stimulus or

$$S = k \log I$$

Fechner's law states that the subjective magnitude or sensation (S) is proportional (k, a constant, which includes the Weber fraction) to the logarithm of the physical intensity of the stimulus (I).

Just as the Weber ratio holds only within limits, Fechner's law also is only an approximation of the relationship of sensory magnitude to physical magnitude. In fact, not all jnd's are found to be subjectively equal. For example, a tone 20 jnd units above the absolute threshold sounds more than twice as loud as one 10 jnd units above the absolute threshold. However, according to Fechner's statement, "twice the loudness" is the only appropriate judgment.

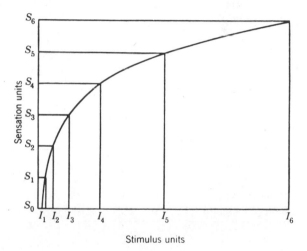

FIGURE 2.6.   The relationship between the sensation continuum and the stimulus continuum according to Fechner's law. Notice that larger and larger differences between stimulus units (I) are required with increases in the stimulus continuum in order to maintain equal differences between sensation units (S) on the sensation continuum. That is, as the sensation increases in equal steps (arithmetically), the corresponding stimulus continuum increases in physically unequal but proportional or ratio steps (geometrically). Thus, equal stimulus ratios, $I_2/I_1 = I_3/I_2 = I_4/I_3$, and so on correspond to equal increments on the sensation scale. A logarithmic function represents the relationship between an arithmetic and geometric series; hence, $S = k \log I$. (Based on J. P. Guilford, *Psychometric Methods*, McGraw-Hill, New York, 1954, p. 38.)

STEVENS' POWER LAW

More recent considerations of this issue contend that the relation between stimulus magnitude and sensory magnitude is not logarithmic. Indeed, one paper disputing Fechner's logarithmic equation is pointedly titled, "To honor Fechner and repeal his law" (Stevens, 1961). The mathematical relationship called the **power law** or **Stevens' power law** (after S. S. Stevens, its originator and until his death in 1973, its principal proponent) shows a reasonably good fit for a wide range of data relating the magnitude of the stimulus dimension to the magnitude of sensation. Some of the sensory and perceptual phenomena that conform to a power law relation are shown in Table 2.6. According to the power law, sensory or subjective magnitude grows in proportion to the physical intensity of the stimulus raised to a power or mathematically stated,

$$S = kI^b$$

where b is an exponent that is constant for a given sensory dimension and set of experimental conditions, and S, I, and k stand for sensation, intensity, and a constant (a scale factor that takes into account

Table 2.6
Representative Exponents of the Power Functions Relating Psychological
Magnitude to Stimulus Magnitude

Continuum	Measured Exponent	Stimulus Condition
Loudness	0.6	Binaural
Loudness	0.54	Monaural
Brightness	0.33	5° target, dark-adapted eye
Brightness	0.5	Very brief flash, dark-adapted eye
Smell	0.55	Coffee
Smell	0.6	Heptane
Taste	1.3	Sucrose, human subjects
Taste	1.13	Sucrose, based on consumption by rats[a]
Taste	1.3	Salt
Temperature	1.0	Cold on arm
Temperature	1.6	Warmth on arm
Vibration	0.95	60 Hz on finger
Vibration	0.6	250 Hz on finger
Duration	1.1	White noise stimuli
Finger span	1.3	Thickness of blocks
Pressure on palm	1.1	Static force on skin
Heaviness	1.45	Lifted weights
Force of handgrip	1.7	Hand dynamometer
Electric shock	3.5	Current through fingers
Tactual roughness	1.5	Rubbing emery cloths
Tactual hardness	0.8	Squeezing rubber
Visual length	1.0	Projected line
Visual area	0.7	Projected square
Angular acceleration	1.41	5-second stimulus

Source: Based on Stevens (1961, 1970, 1975).
[a] See Flaherty and Sepanek (1978).

the choice of units used in the intensity dimension), respectively. By using a power law formulation, it is possible to show that the sensory modalities and perceptual tasks differ from each other in the extent to which the rate of sensation changes with changes in intensity. It is the exponent of the equation—b—that reflects this particular feature of the relation between sensation and stimulation. For example, for the judged length of a line, the exponent is very close to 1.00 and the power equation reduces to $S = kI$. This means that apparent length grows very nearly in direct proportion to physical length. This is depicted in Figure 2.7 as a straight 45° line. Thus, a 20-cm line looks about twice as long as one 10 cm long. For brightness the exponent is about 0.33, and when a **power function** is plotted in arithmetic or linear coordinates, the line representing the function is concave downward. This means that to double the brightness of a light a considerable amount of stimulus energy, clearly in excess of a doubling of the stimulus magnitude, must be expended. In short, brightness grows much more slowly than does stimulus intensity.

In contrast, the exponent for the apparent intensity of electric shock applied to the fingers is about 3.5, and as shown in Figure 2.7 its power function is

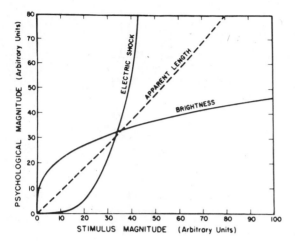

FIGURE 2.7.   Power functions plotted in linear coordinates. The apparent magnitude of shock, length, and brightness follow different growth curves because their power law exponents are 3.5, 1.0, and 0.33, respectively. Notice that when plotted in linear coordinates the curve is concave upward or downward depending on whether the exponent is greater or less than 1.0. The power function for apparent length is almost straight in linear coordinates because its exponent is close to 1.0. The units of the scales have been chosen arbitrarily to show the relative form of the curves on a single graph. (Reprinted from S. S. Stevens, "Psychophysics of sensory function," in W. A. Rosenblith (Ed.), *Sensory Communication*, 1961, by permission of the M.I.T. Press, Cambridge, Mass.)

represented by a curve that is concave upward. Clearly, a doubling of the electric current flow through one's finger results in considerably more than a mere doubling in the reported sensation (more like a 10-fold increase). In general the exponent of the power function determines its curvature. An exponent close to 1.00 results in a straight-line curve; a power function with an exponent greater than 1.00 is represented by a curve that is concave upward, whereas if the exponent is less than 1.00, the curvature is concave downward.

In logarithmic form the power law reduces to $\log S = b \log I + \log k$. When plotted in log-log coordinates (logarithmic scales on both axes), this

equation describes a straight line whose slope (or measure of steepness) is b. That is, when both the ordinate (S) and abscissa (I) are plotted in logarithmic scales, the curvature disappears and the slope of the resultant straight line becomes a direct measure of the exponent. Accordingly, as shown in Figure 2.8 when the power function curves of Figure 2.7 are replotted in log-log coordinates, they become straight lines whose slopes are the exponents of the power equation. In log-log coordinates the high exponent for the sensation of electric current gives a steep slope, visual brightness gives a flat slope, and the nearly linear function for perceived length results in a slope close to 1.00.

A number of methods are available for determining the power function for a given sensory dimension. One of the most often employed methods, called **magnitude estimation,** requires the random or irregular presentation of a series of stimuli that vary only along a single dimension, say, physical intensity. The experimenter (or the subject) assigns a number to a standard stimulus (called the **modulus,**

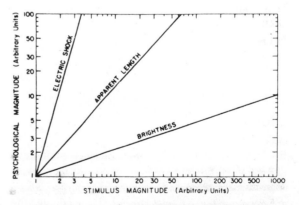

FIGURE 2.8.   Power functions placed in logarithmic coordinates. When the curves in Figure 2.7 are plotted in log-log coordinates, they become straight lines. The slope of the line corresponds to the exponent of the power function governing the growth of the sensation. (Reprinted from S. S. Stevens, "Psychophysics of sensory function," in W. A. Rosenblith (Ed.), *Sensory Communication*, 1961, by permission of the M.I.T. Press, Cambridge, Mass.)

a value of moderate intensity relative to the series), say, 10 or 100, and the subject is required to produce numbers that express his or her judgment of the stimuli relative to the standard or modulus. For the example of loudness, if a stimulus in the series seems 10 times as loud as the modulus, the subject assigns a number 10 times as large. If it appears one-fourth as loud, the subject assigns a number one-fourth as large as the modulus, and so forth. In short, the subject attempts to match the perceived intensity of each stimulus with a number relative to the modulus. Because there is but a short step between the observer's judgment and the final scale, such techniques are often referred to as "direct methods."

Based on a vast body of research, this procedure yields a clear estimate of the relation between subjective experience (sensation) and physical stimulation. Indeed, the method of magnitude estimation was used to obtain most of the exponents listed in Table 2.6. Although it is not unanimous (e.g., Warren & Warren, 1963; Weiss, 1981), there is general agreement that for many scaling tasks Stevens' power law is a better representation than Fechner's logarithmic equation. In nearly all domains one finds an application of the power law. We shall note this on many occasions in the chapters that follow.

THE RELATIVITY OF PSYCHOPHYSICAL JUDGMENTS

It can be argued that the perception of a stimulus depends not only on its isolated stimulation, but on comparative relations between the stimulus and its apparent context or background. For example, the horizontal center line in *a* of Figure 2.9 appears shorter than the one at *b*, but physically the two lines are equal. In fact they are vertically aligned, so that the identity of the two lines should be obvious, yet the center line at *b* still appears longer. Clearly the flanking boxes of each center line exert an appreciable effect on the apparent line lengths, and this gives rise to a perceptual distortion. This points out that we

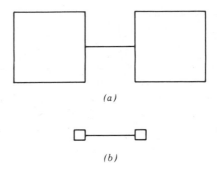

FIGURE 2.9. The effect of context on apparent length. The center lines at (*a*) and (*b*) are equal, but because of contextual stimuli—the different-sized flanking boxes—the line at (*b*) appears longer.

cannot neglect or discount the influence of **context** —the effect of surrounding (or preceding or subsequent) stimuli upon the perception of a focal stimulus (an early comprehensive theoretical approach to this issue can be found in Helson, 1964).

This merits a general principle in perception, namely, that the perception of a stimulus depends not only on absolute, immediate factors but also upon relative, contextual ones. In the pages to follow we will encounter many instances of the relational character of the perception of stimuli.

Interestingly, this phenomenon is not restricted to humans. Flaherty and his colleagues (e.g., Flaherty, 1982; Flaherty & Grigson, 1988) have demonstrated that certain forms of consummatory behavior in rats are also influenced by context and contrast effects. One of the dramatic forms of this relativity phenomenon is called *successive negative contrast*. For example, rats are exposed to one reward level (e.g., a high concentration of a sweet solution) and then shifted to a lower level of reward (low concentration). The performance of the shifted animals rapidly becomes poorer than that of a control group that had been exposed to only the lower level of reward. In other words, the *contrast* between the concentrations of the two rewards exaggerates the reduced sweetness of the lower level of reward, thus reducing only the shifted groups' performance.

SUMMARY

The objective of this chapter was to outline some of the main issues of psychophysics—the relation between the physical dimension and subjective experience. To this end notions of both the absolute and differential threshold were described. The absolute threshold is traditionally and generally defined as the minimum amount of stimulus energy required for the detection of a stimulus. Although there is a vast literature on the absolute threshold, there are many factors that make a notion of a single immutable stimulus value for stimulus detection untenable. Pertinent to this change in the assumption about the nature of a psychological threshold notion was an outline of the Theory of Signal Detection (TSD). This stressed that an observer's response bias, owing to many nonsensory factors such as expectation and motivation, determines the criterion exercised by that observer in the report of whether or not a stimulus (signal) was detected. Furthermore, the TSD makes possible the isolation and evaluation of the separate effects of the observer's sensory capacity and response bias on his or her performance.

The controversial concept of subliminal perception—the pickup of stimuli whose magnitude lies below a level of detection—was introduced. Two sorts of experiments were discussed in which stimulation of which the observer is unaware exerts a measurable influence upon his or her behavior. It was concluded that in certain conditions, weak sensory information, below an intensity or duration range necessary for detection, may be registered by the observer and influence the detection or recognition of subsequent stimuli.

The differential threshold refers to the amount of change in stimulus energy necessary to produce a detectable difference between two stimuli. This led to Weber's fraction, which states that the amount of change in a stimulus necessary to detect it as different is proportional to the magnitude of the stimulus. Fechner extended Weber's work and formulated a mathematical equation linking sensation to stimulation. Fechner's equation states that the magnitude of a sensation is proportional to the logarithm of the physical intensity of the stimulus. Although both Weber's fraction and Fechner's equation have been questioned, their impact on measurement in psychology in general has been significant.

An alternative to Fechner's law was presented: Stevens' power law holds that the relation between sensation and stimulation for many kinds of sensory and perceptual phenomena conforms to an exponential expression; that is, sensation grows in proportion to the physical intensity of the stimulus raised to a power. This formulation probably expresses the relationship between sensation and stimulation that has the greatest degree of recent application in many diverse domains of psychology.

Finally, we noted that judgments about a stimulus do not occur in isolation. We described the notion that judgments in psychophysical tasks are relative by outlining the role played by the context or the background of a stimulus. A general perceptual principle was presented: the perception of a stimulus depends not only on absolute, immediate factors, but also upon comparative relations between the stimulus and the context in which it appears. That is, the perception of a stimulus may be markedly influenced by what precedes it, what follows it, and what serves as its background.

KEY TERMS

Absolute threshold (limen)

Context

Correct rejection

Criterion

d'

Differential threshold

False alarm

Fechner's law

Hit

Jnd

Limen

Magnitude estimation

Method of adjustment

Method of constant stimuli

Method of limits

Miss

Noise

Point of subjective equality (PSE)

Power function

Power function modulus

Psychophysics

ROC curve

Semantic priming

Signal

Theory of Signal Detection (TSD)

Stevens' power law

Subliminal perception

Subthreshold (subliminal)

Suprathreshold (supraliminal)

Weber's fraction (or ratio)

STUDY QUESTIONS

1. What is psychophysics? What does the use of psychophysical techniques enable psychologists to determine about the state of subjective experience?

2. What is the absolute threshold? How can it be assessed? What methods are used to determine the absolute threshold?

3. Consider alternatives to the notion of an absolute threshold.

4. What is the signal detection technique? How does it relate to the traditional notion of an absolute threshold?

5. How do signal detection techniques include the observer's decision criteria and various nonsensory factors in assessing an observer's sensitivity?

6. Enumerate factors that enter into an observer's judgment concerning a decision as to whether a stimulus is present or not.

7. What is meant by the decision-making strategy of the observer in a typical signal detection task?

8. What does the value of d' represent? How is this illustrated by the ROC curve? What factors increase the probability of a hit, a false alarm?

9. What is subliminal perception and how can it be demonstrated? How does research on semantic priming bear on subliminal perception? Why is subliminal perception a controversial research area?

10. What is the differential threshold and how can it be demonstrated? What is the relation of the differential threshold to the observer's ability to discriminate between stimuli? How is the differential threshold affected by the magnitude of the stimulus intensity that is under observation?

11. Consider the relation of Weber's fraction to the notion of a jnd.

12. What is Fechner's law or equation? What does it state concerning the relation of stimulation to sensation? How is it related to Weber's fraction?

13. How does Stevens' power law relate sensation to stimulation? How does Stevens' power law differ from Fechner's equation?

14. What is a power function? What are some methods used to scale sensation using Stevens' power law? What does the exponent of a power function represent concerning the relation of sensation to stimulation?

15. Why is the judgment of various aspects of a stimulus a "relative" matter? What factors in addition to the stimulus enter into its perception?

3

THE ORIENTING SYSTEM

To survive, most organisms must move about and maintain a particular physical orientation to their surroundings. To locomote effectively and to orient themselves to their environment most animals, whether they are terrestrial, avian, arboreal, or aquatic, must possess positional information on their body in space.

It is likely that for all animals gravity serves as the basic plane of reference. Organs and receptors sensitive to gravitational force are very old in the evolutionary scale. They are found in every animal phylum, and their general mode of functioning is quite similar. The receptors share in common the fact that their excitation is dependent on mechanical

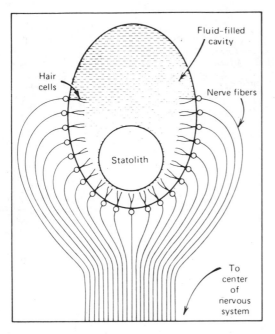

FIGURE 3.1a. Highly simplified schematic drawing of a statocyst cavity, statolith, receptive hair cells, and a set of nerve fibers.

deformation. Accordingly, they are called **mechanoreceptors.** In their simplest form, in invertebrates, gravity detectors are known as **statocysts,** and they are perhaps the earliest specialized sense organs to develop in the entire animal kingdom. Although the physical mechanisms of statocysts observed among animal groups are anatomically diverse, their general sensory equipment operates on the same basic principle. Anatomical structures, generally free moving, called **statoliths,** lie within the statocyst cavity (see Figure 3.1a). The statoliths are heavier than the material (generally a fluid) of the statocyst cavity and are relatively free to move. Due to intertial or **gravitoinertial** force (gravity and acceleration), linear bodily movements produce a shifting or displacement of the statolith relative to a sheet of receptor tissue lined with ciliated receptors or hair cells (see Figure 3.1b). The statoliths thus react to gravity or linear movement—up–down, forward–backward, and left–right—and exert pressure on sensory receptors. The general anatomical structures and principles are similar in vertebrates. The gravity detectors are called **otocysts** in vertebrates, and **otoliths** (*oto* =

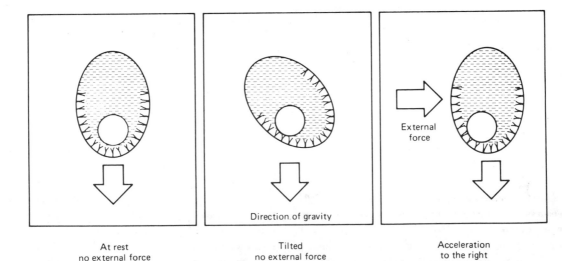

FIGURE 3.1b. The statocyst in three conditions. Movement causes the statolith to stimulate different hair cells

and, accordingly, register changes in position and linear acceleration.

ear, *lith* = bone) or **otoconia** lie within the otocyst cavity and similarly react to gravity or linear movement.

An interesting example of the operation of a statocyst is provided by observing some crustacea. The crayfish regularly molts (sheds) the lining of its statocyst along with the rest of its exoskeleton (external covering). The statoliths, which for the crayfish are grains of sand, are also shed. After the molting process is complete, the crayfish, with its claws, places new grains of sand within the new statocyst cavity. As with all statoliths, the grains of sand react to inertial forces and serve to stimulate the sensory cells as the crayfish moves about. If the only replacement statoliths provided are iron filings, the crayfish will place them in its statocyst cavity. If a magnet is now moved about the head of the crayfish, the replacement statoliths will be correspondingly attracted, and the crayfish will alter its bodily orientation accordingly (the classic demonstration is by Kreidl in 1893; see Howard, 1982, p. 354).

THE MAMMALIAN ORIENTING SYSTEM

The evolution of the organ for detecting orientational information probably proceeded from primitive organs consisting of cells covered with sensory cilia (hairlike structures) located in pits in the skin of aquatic animals. These were receptive to mechanical stimulation; that is, they were sensitive to movements and vibrations of the fluids filling the depression. In evolution these depressions became specialized and account for the bony cavities of the inner ears of mammals (sometimes called the **labyrinth**). The advanced development of the statocyst or otocyst mechanism is seen in the mammalian structures, the **saccule, utricle,** and **semicircular canals,** collectively labeled the **vestibular organs** (see Figures 3.2*a* and *b*).

The utricle and saccule are fluid-filled membranous sacs that act as otocysts. The receptor organ of the utricle and saccule is called the *macula;* it is composed of sensory hair cells imbedded in the inner

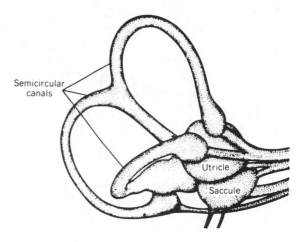

FIGURE 3.2*a*.   A drawing of the human vestibular organs. (From C. G. Mueller, *Sensory Pyschology,* © 1965. Reprinted by permission of Prentice Hall, Englewood Cliffs, N.J.)

surface of the utricle and saccule (see Figure 3.2*c*), which extend to the brain. In the adult human there are about 33,000 hair cells in the utricle and about 19,000 in the saccule (Howard, 1986), with the

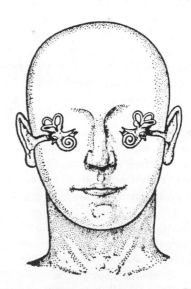

FIGURE 3.2*b*.   Position of vestibular apparatus in head. (Based on D. Krech and R. S. Crutchfield, *Elements of Psychology,* Alfred A. Knopf, New York, 1958, p. 187.)

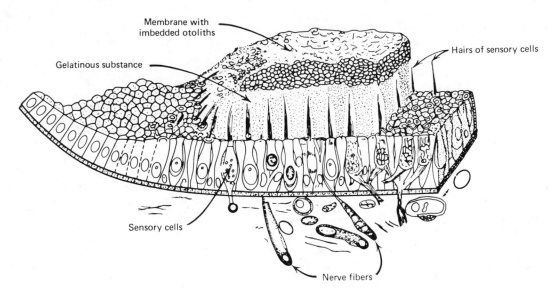

Membrane with
imbedded otoliths

Hairs of sensory cells

Gelatinous substance

Sensory cells

Nerve fibers

FIGURE 3.2c. Structure of the macula in cross section.

number decreasing with age (Johnsson & Hawkins, 1972).

The otoliths in the utricle and saccule sacs are loosely attached to the surface of a gelatinous mass that lies within the sac. The otoliths are calcium carbonate crystals that are quite dense, having almost three times the density of water (Parker, 1980). In operation the hair cells are bent by the otoliths in accordance with the extent and direction of linear displacement and bodily position with respect to gravity. Presumably when the body is speeding up or slowing down in a straight-line motion or when the head is tilted, that is, with linear acceleration (*changes* in the rate of motion), the inertia of the otolith particles brings about a bending of the hair cells with a consequent discharge by attached nerve fibers.

The functioning of the utricle and saccule overlaps with the operation of a second dynamic vestibular organ whose primary function is to register the direction and extent of *rotary acceleration* about any head axis. (Theoretically, the otocysts can register rotary motion as well as linear motion, but functionally this would produce a very complex pattern for a single receptor organ. The addition of a second receptor system for rotary motion enables the separation of functions and yields a greater sensitivity to movement.) The detection of rotary acceleration is available to few invertebrates, but most vertebrates from fish upward have developed specialized structures for its detection called semicircular canals. The semicircular canals are fluid-filled enclosures that lie at approximately right angles to each other (see Figure 3.3) and share a common cavity in the utricle. Each canal, functionally a complete and independent fluid circuit, relates to a major plane of the body. Thus together the canals form a three-coordinate system to which gross bodily motion of a rotary nature can be referred (see Figure 3.4). Within each canal is a set of sensory hair cells. Each canal widens at its base into a somewhat spherical, fluid-filled chamber called an *ampulla*, which contains the vestibular receptors (see Figure 3.5). Each of the ampullae contains a tongue-shaped protuberance, a sensory structure called the *cupula*. It is composed of crests of hair tufts from the vestibular nerve and is encased in a gelatinous mass (see Figure 3.6a). The cupula is fixed at its base, the *crista* (which houses the hair cells and the terminations of the vestibular nerve), but it swings freely into the ampullar cavity

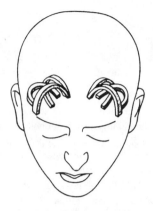

FIGURE 3.3.   Highly schematic drawing of semicircular canals. The semicircular canals in the head are at approximately right angles to each other. (From C. G. Mueller, *Sensory Psychology* © 1965. Reprinted by permission of Prentice Hall, Englewood Cliffs, N.J.)

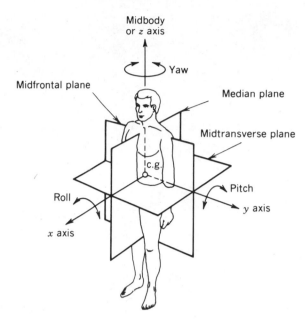

FIGURE 3.4.   Coordinate system of the human body specifying the principal planes, axes, and rotations. The vertical *midbody* or z axis passes down the length of the body through the center of gravity (c.g.). The x axis runs from front to back, and the y axis runs side to side, both through the c.g. The *median* plane is the plane of bilateral body symmetry containing the z and x axis. The *midfrontal* plane lies at right angles to the median plane and contains the z and y axis. The *midtransverse* plane lies at right angles to both the midfrontal and median planes and passes through the center of gravity.

Rotation of the head or body about the z axis is known as *yaw;* rotation about the x axis is called *roll*, and rotation about the y axis is called *pitch*. (From I.P. Howard, *Human Visual Orientation*, Wiley, New York, 1982, p. 6. Reprinted by permission of the publisher.)

and is capable of being bent by pressure of the fluid. This movement at the crista stimulates the hair cells, which transmit a series of impulses to the brain. Indeed, this is what occurs during rotary acceleration such as when the head is turned or rotated on a given axis (see Figure 3.6b). The endolymph fluid of the canals circulates and becomes displaced appropriate to the head rotation, creating hydraulic pressure. This resultant pressure causes a bending of the cupula, its deflection being proportional to the force of the head turn. The rotary acceleration thus causes differential deformation of the hair-cell receptors and is analyzable into its spatial components. When the rotation ceases or its rate stabilizes, the deflection is canceled and the cupula returns to its normal position. In contrast, linear acceleration and gravitational force have little effect on the cupula.

The movements of the cupula have been measured directly in fish by dyeing the cupula so it could be photographed (Dohlman, 1935). Injection of a small drop of oil into the fluid of the canal enabled observation of the change in the position of the cupula in response to rotation. As Figure 3.7 shows, angular displacement of the endolymph produces pressure on the cupula and results in its bending.

VESTIBULAR STIMULATION

The basic orienting system evolved as an adaptation to the conditions that normally confront animals, such as active movements and perhaps brief passive movements. It is not surprising, then, that the system is not well suited to cope with novel spatial conditions—ones that rarely or never occur in nature. For example, the vestibular system does not register

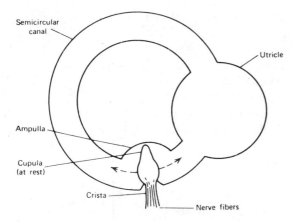

FIGURE 3.5. Schematic of a semicircular canal with ampulla, cupula, and crista. The dashed arrows indicate the potential deflection of the cupula by displacement of the endolymph fluid produced by appropriate rotation of the head.

FIGURE 3.6b. Representation of activity at the crista during various head movements. When the head starts moving or turning, the endolymph liquid of the ampulla at first lags behind, bending the cupula and the hair tufts in the direction opposite to the head movement. As the movement of the head continues, the ampullar liquid and the cupula move at the same rate as the movement of the head, and the hair tufts become erect (which is the case when there is no head movement). As long as the head is moving in a constant direction and at a constant speed, the hair tufts will remain erect. However, when the head movement stops, inertial force of the ampullar liquid carries the cupula forward and the hair tufts are bent in the forward direction. Thus, starts and stops and changes in direction move the liquid in the semicircular canals, bend the cupula, deform the hair tufts, and stimulate the hair cells of the crista, whereas constant motion, as shown in the center figure, produces no deformation and no neural impulses. (From D. Krech and R. S. Crutchfield, *Elements of Psychology*, Alfred A. Knopf, New York, 1958, p. 187. Reprinted by permission of the authors.)

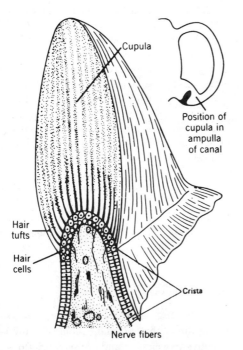

FIGURE 3.6a. Cross section of the cupula, showing the transverse ridge of hair tufts and cells fixed at the base (crista). The small insert shows the position of the ampulla of the semicircular canal.

sustained passive movements at a constant rate. If the velocity is kept stable or uniform, as in high-speed vehicular transport (e.g., trains, planes, or elevators), motion as such is not detectable. This follows from the fact that with constant motion the fluids, otoliths, and receptors will soon all move at the same speed, gravitoinertial forces will be overcome, and there will be no relative movement between the components of the vestibular mechanism, hence no stimulation.

The kinds of motion that the vestibular receptors are responsive to are acceleration or deceleration—changes in rate of motion. In other words, the vestibular organs are suited to detect starts and stops and changes of motion, not constant velocities.

We should note that whereas adequate stimuli for the vestibular organs are head movements, it is possible to stimulate the receptors experimentally by electrical, mechanical, caloric (thermal), and even chemical stimuli. For example, with the caloric method stimulation is produced by irrigation of the external auditory canal with water, either warmer or colder than the canal wall (generally cold water is used). This produces a heat exchange that is readily transmitted to the vestibular organs, particularly to the fluid of a semicircular canal. The heating or cooling of the endolymph, producing expansion or contraction, causes an upward or downward movement of the fluid, which then deflects the cupula (Wendt, 1951).

VESTIBULAR NYSTAGMUS

Stimulation of the vestibular nerve reaches to the lower centers of the brain (medulla and cerebellum) from which connections are made with motor fibers to the neck, trunk, limb, and ocular muscles. The concern in the present discussion is with the relation of bodily position to patterns of ocular reflexes. When an individual is rotated about his or her body axis, stimulation of the vestibular canals and utricle, during the acceleration and deceleration phases,

initiate rhythmic and reflexive movements of the eyes. During acceleration the eyes move slowly in a direction opposite to the movement of the rotation (slow phase) and rapidly back (fast phase); during deceleration the direction of eye movements reverses. This series of fast and slow eye movements is termed vestibular **nystagmus**. When observed directly after the cessation of rotation, these ocular movements are referred to as **postrotational or postrotary nystagmus**. The nystagmic reflex occurs when the individual is in the dark and it is therefore not dependent on vision. However, nystagmic reflexes become complex if vision intervenes. When the eyes are open, objects moving across the visual field may induce another form of nystagmus, called visually induced or **optokinetic nystagmus**, which can become dominant over vestibular nystagmus. Slow movements in pursuit of moving stimuli alternate with quick return jerks. In this case the nystagmus is more geared to the speed at which the visual image moves. Functionally, optokinetic nystagmus has the effect of imaging the same part of the visual field on the eye as long as possible during movements of the whole field of view.

In lower animals, optokinetic nystagmus may be lacking. However, in some instances similar responses to angular acceleration have been observed.

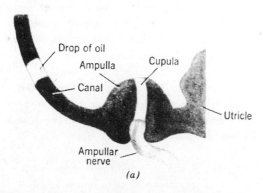

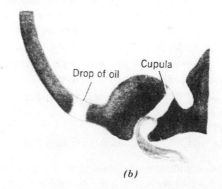

(a)   *(b)*

FIGURE 3.7.   The effect of angular acceleration on the position of the cupula. The displacement of the endolymph was revealed by an injected droplet of colored oil. (*a*) The cupula in its normal position at rest before rotation of the preparation. (*b*) Change in position of the cupula as a consequence of rotary acceleration. (After G. Dohlman, "Some practical and theoretical points in labryinthology," *Proceedings of the Royal Society of Medicine*, 28, 1935, p. 1374. Reprinted by permission of the Proceedings of the Royal Society of Medicine.)

For example, the turtle shows a smooth head-turning response that, upon analysis, occurs reflexively and serves to maintain its eye toward a fixed point in space. A similar phenomenon has been shown with arthropods. When placed within a rotating, vertically striped cylinder, an insect, for example, turns its body in the same direction as the rotation of the cylinder. This response, called the optokinetic reaction, appears to stabilize the stripes in the visual field.

OCULOGYRAL ILLUSION

There are visual effects, often correlated with nystagmic reflexes, that are sensitive indicators of vestibular stimulation. These are most likely to occur in conditions of relatively intense vestibular stimulation. During or just after a period of rapid rotation about the body's longitudinal mid-body axis (see Figure 3.4), objects in the visual field appear to move, either with or against the direction of the rotation of the body. If an observer is rotated in the dark and fixates on an illuminated light source that rotates with him or her so that it is stationary in space relative to the observer, there will be a perceived movement of the light in the direction of the rotation at the start of acceleration. However, the apparent visual movement of the light will cease when the velocity of rotation becomes stabilized and deceleration will reverse the apparent direction of the movement of the light. The result is an illusory perception of movement produced by unusual vestibular stimulation, and it is called the **oculogyral illusion**. It follows that individuals with defective semicircular function are not subject to the oculogyral illusion (Miller & Graybiel, 1975).

VISUALLY INDUCED ILLUSIONS OF MOTION

An illusion similar to the oculogyral effect occurs in which observers report that they are moving when in actuality they are stationary and the visual field is in motion. Perhaps the most common experience of this phenomenon, known as **self-vection,** occurs when an observer, looking from the window of a stationary train and viewing only a nearby moving train, perceives that his or her train is in motion. What occurs is that there is no vestibular stimulation of movement, but there is ambiguous visual stimulation. The visual scene is such that either train can be perceived as moving. Since the tendency is to perceive a consistent stable environment, the viewer attributes the movement to his or her train and perceives the visual field as stationary.

An experiment involving a similar condition was reported by Lee and his colleagues (Lishman & Lee, 1973; Lee & Aronson, 1974), which implicated the compelling role played by vision in the control of posture. They observed that when enclosed in an illuminated box-room whose walls and ceiling could sway back and forth, a physically stationary observer begins to sway in synchrony with the "swinging room." That is, postural sway is imposed by the movement of the visual surroundings and is in the direction the room is moved. This makes sense because the swinging room duplicates the optical stimulation that normally results when our body swings back and forth. Thus when the room moved toward the stationary observer it produced the visual stimulus that would occur if the observer actually was swaying forward; accordingly, as a compensatory adjustment the observer leaned backward. Correspondingly, when the swinging room moved away from the stationary observer, it produced the view that the observer was swaying backward, and appropriate to the view, the observer leaned forward. These effects, involving postural adjustments to a changing visual environment, without any corresponding vestibular stimulation, occurred for infants and for adults; however, the postural sway effects were more pronounced for the infants, often resulting in a loss of balance or even a fall in the direction the room was moved (see also Butterworth & Hicks, 1977).

The observation that in many instances visually induced sensations of motion appear equivalent to those produced from actual bodily motion suggests that movement of the visual scene per se has the same or a similar effect on the individual's nervous system as does stimulation of the vestibular organs. Indeed there is evidence with subprimates that there are cells in the brain that react both to direct stimulation of the vestibular organs *and* to motion of the visual environment (see Dichgans & Brandt, 1978; Daunton & Thomsen, 1979). Thus the apparently equivalent experience of motion from both conditions may depend upon the recruitment and activation of the same underlying neural processes and structures.

Notice should be taken of the fact that, for the most part, the conditions that contribute to visually induced illusions of motion (along with periods of passive linear or rotary motion of the body at a constant velocity) are quite unnatural. Commenting on vestibular illusions obtained in the laboratory, J. J. Gibson (1966) states: "For millions of years animals moved by rhythmic pushes, not as Newtonian bodies and not in railroad cars or airplanes. It is therefore reasonable that an individual should be susceptible to vestibular illusions when passively transported in a vehicle" (p. 69).

The foregoing observations point out the importance of vision in bodily orientation. Indeed the critical role of vision in maintaining postural stability and balance can be easily demonstrated. Stand on one foot, raising the knee of the other foot to about waist level. With your eyes opened you will likely experience little difficulty in balancing on one foot. However, when you try this same demonstration with your eyes closed, maintaining balance becomes noticeably difficult. Of course what this demonstration illustrates is the importance of the visual surroundings in enabling us continuously and smoothly to adjust our musculature so as to maintain our balance.

VESTIBULAR ADAPTATION AND HABITUATION

The vestibular system is subject to **adaptation** and **habituation**. That is, if acceleration of rotation is sustained, the feeling of motion will gradually decrease and eventually may subside. Technically the phenomenon in which vestibular effects decrease for long periods of time with prolonged exposure is termed *vestibular habituation*, while *adaptation* effects are considered to be rapidly induced and dissipated. However, it has been pointed out that the

distinction between the two processes is not clear, and they will be treated here as the same process (Marler & Hamilton, 1966).

Nystagmus may habituate with extended exposure to the abnormal vestibular stimulation that characteristically occurs to individuals who experience durations of continual motion, for example, sailors, aviators, acrobats, and dancers. Other consequences of rotation, such as illusions of movement, vertigo, nausea, and dizziness, also habituate. For example, figure skaters were reported to be able to walk straight after being rotated in a chair. The tendency to veer off had completely habituated out (McCabe, in Marler & Hamilton, 1966).

There are a number of procedures that reduce certain vestibular phenomena even when the body remains in motion. Ballet dancers, for example, are known to reduce nystagmus while spinning by "spotting," that is, by fixating on some distant point generally in the audience. A dancer keeps his or her head pointing to the audience as long as possible and then flicks the head around faster than the body until it again faces the same way. While the body of the dancer is continuously moving, the vestibular organs are stimulated only during the head movement that regains visual fixation on the distant point. This reduces the vestibular stimulation while providing a somewhat stable visual environment. Furthermore, the more or less stable visual input obtained by spotting during rotation ensures that postrotary nystagmus will not occur.

DEFICIENCIES OF THE VESTIBULAR MECHANISM

A cat or rabbit suspended upside down by its paws and then released, whether in a light or dark environment, will usually right itself during the fall and land on its feet (see Figure 3.8). This is known as the **air-righting reflex** (Warkentin & Carmichael, 1939; Howard, 1986). This feat of bodily orientation in midair, physically extremely complex, is controlled by the functioning of the vestibular organs. An animal lacking proper vestibular functioning does not show this adaptive reaction to falling and lands in a heaplike fashion (e.g., Watt, 1976).

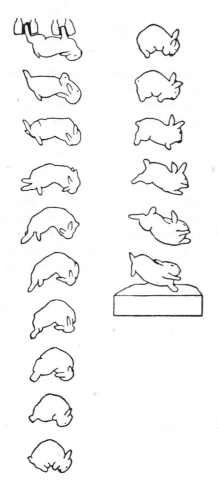

FIGURE 3.8. Tracings of successive frames of a motion picture (64 frames per second) of a 20-day-old rabbit dropped while upside-down. (From G. R. Wendt, "Vestibular functions," in S. S. Stevens, (Ed.), *Handbook of Experimental Psychology*, Chap. 31, John Wiley, New York, 1951; and J. Warkentin and L. A. Carmichael, "A study of the development of the air-righting reflex in cats and rabbits," *Journal of Genetic Psychology*, 55, 1939, pp. 67–80. Reprinted by permission of the Helen Dwight Reid Educational Foundation. Published by Heldref Publications, 4000 Albemarle St., N.W., Washington, D.C. 20016. Copyright © 1939.)

In the human the loss of vestibular function is accompanied by a general disorientation that eventually subsides. Initially the individual cannot stand upright steadily with the eyes closed and may suffer from vertigo. However, with use of vision the individual appears eventually to compensate for the loss. In congenitally deaf individuals, whose vestibular organs may be totally degenerate (due to the anatomical and physiological relationship of the vestibular organs to the auditory ones), equilibrium and postural adjustment are effective. However, when the use of vision is reduced or visual cues are ambiguous, general bodily orientation is sharply reduced. Boring (1942, p. 542) writes that some deaf people do not go under water when swimming because what is "up" and "down" get confused and there is danger of drowning.

Individuals both deaf and blind face a more serious problem in maintaining equilibrium. Of a group of 10 deaf-blind subjects studied with regard to their vestibular functioning, nine were unable to maintain balance more than a second or two when standing on one foot (Worshel & Dallenbach, 1948). Furthermore, the same nine deaf-blind subjects showed no postrotational responses after 30 seconds of rotation in a chair. There was no nystagmus, nausea, dizziness, or illusion of movement. It is likely that the vestibular function was completely lacking in these subjects. It follows that individuals who suffer total loss of vestibular function are not susceptible to motion sickness.

Ménière's Disease Mention should be made of an incurable pathological condition that affects both the vestibular function and hearing. It is held to be due to an overproduction and elevated pressure of the enclosed fluid of the labyrinth (i.e., the inner ear and the vestibular organs). The patient afflicted with **Ménière's disease** experiences episodes of sudden and violent vestibular activity, causing turbulent nystagmic eye movements, extreme vertigo, severe nausea, and often distortions in hearing; high-pitch sounds especially may sound tinny, hollow, or fuzzy.

Ménière's disease is often a progressive disorder; in later stages, hearing and vestibular function may be permanently lost. While there is no cure, surgical procedures are occasionally effective in draining off excess fluid, thereby relieving pressure on the inner ear and reducing the debilitating symptoms. There is also a drastic procedure to alleviate the symptoms that essentially severs the vestibular nerve to the brain.

OTHER MECHANISMS FOR ORIENTATION

Evidence indicates that there is an interaction between the vestibular and visual modalities in the human (e.g., Witkin, 1959). Indeed, as we have previously pointed out, the visual input for the human usually dominates the input from the vestibular mechanism. As we ascend the phylogenetic scale, the vestibular apparatus diminishes in importance as a means of controlling bodily orientation. It follows that damage to the vestibular system of higher mammals is a less serious matter than in lower animals where a substitute mechanism may not be available. On the other hand, there are orientational mechanisms in lower animals that may not be available to humans. For example, modified mechanoreceptors are found in many fish that are receptors ("electroreceptors") specialized for the detection of electric fields and that may be useful for orientation. In addition, fish possess a specialized mechanism that is extremely susceptible to low-frequency vibrations or pressure changes in the surrounding water. It appears as a line running along the side of the body from head to tail and is called the *lateral line*. A small fluid-filled tube that runs under the skin beneath the line contains bundles of sensory cells (*neuromasts*) that respond to faint vibratory stimuli and may contribute to the detection of prey (Montgomery & Macdonald, 1987).

Magnetic Sense   Honeybees seem to possess a **magnetic sense;** they appear to orient to the earth's magnetic field aided by magnetic material located in the front of their abdomen (Gould, Kirschvink, & Diffeyes, 1978). In addition there is some evidence that the pigeon's homing ability may also be aided by the reception of magnetic field information (Walcott, Gould, & Kirschvink, 1979; Kirschvink, Jones, & MacFadden, 1985). When the pickup of information about the earth's magnetic field was disrupted, such as after small magnets were affixed to their heads, pigeons usually failed to orient properly; this was especially the case when other navigational cues were unavailable (such as on cloudy days). However

other studies with pigeons, employing various experimental procedures have failed to demonstrate a magnetic sense in this species (e.g., Griffin, 1987).

Based on the goal orientation behavior of blindfolded humans over long distances, there is the possibility of a human magnetic sense (Baker, 1980; Baker, Mather, & Kennaugh, 1983). In one experiment (Baker, 1980), 31 blindfolded subjects were driven in a complex, roundabout way 16 kilometers from a home site. Of the total, 15 subjects wore bar magnets fastened at the back of their heads. When tested for their orientation (i.e., to indicate the direction of the home site), the estimations made by subjects who wore magnets were much less accurate than were those who did not. In fact the direction estimates of the group that did not wear magnets were significantly clustered toward the home site. The results, while far from conclusive, lend some support to the possibility of a magnetic sense for goal orientation in the blindfolded human. However, as with the research on pigeons, further confirmation of a magnetic sense for humans (and other mammals) is lacking. (See Gould & Able, 1981, and Adler & Pelke, 1985, for failures to replicate with humans. See Madden & Phillips, 1987, for negative findings with small mammals.) It appears that if a magnetic sense does indeed exist, it is an extremely fragile phenomenon.

MOTION SICKNESS

Whenever we submit ourselves to some vehicle or device that transports us passively we incur the risk of unusual or abnormal vestibular stimulation. Perhaps the most immediate, distressing and debilitating feature of abnormal vestibular stimulation is **motion sickness**. It is a widespread phenomenon that occurs in a number of species as well as the human, including monkeys, sheep, horses, some birds and fish, but apparently not in rabbits or guinea pigs (Treisman, 1977). In the human it is disabling and quite unpleasant, manifesting itself in dizziness, pallor, nausea, vertigo, "cold sweating," and general malaise and often it is accompanied by vomiting.

Because motion sickness is typically a result of unusual vestibular stimulation, individuals lacking vestibular function are not likely to suffer from it (see Reason & Brand, 1975). Situations that provoke motion sickness are often characterized by a condition where motion information signaled by the spatial sense of vision is, in some way, discrepant or mismatched with that signaled by the vestibular sense. In addition it appears that the potentially sickness-inducing motion must involve an acceleration of some kind. Thus motion sickness does not generally result from being transported at a steady speed regardless of whether the motion is linear or angular.

Some forms of motion are more effective in producing motion sickness than others. Motion sickness can be produced by repeated vertical motion of a relatively moderate frequency—for example, that pattern of motion occurring to the passive, seated passenger in rough air on an aircraft or in transit on a heaving ship in rough water.

Head Movement and Motion Sickness

During rotation of the body the potential for motion sickness is reduced if the position of the head is fixed relative to the body. It is higher if independent head movement is allowed. In the latter case very complex forces act on the vestibular organs due to the interaction of the movements of the rotation and those of the head.

Head movements made in space, where normal terrestrial gravitational force is lacking, provide an unusual challenge to the vestibular organs. Lackner and Graybiel (1986, 1987) studied the effects of certain head movements made during parabolic flight maneuvers on motion sickness (see Figure 3.9). Evidence of motion sickness was observed in various gravitoinertial conditions (such as in zero gravity and greater than normal levels of gravitoinertial force) for all forms of head movements studied; that is, motion sickness was observed, regardless of the level of the nonterrestrial gravitational force field or type of head movement. However there was evidence of a hierarchy in the susceptibility to motion sickness for the different types of head movements evaluated. Regardless of the level of gravitoinertial force, head movements made in *pitch* (refer to Figure 3.4), especially with eyes opened, were most stressful and effective in eliciting motion sickness, followed by

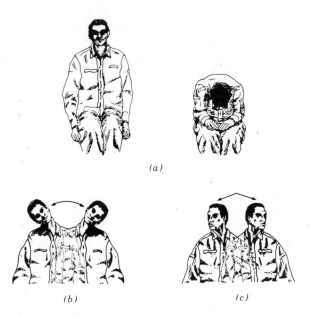

(a)

(b)   *(c)*

FIGURE 3.9.   Types of head movements tested by Lackner and Graybiel (1985, 1986). (*a*) Front-up head and trunk movements, made in pitch; (*b*) shoulder-to-shoulder roll movements; and (*c*) swivel or yaw movements. (Source: Lackner and Graybiel, "Head movements elicit symptoms of motion sickness during exposure to microgravity and macrogravity levels." Proceedings of the VII International Symposium of the International Society of Posturography, 1985, p. 172.)

head movements in *roll; yaw* head movements were the least effective in producing motion sickness.

Active Versus Passive Movement

Another important factor in the initiation of motion sickness, one clearly integral to those just indicated, is whether or not the subject is actively or passively moved. Generally motion sickness does not occur from self-produced movement. Thus a series of short, self-imposed, rapidly repeating movements, as in walking and running, are not effective. Similarly motion sickness is less common and severe even when the subject is passive to the transport, but is somehow in control of the movement. For example, the driver of a car, while still transported passively, is less likely to become physically distressed than is a passenger. Perhaps this occurs because the driver, the more active member, plays a principal role in the induction of the movement and anticipates the movements and makes compensatory motor adjustments toward maintaining proper orientation and matching the visual to the vestibular input.

Other events from common experience even in the absence of actual bodily movement also may cause motion sickness: visual disorientation, visual illusions of movement, unpleasant odors, uncomfortable warmth, drugs (e.g., alcohol, narcotics), inner ear infections, prolonged exposure to loud sounds, and certain emotional factors, such as anxiety, may contribute to motion sickness. Fortunately from an experiential point of view we eventually habituate to stimuli that initially produce motion sickness. Some conditions of motion are habituated to after a brief duration, whereas some require hours or longer. For example, even the motion-induced distress experienced by astronauts in orbit are eliminated after five days of flight (Lackner & Graybiel, 1986). So-called "antimotion sickness" drugs, which have a depressant effect on the central nervous system, such as dramamine, hyoscine, and scopolomine, reduce, inhibit, and may even prevent some of the distressing symptoms of motion sickness (e.g., Graybiel & Lackner, 1987).

Function of Motion Sickness   We must take note of an interesting speculation as to the survival value for some of the more compelling effects of motion sickness, such as nausea and vomiting (Treisman, 1977). Generally, the inputs for the visual and vestibular systems function together and are continuously coordinated with each other in maintaining gross bodily equilibrium and general orientation with the environment. That is, the vestibular and visual systems represent two consistent and closely correlated spatial reference systems. However, if a series of unusual or unpredictable changes are introduced to this correlation, such as those that occur with irregular movements, the effects of motion sickness appear: in particular, the compelling and disturbing effects of a gastrointestinal nature. The speculation given for this is based on the fact that the ingestion of naturally occurring toxins that affect the central nervous system are likely to alter the visual

sensory input and degrade motor coordination. That is, the ingestion of a neurotoxin also produces a disruption of the correlated vestibular and visual inputs. Accordingly, an emetic response to repeated sensory decorrelations would be beneficial and even adaptive for animals that might ingest neurotoxins in vegetation or carrion. Clearly, it would serve as an early warning system for detecting the central effects of neurotoxins and further provides a means of elimination. Supporting this idea is the observation that dogs that have had their vestibular organs removed do not vomit after ingesting poisons (Money & Cheung, 1983). Thus, according to this speculation, it is the avoidance of food poisoning which provides the biological function for motion sickness. Viewed this way the sickness is an adaptive response evoked by an inappropriate stimulus (i.e., motion) and is promoted by those conditions that generate repeated challenges to the two closely correlated and coupled spatial reference systems. It must be stressed, however, that this speculation as to the basis of the symptoms of motion sickness does not provide a full account of its etiology. It should be noted also that the possession of vision is not essential; that is, blind persons are susceptible to motion sickness (Dichgans & Brandt, 1978).

Finally, we must consider the wider biological implications of motion sickness and invoke the obvious: whereas motion sickness is a wretched and debilitating malady, it is also a self-inflicted one. Indeed it is a consequence of accepting the opportunities provided by the tremendous technological successes and advances made in improving human locomotion. In contrast, the human nervous system, along with those of many forms of terrestrial life, remains one of a totally self-propelled animal basically suited to move about in an essentially three-dimensional terrain, subject to normal earth gravity.

SUMMARY

In this chapter we have dealt with the mechanism by which organisms maintain a particular physical orientation to their surroundings. The sensory structures for this mechanism in mammalian forms of life are the utricle, saccule, and semicircular canals, collectively labeled the vestibular organs. The utricle and saccule reacts to gravity or linear acceleration, whereas the semicircular canals register the direction and extent of rotary acceleration.

It was noted that the effective stimulation for the vestibular organs is accelerations or decelerations —changes in the rate of motion; constant or uniform motion is not detectable.

A number of vestibular phenomena were described: vestibular nystagmus, the oculogyral illusion, vestibular habituation, deficiencies of the vestibular mechanism, and finally, motion sickness and its possible causes and implications.

KEY TERMS

Adaptation and habituation

Air-righting reflex

Gravitoinertial

Labyrinth

Magnetic sense

Mechanoreceptor

Ménière's disease

Motion sickness

Nystagmus

Oculogyral illusion

Optokinetic nystagmus

Otocyst

Otolith

Postrotary nystagmus

Saccule

Self-vection

Semicircular canals

Statocyst

Statolith

Utricle

Vestibular organs

STUDY QUESTIONS

1. Identify the organs and structures for registering gravity and general bodily orientation in space. What is their general mechanism?

2. Describe the mechanism used by mammals to register the direction and extent of rotary acceleration. What general principle do the saccule and utricle share with the semicircular canals?

3. The vestibular system is best suited to detect what kinds of environmental movement? It is least suited to register what sorts of movement?

4. Describe nystagmus. Consider the kinds of motion that initiate it. How can it be reduced?

5. Can changes in the visual environment, without corresponding vestibular stimulation, produce sensations of motion? Explain this phenomenon, drawing upon the research of the swinging-room. Consider the significance of the observation that maintaining one's balance on one foot with the eyes closed is quite difficult, whereas with the eyes opened it is not. What do these phenomena signify concerning the role of vision in maintaining balance?

6. Is the vestibular system subject to adaptation? What are some of the techniques used by persons such as dancers to overcome some of the side effects of sustained motion?

7. Consider some of the effects of defects in the vestibular organs. How do individuals who lack or possess defective vestibular organs react to motion?

8. Are there alternative mechanisms to the vestibular system for gaining information concerning bodily orientation? Which alternative mechanism is used by fish? What is the status of a magnetic sense for spatial orientation?

9. In what ways is motion sickness linked to normal and abnormal vestibular stimulation? Does motion sickness occur in all species? Are animals lacking vestibular organs subject to motion sickness?

10. What sorts of motion are most likely to promote motion sickness? Consider the role of head movements in initiating motion sickness. What kind of head movement is most provocative of motion sickness?

11. Explain why active movement is less likely to promote motion sickness than passive motion.

12. In what ways is motion sickness a result of advances in technology? Describe how motion sickness can be considered a self-inflicted disorder.

13. Explain the effects of motion sickness as an adaptive response to the ingestion of a neurotoxin.

4

THE AUDITORY SYSTEM

The ability to receive mechanical stimulation does not cease with the vestibular system. Indeed, it is from the vestibular structures that the auditory system evolved, carrying with it the general principle of hair-cell stimulation by some mechanical agent.

The purpose of this chapter is to identify the characteristics of auditory stimuli and to describe the sequence of physiological events and processes of the auditory system that ultimately result in the perception of sounds.

THE PHYSICAL STIMULUS

The "sounds" we hear are actually patterns of successive pressure disturbances occurring in some molecular medium, which may be gaseous, liquid, or solid; they cannot exist in the absence of a medium, that is, in a vacuum. If a guitar string is plucked, it vibrates back and forth compressing the air. Successive vibrations produce a pattern of periodic compressions and rarefactions of the surrounding air (see Figure 4.1). The pressure variations generated by vibrating bodies travel in wave form within the medium. The simplest kind of sound wave is one that causes successive pressure changes over time in the form of a single repeating sine wave. A graphic plot of the periodic compressions and rarefactions of a simple sound wave passing by a given point is shown in Figure 4.2. Though sound waves move progressively from place to place within the medium, the medium itself does not necessarily move. A visual analogy to sound wave propagation occurs when the surface of a pond is observed after throwing a rock into it. The entry of the stone causes disturbances that are seen as radiating circles of ripples that move progressively from place to place in the water without carrying the water with them.

The velocity of sound (v) is calculated by measuring the time required for a compression to move a known distance. The velocity of sound propagation varies with the physical characteristics of the medium. For example, at 15°C, the rate of sound transmission in air is about 1100 ft/sec (335 m/sec), about four times this in water, and another four times as fast in steel or glass. In general, the velocity of sound is inversely proportional to the compressibility of the conduction medium. The velocity of sound transmission also changes with temperature variation: in air, it increases about 2 feet (61 cm) per second for every degree centigrade rise in temperature.

The principal physical properties of sound waves may be characterized by their frequency, amplitude or intensity, and complexity.

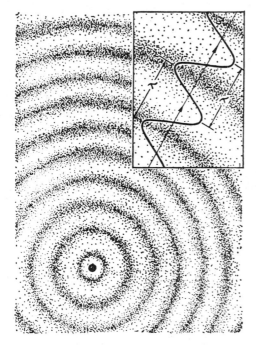

FIGURE 4.1.   The molecules of air around a sound source are distributed as in the figure. Some molecules are grouped closely and some loosely, representing compression and rarefaction of pressure, respectively. A graph of this variation in pressure, shown in the insert, appears as a sine wave. The Greek letter λ represents wavelength. (From D. R. Griffin, *Echoes of Bats and Men*, Anchor Books/Doubleday, Garden City, N.Y., 1959, p. 39. Reprinted by permission of the author.)

FREQUENCY

It is conventional in acoustics to characterize sound waves by the number of cycles or pressure changes completed in a second, that is, how rapidly the pressure changes. The measure is referred to as **frequency (f)**. The auditory sensation or psychological attribute most closely associated with variation in frequency is called **pitch.** (However, we will soon note that variation in other physical dimensions of sound pressure waves can also cause perceived changes in pitch.) The number of cycles per second is usually denoted by the term, **Hertz (Hz),** named for the nineteenth-century German physicist Heinrich

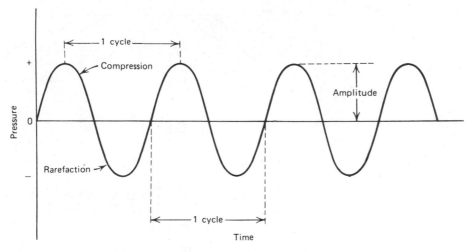

FIGURE 4.2.   A graphic sinusoidal representation of pressure variations—successive compressions and rarefactions—produced by a simple acoustic wave. The graph describes the pressure variations passing by a given point at a fixed distance from the sound source as a function of time. Notice that the *x* axis plots time. Shown are two examples of the length of time for a cycle to pass by a particular point in space. For example, the interval from wave peak to wave peak specifies the time needed to complete one cycle. The frequency of the sound wave is the number of cycles or pressure changes completed in a second. The amplitude of the sound, shown as the height of the wave, indicates the degree of compression (or rarefaction) of the sound wave.

Hertz. It is generally accepted that the range of hearing in the human young adult extends between 20 and 20,000 Hz.

The linear distance between two successive compressions is called the **wavelength** (λ, see Figure 4.1). Wavelength and frequency are inversely related in that wavelength equals sound propagation velocity divided by frequency or $\lambda = v/f$ (see Figure 4.3). Thus a 1100 Hz sound wave traveling at 1100 ft/sec (335 m/sec) has a wavelength of 1 foot (30.48 cm). A higher frequency means more pressure changes occur in a given unit of time and occur closer to each other in space, thus producing a shorter wavelength. Normally the maintenance of a sound of constant frequency is unexpected. Rather, sounds emitted from the environment, in particular animal vocalizations and speech, manifest patterned changes in frequency. Changes in the frequency of a continually vibrating body are referred to as **frequency modulations.** The frequencies of some familiar sound sources are indicated in Figure 4.4.

AMPLITUDE

As Figure 4.2 indicates, sound waves also vary in their **amplitude,** which refers to the extent of displacement of the vibrating particles in either direction from the position of rest. The psychological attribute of **loudness** depends to a great extent on the amplitude of the sound waves. (Although again, this is not an exclusive relationship and variation on other physical dimensions, such as frequency, for example, can produce changes in loudness.) Amplitude, which corresponds to the intensity of the vibration, is a function of the force applied to the sound-emitting source; in practice, the fundamental measure of amplitude is pressure variation. (Technically, the **intensity** of a sound can be measured in terms of pressure, power, or energy which are related to one another. Thus, each measure provides a basic description of the vibration of an object.) **Pressure** is force per unit area and sound pressure can be expressed in a number of different units. Tradition-

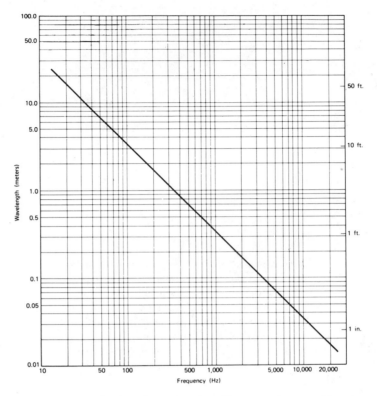

FIGURE 4.3. Wavelength as a function of frequency (measured in air at 15°C).

ally, it is measured in dynes per square centimeter (dynes/cm²); sometimes sound pressure is stated in the equivalent unit microbar (μbar). More recently employed units of pressure variation are Newtons per square meter (N/m²) and the microPascal (μPa).

The ear is sensitive to an enormously wide range of pressures. The range in sensitivity from the strongest to the weakest sound that the human can hear is of the order of billions to 1. Because of this immense range it has been found convenient to use a logarithmic scale of pressures called the **decibel (dB)** scale, named in honor of Alexander Graham Bell. In essence the scale compresses or abbreviates the tremendous range of possible values so that the entire auditory amplitude scale is contained within a range of values from 0 to 160, approximately. The decibel is defined as one-tenth of a *Bel*, which, in turn, is

defined as the common logarithm of the ratio between two powers or energies. The number of decibels is thus defined as 10 times the logarithm of the ratio of two energies. However, decibels can also be used to express the ratio of two pressures. Specifically, in a sound wave, power is proportional to the square of the pressure. The decibel formulas for sound pressure are

$$N_{dB} = 10 \, \log_{10} \frac{P_1^2}{P_2^2}$$

or

$$N_{dB} = 20 \, \log_{10} \frac{P_1}{P_2}$$

where N_{dB} is the number of decibels, P_1 is the sound pressure to be measured, and P_2 is a standard reference pressure, (0.0002 dynes/cm² or 20 μPa),

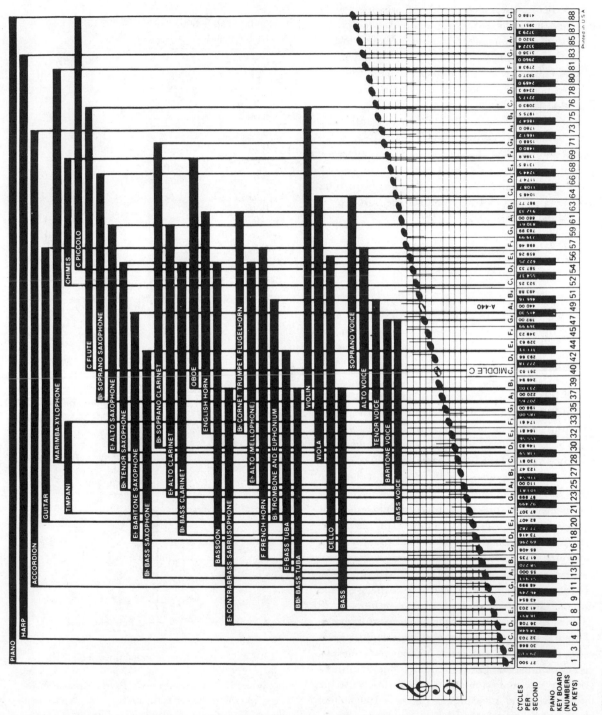

FIGURE 4.4. Tonal frequencies of keyboard, the human voice, and various orchestral instruments. (Courtesy of Conn Ltd., Oakbrook, Ill.)

51

chosen because it is close to the average threshold of human hearing (for a 1000-Hz tone). (Notice that the logarithm of any number squared is equal to two times the logarithm of the number; accordingly in the second equation, we have transposed the 2 from the exponents of the pressures to the coefficient of 10.) Stimulus amplitude, utilizing the reference pressure of 0.0002 dynes/cm^2 or 20 μPa, is conventionally termed **sound pressure level (SPL).** Use of the decibel scale eliminates any absolute zero reference point; the threshold level is taken as the starting level. As an example, a sound with a pressure of 0.02 dynes/cm^2, 100 times the reference pressure, corresponds to 40 dB since

$$N_{dB} = 20 \log_{10} \frac{0.02 \text{ dynes/cm}^2}{0.0002 \text{ dynes/cm}^2}$$
$$= 20 \log_{10} 100 = 40 \text{ dB}$$

Accordingly, a sound with a pressure of 0.002 dynes/cm^2 equals 20 dB, and a sound whose pressure level is 0.2 dynes/cm^2 equals 60 dB. Thus a sound 10 times the reference pressure corresponds to a difference of 20 dB, a sound 100 times the reference pressure corresponds to a difference of 40 dB, and a sound 1000 times the reference pressure corresponds to a difference of 60 dB. In other words, for each tenfold increase in sound pressure, we must add 20 dB. Table 4.1 shows the relationship between sound pressure ratios (SPL) and decibel values. Some common sound sources and their decibel values are given in Figure 4.5.

It should be stressed that the critical component in the calculation of the decibel is the reference pressure against which other sound pressures are compared. We have described decibels with respect to a reference pressure that approximates the least pressure necessary for the *average* human observer to hear a 1000-Hz tone [i.e., 0.0002 dynes/cm^2 or 20 μPa (SPL)]. Another reference employed is the value of the threshold pressure for hearing at the frequency of the tone. That is, the sound pressure for a tone of a given frequency is specified relative to the threshold pressure for that frequency. Notice that because the threshold sound pressure varies as a function of frequency, a different reference pressure is neces-

Table 4.1
Relation between Sound Pressure Ratios (SPL) and Decibel Values

Pressure Ratios (P_1/P_2)	Decibels (SPL)
0.0001	−80
0.001	−60
0.01	−40
0.1	−20
1.0	0
2.0	6.0
3.0	9.5
10.0	20
100.0	40
1000.0	60
10,000.0	80

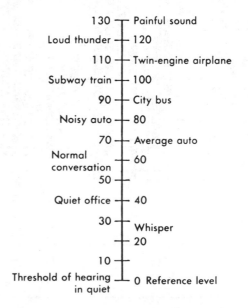

FIGURE 4.5. Approximate sound pressure levels in decibels (SPL) of various common sounds. (From S. S. Stevens and H. Davis, *Hearing: Its Psychology and Physiology*, John Wiley, New York, 1938, p. 31. Reprinted by permission of the publisher.)

sary for each frequency. When the threshold for each frequency is used as a reference, the sound pressure ratio in decibels is referred to as the **sensation level** or **SL.** The point of this, of course, is that the reference pressure should be given in order for the decibel to have precise meaning.

COMPLEXITY

The sounds that occur in nature rarely if ever possess the simple sinusoidal form of Figure 4.2. Indeed, a sound described by a perfect sine curve is usually a laboratory achievement requiring special equipment such as tuning forks or an audio oscillator. Most natural sound-producing sources emit sounds that possess a complex waveform. The psychological dimension corresponding to the sound's complexity is termed **timbre.** The **complexity** of sound results because vibrating bodies do not do so at a single frequency. In general, a body vibrates simultaneously at frequencies that are multiples of the **fundamental tone** or **first harmonic,** that is, the lowest tone of a series of tones. If a violin string is plucked, it vibrates as a whole, alternately compressing and rarefying the air molecules. However, in addition to the full length of vibration (the fundamental tone) there are simultaneous vibrations of shorter lengths (**overtones** or **harmonics**) that are precise divisions of the string's length (see Figure 4.6). It is partly on the basis of tonal complexity that we are able to differentiate between musical instruments that emit tones at the same frequency and amplitude.

Some examples of complex waveforms are shown in Figure 4.7.

Fourier Analysis   One of the tools of complex sound wave analysis is based on a mathematical theorem devised in the early nineteenth century by the French physicist-mathematician, Jean Baptiste Fourier. Briefly, Fourier's theorem states that it is possible to express any complex periodic wave form as the sum of a discrete series of simple sine waves, each with its own frequency and amplitude. The breakdown of a complex waveform into its components is called **Fourier analysis.** The construction of a complex waveform from a series of sinusoidal components is called **Fourier synthesis.** As an example of how a complex wave is so constructed, examine Figure 4.8. A complete cycle of the complex wave is shown at the lower right (roughly a square

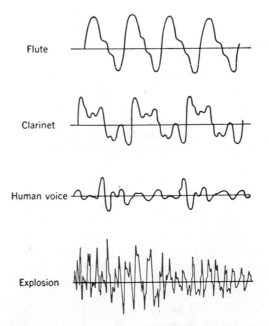

FIGURE 4.7.   Typical sound waves. The first three are periodic waves, repeated regularly. The last is highly irregular. (From E. G. Boring, H. S. Langfeld, and H. P. Weld, *Foundations of Psychology*, John Wiley, New York, 1948, p. 315. Reprinted by permission of the publisher.)

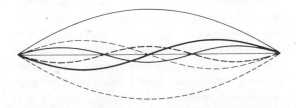

FIGURE 4.6.   The figure shows the complex way in which a plucked string vibrates. In addition to the full-length vibration, which produces the string's fundamental tone, there are simultaneous vibrations of shorter lengths (harmonics) that are precise divisions of the string's length—in this example, one-half and one-third.

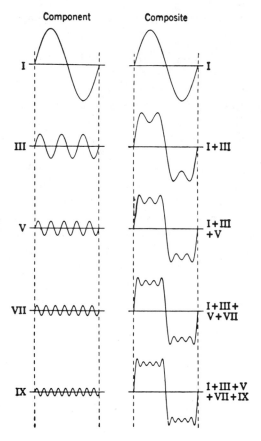

Component   Composite

I

III   I+III

V   I+III
             +V

VII   I+III+
             V+VII

IX   I+III+V
             +VII+IX

FIGURE 4.8. Simple waves add up to a complex wave. The first five harmonic components of a single cycle of a "square wave" are shown in the left column. The column at right shows the progressive change from a simple sine wave as each component is added. The relative frequency of each component corresponds to the numbers I, III, V, VII, and IX, to the left of each line. If enough additional odd harmonics were added, the "square wave," a rectangular form that is already apparent in the form at the lower right corner of the figure, would be even more closely approximated. (From E. G. Boring, H. S. Langfeld, and H. P. Weld, *Foundations of Psychology*, John Wiley, New York, 1948, p. 316. Reprinted by permission of the publisher.)

wave produced by some sirens). A Fourier analysis of this tone reveals that five components, illustrated by the left column of Figure 4.8, comprise it. In the right column are shown the composite waveforms as each

component is added in successive steps. Mathematically, Fourier analysis begins with a fundamental frequency that is the same as the frequency of the complex wave. To the fundamental frequency are added sine waves of higher frequencies that are multiples of the fundamental frequency.

The ear appears to be able to perform a crude Fourier analysis on a complex wave and sends information about which frequencies are present to higher auditory centers. As a consequence, we are able to detect in a complex tone many of its frequency components. This fact, known as **Ohm's acoustical law,** states (with certain qualifications) that when exposed to a complex sound created by mixing several tones, we have the capability to hear each tone separately. In practical terms, Ohm's law refers to a true aspect of hearing. For example, individuals who can identify two notes of a piano when they are sounded one at a time may identify the two notes when they are simultaneously sounded.

The component sine waves of the complex wave forms that represent a musical note, then, bear a simple relationship to each other. Each is an overtone or harmonic of the fundamental note, and the frequency of each overtone is a multiple of the fundamental frequency. However notes of musical instruments are complex in different ways. Both the number of overtones and their amplitudes are determined by the physical properties of the vibrating body and the forces acting upon it.

RESONANCE

Most solid objects vibrate at a specific frequency when struck or driven with the necessary force. The frequency at which the object vibrates is called its *natural* or *resonant* frequency, and it is a function of the mass and stiffness or tension of the object. Many different driving forces, including sound pressure, can cause an object to vibrate sympathetically or to *resonate*. The phenomenon of causing an object to vibrate when the frequency of a sound-emitting source matches the natural or resonant frequency of the object is referred to as **resonance.** Generally the ease with which the resonant vibration or frequency enhancement occurs depends upon how closely the driving frequency matches the object's resonant frequency. An emitted sound having the same frequency as the resonant frequency of an object will be most likely to set the object into sympathetic vibration. The notion of resonance will become significant when we discuss sound waves entering the ear, since the outer ear and ear canal resonate to particular frequencies and thus favor and amplify specific sounds entering it.

PHASE

A complete sound pressure wave or cycle extends from a position of rest to compression to rest to rarefaction and to rest again (refer to Figure 4.2). A complete cycle, or phase, is specified as extending for 360°. The beginning is taken as 0°, the first compression peak as 90°, rest as 180°, rarefaction peak as 270°, and rest again as 360°. **Phase** refers to that part of the cycle the sound wave has reached at a given point in time. Two sounds of the same frequency, simultaneously sounded, will move alike at every instant and their waveforms will be "in phase." However, if two sounds are produced of the same frequency but displaced slightly in time, their waveforms will differ in the time at which the waves rest or reach compression. For example, the same tone emitted from two separate speakers may differ in phase if they must travel different distances to reach a listener's ear. Alternatively, a tone from a single speaker may have to travel different distances to reach each of the two ears of a listener, causing a difference in arrival time (and, therefore, phase) at the two ears. These sounds will be "out of phase" and the phase difference is expressed in degrees. Some examples of phase differences are given in Figure 4.9. If one sine wave is in compression one-quarter of a cycle sooner than another, the waves are 90° out of phase (Figure 4.9, wave *B*). If one wave occurs one-half of a cycle sooner than the other, they are 180° out of phase (Figure 4.9, wave *C*). In this case, if both waves have the same frequency and amplitude, they would exert opposite effects on the air pressure, canceling each other's effects, and no sound would be heard. With respect to Figure 4.9, wave *C*, which appears as a "mirror image" of wave *A*, is said to have the "reverse" phase of wave *A*.

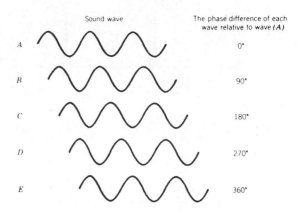

FIGURE 4.9.   Phase differences. The phase difference between two waves is produced by differences in the time at which the waves reach compression. In this example, the phase differences are calculated relative to wave *A*. For example, wave *B* reaches its peak compression 90° after wave *A*, wave *C* reaches compression 180° after wave *A*, and so on. (From W. A. van Bergeijk, J. R. Pierce, and E. E. David, Jr., *Waves and the Ear*, Anchor/Doubleday, Garden City, N.Y., 1960, p. 85. Reprinted by permission of Doubleday & Company, Inc.)

Although in certain instances we may be aware of the vibratory nature of sound (e.g., a very low-frequency note of a pipe organ), we do not generally perceive the time of arrival of compressions of high-frequency waves. However, there is a perceptible effect of phase with complex sounds. In part, the waveform of a complex sound depends on the relative times of arrival of the wave crests of the component frequencies comprising it (see the example of Figure 4.10). Although the frequencies and intensities of the components remain constant, altering the relative phases of the components—having their compressions occur at different times relative to one another—alters the waveform and the quality of sound.

ANATOMY AND MECHANISMS OF THE EAR

We now turn to an analysis of the mechanisms of the ear that enable the complex pressure variations just described to produce the perception of sound. Spe-

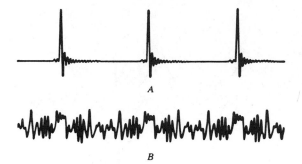

FIGURE 4.10. The effect of phase difference on complex sounds. The waveforms for two complex sounds are shown by *A* and *B*. Each complex wave is the result of the same 32 component sine waves of different frequencies. However, the complex wave forms differ because the peaks of the component sine waves for each complex wave have different relative phases. Thus, the relative phases of the component sine waves were adjusted so that their arrivals were at different times relative to one another, and the complex sound waves are heard as very different. The upper wave, *A*, sounds harsher, lower in pitch, and somewhat louder than wave *B*. (From W. A. van Bergeijk, J. R. Pierce, and E. E. David, Jr., *Waves and the Ear*, Anchor/Doubleday, Garden City, N.Y., 1960, p. 86. Reprinted by permission of Doubleday & Company, Inc.)

cifically, our concern is with the receptor organs and mechanisms that transduce sound energy into nerve impulses and how these organs function. Though there are numerous structures in nature for picking up acoustic energy, we will focus primarily on the human ear (Figure 4.11*a*). As shown in Figure 4.11*b*, this auditory system can be grossly divided into three major structural components: the outer ear, the middle ear, and the inner ear.

THE OUTER EAR

The outer ear of mammals consists of an earflap called the **pinna** or **auricle,** the **external auditory canal** (or the **external auditory meatus**), and the **eardrum** (or **tympanic membrane**). The pinna, a wrinkled or convoluted vestigial flap that lies on the side of the head, functions to protect the sensitive and delicate inner structures, to prevent foreign bodies from entering the ear passage, and to collect and funnel air vibrations into the external auditory canal. The shell-like folds of the pinna serve to amplify high-frequency sounds of around 5000 Hz; this increase in sound intensity is due to resonance effects. It has been reported that pinnae may aid slightly in the localization of sounds (e.g., Batteau, 1968; Freedman & Fisher, 1968). Although the human normally does not have functional control over the muscle system that controls the pinnae, many mammals do; it is common to observe many lower mammals orient their pinnae toward the direction of a sound source. Pinnae are not found in all mammals. Sea-dwelling mammals such as the dolphin and whale do not possess pinnae perhaps because water-born sound waves would tend to pass directly through them; moreover, the protuberance created by earflaps would undermine the streamlining of their outer body surface and hinder mobility. This may also be the reason lower vertebrates such as frogs, reptiles, and birds lack pinnae. In fact, some birds have a covering of feathers over their ear passage that may even hinder their hearing, but it is required to reduce wind noise during flight (Marler & Hamilton, 1966).

The external auditory canal is a cylindrical cavity about 2.5 to 3 cm long and 7 mm in diameter, open on the outside and bounded on the inside. It functions primarily to conduct vibrations to the eardrum, but it also acts as a protective device against foreign bodies and it serves the purpose of controlling the temperature and humidity in the vicinity of the eardrum. The auditory canal acts like a horn, especially for sound frequencies around 3000 Hz, reinforcing, amplifying, and prolonging the sound pressure by induced vibrations or resonance. At this resonant frequency the sensitivity of the ear can be increased by as much as 8 to 10 dB (Békésy & Rosenblith, 1951; Gulick, 1971). Of interest is the fact that in the human this frequency corresponds closely to the frequency to which the auditory system is most sensitive. Because of the combined resonance effects of the pinna and external auditory canal, there is a 10- to 15-dB gain for frequencies that range from 1500 to 7000 Hz.

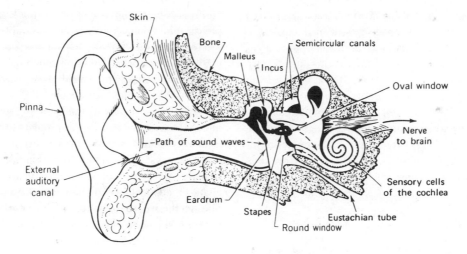

FIGURE 4.11a. A semischematic drawing showing the gross anatomy of the ear. Vibrations entering the external auditory canal affect the eardrum. Vibrations of the drum are transmitted through the middle ear by the chain of bones—malleus (hammer), incus (anvil), stapes (stirrup). The foot of the stapes carries the vibration to the fluid of the cochlea. (Source: H. Davis, *Hearing and Deafness: A Guide for Laymen*, 1947, Murray Hill.)

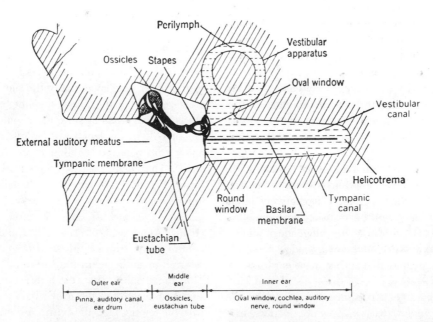

FIGURE 4.11b. Schematic drawing of the ear. Notice that the cochlea is uncoiled in this drawing (as Fig. 4.11c illustrates). When the footplate of the stapes moves inward, the fluid inside the cochlea flows in the direction of the helicotrema and makes the round window membrane bulge outward. (From G. von Békésy and W. A. Rosenblith, "The mechanical properties of the ear," in S. S. Stevens (Ed.), *Handbook of Experimental Psychology*, John Wiley, New York, 1951, p. 1076. Reprinted by permission of the publisher.)

The eardrum, a thin, fibrous membrane pulled slightly inward at its center, is stretched across the inner end of the auditory canal and seals off the cavity of the middle ear. The eardrum vibrates in response to the pressure waves of sound. It is at the eardrum that pressure variations are transformed into mechanical motion. The displacements of the eardrum by pressure waves required to produce hearing are minute. It has been cited that for the detection of some sound frequencies near 3000 Hz the vibrations of the eardrum are as small as one-billionth of a centimeter.

THE MIDDLE EAR

The general function of the middle ear is to transmit the vibratory motions of the eardrum to the inner ear. The eardrum closes off the air-filled cavity of the middle ear. Attached to the eardrum and vibrating with it is the **hammer** or **malleus,** the first of a chain of three small bones (the smallest bones in the human body) called **ossicles** (known by both their English and Latin names) that link the inner ear to the middle ear. The hammer connects to the **anvil** or **incus,** which in turn connects to the **stirrup** or **stapes,** whose footplate finally connects to the **oval window** of the inner ear. The ossicles, which have a total length of about 18 mm, are firmly connected by ligaments and transmit the vibrations acting on the eardrum by a lever system—with the motion of the stapes footplate acting as a piston—to the oval window.

The eardrum (with an average area of about 70 mm^2) is considerably larger than the area of the foot of the stapes (3 mm^2). Thus, comparatively large motions at the eardrum are transformed to smaller motions at the oval window. This difference produces an increase in pressure on the oval window about 25 to 30 times as great as that acting on the eardrum. In brief, small air pressure variations, distributed over the relatively larger eardrum, are concentrated on the smaller oval window with an increase in pressure. Notice that this increase in pressure is a requirement owing to the change in sound wave medium from the aerial vibrations of the middle ear cavity to the fluid-filled inner ear chambers. In other words, the eardrum vibrates in response to small changes in pressure in the air, an easily compressible medium, whereas the oval window must move against the fluid of the inner ear, which requires much more pressure to be set in motion, since fluid is considerably more resistant to movement than is air.

In addition to making the incoming sound waves more effective, the middle ear protects the inner ear from very intense sounds (hence very intense pressure changes). The middle ear chamber, though sealed off from outside atmospheric pressure changes, connects with the back of the mouth cavity through the **Eustachian tube.** This connection permits pressure from the outside to be equalized with air pressure in the middle ear. When the mouth is open, air pressure on both sides of the eardrum is equalized. Extreme pressure differences on both sides of the eardrum may produce abnormal and painful membrane displacements. When one is confronted with extremely loud sounds or abrupt air pressure changes as from altitude changes, the sudden pressure change may burst the eardrum unless the mouth is kept open.

THE INNER EAR

Next in the relay of pressure variations is movement in the inner ear, specifically the movement of the stapes exerted on the fluid of the inner ear. The inner ear is a small, tubular structure about 25 to 35 mm (about $1\frac{1}{2}$ in.) in length, resembling a snail shell, and for this reason it is called the **cochlea** (Latin for snail). The cochlea is coiled on itself about three turns. Figure 4.11c shows a schematic of the cochlea, uncoiled to show the parts (see also Figure 4.11d). The cochlea contains three chambers or canals. Along most of its length it is divided by its central canal, the **cochlear duct** or **canal** (also referred to as the **scala media**) into two chambers. The upper canal, the **vestibular canal** (or **scala vestibuli**), starts at the oval window and connects with the lower canal, the **tympanic canal** (or **scala tympani**), at the tip or apex of the cochlea by way of a small opening called the **helicotrema.** A membrane-covered opening called the **round window,** which expands to accommodate fluid displaced by

Cochlea

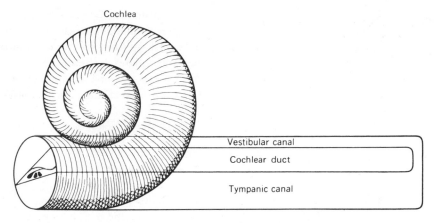

Vestibular canal

Cochlear duct

Tympanic canal

FIGURE 4.11*c.*   Schematic of the cochlea uncoiled to show the canals.

the stapes against the oval window, is found at the basal part of the tympanic canal. The vestibular and tympanic canals are fluid-filled. The cochlear duct is also fluid-filled, and it does not directly communicate with the other two canals. The cochlear duct is bounded by two membranes. It is divided from the vestibular canal by **Reissner's membrane** and it is

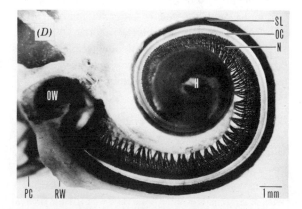

FIGURE 4.11*d.*   Photograph of the human cochlea structure. H—helicotrema, OC—organ of Corti, N—auditory nerve fibers, OW—oval window, RW—round window. (From L. G. Johnsson and J. E. Hawkins, "Sensory and neural degeneration with aging, as seen in microdissections of the human inner ear," *Annals of Otology, Rhinology and Laryngology, 81,* 1972, p. 181. Reprinted by permission.)

divided from the tympanic canal by the **basilar membrane,** a tough but flexible membrane anchored to a bony shelf on one side of the wall of the cochlea and by a ligament on the other. It is the basilar membrane that is considered to differentially displace in response to the frequency of the sound. Whereas the cochlea narrows toward the apex, the basilar membrane becomes progressively wider (see Figure 4.12). At the base, near the stapes, it measures less than a tenth of a millimeter in width; near the apical or helicotrema end it broadens to about half a millimeter. In addition, the basilar membrane at the base of the cochlea is about 100 times stiffer than it is at the apex.

It is within the cochlear duct that the specialized sensory structures, nerves, and supporting tissues for transducing vibrations to nerve impulses are found. Collectively these form a receptor structure called the **organ of Corti,** which rests on and extends along the basilar membrane. The organ of Corti is shown in Figure 4.13. It contains columns of specialized hair cells arranged in two sets, divided by an arch (Tunnel of Corti), that are called the **inner hair cells** and the **outer hair cells** and number about 3500 and 20,000, respectively. In turn, each hair cell has up to 100 cilia (Flock, 1977). The inner set has a single column of hair cells, whereas the outer set has three columns. There are some 50,000 auditory nerve fibers that connect with the inner and

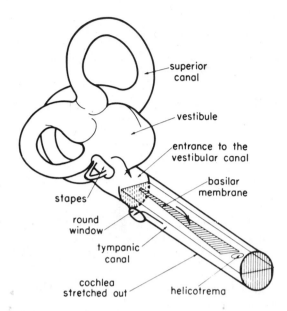

FIGURE 4.12. Schematic drawing of the inner ear with the cochlea uncoiled. Notice that the basilar membrane increases in width as it extends toward the helicotrema. (From G. von Békésy, "Experimental models of the cochlea with and without nerve supply," in G. L. Rasmussen and W. F. Windle (Eds.), *Neural Mechanisms of the Auditory and Vestibular Systems*, Charles C Thomas, Springfield, Ill., 1960; also see G. von Békésy, *Sensory Inhibition*, Princeton University Press, Princeton, N.J., 1967, p. 137. Reprinted by permission of the publisher.)

outer hair cells, but the distribution is neither equal nor proportional to the number of inner and outer hair cells: about 90 to 95% of the auditory nerve fibers make contact with the relatively sparse inner hair cells, whereas the remaining 5 to 10% of the nerve fibers link with the more numerous outer hair cells. These sensory hair cells are the ultimate transducers of mechanical vibrations into nerve impulses. The longer filaments or cilia of the outer hair cells attach to an overhanging **tectorial membrane.** The tectorial membrane is attached at only one end and the other end extends partially across the cochlear duct. Motion of the basilar membrane that occurs in response to vibrations produced in the cochlea, initiated by movement of the stapes against the oval

window, bend the cilia of the hair cells against the tectorial membrane in a shearing action (see Figure 4.14). This produces stimulation of the nerve endings and initiates the first stage in the neural conduction process whereby mechanical energy in a vibratory form is transformed into the nerve impulse.

THE AUDITORY NERVE

Nerve fibers from the hair cells of the organ of Corti originate all along the basilar membrane and make up the auditory nerve. The separate fibers are bundled together in such a way that fibers from neighboring regions on the basilar membrane tend to remain together as they ascend to the major divisions of the cochlear nucleus leading to the brain. There is a functional significance to this. The apex of the basilar membrane near the helicotrema seems to be particularly concerned with encoding low-frequency sound waves into neural responses, while successively higher frequencies stimulate neurons progressively closer to the base near the stapes (see Figure 4.15). Therefore, this spatial arrangement of neural elements, corresponding to the separation of different frequencies—called **tonotopic** organization—is a systematic way to keep information about similar frequencies represented in adjacent neural areas. Thus, a particular part of the auditory cortex is selectively responsive to particular frequencies. In fact specificity in response to frequency appears evident at all levels of the auditory system.

Microelectrode Recording of the Auditory Nerve Measures of the electrical activity of the individual fibers of the auditory nerve in response to various sounds indicate that a form of specificity exists within the auditory nerve. Although many fibers react to various sound characteristics, there is a dominant class of fibers sometimes referred to as **tuned fibers** that are frequency selective; that is, they are maximally sensitive to sounds over a very narrow range of frequencies. As outlined in the **frequency tuning curves** of Figure 4.16, each tuned fiber has a **characteristic** or **best frequency** to which it is most sensitive—a frequency where the intensity necessary to reach its absolute threshold is at a

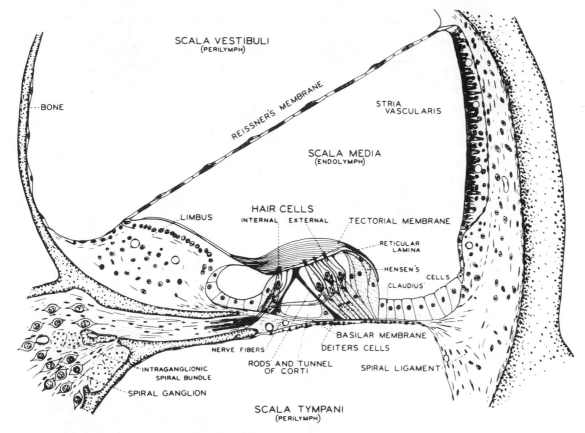

FIGURE 4.13. Diagrammatic cross section of the canals of the cochlea. The cochlear duct, bounded by Reissner's membrane, contains the organ of Corti with its inner (labeled "internal") and outer ("external") hair cells that are the receptors for hearing.

minimum. Thus, by varying frequency, it is possible to determine the best or characteristic frequency of an auditory fiber. It follows that the sensitivity of the fiber decreases and its absolute threshold rises with changes from the best frequency in either direction.

From such measurements, it has been established that the auditory nerve possesses fibers that are selectively and rather sharply tuned to frequencies extending over the entire range of audibility. It is assumed that the finely tuned nature of the fibers is due, in part, to the mechanical properties of the basilar membrane. We will return to the role played by the auditory nerve on frequency and intensity response in a forthcoming section.

BONE CONDUCTION

An alternative route of sound transmission is available, called **bone conduction.** This involves transmission contact between the head and a vibrating body bypassing the eardrum, ossicles, and other middle-ear structures. In bone conduction, the vibration of the skull produces compression in the bones and stimulates the cochlea directly. However, bone conduction is very inefficient relative to normal middle-ear conduction.

It is quite easy to experience the effects of bone conduction: close the auditory canal with ear plugs or even the fingertips and hum or speak. The

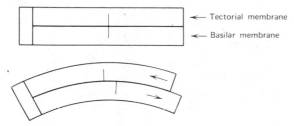

FIGURE 4.14. Schematic of shearing action between the tectorial membrane and the basilar membrane. Shearing action occurs when two flexible strips are joined at one end and then bent; the strips move in opposite directions relative to each other. It is the operation of this principle that produces the shearing action within the cochlear duct. That is, the motion of the basilar membrane produces a bending of the cilia of the hair cells against the tectorial membrane in a shearing action.

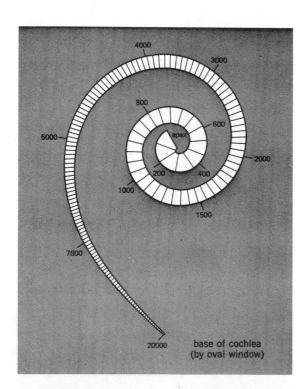

FIGURE 4.15. Map of frequency analysis on basilar membrane. Presumed location on the basilar membrane that is maximally stimulated depends on the frequency of the sound. (After McClintic, 1978, p. 230.)

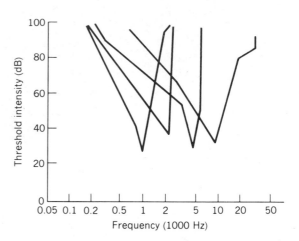

FIGURE 4.16. Frequency tuning curves for four different auditory nerve fibers. Observe that the response of a given fiber varies with stimulus frequency. Each curve is generated by determining the lowest intensity of a tone of a specific frequency necessary to produce a detectable or threshold response. The frequency of the tone to which the absolute threshold of a given fiber is at a minimum is called its characteristic or best frequency. Thus, for example, the second fiber yields a threshold response when stimulated by its best stimulus of about 2000 Hz, that is, 2(1000 Hz), at about 38 dB. Observe that for a given nerve fiber its threshold increases with a change in frequency from its best stimulus in either direction.

Note that the frequency axis is plotted on a logarithmic scale. (Based on data of Katsuki, Watanabe, & Suga, 1959; Katsuki, 1961).

vibrations of the air in the oral cavity are transmitted to the cheeks and from there to the lower jaw. The sounds heard are bone-conducted sounds that have reached the cochlea without access to the outer portions of the auditory system. This explains why the playback of a tape-recorded voice sounds strange and less familiar to the speaker than to his or her friends. Actually, it is not the voice that one usually hears when speaking. Normally the speaker hears not only the air-conducted sounds that others hear but also the sounds transmitted by bone conduction; however, only air-conducted sound has been recorded.

Animals living close to the ground like the snake, who is without eardrums, and some amphibia, have little need for the reception of airborne sounds; however, low-frequency vibrations from the ground are received by these animals by a form of bone conduction.

FUNCTIONING OF THE INNER EAR

The chain of vibration transmission that produces the phenomenon of hearing normally proceeds from the eardrum to the ossicles to the oval window and then to the cochlea. However, it is the movement of the cochlear duct that activates and differentially affects the sense cells and associated nerve fibers. Thus, to understand the production of auditory messages we must primarily focus on how the basilar membrane and the organ of Corti respond to incoming sound waves.

There are two main theories to account for the way in which the sensory structures of the ear function to enable frequency reception. Although there are a number of variations, they are conventionally referred to as the place theory and the frequency theory.

THE PLACE THEORY

The **place theory** assumes that the organ of Corti is organized in a tonotopic fashion, that is, that there is an orderly spatial representation of stimulus frequency on the basilar membrane (see Figure 4.15). Specifically, sensory cells near the base of the basilar membrane are more affected by tones of high frequency, and sense cells located near the apex or helicotrema are more likely to be stimulated by low-frequency tones. Moreover, as we have noted, the nerve fibers from the basilar membrane to the auditory cortex are organized in accordance with the part of the basilar membrane they innervate. Place theories thus maintain that different regions of the basilar membrane are stimulated by different frequencies—in short, different frequencies excite different auditory nerve fibers.

An early version of a place theory was proposed by Hermann L. F. von Helmholtz in 1863 based on assumed resonance properties of the cochlea. However, the major contemporary proponent of a place theory is Georg von Békésy, the Nobel laureate (1961, for medicine and physiology). Békésy has traced and documented the operation of the inner ear and has reported a number of research findings that support a place theory of hearing.

Traveling Wave Motion in the Cochlea Békésy's fundamental research findings concern the hydrodynamics (i.e., transmission in a fluid medium) of the inner ear. The basilar membrane is a flexible membrane not under tension. When vibrated by fluid motion, it shows **traveling wave** motion. As Figures 4.17a and 4.17b show, a traveling wave is a wave form whose point of maximal displacement moves within an envelope. According to Békésy, the general operation of the auditory process is that a traveling sound wave of fluid-conducted displacement, produced at the oval window by the action of the stapes, begins in the stiffer, narrow region of the basilar membrane and travels to the broader, less stiff portion of the basilar membrane. On route the wave stimulates the cochlear canal and displaces its components, in particular, the cilia of the hair cells. High-frequency vibrations create traveling waves whose points of maximal displacement are near the

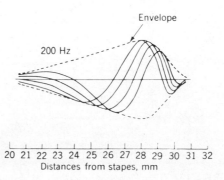

FIGURE 4.17a. Various momentary positions within a cycle and the envelope formed of a traveling wave along the basilar membrane for a tone of 200 Hz. (From Békésy, 1953.)

Organ of Corti

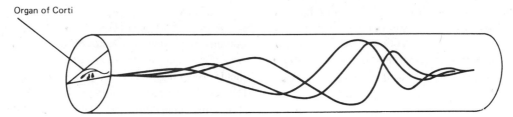

FIGURE 4.17*b*. A traveling wave is described within the schematic cochlea. The cochlea is shown uncoiled to

indicate how the points of maximal displacement of the waveform moves within the cochlea.

stapes and then quickly dissipate (see Figure 4.17*c*), whereas low-frequency vibrations produce traveling waves with peaks near the helicotrema. Thus, the differential action of the basilar membrane provides the basis of a frequency analysis.

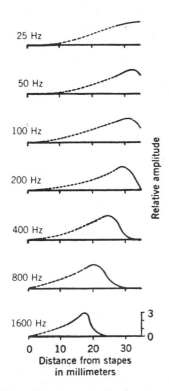

FIGURE 4.17*c*. Envelopes of vibrations for various frequencies over the basilar membrane in a human cadaver. The maximum displacement amplitude moves toward the stapes as frequency is increased. (From Békésy, 1949.)

A number of ingenious experiments by Békésy supports the notion of the transport of vibrations by traveling waves. The sensory effects of much of the physical activity that occurs in the cochlear duct has been verified by a series of mechanical models designed by Békésy (1955) that accurately reproduce many of the elastic properties and couplings among components of the ear.

In addition to his construction of mechanical models, Békésy attempted to observe the activity of the cochlea directly. Békésy observed wave motion in the basilar membrane in fresh and preserved specimens of human and animal cochleae. In some investigations he placed particles of fine metals or carbon in the cochlea and observed their movements during stimulation under magnification. He also cut windows into the human cochleae at various locations and noted the vibration pattern of the basilar membrane for selected frequencies. The results of some of these investigations are presented in Figure 4.17*c*. The patterns of movements were in close correspondence with those obtained with the mechanical models. In short, the locus of maximal displacement of the basilar membrane varies progressively with changes in the frequency of stimulation at the oval window.

In addition to accounting for frequency reception, a place theory explanation has also been proposed to explain how intensity (hence loudness) is registered on the basilar membrane. It assumes that the more intense a sound, the larger the proportion of basilar membrane called into action (e.g., Glaser & Haven, 1972). More specifically, the loudness of a tone depends on the number of hair cells and nerves stimulated, regardless of the location of the displacement along the basilar membrane.

Physiological Analysis of Frequency and Intensity   Overall the way in which responses of the auditory nerve fibers depend upon frequency and amplitude can be described on the basis of the displacement pattern on the basilar membrane as measured by Békésy (see also Khanna & Leonard, 1982). But this serves only as an early stage in frequency analysis and, by itself, is insufficient to account for the sharp tuning of frequency observed in the organ of Corti and higher regions of the auditory pathway (e.g., Zwislocki, 1981; Kiang, 1984). As we noted earlier in the section on the auditory nerve, microelectrode recordings reveal that sharp frequency responses occur at a number of regions, from the finely tuned auditory nerve fibers to their representation in the auditory cortex. Recall also that the organ of Corti includes two sets of hair cells that are distributed along the length of the basilar membrane and are, in large part, innervated by basilar membrane activity. It has been proposed that the more numerous outer hair cells have a different response threshold for innervation than does the inner set: the inner hair cells require considerably more intense stimulation for activation than do the outer hair cells, whereas the outer hair cells respond at minimum intensity levels. The basis of this difference in innervation between the inner and outer hair cells is due to the different neural connections they make with the auditory nerve. Recall that 90 to 95% of the more than 50,000 auditory nerve fibers make contact with the relatively sparse inner hair cells, whereas the remaining 5 to 10% of the nerve fibers connect with the numerous outer hair cells. Thus in the case of the outer hair cells, the neural activity of a large population of receptors is pooled and collectively stimulates a very few nerve fibers. According to Scharf and Buus (1986) about 10 outer hair cells are served by a single nerve fiber. Put in other words, the signal strength from a number of outer hair cells are pooled and converge onto a small number of nerve fibers, thereby increasing their capacity to respond to low sound intensity levels. This "many-to-few" neu-

ral connection of outer hair cells to nerve fibers brings with it a gain in the ability—the sensitivity—of the outer hair cells to register the presence of weak signals.

However, this advantage to detecting weak signals occurs at a sacrifice to the reception of specific information concerning the location on the basilar membrane where the maximum stimulation of hair cells occurs. Indeed the pooling and summation of neural information from a large number of receptor hair cells essentially eliminates the possibility of specifying which receptors were stimulated. In short, an individual nerve fiber connected to a number of outer hair cells cannot resolve information about the *locus* of stimulation of the individual outer hair cells. On the other hand, the inner hair cells, which make connections with the vast majority of the auditory nerve fibers, exhibit little if any of the pooling and convergence of neural activity of individual nerve fibers that is typical for the outer hair cells. In fact Scharf and Buus (1986) note that about 20 nerve fibers innervate each inner hair cell. Accordingly, while they are relatively incapable of registering the presence of weak auditory signals, the inner hair cells are able to resolve and register the region of the basilar membrane that is maximally displaced; that is, the locus-of-innervation information registered by each stimulated inner hair cell is much more likely to be neurally retained, owing to its lack of neural pooling. Thus the "few-to-many" neural connections of the inner hair cells to nerve fibers are well suited for specifying the region of the basilar membrane that is displaced, and as we noted, the region of the basilar membrane maximally stimulated is determined by the frequency of the sound.

There is additional evidence that the inner hair cells are functionally important for frequency discrimination. When lesions were made selectively of inner and outer cochlear hair cells, it was found that frequency discrimination was unaffected by a complete loss of outer hair cells provided that at least 50% of the inner hair cells were left intact (Nienhuys & Clark, 1978). This suggests that the inner hair cells are critical for frequency discrimination and that they can continue to function effectively even with the total loss of the outer hair cells. In contrast, there is evidence suggesting that the outer hair cells register weak sounds and are essential for sound detection close to the absolute threshold (Prosen et al., 1981).

In summary, frequency analysis and the perception of pitch not only depend upon differential activity of the basilar membrane but on innervation of specific inner hair cells; similarly, an explanation of the detection of intensity and the resultant sensation of loudness is based on the number of nerve impulses generated by basilar membrane displacement and on activity of the outer hair cells.

THE FREQUENCY THEORY

The major alternative to the Békésy place theory is called the **frequency** or **periodicity theory** (Wever & Bray, 1930). It holds that the basilar membrane vibrates as a whole reproducing the vibrations of the sound. Frequency thus is transmitted directly by the vibrations of the cochlea elements much like the telephone or microphone diaphragm transduces sounds. The pitch heard, according to this theory, is determined by the frequency of impulses traveling up the auditory nerve, which in turn is correlated with the frequency of the sound wave. The brain, then, serves as the analyzing instrument for pitch perception.

Reliable evidence exists in support of a frequency notion for coding moderately low frequencies, that is, the firing pattern of nerve fibers is in close synchrony with the frequency of the stimulating tone (Rose et al., 1967). As an example, in response to a 250-Hz tone, a fiber might fire every 4 msec, or 250 times per second. Its neural discharge would thus be time-locked to the 250-Hz tone; that is, the successive discharges of the fiber would be regular and locked in time to the frequency of the tone. Accordingly, information about the tone's frequency can be encoded and transmitted by the pattern of the fiber's activity over time. Interestingly, some evidence in support of a frequency theory comes from studies on pitch discrimination in fish, an animal lacking peripheral frequency analyzers such as a cochlea or basilar membrane. Results indicate that fish do possess this discriminative capacity (Fay,

1970). On the basis of such findings we may conclude that a frequency or periodicity mechanism serves to complement the place notion.

Volley Principle   A major criticism of the frequency theory is that a single nerve fiber cannot directly respond more than 1000 times per second —hence, transmit frequencies above 1000 Hz—so it certainly cannot transmit all the frequencies within the audible range. Modifications by Wever and Bray (1937) of the frequency theory have been made under the assumption that every nerve fiber does not fire at the same moment, but rather the total neural activity is distributed over a series of auditory nerve fibers (see Figure 4.18). It is held that a cooperation exists between fibers so that squads or volleys of fibers fire at different times; the overall effect is that the neural pattern of firing is in direct correspondence to the frequency of the stimulus. Thus, groups of fibers that have a staggered discharge rate together yield impulses synchronized with the frequency of the stimulus. This explanation is called the **volley principle** (see Wever, 1949). Some sort of volley phenomenon has been reported from the responses of single neurons (e.g., for frequencies up to 1050 Hz; Galambos & Davis, 1943).

Loudness is explained by increased firings in each volley: more fibers may enter in the volleys and fibers may fire more frequently. The total effect of increasing intensity is to produce more impulses per volley without changing frequency.

It should be noted that whereas the final word on a theory of pitch perception has yet to be written, modern hearing theory generally draws from aspects of each theory. That is, pitch may be mediated by two neural mechanisms. E. G. Wever (1949), a major proponent of the frequency theory, has written: "the low-tone region is that in which frequency holds sway, the high-tone region that for place representation, and the middle-tone region one where both frequency and place work side by side" (p. 190). Békésy (1963) has likewise commented that only the frequency mechanism is active below 50 Hz, the place mechanism alone signals pitch above 3000 Hz, and between 50 and 3000 Hz, both appear to play a role.

Of interest is research that supports this compro-

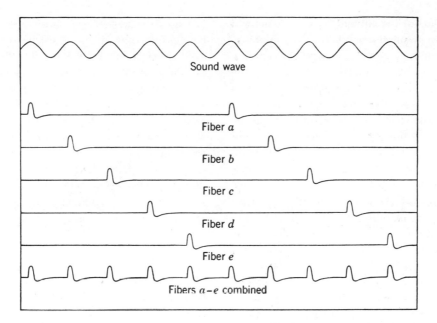

FIGURE 4.18.   The volley principle. Each fiber responds to certain of the sound waves, and their total responses (fibers *a* to *e*, combined) represent the full frequency of the wave. (From E. G. Wever, *Theory of
Hearing*, John Wiley, New York, 1949, p. 167.
Reprinted by permission of the publisher.)

mise. For example, Simmons et al. (1965) implanted
electrodes in different parts of the auditory nerve of a
subject's deaf ear and found that different pitch
effects were produced from differently located electrodes; that is, in support of a place mechanism,
pitch effects were produced that correlated with the
place of stimulation. However, support of a frequency mechanism also occurred in that variations of
stimulus frequency from about 20 to 300 Hz, independent of electrode location, produced changes in
the pitch of the resulting sound (see also Rose et al.,
1967).

AUDITORY PATHOLOGY

Auditory pathology may take a number of diverse
forms—from various hearing impairments that produce systematic distortions to a complete failure of
the auditory mechanism to respond to acoustic energy. In this section we can consider only some of the
major forms of pathology of the auditory system.

TINNITUS

Tinnitus is a condition in which the patient reports
that a tone or a noise is continuously heard in the
absence of an external acoustic stimulus. The most
obvious manifestation of tinnitus is a ringing in the
ears, usually of a relatively high pitch. It may have a
variety of causes and may also occur in the absence of
pathology. Tinnitus is often encountered clinically as
a prominent symptom of a number of ear disorders,
accompanying infections and high fevers, and often it
follows cochlea damage caused by mechanical injury
or certain drugs.

PRESBYACUSIS

Hearing loss attributed to the effects of aging is
known as **presbyacusis, presbycusis,** or **presby-
cusia,** from the Greek *presbys* for "old" and *akousis*
for "hearing". Advancing age is by far the most
common cause of inner-ear hearing deficiencies and
either directly or indirectly is probably the leading
cause of all hearing loss. A number of different
effects due directly to age may play a role: various

forms of middle-ear impairment, loss of elasticity of the basilar membrane, restriction in the vascular flow to auditory structures overall, and the loss of sensory elements in the central nervous system and the cochlea in particular. Age-related hearing loss appears somewhat selective and specific. There is a progressive loss of sensitivity to high-frequency sound with increasing age. Although the upper limit for frequency reception may be beyond 23,000 Hz in children, it decreases with age. In one citation, individuals in their forties were observed to drop in a regular fashion 80 Hz from their upper limit of hearing every six months (Békésy, 1957). In support of a place theory of hearing is the observation that nerve degeneration characteristic of presbyacusis is mainly at the basal end of the cochlea—presumably the region responsible for the reception of high-frequency sounds (e.g., Johnsson & Hawkins, 1972). Whether presbyacusis occurs as a result of deterioration in neural and other supporting structures directly related to the biology of the aging process, or only indirectly due to aging—that is, from the collective influence of infection, occasional abnormal noise exposures and other damaging events that occur in the course of one's life—is unclear. However, the latter is quite possible since some individuals reach an advanced age without significant deterioration of their hearing.

Finally, in this context, notice should be taken of an effect of gradual age-related hearing loss that may play a role in psychopathology. Clinical and audiometric assessments of the elderly mental patient population reveals that hearing loss and deafness are especially prevalent among those diagnosed as paranoid relative to patients with other forms of psychopathology (e.g., Zimbardo, Anderson, & Kabat, 1981). One process by which significant hearing loss and deafness in the aged may contribute to paranoia is based on the gradual onset of the impairment. Indeed owing to the gradual nature of the deficit, a person may be totally unaware that his or her hearing is affected. Thus a person, not recognizing a hearing loss, continually confronts such perceptually anomalous situations as not hearing what others are apparently saying. Nearby individuals, in

fact speaking at a general conversational level, may be interpreted by the aged hearing-deficient person as whispering. In turn, the denial by the individuals that they are whispering may be judged by the elderly person as a lie since it is so clearly at variance with what is apparent, that is, individuals in typical animated conversation, but held at an inaudible level. Uncorrected, this kind of interpretation and resultant interaction can lead to frustration and expressions of hostility; over time it promotes a deterioration of social relationships and eventually isolation, thereby eliminating the essential social feedback required to correct or modify false beliefs.

HEARING LOSS

The term "deafness" refers to hearing threshold levels for speech reception greater than 92 dB (Davis & Silverman, 1978). At these levels normal auditory communication is almost impossible. Hearing loss refers to a measurable loss of sensitivity that does not prevent auditory communication. Generally we will restrict our discussion to hearing loss.

There are two main types of hearing loss: **conduction** or **transmission hearing loss,** and **nerve** or **sensorineural hearing loss.** Conduction hearing loss results from deficiencies in the conduction mechanism of the auditory system particularly involving the structure and function of the external auditory canal, the eardrum, or the ossicles. Nerve hearing loss occurs from deficiencies or damage to the auditory nerves or to the basilar membrane or other closely linked neural connections in the cochlea.

An important instrument for studying hearing loss is the **audiometer.** It usually consists of a tone generator that provides pure tones at a number of different frequencies and allows for setting the intensity at levels at which the tone is just audible. At each test frequency, the intensity necessary for the tone to be barely audible is measured and is compared with previously established standards. The resulting graph from the manipulations is called an **audiogram** and shows any departure from normal sensitivity, that is, hearing loss, in decibels, for the different

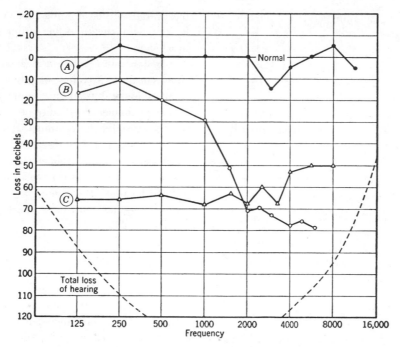

FIGURE 4.19.   Typical audiograms. Normal is the line at zero level near the top. The straight line for zero hearing loss represents the average results obtained from a great many individuals. Curve *A* lies within the normal limits of these average data. Complete loss of hearing is shown by the dashed line near the bottom. (*A*) Typical normal ear. (*B*) Sloping loss, maximal in high frequencies typical of sensorineural hearing loss. (*C*) Flat loss with all frequencies cut down nearly the same, characteristic of conduction hearing loss. (Modified from E. G. Boring, H. S. Langfeld, and H. P. Weld, *Foundations of Psychology*, John Wiley, New York, 1948, p. 340. Reprinted by permission of the publisher.)

test frequencies. Typical audiograms are given in Figure 4.19. The curve for a person with normal hearing (shown by curve *A*) remains close to zero in hearing loss in all frequencies. However, the other curves are typical ones for persons with hearing deficiencies. Curve *B* in the figure is an example of the hearing loss for a person with sensorineural hearing loss. It is characteristic of this form of auditory pathology for hearing loss to be very pronounced in the high frequencies and much less for the lower frequencies. Curve *C* is an example indicative of a person with conduction hearing loss. The curve shows that the person has approximately the same severe hearing loss at all frequencies.

The audiogram or audiometric function shown in Figure 4.20 is based on a somewhat different procedure for assessing hearing loss, as well as for establishing a subject's threshold level for various frequencies. The procedure is sometimes referred to as the **Békésy tracking procedure:** the frequency of the signal or test tone is automatically and gradually advanced. The subject presses a button when a tone is heard, which serves to decrease the intensity of the tone gradually until it fades away and is no longer audible. At this point the subject releases the button, whereupon the tone increases gradually in intensity until the subject hears the tone again, and again presses the button. Thus the intensity of the tone

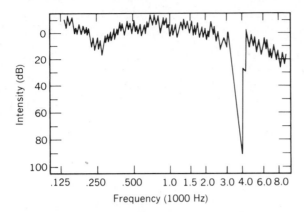

FIGURE 4.20.   Audiometric function generated by the Békésy tracking procedure. The curve shows threshold intensity as a function of frequency. Note that the curve reveals a tonal gap—an insensitivity to a band of tonal frequencies—at about 4000 Hz.

tends to vary around the subject's threshold for each frequency. The output of the procedure, that is, the audiometric function, is generated by a pen moving along a chart. As the subject tracks the tone, the pen runs up and down across the chart reversing its direction each time the button is alternatively pressed or released, accounting for the rather ragged or zigzag curve. This procedure is quite useful clinically as it can reveal **tonal gaps**—narrow ranges of frequencies which are inaudible to the subject.

The causes of hearing loss and deafness vary. They may involve chronic infection of the middle and inner ear, particularly of a viral nature, acoustic trauma, and the use of certain antibiotic medications in high dosages, such as streptomycin, neomycin, and kanamycin. The pathological effects of some antibiotics are so robust and predictable that they have been used in studies examining the effects of selective destruction of the hair cells of the organ of Corti (e.g., Cazals et al., 1980; Prosen et al., 1981). In addition to antibiotics, other drugs and chemicals, such as aspirin, quinine, certain diuretics, carbon monoxide, lead, mercury, and tobacco may contribute to hearing loss (e.g., McFadden & Plattsmier, 1983; Zelman, 1973). Certainly we must consider

the overall effects of aging that may contribute to hearing deficiency (see the earlier section on presbyacusis).

One result of abnormal exposure to intense sounds or noise is called **sound- or noise-induced hearing loss.** Exposure to excessive and prolonged acoustic stimulation—"noise pollution"—can produce severe effects on hearing that may be temporary or permanent. Indeed the structural changes caused by exposure to intense noise can be seen clearly in preparations of the guinea pig cochlea. Exposure to 140 dB for only 30 seconds produces gross distortions of the outer hair cells and tears them off the basilar membrane (*Lancet*, 1975, p. 215). Included here also are the deleterious effects of exposure to the typical loudness levels of amplified music (Hanson & Fearn, 1975).

The effects of intense sounds may be specific to the frequency of the sound (e.g., intense high-frequency tones may produce damage near the basal end of the cochlea, as a place theory would predict). However, it has been noted that impairment effects of intense stimulation to one tone, particularly a low-frequency tone, may uniformly occur to the perception of all frequencies, regardless of the specific frequency of the insulting tone (Gulick, 1971).

COMPARATIVE AUDITORY STRUCTURES

The functioning of the ear and its psychological consequence, hearing, is more fully understood when considered in a general biological context. To do this it is necessary to consider hearing from a comparative view. This can be very useful since the widely different degree of structural elaboration in the auditory mechanisms of vertebrates enables many properties of hearing to be analyzed with respect to anatomy.

The vestibular and auditory structures of a turtle, a bird, and a mammal are sketched in Figure 4.21. Shown are the semicircular canals, the otocysts and the otoliths, and the auditory nerve endings along the basilar membrane. From an evolutionary

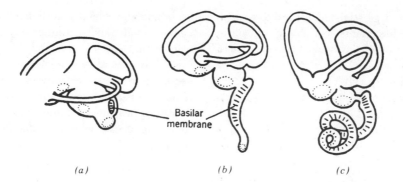

(a)   (b)   (c)

FIGURE 4.21.   The vestibular and auditory organs of a turtle (*a*), a bird (*b*), and a mammal (*c*). The length of the basilar membrane shows a decided increase from the turtle to the mammal. The dotted ellipses represent otolithic organs; the parallel dashes represent the auditory nerve endings along the basilar membrane. (From G. von Békésy, "Frequency in the cochlea of various animals," in E. G. Wever (Trans. and Ed.), *Experiments in Hearing*, McGraw-Hill, New York, 1960; and G. von Békésy and W. A. Rosenblith, "The mechanical properties of the ear," in S. S. Stevens (Ed.), *Handbook of Experimental Psychology*, John Wiley, New York, 1951, p. 1102, Reprinted by permission of the publisher.)

perspective, the semicircular canals appear invariant with phylogenetic ascension whereas there is an increase in the length of the basilar membrane. As Figure 4.21 shows, the increase in length of the cochlea in birds and mammals (*b* and *c*) appears as an elaboration of the lowest otolithic structure seen in the turtle (*a*).

The size of the cochlea and especially the length of the basilar membrane within it can be related to some aspects of auditory reception. Elongation of the basilar membrane presumably occurred in the evolution of avian and mammalian life. Generally the basilar membrane is shortest in amphibia and reptiles, somewhat longer in birds, and it is longest in mammals (Manley, 1971). A conjecture as to the significance of these phylogenetic differences is given by Masterton and Diamond (1973): "Because sounds of different frequencies result in stimulation at different places along the basilar membrane, this lengthening of the receptor organ almost certainly means that there existed a strong and persistent pressure on the ancestors of mammals for wider range and finer discrimination of frequency" (p. 411).

Structures other than those of the inner ear are important to the audible range of hearing. Masterton, Heffner, and Ravizza (1968) have pointed out that high-frequency hearing (above 32,000 Hz) is a characteristic unique to mammals and due to the evolution, in mammals only, of the middle-ear ossicles.

Of interest to the present discussion is the relationship of hearing to gross bodily dimensions. Békésy (1960) has surmised that the physical size of the animal bears some relationship to the minimum frequency that is detectable. Specifically, he has suggested that the lower-frequency limit is shifted downward with increases in animal size. This is related to the general enlargement of the ear. When sound is transmitted along the ear's main surfaces, the sound absorption is less for low-frequency tones than for high ones. Accordingly, when auditory passages are relatively large, there is an advantage to the reception of low-frequency tones. According to Békésy and Rosenblith (1951), the favoring of low-frequency tones offers an ecological advantage to large animals: "The wisdom of nature is evident in all this, because it is certainly important for large animals to hear over great distances. If the sound is propagated along the ground, the absorption will in general affect low-frequency sounds less than high-frequency sounds. Hence the usefulness of favoring the low frequencies" (p. 1104).

It has also been suggested that mammals with a small interaural distance (i.e., the functional distance between the two ears) have been subjected to more selective pressure to hear high frequencies than mammals with more widely set ears; that is, the ability to hear high-frequency sounds is inversely related to the distance between the two ears. As we will acknowledge in Chapter 6, because of the shorter wavelengths involved, high-frequency hearing for small mammals is especially important for the task of sound localization. Generally mammals with large heads and wide-set ears have a more restricted high-frequency limit than do those with small heads and small interaural distances. Thus, while the average mammalian high-frequency hearing limit is of the order of 55 kHz (k = kilo, or thousand), the upper limit for mammals with large physical dimensions such as the elephant is relatively small, about 10 kHz (Heffner & Heffner, 1980).

An additional observation concerning the audible frequency range for mammals bears examination. Heffner and Heffner (1983a, b) have analyzed evidence documenting the frequency range of audibility for various mammalian species and have observed an overall trend. Generally speaking there is a trade-off between high- and low-frequency hearing: across mammalian species, low-frequency hearing improves as the ability to hear high frequencies declines. In short, mammals that have good high-frequency hearing have somewhat restricted low-frequency hearing, and vice versa. Table 4.2 gives some approximate but representative values illustrating this trend.

SUMMARY

In this chapter we described the physical characteristics of the auditory stimulus and its representation in waveform. The principal physical properties of sound waves are characterized by their variation in frequency, amplitude or intensity, complexity, and phase.

The main anatomical structures and mechanisms of the three main divisions of the ear (the outer, middle, and inner ear) were identified and the sequence of physiological events and processes of the auditory system that result in the perception of sound were discussed. In the context of describing the functioning of the inner ear we considered two main theories of pitch perception: Békésy's place theory and the frequency theory (and volley principle); in

Table 4.2
Range of Audible Sound Frequencies (Hz) for Various Mammalian Species

	Low-Frequency Limit	High-Frequency Limit
Elephant	17	10,000
Human	20	20,000
Cattle	23	35,000
Horse	55	33,500
Dog	60	45,000
Monkey	110	45,000
Rat	650	60,000
Mouse	1000	90,000
Bat	3000	120,000

Source: Approximated from Heffner and Heffner (1983a, b).

addition we presented some of the significant findings that bear on these. We noted that a compromise is possible in that the reception of low-frequency tones may be explained by a frequency notion and high-frequency reception by a place theory.

Some common conditions of auditory pathology were outlined: tinnitus, presbyacusis, and certain forms of hearing deficiencies.

Finally, a brief section was given on comparative auditory structures. We noted that increased length of the basilar membrane evolved with phylogenetic ascension. In addition, some trends were observed: for mammalian species the ability to hear high frequencies appears to be inversely related to the distance between the two ears; it was also noted that for mammals, high-frequency hearing occurs at a sacrifice in the ability to hear low frequencies, and vice versa.

KEY TERMS

Amplitude

Anvil (incus)

Audiogram

Audiometer

Basilar membrane

Békésy tracking procedure

Best (characteristic) frequency

Bone conduction

Cochlea

Cochlear duct (scala media)

Complexity

Conduction (transmission) hearing loss

Decibel (dB)

Eardrum (tympanic membrane)

Eustachian tube

External auditory canal (meatus)

First harmonic (fundamental tone)

Fourier analysis

Fourier synthesis

Frequency

Frequency modulation

Frequency (periodicity) theory

Frequency tuning curves

Hammer (malleus)

Helicotrema

Hertz (Hz)

Inner hair cells

Intensity

Loudness

Nerve (sensorineural) hearing loss

Ohm's acoustical law

Organ of Corti

Ossicles

Outer hair cells

Oval window

Overtones (harmonics)

Phase

Pinna (auricle)

Pitch

Place theory

Presbyacusis

Pressure

Reissner's membrane

Resonance

Round window

Sensation level (SL)

Sound- (noise-) induced hearing loss

Sound pressure level (SPL)

Stirrup (Stapes)

Tectorial membrane

Timbre

Tinnitus

Tonal gap

Tonotopic

Traveling wave

Tuned fibers

Tympanic canal (scala tympani)

Vestibular canal (scala vestibuli)

Volley principle

Wavelength

STUDY QUESTIONS

1. Describe a "sound" on the basis of its physical and psychological dimensions. Consider its frequency, amplitude or intensity, and complexity, linking these to the appropriate subjective dimensions of pitch, loudness, and timbre. What is the relation of resonance and phase to the frequency and intensity of a sound?

2. Consider what factors affect the amplitude of a sound. How is it measured? What is the advantage of using a decibel scale?

3. What is the role of a Fourier analysis in understanding the components of a complex sound?

4. Distinguish among the major anatomical components of the outer, middle, and inner ear. Trace the route of a sound from the environment to the transducers of the inner ear.

5. How do the bones or ossicles of the middle ear affect incoming sounds? In particular, consider the role of the stapes in sound transmission from the middle to the inner ear.

6. Outline the main components of the inner ear and indicate their function in sound reception. Focus your answer especially on the structures of the organ of Corti, including the basilar membrane and the specialized hair cells it supports.

7. Consider what kinds of specificity exists within the auditory nerve. How does the observation that nerve fibers may be selectively and sharply tuned to frequency apply to pitch perception?

8. Compare and contrast the place and frequency theories of pitch perception. Indicate their major differences and summarize your answer by indicating how they complement each other. What is the contemporary status of theories of pitch perception? Outline evidence that supports the place theory. Outline evidence in support of the frequency theory, making note of the modification introduced by the volley principle.

9. Indicate how the place theory and the frequency theory register intensity.

10. Distinguish the anatomical and functional differences between the inner and outer hair cells. Explain how the neural connections of the inner and outer hair cells to the auditory nerve fibers may account for the coding of frequency and intensity, respectively.

11. Outline some of the major disorders of the auditory system. Distinguish between disorders due to illness and disease and those due to aging.

12. Consider some of the differences in the range of audibility that are related to a species' anatomy. What anatomical characteristics favor the reception of high- and low-frequency sounds?

5

COMPLEX AUDITORY PHENOMENA I: PSYCHOACOUSTICS

PERCEPTION OF INTENSITY
Intensity Discrimination
Loudness
Loudness and Frequency
PERCEPTION OF FREQUENCY
Frequency Discrimination
Pitch
Pitch and Intensity
HEARING AND TEMPORAL EFFECTS

EFFECTS OF MULTIPLE TONAL STIMULATION
Beats
Combination Tones
Masking
Sound-Induced Hearing Loss (Auditory Fatigue and Adaptation)
SUBJECTIVE TONAL ATTRIBUTES
Volume and Density
Consonance and Dissonance
SUMMARY

In this chapter our focus is on the perception of certain psychophysical features of auditory phenomena. In particular, much of our discussion concerns the relationship of the subjective dimensions of hearing to the measurable physical events that produce them. We have briefly noted that the psychological dimensions of hearing are loudness and pitch; these are functionally related to the physical dimensions of intensity and frequency, respectively. We now turn to some of the quantitative relationships between these dimensions.

PERCEPTION OF INTENSITY

The sensitivity of the vertebrate auditory system to the intensity of a sound is extraordinary. The human threshold—the lowest intensity level that produces a sensation of hearing—at frequencies around 3000 Hz begins to approach the reception of the sounds made by random movement of air molecules (Békésy & Rosenblith, 1951).

Figure 5.1 shows the results of monaural (one ear) and binaural (two ears) measures of the thresholds of intensity as a function of frequency for the human. Depending upon the frequency tested, the binaural threshold may be from 3 to 6 dB lower than that for the monaural threshold (Stevens & Davis, 1938; Reynolds & Stevens, 1960). For the practical purpose of obtaining precise threshold measurements listeners are sometimes tested in specially constructed environments, totally without sound-reflecting objects. One such room is called an **anechoic chamber** (i.e., free of echoes) in which all walls, ceilings, and floors are covered by a highly absorbent material to eliminate sound reflection. Thus the sound pressure level in any given direction from the sound source can be measured without the presence of interfering reflections.

It is clear from Figure 5.1 that the human ear is differentially sensitive to pure tones of different frequencies; thus each frequency has its own threshold value. As a general statement, maximal sensitivity is for those frequencies in the region of 3000 Hz. With intensity held constant, a sound of 3000 Hz sounds louder than other frequencies. This corresponds to the natural resonance of the external ear canal noted earlier. From an ecological perspective the benefit to the human of this particular frequency-

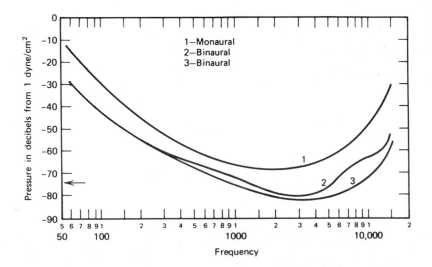

FIGURE 5.1.   Auditory threshold as a function of frequency. Curve 1 represents the threshold of hearing when measurement is made of sound pressure at the eardrum. Curve 2 represents the threshold intensities of a sound field when the observer faces the source and listens with both ears. Curve 3 represents threshold values when the sound reaches the observer from all sides. Note that sounds below a given curve are inaudible. (Notice that the ordinate is plotted in decibels from 1 dynes/cm². The arrow at −73.8 dB shows the standard reference pressure. After Sivian and White, 1933.)

related sensitivity lies perhaps in the alarming and piercing quality of a cry that occurs in the 3000-Hz range. Perhaps as Milne and Milne (1967) speculate, we have a "channel open—as though reserved for emergencies—for any high-pitched scream" (p. 43).

INTENSITY DISCRIMINATION

An important aspect of intensity reception concerns the degree to which the stimulus intensity of a sound must be changed, either increased or decreased, in order to perceive a discriminable difference (referred to as the differential threshold or limen, often noted as ΔI, see Chapter 2). Not unexpectedly, the ΔI is dependent on a number of factors, chiefly among them the frequency, duration, base intensity level, and kind (e.g., pure or complex sounds, noise bursts) of sounds on which the measurement is made. For example, for frequency, empirical determinations of the differential sensitivity indicate that when the base intensity is below 30 dB, the frequency range in which the differential sensitivity is greatest is also approximately that frequency region (2500 to 3000 Hz) in which maximal sensitivity occurs, and it becomes progressively worse as frequency is raised or lowered. In short, the frequency region that requires minimal intensity for threshold detection is also the frequency range with the greatest differential sensitivity. As we shall note in Chapter 6, the functional significance of intensity discrimination is in its contribution to localizing sounds.

LOUDNESS

Loudness refers to a psychological dimension of audition—an aspect of experience which is the perception of intensity—and as we have previously noted, loudness is generally determined by the physical intensity or pressure of the sound. However, the relationship between loudness and intensity is an imperfect and complex one in that loudness does not correspond solely to physical intensity.

A method used to investigate this relationship is Stevens' magnitude estimation (described in Chapter 2). A subject is given a standard stimulus tone and

a set of tones that vary in intensity, but all tones are presented at the same frequency (1000 Hz). The standard is assigned a modulus value, say, 10 or 100, and the subject's task is to assign numbers to the variable tones that reflect its sensory magnitude in proportion to the standard. The result is the construction of a subjective scale of loudness that is a power function of physical intensity. Specifically, Stevens (1956) has shown that the psychological dimension of loudness (L) is related to the physical intensity of the sound (I) (times a constant, k), by a power law of the form

$$L = kI^{0.3} \qquad \text{or} \qquad L = kP^{0.6}$$

where P is sound pressure.

This means that loudness increases approximately as the cube root of sound intensity. Since the exponent is less than 1.0, increases in intensity produce lower proportional increases in loudness. In other words, loudness grows more slowly than intensity.

It has been useful to adopt a standard unit of loudness. Stevens and Davis (1938) used the term **sone**, one sone defined as the loudness of a 1000 Hz tone at a 40-dB SPL intensity level. Both the term and its referents have been universally adopted as the standard of loudness. A function relating intensity level to the sone scale is given in Figure 5.2. Notice from the figure that loudness doubles when the sound intensity level increases by 10 dB (which corresponds to about a tripling of intensity). In other words to double the loudness of a sound, its intensity must be approximately tripled.

LOUDNESS AND FREQUENCY

Specifying only the decibel level of a sound will not fully describe its loudness. Loudness is not solely a matter of physical intensity but it is also dependent on the frequency of the sound. The dependence of loudness on frequency is apparent when two tones whose frequencies differ are matched for loudness and their respective intensities are compared. Using psychophysical methods, it is possible to specify the different frequencies and intensities of sounds that are perceived as equally loud. For example, a subject

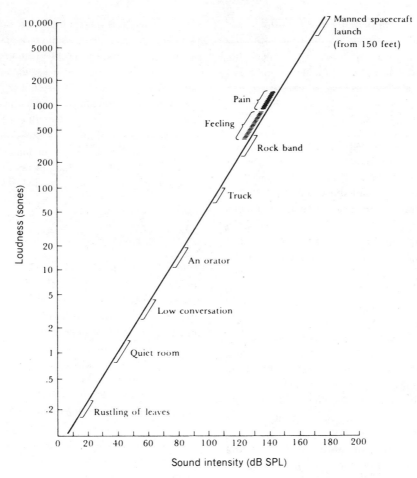

FIGURE 5.2. Relationship between intensity level (decibels) and loudness (sones). Notice that in this function a 10-dB increase in the intensity scale increases loudness by a factor of 2. Note that loudness and intensity are scaled logarithmically. (From Lindsay and Norman, 1972, p. 257. Reprinted by permission of the publisher.)

listens to two tones that differ in frequency and intensity. One has a fixed frequency and intensity, and it is called the standard tone. A second, comparison tone is presented at a different frequency and intensity, and the subject's task is to listen alternately to the standard and comparison tones and adjust the intensity of the comparison until it matches the loudness of the standard tone. When this is done for a number of comparison tones, a curve may be plotted that describes the intensity at which tones of

various frequencies appear equally as loud as the standard tone. Each curve of Figure 5.3 shows the result of such a procedure for a different standard. The family of curves relate perceived loudness to intensities and frequencies and shows to what extent loudness is affected by frequency. The curves are labeled in **phons,** a measure of the loudness level of a tone specified as the number of decibels of a standard 1000-Hz tone of equal loudness. That is, the number of phons of a tone is numerically equal to

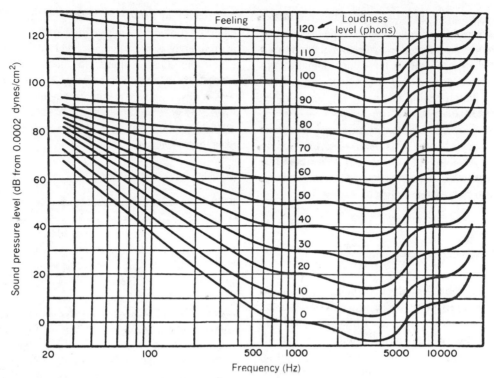

FIGURE 5.3.   Equal-loudness contours. The values by each curve refer to the loudness levels in phons. The bottom curve—0 phons—shows the absolute sensitivity of the ear as a function of frequency. Presumably tones below this curve are not audible. (From H. Fletcher and W. A. Munson, "Loudness, its definition, measurement, and calculation," *Journal of the Acoustial Society of America*, 5, 1933, pp. 82–108. Reprinted by permission of the American Institute of Physics.)

the number of decibels of a 1000-Hz tone that sounds equally as loud as the tone. For example, consider the curve labeled 30 on Figure 5.3. Any sound whose frequency and intensity lies on this curve appears equally as loud as any other sound on the curve although their frequencies and intensities will differ. It follows that a 300-Hz tone at a 40-dB intensity level appears equal in loudness to a 1000-Hz tone at a 30-dB (or 30-phon) intensity level and a 6000-Hz tone at a 35-dB intensity level. Thus, the 300- and the 6000-Hz tones at 40 and 35 dB, respectively, have a loudness level of 30 phons, and any sound whose frequency and intensity falls on this curve (i.e., 30 phons) has a loudness level of 30 phons. Appropriately the curves of Figure 5.3 are called

equal-loudness contours (or **isophonic curves** or sometimes **Fletcher—Munson curves**).

Figure 5.3 points out a number of important facts about the perception of loudness. The effect of frequency on loudness is greatest at low levels of intensity; at high intensity levels frequency does not play a significant role in the perception of loudness and the equal-loudness contours are relatively flat. In other words, if tones are sufficiently intense, they tend to sound equally loud, irrespective of frequency. At relatively low intensity levels, frequencies lower than about 1000 Hz and higher than 4000 Hz sound softer than do intermediate frequencies for the same intensity level. The bow-shaped curves indicate how low and high frequencies must be boosted in intensity in order to maintain a constant loudness level. This relationship appears not only with laboratory-produced sounds but occurs in ordinary listening experiences. For example, many high-fidelity amplifiers possess a compensatory adjustment circuit for listening at low intensity levels called a "loudness compensator" (or simply "loudness"), which overemphasizes the very high and especially the low frequencies. It is necessary because in turning the "volume" (a misnomer) of the amplifier down the relative loudness of various frequencies is changed in the manner shown by Figure 5.3.

PERCEPTION OF FREQUENCY

Although the perception of a sound involves the interaction of intensity and frequency, there are a number of aspects of frequency reception that bear analysis. In the case of "normal" human hearing, the limits of hearing for frequency extend between 20 and 20,000 Hz. Below 20 Hz only a vibration feeling or a "fluttering" sound is perceived, whereas above 20,000 Hz perhaps only a "tickling" is experienced. We have seen from Figures 5.1 and 5.3 that the threshold of hearing varies with both intensity and frequency and that at the extremes of frequency the sounds must be quite intense in order to be audible.

FREQUENCY DISCRIMINATION

The discrimination question raised for intensity can also be asked for frequency; namely, how much of a change in frequency (Δf) must occur in order to be detected by the observer? Some findings indicate that the human observer can detect a change in frequency of about 3 Hz for frequencies up to about 1000 Hz (Harris, 1952). For frequencies between about 1000 and 10,000 Hz, over a wide range of intensities, frequency discriminability, as derived from the Weber fraction, can be specified as a constant and small fraction of the frequency to be discriminated ($\Delta f/f$ approximates 0.004). For example, at about 10,000 Hz a 40-Hz change is required for a change to be perceived.

Important among the variables that affect the determination of the minimal discriminable change in frequency is the intensity level of the sounds at which the measurements are taken. The Δf for frequency increases with decreases in stimulus intensity (especially for high frequencies). In other words, as a sound appears softer it becomes more difficult to detect it as different from other sounds close in frequency.

PITCH

Pitch is a subjective dimension of hearing that refers to how high or low a sound appears, and it is principally but not exclusively determined by the frequency of the tone reaching the ears. Typically, high-pitch sounds are heard from high-frequency tones, low-pitch sounds result from low-frequency tones, but the correspondence is not precise. The dimension of pitch has been scaled using an arbitrary unit called the **mel.** By definition the subjective pitch of a 1000-Hz tone at 40 dB is assigned a value of 1000 mels. The relationship between pitch and frequency was determined by the employment of a psychophysical procedure called the method of **fractionation.** For example, an observer was presented alternately with two tones at a constant intensity level but only one tone at a fixed frequency. The other tone was varied in frequency by the observer until its pitch was perceived to be one-half of the pitch of the fixed tone. In this case the number 1000 mels was assigned to the pitch of a 1000-Hz tone and the number 500 mels to the frequency of the tone that sounded half as high in pitch. Similarly, a sound that appeared twice as high in pitch as the 1000-Hz tone was assigned a value of 2000 mels. Extending this procedure for other frequencies and extrapolating the results produced the numerical pitch scale of Figure 5.4. The curve of Figure 5.4 expresses the relationship between the pitch and frequency at a constant 40-dB level. Observe that only at 1000 Hz does the numerical value of frequency equal the number of mels. Pitch increases more rapidly than frequency below 1000 Hz and increases in frequency above 1000 Hz produce lower proportional increases in pitch. Figure 5.5 shows how a piano keyboard would appear if each

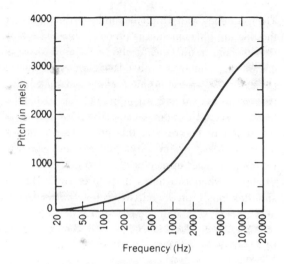

FIGURE 5.4. The frequency–pitch function. The curve shows how the perceived pitch of a tone in mels changes as a function of the frequency of the stimulus. This pitch-function was determined at a loudness level of 40 dB. (After Stevens and Volkmann, 1940.)

key were adjusted in size to represent the number of mels it includes.

PITCH AND INTENSITY

Intensity has a measurable effect on the pitch of relatively pure tones. In a classic study, Stevens (1935), using a single trained observer, determined the effect of intensity on the pitch of tones for 11 frequencies ranging from 150 to 12,000 Hz. Two tones of slightly different frequencies were presented in succession to the observer who adjusted the intensity of one of the two tones until both were perceived as equal in pitch. In short, the observer compensated for frequency differences by means of a difference in intensity. For high frequency tones (3000 Hz and above), a constant pitch is maintained by decreasing the intensity of a tone; similarly for low frequency tones (500 Hz and lower), a constant pitch is maintained by increasing intensity. Stated differently, when intensity is increased the pitch of high tones increases and the pitch decreases for low tones. For frequencies in the middle range (1000–2000 Hz), the effect of intensity on pitch is minimal (see also Gulick, 1971).

HEARING AND TEMPORAL EFFECTS

Since hearing is largely a matter of stimulus reception over time, we would expect certain temporal factors to influence the perception of sound. Indeed, recognizable tonal quality requires some minimal duration of the acoustic stimulus. For example, if a tone of an audible frequency and intensity is presented for only a few milliseconds, it will lose its tonal character and either be inaudible or be heard as a "click." According to Gulick (1971) the length of time a given frequency must last in order to produce

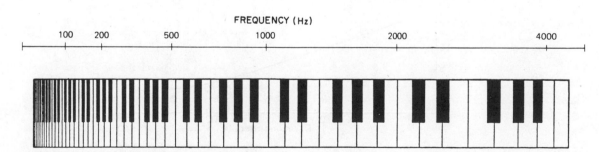

FIGURE 5.5. The mel keyboard. The piano keyboard is distorted so that equal distance represents amounts of pitch rather than equal units on the musical scale. This shows why melodies are so much clearer when played in the treble than when played in the bass. (From E. G. Boring, H. S. Langfeld, and H. P. Weld, *Foundations of Psychology*, John Wiley, New York, 1948, p. 323. Reprinted by permission of the publisher.)

the experience of a stable and recognizable pitch for tones above 1000 Hz is 10 msec. In the case of loudness, as durations become progressively briefer than 200 msec, intensity must be increased to maintain a constant level of loudness (see Figure 5.6). It is also worth noting that for tonal intervals less than 200 msec, the absolute threshold for the tone's detection increases; for durations exceeding 200 msec thresholds remain constant (Scharf & Buus, 1986). Thus although the sound heard depends primarily on the frequency and intensity of the sound, both its pitch and loudness are secondarily affected by the duration of the exposure. Within limits, the loudness and pitch increase as a brief burst of sound is lengthened.

EFFECTS OF MULTIPLE TONAL STIMULATION

BEATS

When simultaneously listening to two tones that are of similar intensity but slightly different in frequency, one may perceive the occurrence of **beats** —perhaps best described as a perception of a single throbbing tone with a single pitch midway between the two tones but periodically varying in loudness: in short, an alternate waxing and waning in loudness.

The frequency with which the loudness fluctuates for the beating phenomenon is precisely the difference between the frequencies of the two sounds that are combined. The reason that beats occur is purely physical: there is a continuous change in the relative phase of two simultaneously applied tones so that the tones alternately reinforce and cancel each other. As illustrated in Figure 5.7, this produces a complex tone that varies in intensity at a frequency equal to the frequency difference of the two tones. Thus, for example, when two tones that differ by 2 Hz are simultaneously produced, the sound waves generated by each will be in compression at the same time two times each second and be exactly out of phase at the same time two times each second; that is, the tones will systematically vary between reinforcing and canceling each other two times a second. The ear hears this phase alternation as periodic variations in loudness, that is, as beats. Indeed, one tone is said to be "beating" against the other.

As the difference between tones increases, beats become faster and they soon lose their individuality. With sufficient increases in the frequency difference (at about 30 Hz), the resultant sound begins to assume a "roughness." The upper limit for the perception of beats is dependent on the absolute frequencies and intensities of the tones, but under proper circumstances tones separated by as much as 250 Hz may produce beats (Geldard, 1972).

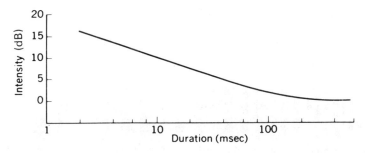

FIGURE 5.6. Equal-loudness contour for middle-frequency tones showing the changes in intensity required to maintain a constant loudness as a function of tonal duration. Intensity is expressed in decibels relative to a standard tone of long duration. As durations become briefer than 200 msec, intensity must be increased to maintain constant loudness. Note that the time axis is plotted on a logarithmic scale. (From W. L. Gulick, *Hearing: Physiology and Psychophysics*, 1971, p. 148. Reprinted by permission of Oxford University Press, New York.)

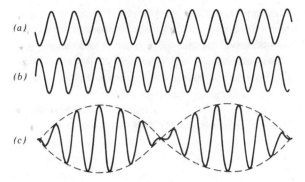

FIGURE 5.7.   The sound waves, *a* and *b*, of two tones, where *b* is slightly higher in frequency than *a*. When sounded together, the waves interact to form a complex tone that varies in intensity at a rate equal to the frequency difference of the two tones. The variation in intensity is called the beat frequency and is shown by the dotted enclosing segments in *c*. (From M. Mayer, *Sensory Perception Laboratory Manual*, Wiley, New York, 1982, p. 91. Reprinted by permission of the publisher.)

COMBINATION TONES

When the frequency difference between the two tones is sufficiently great to eliminate beating phenomena, other tones in addition to the primary pair may be heard. The frequencies of these tones are the sums and differences of the frequencies of the primary tones and their simple multiples. These are termed **combination tones,** and they are of two types—**difference tones** and **summation tones**—both of which may occur from the simultaneous stimulation of the ear by two pure tones. The sound of a difference tone has the pitch that corresponds to the frequency difference of the two primary tones, whereas summation tones occur from the frequency summing of the two primary tones. Unlike beats, the basis for the occurrence of combination tones is not in the physical stimulus; rather, they are a result of the ear's distorting action. In particular, combination tones originate within the cochlea and appear to be due to basilar membrane activity (Hall, 1974).

Many combination tones may result from two primary frequencies and their resultant harmonics.

For example, an examination of the combination tones present in the cochlear response of a cat stimulated by a 700- and 1200-Hz tone at 90 dB yielded 66 different tones, that is, various combinations of the two tones and their upper harmonics (Stevens & Davis, 1938). Note, however, that the amplitude of the resultant combination tones that are higher in frequency than the primary tones are estimated to be about 20 to 40 dB below the amplitude of the primary tones (Zurek & Sachs, 1979).

MASKING

When two tones close in frequency are sounded, but one is of greater intensity, the more intense tone will reduce or eliminate the perception of the softer one. Indeed it is familiar to experience one sound drowning out another. This phenomenon is termed **masking** and is defined as the rise in the threshold of one tone (test tone) in the presence of a second (masker) tone.

The classic study of masking is by Wegel and Lane (1924); Zwicker and Scharf (1965) have also provided the findings summarized in Figure 5.8. The figure shows the masking effects of a narrow band of frequencies centered at a 1200-Hz band of noise (the masker) sounded at three sample intensity levels upon tones of various frequencies. Each curve represents the degree of masking, measured as the rise in the intensity level from threshold necessary for test tones (whose frequencies are distributed along the abscissa) to be heard, in the simultaneous presence of the 1200-Hz masker. As the figure shows, a masking tone raises the threshold of hearing by an amount that varies with intensity and frequency. More specifically, tones close in frequency to the masker are more strongly masked than those far removed in frequency. That is, the masker must lie in the general proximity of the frequency of the test tone if masking is to result. By examining the collective results for the three sample intensity levels of the masking tone, it is clear that a greater amount of masking results when the masker is made more intense.

Also apparent from the figure is the asymmetry of the 80- and 110-dB curves with respect to the

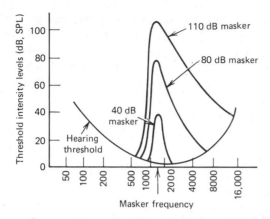

FIGURE 5.8. Representation of masking. Shown are thresholds for tones in the presence of a narrow band of frequencies (masker) centered at 1200 Hz and at three intensity levels. The intensity of the masker is given on each curve in decibels. The magnitude of masking is shown by the height of the threshold curves. The higher the curve, the greater the masking effect. For maskers greater than 40 dB, tones higher in frequency than the masker are clearly affected whereas those lower are not. (Based on Zwicker and Scharf, 1965.)

frequency range of the masking effects. This indicates that the effect of masking is greater on test tones whose frequencies exceed the masker than for those below it. That is, lower frequencies mask higher-frequency sounds more effectively than the reverse. Clearly, the effect of the masker on frequencies below it are very slight even for the 110-dB masker. Observe also in the figure that this general trend in the asymmetry in masking effects applies only at masker levels above about 40 dB SPL. Indeed the effect of the 40-dB masker appears somewhat symmetrical.

Much of the masking phenomenon may be explained in a very simplified fashion by an analysis of the interaction and the interference of patterns of displacement on the basilar membrane. This takes the form of an explanation sometimes referred to as the **line-busy hypothesis** (e.g., Scharf & Buus, 1986). The line-busy hypothesis assumes that to mask the test tone, the masker excites the same restricted group of fibers, thus preventing them from responding to the test tone. In short, masking occurs when the neural elements that normally respond to a given tone are kept too "busy" by the masker to respond adequately to the test tone. Support for the line-busy hypothesis comes from a consideration of the displacement pattern on the basilar membrane. Recall that there is evidence of a spatial representation of frequency on the basilar membrane (see Figures 4.15 and 4.17c). Note further from Figure 4.17c that there is an asymmetry in the spread of displacement along the basilar membrane: low-frequency tones produce a relatively broad displacement pattern extending over much of the membrane whereas tones of high frequency produce patterns of displacement of the basilar membrane that are somewhat sharper, more restricted in area, and have peaks that lie close to the stapes and oval window. When the masker is of a higher frequency and more intense than the test tone, its pattern of displacement on the basilar membrane only extends part way along it. Since the lower-frequency test tone produces displacement in a separate, nonoverlapping region, the interference by the masker is relatively slight and the test tone is detectable (see Fig. 5.9a). In contrast when the masker is a lower frequency than the weaker test tone, the masker's displacement pattern tends to engulf or cover that of the test tone and the detectability of the test tone is reduced or eliminated (Fig. 5.9b). The test tone becomes audible when made sufficiently intense so that its basilar membrane activity overcomes the basilar membrane activity produced by the masker. Accordingly, the intensity of the higher-frequency test tone, in the presence of the lower-frequency masker, must be increased in order to be detected (Fig. 5.9c).

It should be noted here that masking is not restricted to the simultaneous presentation of masker and test tone. Interference effects can occur when the masker precedes (forward masking) or follows (backward masking) the test tone. For example, in backward masking, a test tone, followed after a brief interval, say, 50 msec, by a more intense masker tone, may make the prior sounded test tone inaudible.

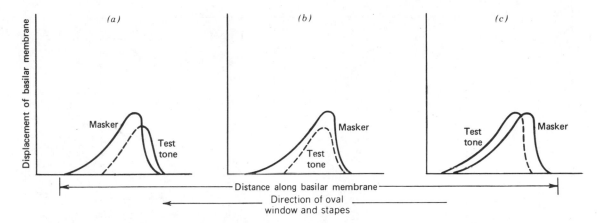

FIGURE 5.9.   Figure (a) shows a masker that is more intense and whose frequency is higher than the test tone. As shown, the lower frequency test tone produces displacement in a nonoverlapping portion of the basilar membrane in a direction away from the stapes and oval window. Thus the interference by the masker is not complete and the test tone is detectable. Figure (b) illustrates a masker that has a lower frequency and is more intense than the test tone. Here the interference effect of the masker's displacement pattern on the test tone is strong rendering it inaudible. Thus the basilar membrane displacement of the test tone is not distinguishable from that of the masker. Figure (c) also shows a masker with a lower frequency than the test tone. But here the intensity of the test tone is increased sufficiently to be detected as a separate tone.

In addition a sound delivered to one ear may mask a weaker sound sent to the other—an effect called **interaural masking.** It is held that the site of the source of interference for interaural masking is centrally located within the auditory nervous system.

SOUND-INDUCED HEARING LOSS (AUDITORY FATIGUE AND ADAPTATION)

The effects of masking on threshold levels of hearing are not necessarily eliminated when the masking tone is terminated. Ordinarily normal threshold sensitivity to a premasking threshold level is restored very soon after the termination of the masking tone. However, when very intense masking stimulation has been applied for long durations, the effects may extend for a number of hours or days. To the extent that the threshold remains elevated above a premasking threshold *after* termination of the masking stimulus, we have a measure of sound- or noise-induced hearing loss (introduced in Chapter 4). These effects are sometimes called **auditory fatigue** or **adaptation.** Like the effects of masking, this form of hearing loss is manifested by an upward shift in the threshold for a given tone or a reduction in its loudness. However, masking is a temporary loss in sensitivity to a tone *during* (or just after) exposure to another tone, whereas the sound-induced effect is a loss in sensitivity to a tone only *following* exposure to another tone. Not unexpectedly, the length and severity of the hearing loss or fatigue depend on the duration and intensity of the inducing tone.

This is observed when the ear is subjected to intense acoustic stimulation. In principle, the hearing loss or change in threshold sensitivity (called **TTS** for **temporary threshold shift**) at a number of frequencies, measured immediately following exposure to the intense sound, is compared with preexposure measures of threshold sensitivity. The shift in threshold at different frequencies is taken as the measure of temporary hearing loss. Figure 5.10 shows the amount of hearing loss induced by prior

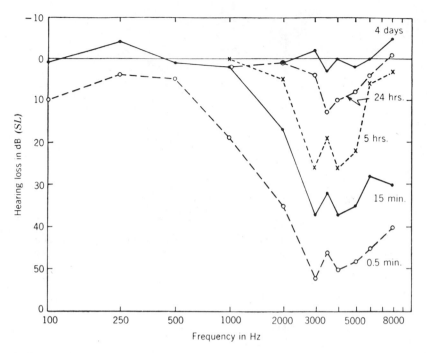

FIGURE 5.10. Audiogram showing changes in auditory sensitivity as a result of exposure to intense noise (115 dB) for 20 min. The curves specify the temporary shift in sensitivity (hearing loss) for various rest periods following exposure to the intense noise. (From Postman and Egan, 1949, p. 72.)

exposure to *white noise* (a form of noise containing a mixture of a wide range of audible frequencies of various intensities). The horizontal zero line represents the preexposure sensitivity of the ear. The curves specify temporary hearing loss for various rest periods after exposure to the noise. The figure shows clearly that temporary hearing loss due to exposure to the intense noise is more pronounced for high frequencies (between 2000 and 6000 Hz), and, as the rest period increases, hearing sensitivity approaches normalcy.

There is also a type of induced threshold shift that is permanent; that is, the individual's threshold never returns to its preexposure level. This **permanent threshold shift** or **PTS** usually results from years of exposure to the intense, chronic noise of the sort observed in certain industrial environments (see the section on hearing loss in Chapter 4). Hearing loss owing to PTS appears to fall primarily within the range of 3000 to 5000 Hz.

SUBJECTIVE TONAL ATTRIBUTES

VOLUME AND DENSITY

The literature on psychoacoustics contains reference to qualities of pure tones that cannot be accounted for by only pitch and loudness. One of these characteristics is termed **volume,** which refers to the size, expansiveness, or voluminousness of a tone. It is based on the assumption that certain sounds, independently matched in pitch and loudness, appear to occupy more space than others. (Notice that the term "volume" as used here is different from the misnamed "volume" control found on radios, receivers, and amplifiers.) When observers are required to order tones along a large–small dimension, considerable agreement occurs in that tones of high-frequency sound smaller or less "voluminous" than tones of low frequency.

Another tonal quality also has been reported called **density.** Density refers to the compactness or tightness of a sound, and greater density occurs with tones of high frequency. Density appears to be reciprocally related to volume with the exception that both increase with increases in intensity, that is, with sufficient increases in intensity a low-frequency tone can be matched in density with a high-frequency tone (Guirao & Stevens, 1964).

CONSONANCE AND DISSONANCE

For most observers, when two tones are sounded together, the resultant combination sounds either pleasant or unpleasant. Those combinations that sound pleasant—that tend to fuse or blend well together—are characterized as **consonant.** Those combinations that sound discordant or harsh are termed **dissonant.** Although it is likely true that nonauditory attributes such as custom, culture, and related learning factors have a role in the consonance–dissonance attribute of combined tones, other auditory processes are also involved.

An important acoustic consideration as to whether two sounds are heard as consonant or dissonant is their frequency difference. One explanation is that dissonance occurs when the upper harmonics of the two fundamentals are close in frequency so as to produce a roughness in the sound (the basis for this was described in the section on beats; see Terhardt, 1977), whereas consonance occurs when the harmonics of the two fundamentals differ sufficiently in frequency to be heard as distinct sounds or they coincide and reinforce each other.

We have outlined a number of significant facts about psychoacoustics. However, we must note that most of this vast body of research, although extremely useful and informative, has been performed in laboratory settings using precisely controlled tones—

usually relatively long-duration pure tones—quite unlike those that ordinarily occur in nature. Perhaps the greatest departure of these laboratory tones from natural ones lies in their purity and duration. Clearly, long-duration pure tones are an infrequent natural occurrence. As put by Masterton and Diamond (1973), "most natural sounds and almost all natural sounds that warn an animal of a potentially dangerous intruder are very brief sounds . . . made up not of enduring pure tones or even their simple combinations, but instead, of sounds such as snaps, pops, crackles, thumps, and thuds" (p. 419).

SUMMARY

By way of summary, we described some of the relationships of the subjective, psychological dimensions of sounds to the physical dimensions of tones. The psychological dimensions of hearing are loudness and pitch, and these are principally determined by the physical dimensions of intensity and frequency, respectively.

The measurement of intensity, intensity discrimination, loudness, and the effect of frequency on loudness were described. Some of the main findings for the human are that, with intensity held constant, sounds in the neighborhood of 3000 Hz sound louder than sounds of other frequencies; differential sensitivity is also greatest in that frequency region.

Frequency, frequency discrimination, pitch, and the effect of intensity on pitch were discussed. Pitch refers to how high or low a sound appears, and it is primarily determined by the frequency of the tone reaching the ear.

Finally, a number of phenomena and variables integral to understanding the perception of sound were discussed: the effects of the duration of a tone, the perception of beats, combination tones, masking, sound-induced hearing loss (auditory fatigue and adaptation, TTS, PTS), and the subjective tonal attributes, volume, density, consonance, and dissonance.

KEY TERMS

Anechoic chamber

Auditory fatigue

Beats

Combination tones

Consonant tones

Density

Difference tones

Dissonant tones

Equal-loudness contours (isophonic contours, Fletcher-Munson curves)

Fractionation

Interaural masking

Line-busy hypothesis

Masking

Mel

Permanent threshold shift (PTS)

Phons

Sone

Summation tones

Temporary threshold shift (TTS)

Volume

STUDY QUESTIONS

1. Describe the change in audibility—threshold levels—as frequency is varied.

2. What are some of the variables that affect the differential threshold of sound intensity? What frequency range yields the greatest differential sensitivity?

3. Describe the relation of loudness to the physical intensity of sound. To what extent is loudness affected by intensity level?

4. Describe the effect of frequency on loudness, making use of equal-loudness contours.

5. What are the general trends observed in the discrimination of frequency? What frequency range yields the greatest discriminability? As stimulus intensity decreases what is the general effect on the discrimination of frequency?

6. Indicate the general relation between frequency and pitch, making use of the mel scale.

7. How is the perception of pitch affected by intensity?

8. To what extent is audibility affected by the duration of a tone? How does the duration of a tone affect the perception of its loudness and its pitch?

9. Describe the phenomenon of beats and consider the role of phase and frequency differences in producing them.

10. What are combination tones and how do they differ from beats?

11. Describe auditory masking and outline the conditions that produce masking. Explain masking by an analysis of interference effects on the basilar membrane, drawing upon the notion of the line-busy hypothesis.

12. Enumerate the effects on auditory sensitivity, especially threshold levels, as a result of exposure to intense sound for an extended duration.

13. Describe the subjective tonal characteristics of volume and density. How do frequency and intensity affect each?

14. What is consonance and dissonance? What determines whether a combination of tones sounds consonant or dissonant? Examine the role of frequency in producing consonance and dissonance.

6

COMPLEX AUDITORY PHENOMENA II: SOUND AS INFORMATION

In this chapter we are concerned with the reception of sound as meaningful stimulus information. Sounds in nature may provide sufficient information to enable the perception of features of distant vibratory events, such as their location and identification. The pickup of meaningful sounds also supports two cognitive skills: it enables the perception of music, and it allows a form of vocal-auditory behavior—verbal communication or speech.

We must emphasize that meaningful natural sounds manifest a vast number of elaborate and complex variations. These variations are far more complex than those observed with the precise experimental manipulations of certain isolated dimensions of laboratory-produced sound stimulation (e.g., frequency and intensity) that we discussed in the preceding chapter.

CEREBRAL DOMINANCE AND HEARING

In the main we have described the functioning of the auditory mechanism as if it consisted of a single unit—the ear. However, normally one ear is but one-half of the listening apparatus. Moreover, the possession of two ears does not merely reflect a duplication of structure; we cannot assume that the ears function independently of each other. Indeed, the auditory nerves that originate from each ear do not necessarily make independent connections with the sound-receiving part of the brain (auditory cortex). The general scheme of connections is sketched in Figure 6.1. After leaving the ear, the fibers of the auditory nerve make a series of connections at various relay stations along the pathway to the brain. Some of the fibers leaving the internal ear to the brain, aside from connecting with other structures, remain on the same (*ipsilateral*) side and interact with fibers from the opposite ear. However, the majority of nerve fibers from one ear (about 60%) cross over to the opposite side. Indeed, this largely *contralateral* connection of neural elements from one side of the body to the opposite side or hemisphere of the brain is characteristic of most of the neural systems of the

body. The auditory cortex is primarily dominated by the fibers that cross—conduction is faster and greater for the crossed pathways—so that each ear is better represented on the opposite cerebral hemisphere of the brain (Rosenzweig, 1961). The effect of this for hearing is that the neural message originating from the right ear is predominantly registered on the left side of the brain and that a message from the left ear is principally registered on the right side of the brain. In operation this means, of course, that a sound produced on one side of the body results in greater cortical activity on the opposite hemisphere.

Another lateral difference in the auditory pathways is that the left and right hemispheres of the brain predominate in different functions. Specifically the two hemispheres differ in the perception of certain broad characteristics of sound stimulation and may differ in the modes of processing information—a functional distinction in its most general sense referred to as **cerebral dominance** or brain asymmetry. The results of a number of studies have indicated that the auditory cortex of the left hemisphere of the brain predominates in the perception of speech and language-related stimulation whereas the right side of the auditory cortex is more functional in the perception and processing of certain nonverbal sounds. There is evidence that structural differences between the hemispheres may underlie functional cerebral dominance (Witelson, 1985). The functional difference has been demonstrated with an auditory technique called **dichotic listening** (different stimulation delivered to each ear is termed *dichotic*). Basically, an observer wearing an independently driven earphone over each ear simultaneously hears two separate messages—a different message to each ear. In one of the initial studies different digits, presented in pairs spaced one-half second apart, were heard by the two ears. When the subjects reported what they heard, more of the digits that had entered the right ear (and as we indicated, primarily registered in the left hemisphere) were correctly reported than were digits delivered to the left ear (Kimura, 1961). These general findings have been extensively replicated and extended (e.g., Bradshaw & Nettleton, 1983; Springer & Deutsch, 1985).

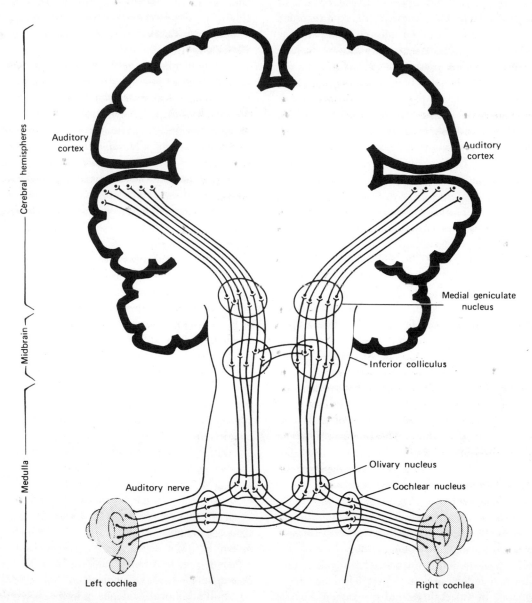

FIGURE 6.1. Semischematic diagram of the conduction pathway of auditory stimulation from the cochlea of each ear to the cerebral cortex. At the olivary nucleus (a relay station), some of the nerve fibers from the cochlear nuclei of both ears converge on the same nerve and thus transmit messages from both ears. At still higher levels there is increasing convergence and interaction between messages from the two ears. Notice, however, that more nerve pathways originating in one cochlear nucleus cross to the opposite side of the brain than remain on the same side.

Interestingly, even when speechlike sounds such as those produced by the reverse playback of recorded speech are presented to the left and right ears, the sounds arriving at the right ear are more accurately identified than those arriving at the left (Kimura & Folb, 1968). On the other hand, for musical stimulation (solo instrumental passages), a reversal in ear dominance occurs: melodies delivered to the left ear were better recalled than similar musical stimuli sent to the right ear (Kimura, 1964, 1967; Johnson & Kozma, 1977). This was also the case for chords and notes from musical instruments (Sidtis & Bryden, 1978) and pure tones (Spreen, Spellacy, & Reid, 1970). Moreover, reaction times to musical sounds were faster when delivered to the left ear than to the right ear (Kallman & Corballis, 1975).

For nonmusical sounds a left-ear dominance was also observed with environmental noise [e.g., a phone ring, dog bark, and clock tick (Curry, 1967; Knox & Kimura, 1970)]. Furthermore a left-ear superiority was reported for nonverbal vocalization [e.g., a cry, sigh, and laugh (Carmon & Nachshon, 1973)]. It appears that for verbal stimuli the right ear is dominant, that is, has a better path to the speech-processing area of the left cerebral hemisphere, whereas for nonverbal stimuli the left ear (and right cerebral hemisphere) is more important. It also should be noted that these hemispheric differences occur early in development: MacKain et al. (1983) have reported that the left hemisphere plays a dominant role in language processing in infancy.

There is evidence suggesting that one of the critical factors promoting right-ear dominance relates to the rapidly changing acoustic stimuli typical of speech (Schwartz & Tallal, 1980). That is "the superiority of the left hemisphere for linguistic processing may reflect, at least in part, left-hemispheric dominance in processing rapidly changing acoustic events, which is critical for the processing of fluent speech" (p. 1381). However, it cannot be concluded that it is merely something inherent in the nature of verbal stimuli per se that accounts for left-hemisphere dominance. There is evidence that it is the kind or level of analytic processing characteristic of verbal or language-related stimuli that is crucial.

Thus Bever and Chiarello (1974; Kellar & Bever, 1980) have reported that musically experienced listeners recognize simple melodies better when sent to the right ear (hence dominant processing by the left hemisphere) than when presented to the left ear, whereas the reverse is the case for naïve listeners. They propose that experienced musicians employ different listening strategies for music; that is, they perform a level of analysis on the melodic information similar to that typically required for speech perception. Thus the musically experienced "have learned to perceive a melody as an articulated set of relations among components, rather than as a whole," whereas musically naïve listeners, "focus on the overall melodic contour"; that is, they "treat melodies as unanalyzed wholes" (p. 538).

A specific case history bearing on this hemispheric structural–functional issue is that of the French composer Maurice Ravel, who at the age of 56, at the peak of his career, suffered severe damage to his left hemisphere (Alajouanine, 1948). Subsequently, he was able to recognize and appreciate music much like a naïve listener, but most of his highly sophisticated analytical skills with music were lost, and he was never able to deal with music as a highly trained musician: he could no longer read or compose in musical notation, play the piano, or even sing in tune.

These behavioral findings bearing on stimulus content and ear–hemisphere dominance have also been given a firm physiological base. Recording auditory responses of the human cortex, Cohn (1971) reported that click noises showed a relatively greater response amplitude over the right cerebral hemisphere and that verbal stimuli produced either an equal or higher response amplitude over the left hemisphere (see also Papanicolaou et al., 1983).

Still additional evidence of hemispheric asymmetry is given by the studies of people who have had large portions of the brain or a single lobe removed to relieve some of the effects of epilepsy. If the left temporal lobe is removed, the patients show very marked difficulties with verbal-related tasks such as comprehending and remembering verbal stimuli. In contrast, lesions of the right temporal cortex lead to difficulties in the perception of nonlinguistic stimuli (e.g., Warrington, 1982). Similarly, patients who have had the connections between the two halves of their brain severed were not able to respond appropriately to verbal stimuli that were presented only to the right hemisphere (e.g., Gazzaniga & Hillyard, 1971). (We should note that the foregoing discussion of cerebral dominance applies primarily to the right-handed majority. The pattern of dominance for left-handed individuals is not nearly as clear; see, e.g., Annett, 1985.)

AUDITORY SPACE PERCEPTION

Functionally the auditory system serves to localize sounds in space. In order to do this precisely both the *direction* and the relative *distance* of sound-emitting stimuli must be perceived and these are given by **monaural** (one-ear) and by **binaural cues.**

MONAURAL CUES

For the most part, monaural cues may be useful for evaluating an object's relative *distance* (although some coarse sound *localization* is possible with monaural hearing; see Oldfield & Parker, 1986). Certainly an important characteristic in judging the distance of a sound source is given by the *intensity* or loudness experienced from the sound wave reaching the ear. The louder the sound, the closer the object appears to be. If two sounds are heard, ordinarily the louder one is perceived as closer. If the intensity of a single sound gradually changes, the perception correspondingly changes. The sound is perceived to approach if it gradually grows louder, and it is perceived to recede if it grows softer. The changing intensity, and corresponding loudness of a siren's wail as a cue to the changing distance of an emergency vehicle in transit relative to a stationary observer, is a familiar example.

Doppler Shift   Another cue to the changing distance of a moving object is given by the shift in the frequency (and pitch) emitted by a sound source moving in relation to a stationary listener. It is called the **Doppler shift,** named after its discoverer, a nineteenth-century Austrian physicist, Christian Doppler. The basis of the shift is that as a sound-emitting object moves, each of its successive sound waves is emitted slightly farther ahead in its path. However, the waves, though moving in all directions at a constant speed, do not share a common center (as would be the case with a stationary sound source). Instead, the sound waves tend to bunch up in front of the moving sound source—that is, there is a lessening of the distance between waves, hence an increase in frequency. The perceptual result is that as the frequency of the sound waves that pass a given point increases, the pitch heard at that point increases. After the object passes, a reversal in pitch occurs; that is, the distance between waves is stretched, frequency decreases, and to the listener, the pitch lowers.

BINAURAL CUES

Although relative distance information is available monaurally, the ability to perceive the direction of a sound is seriously affected when using only one ear. To a monaural listener the physical information from a sound-emitting object could specify the sound lying at any number of undifferentiated locations. It appears that localization depends on the relative stimulation of the two ears—on binaural cues. That is, the auditory system makes use of the physical differences in stimulation that arise between the two ears because of their separation in space.

Time   The information contained in dichotic binaural stimulation enables sound localization. One such cue, called **interaural time differences,** is the slight time differences produced when a sound, especially one with a sharp onset such as a click, reaches one ear before it reaches the other. As shown in Figure 6.2, any sound from source *(B)* in the head's median plane (the plane passing through the middle of the head from front to back) will produce equal effects on the two ears (called *diotic* stimulation). In contrast, a sound arriving from a lateral location, as from source *(A)*, will travel farther to

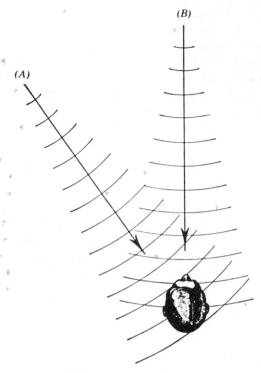

FIGURE 6.2. Binaural cues for sound localization. Sound waves coming from source *B* in the median plane affect both ears equally. A sound from source *A* reaches the left ear before the right ear, and it is more intense because the right ear is slightly "shadowed" by the head.

reach the right ear than the left. It follows that the sound waves from *(A)* will have a later time of arrival at the right ear than the left. In general, a sound source located closer to one ear than the other sends off waves that reach the nearer ear sooner than the farther one. The difference may be slight, but under certain circumstances it is sufficient to locate the sound source (see Wallach, Newman, & Rosenzweig, 1949). It has been stated that sounds whose time of arrival differ by as little as 0.0001 second or even less (without accompanying intensity differences) are sufficient to serve as cues for localizing sound in space; this must be accomplished neurally because such an interval is too small to allow the

sounds to be heard as separate stimuli (Rosenzweig, 1961).

Rosenzweig (1951, 1954, 1961; see also Yin, Kuwada, & Sujaku, 1984) has demonstrated with anesthetized cats that such small differences produce differential responses in the auditory cortex. Tiny electrodes placed at various points along the auditory neural pathway, including the auditory cortex, recorded signals produced by independent earphones, one on each ear. Although responses occurred at both sides of the auditory cortex, when only the right ear was stimulated, the responses at the left side were stronger. When both ears were stimulated but with a small time interval between stimuli (clicks), the resultant cortical responses resembled the responses to the single stimulus. For example, when a click to one ear preceded one to the other ear by, say, 0.0002 second, the amplitude of the cortical response from the initially stimulated ear was slightly larger than that from the other ear. Of course, as previously described, this is based on the fact that each ear is better represented in the opposite side of the brain; thus a sound delivered to one ear prior to the other produces more neural activity in the side of the brain opposite to the ear first stimulated and partially inhibits the response to the later one. The neural response pattern therefore reflects the temporal differences in the pattern of stimulation.

The Precedence Effect This phenomenon of suppressing later-arriving sound is termed the **precedence effect.**

The effect can be partly demonstrated by employing two speakers of a home stereo system set to monaural or "mono" so that the speakers will deliver identical acoustic stimuli. If you are seated equidistant from the two speakers, you will hear the sound from both speakers simultaneously. However, if you move to the left or right, only one of the speakers will appear to be sounding. That is, the nearer speaker will appear to be the only active sound source. The sound reaching the ears from the farther speaker may be delayed only a few milliseconds (and may be only slightly less intense) relative to the sound of the nearer speaker. However, this relatively slight time difference is sufficient to suppress the sound of the farther speaker, at least with respect to its apparent locus. In fact, you may even need to verify that the other speaker is still "on." The sound from the farther speaker, though apparently inaudible, does affect the quality of the sound coming from the nearer speaker. When the farther speaker is turned off, the sound from the nearer, audible speaker will seem weaker and less expansive. This observation suggests that the auditory system weighs the first sounds more heavily and tends to suppress later-arriving sounds (Wallach, Newman, & Rosenzweig, 1949). Indeed, in an environment with prominant echoes, the first waveforms or sounds contain the most accurate information concerning the locus of the sounds. Later-arriving waveforms generally give a false impression of locations since they originate from objects that have reflected the first waveforms (Green, 1976).

Phase Under certain conditions, especially for low frequencies, sound localization may be effected by detecting a difference in phase between the sounds reaching the two ears. Sounds of low frequencies have wavelengths that are longer than the diameter of the head; such sounds are diffracted around the head and may produce phase differences. That is, the waveform of the sound reaching one ear may be in a different part of its compression–rarefaction cycle than the waveform of the sound arriving at the other ear. However, above about 1000 Hz, phase differences are not significant for sound localization (Oster, 1973).

Intensity Another binaural cue, called **interaural intensity differences,** results from the intensity difference between the sounds reaching each ear. A sound, nonequidistant from the ears, not only strikes the nearer ear first but it also delivers a slightly more intense sound to that ear. This is because the head becomes an acoustic obstacle, that is, the head casts a sound "shadow" and the ear opposite to the sound source lies in this shadow (see Figure 6.2). Hence, sound waves that must pass around the head are disrupted and reach the farther

ear with a weaker intensity than the nearer ones. Because the long wavelengths of low-frequency sounds tend to bend around the ear, the influence of sound shadows on interaural intensity differences are greater as frequency increases (i.e., wavelength decreases). In other words, interaural intensity differences are most effective as cues for localization at high frequencies.

Relevant to localization based on interaural intensity differences is the fact that when a tone is presented to both ears simultaneously but made more intense to one ear, the listener hears the tone as coming only from the direction of the more intensely stimulated ear. In a phenomenon analogous to the precedence effect discussed earlier, the tone appears to stimulate only the ear receiving the more intense signal. However, the weaker signal, although not audible, contributes to the overall loudness of the more intense tone in that if the weaker tone is eliminated the more intense tone appears to decrease in loudness. Thus for localization the auditory system tends to maximize the more intense stimulus.

The localization effect based on the interaural intensity difference can be easily experienced using earphones with a home stereo system. While wearing the earphones, manipulate the "balance" control (which modulates the intensity of the sound reaching the left and right ear, individually) just until the sound appears to come from only one earphone. By listening individually to each earphone, you will observe that there is actually sound coming from the other, less intense earphone.

Using this demonstration we can better understand the following historical anecdote on auditory localization. According to Rosenzweig (1961), shortly after 1900 the German physician Stenger devised a clinical test to expose individuals feigning deafness in one ear. The test, which is still used, is based on some of the points made in the text and in this demonstration. For example, a person who pretends to be deaf in his or her left ear will report hearing a tone if it is presented to the right ear through an earphone. What happens if the same tone is now presented to the right ear and *simultaneously, but more intensely* to the left ear? According to the demonstration and the text, the listener with normal hearing will hear the sound as coming only from the left. Of course a person truly deaf in the left ear will hear only the less intense tone sent to the right ear. In contrast, the malingerer (who has normal hearing) will betray himself or herself by stating that he or she does *not hear any* sound, in spite of the fact that sound of an audible intensity level is being delivered to the admittedly normal right ear. According to Rosenzweig, "The effectiveness of this test makes it clear that the listener hears only a single localized sound and does not compare separate sensations arising at the two ears" (p. 132).

Head Movements   To binaural listeners the location of sound sources in the horizontal plane is possible, but vertical location (i.e., the location of a sound above versus below the observer) poses a problem. Furthermore, if a sound source is located in the median plane (the vertical plane passing through the middle of the head from front to back), its direction cannot be correctly determined by a stationary observer. Similarly, a listener may experience confusion in the localization of sounds originating on the surface of a **cone of confusion,** as illustrated in Figure 6.3, when the sounds are parallel to the median plane. The listener can tell from which side the sounds come (i.e., left or right). However, confusion in these cases results because no matter where the sounds originate on the median plane, or parallel to it on the conical surface, they are always the same distance from each ear, thereby producing the same degree of interaural time and intensity differences. These problems of location can be solved by allowing free movement of the head: when an organism moves its head, temporal and intensity changes in sound reception are produced. It follows, then, that if the head turns to the left of the midline, a sound directly behind is heard sooner and louder by the left ear than by the right ear. Moreover, by moving the head up and down sound-emitting stimuli in the vertical plane can be located.

We should note in this context that the complex surface created by the folds and corrugations of the

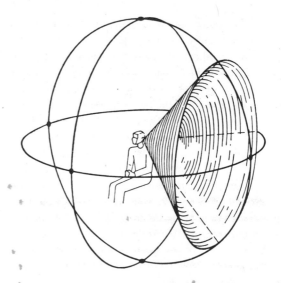

FIGURE 6.3.   Cone of confusion. The conical surface on the side of the median plane is called a cone of confusion because the listener cannot discriminate among sounds located on the surface when they are parallel to the median plane, although the listener can tell from which side—left or right—the sound comes. Confusion results because sounds originating at any location on the surface of the cone and parallel to the median plane will provide the same difference in stimulation at the two ears. The circles indicate possible positions of the sound source in the three principal planes of the head.

pinna (i.e., the external ear flap) modify and reflect the spectrum of a sound (especially of a high frequency) prior to entering the external auditory canal and, along with head movements, may provide cues to the sound's localization (e.g., see Batteau, 1967, for monaural, and Oldfield & Parker, 1986, for binaural localization). In action the wrinkles and convolutions of the pinna may act like small reflecting surfaces that create different patterns of echoes for sound sources that lie at different directions from the listener; thus sounds originating in front of the listener in some situations may be heard as different from those located behind the listener. In one investigation, when the pinna was rendered ineffective by functionally smoothing out its irregularities and hence its sound reflecting properties, accuracy in localization was measurably reduced (Gardner & Gardner, 1973).

Much of the foregoing relates to animals with symmetrical ears. However, the ears of the owl, unlike those of all other vertebrates, are not symmetrical. Because of this, the owl can easily locate horizontal and vertical sound sources (Matthews & Knight, 1963). Thus, to the owl a sound heard in the median plane reaches one ear first, whereas in most other vertebrates both ears would receive the sound at the same instant. No doubt we can assign the asymmetrical placement of the owl's ears as a special adaptation: characteristically the owl stalks its prey (generally small rodents and insects) on the wing at night, and must locate it primarily on the basis of faint and brief transient sounds. This adaptation is extended to the unique organization of the owl's auditory cortex, which has specialized neurons that react to sounds only when they originate from certain spatial regions, thus creating a neural map of auditory space (Knudsen & Konishi, 1978).

Stereophonic Listening   Almost all individuals are familiar with the striking auditory effects produced by stereophonic recordings that employ a playback system of two loudspeakers. The basis for the stereophonic experience is binaural hearing. **Stereophonic listening** is produced by dichotic stimulation and results in an experience of aural space. At their simplest, stereophonic recordings are made by recording the same acoustic event with two microphones placed at different locations in order to simulate partly the difference in sounds received by the two ears. Upon playback, these two sound sources are each delivered to a separate speaker so as to produce a mild form of dichotic stimulation for the listener. (Actually, modern techniques of stereophonic recording make use of more than two microphones.)

However, with the simplest technique of stereophonic recording, stereophonic listening cannot properly replicate the full aural space or sonic ambience experienced at a live performance in a large auditorium. This is owing, in part, to the fact that in a sizable auditorium sound reflections strike the listener from all directions (and at slightly different times) but largely from the rear. Although some of these reflections may be captured on a stereophonic recording, they are delivered typically by speakers located in front of the listener. Thus, an element of ambient sound is lost.

A very realistic sound experience can be achieved by placing a recording microphone close to the auditory canal of each ear. The sounds thus recorded preserve all the binaural differences that are ordinarily heard. On playback, wearing stereophonic headphones, the recording sounds strikingly like what was originally heard. Stereophonic effects can be manipulated by a number of factors, such as by changing the microphone placement at the recording site and by varying the location of and the intensity difference between the playback loudspeakers in the listening environment. Reproduction systems using four speakers (so-called "quadraphonic" or four-channel sound systems), tend to produce a more displaced and enlarged sound space than that offered by the two loudspeakers of stereophonic sound systems. In quadraphonic sound systems, two of the speakers are placed in back of the listener to supplement the sound heard from the front.

An innovation in simulating the reflections of sonic ambience is the use of a four-speaker system coupled with an ambience synthesizer that can selectively produce time delays. The time-delay device holds the sonic signal for a fraction of a second and then feeds it to a pair of speakers located in back of or at the sides of the listener, while the undelayed portion of the signal goes to the front speakers. Accordingly, by altering the delay, the auditory system may register the sounds of an enlarged, though nonexistent environment. Thus, increasing the delay of the sounds delivered to the rear of the listener expands the apparent size of the auditory space—a *trompe d'oreille*. However, most time-delay systems, while useful in offsetting the acoustic limitations of small rooms by creating a more spacious sonic impression, may contribute very little to the authenticity of sound and may even result in some loss of clarity and fidelity.

ECHOLOCATION

The natural habitat of a number of nonterrestrial mammals, including bats, whales, porpoises, and perhaps some small terrestrial rodents, requires activity in places where the use of vision is severely reduced or eliminated. For example, bats are active at night and in conditions where the amount of light is negligible; whales and porpoises may dwell in murky waters and at depths to which light does not easily penetrate. Functionally speaking, to locomote effectively in visually impeded environments, these animals have evolved the ability to evaluate the reflection or echoes of their own sounds from objects in their surroundings. The result is that they gain information about the range and direction (and perhaps the velocity, size, and shape) of objects at a distance. In short, they are made aware of the location of objects that they cannot see by means of self-emitted sound waves reflected by them. The use of self-produced echoes to gain biologically significant information such as object range and direction is termed **echolocation.**

Most of the research on echolocation has been done with bats, whose principal sensory modality appears to be audition. It is estimated that there are about 600 living species of bats that pursue prey guided by echolocation (Simmons, Fenton, & O'Farrell, 1979). We will briefly focus on the bat's echolocating mechanism. The bat avoids obstacles when flying in the dark, and it can locate and capture prey with near perfect accuracy while it and its prey fly at relatively high speeds. Bats perform these feats by producing and receiving the echoes of extremely brief *ultrasonic* cries or pulses (i.e., sounds above the frequency limit of human hearing) whose frequencies are in excess of 100 kHz (see Figure 6.4). The number of pulses emitted varies with the bat's activity. During searching flight, only 10 pulses per second are emitted, whereas during interception maneuvers as many as 200 of these pulses may be produced in a second (Novick, 1971).

The production and reception of ultrasonic sounds are necessary for bats to identify and track prey and avoid obstacles. This is due to several physical considerations of sound transmission: high-frequency sounds are reflected less diffusely than low-frequency sounds. In addition, to be reflected from an object and thus to carry information about it, the sound must have a wavelength smaller than the object. For the bat, small insects are the objects to be localized, so high-frequency sounds (i.e., short wavelengths) are most important. This points out the biological value of the bat's extended upper limit of hearing.

Indeed, there are structural peculiarities of the bat's auditory and vocal anatomy that facilitate the reception of high frequencies. For example, the region of the cochlea concerned with high-frequency reception, nearest the middle ear, is unusually large in bats. Furthermore, the bat's vocal structures are well engineered for producing ultrasonic pulses (Griffin, 1958, 1959).

The design of ultrasonic pulses for bats varies with family. For example, *horsehoe* bats emit sounds of nearly a single frequency of about 83 kHz—followed by a sweep down to 65 or 70 kHz (Simmons, 1971). The individual sounds may last from 50 to 65 msec. The small brown bats, common to the United States, begin their pulses at 90 kHz and end up at 45 kHz. Their pulse duration lasts only about 2 msec, which means that there is a very rapid frequency change. This type of sound emission is called *frequency modulation* or *FM*. FM pulse emission can serve as a very sophisticated range-measuring mechanism. The utilization of a pulse whose frequency changes means that echoes returning from targets located at different distances are heard at different frequencies. In the case of a single echo, if it reached one ear prior to the other, it would be heard at a different frequency in each ear.

In general, different species of bats have evolved with differences in their echolocating systems to meet the demands of their particular acoustic environment. However, the general mechanism of bat echolocation utilizes an emission of a series of short ultrasonic orientation pulses and a comparison of their echoes with respect to the original pulses. This may involve the evaluation of temporal, intensity, and frequency differences between the emitted pulse bursts and the reception of their echoes. In many respects this mechanism is similar to the

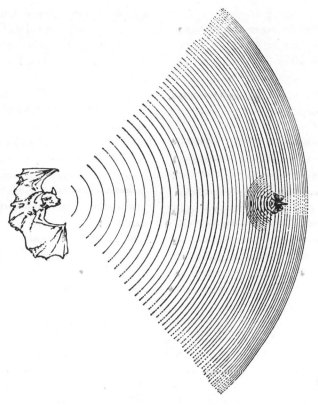

FIGURE 6.4. A flying bat and a representation of its emitted ultrasonic pulse. The curved lines represent individual sound waves in a single pulse. The frequency and wavelength of a bat's sound may vary during each pulse. The figure, which according to its author is drawn to scale, illustrates the small amount of sound reflected by one insect. In searching flight, bats may emit about 10 pulses per second. The pulse rate is increased to between 25 and 50 per second during a phase in which the bat appears to identify a target. During an approach or interception phase, the rate may be increased to 200 or more pulses per second (Novick, 1971). (From D. R. Griffin, *Echoes of Bats and Man*, Anchor Books/Doubleday, Garden City, N.Y., 1959, p. 86. Reprinted by permission of the author.)

technical instruments for sound navigation in water (i.e., *SO*und *N*avigation *A*nd *R*anging, hence the term **SONAR**). Thus for the bat and other animals, we may use the term **biosonar** to characterize their functional employment of echoes.

OBSTACLE PERCEPTION BY THE BLIND

Blind individuals are often able to avoid walking into obstacles. Several theories have attempted to account for this ability. A prominent one held that the touch and temperature senses developed sufficiently in certain of the blind to enable them to feel air currents as they are affected by the proximity of obstacles. The locus of this ability was attributed to the face, hence the term "facial vision." Auditory cues in the form of echoes from objects have provided another explanation for the perception of obstacles by the blind. A series of experiments in the 1940s was undertaken to choose between these two explanations.

Using blindfolded normally sighted and blind

subjects, Supra, Cotzin, and Dallenbach (1944) tested the effectiveness of auditory cues for obstacle perception. A subject was instructed to walk down a hallway and to indicate when he thought he was approaching a wall and to walk up as close as possible to it without striking it. When sound cues were reduced—such as by having subjects walk in their stocking feet over thick carpeting or by stopping their ears—obstacle avoidance was poor or eliminated. In most instances this result occurred although potential sources of touch stimulation were available, that is, the head, arms, and hands were open to stimulation. This indicated that touch is not sufficient for the perception of obstacles at a distance. Moreover, when subjects wore earphones that presented a masking tone but were also provided with potential touch stimulation, no obstacle avoidance was observed. Indeed, that sound alone is critical for obstacle avoidance is given in the following experiment in which all sensory channels of stimulation except the acoustic one were eliminated. Subjects were placed in a soundproof room and were instructed to judge the experimenter's approach to an obstacle by means of the experimenter's footsteps. The sounds of the experimenter's footsteps were picked up by a microphone carried by the experimenter at ear height and transmitted to the subject through an amplifying system and earphones. Under these conditions, all subjects tested were able to perceive the experimenter's approach to the obstacle and their ability to do so was only slightly inferior to their performances when they themselves walked toward the obstacle. Clearly, these experiments show that blind subjects perceive obstacles on the basis of sound information.

Several questions arise: How accurate are sound cues for spatial perception? What additional spatial abilities are possible using sounds? Some research on this has been attempted by Kellogg (1962), who compared the performance of the blind with that of blindfolded normally sighted control subjects in a number of spatial tasks. Of particular interest is that subjects were informed that they could make any sound they wanted for the purpose of producing echoes. Although the subjects sometimes employed tongue-clicking, finger-snapping, hissing, or whistling, coupled with headbobbing, the preferred source of self-produced sound was the human voice used in a repetitive fashion—that is, vocalizing the same word over and over.

In a series of tasks, Kellogg (1962) found that blind subjects were able to derive distance and size information on the basis of self-produced sounds, whereas the performance of the blindfolded normal subjects was at about a chance level. Blind subjects also were able to discriminate between different texture surfaces such as metal, glass, wood, denim and velvet whereas blindfolded normal subjects could not. The conclusion is that the perception of echoes reflected from objects provides sufficient information for object detection and avoidance in the human blind. A striking nonlaboratory demonstration of the use of reflected sound for deriving location information is that by a nationally ranked intercollegiate equestrian who has been blind since birth. Her ability to navigate the corners and winding turns on the course during competition are based on the reflected echoes produced by the sounds of her ride. As she describes it, "I can hear my horse's hooves echo off the rails when they hit the ground" (Knouse, 1988, p. 8).

As to the stimulus factors used for auditory localization and the perception of obstacles, it has been found that changes in the pitch rather than the loudness of echoes are the basic cues (Cotzin & Dallenbach, 1950). Moreover, Rice (1967) found that self-produced sounds of moderately high frequency are most effective in object localization. It is probable that high-frequency sounds are most useful because the higher the frequency, the shorter the wavelength and the better the reflection. Furthermore, as we have previously noted, wavelength size also specifies another limitation: an object must have a size at least as large as a single wavelength in order to reflect an effective echo.

Finally, it is worth noting in this discussion that a factor contributing to the successful spatial localization and environmental orientation for the blind concerns the time at which blindness occurred in an individual's life span. Individuals who have had early visual experience in orientation prior to losing their sight are subsequently more effective in tasks involving object localization and orientation than are individuals who have been blinded early in their life and thereby deprived of visual experience (Veraart & Wanet-Defalque, 1987; Hollins & Kelley, 1988). That the amount of early visual experience can play a significant role in achieving auditory spatial localization for the blind applies especially for judging distance (Veraart & Wanet-Defalque, 1987). It has been proposed that some early visual experience enables the blind person to have a better grasp or mastery over the notion of spatial representation. That is, prior visual experience could facilitate the blind individual's coordination and use of nonvisual external reference cues in deriving and constructing an accurate spatial framework, thereby promoting more successful environmental interactions.

THE PERCEPTION OF MUSIC

Thus far in our discussion of sound and audition, we have uncovered a wide range of psychoacoustic principles, processes, and facts, for the most part concerning the reception of relatively simple laboratory sounds. However we are also capable of experiencing the succession of sounds that vary in frequency, intensity, complexity, and duration in a very unique way—as *music*.

Whereas the general nature and transmission of musical sounds follow the facts we have outlined in Chapters 4 and 5, it must be stressed that music is a very special and complex kind of acoustic information. Clearly the characterization of musical tones solely on the basis of their physical attributes and properties is not sufficient to explain the experience of those tones as heard within a musical context. First, we perceive music as more than merely a succession of discrete sounds; rather, the sounds are integrated and heard as organized, well-formed, coherent patterns that may be recognized as musical phrases or *melodies*. Indeed a melodic pattern may be so compelling, so evocative to the listener, that often,

after hearing it only once, it may be reproduced from memory. Moreover, we recognize that the succession of tones comprising the melody also has a beat, a rhythm, and a cadence.

For our purposes we may characterize the perception of music as a psychological experience that is generated by the relationship of tones to each other and to the context of which they are a part. Different contexts initiate different listener strategies and frameworks, which may lead to quite different perceptions of the same physical sounds. The performance of tasks that are musically meaningful, such as the recognition of melodies and harmonies, greatly influences how tonal sequences are processed and heard. Thus recognizing a *musical context* tends to induce, within the listener, a particular mental mode or cognitive framework within which tones are perceptually interpreted.

ACOUSTIC DIMENSIONS OF MUSIC

A fundamental understanding of the perception of music requires a discussion of a number of technical details that extend considerably beyond the scope of this chapter. We can, however, draw upon our earlier discussion of psychoacoustics and outline some of the basic experiential phenomena and relationships that exist between certain of the physical characteristics of musical tones or notes and some processes that contribute to their perception as music.

We noted in Chapters 4 and 5 that pitch is principally related to frequency, but as we observed when describing the mel scale (Figure 5.4), the higher-pitch tones (or notes) appear to include more psychological or mel units than the lower notes. In practice, melodies played in the treble (e.g., on a piano) are much clearer than when they are played in the bass. That is, it is as if the psychological distance between the piano keys on the high end is greater than on the low end (see Figure 5.5).

OCTAVES, MUSICAL NOTATION, AND SCALES

The sixth-century Greek mathematician and philosopher Pythagoras (472–497 B.C.) uncovered the simple numerical relationship of musical sounds from which modern Western musical scales derive; he observed that the pitch of a sound from a stringed instrument depends upon the length of the string that produces it. He noted further that when one string is exactly twice the length of another equally taut string it produces pitches corresponding to an **octave** difference. In other words, an octave is the interval between any two tones, one of which is exactly twice the frequency of the other; moreover such tones possess a strong psychological similarity. Thus a tone whose frequency is 880 Hz (i.e., A_5, in musical notation described shortly) is one octave higher than a tone whose frequency is 440 Hz (A_4). However, even though the first tone sounds higher in pitch, it is heard as very similar to the second tone. In fact, tones that are exactly one octave apart seem more similar to each other than do sounds separated by less than an octave. As an example the two tones whose frequencies are 261.63 and 523.25 Hz (i.e., C_4 and C_5), respectively, sound closer to each other than do the two tones corresponding to 261.63 and 392 Hz (i.e., C_4 and G_4).

In Western musical notation, a tone is represented by a letter that specifies its position within the octave, along with a number that indicates the particular octave in which it occurs. Thus the letters used for tones *within* a given octave are C, D, E, F, G, A, B, and C and, for example, the numerically notated letters C_3, C_4, C_5, represent tones that stand in an octave relation to each other. Technically each octave is divided into 12 parts (actually 12 equal ratio intervals) called **semitones.** Consider the segment of a piano keyboard that spans a full octave, sketched in Figure 6.5. If one starts at middle C on the piano and plays every note, white and black keys, to the C above middle C—that is, an octave range—one has played a **chromatic scale.** If only the white keys are played, the familiar "do-re-mi-fa-so-la-ti-do" sequence is heard, called the C-major or major diatonic scale. Observe from the piano keyboard that there is no black key between E and F or between B and C. The intervals between these two steps is a semitone, whereas all other steps are separated by a whole tone. Thus an octave consists of 12 semitones, and the pitch of a given tone can be described based on which octave and where within that octave it lies.

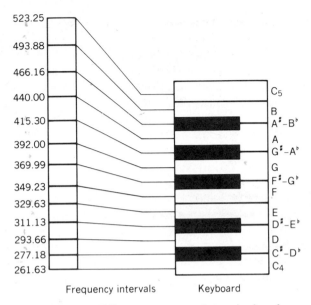

Frequency intervals   **Keyboard**

FIGURE 6.5.   Full-octave segment of piano keyboard matching the tones with their frequencies. The octave interval between C_4 and C_5 is divided into white keys, which sound the notes of the C-major or major diatonic scale, and black keys, which produce the in-between tones called sharps and flats: a sharp (♯) is a half-step up from a white note, a flat (♭) is a half-step down. Playing every key, white and black, of the octave interval, sounds the notes of the chromatic scale.

The unique structure that characterizes the relation of each tone to each other tone within a given octave is invariant across changes of octave. For example, whereas E_4 sounds similar but lower in pitch than E_5, the relation of E_4 to D_4 and F_4 is the same as is the relation that E_5 is to D_5 and F_5. The perceptual similarity of tones that stand in an octave relation, referred to as **octave equivalence,** requires that pitch be analyzed in more than a unitary dimension. This can be illustrated by the use of an unusual configuration, similar to an old-time barber pole, shown in Figure 6.6, that deforms the scale of pitch into the spiral shape of a helix (this configuration is based on a scheme proposed by M. W. Drobisch in 1846, cited in Ruckmick, 1929). The vertical dimension, termed **tone height,** specifies overall pitch level (i.e., reflects the sense of high

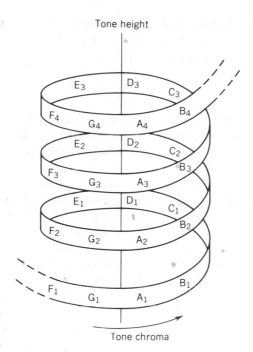

Tone height

FIGURE 6.6.   Bidimensional representation of pitch: *tone height* represents overall pitch, which depends upon stimulus frequency; *tone chroma* represents the position of a tone within a given octave. Observe that the spacing between tones, representing their relative positions, remains the same within each octave and that tones that stand in an octave relation to each other, for example, G_2, G_3, G_4, and so on are aligned with each other within each turn of the helix. (Based on Boring, Langfeld, and Weld, 1948, p. 320.)

and low pitch) and varies with stimulus frequency; the circular plane, called **tone chroma,** represents the relative position of a tone within a given octave. A complete turn or rotation of the helix in the horizontal plane accommodates a single octave. Notice that within each turn of the helix, tones standing in an octave relation to each other appear to lie relatively proximal on the vertical axis.

In addition to octave similarity, there are other relations between musical tones that possess perceptual significance. For example, when one tone is 1.5 times the frequency of the other (i.e., a 3-to-2 ratio, a perfect fifth) or a 4-to-3 ratio, the two tones are more

pleasing or consonant when sounded together than are tones separated by other frequencies (with the exception of the 2-to-1 frequency ratio of the octave interval; see Roederer, 1973, and Krumhansl & Kessler, 1982).

ABSOLUTE OR PERFECT PITCH

An aspect of pitch perception that bears discussion concerns the ability of some individuals to identify and even to reproduce isolated musical notes without any apparent musical reference or standard. This ability, which is relatively rare even among professional musicians, is called **absolute** or **perfect pitch.** Although individuals with perfect pitch can readily identify a musical note, they may be somewhat prone to misidentify the octave in which the tone is located. An unusual anecdote concerning absolute pitch is attributed to the musical prodigy Wolfgang Amadeus Mozart (Stevens & Warshofsky, 1965). At the age of seven Mozart was able to discern that his violin was tuned "half a quarter of a tone" sharper than his friend's violin, an instrument that he had last played days earlier. Whereas prolonged training appears to enhance overall skill in pitch recognition, perfect pitch appears to be a genetically derived ability that requires proper exposure and training during early development for it to be realized fully (e.g., Miyazaki, 1988).

PERCEPTION OF PITCH SEQUENCES: MELODIES

When played in different keys or on different instruments, or even when sung by different voices, melodies retain some invariant characteristics and continue to sound the same or very similar. That is, melodies appear to retain their perceptual identities when they are systematically altered, such as when tones are transposed to different pitch ranges, provided that the relationships between the successive tones and their pitches comprising the melody remain unchanged. This underscores the idea that melodies are heard not based on the sequential reception of a series of specific notes, but rather due to the perception of a unique overall relation or pattern among notes. That is, when listening to music, one attends to pitch *relations*, not to absolute pitch sounds. Part of the explanation of this is based on the fact that a sequence of tones comprising a musical passage possesses certain invariant global features that assign to it a particular musical character and, accordingly, contribute to its perception as music. Principal among these is the recognition of the spacing between discrete notes and the sequence of pitch changes between successive notes—that is, the pattern of peaks and troughs of frequency that characterize a particular melody—that create a musical context. The latter refers to the melodic *contour* of the passage and serves to define the melody (e.g., Dowling, 1978). Indeed as D. Deutsch (1978, 1986) observes, for the most part, melodies may be recognized on the basis of contour alone.

The perception of the contour of a musical sequence of notes appears to occur on the basis of certain organizing tendencies. These organizing tendencies resemble the grouping processes that occur in vision (codified as Gestalt principles, particularly applicable to form and pattern perception in vision, described in Chapter 14). Several of the fundamental principles governing these grouping tendencies in musical audition can be noted here: for example, notes within a sequence that appear close to each other in time (i.e., contiguous in time of note onset) and pitch tend to be perceived or grouped as being part of the same musical unit (Monahan, Kendall, & Carterette, 1987). When adjacent tones in a sequence combine to form changes in the pitch pattern —rising and falling together—they are likely to be perceived as a group. Also, repetition of a particular subsequence within a musical sequence induces in the listener the tendency to group the elements comprising the subsequence together as a unit, distinct from the remainder of the overall sequence (For theory and evidence on the perceptual grouping of musical elements, see, e.g., Deutsch, 1982; Sloboda, 1985; and Delierge, 1987).

TEMPORAL ORGANIZATION

Characteristics such as rhythm, meter, tempo, and temporal accent, collectively, refer to the various temporal orderings, intervals, and proportionalities in the time spans that occur between musical elements in a given sequence (see Jones, 1987). Variation of temporal relationships—for example, the imposed rate or timing at which tones within a sequence are presented—can affect the perception of the sequence in a number of ways. Indeed, most musical passages have internal durational properties or rhythmic structure that may provide the basis as to how the listener hears groups of tones as forming a perceptual unit. As an example, the perceptual grouping or segmenting of tonal sequences may be accomplished on the basis of temporal proximity: thus temporally accenting, such as producing a gap between equally spaced elements of a tonal sequence promotes, spontaneously, the hearing of segments of tones as discrete and cohesive musical groups, distinct from other groups in the sequence. In brief, the coding of temporal sequences or patterns and the apparent spontaneous rhythmic organization appears to conform to certain internalized principles of grouping that we addressed with respect to melodic contour (e.g., Povel & Essens, 1985; Monahan, Kendall, & Carterette, 1987). It should be noted also that durational organization and melody are not psychologically independent dimensions; indeed, in tasks that require the processing of musical sequences, such as with melody recognition, there are significant interactive effects of rhythmic with melodic features (e.g., Jones, 1987).

CHROMESTHESIA AND MUSIC

Synesthesia is a phenomenon in which stimulation of one sensory modality almost simultaneously evokes an experience in a different sensory domain (Marks, 1975, 1978). **Chromesthesia** (also termed chromaesthesia, or color hearing) is a specific form of synesthesia in which sounds not only register an aural sensation but produce vivid color sensations as well. This interplay of sensory experience is especially prevalent in the case of musical sounds. Whereas there is considerable variation among individuals, the tone–color relationship does manifest certain general uniformities and trends: for example, Langfeld (1914) reported the synesthetic responses of a musician-composer when she was 23 and 30 years of age and observed that treble notes resulted in relatively stable sensations of lighter colors and bass notes induced darker colors. Moreover, the results, spanning over a seven-year period, were quite similar. Remarkably, the subject could sense or "see" the color at the mere mention of the musical note.

More recently, Cutietta and Haggerty (1987) investigated the colors associated with auditory sensations (a phenomenon they label "color association," rather than true chromesthesia) to determine whether or not the effect is due to experiential conditioning. Because of the extensive subject population used, it is of interest to consider their procedure: they examined the color associations of 1256 subjects, ranging in age from 3 to 78 years. Subjects were instructed to listen to three tape recorded musical passages. The particular musical examples were selected because each possessed a distinctive and unique overall musical quality. They were (1) a "majestic and vigorous" passage (Gustav Holt's *Suite No. 1 in E flat major*, third movement, "March"), (2) a "plodding and laboring" passage (Moussorgsky's, *Picture at an Exhibition*, fourth movement, "Bydlo"), and (3) a "lively, dancelike piece," played by a trio of woodwinds, (Handel's *Music for the Royal Fireworks*, "Bourrée," measures 11–26). While listening to each music passage, subjects were instructed to indicate the colors of which the music "reminded them or made them think, or that they associated with the music." While there was significant variation, there was also overall consistency in color responses. The "majestic" example (1) was primarily associated with the color red, the "plodding" example (2) tended toward associations of blue, and the "lively" example (3) was associated with yellow. Consistency of color associations to the music passages was noted in children at about age 9; this consistency was similarly observed in those whose age ranged into early adulthood. However, for subjects in their forties and fifties, greater variability was found. While the findings are clear that across many age groups there are consistent color–music associations, the origin and basis of the link is elusive. According to Cutietta and Haggerty, if individuals are conditioned in childhood

to make certain color associations to music, then it should follow that the association responses should occur gradually and should grow more consistent with age and the corresponding gain in experience. However, such results were not found; thus the consistency of color–music associations observed in the young subjects and the increasing variability in associations noted in the older adults tested argues against an experiential conditioning explanation.

FUNCTION OF MUSIC PERCEPTION

Finally, we may consider the status of music perception in the overall context of general auditory system function. Clearly, music may provide intensely experienced aesthetic pleasure. The amalgam of complex, but ordered patterns, intertwined with emotion, tension, change, uncertainty, and even surprise, common to most aesthetic experience, is probably basic to its intrinsic appeal. Indeed, music has been characterized as "designed uncertainty" (L. B. Myers, cited in Smith, 1987). Clearly, by almost any criterion music ranks as a highly evolved art form and stands as a prominent part of the human cultural endeavor and heritage. However, from a more biological context, consider the proposal by the physicist J. G. Roederer (1973) that in the course of evolution, the attainment of music perception occurred as an incidental consequence dictated by the tremendous complexity demands placed on the auditory system, to serve, first, as a distance and locus detector and, later, as a communication system.

THE PERCEPTION OF SPEECH

An important behavioral function of the auditory system is its role in the form of human communication called speech. Obviously, the perception of speech begins with stimulation of the ear. However, as with music, speech perception involves an enormous number of complex psychological variables so that we can only briefly outline the processes involved. Consider how remarkable this ability is. It requires the ability to make very fine discriminations between sounds. For example, a spoken word consists of a short pattern of sounds lasting less than a second. Moreover, the perception of speech persists when the sounds comprising words undergo a number of marked changes. That is, words retain their identity and are perceived accurately under a number of distorting conditions: for example, varying accents, dialects and voice qualities, masking background noises and sound omissions, and distortions produced by electrical means such as by telephones or other mass communications systems. Indeed, even when most physical characteristics of speech sounds have been changed to some degree, intelligibility may still persist. That meaningful speech occurs under these conditions points out a striking perceptual achievement.

The range of actual speech sounds is limited by the anatomy of the vocal apparatus rather than by the potential of the ear to hear. Human speech is produced by the mechanics of the vocal cords and the variably resonant vocal tract, which includes cavities of the mouth, throat, and nose. The air in the cavities is set into vibration by movement of the vocal cords producing sound waves. Different frequencies may be produced by the combined action of the vocal tract and the relative positioning of the tongue, lips, cheeks, and jaw. The potential for varying frequency is determined by a number of factors. The resonant frequency of the oral cavity is governed by the physical length of the tract and the mass of the vocal cords. For the average man this frequency is close to 500 Hz; for women, 727 Hz; and for children, 850 Hz (Bergeijk, Pierce, & David, 1960). As Figure 6.7 shows, the highest useful frequencies for speech production lie close to 6500 Hz. Thus, speech sounds occupy about a third of the total range of frequencies audible to humans. Note also from Figure 6.7 that although a major part of speech energy occurs at comparatively low frequencies (where the

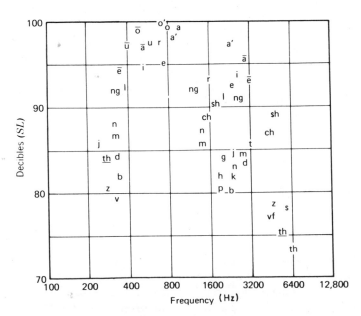

FIGURE 6.7. Frequency and intensity characteristics of the fundamental speech sounds. Those sounds having more than one principal frequency component appear at more than one location on the figure. (From Harvey Fletcher, *Speech and Hearing*, rev. ed., D. Van Nostrand Company. Copyright © 1952.)

human is less sensitive), the frequencies containing the defining characteristics for the majority of consonants, which are critical for speech perception, are in the range of 1000 to 5000 Hz (where the human is most sensitive). The range of produced intensities is likewise narrow. Between the softest sounds (whispers) and the loudest sounds (shouts) that may naturally occur from the human voice is a range of about 70 dB. The energy levels at both these extremes are far from the limits of human audibility.

SPEECH SOUNDS

To comprehend the fine discriminations perceived between words, we must focus on the individual sounds upon which a language is built. A major unit of speech is the **phoneme,** which is the smallest unit of the speech sounds of a language that enables one

utterance to be distinguished from another (see Table 6.1). Phonemes generally serve to classify sounds on the basis of their physically distinguishing features. The English language uses about 40 phonemes, whereas some languages use as few as 20 and some use as many as 60 (Bergeijk, Pierce, & David, 1960).

Another means of classifying speech sounds is based on the distinctive features associated with their vocal means of production, that is, how the vocal apparatus is used in producing the vowels and consonants that comprise phonemes. Vowels are sounds produced by the vocal cords, the resonance of the throat cavities, and the open mouth. Consonants are produced by constriction of the passage through the throat and mouth. Vowels are louder than consonants although some consonants are much louder than others. The energy in vowel sounds is almost entirely in the frequencies below 3000 Hz, whereas

Table 6.1
The Phonemes of General American English[a]

Vowels	Consonants	
ee as in h*ea*t	*t* as in *t*ee	*s* as in *s*ee
I as in h*i*t	*p* as in *p*ea	*sh* as in *sh*ell
e as in h*ea*d	*k* as in *k*ey	*h* as in *h*e
ae as in h*a*d	*b* as in *b*ee	*v* as in *v*iew
ah as in f*a*ther	*d* as in *d*awn	*th* as in *th*en
aw as in c*a*ll	*g* as in *g*o	*z* as in *z*oo
U as in p*u*t	*m* as in *m*e	*zh* as in gar*a*ge
oo as in c*oo*l	*n* as in *n*o	*l* as in *l*aw
Δ as in t*o*n	*ng* as in si*ng*	*r* as in *r*ed
uh as in th*e*	*f* as in *f*ee	*y* as in *y*ou
er as in b*ir*d	θ as in *th*in	*w* as in *w*e
oi as in t*oi*l		
au as in sh*ou*t		
ei as in t*a*ke		
ou as in t*o*ne		
ai as in m*i*ght		

[a]General American is the dialect of English spoken in mid-western and western areas of the United States. Certain phonemes of other regional dialects (e.g., Southern) can be different. The phonemes of General American English include 16 vowels and 22 consonants as shown above.
Source: Denes and Pinson (1973, p. 15).

the energy in a *ch* or *s* consonant sound, for example, lies above 3000 Hz.

Speech sounds do not consist of pure or even simple tones. Indeed, to account for the discrimination between the various phonemes and their distinctive features on the basis of the physical sound waves turns out to be quite difficult. Most speech sounds represent a complex pattern of intensities and frequencies over time. A record that indicates the changes in the intensity and frequency pattern of utterances over time is called a sound **spectrogram.** A characteristic spectrogram is shown in Figure 6.8. Time is plotted along the abscissa, frequency on the ordinate, and the darkness of the record indicates intensity. The concentrations of acoustic energy that appear in the display as dark bars are called *formants*. Note that, in general, there is little apparent connection between the breaks in the speech record and the boundaries between individual words as shown on a typical spectrogram; we will return to this point later in the chapter.

SPEECH PERCEPTION WITH SOUND DISTORTION

FREQUENCY CUT-OFFS

The perception of a stream of sounds as a related sequence of words requires the operation of a complex cognitive integrative mechanism. That speech perception involves considerably more than mere sound reception is indicated by the ability to perceive meaningful speech when the flow of acoustic energy is distorted, say, when ranges of frequencies are eliminated. The elimination of ranges of frequencies is referred to as **frequency cut-offs.**

In one study, whole bands of frequencies were completely removed from speech. When frequencies above 1900 Hz were filtered out from speech, about 70% of the words were intelligible. Furthermore, the same result was obtained with the elimination of all sounds below 1900 Hz (French & Steinberg, 1947). In other words, as much of the total intelligibility is

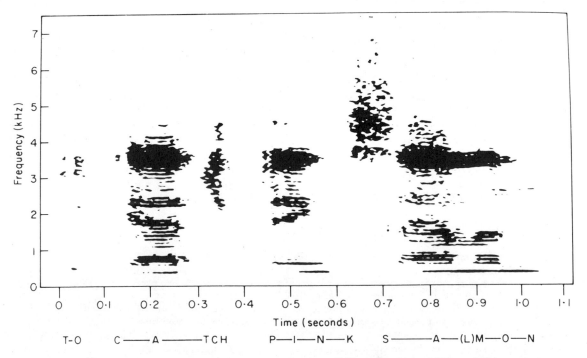

FIGURE 6.8.   Spectrogram of the utterance: "to catch pink salmon." (From Mattingly, 1972, p. 328.)

carried by frequencies below 1900 Hz as is carried by frequencies above 1900 Hz. There is a trade-off in information retained and removed: eliminating the high frequencies affects the perception of consonants more than vowels, whereas filtering out the low frequencies affects vowels more than consonants. Thus, neither all the high- nor low-frequency speech components are necessary for a reasonable degree of intelligibility.

CONTEXT

The meaningful perception of the incoming pattern of stimulation is dependent on expectations of what the stimulations should be. That is, a form of extra information is provided by the context in which sounds are heard. The importance of verbal context for speech perception is obvious in the following example of a phenomenon called the **phonemic restoration effect** (Warren, 1970; see also Warren & Warren, 1970). A missing speech sound (phoneme), represented by the blank space in the following spoken sentence, was replaced by a loud cough. "It was found that the ( )eel was on the orange." The blank before the word fragment "( )eel" can be determined by the context provided by the last word in the sentence—namely, the listener hears the word "peel." Other words that could complete the sentence and alter the context are "axle" and "shoe." Each would indicate a different speech sound for the preceding word fragment, that is, "wheel," and "heel," respectively. Thus *phonemic restoration* conforms to the context provided. Notice that the perception of the missing sound was aided by words that occurred *after* the cough. This indicates that the listener must be storing incomplete information until the necessary context is established. Interestingly, the missing sound was "heard" clearly, although perception of where the cough occurred was poor. When a silent gap rather than a cough replaced the missing phoneme, the gap could be located.

The role of context may also reduce inaccuracies or "slips of the ear" in the perception of fluent conversational speech. This is especially the case when the acoustic input is ambiguous or the same utterance has readily accessible alternative perceptions. That is, the same acoustic input, received phonetically in the same manner, may be perceived quite differently depending upon the context in which the input occurs: thus within the childhood chant "I scream, you scream, we all scream for ice cream," one hears the words, "I scream" and "ice cream," appropriate to their respective context. Compare the term "euthanasia" versus the almost phonetically identical phrase, "youth in Asia." An often cited and particularly interesting and amusing inaccuracy in speech perception, presumably owing to the *lack* of context, was described by *The New York Times* columnist, William Safire (1979), about a woman who upon hearing some lyrics of the well-known Beatles' song "Lucy in the Sky with Diamonds," perceived ". . . the girl with kaleidoscope eyes" as, "the girl with colitis goes by." In this example, the context (or the lack of context) contributes to the manner in which sounds were bounded or segmented into discrete words.

Clearly, the context plays an important role in the processing and perception of speech signals, especially in tasks such as establishing word boundaries and generally in conditions where there is ambiguity in the speech input (see Garrett, 1982).

Finally, it should be noted that even the perception of small units of speech such as vowels are influenced by their context. Rakerd (1984) reported that vowels heard in the presence of neighboring consonants—"consonantal context"—are perceived quite differently (i.e., more linguistically) than when they are presented in isolation.

SPEECH BLANKING

A result similar to the filling-in effect produced by context occurs when sections of the flow of speech are eliminated by periodically turning the speech on and off by mechanical means in **speech blanking.** When conversation was blanked out for 50% of the time, speech quality was altered but only 15% of the words were lost (Miller, 1947). The general trend for blanking proportions is shown in Figure 6.9. Thus, under certain conditions speech perception is quite

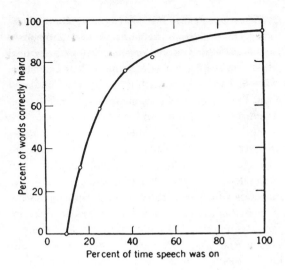

FIGURE 6.9. Intelligibility of blanked speech. Speech was turned on and off nine times per second. Quite short bursts of speech are enough to give good intelligibility. (From Boring, Langfeld, and Weld, 1948, p. 349; after Miller, 1947).

good even though the auditory systems hears the speech only half the time (see also Licklider & Miller, 1951).

> To approximate the effect of speech blanking, rapidly adjust the volume or loudness control while listening to a radio during a news broadcast. Turn the dial rapidly back and forth in such a way that silence alternates with audible speech. The intelligibility of the news broadcast should depend upon the speed with which you turn the dial and how long you pause for silence or speech.

SEGMENTED SPEECH

In a procedure similar to speech blanking, Huggins (1964) segmented the speech flow by inserting silent intervals in continuous speech. This procedure of segmentation differs from speech blanking in that no speech stimuli are eliminated; instead, intervals of silence are used to separate the intact speech sounds. One general finding of **segmented speech** was that there is a critical silent interval of about 60–120

msec, which, when exceeded, reduced intelligibility. That is, too long a silent interval (or too short a speech segment) effects a measurable reduction in speech intelligibility. Successive speech segments must follow each other with gaps of silence *less* than those in the critical silent interval in order to retain intelligibility.

THEORIES OF SPEECH PERCEPTION

One of the fundamental issues and major difficulties facing an understanding of speech perception is explaining how we perceive the sequence of sounds comprising the spoken message as distinct, well-articulated words when in fact there is little present in the physical signals to segment or partition the verbal message properly into discrete words. As we noted earlier, even the breaks between words are not indexed by gaps in the spectrogram. Indeed, successive phonetic segments often merge into one another. A stranger to a language perceives this segmentation difficulty immediately. A truly foreign language is heard as a rapid and continuous stream of utterances, and for the naïve listener, it is impossible to identify discrete words based only on their sounds. In fact, as Jusczyk (1986) observes, "Given the continuous nature of the signal, perhaps it is not surprising that nonnative listeners have difficulty in pinpointing word boundaries and that they complain that English is spoken too rapidly by native speakers. Rather, the real surprise is that native speakers *do* hear this continuous signal as a series of discrete word-size units" (p. 27-3).

MOTOR THEORY OF SPEECH PERCEPTION

One explanation for the perception of word boundaries is that the perceptual system must know what the word is before it can be properly segmented and perceptually bounded as a distinct word. According to one group of researchers, the perception of spoken language occurs as a result of a subtle unconscious form of articulation mimicry or covert speech performed prior to speech recognition. This has formed the basis of a theory whose key assumption is "that the sounds of speech are somehow perceived by reference to the ways we generate them" (Liberman et al., 1967a, p. 70; see also Liberman & Studdert-Kennedy, 1978). It is a **motor theory** in that listeners are held to make use of their knowledge of the articulatory gestures that are ordinarily involved in the production of speech. In other words, an integral part of the process of speech recognition is speech production—the hearer is also a speaker.

Categorical Perception   Some supportive evidence for a link between speech perception and production, that is, for the motor theory comes from the discontinuous or **categorical perception** of certain speech sounds. In general terms, categorical perception is said to occur when the ability to discriminate among members of the *same* category is substantially inferior to the ability to discriminate between members of *different* categories (e.g., Jusczyk, 1986). As applied to speech sounds, categorical perception holds that the discrimination between two different linguistic sounds, such as the consonants, /p/ and /b/ (or /d/ or /t/) should be easier than the discrimination between different forms of /p/ or different forms of /b/. Consonant sounds such as /p/ and /b/ are produced differently. Both sounds are produced by closing the lips, then opening them and releasing air, and by vocal cord vibration (*voicing*). However, in producing /b/, the vocal cords begin vibrating nearly simultaneously with the release of air, whereas for the /p/ there is a short latency between the air release and vocal cord vibration; the vocal cords vibrate about 50 to 60 msec after the release of air. Of interest to our present discussion is that listeners make use of the latency between the release of air and the onset of the vocal cord vibration or voicing as a cue in determining whether a /b/ or a /p/ sound has been uttered. The time between air release and voicing is referred to as **voice-onset time** (or **VOT**).

In a basic experiment on consonant discrimination (using synthesized speech sounds), the VOT is systematically varied in small increments, and the listener's task at each step is to indicate whether a /b/ or a /p/ sound is heard. In our example of distinguishing between /b/ and /p/, listeners will initially hear /b/, which remains invariant with incremental changes in VOT, until the VOT reaches a certain point—the **phonetic boundary**—whereupon a /p/ sound will be heard. That is, upon crossing the phonetic boundary, the perception abruptly changes consonant category. Increases in the VOT of sounds beyond this point continue to be heard as /p/. Thus even though the VOT has been changed considerably on either side of the phonetic boundary, the listener identifies only two categories of sounds: /b/ and /p/. This phenomenon of hearing only /b/ on one side of the phonetic boundary and only /p/ on the other side is an instance of categorical perception. In other words, we have difficulty making acoustic discriminations between members of the same phonetic category, but can easily discriminate phonemes if they are members of different categories, that is, if they fall on opposite sides of the phonetic boundary.

For proponents of the motor theory, categorical perception illustrates a close relationship between the perception of certain speech sounds and the way they are produced. That is, "perception appears to be tied to articulation" (Liberman et al., 1967b, p. 453). That we perceive sounds discontinuously—for example, /b/ *or* /p/ is perceived in only one way—is paralleled by the way we produce these sounds. In natural speech considerable variation in VOT may occur yet we continue to hear the same consonant, /b/; then, at the phonetic boundary, where the speaker produces a specific VOT, perception abruptly changes, and we hear /p/. Thus a particular change in articulation produces a corresponding change in perception.

The notion that speech perception and production may involve similar mechanisms is argued persuasively by Liberman et al. (1967b): "It seems unparsimonious to assume that the speaker-listener employs two entirely separate processes of equal status, one for encoding language and the other for decoding it. A simpler assumption is that there is only one process" (p. 452). As to the processes involved, Phillip Lieberman (1968) proposes that

The listeners "decode" the input speech signal by using their knowledge of the constraints that are imposed by the human articulatory "output" apparatus. In a sense we have proposed a "motor" theory of speech perception since we have suggested that there is a close relationship between the inherent properties of the speech output mechanism and the perceptual recognition routine. (p. 162)

It is further contended that because speech perception is so quick and so well established the requirement of actual motor responses is rendered minimal or nonexistent. The central nervous system, using feedback from previous experiences along with the basic knowledge of the grammar of the language, may function to eliminate the need for actual motor responses. The basic argument is that in the process of speech perception the brain in some way is able to make use of the results of associations with prior articulatory movements without recourse to actual articulation. Liberman et al. (1967a) assume "that somewhere in the speaker's central nervous system there exist signals which stand in a one-to-one relation to the phonemes of the language" (p. 77).

The motor theory of speech has greatly influenced the scope and direction of much of the research in speech perception. Moreover, it has provided a useful strategy addressed to the basic issue of the relation of speech perception to speech production. However, in the final analysis, it may have raised more questions than it has answered. It cannot, for example, account for cases of individuals who are incapable of producing speech, but who can understand speech (e.g., Lenneberg, 1962). Furthermore, a significant body of research with infants indicates that the perception of a phonemic distinction ordinarily *precedes* the ability to produce the distinction (e.g., Eimas et al., 1971; Strange & Jenkins, 1978); that is, infants are able to perceive and to discriminate between speech sounds well before they are capable of producing the sounds. Although these issues do not cause us to reject the motor theory, they are serious ones and remain unresolved.

Before leaving this topic we will consider two additional approaches to explaining speech perception; one assumes that there are detectors in the auditory system specialized or tuned to respond to distinctive features of speech sounds (i.e., linguistic feature detectors), and another notion proposes that there is a unique speech mode of perception employed for processing the acoustic input recognized as speech.

LINGUISTIC FEATURE DETECTORS

Another theory that attempts to explain the complexities involved in speech perception assumes the existence of feature detectors that are specialized for the analysis of specific human speech sounds. That is, there are **linguistic feature detectors** fine-tuned to respond exclusively to specific characteristics and features of the speech signal. One means of demonstrating the existence of specific feature detectors for speech stimuli is to employ a **selective adaptation** procedure that essentially fatigues or adapts a specific linguistic feature by a controlled form of overexposure. If there is a specific linguistically based detector for a given feature of speech, then following repeated exposure of this feature listeners should be less likely to hear that particular speech sound. In one now classic experiment Eimas and Corbit (1973) prepared a series of computer-generated, synthetic speech sounds; among the stimuli were the two pairs of consonants, /t/, /d/ and /b/, /p/, as well as some intermediate speechlike sounds for each pair that were sufficiently ambiguous so that either /t/ or /d/ (or /b/ or /p/) could be heard from the same synthesized speech signals. In other words, along with distinctive consonant sounds of /t/, /d/ and /b/, /p/, speech sounds were synthesized that appeared to lie at the linguistic boundary between two distinct consonant categories, that is, /t/ *or* /d/ (and /b/ *or* /p/). The researchers then had subjects repeatedly hear the unambiguous consonant, /d/, for two minutes. This served to adapt selectively a presumed /d/ detector. It followed that when exposed to the appropriate ambiguous consonant (originally heard as *either* /t/ or /d/), the subject was less likely to hear the consonant that was repeatedly exposed, that is,

/d/, and tended to hear /t/. The same procedure yielded similar results for the /b/–/p/ pair. That is, the effect of repeated presentation of the linguistic feature (to which a presumed given detector is sensitive) fatigued the detector and accordingly reduced its perception. In short, the findings were taken to support the existence of distinctive linguistic feature detectors.

While this conclusion is appealing, subsequent research reduced its generality and its impact. One of the problems faced by proposing specific feature detectors as a primary process mediating speech perception is the enormous number of distinct linguistic detectors necessary to account for even the simplest forms of speech recognition. Thus, a separate linguistic feature detector would have to be assumed for each of the enormous number of possible speech events. Moreover, it appears that there is nothing inherent in the *linguistic* character of the acoustic input that produces selective adaptation; that is, selective adaptation also occurs readily for nonspeech sounds (e.g., Sawusch & Jusczyk, 1981). In general, the effects of selective adaptation are dependent upon the acoustic characteristics of the auditory stimulus rather than on its phonetic or linguistic properties (e.g., Jusczyk, 1986). That is, the overall effects of selective adaptation can be fully accounted for on the basis of the psychoacoustic structure of the speech signal, without recourse to specialized detectors for speech. Thus the conclusion that the perception of speech is due to the exclusive activity of detectors restricted to processing features of speech alone is unwarranted.

SPEECH MODE OF PERCEPTION

Another form of theorizing about speech perception stresses the manner in which the human auditory system is most likely to respond to speech. Certainly, the observation that speech sounds are in fact complex symbols demands that they must undergo some form of special processing to uncover the message they contain. What is proposed is that there is a special **speech mode** of perception such that acoustic input recognized as speech undergoes this unique

form of specialized processing: in short, the input is treated as speech rather than as psychoacoustic signals.

The most convincing evidence that there is a special speech mode emerges from research indicating that the same set of acoustic signals is processed and perceived quite differently depending upon whether the listener treats them as speech or as nonspeech information. That is, listeners appear to employ different strategies and criteria for evaluating sounds they perceive to be speech than for those they perceive to be nonspeech (Reméz et al., 1981; Best, Morrongiello, & Robson, 1981).

In addition to studies demonstrating that the same speech sounds may be perceived on different occasions as speech or as nonspeech, there are also special circumstances in which the same physical stimulus can simultaneously evoke a psychoacoustic or nonspeech mode and a phonetic or speech mode. This effect of hearing sound signals simultaneously as speech and as nonspeech is called **duplex perception.** It is proposed that duplex perception reflects mutually distinct auditory and linguistic ways of perceiving the same stimulus. In one demonstration of this phenomenon reported by Whalen and Liberman (1987), complex computer-generated sounds were synthesized that were heard as /da/ and /ga/ at relatively low intensity levels, but when presented at higher intensities, duplex perception occurred. That is, with an increase in the intensity level of the same acoustic input, subjects heard not only the /da/ and /ga/ sounds, but they also simultaneously heard a nonspeech whistle sound component. According to the researchers the speech processing mode takes priority over the nonspeech mode, and only when the signals are made sufficiently intense does the nonspeech mode enter: "the duplex phenomenon supports the hypothesis that the phonetic mode takes precedence in processing the (input signals), using them for its special linguistic purposes until, having appropriated its share, it passes on the remainder to be perceived by the nonspeech system as auditory whistles. Such precedence reflects the profound biological significance of speech" (p. 171).

The acquisition of the speech mode appears to occur in a gradual manner beginning in infancy. Whereas infants initially process speech in terms of its physical properties, they appear to be endowed with a predisposition to discriminate between sounds that correspond to different phonemes and to learn the particular phonemes that are relevant to advancing their communicative skills (e.g., Kuhl, 1983; MacKain et al., 1983. Note however, that significant controversy exists as to whether infants possess specialized speech perception capacities; see Jusczyk, 1986). At some point during the course of language acquisition infants begin to take into account the phonological structure and other general linguistic rules of the language they are acquiring and, correspondingly, begin to process the same input differently; that is, the basis for the infant's classification of speech sounds shifts from classifying and processing sounds on their physical basis to their linguistic relevance. Thus the speech mode develops as a consequence of acquiring language skills and attempting to attach linguistic meaning to the acoustic input relevant as speech.

Our brief discussion of theories of speech perception underscores the enormity of the task of arriving at a useful and reasonably complete explanation. Perhaps as with other sorts of complex human activities and capacities, there is more than one method or strategy by which speech perception can be achieved. In any event, it should be clear that an understanding of speech perception extends well beyond the boundaries of the physical dimensions of the speech waveform and sound reception in the ear.

ANIMAL COMMUNICATION

Although it is generally agreed that linguistic behavior is afforded only to humans, we should note that the sounds produced by many animals, ranging from insects to primates, including fish, amphibia, and birds, may be used for the purpose of a form of intraspecies information exchange.

For the most part, communicative behavior patterns are highly characteristic for the species, both in their production and in the sorts of information they convey. Insects such as the cicada, katydid, and cricket (especially the male), for example, use signals to convey information as to courting and other mating-related activities and for maintaining contact with each other. Birds use sound signals—calls or songs—for such diverse activities as territorial defense, nesting, parental recognition, and the establishment and maintenance of pair bonds. For example, the extensive song repertoire and mimicry of the northern mockingbird appears to be exploited for attracting mates. Indeed, unmated males sing significantly more than do mated males; moreover they are more active than the mated, flying from perch to perch so as to deliver their song from a number of different locations and, hence increase the likelihood of attracting a mate (Breitwisch & Whitesides, 1987; Lewin, 1987).

Mammals also make extensive use of vocalization for within-species communication. By howling, wolves communicate information of their identity, their location, and perhaps something of their emotional state (Theberge, 1971). Primates also exchange acoustic signals in an informative way. Perhaps the most closely studied group has been the rhesus monkey. Rowell (1962) described distinct calls or cries produced by the rhesus that express some aspect of the animal's condition in certain types of situations. For example, a long, fairly loud roar is made by a very confident rhesus monkey when threatening another of inferior rank. In contrast, a short, very high-pitched squeak is made by a defeated animal at the end of a fight.

Evidence also exists that vervet monkeys make acoustically distinct and different alarm calls to at least three different classes of predators: leopards, eagles, and pythons (Seyfarth, Cheney, & Marler, 1980). Field recordings made in Kenya yielded the following: leopard alarms were "short tonal calls, typically produced in a series of both exhalation and inhalation," eagle alarm calls were "low-pitched, staccato grunts," and the python alarm calls were "high-pitched 'chutters'." Moreover, these calls appear to contribute to a form of communication. When recordings of the alarms were played back in the absence of actual predators, adult vervet monkeys displayed apparent adaptive activity specific to the hunting behavior of the predator represented by the recording. Thus, when the monkeys were on the ground, the sounding of the leopard alarm was likely to cause them to climb up into trees (thus apparently rendering them safest from the ambush type of attack typical of leopards). Eagle alarm calls caused the monkeys to look up or run into cover. Python alarm calls caused the monkeys to look down at the ground around them. "Such responses suggested that each alarm call effectively represented, or signified, a different class of external danger" (p. 802).

It is of interest to consider the evolution of language from the general perspective of animal communication. It is held that the principal factor in the development of language is the unusual intellect that is uniquely human, that is, language reflects the human intellect and accordingly is afforded only to the human (see Lenneberg, 1967). Furthermore, it has been argued that the human vocal tract evolved from something like that of a chimpanzee (e.g., Lieberman & Crelin, 1971; Lieberman, Crelin, & Klatt, 1972). Thus, the attainment of human spoken language must be viewed as the product of a long evolutionary process that involved changes in anatomical structure through mutation, successive variation, and natural selection, which enhanced vocal communication.

SUMMARY

This chapter has focused principally on the informational aspects of acoustic energy, such as object detection, and localization and speech perception. First, we introduced the notion of cerebral dominance and hearing. It was noted that the neural message originating in the right ear is predominantly registered in the left hemisphere of the auditory brain, and the message from the left ear is principally registered in the right hemisphere of the brain. Furthermore, a number of studies indicate that the auditory cortex of the left hemisphere of the brain predominates in the perception of language-related stimulation and in sequential, analytic processing in general, whereas the right hemisphere is dominant in the reception of such forms of stimulation as pure tones and music.

The phenomena of auditory space perception—the localization and identification of sounds in space—were discussed for both monaural and binaural hearing. Monaural hearing can enable the evaluation of a sound-emitting object's relative distance; this is based mainly on the intensity of the sound source. However, for the precise localization of an object, binaural hearing is necessary. The cues afforded by binaural hearing are the interaural time and intensity differences between the stimuli reaching each ear. That is, a sound closer to one ear reaches it sooner and with greater intensity than it does to the other ear. A number of phenomena relevant to sound location were discussed, such as the Doppler shift, the role of the pinna, stereophonic listening, and echolocation. The concepts discussed in auditory space perception were brought to bear on the striking ability of bats and the human blind to avoid obstacles.

The psychology of music was introduced; music was characterized as a psychological experience produced by the perception of the relationship of tones to each other in a particular context. Phenomena and capacities relevant to a basic discussion of the perception of music were outlined such as elementary musical notation, absolute pitch, and the octave relationship. In light of the notion of octave equivalence the necessity of an analysis of pitch on a bidimensional scale was noted. It was observed that the perception of melodies and their temporal properties is based upon the recognition of certain invariant global features inherent within a musical passage; that is, the perception of musical characteristics appears to occur on the basis of certain organizational tendencies. Finally, we ended with a brief section on the functions and origins of music perception, speculating that perhaps it evolved from the perception of speech.

The role that the auditory system plays in human speech communication was outlined. The physical characteristics of the sounds used in speech were identified and the perception of speech under a number of conditions of distortion was discussed; these were frequency cut-offs, phoneme omissions, speech blanking, and segmented speech.

Several theories of speech perception were considered: a motor theory, according to which the perception of speech is intimately linked to knowledge of the subtle articulatory motor gestures involved in the production of speech; a theory that assumes the existence of linguistic feature detectors that are specialized and tuned to react exclusively to specific features of human speech sounds; and, finally, a theory that proposed that speech perception involves a special speech mode such that the acoustic input, recognized as speech, undergoes a unique form of specialized processing and analysis.

Lastly, the evolution of language communication was briefly discussed within the context of animal communication. It was suggested that the attainment of human language is the product of a long evolutionary process.

KEY TERMS

Absolute (perfect) pitch

Binaural cues

Biosonar

Categorical perception

Cerebral dominance

Chromatic scale

Chromesthesia

Cone of confusion

Dichotic listening

Doppler shift

Duplex perception

Echolocation

Frequency cut-off

Interaural intensity difference

Interaural time difference

Linguistic feature detectors

Monaural cues

Motor theory

Octave

Octave equivalence

Phonemes

Phonemic restoration

Phonetic boundary

Precedence effect

Segmented speech

Selective adaptation

Semitone

Sonar

Spectogram

Speech blanking

Speech mode

Stereophonic listening

Synesthesia

Tone chroma

Tone height

Voice-onset time (VOT)

STUDY QUESTIONS

1. Trace the neural connections of the auditory nerve from the ear to the brain and describe how the connections may contribute to sound localization.

2. What sorts of evidence indicate that the two cerebral hemispheres of the brain are dominant in different auditory functions? What are some of the different functions?

3. Enumerate the monaural and binaural cues for auditory space perception. Describe how interaural time differences and interaural intensity differences contribute to auditory localization. How does the use of head movements resolve localization ambiguity such as when sounds occur in the median plane or on the cone of confusion?

4. How can you determine whether someone who claims to be deaf in one ear is feigning? Consider the implications of your procedure for auditory localization and stereophonic conditions of listening.

5. How does the pinna contribute to auditory localization?

6. What is echolocation and how is it employed in different species? What evidence suggests that humans may be capable of echolocation?

7. Describe the role that sounds and their echoes play in the spatial perception of the blind. What aspects of the sounds are most informative for sound localization?

8. In what ways are musical sounds different from nonmusical sounds? What are the tonal properties and acoustic dimensions that enable a succession of sounds to be characterized as musical sounds?

9. Identify the notation used to describe musical sounds. Indicate the significance of the octave relationship to the psychology of music. Examine the notion that requires that pitch be analyzed in terms of both tone chroma and tone height.

10. What is unique about a melody? Consider why melodies remain unchanged in spite of changes in the pitch range of the tones conveying a melody. What are some global features that enter into a melody?

11. Describe chromesthesia and indicate how it can be demonstrated.

12. Consider the difficulties involved in the perception of acoustic stimulation as speech and discuss the proposition that the perception of speech is a remarkable ability.

13. Enumerate the sorts of acoustic distortions that do and do not eliminate the perception of speech. Consider the effects of eliminating selected frequencies, blanking speech, and segmenting speech on the intelligibility of speech.

14. Outline the human vocal apparatus and its operation in producing speech. What are the physical ranges of speech sounds? Define the basic speech units.

15. Discuss the difficulty in characterizing speech only on the basis of its physical dimensions.

16. Discuss the contribution made by the context in which sounds are heard for speech perception.

17. Outline and compare the major theories of speech perception. What evidence supports a motor theory of speech perception? Examine the significance of categorical perception for the motor theory. What problems are there with this theory?

18. What are linguistic feature detectors? How does the procedure of selective adaptation support the notion of linguistic feature detectors? What aspects of speech perception are especially difficult for linguistic feature detectors to explain?

19. Examine the speech mode of perception, taking into account the phenomenon of duplex perception. Consider how the speech mode develops.

20. What evidence supports the proposition that animals other than the human use forms of vocalization for communication? What kinds of behaviors and environmental events are especially relevant to animal communication?

7

SOMESTHESIS I: KINESTHESIS AND CUTANEOUS SENSE

This chapter and the one following are concerned with the two main topics that are collectively labeled **somesthesis:** *kinesthetic* sensitivity, which refers to spatial position and movement information occurring from mechanical stimulation of the mobile joints, muscles and tendons, and *cutaneous* sensitivity, or skin sensitivity to touch or pressure, temperature, and pain. In the present context kinesthesis and the cutaneous sense are considered subsystems whose complex functional interactions provide information about the environment immediately adjacent to an organism. The mechanisms and phenomena of kinesthesis are described first, followed by the cutaneous sense of pressure or touch. In the next chapter, the cutaneous senses of temperature and pain are discussed.

KINESTHESIS

Kinesthesis or kinesthesia (from the Greek *kineo*, "to move") refers to the reception of body part position and movement—information about the posture, location, and movement in space of the limbs and other mobile parts of the jointed skeleton (e.g., fingers, wrist, limbs, head, trunk, vertebrate column). At least two sources of stimulation have been proposed to contribute to the kinesthetic sense: in particular, those from the joints and those from the muscles and tendons. The mechanoreceptors for joint information are **Pacinian corpuscles,** which lie in the mobile joints of the skeletal system, and Ruffini endings and Golgi organs which lie in the connective tissue of the joints. The receptors are stimulated by contact between the parts of the joint surfaces. Thus, stimulation occurs with changes in the angles at which the bones are held. In a sense, these mechanoreceptors are subcutaneous pressure receptors.

Another source of information that contributes to the perception of body-part location or kinesthesis results from innervation of muscles. Muscles and their attached tendons are well supplied with sensory nerves that respond to changes in tension when the muscle fiber is stretched or contracted. Stimulation of the appropriate receptors produce patterns of excitation that may lead to the perception of stretch and strain, such as that occurring when weight is supported; that is, a feeling of strain becomes part of the total kinesthetic information when there is resistance to limb movement. In addition, the receptors from muscles and tendons may contribute to the control of postural reflex actions, automatically adjusting tension to the needs of the limbs.

Although kinesthetic stimulation does not result in a distinct perceptual experience such as hearing a sound, the kinesthetic system continually provides a source of important information. Without any difficulty we know the position, posture, and the direction of the movement of our limbs in space. We scratch an itch we cannot see; we walk safely down a flight of stairs without directly gazing at our feet; and, in general, we may accurately touch any part of our body in the dark. In the laboratory, experiments have shown that a person is capable of accurately pointing with the limbs without using vision (e.g., L. A. Cohen, 1958; Wood, 1969). When an individual is instructed to point with a hand-held rod to the gravitational vertical or horizontal, the average error is only a few degrees (Gibson, 1966; Rymer & D'Almeida, 1980). The ability of the receptors at the joints to supply quantitative information about angles and distances is seen when a person accurately uses the distance between the two palms to mark off length no matter if the eyes are opened or closed. The main receptors for this particular action reside in the shoulder joints and associated musculature. Similarly, the gap spanned by the index finger and its opposable thumb is accurately used to mark off width or short distances. Here the receptors are in the knuckle and wrist joints. The accuracy of these abilities have been demonstrated in the laboratory (e.g., Wertheimer, 1954; Teghtsoonian & Teghtsoonian, 1970). No doubt it is this activity that is referred to when we say we can measure an object or compare two objects on the basis of "touch."

THE SKIN AND CUTANEOUS EXPERIENCE

The human skin, viewed as a protective surface and as a sensory organ, is remarkable. It is by far the largest organ, forming a covering for the entire body. A person 6 feet (1.83 meters) tall and of average weight and body build has about 3000 square inches (1.93 square meters) of skin area (see Figure 7.1).

The skin is also the most versatile sensory organ of the body, serving as a flexible shield against many forms of foreign agents and mechanical injury. It holds in vital body fluids. It serves to ward off the harmful light waves (ultraviolet and infrared radiations) of the sun and, by means of its pigmentation, the skin protects against the loss of light-sensitive vitamins and metabolites (Branda & Eaton, 1978). When appropriate, it stabilizes body temperature (in birds and mammals), either cooling the body or retarding heat loss. It also has a role in regulating the pressure and direction of the blood flow. Finally, the skin has nerve endings embedded within it that can be stimulated in a variety of ways to mediate different sensations. The experiential result of skin stimulation is termed **cutaneous sensitivity.** Four basic qualities or sensations of cutaneous stimulation have been identified: pressure or touch, cold, warmth, and pain.

Externally viewed, the skin appears as a highly irregular surface, manifesting distinct surface qualities and extensions—hairs, feathers, scales, creases, colorations, thicknesses—in different regions. However, the skin is not a single structural unit but is composed of layers. These layers, along with the sensory nerve endings, are identified and shown in cross section in the composite drawing of the skin in Figure 7.2. Although it is held that the nerve endings found in the skin are the receptors for cutaneous experience, it has not been established clearly that stimulation of a particular type of receptor exclusively initiates a certain cutaneous experience.

The sensations of pressure, cold and warmth, and pain have been based on subjects' responses rather than on the identification of anatomically distinct fibers. That is, evidence for the existence of distinct cutaneous sensations is accessible principally through subjective report. Thus we will examine some of the perceptual phenomena associated with cutaneous experiences.

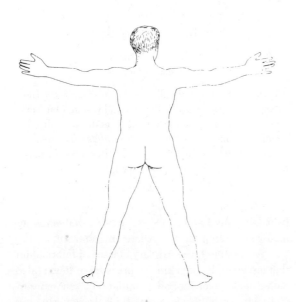 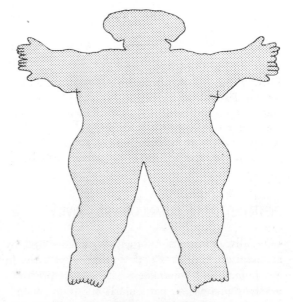

FIGURE 7.1.   Total surface area of the skin, which seems surprisingly large in contrast to the outline of the human figure (left), is calculated by adding the areas of a series of cylinders constructed from an average of leg, arm, and torso circumferences. (From W. Montagna, "The skin," *Scientific American, 11,* 1965, pp. 58–59. Copyright © 1965 by Scientific American, Inc. All rights reserved.)

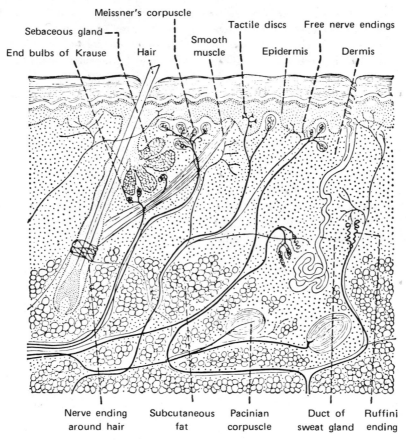

FIGURE 7.2.   Composite diagram of the skin in cross section. The chief layers—epidermis, dermis, and subcutaneous tissue—are shown, as are also a hair follicle, the smooth muscle that erects the hair, and several kinds of nerve endings. In the epidermis are to be found tactile discs and free nerve endings; in the dermis are Meissner corpuscles, Krause end bulbs, and Ruffini endings. The subcutaneous tissue is chiefly fatty and vascular but contains Pacinian corpuscles, the largest of the specialized endings. (From E. Gardner, *Fundamentals of Neurology*, W. B. Saunders, Philadelphia, 1947. Reprinted by permission of the author and publisher.)

DISTRIBUTION OF CUTANEOUS SENSITIVITY

Generally cutaneous information is registered by mechanical stimulation of the surface of the body. In the human this information is received predominantly from the skin, particularly of certain appendages. Cutaneous information is not only picked up directly by the skin but also indirectly by other surface structures such as hairs and nails, and in other animals by claws, hooves, horns, vibrissae (whiskers), and antennae—structures that separate an organism from its immediate environment.

As we noted, the primary classes of information that are given by the skin are pressure or touch (also called contact or tactual stimulation), temperature (cold and warmth), and pain. If we drew a grid on a part of the skin of a blindfolded subject and systematically explored the squares of that grid in turn with a heated rod and a cold rod, a hair, and a needle point, it is likely that our subject would report the cutaneous experiences of warmth, cold, pressure, and pain, respectively. A plot of the distribution of sensitive "spots" would provide us with a map of cutaneous sensitivity. In mapping all the spots for which temperature, pain, and pressure are represented, we find that regions of the skin are not uniformly sensitive to all stimuli. Some areas may be sensitive to slight contact only, some to temperature only. In other words, there is a distribution of distinct areas sensitive to different kinds of stimuli.

THE SKIN AND THE BRAIN

The relationship between the skin and nerve pathways to the brain is linked to two major neural systems—the **lemniscal** and the **spinothalamic** —and each transmits different classes of information to the brain. Nerve fibers that make up the lemniscal system are relatively large and fast conducting and transmit precise positional information about touch and movement stimulation. It should be noted that the cutaneous input carried by the lemniscal system for the left side of the body terminates in the right side of the brain (i.e., the somatosensory cortex), and cutaneous input for the right side of the body terminates in the left side of the somatosensory cortex. The fibers of the spinothalamic system are of small diameter and relatively slow conducting and carry input concerning nonlocalized touch, temperature, and pain to both sides of the brain. Another difference between the two systems is in terms of the receptive fields of nerve fibers subserving a particular skin region.

RECEPTIVE FIELDS

The human achieves an extraordinary degree of tactual sensibility; this is due, in large part, to the manner in which the skin is topographically projected and arranged in the sensory cortex. That is, underlying nerve fibers from each part of the body surface of the skin are systematically represented in a particular part of the somatosensory cortex. Some

areas of the skin, such as those of the fingers, lips, and tongue are more densely supplied with nerve fibers; hence, they are more easily innervated, are more sensitive than other areas, and are correspondingly represented by larger areas of the somatosensory cortex. This is shown by the distortion obvious in the sensory **homunculus** (a topographic representation of the relative amount of brain devoted to various parts of the body) of Figures 7.3a and b. For example, the muscles controlling very fine movements are represented by more area of the somatosensory cortex than are the muscles controlling coarse movements. Notice that we have much finer control over moving our fingers than over moving our toes. Correspondingly, a larger area of the somatosensory cortex is devoted to controlling the fingers than the toes. In general, the finer the muscle control, the greater its representation in the somatosensory cortex.

In addition to the degree of representation, the activity of neurons in the somatosensory system appear to be quite specific to skin region. Indeed for each neuron of the somatosensory cortex, there is a precise area or region of the skin—called its **receptive field**—that, if appropriately stimulated, can alter the neuron's firing rate. The receptive field is a specific area on the skin that when stimulated will either excite or increase (or inhibit or decrease) the firing of a specific neuron of the somatosensory brain. In other words, location differences in neural excitation correspond to the excitation of different skin regions.

Variation in the *size* and the *density* of the receptive fields reflect differences in the functioning of the lemniscal and spinothalamic systems. The receptive fields for neurons in the lemniscal system are more numerous and smaller (i.e., each represents a relatively small area of skin surface), whereas receptive fields of neurons of the spinothalamic system are fewer, with each covering relatively large regions of skin (see Figure 7.3c). The receptive field organization for the lemniscal system is clearly an aid to tactual acuity and the resolution of fine spatial detail. Having numerous receptive fields that each represent only a small area of the skin and having them densely packed enables finer tactual discrimi-

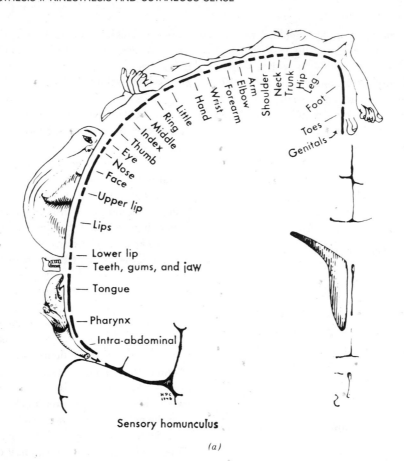

Sensory homunculus

(a)

FIGURE 7.3.   Two versions of the sensory homunculus and typical receptive fields on the hand and arm. (*a*) The projection of various human body regions on the sensory cortex. The length of each line represents the proportion of the somatosensory cortex devoted to the body part indicated by the adjacent label. The caricatures of the body parts are drawn in about the same proportion as the lines. (Based on McClintic, 1978, p. 205.) (*b*) The completed homunculus depicts the body surface with each part drawn in proportion to the size of its representation in the somatosensory cortex. (Modified from Rosenzweig and Leiman, 1982, p. 293.) (*c*) Highly schematic receptive fields on hand and arm. Receptive field size is indicated by the spots and areas of shading on the limb. Very sensitive body regions, such as the fingers, have very small receptive fields, while less sensitive regions, such as the back of the hand and forearm, have large receptive fields.

(b)

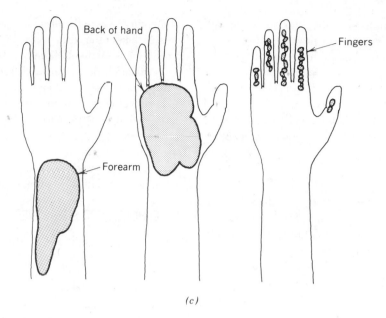

(c)

FIGURE 7.3   *(continued)* Schematic receptive fields on hand and arm.

nations to be made by stimulation of such skin regions. Indeed the cortical cells for areas of the skin that are most sensitive to touch, and accordingly have the greatest cortical representation—the tongue, lips, and fingertips—have the smallest receptive fields and the largest number of receptive fields per unit area of skin.

In addition to neurons that fire to simple tactual stimulation, there are cortical neurons of a more complex nature in that they fire only to relatively specialized stimulation applied to the skin. For example, there are cells whose receptive fields do not react well to mere touch or pressure, but do respond vigorously to movement of a textured surface in a specific direction on the skin. That is, there are neurons that are directionally sensitive, that react best to movement along the skin in only one direction (e.g., Costanzo & Gardner, 1980; Darian-Smith et al., 1982). Still other cells may respond best to stimulation provided by an edge placed on the skin and moved in a particular direction. Clearly complex cells contribute to the ability of the skin to tactually explore, pick up, and process environmental infor-

mation, for example, to identify and differentiate between textured surfaces and to recognize the shape of an object. Of course we have only introduced a very small part of the neural complexities linking the skin with the brain. Moreover, the tactual perception of the immediate environment is an attainment that involves a tremendous degree of integration and association within the cortex that also incorporates the input from more than a single sense modality. Typically tactual stimulation interacts with position (i.e., kinesthesis) and visual information to provide a sense of awareness of the environment immediately surrounding the organism.

PRESSURE AND TOUCH

A number of distinctions have been made in the treatment of tactual perception. One of the major distinctions is that between *passive* touch (in which the observer exerts no control over the reception of stimulation) and *active* touch (in which the observer exerts active control over the pick up of tactual information, such as with self-produced touch; e.g., Gibson, 1962, 1966). In addition, Loomis and Lederman (1986) use the term "tactile" perception to refer to tactual perception mediated solely by cutaneous stimulation and reserve the term "haptic" perception for tactual perception in which concurrent cutaneous and kinesthetic information is picked up. Where relevant and possible, we shall attempt to conform to these distinctions. Much of the psychophysical findings discussed in the paragraphs that follow concern stimulation imposed on the subject in the determination of cutaneous thresholds and related basic phenomena; these findings fall under the rubric of passive tactile perception. Later sections deal with active touch and haptic perception. (Notice should also be taken that in some sources "touch" applies to stimulation produced by displacement of hairs on the skin, whereas the term "pressure" refers to displacement of the skin surface; generally we will use touch and pressure interchangeably.)

A good part of the outer surface of the skin responds to the pressure or touch of the environment. In the human, the guiding and exploratory parts of the body—the fingers, the hands, parts of the mouth, and the tip of the tongue—are most sensitive to those mechanical encounters with the environment that provide pressure or touch stimulation. Less sensitive areas, with fewer pressure spots, are the legs, arms, and trunk—areas where less important mechanical events occur. It is sometimes held that the underlying receptors for pressure are Pacinian corpuscles (held to be the skin's as well as the joints' primary receptor for mechanical distortions), **free nerve endings** (called "basket cells," in hairy regions of the skin), and **Meissner corpuscles** (in hairless or glabous skin regions); however, direct evidence in support of this is not substantial.

The adequate stimulus for touch or pressure is a mechanical deformation of the skin, that is, a change of shape or pressure differential. Uniformly distributed pressure or continuous gradations of pressure are not deforming, hence not mechanically stimulating. Consider the situation posed by Geldard (1972) in which a finger is immersed in a heavy liquid such

as mercury, where the pressure deep in the liquid is greater than at the surface (see Figure 7.4). There is a continuous gradient of uniform pressure both from the surface on downward and from the surface upward; hence, these gradients are not deforming ones and are ineffective stimuli. The pressure is felt only at the boundary—the *discontinuity*—between liquid and air, and it is this discontinuity that provides the adequate stimulus. In general, discontinuities are the important stimulus events for the organism, not continuous gradations of stimulation.

THRESHOLDS FOR PRESSURE

Under certain conditions of stimulation, displacements of the skin less than 0.001 mm (0.00004 in.) are sufficient to elicit a pressure sensation (Verillo, 1975). However, the sensitivity to pressure stimulation varies not only with the strength of the mechanical stimulus applied but also with the region of the skin stimulated. Using nylon filaments, whose force could be precisely calibrated in milligrams, Weinstein (1968) tested various body parts of right-handed

FIGURE 7.4.   A finger immersed in mercury. Although the pressure deep in the liquid is much greater than that at the surface, only the discontinuity produced at the boundary between liquid and air is perceived.

subjects for threshold levels of pressure or touch. The results for the right and left sides of the body, shown in Figure 7.5, indicate that the face is the most pressure-sensitive part of the body. The trunk is next, followed by the fingers and arms. The least sensitive body parts for pressure are found in the lower extremities. Males and females show about the same trend in sensitivity, but in general, women manifest lower thresholds, that is, they appear more sensitive to touch than males.

POINT LOCALIZATION FOR PRESSURE

It is possible to localize pressure sensations on the region of the skin where stimulation is applied; however, this ability largely varies with the region of the body stimulated. For example, stimulation ap-

plied to the fingertip or the tip of the tongue is well localized (the average error is of the order of a millimeter). In contrast, stimulation of the upper arm, thigh, or back produces an error of localization of more than a centimeter. Generally, the more mobile the skin region stimulated (e.g., hands, feet, mouth), the more accurate is the point localization (see Figure 7.6). Clearly, accuracy of localization at various skin sites is highly correlated with the amount of cortical representation devoted to the skin receptors of that body region.

TWO-POINT THRESHOLD

Another important measure of the localizing capability of the skin is called the **two-point threshold,** which refers to the separation of two points of concur-

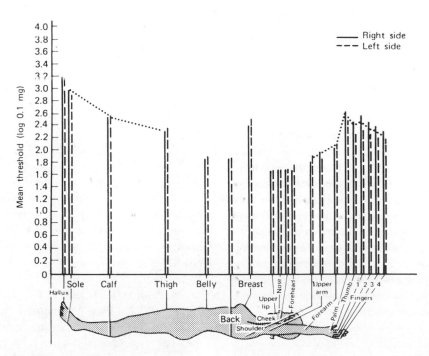

FIGURE 7.5.   Thresholds for pressure. The ordinate represents the force necessary for perception at the threshold. The figure is for females, but corresponding thresholds for males are similar. (From S. Weinstein, "Intensive and extensive aspects of tactile sensitivity as a function of body part, sex, and laterality," in D. R. Kenshalo (Ed.), *The Skin Senses,* Charles C Thomas, Springfield, Ill., 1968, p. 201. Reprinted by permission of the author and publisher.)

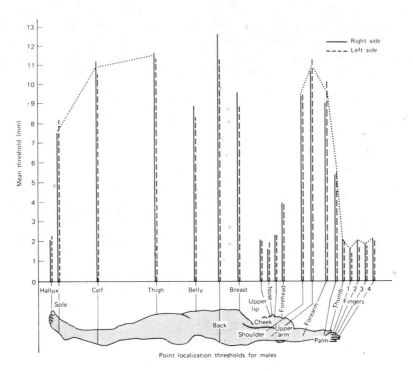

FIGURE 7.6. Point localization thresholds. The ordinate represents the distance between the body point stimulated and the subjects' perception of where stimulation occurred. (From S. Weinstein, "Intensive and extensive aspects of tactile sensitivity as a function of body part, sex, and laterality," in D. R. Kenshalo (Ed.), *The Skin Senses*, Charles C Thomas, Springfield, Ill., 1968, p. 204. Reprinted by permission of the author and publisher.)

rent stimulation on a region of the skin that just gives rise to two discrete impressions of touch; if the points are brought any closer together and simultaneously applied, they elicit a unitary touch impression. Thus the two-point threshold represents the smallest separation of two points of stimulation that produces two distinct impressions of touch. Like the localization of a single stimulus, the more mobile the region stimulated, the lower the two-point threshold.

ARISTOTLE'S ILLUSION

A unique tactual experience attributed to Aristotle (e.g., Benedetti, 1985)—**Aristotle's illusion** —bears on some of the phenomena just described, especially tactual localization. According to Benedetti (1985), Aristotle noted that if two adja-

cent fingers are crossed (most easily accomplished with the index and middle finger), creating a "V" by the fingertips, and if the V of the two crossed fingers is stimulated by a small object such as a bead, a sensation of touching two beads will result. A version of this is illustrated in Figure 7.7.

According to Benedetti's analysis (1985, 1986a, 1986b, 1988), the unusual experience of sensing two stimuli from a single stimulus when the fingers are crossed (Figure 7.7b) follows from the fact that the cutaneous areas of the two fingers that are simultaneously stimulated (i.e., their outsides) are the ones that ordinarily require the application of two stimuli. That is, it is not usually possible for a single object to stimulate the out-

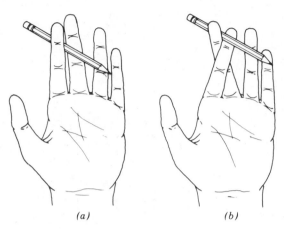 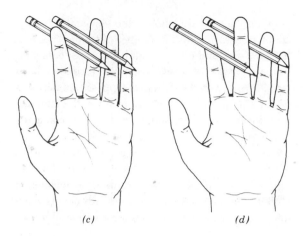

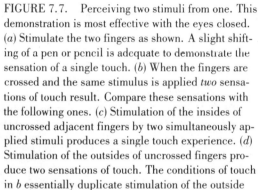

(a)   (b)   (c)   (d)

FIGURE 7.7.   Perceiving two stimuli from one. This demonstration is most effective with the eyes closed. (a) Stimulate the two fingers as shown. A slight shifting of a pen or pencil is adequate to demonstrate the sensation of a single touch. (b) When the fingers are crossed and the same stimulus is applied *two* sensations of touch result. Compare these sensations with the following ones. (c) Stimulation of the insides of uncrossed adjacent fingers by two simultaneously applied stimuli produces a single touch experience. (d) Stimulation of the outsides of uncrossed fingers produce two sensations of touch. The conditions of touch in b essentially duplicate stimulation of the outside areas of the uncrossed fingers in d, but the latter requires the simultaneous application of two stimuli, as indicated.

Observe that although conditions b and d are similar with respect to stimulation of the outsides of both fingers, there are cutaneous and kinesthetic stimulation differences: when the fingers are crossed, it is difficult to stimulate exactly the same cutaneous areas of both fingers that are stimulated when they are uncrossed. In addition when the fingers are crossed, they are in different relative positions to one another, producing kinesthetic stimulation that is lacking when they are uncrossed.

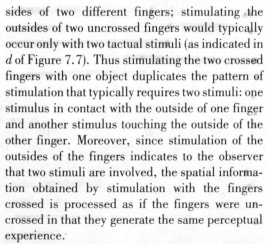

sides of two different fingers; stimulating the outsides of two uncrossed fingers would typically occur only with two tactual stimuli (as indicated in d of Figure 7.7). Thus stimulating the two crossed fingers with one object duplicates the pattern of stimulation that typically requires two stimuli: one stimulus in contact with the outside of one finger and another stimulus touching the outside of the other finger. Moreover, since stimulation of the outsides of the fingers indicates to the observer that two stimuli are involved, the spatial information obtained by stimulation with the fingers crossed is processed as if the fingers were uncrossed in that they generate the same perceptual experience.

Coren, Porac, and Ward (1984) suggest a neural organization that coincides with the foregoing description. They argue that when an object stimulates the insides of two adjacent fingers (i.e., a of Figure 7.7), the touch information is sent to two related or overlapping areas of the touch sensory cortex, resulting in a single touch sensation. In fact, as indicated in c of Figure 7.7, the cutaneous experience created by two concurrently applied stimuli to adjacent skin regions is of a single touch. However, when the fingers are crossed and a stimulus contacts the outsides of the two fingers (b of Figure 7.7), the information is sent to two separate, unrelated areas of the sensory cortex, producing a double touch sensation.

ADAPTATION TO PRESSURE

The result of continued pressure stimulation may be a decrease or even a complete elimination of its sensory experience: pressure sensibility undergoes adaptation. As with thresholds, the temporal course of adaptation varies with a number of factors, particularly the size and intensity and skin area contacted. The time taken for the sensation produced by a weight resting on the skin to disappear completely is directly proportional to the intensity of the stimulus and inversely proportional to the area contacted (Geldard, 1972). The sensation, however, can be quickly restored by a brief movement of the stimulus or some other form of abrupt change in the stimulation to a given skin area. Continuous change in stimulation, of course, is what normally occurs when the perceiver *actively* touches surfaces and objects.

COMPLEX TOUCH PHENOMENA

READING WITH THE SKIN

The Braille System   We have noted that the fingers are quite sensitive to point localization and two-point discriminations. It is not surprising, then, that some sort of complex information extraction of a communicative form can occur from active touch stimulation. One example is the well-known **Braille system** devised by Louis Braille in the nineteenth century. The Braille alphabet is actually a reading system composed of dots embossed on a surface that can be "read" by the skin, usually the tips of the fingers. As shown in Figures 7.8a and b, various combinations of dots are used to represent letters and words. By moving the finger over the raised surfaces of Braille, the experienced adult Braille reader can reach 100 words per minute (Foulke & Berlá, 1978; Kennedy, 1984).

Because Braille is displayed in a manner similar to print symbols, the Braille code retains many of the advantages of the print code: for example, the Braille reader can vary the reading rate and can retrace ambiguous material. Since Braille symbols are displayed spatially, the Braille reader can also extract such features from the display as paragraph indentation and centered headings. Moreover, the same basic cognitive mechanisms may be involved in

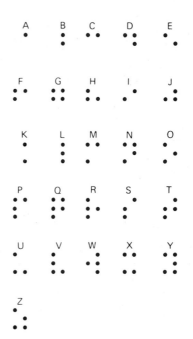

FIGURE 7.8a.   The Braille alphabet. Various combinations of from one to six embossed dots are used to represent letters and short words. Each dot stands 1 mm above the surface and dot separations are 2.3 mm (From Kenshalo, 1978).

processing printed visual text and Braille tactual text. Krueger (1982b; Krueger & Ward, 1983) found that Braille letters (like print letters) are detected more rapidly and accurately when embedded in words than in nonwords (see also Heller, 1980).

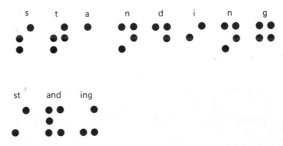

FIGURE 7.8b.   The word "standing" written in Braille symbols (top) and written in a contracted form (bottom) in which frequently recurring letter groups are assigned specific patterns. (After Foulke and Berlá, 1978.)

The Optacon   More recent is an electronic reading aid called the **Optacon,** (*O*ptical-to-*ta*ctual *con*verter), which converts the visual image of a printed character directly into a tactual one for the fingertip. Users are able to read these tactual images at a rate of 60 words per minute (Bliss, 1971). Moreover, devices such as the Optacon allow the blind reader access to most printed materials, not just those materials that have been translated to Braille.

There are also devices available that enable blind individuals to make use of computers, that is, to "read" characters directly from a computer screen. One device (by IBM) is a kind of hand-guided, Braille "mouse" pointer, linked to the computer screen and modified with six independently driven tiny pistons that fit against the index finger; the pistons rise and fall, successively forming patterns of cutaneous stimulation for the standard Braille characters like those felt on a printed page. By hand-guiding the mouse pointer and feeling the corresponding characters formed on the fingertip, the blind user can perceive the material on the screen.

Vibratese and the Optohapt System   Communication of letters and words by touch is not limited to the skin of the fingers. If a letter is slowly traced on the wrist, palm, or back of the hand, it is not difficult to recognize the letter. It is known that it is possible to make discriminations between stimuli that vary in intensity, temporal length of the stimulation (duration), rate at which successive impacts are delivered to the skin (frequency), and loci of skin sites stimulated (Geldard, 1960; see also Sparks, 1979). By placing small contact vibrators that could be varied in these dimensions on the chests of subjects, Geldard (1966, 1968*b*) devised a language for use on the skin called **Vibratese.** It was constructed as follows: three levels of intensity (weak, medium, and strong) at three durations (0.1, 0.3, and 0.5 seconds) were delivered to five different locations on the chest, resulting in 45 separate signals. Each letter of the alphabet was assigned a signal that was its own combination of duration, intensity, and location. The most frequently occurring language elements were

assigned shorter durations enabling users of the system to proceed at a rapid pace. Geldard reported that the Vibratese alphabet could be mastered in only a few hours, and eventually whole words and meaningful sentences were perceived. One subject successfully received signals at a rate of about twice that of proficient Morse code reception. (Military standards for the proficient Morse code receiver are 18 words per minute.) Reception of Vibratese was limited by the speed of the sending equipment.

Subsequent research focused on increasing the potential input of printed characters by using vibrators scattered over the body, two on each arm and leg and one on the abdomen. The **Optohapt** system consists of an optical scanning device which converts printed material into touch stimulation. The material to be read is scanned by an electronic circuit; these, in turn, control a series of vibrators located on the body whose activation provides the meaningful touch stimulation. As shown in Figure 7.9, distinctive time–space patterns of vibratory bursts were as-

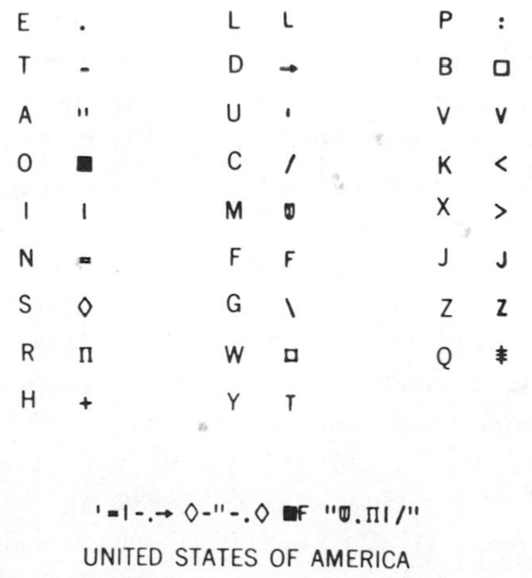

E	.	L	L	P	:
T	-	D	→	B	□
A	"	U	ı	V	v
O	■	C	/	K	<
I	ı	M	⍉	X	>
N	=	F	F	J	J
S	◇	G	\	Z	z
R	π	W	◻	Q	ǂ
H	+	Y	T		

'■I-.→ ◇-"-.◇ ■F "⍉.πI/"

UNITED STATES OF AMERICA

FIGURE 7.9.   Optohapt alphabet. The symbols, listed to the right of the alphabet, can be rapidly sent to and "read" by the skin. (From F. A. Geldard, "Pattern perception by the skin," in D. R. Kenshalo (Ed.), *The Skin Senses*, Charles C. Thomas, Springfield, Ill., 1968, p. 318. Reprinted by permission of the author and publisher.)

signed an alphabetic coding. The stimuli chosen for the alphabet were punctuation marks, numerals, literary and business symbols, and certain letters of the alphabet—characters chosen for their ease of discriminability. According to Geldard, an optimal presentation speed is at a rate of 70 characters per minute. The essential mode of operation of the Optohapt is to represent the symbol directly on the skin surface; the letter "V," for example, produces a rapid sweep from the topmost vibrator to the bottom one and then reverses the sequence. It is as if the Optohapt "writes" on the skin surface with the vibrators in, as Geldard (1968a) puts it, "body English."

THE TADOMA METHOD

That cutaneous stimulation can also be used to communicate speech is demonstrated by the success of some individuals that are both blind and deaf, using the **Tadoma method** of speech reception (Reed, Doherty, Braida, & Durlach, 1982). In the Tadoma method the listener places his or her hand in contact with specific parts of the speaker's lips, face, and neck so that the hand receives some of the complex spatiotemporal patterns of movement stimulation produced by the speaker's articulatory activity while speaking (see Figure 7.10). If the rate of speech is moderated and if the listener is well experienced, use of the Tadoma method permits a reasonable level of speech comprehension.

It is interesting to note in this context that the hand, held against the vocal apparatus of the speaker in using the Tadoma system, is receiving an informative pattern of pressure changes, that is, vibrations. However, the general technique is not confined to receiving stimulation directly from the vocal apparatus. Krueger (1982a) cites the case of a deaf girl who ". . . could understand what a normal girl was saying in a dark room if she laid her hand on the breast of the speaking girl. Another deaf person could 'listen' to and understand vibrations transmitted from the speaker by means of a billiard cue stick or a bowed piece of paper" (p. 13). By placing their hand on an audio speaker this technique of vibration transmission is also used by the deaf to "listen" to music.

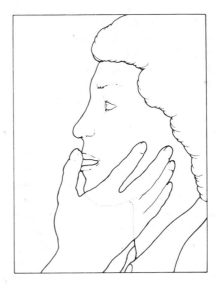

FIGURE 7.10.   Representation of hand placement using the Tadoma method of speech perception. The deaf-blind "listener's" hand is placed on the speaker's face and neck. The thumb is placed vertically with its tip over the speaker's upper lip, the little finger is placed over the jaw with its tip against the jaw (i.e., the temporal-mandibular) joint, and the remaining fingers fan out over the speaker's cheek. As the speaker talks the listener can directly pick up information that is closely tied to articulation, that is, stimulation from lip and jaw movements, laryngeal vibrations and oral air flow. (From J. M. Loomis and S. J. Lederman, "Tactual perception," in *Handbook of Perception and Human Performance*, Volume II, Wiley, New York, 1986, p. 31-19. Reprinted by permission of the publisher.)

PRESSURE PHOSPHENES

Other means of producing an alphabetic coding from touch stimulation have been attempted. One possibility has its basis in **pressure phosphenes,** the subjective lights and images resulting from pressure stimulation of the eye. Although not utilizing the skin surface, the use of pressure phosphenes has some relevance in this context. Typically, phosphenes are produced by applying pressure on the closed eyelid (Oster, 1970). Although they may appear to be completely random, in fact many of their characteristics such as their duration and location in the visual field can be controlled. Furthermore, the production of phosphenes does not require that pressure be applied directly to the external anatomy of the eye. It is possible to stimulate the visual area of the brain directly to produce phosphenes (e.g., Dobelle, Mladejovsky, & Girvin, 1974). Thus, the experience of phosphenes is available to persons who do not possess an intact visual system. One potential function of cortically produced phosphenes is for developing a visual prosthetic device. It may be possible by directly stimulating the brain to produce meaningful images. They would not necessarily be topographically similar to alphabet characters but as in the case of the symbols for the Optohapt, subjects could learn to associate a particular pattern of phosphenes with certain letters.

SEEING WITH THE SKIN

Another possibility for a means of cutaneous communication is to use the skin surface as a direct channel for pictorial material. A group of researchers (White et al., 1970; Collins, 1971) have developed a **vision substitution system** with the purpose of converting a visual image into a direct cutaneous display. The apparatus for this is shown in Figure 7.11. It consists of a tripod-mounted television camera—the "eye" of the system—that is connected to a 20×20 matrix of 400 vibrators mounted on the back of a stationary dental chair (see Figure 7.12). The video image is electronically transformed so that a vibrator is active when its locus is within an illuminated region of the camera field. The subject seated in the chair with his or her back against the vibrators is appropriately stimulated when the camera picks up an image. Thus, when a subject moves the television camera across a scene, patterns of light intensity in the visual field are reproduced in successions of tactual impressions on the skin surface of the back.

The results from presentation of this relatively coarse tactual image are remarkable. Subjects, both blind and blindfolded normally-sighted, were able to perceive some simple displays very soon after they had been introduced to the system. Simple geometric

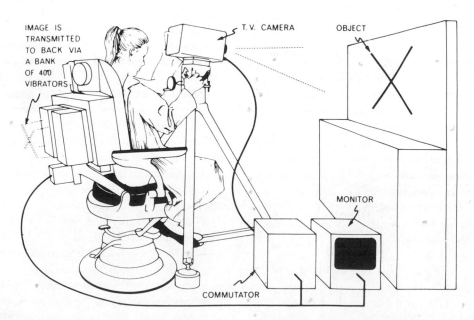

FIGURE 7.11. Schematic drawing of the vision substitution system. (From B. W. White, F. A. Saunders, L. Scadden, P. Bach-y-Rita, and C. C. Collins, "Seeing with the skin," *Perception & Psychophysics*, 7, 1970, p. 23. Reprinted by permission of Psychonomic Society, Inc.)

FIGURE 7.12.   The vibrator array mounted in the back of the chair. (From B. W. White, F. A. Saunders, L. Scadden, P. Bach-y-Rita, and C. C. Collins, "Seeing with the skin," *Perception & Psychophysics*, 7, 1970, p. 26. Reprinted by permission of Psychonomic Society, Inc.)

shapes—a circle, a triangle, and a square—were accurately identified when subjects were allowed to scan the figures by moving the television camera and were given immediate correction after a wrong response. With sufficient experience, a collection of 25 complex items (e.g., coffee cup, telephone, stuffed animal) were identifiable. Furthermore, experienced subjects were also able to identify the objects and describe their arrangements on a table when the objects were viewed by the camera from slightly above (an angle of 20° off the horizontal). The fact that some objects at the rear were partially occluded by those in front suggests that some of the depth and distance information of the visual scene is provided in the corresponding cutaneous image. One such cue for the location of an object in depth was its vertical position on the cutaneous display—the farther back its location on the table top, the higher up on the display. A second

cue for tactually perceiving depth is based on the inverse relationship between the projected size and distance of an object. The change in the image size normally projected on the eye as the object distance is varied also occurred on the skin surface in this arrangement. One of the subjects was a blind psychologist who has taught this relationship (i.e., an inverse relation between the projected size of an object and its physical distance from an observer) to his classes for several years, but obviously he had never directly perceived it. His experience of the increase in the size of a tactual image, as an object was brought closer and closer to the camera and a decrease in image size as object distance from the camera was increased, produced in him a sort of insightful perceptual realization about the relation between projected size and physical distance—"a genuine 'aha' experience."

Some variables are critical. It appears to be particularly important that the television camera not be kept in a fixed position and that the subject actively control the movement of the camera. It appears that enabling subjects to perform self-generated explorations of figures by sweeping the camera over the display results in the kind of successive changes in the activity of the vibrators that are necessary for meaningful tactual images to be perceived.

Subsequent development of the visual substitution system has been toward portability and increasing the amount of information received. As the authors comment, "the limitations of this system are . . . more attributable to the poverty of the display than to taxing the information-handling capacities of the epidermis" (White et al., 1970, p. 27). Other versions of tactual displays have been employed, but especially modified for use with different regions of the skin, such as the abdomen and the forehead (e.g., Cholewiak & Sherrick, 1981).

Within this context, we should take notice of the evidence that, on the basis of touch, the blind can understand many "visual" spatial concepts. By running their hands over "pictorially correct" raised surfaces, representations of depth and distance, relative size, and certain figural relationships (e.g., figure–ground or foreground–background) are readily perceived by the blind (see Kennedy, 1983; Kennedy & Campbell, 1985). In fact there are complex and spatially detailed artworks, including representational sculpture and bas relief murals, that are especially designed for the tactual perception of the blind (e.g., Good, 1988).

THE HAPTIC SYSTEM

As we noted in an earlier discussion, the combined input from the skin and from kinesthesis provides the basis of a perceptual channel called the **haptic system** (from the Greek, "to lay hold of"). According to J. J. Gibson (1966), who most clearly identified and stressed the importance of this channel, the haptic system is the perceptual system by which organisms are literally in touch with the environment. (Credit for recognizing the role of the haptic system must also be given to David Katz; see Krueger, 1982a). Consider some of the many functions of haptic perception:

> the sensing of fabrics by the hand; the sensing of food texture by the mouth; the sensing of vibrations in machinery that signify normal or abnormal operation; the identification of solid objects and their spatial arrangement; the sensing of imperfections and dirt on the surfaces of objects; the examination of internal organs of the body by palpation; the examination of unseen portions of the teeth using dental probes; and the sensing of weight, center of gravity, and the moment of inertia of hefted objects. . . . For humans . . . it contributes much to social and sexual communication, to individual development, and to the aesthetic appreciation of both art and daily life. (Loomis & Lederman, 1986, p. 31-26)

Thus, haptic perception normally results from a broad range of contacts between the environment and the organism's body. Indeed, most self-produced,

perceptual–motor encounters produce combined kinesthetic and cutaneous stimulation. For example, when we perform the common act of identifying an object on the basis of handling it, we simultaneously obtain information about the shape from the position of our fingers and from skin contact. Anatomically distinct receptors act in conjunction to produce what is clearly a unitary experience. Furthermore, the nerve pathways for the cutaneous sense and kinesthesis are very similar: they are both projected to the same area of the somesthetic cortex, and as a matter of experimental convenience, they have usually been investigated together. In brief, kinesthetic and cutaneous inputs combine to act as a single functional perceptual system.

It should be stressed that it is not passively applied cutaneous and kinesthetic stimulation that provides and registers the necessary information for haptic perception but "active touch": that is, concurrent cutaneous and kinesthetic stimulation that results from self-produced exploratory and purposive environmental encounters by the body. One product of this obtained coincident stimulation is the perception of the spatial features of objects and surfaces. No doubt it is the gathering of such stimulation that we actually refer to when we say we "touch," "feel," or "hold" something with our fingers or hands. A commonplace example of such a haptic ability is tactual stereognosis.

TACTUAL STEREOGNOSIS

Tactual **stereognosis** refers to the familiar ability to perceive three-dimensional shapes by palpation or exploratory manipulation of the hands. It appears to be also a very accurate ability. In one investigation, Klatzky, Lederman, and Metzger (1985) studied the ability of 20 subjects to identify common objects on the basis of touch alone. Blindfolded subjects handled 100 common objects, each easily identifiable by name, for example, toothbrush, onion, paperclip, screwdriver, fork. The results were impressive in terms of subjects' accuracy and overall competence in tactual exploration: out of a total of 2000 responses, approximately 96% were correct and 94% of the correct responses occurred within 5 seconds of handling by the subject.

Active touch need not be restricted to the hands and fingers. As we noted earlier with the vision substitution system, the surface of the back may be quite informative if stimulation is actively obtained rather than imposed. Indeed various parts of the body surface may be quite informative if stimulation is properly obtained. In fact there is a prosthesis called "sensate hand prosthesis" available for artificial hands that enables the wearer to obtain a sense of "touch" from its fingers. Contact sensors are built into the fingertips of the artificial hand that are capable of generating recognizable signals in the form of high-frequency vibrations. The thumb and index finger each transmit vibrations at a distinctive frequency, whereas the other three fingers generate a third frequency. Upon contact of the fingers, the vibrations are transmitted to the base of the artificial hand that adjoins the bony stump of the natural limb, and the wearer feels the vibrations in the arm. According to the inventor, a plastic surgeon (V. C. Giampapa, 1989), wearers quickly learn to distinguish the three signals from the different fingers and, to an extent, are provided with a source of tactual information concerning the objects and surfaces in direct contact with the fingers.

ROUGHNESS ENHANCEMENT

We note here the interesting observation of an enhanced sensitivity of the skin to actively self-imposed pressure or touch stimulation when using a simple surface aid. An individual may detect the surface undulations of an object more accurately when he or she moves a thin, intermediate sheet of paper across the surface than when the bare fingers are used (Gordon & Cooper, 1975). This method of "feeling," referred to as **roughness enhancement** (see Loomis & Lederman, 1986), has long been employed by craftsmen and autobody shops to examine the "smoothness" of the finish on repaired or reworked surfaces. According to Lederman (1978), as the bare fingers are moved over certain textured surfaces,

lateral (or shear) forces are applied to the skin of the finger tips; such forces serve to mask some of the critical skin deformation stimuli for roughness that are produced, in part, by normal (or downward) force. When an individual moves the intermediate sheet of paper across the surface, the paper reduces the shear force, which also reduces the interfering masking. The result is an increase in sensitivity to the roughness of a surface when felt through the sheet of paper moving with the fingers, relative to that experienced with the bare fingers.

The phenomenon of roughness enhancement can be demonstrated. Rub your fingers over the glazed surface of an apparently smooth piece of ceramic pottery. [An alternative surface is an auto body. Note that the choice of surface used is important. As Green (1981) points out, roughness enhancement will not occur with all textured surfaces.] Then place a piece of very thin paper (such as "onion skin" or the kind of paper attached to a carbon) and rub the paper over the same surface with your finger. When the ceramic surface is rubbed with the paper over it, it will feel slightly rougher than when the surface is felt by only the skin of the fingertip.

Finally it is worth noting that we can also make accurate judgments concerning the relative hardness of a surface using self-imposed touch stimulation. Even with reflected sound cues (as echoes) excluded, briefly tapping a surface with the fingernail is often sufficient to determine whether the surface is made of wood, metal, or plastic (Geldard, 1972).

SUMMARY

This chapter has focused on kinesthesis and on an introduction to cutaneous sensitivity. Kinesthesis refers to position and movement information registered from activity of the mobile parts of the jointed skeleton. It was noted that stimulation from the muscles, tendons, and joints provide information about the position, posture, and direction of the limbs in space.

Next the skin and the cutaneous sense of touch or pressure was discussed. It was observed that, whereas the sensation of touch is registered by mechanical stimulation of the surface of the skin, not all regions of the skin are equally sensitive to touch stimulation. Similarly, some regions are more sensitive to either thermal or pain stimulation than others. In short, there is a distribution of distinct areas sensitive to different kinds of cutaneous stimuli. However, there is no substantial evidence that each area is served by an identifiable and/or a distinct receptor.

The adequate stimulus for touch or pressure is a deformation of the skin or a pressure differential between one part of the skin and another. Uniform or continuous gradations of pressure are not effective forms of stimulation.

The relation between the skin and brain was outlined. It was noted that the skin is topographically projected onto the somatosensory cortex. Some of the differences between the two major nerve pathways to the brain, the lemniscal and the spinothalamic systems, were identified. In particular the difference between each system with regard to receptive fields of the skin was discussed. It was observed that the receptive field of a neuron of the somatosensory cortex is a specific area on the skin that when stimulated will alter the firing rate of the neuron. Receptive fields for neurons in the lemniscal system are more numerous and smaller than those for the spinothalamic system, and this enables finer tactual discriminations.

With respect to absolute threshold values for pressure, regions of the face and the fingers are the most pressure-sensitive parts of the body. With regard to localizing the point on the skin where the pressure stimulus is applied, it is generally the case that the more mobile the skin region stimulated (i.e., the mouth, the hands), the more acute the point localization. This also applies to the two-point threshold.

Finally a number of complex touch phenomena were identified and described: the Braille system, the Optacon, Vibratese, the Optohapt system, the Tadoma method of speech reception for the deaf-blind, and pressure phosphenes. The vision substitution system was discussed, and it was observed that the application of complex patterns of pressure on the skin enables the conversion of a visual image into a meaningful cutaneous experience that is directly linked to the visual image. Finally a brief discussion was given of haptic perception and the haptic capacities of roughness enhancement and tactual stereognosis: the latter refers to the ability to perceive three-dimensional shapes by manipulation of the hands.

In the next chapter we continue our discussion of the cutaneous modalities, introducing the temperature and pain senses.

KEY TERMS

Aristotle's illusion

Braille system

Cutaneous sensitivity

Free nerve endings

Haptic perception

Homunculus

Kinesthesis

Lemniscal system

Meissner corpuscles

Optacon

Optohapt

Pacinian corpuscles

Pressure phosphenes

Receptive field

Roughness enhancement

Somesthesis

Spinothalamic system

Stereognosis

Tadoma method

Two-point threshold

Vibratese

Vision substitution system

STUDY QUESTIONS

1. Identify and indicate the role played by kinesthesis in registering information about body position.

2. Identify the basic cutaneous sensations and describe the distribution of cutaneous sensitivity over the skin surface of the body.

3. Compare the lemniscal neural system with the spinothalamic system, indicating the different kinds of stimulation each transmits. Discuss the two systems with particular reference to the receptive fields of the skin. Indicate how the size and density of receptive fields contributes to tactual sensitivity.

4. Describe the different kinds of thresholds that exist for pressure. Indicate the general relation concerning skin region location and pressure sensitivity.

5. In what ways does the pattern of pressure changes on the skin enable a form of communication? Consider such phenomena as Braille, the Tadoma method, and devices such as the Optacon, the Optohapt system, and the vision substitution system as enabling alternative forms of communication.

6. Consider the manner and extent to which the blind can use touch to inform them of the spatial environment.

7. What is the haptic system and how does the combined use of kinesthesis and cutaneous experience enable tactual stereognosis?

8

SOMESTHESIS II: TEMPERATURE AND PAIN

We continue our discussion of somesthesis in this chapter with the primary emphasis on temperature and pain reception. Although temperature and pain refer to independent cutaneous modalities, they both differ from pressure in that their effective stimulation generally involves more than mechanical encounters and events.

In introducing the perception of thermal quality, we must make note of its adaptive behavioral contribution to the body's homeostatic temperature regulating system. Clearly, it is of survival significance for organisms to be aware of the rate at which their bodies are gaining and losing heat; most animals cannot live at the extremes of temperature. In nature, when heat loss is too great (and cold bodily sensations occur), an organism must seek some means of reducing it, such as seeking shelter or insulation or the proximity of a direct source of heat like sunlight or a fire. Similarly, if the heat gain is too great (and warm sensations result), a cooler environment is sought, such as shade or perhaps a brief immersion in water. Thus we may view a sensory system for the pickup and perception of thermal information as an adaptation that helps the organism avoid environmental extremes and contributes to the attainment of thermal equilibrium.

TEMPERATURE

The sensation resulting from the temperature of a surface that is in contact with the skin is registered by a form of cutaneous stimulation although its mechanism is far from clear. Thermal sensitivity is irregularly distributed in spots over the skin surface. Exploration with warm or cold stimuli reveals that some spots are especially sensitive to warmth, other more numerous spots are more sensitive to cold stimulation. As shown in Figure 8.1, the sensitivity of a given thermal spot may vary markedly over time. Like touch, the number of thermally sensitive spots depends on the intensity of the stimulus applied. Part of the experience of thermal variability may be due to temperature shifts within the skin itself, that is, to normal heat interchanges occurring at the site of nerve stimulation. The skin tissue is continually undergoing thermal variations owing to heat radiation, conduction, and convection, from moisture evaporation and dilation or constriction of the blood vessels of the subcutaneous tissue. In general, however, the body surface remains in a relatively stable thermal equilibrium with its immediate surroundings. Over the clothed areas of the body and the face, the skin temperature is close to 35°C (95°F) on the

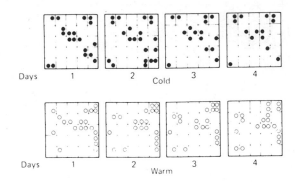

FIGURE 8.1. Successive mappings of cold and warm spots. The same region (1 sq cm) of the upper arm was mapped with a 1-mm-diameter cylinder for thermal spots on four different days. Observe that the distribution of spots shifted somewhat from mapping to mapping, but considerable stability of spots is also apparent. (From K. M. Dallenbach, "The temperature spots and end-organs," *American Journal of Psychology*, 39, 1927, p. 121. Reprinted with permission of the publisher, University of Illinois Press.)

hands and arms at about 33°C (91°F), and, of course, under the tongue at 37°C (98.6°F). Where blood flow is sluggish, as in the case of the ear lobe, the temperature may be significantly lower (20°C or 68°F). However, the temperature of the skin per se as we shall see is not a good predictor of thermal experience.

THERMAL ADAPTATION

Thermal sensations from the skin undergo adaptation. Initial exposure to a moderately cold or warm environment, as in the case of a swimming pool or bath, may initially result in very cold or hot experience, but eventually the thermal sensations will diminish and the water will feel slightly cool or warm. Prolonged warm or cold stimulation is likely to reduce the thermal sensitivity (raise the threshold values) for warmth and coldness, respectively. Although this is demonstrated readily for both warm and cold stimulation, perceived cold follows skin temperature to a greater extent than does warmth

(Marks & Stevens, 1972). Moreover, both warm and cold sensitivities are simultaneously affected by warm or cold stimulation. Adaptation to a warm stimulus also produces a lowering of the threshold for cold. Similarly, prolonged cold stimulation reduces the threshold for warmth, so that lower than normal temperatures are sufficient to produce a sensation of warmth.

Physiological Zero   A unique aspect of complete adaptation to thermal stimulation is that the thermal quality of the adapting stimulus is not experienced. The narrow range of temperatures to which a response of neither warm nor cold occurs—a neutral zone of complete thermal adaptation or thermal indifference—is called **physiological zero.** The size of the neutral zone varies with a number of factors but it can be as small as 0.01°C or as large as 8°C. A change in temperature from physiological zero is required to produce a thermal experience whose quality varies with the direction of the temperature change. Normally, physiological zero corresponds to the skin temperature at 33°C (91°F). The skin temperature for effecting physiological zero, however, can undergo variation. The demonstration attributed to John Locke in 1690 is appropriate here. If prior immersion of one hand is in a 40°C (104°F) basin of water, the other in a 20°C (68°F) basin and then both hands are shifted to a 33°C (91°F) basin of water, the water in the 33°C basin will now feel distinctly cold to the hand that was in the warm water and warm to the hand originally in the cold water. Physiological zero has shifted as a consequence of adaptation. This relationship of the adapted skin temperature to the temperature of a new thermal environment, as schematized in Figure 8.2, also demonstrates that the skin does not furnish accurate absolute temperature information. As indicated, the same physical temperature can feel cold to one hand and warm to the other. Thus, thermal experience occurs as a result of the *relation* of the temperature of the skin surface to its surroundings rather than from physical temperature itself. This explanation also applies to the familiar experience of briefly feeling cold after coming out of a heated swimming pool, or

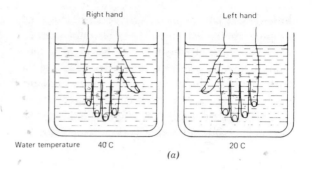

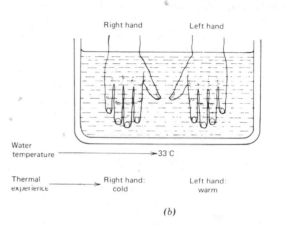

FIGURE 8.2.   Effects of thermal adaptation. (*a*) Each hand is placed in a separate basin of water and is thermally adapted to a different temperature. (*b*) When both hands are then placed in the 33°C water, the hand previously adapted to warm water feels cold, and the hand previously adapted to cold water feels warm. These effects of adaptation point out that the skin is not a good indicator of physical temperature.

even a hot bath or shower, during summer warm weather. Of course what has occurred is that the skin has adapted to the water temperature of the pool or bath. Thus even though the air of the poolside or bathroom environment is quite warm, relative to the temperature of the previously exposed water the air is "cool"; accordingly, the temperature differential —like that affecting the right hand in part *b* of Figure 8.2—promotes a brief cooling sensation.

In general, the more extreme the temperature,

the longer the time required for adaptation. However, complete thermal adaptation occurs only within a restricted range of temperatures. Extremes of temperature do not completely adapt. Immersion of the hands, for example, in very cold or very warm water will produce persistent cold and warm sensations. The temperature range for thermal indifference, within which total elimination of thermal sensation occurs, is generally put at 16°C to 42°C (61°F to 108°F). However, these limits have been shown to vary with the method of measurement and with the bodily region stimulated. In one study using the skin of the forearm, a very narrow range of thermal indifference was observed—between 29°C (84°F) and 37°C (99°F) (Kenshalo & Scott, 1966). It was found that temperatures between these rather moderate extremes reached physiological zero relatively rapidly. Temperatures below or above these values did not undergo complete adaptation but continued to elicit the experience of coldness or warmth.

TEMPERATURE DISCRIMINATION

Differential sensitivity determinations for temperature (minimal discriminable changes in temperature, ΔT) are quite difficult to obtain, due in large part to problems of experimental procedures. In general, minimal discriminable differerences in temperature —the difference threshold—vary with the conditions under which they are measured. Some of these are the region of the skin surface stimulated, the previous thermal state to which the skin is adapted (physiological zero), the rate of thermal change, and the size of the region stimulated. These are further affected by the fact that adaptation to coldness or warmth influences the ΔT for warmth or coldness, respectively. However, some general statements on difference thresholds can be offered. When thermal change (addition or withdrawal of heat) occurs slowly, larger deviations from skin temperature are required to produce a discriminable difference than if the temperature change occurs rapidly. Furthermore, the sensitivity to thermal change increases with increases in the size of the exposed skin surface. Thus, the palm of the hand in contact with the surface

of an object provides a better impression of the temperature of an object than does the fingertips. The notion that general thermal experience is more accurate when larger regions of the skin are stimulated (temperature held constant) has been termed **spatial summation,** and it implies that the activation of individual temperature receptors sum together to augment the intensity of the thermal experience (Kenshalo & Gallegos, 1967; Kenshalo, 1970). This is consistent with the observation that in comparison to the localization of tactual stimulation, the spatial localization of thermal stimulation is poor (Green, 1977).

PARADOXICAL THERMAL SENSATIONS

It has been reported that spots sensitive to cold will, under certain conditions, result in a cold impression although stimulated with a hot stimulus (45°C or 113°F). This phenomenon, termed **paradoxical cold,** is of course, paradoxical in that a stimulus of fairly high temperature produces a cold sensation. Related to this is the psychological experience of "heat." If a stimulus in the neighborhood of 45°C or greater is applied to a small region of the skin surface that is sensitive to both warm and cold stimulation, the experience of "heat" occurs. Warm spots are appropriately activated by the warm stimulus and cold spots are simultaneously and paradoxically activated. The assumption is that the warm and cold sensations fuse and produce an overall sensation of intense heat.

It is possible to simulate heat experience by simultaneously applying warm and cold stimulation to neighboring warm and cold spots on the skin. One approach is to use the "heat grill" sketched in Figure 8.3. Each set of tubes represents markedly different thermal ranges (the cold coil at, say, 20°C or 68°F and the warm coil at 40°C or 104°F). The thermal impression from touching the heat grill with a region of the arm containing both warm and cold spots is of intense heat, enough so that the limb is quickly withdrawn from the grill as if to avoid a burn though the grill is not physically hot. It should be noted that this demonstration is not always successful, which

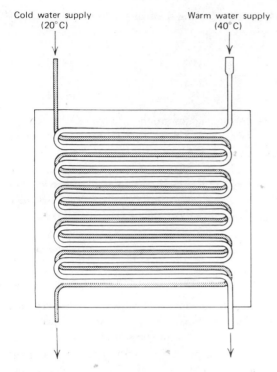

Cold water supply
(20°C)

Warm water supply
(40°C)

FIGURE 8.3.   The "heat" grill. Cold water circulates through one coil, warm water circulates through the other coil. If a skin area is placed firmly against the grill, the experience of "heat" results, although neither of the coils is "hot."

underscores the subjective nature of the thermal modality and its experiences (e.g., Geldard, 1972; Sherrick & Cholewiak, 1986).

Keep in mind that we are describing thermal sensations and impressions, and as such, it is debatable whether heat is a separate and uniquely different perception occurring from the fusion of warmth and cold, or whether it is experienced as intense warmth with the addition of a slight quickly adapting stinging sensation. The phenomenon of paradoxical cold and the cutaneous experience of heat has theoretical implications for understanding thermal perception. However, a fully acceptable explanation for their occurrence has yet to be given.

THEORIES OF THERMAL PERCEPTION

There are two main contending theories for explaining thermal sensitivity. The **specific receptor theory** assumes that specific and distinct receptors exist for warmth and cold. Although this theory has had many important supporters, it is generally attributed to Max von Frey (1852–1932). He argued that two separate types of receptors, *Krause end bulbs* and *Ruffini cylinders*, mediate the sensations of cold and warmth, respectively. Support for this contention comes from a number of sources that show that certain structural and functional differences exist between the effecting of warm and cold experiences. Application of warm or cold stimuli results in different latencies of thermal response. That is, a cold sensation occurs sooner after stimulation than is the case for a warm sensation. Further evidence was shown in Figure 8.1, which describes certain spots of the skin sensitive to only one or the other thermal extreme. The number of warm and cold spots appears to vary independently of each other, producing variable temperature sensitivities throughout the body. Additional evidence for receptor specificity comes from the fact that different thermal sensations can be actuated by different chemicals. Cold sensations may be produced by a number of chemicals applied directly to the skin; menthol is a familiar example. There is a class of synthetic compounds called *icilins* that produce sensations of cold by exerting selective stimulation on peripheral skin receptors (Wei & Seid, 1983). Other familiar chemicals such as ether, alcohol, and gasoline also produce only cool sensations when they are applied to the skin surface and then allowed to evaporate. On the other hand, there are chemicals such as carbon dioxide (when its evaporation is prevented), and capsaicin (the main pungent component of hot pepper) that produce sensations of warmth when applied to various parts of the body. They produce a very mild irritation that brings blood to the skin surface, and an intense feeling of warmth results.

Although it is possible that specific receptors such as Krause end bulbs and Ruffini cylinders are especially sensitive to temperature stimulation, it is unlikely that they are the only receptors. Thermal experiences occur from regions of the skin where these receptors occur very sparsely or do not occur at all. It has often been cited (and often contested) that the range of cutaneous sensations—pressure, warmth, coldness, and pain—occurs from appropriate stimulation of the cornea of the eye, a structure containing only free nerve endings (see Lele & Weddell, 1956). At present we must conclude that evidence for a distinct sensory nerve ending whose firing rate shifts only and directly as its temperature is increased or decreased—that is, a *caloriceptor*—has little support.

A second formulation, the **vascular theory** of thermal sensation proposed by Nafe and Kenshalo (Nafe, 1934; Kenshalo & Nafe, 1962) does not hold that specific nerve fibers in the skin are directly sensitive to warming or cooling or that there are separate systems for the two thermal impressions. Instead, a single mechanism for thermal sensibility is proposed: both warm and cold sensations are mediated by activity of the neurovascular system. It is argued that specific thermal sensations are a matter of the characteristics of the nonneural vascular tissue in which sensory nerve endings are imbedded. More specifically, thermal sensations occur from constriction and dilation of the smooth muscle walls of the blood vessels of the skin. The smooth muscles of the vascular system contract when cooled and relax when warmed. The direct responses of smooth muscle tissue producing size changes of the vessels initiate activity in the sensory nerve endings that are connected to the muscle walls, resulting in a thermal experience.

There are shortcomings in the vascular theory. For example, the vascular theory cannot account for the relative distribution of warm and cold spots. Warm spots frequently exist in skin areas separate from cold spots. If indeed there is only one mechanism underlying both warm and cold thermal experiences, then they should not manifest such divergent distributions on the skin. In general, neither the specific receptor theory nor the vascular theory is adequate to account for all the findings—and the

issue of explaining thermal experience remains unresolved.

PAIN

It is obvious that toward the extremes of temperature —freezing and boiling—thermal experience merges with pain. This is an adaptive association because intense thermal stimulation can produce tissue damage. As painful stimuli are unequivocally reacted to, this serves to protect the organism against harmful and perhaps even lethal thermal extremes. This points out that a significant benefit from the reception of pain is warning of potential biological harm.

FUNCTION OF PAIN PERCEPTION

Although tissue damage is neither a necessary nor a sufficient condition for the experience of pain, as a trend, most forms of pain-producing stimuli are potentially damaging: intense thermal, acoustic, photic, and electrical stimulation, under certain conditions, can result in serious bodily harm. There are exceptions, of course, but in the general case, from an evolutionary point of view, the perception of pain offers an important biological advantage for the survival of the organism. Failure to perceive pain is extremely maladaptive. Indeed some of the pernicious physical effects occurring to individuals who lack the sense of pain provide convincing testimony of its value to the organism. Reports of self-inflicted injury due to pathological pain insensitivity have included serious injuries of the skin, flesh, and bones, burns from hot surfaces and liquids, and even chewing off the tip of the tongue (e.g., Cohen et al., 1955).

In one clinical study of pain-insensitive children it was noted that on occasion they have pushed their eyeballs out of their sockets, pulled their teeth out, and had their fingernails pulled off with almost no discomfort; quite striking was the observation that males were indifferent to testicular compression (Jewesbury, 1951). Certainly among the most well-documented and dramatic instances of chronic insensitivity to pain, and one that illustrates the need for pain mechanisms and perception, is the clinical case reported by Baxter and Olszewski (1960).

The patient, the daughter of a physician, was a young Canadian student at McGill University in Montreal. According to extensive psychological testing, she was highly intelligent and seemed normal in all ways except that she had never experienced pain. Her apparent insensitivity to pain was noted at an early age. She bit her tongue on so many occasions that it was permanently deformed. Early childhood injuries involving numerous cuts, bruises, and abscesses (and their incisions) were experienced without any pain. At the age of 3 she sustained a third-degree burn while kneeling on a hot radiator and offered no complaint of pain. Similarly, an occasional sunburn never caused any discomfort. During the winters her extremities were frostbitten on several occasions, but this was never associated with pain. In addition she denied any pain from headache, toothache, earache, or stomache ache and apparently had never experienced the sensations of itching (even during an attack of the hives) or tickling. By the age of 8 she had been hospitalized on three occasions for orthopedic problems, which were to continue into her adult years. By this age she was aware of her unusual insensitivity to typically painful, tissue-damaging incidents and learned to take certain precautions. For example, she inspected her feet after a day at the beach to be sure that she had not sustained any unnoticed, but serious lacerations.

At the age of 22 she underwent extensive neurological examinations and appeared insensitive to the administration of any noxious stimuli. For example, she experienced no pain to prolonged ice baths (0°C or 32°F, for 8 min) or to immersion in hot water (50°C or 122°F, for 5 to 8 min); in fact, attempts to establish a pain threshold for warmth was aborted when the patient failed to experience any pain despite thermal stimuli sufficient to cause skin blistering. She received no pain sensations from the insertion of a hypodermic needle into her skin or from the administration of series of electric shocks. A stick could be inserted up through her nostrils without causing any discomfort or even the tendency to sneeze. The

injection of histamine intravenously (which normally produces intense pain) merely produced throbbing sensations. Furthermore, the corneal reflex (movement of the eyelid to protect the eyes) was absent and the gag reflex could be elicited only with great difficulty. Of interest is that she failed to show typical physiological reactions to pain, such as changes in pulse rate, blood pressure, and respiration. In contrast she did exhibit the expected variations in these measures when subjected to stressful psychological tests that did not make use of physically noxious stimuli.

Despite her pain insensitivity she was reasonably well-coordinated, could experience and localize touch, and could distinguish between hot and cold objects anywhere on the body surface, even when the difference between two temperatures was small. Overall her neurological examination did not reveal any evidence of organic neurological disease. However her life-long orthopedic problems became more severe. At age 23 she began to limp and exhibited pathological changes in her hip-joint and spine, which were soon followed by numbness and a marked muscle weakness in her lower extremities. Several orthopedic operations, including spinal decompression and fusion, were performed but without success. According to Melzack's (1973) analysis, the pathological changes were "due to the lack of protection to joints usually given by pain sensations. She apparently failed to shift her weight when standing, to turn over in her sleep, or to avoid certain postures, which normally prevent inflammation of joints" (p. 16).

The patient died at the age of 29 due to intractable massive infections to her hip. During her last month she finally complained of pain in the region of her left hip, and the pain was relieved by analgesic tablets. According to Baxter and Olszewski (1960), "Her lack of pain appreciation was so great that she suffered extensive skin and bone trauma which contributed in a direct fashion to her death" (p. 392).

PAIN DUE TO OVERSTIMULATION

Although we know that pain may be evoked by many sorts of stimuli, the exact characteristics of the stimuli that excite the receptor cells are not determined. An early hypothesis for pain perception was that sensory receptors for pain are not specialized to react to a simple form of energy. Since pain is an accompaniment of most intense forms of stimulation, it was conjectured to be produced by *overstimulation* of the cutaneous receptor. However, overstimulation in itself is insufficient to account for the production of pain, because pain can occur without intense stimulation and pain may not necessarily occur with it.

THE NOCICEPTOR

Another alternative is to assume that pain is a unique perceptual experience resulting from the excitation of a specialized receptor—a **nociceptor** (from the Latin, *nocere*, "to injure"; a receptor whose effective stimulation produces injury to the body and whose sensations are unpleasant)—that can be triggered by a wide range of stimuli. This is supported by the fact that, using mapping techniques, there are regions or spots of the skin the stimulation of which yields only the sensation of pain. Of interest is that pain spots are more numerous than pressure and thermal spots, and their distribution appears to be quite diffuse. Further evidence for pain as a separate sense modality comes from measurements taken when the skin is made insensitive by the use of morphine. Morphine renders the skin insensitive to pain but has little effect on the other cutaneous systems. Indeed in the dramatic case of congenital pain insensitivity noted earlier, the woman was able to perceive pressure and to make thermal discriminations (Baxter & Olszewski, 1960). Also the thresholds for pain and touch have been shown to differ on a number of quantitative dimensions (Gibson, 1968).

The identification of a specialized receptor for pain has been a problem for the nociceptor notion. Based on the observation that **free nerve endings** are ubiquitously distributed throughout the skin as well as in much of the internal anatomy, muscles, tendons, joints, and connective tissue of the viscera, they are often the proposed candidate for the nociceptor.

THE QUALITIES OF PAIN

It is possible to distinguish pain from most other sensory experiences and even to distinguish between classes of pain. Brief skin pain may be characterized as "sharp" or "bright." It is well localized and causes an immediate reaction. It is experienced as being quite different from so-called "dull" pain originating from deep within the body (the chest and abdomen), which may produce other bodily reactions (e.g., sweating, palpitations) and in general is poorly localized (Békésy, 1971).

In keeping with tradition, we have stressed the skin as a primary receptive surface for pain. Obviously, however, the locus for pain is not so confined. Pain can result from the effective stimulation of almost any body region, internal as well as on the surface.

At times pain originating from internal organs may appear to occur from another region of the body, usually the surface of the skin. Such phenomena are called **referred pain.** For example, the intense pain arising from the heart associated with *angina pectoris* appears to come from the chest wall and a skin region lying on the inner surface of the upper arm.

Under certain circumstances, *double pain* may be experienced. That is, two kinds of pain, "sharp" and "dull" occurring from the same stimulation, may be distinguished. The sharp pain is rapidly aroused and is gradually followed by a more persistent dull pain. Other pain sensations are those of "pricking" pain, a pain produced by a very brief skin surface contact, and "burning" pain, where the pain-producing stimulus is of greater duration. The list of pains can be further extended to include irritations. For example, *itch*, produced clinically by mechanical and chemical means, is considered a low-grade pain (Geldard, 1972).

THE PAIN STIMULUS AND PAIN THRESHOLDS

It is generally agreed that when the skin is mechanically stimulated the appropriate stimulus for pain is the lengthwise stretching of the skin. This is supported by the observations that injury to the skin such as cutting will be painful if, in the process, the skin is stretched. If cutting is done on skin that is rendered immobile, little or no pain is experienced.

Because of marked individual differences in pain experience, general statements about the psychophysics of pain are difficult to make. This difficulty is compounded by the fact that pain can be elicited by very different stimuli which may not uniformly produce the same pain quality. Also the same stimulus at different intensities can produce different painful experiences. Furthermore, if tissue damage occurs, subsidiary effects, such as inflammation and swelling, provide a further complexity in evaluating the pain experience.

Pain thresholds may be affected not only by the amount of painful stimulation but by how that stimulation is distributed. Messing and Campbell (1971) demonstrated with rats that when electric shock (presumably painful stimulation) was divided over two anatomically distinct and widely separated loci (neck *and* tail) the avoidance response was less than when the same amount of electric shock was applied to a single anatomical region (neck *or* tail), that is, "Rats preferred shock in two (anatomical) locations to an equal amount in one location" (p. 225).

There are also gender-related effects and gender differences in pain sensitivity and thresholds. Goolkasian (1980) reported that women with normal menstrual periods experienced a heightened sensitivity to pain during ovulation. In contrast, for women in whom ovulation was inhibited (by the use of oral contraceptives), there was no change in pain sensitivity across the menstrual phase. There is also evidence of gender differences in reaction to pain. Using electrocutaneous shock as the noxious stimulus, Jones and Gwynn (1984) reported that females typically rated the same shock intensity as more painful than did males. Similarly, Rollman and Harris (1987), also employing electric shock as the pain stimulus, observed that females had significantly lower pain thresholds. Thus there appears to be a general sex difference in response to electrocutaneous shock.

SUBJECTIVE FACTORS IN PAIN EXPERIENCE

Pain is a subjective experience, and, as such, it is subject to more than the administration of a noxious stimulus. Psychological factors such as expectation and attitude, attention and suggestion, motivation, various ongoing emotional states and cognitive processes, and the meanings that one attaches to the source of the pain may exert a significant effect on the intensity and the quality of the pain experienced. Indeed the observation of a uniform sensation threshold that is exclusively dependent upon and directly proportional to the amount of pain stimuli applied, is for the most part restricted to laboratory observation. In the more natural environmental encounters that may produce pain, psychological factors can radically modify the experience. A pain stimulus that is extremely unpleasant in one situation may not be in another. Thus, an injury sustained in battle or competitive sports may not elicit the same degree of pain as when it is experienced in a more tranquil setting. Moreover it is entirely possible that the same injury can produce different effects in different persons.

From time to time, various sociocultural and ethnic effects have also been proposed to affect pain thresholds directly (e.g., Hardy, Wolff, & Goodell, 1952), and pain tolerance levels (Sternbach & Tursky, 1965). Melzack (1973) describes several culturally based initiation rites and rituals (of India and of the North American Plains Indians) that involve suspending and swinging "celebrants" by skewers and hooks that are inserted into their chest and backs as part of religious ceremony. Rather than showing the effects of pain, the celebrants appear more in a state of exaltation and ectasy. That the range of pain tolerance may be linked to culture is further supported by some clinical observations following major surgery. H. Keim (1981), an orthopedic surgeon, reports that he has performed spinal grafts or fusions (in which bone fragments are chipped from regions of the pelvic bone and placed over vertebrae) on Canadian Indians on one day, and on the next day they walked about as if without any pain. Such stoic behavior was rarely observed with members of other cultural groups.

Overall we may conclude that psychological variables can exert potent effects on pain experience and account for a high degree of variability in perceived and reported pain. It is worth noting that pain is not a single sensation produced by a single or specific stimulus; rather pain may encompass a range of different, unpleasant experiences produced by a large set of potentially noxious events that are linked to one's personal history.

PAIN ADAPTATION

Most people who have suffered prolonged conditions of pain—toothache, headache, burn, nerve trauma —concur that the pain seems to extend indefinitely; that is, it does not adapt. Moreover, from an evolutionary point of view, it could be argued that the sensation of pain should not undergo adaptation for then it would not have survival value. However, the profound biological benefit of pain is seen in its initial effect. So long as the initial stimulation is perceived and reacted to there is no need for continued stimulation. Hence pain adaptation is not maladaptive. Indeed, because of the very urgent, almost primordial nature of pain experience, it usually effects an immediate response. Furthermore, in those cases where pain does not appear to adapt, it is not clear if the stimulus and receptor conditions at the region of injury are held constant. Most painful conditions occur with continual variations at the site of injury, "chiefly rhythmic ones based on circulatory events" (Geldard, 1972, p. 327). Thus, pain may not *appear* to undergo adaptation because different regions are continually being stimulated, or because the stimulation at a single region is, in fact, varying.

The evidence strongly favors the notion that within limits cutaneous pain does adapt. Depending on the stimulus conditions, the skin adapts to the pain of thermal extremes. Complete pain adaptation, for example, occurs within 5 minutes when the hand is immersed in 0°C water. The rate of adaptation varies with the amount of skin involved, because with a smaller area adaptation occurs sooner. Similarly, the pain occurring from temperatures up to about 47°C (117°F) may be adapted to also, although the pain from temperatures above this, which are in the range of tissue damage, appear nonadapting (Kenshalo, 1971; Hardy, Stolwijk, & Hoffman, 1968). In general, the smaller the region to which the painful

heat stimulation is applied, the more likely is adaptation to occur.

Pain induced by mechanical stimulation is adapted to not because of neural fatigue due to continual stimulation but because of a lack of effective stimulation. The pain produced by insertion of a needle soon adapts, but recurs when the needle is withdrawn. It is the tissue movement that is the painful stimulation, and a lack of stimulation creates the condition for adaptation.

Adaptation to pain provides further evidence in support of the view that pain is a distinct and separate sense rather than a secondary sensation resulting from overstimulation of one of the cutaneous receptor mechanisms. For example, in the course of pain adaptation to, say, intensely applied cold stimulation, the feeling of pain gradually subsides leaving only a cool feeling. In general, residual effects, specific to the stimuli applied, replace the pain. These are the results that would be expected if pain is a distinct cutaneous modality; that is, it adapts independently of the other skin senses.

THEORIES OF PAIN

In the preceding discussions, we have introduced a specificity theory that proposes that pain is a distinct and separate sensory modality with its own set of specific peripheral pain receptors in the body—free nerve endings—that project to a central pain center in the brain. **Pattern theory,** in contrast, ignores physiological specialization and assumes that general stimulus intensity or the summation of neural impulses by a central mechanism are the critical determinants of pain.

SPINAL GATE CONTROL THEORY OF PAIN

A third, eclectic theory has been proposed that is, in part, a specificity theory and, in part, a pattern theory. Melzack and Wall (1965; see also Melzack, 1973) have described a **spinal gate control theory** of pain reception that focuses on nerve impulse transmission from the skin to the spinal cord. It is a theory that assumes a competitive interaction between two different kinds of nerve fibers reaching the first central transmission (T) cells of the spinal cord. The theory further assumes that there exists a neurological gate control system within the spinal cord that modulates or "gates" the amount of nerve impulse transmission from peripheral fibers of the skin to the T cells and that pain results when the output of the T cells reaches or exceeds a critical level. Several structures play a role in determining what transmission there will be from the central T cells. The gate control system is primarily affected by the inhibitory effect on T cell stimulation of the *substantia gelatinosa*, a highly specialized structure composed of small, densely packed cells that form a functional

unit extending the length of the spinal cord. The factors involved in the transmission of impulses from peripheral nerves to T cells in the spinal cord are schematically diagrammed in Figure 8.4.

Crucial to the theory is the kind of fibers making connection to the substantia gelatinosa. Pain is carried by at least two different types of nerve fibers: large-diameter, myelinated (sheathed), rapidly-conducting fibers (L fibers in the figure) convey "sharp" pain as well as other sensory events, and small-diameter, unmyelinated, slow-conducting fibers (S fibers in the figure) convey dull or "burning" pain. (Recall from Chapter 7 that fast-conducting, large-diameter fibers are part of the lemniscal system

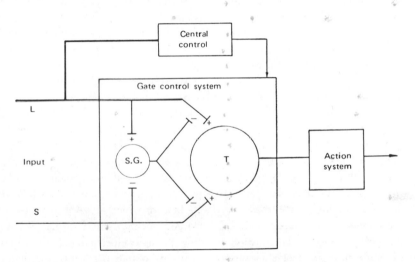

FIGURE 8.4.   Schematic of the spinal gate control theory of pain: L, the large-diameter fibers; S, the small-diameter fibers. The plus sign (+) signifies neural excitation; the minus (−) indicates neural inhibition. The L and S fibers project to the substantia gelatinosa (S.G.) and to the first central pain transmission (T) cells. Both L and S fibers have a direct effect on the T cells and contribute to the transmission of pain. However, the activity of L and S fibers each functions differently in reducing or inhibiting pain transmission. The L fiber activity excites (+) the S.G., whereas the S fibers activity inhibits (−) the S.G. When the L fibers stimulate the S.G., an hypothesized pain "gate" (shown as the branch connected to the right of the S.G.) is *closed* and an inhibitory (−) effect is applied to the T cells. The result is a reduction in pain transmission. In contrast when S fiber activity is increased, the S.G. is inhibited (−), the gate is *opened*,

and little inhibition is sent to the T cells. The result is that the T cells are more active and pain transmission is increased. Thus the pain gate is part of the S.G. and directly affects the activity of the T cells: activity of L fibers closes the gate and inhibits pain, whereas activity of S fibers opens it and increases pain transmission.

Notice that the L fiber system is connected to a central control mechanism, which in turn, projects back to the gate-control system. It is by this mechanism that the brain exerts influence on the gate-control system. That is, the central control is the mechanism that enables cognitive control of pain experience by way of past experience, emotions, cognitions and perceptions, and the like. (From R. Melzack and P. D. Wall, "Pain Mechanisms: A New Theory," *Science, 150,* 1965, p. 975. © 1965 by the American Association for the Advancement of Science.)

and the slow-conducting, small-diameter fibers are from the spinothalamic system.) Both types of fibers have branches going to the substantia gelatinosa. As shown in the figure, the L fibers excite the substantia gelatinosa, which in turn blocks the effect of L fibers on the T cells. That is, although nerve impulses in large fibers are extremely effective in initially activating T cells, their later effect is reduced in that L fibers act to inhibit themselves by a feedback mechanism. Large fibers also act to block the slower acting small-diameter fiber inputs by way of the substantia gelatinosa—in short, by stimulating the substantia gelatinosa they close the theorized gate and inhibit pain transmission. In contrast, S fibers inhibit the substantia gelatinosa. This reduces the inhibitory action of the substantia gelatinosa on the T cells and thus allows the T cells to transmit the S fibers' pain information. That is, the inhibitory action of the S fibers causes the substantia gelatinosa to hold the pain gate in a relatively open position and pain transmission is increased. At levels of high stimulation that accompany injury, bursts of S fiber input will reduce the inhibitory effect of the substantia gelatinosa and allow the T cells to be stimulated at a high rate, which results in pain. If a gentle stimulation is applied to the skin, however, the transmission will contain large-fiber impulses that will partially close the gate. As the stimulus intensity of the injury is increased, more receptor units are recruited and the resultant positive and negative effects in the large and small fibers will tend to counteract each other—the inhibitory effect of the substantia gelatinosa is negated—with the net result of increased stimulation of the T cells. Furthermore, when stimulation is prolonged, the large fibers adapt, producing a relative increase in small-fiber activity—the gate is opened further. Thus, the total number of active fibers and the relative balance of activity in large and small fibers at the point of the spinal gate determines the excitatory effects at the T cells. When the arriving impulses reach a critical level, there is a firing of the T cells that in turn activates the neural mechanism of a postulated central decoding system. This system is assumed to be sensitive to the firing frequency of the T cells in that when the frequency is low, the stimulation is interpreted as nonpainful, but a high

frequency is interpreted as pain. This theory explains pain as a result of an increase in the activity of S fibers or a decrease in activity of L fibers.

Notice that the theory also provides for a cognitive-motivational-emotional dimension of pain. The central control in the figure is the mechanism whereby general excitement or emotion, attention, attitude, and prior experiences exert control over the sensory input and modulate pain reception through the gate control system. That is, the central control exerts its influence on the activity of T cells by sending messages from the brain *downward* by way of neural pathways. Thus input from the brain of a cognitive nature (or even by direct stimulation) can open or close the gate and affect the perception of pain.

Although there is little direct physiological evidence, there is some empirical support for this theory. One testable implication for this theory is that pain relief should be achieved by decreasing the input of the small fibers and increasing the input of the larger fibers. The latter was essentially performed by Livingston (1948) who observed that *causalgia* (a severe and prolonged burning pain produced by lesions to peripheral nerves) could be effectively controlled by therapy such as bathing the injured region in gently moving water followed by massage—both of which serve to increase the input in the large fiber system. Wall and Sweet (1967) applied low-intensity electrical pulses—experienced as "tingling"—to patients with chronic cutaneous pain. These stimuli produced impulses only in large-diameter fibers. Patients with peripheral nerve diseases experienced some relief of their pain after such electrical stimulation.

The gate control theory also provides for speculations on the basis of **phantom limb pain**—apparent pain in the amputated limb. Although usually phantom limb pain tends to decrease and eventually disappear, there are cases where the pain intensifies over time. It is difficult to account for such pain because the peripheral pain receptors are removed along with the limbs. However, Melzack (1970) has noted that when a limb is amputated, about half of the cut nerve fibers that still remain in the stump die. The rest regenerate and grow into stump tissue, and these fibers are usually of small diameter and slow conducting. Thus, the full range of fiber sizes is missing. Most critical and relevant to our present discussion is that a lack of large-diameter fibers means that there is a corresponding lack of inhibitory effect in the sensory pathway from the spinal cord to the brain. That is, the spinal gate is opened and in some cases, pain is the result. It must be noted that although the spinal gate control theory has come under criticism, it remains the most influential and important current theory of pain perception.

ACUPUNCTURE

Mention must also be made of the striking and profound anesthetic effects produced by the traditional Oriental therapy for the general treatment of disease and control of pain, **acupuncture** (from the Latin, *acus* for "needle" and *pungere*, "to sting"). We are not here concerned with the merits of acupuncture for the treatment of disease but with its application to pain. In most cases needles, electrified, set in movement ("twirled"), and often heated, are inserted at various bodily loci. The potential needle sites are charted precisely and vary with the pain site. Although Western medicine has been cautious in accepting acupuncture as valid, the reporting thus far has been mainly, though not exclusively, positive (e.g., Gwei-Djen & Needham, 1979). Precisely how acupuncture works to eliminate pain is still a matter of conjecture. However, the gate control theory does provide a reasonable explanation. The sensory input appears to be a critical factor. Perhaps electrifying, twirling, and heating the needle produce a stream of nonpainful sensations that selectively stimulate the large-diameter fibers (L) of the sensory nerves, which close the hypothesized gate in the spinal cord. Accordingly, the needles, by selectively and continuously stimulating the large-diameter nerve fibers, initiate the inhibitory influence of the substantia gelatinosa and hence block pain impulses that travel along the small diameter nerve fibers. This, of course, does not explain the full range of anesthetic effects produced by acupuncture, such as inserting needles in the arm to allow painless dental extrac-

tions. Obviously, we are at the very beginnings of understanding this unusual means of pain control.

ENDORPHINS AND ENKEPHALINS

Acupuncture may induce the secretion of an endogenous pain suppressor, a neurally secreted opiatelike chemical. Indeed, chemicals—endogenous opioids—have been isolated called **enkephalins** (from the Greek, *kephalé*, meaning "head") and **endorphins** (from "endogenous morphine"). These chemicals appear to be neurotransmitters for events relating to pain and perhaps other bodily processes (Marx, 1979; Wasacz, 1981). Although endorphin is used as the general term to describe both normally occurring opiatelike substances, endorphins are found in high concentrations in the pituitary, whereas enkephalins are found broadly and unevenly distributed in the brain, spinal cord and intestines (e.g., Akil et al., 1978; Lewis et al., 1981). Endorphins appear to have specific binding sites or receptors (Pasternak, Childers, & Snyder, 1980), which in some cases are the same as the binding sites of the opiates (e.g., morphine and heroin). It is a reasonable speculation that specific binding or receptor sites did not evolve in the human for the singular purpose of receiving external chemical stimuli, such as the opiates; that is, these receptor sites must have developed for substances produced within the body (Wasacz, 1981). It is of interest that one form of brain endogenous opiate labeled β-endorphin shows an even higher affinity for the body's opiate receptor sites than does morphine and it has stronger analgesic properties: according to Kelly (1984) it is many times more potent than morphine. As is the case with exogenous opiates, chronic administration of β-endorphin produces drug tolerance (i.e., progressive weakening of its analgesic effects), and its abrupt withdrawal initiates the range of distressing effects of morphine addiction.

Of interest to the preceding discussion on the spinal gate control theory of pain is that the substantia gelatinosa of the spinal cord is highly enriched in both opiate receptors (Yaksh, 1978) and endorphin-containing neurons (Snyder, 1977; Neale et al.,

1978). Accordingly, endorphins may act by inhibiting the release of excitatory substances for neurons, especially those carrying information about pain. That is, endorphins may "close" the spinal gate and thus suppress pain.

Endorphins and Stress   Certain forms of severe stress may promote the activation of an endogenous analgesia system, suggesting that endorphins may serve a biologically significant role in pain management and control (e.g., Terman et al., 1984). However, as we emphasized earlier, the perception of pain provides an immense biological advantage to the organism: indeed, pain normally demands immediate attention, and it may initiate adaptive action necessary for survival. Accordingly a system that suppresses pain awareness should be activated only in emergency situations where the normal reaction to pain could disrupt effective coping strategies and hence be seriously disadvantageous or even maladaptive to the organism. That is, perhaps there are conditions where the suppression or reduction of pain enables the organism to perform biologically adaptive activity (e.g., Willer, Dehen, & Cambier, 1981).

Laboratory studies of animals confronting stresslike conditions tend to support this notion. Thus, for example, endorphin system activity has been observed during pregnancy in rats (Gintzler, 1980), and in conditions of food deprivation (McGivern & Berntson, 1980; Gambert et al., 1980; Mandenoff et al., 1982). It has been reported that the pain produced by exposure to inescapable foot shock, administered to rats intermittently for 30 minutes, caused significant analgesic effects (Lewis, Cannon, & Liebeskin, 1980; see also Herman & Panksepp, 1981; Grau, 1984). It has also been reported that after repeated exposure to physical attack, defeated mice secrete endorphins and show effects of pain suppression (Miczek, Thompson, & Shuster, 1982). Associated with these analgesic effects are displays of submissive behavior and the typical posture of defeat in mice, characterized by an upright position, limp forepaws, upwardly angled head, and retracted ears. Finally, it should be noted that whereas severe stress appears to trigger pain

suppression through endorphin activity, identification of the essential mediating mechanisms remains elusive.

SUMMARY

In this chapter we have continued our discussion of somesthesis focusing on the cutaneous senses of temperature and pain. Sensations of temperature —warmth or coldness—result from skin contact with thermal stimuli; however, the thermal experience occurs as a result of the relation of the temperature of the skin surface to that of its surroundings rather than from the physical temperature of the surroundings alone. That is, skin temperature itself is not a good indicator of thermal experience. Within limits, if the thermal environment is held invariant, the sensory experience of either warmth or coldness diminishes until complete adaptation of thermal sensation results. The temperature range of stimuli to which a response of neither warmth nor coldness occurs is called physiological zero.

There are a number of theories of thermal sensitivity. One holds that there are specific and distinct receptors for warm and cold sensations. A vascular theory contends that there is a single mechanism mediated by the activity of the neurovascular system. It holds that thermal sensations result from the constriction and dilation of the smooth muscle walls of the blood vessels of the skin; the smooth muscles of the vascular system constrict when cooled and relax when warmed. The sensory nerves imbedded in the vascular tissue register the size changes of the blood vessels of the skin (dilation or constriction), which gives rise to the thermal experience. Inadequacies of both theories were noted. In general, the issue of explaining the temperature sense is unresolved.

The sensory modality of pain was introduced, and its functional, informative role, as well as its overall benefit for the survival of the organism, was stressed. It was noted that the sensation of pain may be invoked by many kinds of stimulation. There was discussion of the conditions that modify the experience of pain, such as adaptation, gender, and various psychological factors, such as suggestibility, expectation, and the motivational, cognitive, and emotional states of the individual. One explanation of pain reception is that since pain is an accompaniment of most intense forms of stimulation, it is thereby produced by overstimulation of any cutaneous sensory receptor. An alternative explanation posits the existence of a nociceptor, a specific receptor that can be activated by a wide range of stimuli and that produces the painful sensation. The receptors proposed for this are the free nerve endings. A third theory, the spinal gate control theory, contends that pain is the result of the relative nerve impulse transmission from the skin to the spinal cord. Fast-conducting, large-diameter fibers in the sensory nerves running from the skin to the central nervous system close the "gate" in the pain-signaling system and thus reduce the degree of pain received; slow-conducting, small-diameter fibers open the spinal gate and increase the pain signals reaching the brain. Some empirical studies lend tentative support to this theory. In addition, a number of phenomena related to pain sensitivity were discussed: the qualities of pain, thresholds, acupuncture, and endorphins.

KEY TERMS

Acupuncture

Endorphins

Enkephalins

Free nerve endings

Nociceptor

Paradoxical cold

Pattern theory

Phantom limb pain

Physiological zero

Referred pain

Spatial summation

Specific receptor theory

Spinal gate control theory (Melzack & Walls)
Vascular theory

STUDY QUESTIONS

1. Consider the biological function of a sensory–perceptual system that provides sensations of warm and cold.

2. What is the general relationship between skin temperature and thermal experience? Consider whether the physical temperature of the skin is effective for eliciting thermal sensations.

3. How can the skin be thermally adapted? What are the ranges and limits of thermal adaptation? How well can temperature change be discriminated?

4. What is "heat," and how can the sensation of heat be produced from the stimuli that produce the sensations of warm and cold? How does the phenomenon of paradoxical cold bear on the sensation of heat?

5. Outline the main theories of thermal perception. What evidence opposes the notion that there are specific receptors or caloriceptors for the registration of warm and cold? Consider evidence that is counter to the vascular theory.

6. Discuss the adaptive role played by pain. Specify the general environmental conditions that produce pain.

7. Examine the notion that pain is a result of sensory overstimulation and compare this with the view that pain is due to stimulation of a specialized receptor or nociceptor.

8. What role does gender play in the threshold for pain? Consider the effects of subjective-psychological factors, such as expectation, attention, suggestion, and culture, on pain perception.

9. Consider whether the sensation of pain can be adapted. Examine the notion that pain repre-

sents an independent, separate cutaneous sensation, distinct from the extremes of pressure and thermal sensations.

10. Outline the spinal gate control theory of pain, indicating the contributions of the lemniscal and spinothalamic neural systems. What sorts of evidence support the theory?

11. Describe acupuncture and assess its status in pain control. What are endorphins? What kinds of environmental conditions promote the activity of an endorphin system? Consider the relation of acupuncture and endorphins to the spinal gate control theory.

THE CHEMICAL
SENSORY SYSTEM I:
TASTE

Our focus in this chapter and the following one will be on the chemical senses: taste (gustation) and smell (olfaction). Unlike the sensory systems discussed in preceding chapters, both taste and smell depend on receptors that are normally stimulated by chemical substances. Accordingly, the receptors are termed **chemoreceptors.** Aside from the fact that the taste and smell systems are both activated by chemical stimuli, they are also functionally related. In the human, the interdependence of smell and taste in the case of food ingestion can be easily demonstrated. If the input for smell is reduced or eliminated by blockage of the air passages of the nostrils, as sometimes happens during a "cold" (in which an overproduction of mucous results in a congestion of the olfactory sensory cells), or by holding the nostrils closed, two different food substances may taste quite similar. For example, under these circumstances, a bite of raw potato does not taste very different from a bite of apple. This indicates that many taste qualities assigned to food are in fact due to their odors. Meat is an instance of this; most of its sensory qualities are olfactory. According to Moncrieff (1951) **anosmic** individuals (lacking a sense of smell) cannot distinguish between meats by taste experience alone. This suggests a diet aid for certain individuals—a reduction in the odor of foods that renders them somewhat "tasteless" may result in a decrease in their appeal, therefore perhaps a decrease in consumption.

It is neither necessary nor even possible to make a distinction between taste and smell for all animals. There is evidence that many forms of aquatic life can detect the presence of chemical substances in their immediate environments. Fish possess a pit resembling a nose lined with chemoreceptors, as well as taste receptors scattered over the surface of the body and mouth. In water the ability to detect the presence of chemical substances is not easily separated into smell and taste, since both give information about chemical substances in a surrounding medium. Perhaps when life emerged from the sea in the form of amphibia, a general chemoreceptive system separated into two anatomically distinct but functionally united mechanisms to take into account the chemical information occurring in two different environmental

media. However, since receptors for taste (taste buds) occur in virtually all vertebrates the attainment of a taste or gustatory system was an early event in the evolution of vertebrate phylogeny. According to Glass (1967), taste has evolutionary priority, preceding smell. Smell developed as a means of extracting chemical information from air—"taste at a distance" —typically occurring as a by-product of breathing and sniffing. It is an active process enabling the detection of events at a distance by means of their odors. In fact, the close relationship between breathing and smelling suggests that a channel of information is continually open and explains the high degree of alertness that many organisms show to the presence of odors. In contrast, the capacity to detect information from liquids became limited to the mouth and tongue; the mouth, being somewhat internalized, retained a liquid base of saliva and moist mucosa. In addition to its set of receptors for perceiving chemical solutions, the mouth also possesses the capacity for perceiving haptic information such as relative location, bulk, texture, and temperature of substances.

As suggested by J. J. Gibson (1966) and others, functionally taste and smell together may be considered a food-seeking and sampling system, consisting of numerous dietary activities—seeking, testing, and selecting or rejecting the food or drink. Of course, smell precedes taste in this process. As Moncrieff (1951) puts it, "Smell is the distance receptor for food and taste gives the food the final check, approving it, or disapproving, such disapproval being the forerunner of disgust" (p. 58). However, for certain environmental events, taste and smell may be independently employed. Smell may be used for the reception of nonnutritive information such as detecting the presence of predator or prey or for sexual activities, whereas taste aids in the regulation of the intake of nutrients and the avoidance of tainted and toxic substances (see Palmerino, Rusiniak, & Garcia, 1980). That is, taste enables an organism to "sample" substances prior to ingestion. For example, taste alone is responsible for certain kinds of dietary preferences, as in the case of the salt-deprived rat, which, when confronted with a series of foods, chooses the salt (Richter, 1942).

THE CHEMICAL STIMULUS AND TASTE EXPERIENCE

The potential stimulus for taste must be a dissolved or soluble substance. Normally, in order to be tasted, a potentially **sapid** or tastable substance must go into solution on coming in contact with saliva, a requirement that limits taste to water-soluble molecules. Accordingly, we do not taste oils. On the basis of human experience, four basic or primary tastes have been distinguished: sweet, sour, salty, and bitter. The commonly accepted model of the four basic tastes proposed by Henning in 1916 is shown in geometric form in Figure 9.1 in his **taste tetrahedron.**

However the existence for the human of four primary taste qualities, though widely accepted, has been questioned. For example, S. S. Schiffman and Erickson (1971) found that the stimuli could be ordered into five groups: salty, sour, bitter, sweet, and an *alkaline* group (the latter as typified by NaOH and Na_2CO_3). From time to time additional basic taste qualities have been proposed. S. S. Schiffman (1974a; Schiffman & Dackis, 1975) has reported some evidence for the existence of a sulfurous and fatty taste. Lawless (1987) notes the possibility of a primary "metallic" taste and an "umami" taste, a basic taste in Japanese psychophysics. **Umami** translates loosely to "delicious taste" and refers to the gustatory sensations elicited by MSG (monosodium glutamate, a substance we will discuss later in the section on taste modifiers). S.S. Schiffman (1988) has also provided evidence for a basic umami taste, not reduceable to the four basic tastes of sweet, sour, salty, and bitter. However, until there is a great deal of empirical substantiation, the vast literature on human taste is likely to recognize the existence of only four primaries (Lawless, 1987; Erickson, 1984).

There has been a good deal of speculation as to the relative significance of these primary tastes to the organism. According to Moncrieff (1951), saltiness and sourness are more basic owing to the evolutionary development of taste from aquatic life: "As we are descended from sea-inhabiting invertebrates we should expect the salt taste to be the most primitive, followed by the acid (sour) taste, which would function chiefly as a warning. These two tastes are more concerned with environment and safety than with food. Later, when bitter and sweet tastes made their appearance they were concerned with nutrition" (Moncrieff, 1951, p. 131). Salt is obviously basic to sea life, whereas sourness may indicate the presence of foul water or corrosion. Sweet tastes, so acceptable to many species, usually accompany substances that have food value. Bitter tastes may signal the potential ingestion of noxious or toxic substances.

An interesting speculation as to the biological incentive for the evolution of a sensitivity to salt is *not* that it evolved as part of an intake mechanism related to the regulation of an adequate sodium diet (with the possible exception of herbivores), but that a sensitivity to salt primarily evolved as a warning against the ingestion of intolerably high concentrations of salt, that is, as a guard against hypersalinity (Dethier, 1977; Denton, 1982). In this light, the sensitivity to salt may be viewed as part of a monitoring and regulatory system capable of detecting the presence of excess salts. It would be especially critical for animals living near maritime shores to detect excessive salt in their dietary water.

However, in spite of a presumed mechanism for regulating salt intake, in the case of the human there is a powerful preference for salt: in the United States, each person consumes an average of 6 to 18 grams of

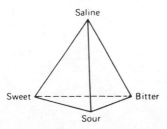

FIGURE 9.1. Henning's taste tetrahedron. The figure is an equilateral tetrahedron with the presumed four principal tastes located at the four corners. Intermediate tastes consisting of mixtures of any two primary tastes are located on the edges, and tastes produced by three primary tastes are located on the surfaces of the geometric form.

salt every day, exceeding by far any nutritional requirements (Beauchamp, 1987; Denton, 1986).

THE CHEMICAL STIMULUS FOR TASTE

As far as specifying the chemical stimulus for taste experience, it is generally noted that sour primarily results from acid compounds. However, not all acids taste sour (e.g., amino acids and sulphonic acids are sweet), and chemical substances other than acids may also taste sour. Salts generally, but not always, taste salty; for example, cesium chloride is bitter. Bitter tastes occur from alkaloids such as strychnine and quinine, but other chemical substances such as potassium iodine and magnesium sulfate also taste bitter. Sweet tastes, generally resulting from nutrients, are associated with organic substances of carbon, hydrogen, and oxygen, such as carbohydrates and amino acids, but at low concentrations the nonnutritional synthetic, saccharin, lead acetate, and beryllium salts also taste sweet. In addition two proteins, found in some tropical fruits, contain no carbohydrates, yet taste intensely sweet (Cagan, 1973).

Adding to the complexity of specifying the adequate stimulus is the fact that for some substances taste quality changes with concentration. Thus the taste of sodium saccharin shifts from predominately sweet to bitter with increased concentration (Bar-

toshuk, 1978). A similar concentration-dependent effect occurs with some inorganic salts. For example, the compound lithium chloride tastes sweet at low concentrations, and changes to sour and salty as the concentration increases (Dzendolet & Meiselman, 1967).

There are too many exceptions to account directly and exactly for all taste on the basis of chemical composition. The fact is that no definitive rules relating taste experience to the chemical composition of substances have been constructed. It is even possible to produce a taste experience by injecting a chemical stimulus directly into the bloodstream. For example, when injected, saccharin produces the taste experience of sweetness. Taste sensations produced by electrical stimulation are also possible. When the tongue is electrically stimulated by a steady direct current, a sour taste results. The taste experienced is dependent on the frequency and intensity of the current. Moreover, alternating and direct current may produce different tastes (Pfaffmann, 1959).

ANATOMY OF TASTE RECEPTION

The basic receptor structures for taste, called **taste buds** (shown in Figure 9.2), are specialized receptor

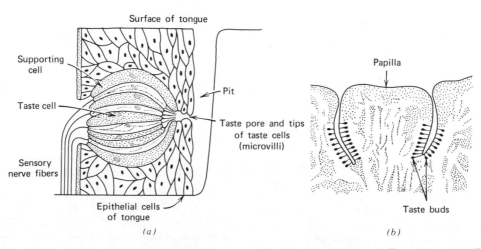

FIGURE 9.2. (*a*) Semischematic structure of an individual taste bud. Sensory nerve fibers connect to the taste cells. The tips of the taste cells project microvilli into the taste pore. (*b*) Clusters of taste buds form papillae.

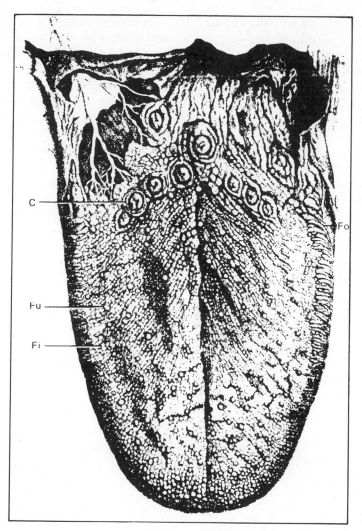

FIGURE 9.3. Distribution of papillae along dorsal surface of tongue: C, circumvallate; Fu, fungiform; Fi, filiform. The foliate papillae (Fo) lie on the lateral surface of the tongue and in the folds along the back sides. (Modified from Geldard, 1972, p. 488.)

organs located in microscopically small pits and grooves of the mouth, soft palate, throat, pharynx, the inside of the cheeks, and particularly along the dorsal surface of the tongue. Taste buds, which number between 9000 and 10,000 in the human, are generally found in clusters lying within small, but visible elevations on the tongue, called **papillae.** Several different types of papillae, distinguished by shape and location, have been identified: *fungiform, foliate, circumvallate,* and *filiform* (see Figure 9.3). The filiform papillae, primarily located in the center of the tongue, are the only ones presumed devoid of taste buds.

Taste receptors have a multiple nerve supply: the *chorda tympani* branch of the facial nerve serves the front part of the tongue, the *glossopharyngeal nerve* serves the back of the tongue, and the *vagus nerve* serves the deeper recesses of the throat, the pharynx, and larynx.

The 50 to 150 cells comprising each taste bud terminate in fingerlike projections called **microvilli** (see Figure 9.2*a*), which extend into taste pores and are in direct contact with chemical solutions applied to the surface of the tongue. Taste cells appear to have a short life of only several days and are renewed constantly. Indeed, the taste cell is one of the fastest aging cells in the body. As the taste cell ages, it moves from the edge of a taste bud toward the center. These findings suggest that differences in cell types within a taste bud actually represent different stages in development, degeneration, and migration of the taste cell. It is proposed that the sensitivity of a taste cell varies with its age. Accordingly, with increasing age of the organism, taste cell replacement becomes slower and the sense of taste diminishes. According to one observation, the taste qualities of sweetness and saltiness appear to show the greatest decrease with age, and bitter and sour tastes are heightened (Schiffman, 1974*b*). However, it is maintained that the sense of smell declines much more rapidly than the sense of taste. "Hence, foods which are bitter but have a pleasant odor (e.g., green pepper, many other vegetables, chocolate) are experienced as just plain bitter by an aged person because the pleasant odor no longer contributes to the flavor" (Schiffman, 1975).

THRESHOLDS OF TASTE

A number of stimulus conditions affect both the absolute and differential thresholds of taste. Some of these are the chemical stimulus and its concentration, the location and size of the area of application, prior chemical condition of the mouth, prior dietary conditions, temperature of the chemical substance, age and species of animal tested, and various procedural variables of testing (e.g., O'Mahoney et al., 1976; Lawless, 1987). As an example, consider temperature: depending on the substance and taste quality examined, hot or cold temperatures, or both,

affect sensitivity. Some of the effects of temperature on thresholds are reported by McBurney, Collings, and Glanz (1973), and are summarized in Figure 9.4. Observe that thresholds for all sample substances, each representing a different taste quality, are lowest for temperatures between 22°C and 32°C (about 72°F to 90°F). This coincides with the generalization by Lawless (1987) that maximal sensitivity to most compounds occurs in the range between room and body temperature. All curves are somewhat U-shaped, but the degree of temperature dependence and the temperature yielding maximal sensitivity differs by substance. In a practical vein we might observe that salted foods taste more salty when they are heated or cooled to the 22°C to 32°C range. Similarly, a hot sweetened beverage tastes sweeter as

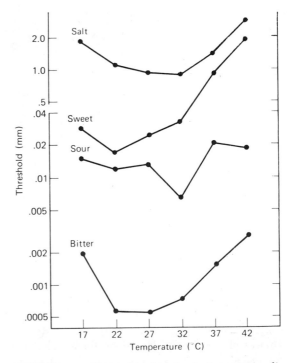

FIGURE 9.4. Threshold values for the four taste qualities, each represented by a different sample compound, taken at six temperatures. (Salt: NaCl; sweet: Dulcin; sour: HCl; bitter: QSO$_4$.) (Based on McBurney, Collings, & Glanz, 1973.)

the temperature of the liquid cools to about 22°C. In general, of course, the cook's caveat applies: food seasoning should be adjusted to the temperature at which the food will be served.

The chemical state of the mouth is also a critical threshold variable. Saliva has a complex chemical composition. It not only contains a weak solution of salt but has constituents of chlorides, phosphates, sulphates, and carbonates as well as organic components of proteins, enzymes, and carbon dioxide (Geldard, 1972). When the tongue is continually rinsed with distilled water, rendering the taste receptors relatively saliva-free, thresholds for salt are significantly decreased (McBurney & Pfaffmann, 1963; O'Mahoney & Wingate, 1974).

Threshold value determinations are also influenced by the differing taste sensitivities in different

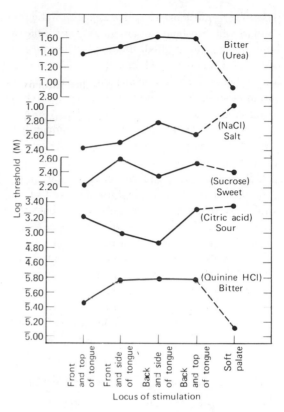

FIGURE 9.5b.   Threshold values for five different taste stimuli applied to four tongue loci and the soft palate. Note the similar response patterns across loci for the two bitter substances, quinine and urea. (The ordinate, in log molar concentrations, is modified so that all taste qualities can be plotted on a single figure; based on V. B. Collings, "Human taste response as a function of locus of stimulation on the tongue and soft palate," *Perception & Psychophysics, 16,* 1974, p. 170. Reprinted by permission of the Psychonomic Society, Inc.)

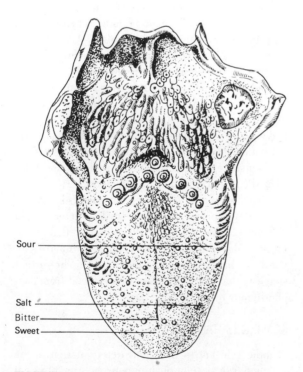

FIGURE 9.5a.   Approximate location on tongue of regions of greatest taste sensitivities for four primary taste qualities. For the bitter taste, the soft palate is the most sensitive region.

regions of the tongue. That is, not all tongue regions are equally responsive to all chemical stimuli. Figures 9.5a and b give a summary of the findings on threshold determination for four regions of the tongue and the soft palate (Collings, 1974). For the sweet taste the threshold was lowest at the front; for sour, the rear sides were the most sensitive; for salt, the front and sides were the most sensitive tongue regions; and for bitter, the front and especially the soft palate were the most sensitive regions. Notice the similarity in thresholds across tongue loci for the two bitter substances studied; this implies that they are coded by a common mechanism.

It should be clear from our brief discussion of the variables affecting thresholds that their measurement is a difficult and often unreliable matter. However, some threshold determinations for the human have been made and are shown in Table 9.1. According to an analysis of threshold measures made by Lawless (1987), a trend exists in terms of the primary tastes: bitter substances tend to yield low threshold values, with sour (acids) next, and salts and carbohydrate sweeteners a bit higher. However, exceptions such as the low threshold for saccharin relative to natural sweet substances and the high threshold for the bitter substance, urea, diminish the strength of any general guidelines for taste sensitivities.

Taste thresholds are also affected by the normal process of aging. For example, on the average, taste

Table 9.1
Absolute Taste Thresholds for Representative Stimuli

Substance	Median Threshold (molar concentration)[a]
Caffeine	0.0007
Nicotine	0.000019
Quinine sulphate	0.000008
Citric acid	0.0023
Acetic acid	0.0018
Hydrochloric acid	0.0009
Sodium iodide	0.028
Sodium chloride	0.01
Sodium fluoride	0.005
Glucose	0.08
Sucrose	0.01
Sodium saccharin	0.000023

[a] Molar concentration represents the number of grams of solute divided by its molecular weight, per liter of total solution.
Source: C. Pfaffmann, "The sense of taste," in J. Field, H. W. Magoun, and V. E. Hall (Eds.), *Handbook of physiology*, Vol. I (Washington, D.C.: American Physiological Society, 1959), Tables 2 (p. 514), 4 (p. 517), 6 (p. 519), and 8 (p. 521).

thresholds for amino acids (Schiffman, Hornack, & Reilly, 1979), sweeteners (Schiffman, 1983), and salt (Grzegorczyk, Jones, & Mistretta, 1979) are two to two-and-a-half times higher in the elderly than in the young. Note also that taste experiences at above-threshold levels are affected also by aging (Murphy & Gilmore, 1989).

TASTE THRESHOLDS AND GENETICS

Taste thresholds for some chemical solutions also vary considerably from taster to taster and for the same taster over time. Two such chemicals are vanillin and the intensely bitter substance, phenyl thiocarbamide (**PTC**). The variability of threshold values for PTC is of some interest because the threshold distribution is bimodal. That is, some individuals have significantly higher thresholds for PTC than do others. The relative lack of sensitivity to PTC for some individuals appears to be due to an inherited (recessive) characteristic, attributed, in part, to the constituents of their saliva. About a third of the Caucasian and Asian populations are nontasters of PTC (who have, for the most part, otherwise normal taste capacities), whereas native inhabitants of Africa and South America are almost all tasters (McBurney, 1978). This "taste blindness" for PTC may also extend to other compounds: Lawless (1987) notes that PTC taste-blind individuals may also be less sensitive to the bitterness of caffeine and relatively high concentrations of saccharin.

The threshold values for saccharin also provides another example of a bimodal distribution for a sapid substance. Bartoshuk (1979) reported that some individuals experience certain concentrations of saccharin as bitter, whereas others do not. She further suggests that the bitter taste experienced from saccharin may have a genetic basis.

SCALING OF TASTE INTENSITY

A topic relevant to threshold determination is the psychophysical relationship between the physical concentration of the taste stimulus and the intensity of the taste experience. An indirect attempt at assessing this has been made by having subjects specify the perceived intensity of different concentrations of the four basic tastes in terms of a standard taste unit called the **gust** (Beebe-Center & Waddell, 1948). A gust is defined as the perceived intensity of a 1% sucrose solution. Thus, the perceived intensity of a solution providing any of the four tastes is expressed in gust units by comparing each solution with the intensity of a sucrose (sweet) standard. It is possible for subjects to choose a salty or bitter or sour solution that tastes half or twice as salty, bitter, or sour or is equal in perceived intensity to the sweetness of the standard solution. In general, the concentration required to match a gust was lowest in a bitter solution, followed by sour and salt.

When scaled by direct methods (i.e., magnitude estimation, see Chapter 2), stimulus concentration and taste intensity are related by a power function in which the exponent varies markedly with the particular solution scaled; for example, for humans the following have been reported: 1.4 for NaCl, 0.8 for saccharin, and 1.3 for sucrose (Stevens, 1961*b*, 1972). Thus, the sweet taste of saccharin intensifies more slowly than does its stimulus concentration, whereas sucrose produces the reverse effect.

TASTE ABNORMALITIES AND DISEASE

Certain diseases, nutritional deficiencies, and drugs can affect taste thresholds and taste experiences. Among the more common malfunctions of taste are **ageusia** (absence of taste), **hypogeusia** (diminished taste function), **hypergeusia** (increased sensitivity to taste), and **dysgeusia** (distortions in taste qualities). According to Lawless (1987) the more common dysgeusic complaints are those of persistent metallic, burning, and sour tastes that are inappropriate to substances in the mouth; paradoxically, responses to the four basic tastes are normal.

Among the proposed causes and exacerbations of taste abnormalities are certain disease states and endocrine disorders, nutritional deficiencies, and drug effects. Diseases that can produce taste malfunctions include Bell's palsy, multiple sclerosis, hepatitis, cirrhosis of the liver, chronic renal failure, and diabetes. Nutritional deficiencies of vitamins

B_{12}, A, niacin, and the mineral zinc have been associated with taste abnormalities. Drugs that can disrupt normal taste function include anesthetics, antihistamines, antibiotics, and diuretics. Also included as possible causes of taste dysfunctions are general malnutrition, head trauma, the administration of radiation to the head region (as in the treatment of cancer), and the general effects of aging. (For a detailed survey and evaluation of the causes of taste disorders, see Schiffman, 1983.)

ADAPTATION

Prolonged exposure of the tongue to an invariant solution results in a decrease in or complete lack of sensitivity to the solution. This decrement in taste sensitivity, which we observed in the other sensory modalities, is due to **adaptation.** Complete adaptation is primarily a laboratory condition since, in the normal course of tasting, tongue and chewing movements result in continual stimulus change. The shifting of chemical substances over different regions of the tongue, stimulating different receptors at different times, prevents the conditions of constant stimulation necessary for complete gustatory adaptation. Adaptation phenomena for taste, however, are shown clearly with isolated papillae.

The adaptation rate—the time required for the disappearance of the taste sensation—is principally, although not exclusively, a matter of the concentration of the adapting solution. The higher the concentration, the greater the time required for the completion of adaptation. Of course, adaptation is also dependent on the chemical nature of the solution producing it.

It should be clear that adaptation involves not only the loss of taste sensation but an increase in the threshold level. During adaptation the absolute threshold increases until it is higher than the concentration of the adapting solution. Thus, at this point adaptation is complete and no taste experience occurs. When the adapting solution is removed, thereby reversing the adaptation process, the threshold falls back to its original value.

ADAPTATION-PRODUCED POTENTIATION

Taste adaptation is a dynamic rather than a static process in that there are various taste interactions and taste shifts that are induced by the adapting process. For example, adaptation to certain chemical substances not only causes changes in the taste of other compounds that are sampled immediately following the adapting solution, but they show that adaptation can also impart a particular taste to water (e.g., Bartoshuk, 1968). Such effects have been termed **adaptation-produced potentiation.** McBurney and Shick (1971) have shown that each of the four primary tastes can be induced by adaptation to certain chemical solutions. The effect of adaptation to bitter substances (e.g., caffeine) was to *potentiate* a sweet taste from water; adaptation to sweet substances (sucrose, fructose, and saccharin) resulted in a sour and bitter taste from water; adaptation to salts potentiated sour, sweet, and some bitter water tastes; and sour (e.g., citric acid) adapting solutions produced sweet water tastes. Of 27 chemical compounds tested, only adaptation to urea (sour-bitter) produced a reliable salty taste from water.

In addition, the taste quality induced by water after adaptation to a chemical solution sums with the taste of another solution having the same quality. For example, adaptation to a normally bitter solution (quinine hydrochloride) produces a sweet water taste. When adaptation to bitter is followed by the administration of a weak sucrose solution, the sucrose tastes sweeter than normal (McBurney, 1969). Similarly, when the tongue is sweet-adapted (producing a sour water taste), the taste intensity of a sour solution is increased.

CROSS-ADAPTATION

There is evidence that different sapid substances that produce the same taste quality can cross-adapt each other. In **cross-adaptation** adaptation to one taste substance reduces the sensitivity to similar taste substances. For example, adaptation to sodium chloride reduces the sensitivity to other salts while not affecting other taste qualities (Smith & McBurney, 1969). Similarly, adaptation to sucrose reduces the sensitivity to other sweet substances (McBurney, 1972). There is also evidence for cross-adaptation for sour. However, cross-adaptation to the bitter taste is more complex; there is evidence of cross-adaptation between certain bitter substances, but not between others (McBurney, Smith, & Shick, 1972; McBurney, 1978). That there is a generalization of adaptation *within* a taste quality suggests that there may be a common receptor–neural mechanism for encoding the stimuli that elicit that quality. Thus, there may be separate mechanisms for coding the salty, sour, and sweet tastes.

TASTE INTERACTIONS

Thus far our discussion has focused primarily on the unitary taste qualities produced by single chemical compounds. However, typically tastes occur in dynamic conditions of stimulation involving interactions between various substances. Numerous complex interactions among the primary taste qualities prevent the predicting of the precise product of taste mixtures. The result of combining two chemical solutions whose single components each appeal to a different taste is a complex psychophysiological event: the solutions do not function independently of each other, but, depending on the chemical substances, may show facilitative or inhibitory effects in combination. Condiments work on this principle, selectively inhibiting and augmenting taste qualities.

A basic rule concerning taste mixtures is that no taste quality occurs from a mixture that is not present in the individual constituents of that mixture. Thus, a mixture of NaCl and quinine will yield only salty and bitter taste sensations but not sweet or sour ones.

There is also evidence that different taste qualities may mutually suppress each other. However, if the two sapid substances of the taste mixture are sufficiently strong, they cannot mutually suppress each other to produce a tasteless mixture. In addition when the components retain their distinct taste quality in the mixture, they are often judged to be less intense than when they are in unmixed solutions. For example, a solution containing 0.3 M sucrose (sweet) and 0.0001 M quinine (bitter) is judged as less sweet than a solution containing *only* 0.3 M sucrose (no quinine), and less bitter than a solution containing *only* 0.0001 M quinine (no sucrose) (Lawless, 1986).

TASTE MODIFIERS

Additional interactions affecting taste experience occur with some drugs and chemical compounds that have different effects on the four basic tastes. That is, there are substances that differentially suppress some taste qualities and enhance others. One such drug that enhances the palatability of food is **monosodium glutamate (MSG),** a chemical commercially sold under several trade names (e.g., Aćcent). It is presumed to act not by imparting its own taste but by modifying the taste receptors to accentuate the taste character of food, hence serving as a taste stimulant. By itself, MSG elicits all four primary tastes, principally saltiness and sweetness, and gives off little or no odor. Mosel and Kantrowitz (1952) studied the effect of MSG on the primary tastes: when present in relatively high concentrations, well above threshold levels, MSG was found to accentuate sweet and salty tastes in food. As we noted earlier MSG appears to have a special status, serving not only as a taste modifier but as a culturally based primary taste quality, that is, "umami" or "delicious taste."

Organic acids from the leaves of the Indian plant, **Gymnema sylvestre,** have been shown to suppress sweetness, without affecting the response to salty, acid, or bitter substances. For example, sugar loses its taste and feels like sand after chewing the plant leaves.

Another chemical that differentially affects taste experience is *Synsepalum dulcificum* or *Richardella dulcifica*, most commonly called **miraculin,** a fruit plant indigenous to tropical West Africa. The plant produces olive-shaped berries, 1 to 2 cm long—so called miracle fruit—that turn red when ripe. The striking effect of the fruit is that while tasteless itself, exposure of the tongue to the thin layer of fruit pulp for at least three minutes causes any sour substance to taste sweet, and this effect can last for several hours. Miraculin somehow converts a sour taste into a sweet one without impairing the bitter, salt, or sweet response (Henning et al., 1969).

MSG, Gymnema sylvestre, and miraculin produce their effects by selectively affecting other tastes: sweet and sour tastes are modified by Gymnema sylvestre and miraculin respectively. In contrast, for some individuals exposure of the tongue to an artichoke (*Cynara scolymus*) can make water taste sweet (Bartoshuk, Lee, & Scarpellino, 1972). Exposure of the tongue to the extract from one-fourth of an artichoke heart makes water taste as sweet as a solution of 2 teaspoons of sucrose in 6 oz of water, and the duration of the effect may exceed 4 minutes. It is suggested that the sweetness induced by the artichoke is not due to mixing of a sweet-tasting additive with the substance to be tasted, but is produced by temporarily altering the tongue so that a normally tasteless substance tastes sweet. As it has been written, the artichoke is a vegetable "of which there is more after it has been eaten."

In addition to the foregoing taste-modifying substances, a number of chemicals have been identified by S. S. Schiffman and her colleagues that selectively enhance or inhibit certain tastes. For example, some chemicals found in coffee, tea, and chocolate enhance taste for certain artificial sweeteners and salts (Schiffman, Gill, & Diaz, 1985; Schiffman, Diaz, & Beeker, 1986; Schiffman, 1987).

NEURAL RECORDING

Electrophysiological methods have enabled the study of gustatory nerve-impulse traffic. When, for example, a microelectrode is inserted into a single taste cell and a taste solution is flowed over the tongue, a measurable change in frequency discharge occurs. Applying various chemical substances to the cell reveals that, in general, a single cell is responsive to more than one specific solution. Some cells respond to a broad range of stimuli, whereas other cells may respond to relatively few. Also evident is that different cells show different sensitivities to the same stimuli.

A similar lack of specificity has been observed in single nerve fiber recordings from the cat's chorda tympani. In general they show that fibers are not specific to different chemical solutions but that most fibers respond to more than a single taste stimulus. Multiple sensitivity to the four basic taste qualities was also demonstrated in single taste buds of human fungiform papillae (Arvidson & Friberg, 1980). In general, the recordings of single cells, taste buds, and nerve fiber stimulation, for a number of species, present little or weak evidence of neural specificity for taste stimuli.

CROSS-FIBER PATTERNING

A lack of specificity of peripheral neural units poses important problems to understanding taste experiences. Pfaffmann (1959, 1964) has proposed an **afferent code** for taste. He argued that taste is based on the relative activity across a population of fibers. Individual fibers fire to more than one taste stimulus, but they do not all have the same pattern of firing. That is, there is considerable diversity in fiber sensitivity to taste stimulation. That each fiber has its own profile suggests that taste quality, rather than being coded by a single fiber or set of specific fibers, is a matter of the *pattern* developed across a great number of fibers. Given a lack of neural specificity, a reasonable speculation is that at least part of the coding of taste occurs at more central levels—in the pathways to the brain or in the brain itself.

A critical question about the recordings of neural activity is what relation these discharge patterns have to the different taste qualities, that is, to the actual tastes experienced. Erickson (1963) developed an interesting behavioral test to investigate **cross-fiber patterning.** He recorded the firings of a

number of individual chorda tympani fibers in response to different salts. Figure 9.6 shows the neural activity of 13 individual taste fibers when stimulated by three different salt solutions: sodium chloride (NaCl), potassium chloride (KCl), and ammonium chloride (NH_4Cl). Clearly, stimulation with ammonium chloride and potassium chloride produces quite similar cross-fiber patterns in rates of firing. In contrast, the neural firing pattern of sodium chloride is quite different. To decide whether these neural similarities and differences relate to actual taste sensations a behavioral test based on taste generalization was used. That is, the question asked was: do ammonium and potassium chlorides taste similar to each other, and does sodium chloride differ from both? Rats were trained to avoid one of the salts by shocking them when they ingested a solution of it. When they showed an avoidance of this test solution, they were tested with the other solutions. This was done for all three salts. One group was shocked for drinking ammonium chloride, one for potassium chloride, and one for sodium chloride. When tested with the two salts for which they were not shocked, the rats showed a significant generalization to the salt most similar in neural response pattern to the salt for which they were shocked. Thus, rats that had been trained initially to avoid ammonium chloride avoided the potassium chloride significantly more than they avoided the sodium chloride. Likewise, rats that had learned to avoid potassium chloride avoided the ammonium chloride much more than they did the sodium chloride. Finally, rats trained to avoid sodium chloride showed relatively little avoidance of either ammonium chloride or potassium chloride.

Therefore, in addition to concluding that there are many fiber types in gustation, one may conclude that the neural message for gustatory quality is a pattern made up of the amount of neural activity across many neural elements. (Erickson, 1963, p. 213)

Thus, according to Erickson's analysis, different firing patterns across taste fibers account for different sensations.

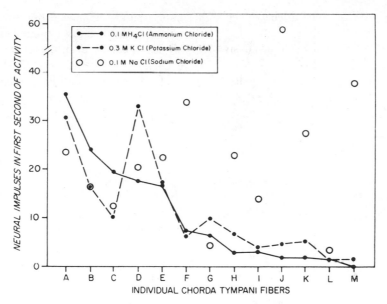

FIGURE 9.6.   The neural response of 13 chorda tympani fibers of a rat's tongue to three salts. The fibers are arranged in order of responsiveness to ammonium chloride. It is clear from the neural cross-fiber patterning in firing rates that the potassium chloride pattern is similar to that of the ammonium chloride, and both patterns differ from the sodium chloride pattern. (Reprinted with permission from R. P. Erickson, "Sensory neural patterns and gustation," in Y. Zotterman (Ed.), *Olfaction and Taste*, Pergamon Press, New York, 1963.)

THE BEST STIMULUS AND LABELED LINES: TASTE RECEPTOR SPECIFICITY

As we noted, most taste fibers are broadly tuned and display multiple sensitivities when presented with sample stimuli from the four taste qualities. However, when one examines a large population of single fibers and samples more widely in species, some fibers do show some bias or selectivity. Usually one class of stimuli will be most effective in eliciting the highest frequency impulse discharge and can be designated as the **best stimulus.** In this light taste receptor specificity can be described as a *relative* rather than an all-or-none response. That is, the differences among responses to stimuli are not so much a distinction between firing and nonfiring, but instead differences in the *amount* of firing.

A possible trend that opposes the almost classical lack of specificity of peripheral neural units has been observed from electrophysiological recordings of single taste nerve fiber responses of the hamster (Frank, 1973, 1977), the squirrel monkey (Pfaffmann, 1974; Pfaffmann et al., 1976), and the rat (Scott & Chang, 1984; see also Nowlis, Frank, & Pfaffmann, 1980). The line graphs of Figure 9.7 show for the hamster the response activity profiles of 20 of 79 chorda tympani fibers sampled that gave the best responses to sodium chloride (*A*), hydrochloric acid (*B*), sucrose (*C*), and quinine hydrochloride (*D*). It is obvious from the figure that some taste stimuli are more effective in eliciting responses in an individual fiber than are other taste stimuli.

Evidence exists for four major clusters of fibers with selective sensitivity for each of the basic taste qualities (see Pfaffmann, 1978; Smith, 1984). Moreover, each of these main clusters provides the basis of a **labeled line** (i.e., specifying or labeling fibers on the basis of the taste quality of their best stimulus). Thus fibers may be classified into categories or

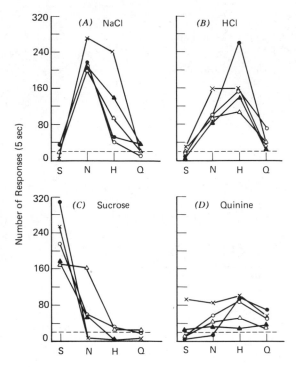

FIGURE 9.7. Response profiles across four tastes: 0.1 M sucrose (S), 0.03 M NaCl (N), 0.003 M HCl (H), and 0.001 M quinine hydrochloride (Q), of 20 hamster chorda tympani nerve fibers. Each graph illustrates the profile for 5 fibers (of 79 fibers sampled) that responded most strongly to NaCL (A), HCl (B), sucrose (C), or quinine (D). The fibers are grouped according to which of the four basic tastes elicited their largest (or best) response. Generally, fibers in the same taste category, salt-best (A), acid-best (B), and sucrose-best (C), show similar response profiles. However, four of the five fibers most sensitive to quinine responded more to acid (H) than to quinine. The response measure is the number of nerve impulses in the first 5 seconds of response. The dashed line at a response level of 20 represents an arbitrary threshold (Frank, 1973).

labeled on the basis of their maximum sensitivities. Hence when the sugar-best cluster is activated, the sensation is of sweetness, or its equivalent.

How are we to resolve what appear to be two incompatible principles mediating taste quality: the cross-fiber patterning of neural activity on one hand and the preferential sensitivity of nerve fibers—the best stimulus or labeled line—on the other? It is quite possible that these two theories of taste coding are not mutually exclusive. Labeled-lines clusters could differentiate between the four primary taste qualities, while cross-fiber patterning could signal differences within a basic taste cluster.

TASTE PREFERENCES AND TASTE WORLDS

Most of our discussion has focused on the taste qualities that are pertinent to human experience. However, taste experience among lower animals is somewhat different. Clearly, under many conditions gustatory stimuli are motivating and can elicit behavior—acquisition or avoidance activity—from an organism. Although for the human sweet and salty solutions are positive "approach-type" stimuli and bitter substances are negative "avoidance-type" stimuli, this is not the case for all species. All animals do not react similarly to a given chemical solution. Generally, the chicken and the cat are indifferent to the sweet stimuli that are readily accepted by most species (Zotterman, 1961; Kare & Ficken, 1963). Sodium chloride preference is also species-specific. Whereas the rat, cat, rabbit, and sheep show strong salt appetites (Denton, 1982), the hamster shows aversion (Carpenter, 1956; Wong & Jones, 1978).

There appears to be no clear line of evolutionary development for taste receptors. Species differ in the type, locus, and number of taste buds. Table 9.2 presents the average number of taste buds for a group of animals. However, there is no obvious relationship between the number of tastebuds and the taste experiences of the animals. Animals with many taste receptors do not necessarily taste more, nor are they more sensitive than those possessing fewer receptors.

The literature on food preferences of animals is quite complex, often equivocal, and sometimes contradictory. However, taste preferences of a species have many corresponding nutritional and metabolic determinants and may also reflect a given species' solution and adaptation to environmental challenges. We can reasonably conclude that there are different taste worlds for each species, and that the taste system of a particular species is adapted to the species' own unique metabolic requirements.

TASTE PREFERENCE AND DEPRIVATION

There are many instances of compensatory taste appetites or cravings that arise from a state of physiological need. A dramatic intake of NaCl follows adrenalectomy (which produces a marked salt deficiency) or controlled dietary restriction of NaCl in the laboratory rat (e.g., Richter, 1939, 1942; Nachman, 1962). Salt-deprived rats show an increased intake at all concentrations, including weak solutions at a concentration level below that normally taken by intact animals (Pfaffmann, 1963; Wolf, 1969). A compensatory preference has also been shown for ruminants (Bell, 1963). Similarly, thiamine-deficient rats show a strong preference for alternative diets as opposed to the experimentally deficient diet (Rodgers & Rozin, 1966; Zahorik & Maier, 1969). In addition to sodium chloride and thiamine, specific appetites have been observed in response to nutritional and metabolic imbalances for calcium, potassium, and sugar (Schiffman, 1983). In general, a deficit induced by food deprivation may amplify the role of taste in the control of food intake (Jacobs, 1967). It is inviting to consider the existence in the human of taste mechanisms that may correct

Table 9.2
The Average Number of Taste Buds for Various Animals

Snake	0
Chicken	24
Duck	200
Kitten	473
Bat	800
Human	9,000
Pig and goat	15,000
Rabbit	17,000
Catfish	175,000

nutritional deficiencies by initiating substance-specific cravings and appetites.

ORIGINS OF TASTE PREFERENCES

Although it is reasonable to assume that for many animals sweet and perhaps salty solutions are attractive and bitter ones are aversive—suggesting a relationship between taste, nutrients, and poisons—the origin of taste preference is not agreed on. However, for some animals, some preferences appear sufficiently early to suggest that they have a biological genesis. Thus, the sense of taste, at least for sweet may be functional at birth, for example, in the rat (Jacobs, 1964), the pig (Houpt & Houpt, 1977), and sheep (Hill, 1987).

Since morphological development of the human taste receptors primarily occurs prenatally, one would assume that the sense of taste is functional at birth and that there is only a brief time course for the attainment and manifestation of reliable taste preferences. Indeed a wide variety of studies show that newborn humans show taste preferences. For example human infants of one to three days of age discriminated a sucrose solution from water and showed a distinct preference for the former (Desor, Maller, & Turner, 1973; see also Beauchamp & Moran, 1982). Human infants also show an aversion to bitter and sour substances (Crook, 1978). However, the taste system for most species of mammals undergoes rapid physiological and functional changes within the first few weeks after birth, and observations of preference behavior parallels some of these changes.

CONDITIONED TASTE AVERSION

In addition to food preferences, when individuals are exposed—even once—to a substance under certain unpleasant conditions a powerful aversion to that substance may be created. Garcia and his colleagues (Garcia, Hankins, & Rusiniak, 1974; Gustavson & Garcia, 1974; Nicolaus et al., 1983) observed that when rats drink a solution of sugar and water containing a poison that makes them sick, they subsequently reject or avoid the sugar solution. That is, a taste, paired with sickness, conditions a taste aversion—a highly adaptive phenomenon called **conditioned taste aversion.**

The ability of animals to form conditioned associations between taste cues and subsequent sickness provides an explanation for the phenomenon of "bait shyness," sometimes observed with animals whose population growth must be controlled through poisons. Thus, for example, wild rats that ingest a nonlethal dose (but sufficient to produce illness) of a food treated with poison, in the future will avoid food laced with that particular poison. To avoid the problem of bait shyness, poisons with novel tastes must constantly be employed.

There are serious consequences to conditioned taste aversions in the human. It has been noted that cancer patients undergoing radiation and chemotherapy treatment (which also induce nausea and sickness), frequently acquire taste aversions and reduced preferences for foods consumed close to the time of therapy (Bernstein, 1978; Bernstein & Webster, 1980). Consequently, they may experience serious weight loss and may even become malnourished. Accordingly it is advisable for the patients that they not eat for several hours before or after treatment; moreover the same food or highly preferred foods should not be consumed consistently close in time to the therapy since aversions may develop with any ingested substance, even for highly favored foods (Schiffman, 1983).

CULTURE AND TASTE PREFERENCES

The cultural basis of taste preferences in the human infant has been assessed by Jerome (1977) in a comparison between cultures that have the custom of feeding dietary sugars soon after birth with those cultures whose infants thrive with a relatively sugar-free diet. Groups with a nonsugar tradition of infant feeding show the usual preference for sweet dietary items after these are introduced to the culture suggesting that a sweet preference is unlearned.

However, it seems clear that both genetic and environmental influences are operative in human taste preferences. In the human the palatability of

certain foods seems partially determined by education and custom. Specific seasonings, spices, and condiments have a basic ethnic origin and their use is culturally linked. That is, we cultivate or acquire a "taste" for certain foods. Who would risk sampling ". . . the coagulated secretion of the modified skin-glands of a cow after it had undergone bacterial decomposition" (Matthews & Knight, 1963, p. 205)? Those who do, have merely sampled cheese. Some cultures and ethnic groups savor food considered inedible by other groups (e.g., brains, insects, octopus tentacles). Certainly, the palatability of some bitter solutions, such as alcoholic beverages, coffee and tea, is acquired. It may be that the foods given us at certain critical times in our formative years determine, in part, many of the foods we subsequently prefer.

TASTE PREFERENCE AND FLAVOR

The hedonic (pleasant–unpleasant) character of taste stimuli for the human is affected by more than a unitary "taste" response. Indeed we should note that the overall palatability of a substance is due to a combination of sensory effects that is termed **flavor.** Flavor may include such factors as a substance's concentration, aroma, texture, temperature, color and even the sound it makes when it is chewed on or bitten (Edmister & Vickers, 1985; Vickers, 1987); moreover it may include some irritability in the oral and nasal cavities (such as with carbonated beverages and spices). All these factors, as well as the dietary history and the hunger state of the taster, in combination, influence the hedonic judgment of the taste of a substance. S. S. Schiffman (1986) has called attention particularly to the textural character of food in affecting its flavor. Consider the following inventory of possible food textures:

hardness (soft, firm), brittleness (crumbly, crunchy, crisp, brittle), chewiness (tender, chewy, tough), gumminess, viscosity (thin, thick), adhesiveness (sticky, tacky, gooey), and fatty (oily, greasy), . . . airy, chalky, fibrous, flaky, fluffy, grainy, granular, gritty, lumpy, powdery, pulpy, sandy, stringy, creamy, doughy, elastic, heavy, juicy, light, mushy, rubbery, slimy, slippery, smooth, spongy, soggy, and springy. (p. 44P)

We have assumed that a significant functional role of the taste system is to regulate the ingestion of nutrients and the rejection of toxic solutions. Although this may be acceptable for animals in the wild, the biological advantage of the taste system for the human must be tempered. A pertinent caveat has been expressed by Glass (1967):

Man himself, the most domesticated of mammals, seems to stand at a fresh crossroad in the evolution of the regulation of eating. Satiety is no longer a sufficient guard against overeating, and hunger is no longer a sufficient bulwark against dietary insufficiencies. Man has provided himself with too many foods unknown in the natural environment, too many natural goods appealing to his appetite but unbalanced or deleterious when consumed in great quantity. Even milk and milk products, as adult foods, come under grave suspicion. Man is too adaptable in diet, in spite of his cultural conservatism in matters of food and appetite, to pick and choose safely on the basis of flavor and appetite as guides to nutrition. (p. vi)

SUMMARY

Functionally, taste and smell together may be considered a food-seeking and sampling system. However, in this chapter we have principally focused on the sense of taste.

The receptors for taste—taste buds—are activated by chemical substances that are soluble; that is, they go into solution upon coming in contact with saliva. On the basis of human experience four primary tastes have been distinguished: salt, sour, sweet, and bitter. However, the exact chemical stimuli for unequivocally activating these qualities have not been identified.

Thresholds for taste vary with the taste quality investigated and are subject to many of the experimental conditions of testing, such as the chemical concentration, the locus and area of application, prior chemical state of the tongue or mouth, and the temperature of the solution. For most sapid substances the thresholds are lowest for temperatures between 22°C and 32°C (about 72°F and 90°F). Additionally, the tongue regions are not equally responsive to all chemical stimuli. Sensitivity to bitter solutions is greater at the front of the tongue and the soft palate, sweet at the front, sour along the rear sides, and salt over much of the tongue surface but best toward the front and sides. However, differential locus sensitivity has not led to corresponding taste bud or papillae (groups of taste buds) specificity.

Taste experience undergoes adaptation (relative lack of sensitivity) when the tongue is subject to prolonged exposure to an invariant solution. A number of factors affect adaptation, especially the concentration of the adapting solution. Moreover, the adaptation of one taste quality affects the taste of certain chemical solutions that are sampled immediately following the adapting solution. Adaptation can also impart a particular taste to water—an effect called adaptation-produced potentiation. For example, adaptation to caffeine (bitter) appears to potentiate a sweet taste from water. The thresholds for some substances vary considerably within the population. In particular, sensitivity to PTC and certain concentrations of saccharin may have a genetic basis.

Several taste dysfunctions were identified, and it was noted that they have various causes including, but not limited to, certain disease states, nutritional deficiencies, drugs, head trauma, and the general effects of aging.

The effects of taste modifiers such as MSG, gymnemic acid (a sweet suppressant), and the so-called miracle fruit (a sweet enhancer) were discussed. Also noted were several chemicals that appear to affect taste experience selectively. In addition, it was noted that exposure of the tongue to the extract from an artichoke heart makes water taste sweet.

The lack of specificity of taste nerve fibers to different chemical solutions has given rise to the proposal of an afferent code for taste quality. As described by Pfaffmann, taste is based on the relative activity across a population of fibers. This corresponds to the observation that individual taste fibers do fire to more than one taste stimulus, but they do not show the same pattern of firing. That is, each fiber has its own firing profile suggesting that taste quality, rather than coded by a single fiber or set of specific fibers, is due to the firing pattern developed across a number of fibers. Some evidence for this notion was summarized. An alternative notion was presented suggesting that taste fibers show selectivity in response to presentation of the "best" stimulus. Electrophysiological recordings of single nerve fibers indicate that maximal responses are elicited for each of the basic taste qualities.

Taste preferences and their origin were discussed. It was noted that different species have quite different taste preferences, which are likely adapted to the species' nutritional and metabolic requirements.

Whereas evidence exists that specific appetites can be initiated in response to nutritional deficiencies, the taste preference for sweet substances, over a number of different species, appears to have a biological basis. Moreover, the possibility of a conditioned taste aversion was noted; that is, a taste paired with sickness conditions a strong taste aversion.

Clearly, in the human the acceptability and palatability of certain foods is, in large part, due to education and custom, as well as to a food's flavor—a combination of sensory effects, including concentration, aroma, temperature, and texture.

KEY TERMS

Adaptation

Adaptation-produced potentiation

Afferent code

Ageusia

Anosmic

Best stimulus

Chemoreceptors

Conditioned taste aversion

Cross-adaptation

Cross-fiber patterning

Dysgeusia

Flavor

Gust

Gymnema sylvestre

Hypergeusia

Hypogeusia

Labeled line

Microvilli

Miraculin

Monosodium glutamate (MSG)

Papillae

PTC

Sapid

Taste buds

Taste tetrahedron

Umami

STUDY QUESTIONS

1. Compare the chemical senses of taste and smell. What are the main differences in the necessary stimuli for each? To what extent do they overlap functionally and serve a complementary role in nutrition?

2. Identify the basic tastes and indicate their general relationship to the chemical composition of stimuli that typically elicit them. Consider what the functional relevance may be to the ability to taste bitter, sweet, and salty substances.

3. What effect does the concentration of a substance have on taste quality?

4. Outline the main anatomical components of the taste system. Indicate what is unique about the life span of taste cells.

5. Identify the main factors that have a significant effect on taste thresholds. What generalization can be made concerning the effect of temperature on taste thresholds? What effect does the part of the tongue stimulated have on each of the thresholds of the basic tastes?

6. Identify the different kinds of taste abnormalities. What sorts of disorders, diseases, and deficiencies produce taste abnormalities?

7. Describe the effects of prolonged exposure to a specific taste on taste experience. Examine the subsequent decrement in taste sensitivity —adaptation—on other similar-tasting substances. Consider the effect that taste adaptation may have on the taste of water.

8. Describe the interactive effects on taste sensation when different tastes are combined. Explain the phenomena that different taste qualities can mutually enhance and suppress each other when combined.

9. How do taste modifiers affect taste? Enumerate some of the major taste modifiers.

10. What does the general pattern of neural activity of taste receptors to each of the four basic tastes indicate about the specificity of taste receptors?

11. How can cross-fiber patterning account for taste quality? Alternatively, examine the notion of a best stimulus and a labeled line for coding taste quality. Consider a compromise that can encompass both the cross-fiber patterning and the specificity of the labeled line to explain the coding of taste quality.

12. Discuss the notion that different sorts of animals possess different basic tastes and different taste preferences. Examine the basis of taste preferences and consider the extent to which they may be biologically or culturally determined.

13. Discuss the possibility that a selective dietary deprivation of a nutrient may promote a compensatory taste appetite.

14. What is a conditioned taste aversion? What does it imply concerning temporary changes in taste preferences?

15. What is flavor? How does it differ from taste?

10

THE CHEMICAL SENSORY SYSTEM II: SMELL

Functionally, the sense of smell or olfaction serves in the reception of information from chemical events that transpire at a distance as well as nearby. Notice the dog's ability to track both air and ground scents. In many lower animals, the sense of smell may be quite necessary for an efficient orientation to their environment. This is especially true for nocturnal animals or those that dwell in poorly lit environments, since their locomotion is dependent on a source of nonvisual information. Animals possessing a keen sense of smell are called **macrosmatic** (cf. **osmics:** the science of odors); animals lacking a keen sense are **microsmatic.** For many animals, smell plays an important role in territoriality, feeding, sexual selection, and mating. Some predators hunt their prey and some prey avoid their predators by smell. There are striking instances where animals utilize the emission and pickup of odors for their survival. For example, the female gypsy moth emits a scent that, with proper wind conditions, can attract the male moth from miles away. The inky secretion discharged by a frightened octopus or squid serves not only to decrease an attacker's vision but to dull the olfactory sensitivity of pursuing predator fish (Milne & Milne, 1967). Olfaction is of lesser importance to avian and arboreal species than to terrestrial and aquatic species. It may be totally absent in some animals, such as the porpoise and perhaps the whale, who as lung-breathing aquatic mammals, cannot use their nose under water to receive odors (Altman, 1966). (Animals totally lacking a sense of smell are called **anosmic.**) As we noted earlier (Chapter 6), in these animals the sense of hearing has evolved to a degree that perhaps serves to compensate for their lack of an adequate smell sense.

The sense of smell for the human is much less important than it is for many other animals: certainly it is not necessary for survival. As Charles Darwin observed in 1871,

> The sense of smell is of the highest importance to the greater number of mammals—to . . . the ruminants, in warning them of danger; to . . . the carnivora, in finding their prey. . . . But the

> sense of smell is of extremely slight service, if any . . . (to man). . . . He inherits the power in an enfeebled and so far rudimentary condition, from some early progenitor, to whom it was highly serviceable, and by whom it was continually used. (pp. 405–406)

However, in combination with taste, smell can aid in food selection (e.g., detection of spoiled food) and maintenance of a clean environment; in the case of certain odors, smell may provide some pleasant aesthetic sensations (e.g., the scent of food and of flowers). The following represents only a sample of the distinctive scents and odors—both natural and the technological products of our society—that one may encounter in an ordinary day: the scents from breath and perspiration, the smells of the toilet (both of bodily wastes and of cleaners and cosmetics), the complex aromas of food and of the kitchen, the smells of auto exhausts, and those of trains and buses, the smell of smoke, and the odors of plants. Certainly some are unpleasant, even foul—more stench than scent—but they are all intimately attached to our daily encounters and, for the most part, inform us by enabling the perception of their sources in the present environment.

The pathologist–essayist, Gonzalez-Crussi (1989) draws our attention to odorant quality in a particularly compelling and somewhat disturbing fashion:

> You know the stubborn quality of a disagreeable smell. It assails you when you least expect it. One day, you stroll casually outdoors, and there it is: the repugnant companion of a revolting object. It hovers invisible over a dead and decomposed animal, a piece of carrion, or a heap of excrement. You turn away from the repelling sight, but it is no use: The smell has taken hold of you and does not leave. Or it diffuses relentlessly, from unseen origins. For it . . . has a presence of its own, and such power as can persecute you, and harass you, like a maddening obsession. (p. 79)

CHEMICAL CORRELATES OF ODOR QUALITY

The potential stimulus for the smell system must be a volatile or readily vaporizable substance. Accordingly, solids and liquids must pass into a gaseous state. Volatility, however, is necessary but not sufficient for stimulation of the smell system since many substances—water, for example—are volatile yet odorless. Potentially odorous substances must also be water and lipid (fatty) soluble in order to penetrate the watery film and lipid layer that covers the olfactory receptors.

In general, the normal chemical stimuli for olfaction are organic rather than inorganic substances. Indeed, under usual circumstances, none of the elements occurring free in nature is odorous in its atomic state. For the most part odorants are mixtures of chemical compounds, often immensely complex: environmental odors emitted by vegetative life (fruits and flowers), decaying matter (flesh and feces), and scent-producing glands of animals. In brief, the natural odors occur as signals for the recognition and location of nutrients, predators, and mates. But overall, the relationship between chemical properties and odor quality is far from clear. It seems most reasonable to conclude that a number of different properties of odor-producing molecules play a role in determining their odor quality.

CLASSIFICATION OF ODOR QUALITY

Unlike taste qualities, the basic smell attributes are far from agreed on. Many classifications of odors have been made on the basis of subjective experience, but a general problem encountered in this task is isolating the basic or primary odors whose mixtures yield the many thousands of possible complex odors. One attempt to establish a classification of odors is based on a geometrical construction—**Henning's**

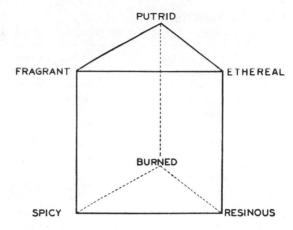

FIGURE 10.1.   Henning's smell prism.

smell prism—shown in Figure 10.1. The triangular prism is supposed to be hollow with six primary odors—fragrant, putrid, ethereal, burned, resinous, and spicy—occupying the corners. Along the surfaces and edges lie the intermediate odors that are blends of several primaries. Other classifications have used fewer or greater numbers of basic odors. The Crocker–Henderson system offers four: burned, fragrant, acid, and caprylic (goaty). However, none of these classifications has met with widespread acceptance.

STEREOCHEMICAL THEORY: LOCK AND KEY

A more recent scheme involving a sevenfold classification attempts to establish direct links between the chemical composition of substances and perceived odors. It is called the **stereochemical** (or steric) **theory** of odors, and it is a modern version of a theory of Lucretius, the first-century (B.C.) Roman Epicurean poet. The development of the theory is as follows: based on the terms most frequently used to describe the odors of organic compounds, the seven odors, shown in Table 10.1, were identified as probable primaries. Using the techniques of stereochemistry, from which it is possible to construct a three-dimensional model of the molecule of any

Table 10.1
Primary Odors with Chemical and Familiar Examples

Primary Odor	Chemical Example	Familiar Example
Camphoraceous	Hexachloroethane, camphor	Moth repellent
Musky	Butylbenzene	Musk, civetone
Floral	Ethyl carbinol	Rose, lavender
Minty	Menthol	Peppermint
Ethereal	Diethyl ether	Cleaning fluid
Pungent	Formic acid	Vinegar, roasted coffee
Putrid	Butyl mercaptan	Rotten egg
	Hydrogen sulfide	

Source: J. E. Amoore, Current status of the steric theory of odor, *Annals of the New York Academy of Sciences, 116,* 1965, 457–476.

chemical compound from its structural formula, it was noted that all the models for molecules of compounds that shared a similar odor had similar geometric properties; that is, they were all of about the same shape and diameter. For example, all chemicals with a camphoraceous molecule were roughly spherical in shape and had the same approximate diameter. This was shown with a degree of success for five of the seven primaries, as shown in Figure 10.2.

The next step involved the assumption that there are different receptor sites or ultramicroscopic slots in the nerve fiber membrane, each with a distinctive size and shape. From a stereochemical analysis, it is possible to synthesize and modify molecules of certain shapes. According to the proponents of the stereochemical theory, it is also possible to predict odors of the resultant molecules on the basis of their geometric properties. Within limits judgments of odor similarity relate reasonably well to molecular shape. It follows, then, that a change in the shape of a molecule changes its odor, and that the empirical or structural formula may differ markedly between molecules, but substances whose molecules have the same shape and size should share the same odor. A complex odor is comprised of more than one primary odor in varying proportions and has molecules which can fit into more than one receptor site. An example cited by the proponents of the stereochemical theory

is almond-scented compounds, which fit into the presumed camphoraceous, floral, and pepperminty sites.

This theory is sometimes referred to as a "lock-and-key" theory: the key is the molecule with certain geometric properties; the lock is an assumed receptor site that accommodates molecules with the geometric properties of the key. Keys are specific to locks and both are specific to odors. In general, the theory has required a number of modifications (Amoore, 1965) and, while demonstrating some relationship between the geometric properties of an odorant's molecule and its perceived odor, the theory does not have wide acceptance (e.g., see Cain, 1978). This is due largely to a lack of clear evidence of distinct and specific receptor sites as well as some disconfirmatory evidence. Thus S. S. Schiffman (1974*b*) has reported that changes in certain molecules which do not alter their size and shape appreciably have a profound impact on smell quality. Generally she did not find clear evidence of similarity in molecular properties of perceptually similar odorants. Based on her findings, she concluded that "There are no clear psychological groups or classes of stimuli, merely trends" (p. 115).

It is apparent that none of the proposed odor categorization or classification schemes is adequate to describe or summarize effectively the subtlety and enormity of odor experiences (see Dravnieks, 1982).

Receptor site   Odorant molecule   Site plus molecule

Ethereal

Camphor-aceous

Musky

Floral

Minty

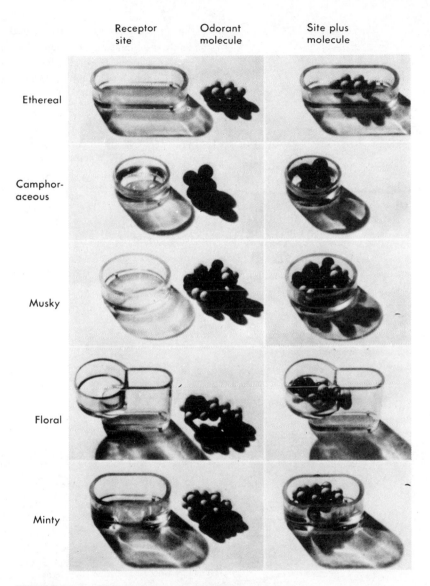

FIGURE 10.2.   Models of olfactory receptor sites and of molecules that "fit" them in the stereochemical theory of odor. (From Amoore, 1964.)

ANATOMY AND PHYSIOLOGY OF THE OLFACTORY SYSTEM

The exact nature of the physiology of the olfactory process is elusive, owing to the inaccessibility of the receptors (see Figure 10.3). The entire odor-sensitive tissue region, called the **olfactory epithelium** or **olfactory mucosa,** occupies a total area of about one square inch. It is located on both sides of the nasal cavity which is divided by the nasal septum.

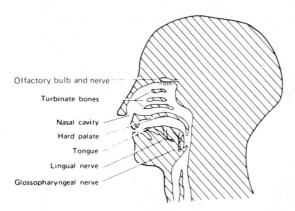

Olfactory bulb and nerve

Turbinate bones

Nasal cavity

Hard palate

Tongue

Lingual nerve

Glossopharyngeal nerve

FIGURE 10.3. The nasal passages. (From F. A. Geldard, *The Human Senses*, John Wiley, New York, 1972, p. 444. Reprinted by permission of the publisher.)

The olfactory receptors are located in the mucous membrane high in each side of the nasal cavity (see inset of Figure 10.4a). They are relatively long, narrow, column-shaped cells surrounded by pigmented supporting cells. There are estimated to be about 10,000,000 olfactory cells in the human (Wenzel, 1973) and perhaps more than 20 times as many in the dog. On one end of the olfactory receptor cells, hairlike projections, the **olfactory cilia,** project down into the fluid covering the mucous membrane of the epithelium (see Figure 10.4a and b). There is evidence that the cilia, and their immediate connections, the **dendritic knobs** and the mucosa, are the receptor sites for odorants and are the structures involved in the initial stage of the transduction process (Getchell & Getchell, 1987).

Extending from the olfactory receptor cells are nerve filaments comprising olfactory nerve fibers,

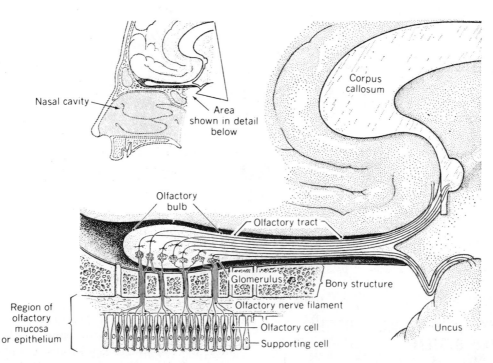

Nasal cavity

Area shown in detail below

Corpus callosum

Olfactory bulb

Olfactory tract

Glomerulus

Bony structure

Olfactory nerve filament

Region of olfactory mucosa or epithelium

Olfactory cell

Supporting cell

Uncus

FIGURE 10.4a. Schematic anatomy of olfactory system. (Modified from D. Krech and R. S. Crutchfield, *Elements of Psychology*, Alfred A. Knopf, New York, 1958, p. 184. Reprinted by permission of the authors.)

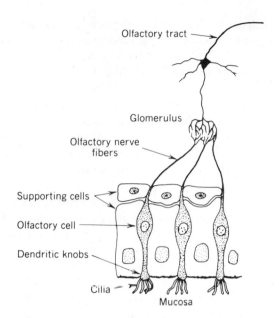

Olfactory tract

Glomerulus

Olfactory nerve
fibers

Supporting cells

Olfactory cell

Dendritic knobs

Cilia

Mucosa

FIGURE 10.4*b*.   Schematic representation of olfactory structures, detailing anatomy at the region of the epithelium. Shown are the dendritic knobs and the olfactory cilia embedded in the mucosa; collectively, these are the assumed structures for the initial transduction stage.

which connect to the **olfactory bulb** of the brain at a relay connection called the **glomerulus,** further connecting with other parts of the brain by olfactory tracts. The receptors thus serve the function of reception and conduction. Geldard (1972) points out that this duality of function is common in the relatively primitive nervous systems of lower vertebrates and here reflects the antiquity of the olfactory system in phylogenetic development.

In the olfactory bulb, a relatively large number of fibers converge on a single cell that, in turn, proceeds rather directly to the higher cortical regions. The activity of many cilia (6 to 12) serving a single olfactory receptor cell, and further neural convergence in the olfactory brain, display a general funneling of neural response (and olfactory information), which contributes to the extreme sensitivity of the olfactory system. It is estimated that at the level of the olfactory bulb there is about a 1000-to-1 reduc-

tion in the nerve fibers to the olfactory tracts conveying sensory information to the brain.

When air is inspired, accompanying gaseous stimuli are carried to the olfactory epithelium by small eddy currents. (Note that odor stimulation may also occur during expiration, especially during eating.) The air stream is warmed and filtered as it passes three baffleshaped *turbinate* bones in the upper part of the nose. The stimuli are dissolved in the olfactory epithelium by its fluid covering. This stimulates the cilia and adjacent structures, and by means of some poorly understood biochemical process provokes the olfactory cells into neural activity. It would seem that the more vigorous the inhalation, as in active sniffing, the more the olfactory epithelium is bathed by the odorant and the greater is the stimulation. However, as noted by Laing (1983), "it is very difficult to improve on the efficiency of sniffing techniques of individuals and that a single natural sniff provides as much information about the presence and intensity of an odour as do seven or more sniffs" (p. 90).

PLASTICITY OF THE OLFACTORY SYSTEM

The olfactory system and its receptor cells, in particular, display a remarkably unique capacity for plasticity. The olfactory receptor cells undergo a continual process of degeneration and regeneration, with the life span for an individual olfactory receptor neuron set at between four to eight weeks. Moreover, following receptor cell damage and destruction due to injury and chemical irritation, they are virtually the only sensory neurons in the adult mammal that can be replaced by new nerve cells (Costanzo & Graziadei, 1987). However despite the continuous process of receptor cell turnover the capacity of the olfactory system remains uninterrupted.

OLFACTORY CODING

The coding of olfactory stimuli—both odorant intensity and quality—begins with the mucosa of the olfactory epithelium. Here the odorant compounds, represented as electrical and chemical signals, diffuse through the mucous layer to bind with chemically receptive membranes of the olfactory receptor cells.

Intensity It is assumed that electrical changes that occur within the olfactory nerves at the surface of the olfactory epithelium serve as a measure of the activity of olfactory receptor cells. The amplitude of these responses increases proportionally to the intensity and the duration of the stimulus. For intense olfactory stimuli the electrical response rises rapidly, peaks higher, and decays relatively slowly in contrast to weak stimuli. In short, the amount of neural activity increases with increases in the concentration of a given odorant; accordingly, the perceived intensity of an odorant is proportional to the number of stimulus molecules interacting with the receptors (Gesteland, 1978; Kauer, 1987).

Quality An understanding of odor quality presents a more difficult problem than intensity. For one thing odor quality cannot be easily characterized on the basis of specific neural activity. Indeed distinctive odorant compounds do not activate highly specific receptor cells. For example, Gesteland (Gesteland et al., 1963; Gesteland et al., 1965), recording from the receptors of the frog's olfactory epithelium, noted that the odor response properties of single receptor cells are not highly specific, but rather that each is broadly tuned and, accordingly, responds to a variety of different odorant compounds; however, there was evidence reported of selective *patterns* of neural activity from the application of distinctive odorants (Gesteland et al., 1963). When tested with 25 different odorants, each receptor whose activity was recorded was responsive to only several, and the magnitude of the response varied from odorant to odorant. Mozell (1964, 1966) recorded the neural traffic from the frog's olfactory nerve branch serving two widely disparate spatial loci of the olfactory epithelium. The result was that differences in the magnitude of the neural discharge from each epithelium location was specific to the odorants. For example, octane affected one location more than the other, whereas citral produced the reverse effect.

Whereas odorants do not activate highly specific receptor neurons that fire exclusively to a particular

compound, there do appear to be coherent differences in receptor cell sensitivity to various odorant compounds that may enable odorant differentiation. Kauer (1987) hypothesizes that there is a coding process that takes into account the broad tuning of receptor cells and enables the perception of olfactory quality. According to Kauer's analysis there are groups or subunits of receptor cells, each having a wide range of sensitivities to various odorants, but overlapping one another. Hence stimulation with one odorant may activate a given subunit of receptor cells yielding a particular *pattern* or response profile for that group of receptor cells; stimulation by a different odorant activates another subset of receptor cells, some of which also respond to the first odorant. That is, the same receptor cells may enter into the coding process for different odorants. What is invariant however, is the relatedness of odor compounds to the response profiles of groups of receptor cells. A schematic example of the pattern of activity among subgroups of receptor cells that can code particular odorants is given in Figure 10.5.

It must be stressed that while there are numerous speculations, hypotheses, and proposals, the mechanisms of olfactory quality coding is not well understood, and few straightforward and conclusive statements can be made on this matter.

THRESHOLDS

Absolute threshold determinations have been made for a number of odorant materials indicating that extremely low concentrations are sufficient. With respect to the concentration of molecules, it has been estimated that olfaction is the more sensitive of the chemical senses—10,000 times as sensitive as taste, according to Moncrieff (1951). A striking example of olfactory sensitivity is given by our sensitivity to **mercaptan,** a foul-smelling compound often added to odorless natural gas as a warning signal of its presence. A concentration of 1 molecule of mercaptan per 50 trillion molecules of air is detected. Another dramatic example is given by skatol, which has an objectionable fecal odor: a single milligram of

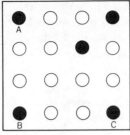 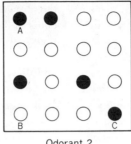 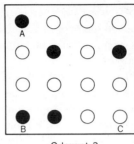

Odorant 1   Odorant 2   Odorant 3

FIGURE 10.5. A schematic description of the firing pattern of a sample of 16 receptor cells for three different odorants. Each circle represents an olfactory receptor cell, and black circles represent those receptor cells that fire in response to a particular odorant. Observe that receptor cell A is activated by all three odorants; receptor cell B is activated by odorant 1 and 3, and receptor cell C by odorant 1 and 2. Thus while individual receptor cells may be activated by several different odorants, each odorant activates a different group or *pattern* of receptor cells. Accordingly, a specific pattern of activated receptor cells signals or codes a specific odorant. (Based on Spear et al., 1988.)

skatol will produce an unpleasant odor in a hall 500 meters long by 100 meters wide and 50 meters high (Moncrieff, 1951). A final unusual example of the extraordinary power of olfactory stimuli and human sensitivity to odorants draws from the procedure used by Gibbons (1986) and Gilbert and Wysocki (1987) for a smell survey published by The National Geographic Society. They employed six "scratch-and-sniff" panels (each about 44 by 31 mm or 1¾ by 1¼ in.), for which less than 27 grams (less than an ounce) was needed of each odorant to microencapsulate it on nearly 11 million copies of the survey.

Indeed, it is because the amounts of the odorous vapor required for the minimal detectible stimulus are so small that very complicated methods of threshold measurements must be employed. Perhaps the most elaborate of all methods of assessing olfactory sensitivity is the *olfactorium*, a glass double chamber that actually is an area where the odor environment is completely controlled. Prior to the administration of the odorant all residual body odor is removed from the subject by bathing. The vapor of the chamber consists of only the odorous chemicals and a known quantity of air at a controlled temperature and humidity (both of which can influence volatility).

In general, threshold measurements are significantly influenced by the methods and procedures used for introducing the odorant to the receptors. A listing of threshold concentrations for some representative odorants are given in Table 10.2. Clearly people are extremely sensitive to minute amounts of certain odorants. As Mozell (1971) points out, the olfactory system can detect the presence of a smaller number of molecules than can most laboratory methods used for the same purpose.

We should make note of the correlation between the number of olfactory receptors and detection thresholds. The dog possesses many times the olfactory cells as the human. Not surprisingly, we find that such animals with a greater number of receptor cells and cilia per receptor show a much keener sense of smell than does the human.

THRESHOLDS AND GENDER

Thresholds for certain odorants may be affected by the interaction of gender and hormonal variation of an individual. It has been reported that the absolute threshold for **Exaltolide**, a musklike synthetic odorant used as a fixative in perfume, varies in the human female according to the stage of the reproductive or menstrual cycle. In a series of studies (Le Magnen, cited in Vierling & Rock, 1967; Good, Geary, &

Engen, 1976), it was noted that most sexually mature women perceived the odor of a sample of Exaltolide as intense, whereas most immature females and males, and mature males either barely perceived it or were insensitive to it. Examination of the perception of the males to Exaltolide revealed that of those studied, half the males were anosmic to Exaltolide, and for the remaining men, their threshold was 1000 times greater than for that of sexually mature women. Subsequent research on the absolute threshold of Exaltolide indicated that peaks in olfactory sensitivity occur at two points in the female reproductive cycle (Vierling & Rock, 1967). These peak times in sensitivity are approximately when estrogen secretion levels also peak, suggesting that the presence of estrogen influences the sensitivity to Exaltolide (Doty et al., 1981). This is given additional support by the findings that women deprived of normal estrogen by removal of their ovaries had higher thresholds than did normal females, but that restoration of the threshold to within a normal range followed the administration of a form of estrogen. Of some further support is the observation that a partially anosmic woman with abnormally low levels of estrogen became increasingly sensitive to the odor of Exaltolide while undergoing estrogen therapy (Good, Geary, & Engen, 1976). It appears, then, that the hormonal status may exercise an effect on olfactory thresholds (see Mair et al., 1978; Doty et al. 1981). We will return to the significance of the sensitivity to Exaltolide in a later section.

It should be noted additionally that females outperform males in the identification of other odors (e.g., Doty et al., 1984). Moreover this superiority for females was also noted between prepubertal girls and boys, questioning the notion that sex differences in olfactory perception is due exclusively to concurrent levels of circulating sex hormones.

THRESHOLDS AND AGE

We noted in the earlier chapter on taste that the sense of smell declines much more rapidly with age than does the sense of taste. Some of the decreased

Table 10.2
Some Representative Odor Thresholds

Substance	Odor	Threshold Concentrations[a]
Carbon tetrachloride	Sweet	4.533
Methyl salicylate	Wintergreen	0.100
Amyl acetate	Banana oil	0.039
N-butyric acid	Perspiration	0.009
Benzene	Kerosiney	0.0088
Safrol	Sassafras	0.005
Ethyl acetate	Fruity	0.0036
Pyridine	Burned	0.00074
Hydrogen sulfide	Rotten eggs	0.00018
N-butyl sulfide	Foul, sulfurous	0.00009
Coumarin	New-mown hay	0.00002
Citral	Lemony	0.000003
Ethyl mercaptan	Decayed cabbage	0.00000066
Trinitro-teritary-butyl xylene	Musk	0.000000075

[a] Milligrams per liter of air.
Source: M. A. Wenger, F. N. Jones, and M. H. Jones, *Physiological psychology*, Holt, Rinehart and Winston, New York, 1956, p. 148.

sensitivities (increased thresholds) with increasing age are rather striking: Kimbrell and Furtchgott (1963) reported approximately a 10-fold increase in threshold from the fourth decade to the seventh decade for certain odorants. Similarly, S.S. Schiffman, Moss, and Erickson (1976), using the odor of select foods, reported that thresholds for elderly subjects (about 81 years of age) were 11 times as high as those for young subjects (about 22 years old).

Doty et al. (1984) studied the odor recognition ability in almost 2000 subjects, ranging in age from 5 to 99 years, and observed clear age-dependent effects: the average ability to identify odors was greatest for those in their third and fourth decade of life (between 20 and 40 years) and declined markedly with older subjects up until the seventh decade. It was also observed that a large number of the elderly experience major olfactory dysfunctions. Moreover, aside from serious olfactory impairments, almost 25% of the persons tested between the ages of 65 and 68, and nearly 50% of the persons tested over the age of 80 years were anosmic (see also Murphy, 1987). Of subsidiary interest is the finding that, at all ages, nonsmokers outperformed smokers.

ADAPTATION

Continued exposure to an odorant results in an increase in the threshold or a decline in sensitivity to that odorant: in short, continued odor stimulation results in **olfactory adaptation.** Depending on the odorant and its concentration, with a sufficient exposure duration, odor experience tends to disappear. Olfactory adaptation is a common experience. The cooking odors initially experienced when first entering a kitchen are quite different after several minutes of exposure. Although it can be advantageous to reduce the sensitivity to certain unpleasant odors, adaptation also has dangerous consequences. Miners once used canaries to detect the presence of lethal methane gas to which their own receptors had adapted before the presence of the gas was noted.

The relative absence of odorants (as with exposure to pure air) can result in increased olfactory sensitivity. The average threshold drop due to prior exposure to pure air may be as much as 25%. However, like the effect of saliva on taste, our odor world is continually filled so that usually we are at least partially odor-adapted.

Olfactory adaptation is a selective phenomenon. Although adaptation is greatest when the adapting and test stimuli are identical (i.e., **self-adaptation**), adaptation to one odorant may affect the threshold of another odor stimulus—an effect called **cross-adaptation.**

ODOR MIXTURES

When two different odorants that do not react chemically are simultaneously administered, several results are possible. The two odorant components may continue to be identified, depending on their initial distinctiveness. However, the more similar the components, the greater is the tendency for the odorants to blend or fuse and yield a third unitary odor. Another possibility of odorant mixtures is **masking,** which typically appears when the concentration of one odor sufficiently surpasses that of the other—an effect that is often erroneously referred to as "deodorization." True deodorization occurs only when the odorous molecules are removed from the olfactory environment. This can be produced by submitting the contaminated air to adsorbants such as activated charcoal. Of course it is possible to eliminate odor quality by chemically producing anosmia. Thus, in weak solution, formalin (formaldehyde) vaporizes to cause temporary anosmia (Leukel, 1972).

ODOR PREFERENCES

As we noted, all animals do not require or possess the same level of olfactory sensitivity, nor do they share the same spectrum of odor detectability. Because olfaction generally serves a biological function, it follows that, depending on species, the odors that are best perceived are those that are biologically relevant.

Odor preference should similarly follow the adaptive trend of odor reception, namely that "Like or dislike of an odor, especially of food, is partly determined by the requirements of the body. What will be good for the body will usually be liked" (Moncrieff, 1966, p. 208). Thus, the odor of carrion, so repulsive to many animals, is attractive to the scavenger.

Moncrieff (1966) has performed an extensive investigation on the relationship of odor preferences to many human personality and constitutional variables that has resulted in a number of generalizations. Using a collection of 132 different odorants, some natural and others synthetic, Moncrieff found that those odorant materials that were best liked were from flowers and fruits and from substances derived from natural products. A second finding of interest to our present discussion is that odor preference is affected by concentration. Many chemicals yield pleasant odors when they are in dilution. In a number of instances the perception of a given odorant will vary from pleasant to unpleasant as its concentration is increased.

Within this context mention should be made of some evidence for own-odor preference. In one study (McBurney, Levine, & Cavanaugh, 1977), odor stimuli were produced by having 11 male donors wear cotton undershirts continuously for 48 hours. When required to rate the pleasantness of the body odors in the unidentified shirts, subject-donors typically rated their own odors (shirts) as more pleasant than did other raters; this occurred even though only 3 of the 11 subject-donors correctly identified their own shirt based on its odor.

IDENTIFICATION AND MEMORY OF ODORS

The human observer appears reasonably capable of identifying the sources of a vast number of familiar odors. Some identifiable sources come from the human body, and apparently the ability to identify some of them occurs at an early developmental stage. Indeed an infant as young as six weeks of age can identify the scent of its mother (Russell, 1976). Evidence has been reported that sex identification is possible based only on the olfactory information in perspiration. Russell (1976) found that subjects could identify the gender of the wearers of undershirts worn by males and females for 24 hours, who neither bathed nor used any deodorant or perfume. Wallace (1977) also observed that subjects could discriminate males from females, with over 80% accuracy by smelling the person's hand. The males and females, whose hands served as the odorant-carrying surface, wore odor-free sterile gloves for 15 minutes prior to testing to promote perspiration. Consistent with some of our earlier discussion, females outperformed males on this task. Aside from the odor of perspiration, Doty et al. (1982) found that subjects were moderately successful in judging a person's gender only on the basis of his or her breath. Again females were more accurate than males.

When the complex odors from familiar inanimate objects and materials are used as stimuli with specific training procedures, identification by adults is quite good. In an investigation by Desor and Beauchamp (1974), the distinct odors of 64 common sources were used (e.g., coffee, popcorn, human urine, molasses). With some laboratory training in identifying odors, subjects approached near-perfect identification. The fact that training enhances odor identification points out the significant role played by learning processes (Rabin, 1988). Indeed, from his investigation, Cain (1979) concluded that successful odorant identification depends on the familiarity of the odorant, the establishment of a long-standing association between an odor and its name, and some aid or prompting in recalling the odorant's name (i.e., hints to individuals when in a "tip-of-the-nose" state. See also Lawless & Engen, 1977; Lawless, 1978).

One of the striking aspects of odor memory is that although the initial identification and recognition of laboratory odors is not nearly as high as for visual stimuli, the memory for odors studied in the laboratory, and **episodic odors** (i.e., odors associated with real-life experiences), are both quite long lasting (see Figure 10.6). That is, although there is only moderate recognition for laboratory odors compared to pictures, the memory of such odors shows relatively little loss over time. Engen and Ross (1973) reported that when their subjects were given a diverse set of 20 laboratory odors of familiar household products, they recognized about 70% when tested immediately after exposure. However, when tested again, 1, 7, 30, and 90 days later, approximately 70% of the original odors were still correctly recognized. Moreover, when about 20% of the original subjects were tested 1 year later, their average recognition score was almost 65%. Coupled with comparable experiments with visual material (Shepard, 1967), this suggests that odor memory may be less influenced by the passage of time than visual

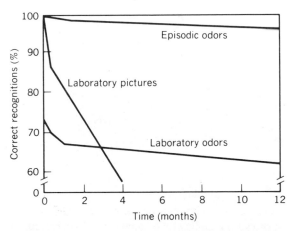

FIGURE 10.6.   Correct recognition of visual stimuli and laboratory and episodic odors (odors from real-life experiences) as a function of time. The memory for episodic odors remains stable and close to its initial high level with the passage of time. However, the memory for pictorial materials, while initially as high as the memory for episodic odors, falls off quite rapidly with time. Laboratory odors, while not well recognized after a short interval of time, like episodic odors show little loss over time. (Based on Shepard, 1967; Engen & Ross, 1973; Engen, 1987.)

memory. A speculation offered by Engen and Ross (1973) is that visual stimuli such as pictures are easily identified after a brief inspection because they contain multiple distinguishable attributes (e.g., shape, size, color) that can be used in an encoding process, whereas odors produce more unitary experiences. Thus, for recognition performance the all-or-none coding of odors may affect initial learning and promote some immediate errors, but its unitary nature also renders odors quite resistant to subsequent confusions.

It is also of interest to note that the presence of odors can facilitate memory for visual stimuli: a visual stimulus associated with a particular odor is more readily recognized in the presence of that odor (Cann & Ross, 1989). We now examine the possibility that the unique relation between odors and emotion may play some role in the memory of odors.

ODORS AND EMOTION

Kirk-Smith, Van Toller, and Dodd (1983) reported that if an unfamiliar neutral odor, even at a very low intensity level, is associated with a stressful emotional event or situation, then at a subsequent time the odor can elicit concomitant mood and attitudinal changes. It is also worth noting in this context that the establishment of some associations between odors and events can occur apparently without the person's awareness (e.g., Van Toller et al., 1983; Kirk-Smith, Toller, & Dodd, 1983). Relatedly, Rubin, Groth, and Goldsmith (1984) note that odors tend to evoke more vivid emotional memories than other types of cues (for example, names or photographs). Such findings suggest that the apparent long-term status of many odor memories stems from their strong, emotionally significant associations. The point made here is that part of the reason that memories of some odors persist is that they tend to have more definite, significant emotional referents—that is, the retention is due, in part, to the profound effect of the memory for emotional events, relatively independent of any special attribute of olfactory stimulation, per se.

However, no matter what is the source that provokes their enduring nature, we must conclude that odors, along with emotions, occupy a special place in memory; clearly their capacity for pervading, even overwhelming one's conscious experience from time to time, is without doubt. Reflecting on our general sensory loss with time, Gonzalez-Crussi (1989) hauntingly observes: "When the features of a loved face will have blurred; when pitch and inflection of a cherished voice will no longer beckon distinctly; what a vivid pleasure, then, to open a flask and inhale the fundamental, irreducible reality of an odor. Oh, for the odor of the absent one!" (p. 92).

OLFACTORY DISORDERS

According to Murphy (1987) there are two main classes of olfactory dysfunctions: physical obstructions of the nasal pathways due to various forms of rhinitis (inflammation of the mucous membranes of the nasal cavity) and a class of disorders that directly affects the olfactory system, such as damage to the olfactory epithelium by major head trauma, certain viral infections (e.g., influenza, hepatitis), bronchial asthma, tumors that exert pressure on the olfactory bulb or tract, burns from the inhalation of certain chemicals (e.g., ammonia, cocaine, and other caustic agents), and the overall degenerative effects due to the aging process (see Schiffman, 1983, for a detailed listing of disorders and drugs that affect olfaction). We also noted in the previous chapter that the sense of smell is considered more vulnerable to aging effects than the sense of taste.

THE ODOR OF DISEASE

It has been long known that for various diseases there are distinctive odors—often malodors—due, in part, to particular classes of metabolic products or bacterial decomposition. These associations were once employed by physicians as a diagnostic instrument. For example, historically, distinctive odor qualities have been attributed to scurvy (putrid), typhoid fever (fresh baked brown bread), and arsenic poisoning (garlic), and a sweet, fruity (like apples) odor has been associated with diabetic coma (see Schiffman, 1983 for more timely references). Some sense of the odors associated with diseased states recorded in eighteenth- and nineteenth-century France is captured by the historian, Alain Corbin (1986):

> what characterized the smell of the atmosphere of the hospital was the complex nature of the putrid odors. Patients' quickened respiration and foul-smelling sweat, their purulent sputum, the variety of pus that flowed from wounds, the contents of buckets and commodes, the pungency of medication, the effluvia of plasters, all amalgamated into stench that the practitioner tried to analyze as fast as possible in order to avert the risk of an epidemic. The sex, age, occupation, and temperment of the patients modified this overall fetidity, from which the effluvia of the dominant disease emerged. The worst was really "hospital fever," the odor of corpses that preceded and foreshadowed death; it rose from gangrenous limbs and from the sweat-impregnated beds reserved for the dying. (p. 51)

PSYCHOBIOLOGICAL FUNCTIONS OF OLFACTION: PHEROMONES

The olfactory system receives biologically useful information although its importance varies with animal groups. For many arthropod and mammalian species, olfaction serves in important survival functions. It enables the perception of the sources of odors—food, sex object, predator—and it conveys information for the performance and perception of certain forms of behavior such as orientation, sexual activity, territory and trail marking, aggression, and species recognition. In certain animal species, olfaction thus enables a form of chemical communication. One process by which this occurs involves the use of chemical communicants or signals called **pheromones** (from the Greek, *pherein*, "to carry," and *horman*, "to excite"). Pheromones are chemical substances secreted to the external environment and exchanged among members of the same species. Unlike hormones, which are secreted in the bloodstream and regulate an organism's internal environment, pheromones are excreted by specialized glands of the skin or in the urine or saliva. These substances produce specific reactions in the behavior or physiology of receptive animals of the same species as the donor.

The mode of influence of pheromones may take either of two general forms. *Releasers* produce an immediate and direct effect (e.g., the attraction of a bitch in heat). A releaser compound has been identified in the vaginal secretions of female dogs in estrus. When small amounts of the releaser pheromone were applied to the genitals of unreceptive or spayed females, males in the immediate vicinity become sexually aroused and initiated mating behavior (Goodwin, Gooding, & Regnier, 1979). That is, the pheromone compound released sexual behavior in the males identical to that released by an estrus female dog. *Primers* act by producing a receptive state or physiological change such as affecting the estrus cycle. Olfactory sex pheromones have been identified for many insects, and synthetic variants are sometimes used for insect control (Silverstein, 1981; Linn, Campbell, & Roelofs, 1987). Pheromones are also used in achieving aggregation in insects. Thus worker honeybees, on finding a source of food, release a scent that attracts other bees. This same species also makes use of chemical signals for colony recognition.

Another function of pheromones is in identifying and marking out one's territory by leaving chemical trails. The dog's vigorous sniffing and urination is an all-too-common example of this. Other means of marking territory also exist. Reindeer have scent glands behind their hind toes that allow them to leave scent trails for herd members; the odor has a "cheesy" smell (Gibbons, 1986).

A number of studies have identified the existence of chemical excretions of the mouse that influence hormonal activity, the estrus cycle, and hence the reproductive physiology and behavior of other mice (e.g., McClintock, 1984). In addition, it has been reported that removal of the olfactory bulb abolishes not only the estrus cycle but eliminates maternal behavior in lactating mice (Gandelman et al., 1971). In a related study, olfactory bulb removal eliminated mating behavior in the male hamster (Murphy & Schneider, 1969). It appears that the ability to smell is a prerequisite for reproductive behavior in many mammalian species. Some of the pheromonal effects are quite stylized. For example, Michael and Keverne (1968) mention that the pheromones excreted by the boar elicit an immobilization reflex in the sow in estrus so that the sow stands rigid while mating. The pheromones promoting this activity have been identified, and they are secreted by the boar's salivary glands (Patterson, 1968). When sexually excited, the boar salivates profusely, thereby providing what is termed the "swine sex odor" (Berry et al., 1971). The reception by an estrus sow of the pheromone odorant present in the boar's saliva is an essential prerequisite before the characteristic immobilized mating stance can be elicited (see also Amoore, Pelosi, & Forrester, 1977).

There are also classes of pheromones that serve to signal the presence of danger—*alarm pheromones*. In one study (Valenta & Rigby, 1968), rats that had been trained to make a single response (bar press) were used. When an air sample taken from the vicinity of rats who were undergoing a stressful exposure (electric shock) was introduced into the test chamber of the trained rats, their responses were interrupted. No such effect occurred when air from unstressed rats was introduced. The indication is that rats who were shocked excreted a detectable chemical—the alarm pheromone—that disrupted the learned behavior of the trained rats (see also Fanselow, 1985).

The role of pheromones in primates is not clear, but it has been noted that among certain lower primates pheromones are used for territorial marking and sexual behavior. In higher primates there is some evidence that the sexual activity of males and females is partially mediated by a sexual pheromone. In one study, experimentally anosmic male rhesus monkeys showed no interest in receptive females until normal olfactory function was restored (Michael & Keverne, 1968). In addition, males with normal olfaction were more sexually responsive to females that were administered estrogen than to females experimentally lacking this hormone. Although these findings suggest that a hormonal-dependent vaginal pheromone may affect primate sexual behavior, there is also evidence that the detection by the male primate of pheromones from the female is not a *necessary* condition either for the occurrence or for the cyclicity of copulatory behavior (Goldfoot et al., 1978).

It should be noted that although pheromones may not play as dominant a role as visual or certain behavioral cues, or even be essential for primate breeding, their presence may confer an advantage in certain environments by identifying the sexually receptive females, thereby increasing the likelihood of fertile matings (see Rogel, 1978).

THE VOMERONASAL SYSTEM

Before leaving the topic of chemocommunication in lower species it should be noted that olfaction is probably not the only sensory system employed for extracting chemosensory signals of a communicative nature from the environment. A system called the **vomeronasal** system appears to be specialized to deal with large, relatively nonvolatile molecules, that generally require physical contact (such as licking) for their reception. The vomeronasal organ is generally organized in parallel with the olfactory organ and in most animals lies above the hard palate of the mouth. The vomeronasal chemicals appear to mediate such activities as aggression, hormonal changes, the modulation of female ovulation cycles, and certain aspects of courtship and reproductive behavior (see Wysocki & Meredith, 1987).

HUMAN PHEROMONES

The existence of pheromones in the human is far from certain, but there are suggestions. As we briefly noted earlier, some evidence exists that olfactory stimuli may enable accurate sexual identification. In the report by Russell (1976) that we previously cited, the gender of wearers of odor stimuli (i.e., worn undershirts) was correctly identified by a significant majority of subjects; in addition the odor stimuli of the male donors were characterized as "musky," whereas those of the female donors as "sweet."

Some indirect hints emerge from applied chemical technology. Perfumers make ample use of certain mammalian sex pheromones such as civetone (produced by the anal glandular pouch of the male and female civet, a nocturnal felid found in Africa and Asia) and musk (from the anal scent glands of the male musk deer), substances used principally as fixatives and extenders. Both pheromones are normally used by their donors for territory markings and as sex attractants. Apart from their practical function of extending the more valued components of commercial perfumes, the odors of sex pheromones of lower mammals appear to have some attraction for the human. We noted earlier that Exaltolide, which is similar in odor and chemical structure to a mammalian sex attractant called muscone (Good, Geary, & Engen, 1976), evokes a threshold response in the human female that varies according to her reproductive cycle. In addition its musklike odor is pleasant and attractive to females ("sweet" and "like perfume" were the most frequent comments in one study; Vierling & Rock, 1967). Of some relevance to our discussion is that a compound found in human urine also has a sharp musklike odor, and the adult male secretes about twice as much as does the adult female (Vierling & Rock, 1967). The conjecture here, of course, is that Exaltolide mimics a sexually relevant human pheromone. In addition, a female vaginal secretion of volatile fatty acids, similar to those possessing sex-attractant properties in other primate species, has been suggested as a possible human pheromone (Michael, Bonsall, & Warner, 1974).

Clearly, the human possesses the necessary glandular and other physiological and structural mechanisms to transmit external chemical signals (i.e., for chemocommunication). For example, the human is amply supplied with apocrine glands that secrete odorants through sweat; moreover, the chemical composition of both secretions and excretions varies with emotional and perhaps mental state. Thus, it has been reported that schizophrenics emit a peculiar and characteristic acidic odor in their sweat, and this substance has been identified (Smith, Thompson, & Koster, 1969).

McClintock (1971) has reported a study on women (all dormitory residents of a women's college) that indicates that the menstrual cycles of close friends and roommates fall into synchrony. The critical factor producing menstrual synchrony, according to McClintock, was that the individuals interact and remain in close proximity to one another. Further studies of menstrual synchrony also show that a significant factor in synchrony is the degree of association between female individuals (Graham & McGrew, 1980; Quadagno, Shubeita, & Deck, 1981). Menstrual synchrony was not affected by the amount or nature of social interaction with males. One explanation for these findings is that the mechanism underlying this menstrual synchrony phenomenon is pheromonal. Indeed there is evidence that a secretion from the axillary (armpit) gland is the chemical that mediates menstrual synchrony through olfaction. Generally, Russell et al. (1980) and Preti et al. (1986) found that when women had their upper lips swabbed three times per week with perspiration extract from the axillary glands of donor women, the women who received the extract began to menstruate in synchrony with the donor women between about their third and fifth menstrual cycle.

Another factor that may influence aspects of menstruation (i.e., length and timing) in humans is that of male axillary secretions. As in the previous study, Cutler et al. (1986) observed the effect of such secretions on females, between the ages of 19 and 30 years, who had somewhat aberrant menstrual cycles (i.e., less than 26 or more than 32 days). After about 14 weeks of having their upper lips regularly swabbed with perspiration extract from the axillary glands of heterosexually active male donors, there was a reduction in the proportion of aberrant length cycles. Thus there is some evidence to assume that for the human, a chemical signal from the male that would normally be transferred only during intimate physical contact, exerts some control on the reproductive physiology of the female.

Whether normal genital secretions of a volatile nature, for both the human male and female, exert sex-attractant influences on humans is not known. If these odorants do play a role, the popularity of deodorants, especially the intimate types for the female genital region, suggests a peculiar deemphasis of a potential sexual attractant in a culture that seems to emphasize sexual attraction in so many other ways.

In conclusion, it must be cautioned that although the notion of a human pheromone is appealing, the supporting evidence is more preliminary and circumstantial than conclusive. Moreover, we must take note of the speculation that in the course of evolution, the human's spectacular potential to verbalize his or her motivational and emotional states may have reduced the need to communicate by olfactory-dependent mechanisms. By the same token, however, the vast research literature on chemical communication systems and pheromones, at least for other species, testifies to the important influence olfaction has on behavior.

COMMON CHEMICAL SENSE

Gustation and olfaction are not the only sensory systems receptive to environmental chemicals. There is a system called the **common chemical sense** (or trigeminal chemoreception) that is stimulated by the action of chemical irritants (e.g., ammonia, pepper, vinegar) on mucosal surfaces (i.e., surfaces found in the nose, mouth, eye, respiratory tract, anus, and genital apertures). Of particular concern to our discussion is chemical stimulation of the **trigeminal** (or Vth) **nerve**, which provides sensory innervation to much of the mucous membrane of the head, including the nasal, oral, and corneal regions, and is the major neural structure mediating the common chemical sense. It has been proposed that the role of the common chemical sense is to protect the organism from potentially harmful chemicals. That is, it serves as an irritant detector or **chemonociceptor** (see Silver & Maruniak, 1981; Silver, 1987). In fact stimulation of the appropriate common chemical sense receptors elicits a wide range of physiological reflexes that appear to reduce the effect of noxious stimuli by tending to remove the organism from the source of the irritant and thereby protecting the organism from further exposure. Indeed certain reflexes elicited by stimulation of the common chemical sense, especially of membrane structures in the nasal cavity, are among the strongest in the body and often are accompanied by stimulus rejection and withdrawal reactions, such as sneezing, increased nasal air flow resistance, tearing, and the inhibition of respiration.

Stimulation of trigeminal receptors of the oral cavity with chemical irritants produces increased salivation, tearing, increased nasal secretions, general vasodilation (flushing of the face, chest, neck, and shoulders and reddening of the conjunctiva—the membranous covering of the eyeball), and perspiration of the head and neck regions. The profuse perspiration and salivary flow that accompanies stimulation of oral chemoreceptors increases with the intensity of the chemoirritant.

It should be stressed that reception by way of the common chemical sense is qualitatively different from taste and smell. Indeed Doty et al. (1978) have reported that subjects lacking olfactory nerve functioning are able to detect certain chemicals in vapor form, that is, based on the irritating properties of the odorants rather than upon their odors per se (see also Mason & Silver, 1983). However stimulation of the trigeminal nerve does appear to have a potentiating or complementary effect on olfaction and makes a contribution to the perception of the intensity of an odorant, especially at high concentrations.

EFFECTIVE STIMULUS FOR THE COMMON CHEMICAL SENSE

Generally speaking, to evoke the common chemical sense, the chemical concentration should be relatively high (i.e., higher than the olfactory threshold for a given chemical; Prah & Benignus, 1984), and it should be lipid soluble in order to reach chemoreceptive trigeminal nerve endings (Silver, 1987). The effective stimuli for trigeminal stimulation of the

nasal cavity include pungent spices and vegetables such as onions, substances that irritate the eyes and produce tearing (lacrimatories), substances that provoke sneezing (sternutatories), tobacco smoke and ammonia (sufficants), and skin irritants (Silver, 1987). Trigeminal chemoreceptors in the oral cavity react especially to such pungent spices as chili or red pepper (in which the irritant capsaicin is found), black pepper (piperine), ginger, mustard, cloves, and horseradish and to such chemicals as menthol (which, of course, produces the sensation of coolness). Of interest is the observation that the sensitivity of the oral cavity to chemical irritation from such trigeminal stimuli as chili pepper or black pepper is a function of the locus of stimulation: Lawless and Stevens (1988) report intense sensations from stimulation of the tip and side of the tongue and posterior palate (all of which contain gustatory receptors) and less intense sensations from the cheek and anterior palate. Also of interest from this investigation is that the perceived intensity of irritation grows over time.

PREFERENCE FOR IRRITATING TRIGEMINAL STIMULI

Finally, we may consider the interesting aspect of both nasal and oral trigeminal chemoreception, that for humans, certain substances that are initially aversive and abruptly rejected, eventually assume a preferred status. Familiar examples include pepper, mustard, horseradish, curry, ginger, vinegar, tobacco, and carbonated beverages. The observation that infants, children, and taste-naïve adults typically find the irritating properties of these substances aversive upon first exposure and reject and avoid them, suggests strongly that they are innately unpalatable. However, in adulthood, many individuals reverse their natural rejection and acquire a preference for at least some of these aversive substances. It has been reported that chemical irritants of the common chemical sense interact with gustatory sensations, particularly bitter and sour tastes (Lawless, 1987). Perhaps in the case of the human the irritating factor serves to augment and enhance the palatability of one's diet. It is possible that it may interact with both taste and smell by adding a crispness or slight pungency to the overall sensory quality of food. At any rate, attempts to reverse the rejection and promote a preference for trigeminal stimuli in animals other than the human, despite intensive and varied training procedures, have been unsuccessful (Rozin, Gruss, & Berk, 1979). Lastly it is of some interest that continued ingestion of certain chemical irritants, such as chili pepper (i.e., capsaicin), renders the oral region relatively insensitive to further chemical irritants. This would coincide with the familiar observation that individuals who frequently eat hot peppers appear less affected by their burn or irritation than does the occasional taster (Lawless et al., 1985; Lawless, 1987).

SUMMARY

In this chapter we have described the processes and phenomena of smell or olfaction. It was noted that although the sense of smell is not necessary for human survival, it does provide crucial biologically relevant information for many species.

The adequate stimulus for smell is a volatile substance that must also be water and lipid soluble. Generally the normal chemical stimuli for the olfactory system are organic substances that are mixtures of chemical compounds.

The basic categories of odors are not agreed upon. However, there are various classifications based on subjective experience. One scheme, called the stereochemical theory, emphasizes the geometric properties—size and shape—of the molecules comprising the odorant. This theory assumes that the molecules of certain sizes and shapes must fit into correspondingly shaped receptor sites of the olfactory membrane, much as a key fits in a lock. When substances of similar molecular construction (keys) stimulate the same receptor sites (locks), they produce similar olfactory qualities. This theory is inconsistent with a number of empirical findings.

The anatomy of the olfactory systems was outlined, and it was noted that the receptors serve the functions of reception and conduction. It was noted that the dendritic knobs and the cilia of the olfactory cells are the structures involved in the initial transduction stage.

Olfactory coding was outlined. For intensity it was observed that the degree of neural activity increases with increases in the concentration of a given odorant. Some of the problems of understanding the coding of olfactory quality were identified. The notion was proposed that different odorants produce coherent and distinctive spatial and temporal patterns of neural activity. That is, response profiles of groups of receptor cells are closely linked to odor compounds.

Threshold measures for olfaction were presented, and it was stressed that extremely low concentrations are sufficient for detection. Some variables critical to thresholds were identified; for example, olfactory sensitivity markedly declines with age.

Phenomena relevant to olfaction, such as adaptation, masking, self-adaptation, cross-adaptation, odor preferences, and memory of odors were discussed. Studies bearing on the recognition of odors were also discussed; it was noted that humans can identify their own clothing on the basis of perspiration, and they can also identify the gender of clothing worn by strangers on the same basis.

The relation between emotion and odors was observed with reference to a number of studies; it was concluded that the memory for some odors is due in large part to their emotional referents and occurrence within emotional contexts. A brief discussion was also presented on disorders of the olfactory system and on the odors of disease.

A means of chemical communication by way of pheromones (and the vomeronasal system) was described. Pheromones are chemical substances secreted to the external environment and exchanged among members of the same species to produce behavioral or physiological reactions in the receptive animals. Pheromonal communication has been shown for a number of animal species including primates but the evidence for a possible human pheromone is not compelling. However there are data that suggest that secretions from the axillary gland of human females and males exert an influence on aspects of the human female menstrual cycle.

Finally, the common chemical sense was discussed. It is a chemosensory system, distinct from taste and smell, which is stimulated by action of chemical irritants over mucosal surfaces (especially in the mouth and nose), and it is mediated by the trigeminal nerve. It has been proposed that the role of the common chemical sense is to act as an irritant detector, that is, as a chemonociceptor, to protect the individual from potentially harmful chemicals. However, the pungency of mild irritants, especially in the oral cavity, such as produced by mustard and the like, appears to add an appealing experience to the palatability of food for the human.

KEY TERMS

Anosmia

Chemonociceptor

Common chemical sense

Cross-adaptation

Dendritic knobs

Episodic odors

Exaltolide

Glomerulus

Henning's smell prism

Macrosmatic

Masking

Mercaptan

Microsmatic

Olfactory adaptation

Olfactory bulb

Olfactory cilia

Olfactory epithelium (mucosa)

Osmics

Pheromones (releasers, primers)

Self-adaptation

Stereochemical theory

Trigeminal nerve

Vomeronasal system

STUDY QUESTIONS

1. Discuss the functional relevance of the smell system to various species.

2. What are the stimulus requirements for the smell system and what are the naturally occurring sources of odorants?

3. Consider the problems involved in identifying and classifying basic odors. Consider the extent to which the classification used by the stereochemical theory is successful in identifying basic odors. In what ways is the theory incomplete or inadequate?

4. Outline the major components of the olfactory epithelium and indicate the probable reception sites for odorants.

5. Outline olfactory coding for both intensity and quality. Indicate how odor quality may be coded by a specific pattern of activity for groups of receptor cells. Consider how the activity of the same receptor cell may enter into the coding of more than one odorant.

6. Discuss the notion that the sensitivity for odors reflects a remarkable ability. Compare the sensitivity of taste with that of smell.

7. What is the effect of gender on the sense of smell? What roles does the chemical Exaltolide play in assessing the effect of gender on thresholds for smell?

8. Describe the effects that aging and smoking have on the sense of smell.

9. Describe the phenomenon of self-adaptation. Examine the possibility of eliminating unwanted odors by the addition of various odorants.

10. What factors determine or have a significant effect on odor preferences?

11. How effective is the human's ability to recognize odors? What characteristics of an odorant are important to its recognition? What aspects of human odors enable gender recognition?

12. Explain the observation that the memory for odors, relative to visual stimuli, shows little loss over time. Consider the difference between visual and olfactory stimuli in explaining the memory difference. Describe the role played by emotions in the memory for odors.

13. What sorts of disease affect the olfactory system? Consider how disease affects one's body odor. What role could body odor serve in medical diagnoses?

14. Describe pheromones and indicate what functions they perform. Describe the kinds of information pheromones transmit.

15. What is the vomeronasal system and what role does it play in chemocommunication?

16. Outline evidence that suggests the possibility of a human pheromone. Indicate the kinds of effects that pheromonal-type chemicals may have on cyclic human physiology.

17. What is the common chemical sense and how does it differ from the taste and smell system? What anatomical regions, served by the trigeminal nerve, are most prone to stimulation by the common chemical sense? What are some characteristic stimuli for the common chemical sense?

18. What is the function of the common chemical sense and what are some typical reactions to the application of chemical irritants? How does the common chemical sense interact with the sense of smell and taste? Explain how stimuli of the common chemical sense may become appealing to the human.

THE VISUAL SYSTEM

In many forms of life, vision is crucial for gaining knowledge about the arrangement of objects and the presence of events in the environment. This knowledge depends on information such as shape and texture, size and distance, brightness, color, and movement. Vision is the dominant sensory system for

the human. This can be demonstrated when vision is put in conflict with another sensory modality. Rock and Victor (1964; see also Rock & Harris, 1967) examined the priority of vision over touch by providing an experimental situation in which a square was made to look like a rectangle whose sides appeared in the proportion of two to one (see Figure 11.1*a*, *b*). When the subject both felt and saw the square through a distorting lens, which produced an optical compression of the height, the square was perceived as a rectangle. That is, the stimulus was perceived on the basis of the distorted visual input rather than the undistorted tactual one. That the object "feels" as if it has the size or shape that is seen is called **visual capture** (e.g., Rock, 1986). Although the results of other studies may not make so compelling a case for the overriding influence of vision when there is a sensory conflict (e.g., Power, 1980; Heller, 1983, 1989), we must agree with Duke-Elder (1958) that, "We are indeed highly visual creatures."

Because vision is so dominant a sense in the human, it has been studied in great detail and more is known of it than the other senses. Accordingly, a major portion of the remainder of this book will be devoted to the visual modality.

THE PHYSICAL STIMULUS

The physical properties of the visual stimulus—**radiant electromagnetic energy**—are compatible with two complementary conceptions of light. Based on the fact that radiant energy is propagated in a continuous wave form, we can describe it by its wavelength (or its reciprocal, frequency). Radiant energy also behaves as if it is emitted as discrete particles or quanta of energy. The quantum unit of photic energy is called a *photon*, and the intensity of a source may be given as the number of photon units emitted. It is agreed that light possesses both wave and particle properties. Indeed, the two are quantitatively related in that the shorter the wavelength, the greater the energy. Suffice it to say, light is generally described by its wavelength and its intensity. *Color* or *hue* is the subjective or psychological correlate to wavelength (discussed in detail in Chapter 13). The **intensity** of light refers to the amount of radiant energy, and its psychological correlate is **brightness.**

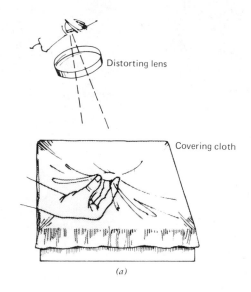

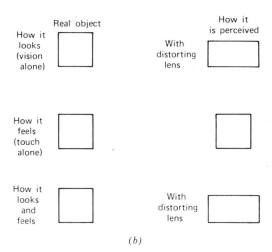

FIGURE 11.1. Experimental arrangement used to present the subject with contradictory information from vision and from touch. The apparatus included a distorting lens, a cloth over the subjects' hands so that they would not deduce from the small appearance of their hands that they were looking through a distorting lens, and a square made of hard plastic. In the experiment depicted, the subject looked at the square and simultaneously grasped it. The lens optically showed a rectangle. The results for this and other conditions are schematized in (*b*).

It is important to distinguish between intensity and brightness. Although brightness typically varies with intensity, the term brightness is restricted to the subjective–perceptual effect resulting from the intensity of light. That is, whereas intensity is a physical property of light, brightness refers to the impression produced by the intensity of light striking the visual system.

WAVELENGTH

Wavelengths of electromagnetic radiation vary from trillionths of a meter to many kilometers in length (see Figure 11.2). However, the wavelengths of radiant energy of significance to the visual systems of most animal species occupy a relatively small region of the total electromagnetic spectrum. Insects and some birds may be sensitive to near ultraviolet radiation; in addition, some snakes possess specialized sense organs for receiving infrared radiations. However, under normal conditions, for most vertebrates, visible radiation-light extends from about 380 nm (**nm, nanometer,** billionth of a meter) to about 760 nm. This range constitutes only a narrow band, about one-seventieth of the total spectrum. Part of the reason for the reception to only a limited portion of the spectrum may be due to the filtering of light energy by the ozone layer (15 miles above the earth) so that eighty percent of the solar energy reaching the terrain lies between 300 nm and 1100 nm. In addition, as light enters water it undergoes absorption, scattering, and, even at moderate depths, extinction. By one accounting, the short ultraviolet waves are almost extinguished in a few millimeters of water, the infrared waves are eliminated in about a meter, thereby leaving the narrow band of the visible spectrum shown in Figure 11.2 (Walls, 1963, p. 373). Thus, aquatic creatures whose vision is adapted to the available light spectrum and those terrestrial animals owing their origins to aquatic forms of life share a similar visible spectrum. There are, however, some notable exceptions to this generalization. The emission of infrared radiation by warm-blooded animals has been exploited by some nocturnal cold-blooded animals: as we noted, snakes such as the pit viper and the rattlesnake hunt for small mammals and birds in the absence of visible light by utilizing specialized organs located along side their eyes that are capable of forming an infrared or "heat" image of the immediate surroundings, especially of their warm-blooded prey.

INTENSITY

The measurement of the intensity dimension of a photic stimulus requires extremely complex procedures, and they are specified in a diverse array of units. Table 11.1 provides a summary of some

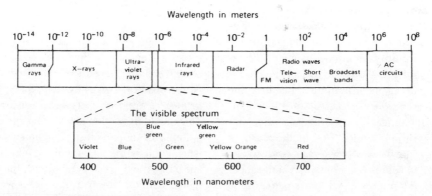

FIGURE 11.2. The electromagnetic spectrum. The normally visible portion of the spectrum is enlarged in the lower part of the figure. (From Geldard, 1972, p. 20; after Chapanis, Garner, & Morgan, 1949.)

Table 11.1
Photometric Terms, Units, and Measures

Illuminance	Foot-candle (ft-c)	The illumination received on a surface 1 foot square located 1 foot from a standard candle.
	Meter-candle (m-c)	The illumination on a surface of 1 meter square located 1 meter from a standard candle. (One meter-candle = 0.0929 foot-candles, or 1 foot-candle = 10.76 meter-candles.)
Luminance	Foot-lambert (ft-L)	The total amount of light emitted in all directions from a perfectly reflecting and diffusing surface illuminated by 1 foot-candle.
	Millilambert (mL)	1 mL = 0.929 ft-L.
	Candela per square meter (cd/m^2) or *nit*	The amount of light given off by a perfectly diffuse reflecting surface illuminated by 1 meter-candle. (One candela per square meter or nit = 0.3142 mL or 0.2919 ft-L.)

often-used photometric measures. However, only two aspects need concern us: the physical intensity of the radiant energy falling on a surface—the amount of *incident light*, and the intensity of the light reaching the eye from a surface—the amount of *reflected light*. The former is called **illuminance.** A common English unit of illuminance is the *foot-candle* (ft-c). A metric unit of illuminance is the *meter-candle* (*m-c*). Of course, the farther away a surface rests from the light source, the smaller is the amount of light reaching it.

Ordinarily we do not look directly at a light source: most of the light that we see is reflected from surfaces. The intensity of the light reflected from an illuminated surface is termed **luminance.** An English unit of luminance is the *foot-lambert* (ft-L). Another common unit of luminance is the *millilambert* (mL). Table 11.2 shows luminance levels for some typical sources of stimulation. Because the visual system can respond to a great range of luminance levels, its range of sensitivity is often described in logarithmic units. As in the case of acoustic energy, the use of logarithms reduces an enormous range of values to a relatively small range. With a base 10, a luminance of 1 converts to a value of 0 in the log scale ($\log_{10} 1 = 0$). Similarly, a luminance of 10 converts to a value of 1 ($\log_{10} 10 = 1$), a luminance of 100 to a value of 2 ($\log_{10} 100 = 2$),

and so on. Observe that a difference of one log unit reflects a 10-fold difference in intensity.

It is useful to summarize several of the features of light specification relevant to our discussion. Consider the characteristics of light necessary to read this book: the amount of light energy emanating from the bulb of your desk lamp specifies radiant energy or *radiance*, the amount of light falling on the page is *illuminance*, the amount of light reflected from the page is *luminance*, and the psychological–perceptual effect of the image of the page on your visual system is *brightness*.

RECEPTION

Radiant energy is informative only when it affects a visual system. In the initial stage of vision, radiant energy must be transduced into a neural form. That is, the physical energy acts on photoreceptive tissue to produce impulses that convey sensory information. The kind of tissue that is responsive to radiant energy is found in the simplest of organisms. Some organisms, such as the single-celled amoeba, possess no specialized light receptors; rather, the entire body is light sensitive. However, most animals have a region on their body that is maximally sensitive to light. Of course, mere responsivity to light is quite a different matter from actually forming a visual image. Indeed,

Table 11.2
Luminance Values for Typical Visual Stimuli

	Scale of Luminance (millilamberts)	
	10^{10}	
Sun's surface at noon	10^9 Damaging	
	10^8	
	10^7	
Tungsten filament	10^6	
	10^5	
White paper in sunlight	10^4	Photopic (color vision)
	10^3	
	10^2	
Comfortable reading	10	
	1	
	10^{-1}	
White paper in moonlight	10^{-2}	
	10^{-3}	Scotopic (colorless vision)
White paper in starlight	10^{-4}	
	10^{-5}	
Absolute threshold	10^{-6}	

Source: L. A. Riggs, in *Vision and Visual Perception*, edited by C. H. Graham, John Wiley, New York, 1965, p. 26. Reprinted by permission of the publisher.

many of the light-sensitive structures of lower forms of life act primarily to concentrate light upon a photosensitive pigment. That is, they serve as *light-gathering* rather than *image-forming* organs. It is from advanced stages of evolution that an image-forming eye developed. The structural transition in light-sensitive organs from simple light gatherer to image former is suggested in Figure 11.3.

According to Wald (1959), only three of the major phyla have developed image-forming eyes: the arthropods (insects, crabs; see Figure 11.4), mollusks (squid, octopus), and vertebrates. Many different optical devices for forming an image have evolved within these phyla. For example, the cephalopod mollusk, Nautilus, has a pinhole eye (a small hole in an opaque surface forms an image on a surface behind it). The tiny arthropod, Copilia, has a lens and a single attached light receptor that moves back and forth scanning the image in a way similar to the method used by a TV camera.

All image-forming eyes have advantages and limitations. The pinhole eye provides an image in focus at all distances from the object viewed. However, it can admit only a small amount of light to its photosensitive tissue. The **compound eye** of arthropods (Figure 11.4) consists of a mosaic of tubular units, called **ommatidia,** that are clustered tightly together and arranged so that the outer surface forms a hemisphere. Each ommatidium registers only the light directly in front of it; this produces a single image constructed from an enormous number of separate signals. The compound eye is especially effective for detecting movement. However, this form of visual system is effective at only a very close object distance. In contrast, the vertebrate eye is quite effective in long-range viewing, but it cannot resolve images at the short distances at which the arthropod eye is effective. However, no matter what design or variation on the basic form of image-forming eye a species had adopted, it is clear that, in general, the eye is adapted in different ways in different species to maximize the capture and the amount of information

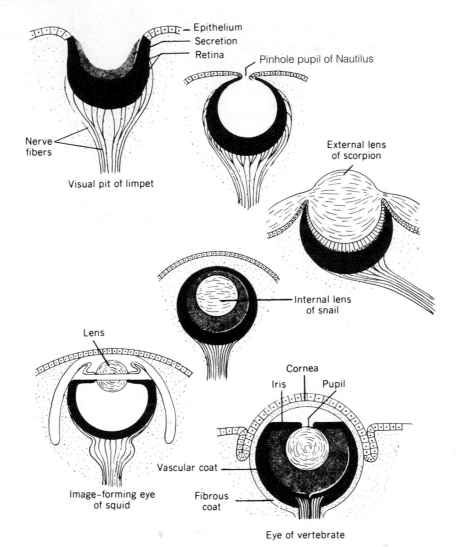

Epithelium
Secretion
Retina

Pinhole pupil of Nautilus

Nerve fibers

Visual pit of limpet

External lens of scorpion

Internal lens of snail

Lens

Image-forming eye of squid

Cornea
Iris
Pupil

Vascular coat

Fibrous coat

Eye of vertebrate

FIGURE 11.3.   Examples of some primitive "eyes." (Source: Gregory, 1973, p. 24. Reprinted by permission of the author.)

in the optic array. In short, the eye of a given species is related to the demands of its environment and its way of life.

ANATOMY OF THE VERTEBRATE EYE

The vertebrate eye is built on a single basic plan: from fish to mammal, all vertebrate eyes possess a photosensitive layer called a **retina,** and a **lens** whose optical properties are such that it focuses an image upon the retina. Figure 11.5 presents a cross-sectional slice of a human eye. We will first describe its major structural components and then discuss several important functional mechanisms. The eyeball, lying in a protective socket of the skull, is a globular structure, just under an inch (about 20 mm) in diameter. The outer covering of the eyeball is a tough white opaque coat called the **sclera** (seen as

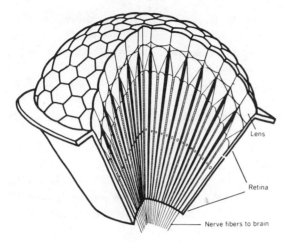

FIGURE 11.4. Three-dimensional cutaway view of compound eye of an arthropod. (From Buchsbaum, 1948, p. 246.)

the "white" of the eye). The sclerotic covering at the front of the eye becomes the translucent membrane called the **cornea.** Light rays entering the cornea undergo **refraction** or are bent by its surface. A second layer of the eyeball called the **choroid** is attached to the sclera. It consists largely of blood vessels and provides a major source of nutrition for the eye. In addition, the choroid layer is heavily

pigmented; this enables the absorption of most extraneous light entering the eye, thereby reducing reflections within the eyeball that might blur the image. However, some animals possess a retinal layer, called the **tapetum,** that reflects back some of the light entering the eye. It is the reflection of light from their retinae that accounts for the "eyeshine" that appears from the eyes of many familiar nocturnal animals. What is occurring, say, when we drive past a cat or dog at night, is that the animal's eyes are reflecting back some of the light of the car's headlights rather than absorbing the light as in the case of the human choroid layer. The function of the tapetum is not clear, though Walls (1963) suggests that it may enhance vision in nocturnal conditions.

In the front of the eye the choroid is modified to form the **iris.** Behind the cornea, lying on the lens, the disklike pigmented or colored iris controls the amount of light entering the eye—a structural analogy to the diaphragm of a camera (see Figure 11.6). When lighting conditions are poor, the iris opens to increase the size of or *dilate* the **pupil**—the round black opening surrounded by the iris (see Figure 11.7). On the other hand, in bright light the iris closes, constricting or reducing the size of the pupil. Generally the pupil's reaction to the overall conditions of lighting is reflexive. Shining a bright light in

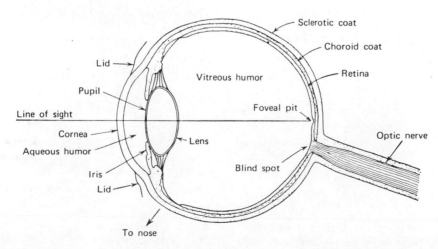

FIGURE 11.5. Gross structure of the human eye. Note that the region labeled "blind spot" is often referred to as the optic disk.

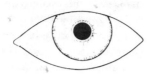

FIGURE 11.6. Optical similarity of diaphragm of camera and iris of eye. Both adjust to the intensity of light.

an individual's eye produces **Whytt's reflex** (a reflex identified by Robert Whytt, in the mideighteenth century): an immediate constriction of the pupil in response to bright light. In fact, Whytt's reflex has important diagnostic value concerning the functioning of the central nervous system in that the inability to demonstrate Whytt's reflex may be indicative of neural injury.

The human pupil is circular but a variety of shapes exists for different species. Figure 11.8 shows the vertical slit pupil of a cat during dilation and constriction. Such a pupil allows an essentially nocturnal animal to hunt in bright daylight (as in the case of the cat) or to bask in the comfort of the sun (e.g., the crocodile) (Duke-Elder, 1958).

In the human the range of pupil size extends from 1.5 to over 9 mm in diameter. Pupil size is controlled by two opposing smooth muscles in the iris, the *sphincter* and the *dilator* (Figure 11.9). The sphincter forms a ring around the pupil and can shorten as much as 87% to constrict the pupil. (We will return to changes in pupil sizes in a later section.)

The crystalline lens of the vertebrate eye divides it into two unequal chambers—a small one in front filled with watery fluid held under pressure, the *aqueous humor*, which helps to maintain the shape of the eye and provides the metabolic requirements of the cornea, and a larger chamber behind the lens filled with a jellylike protein, the *vitreous humor*. These fluids, both transparent, aid in holding the lens in place and allow its housing to be flexible. A set of muscles, the **ciliary muscles,** attached to the lens by ligaments (the zonal fibers of Figure 11.9), controls its curvature, which varies depending on the distance of the object focused. (We will discuss this mechanism in a separate section.) From a comparative viewpoint, lens size bears an interesting relation to the normal lighting conditions of an animal's habitat. Because large lenses can collect more light

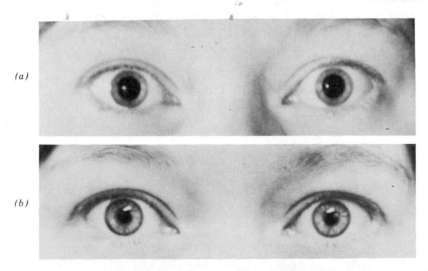

FIGURE 11.7. The size of the pupil changes with the level of light. The photo for (a) was taken in dimmer light than the one for (b) (although they appear about equally bright). Accordingly, the pupils shown in (a) are dilated whereas those in (b) are constricted. (From Buss, 1978, p. 139.)

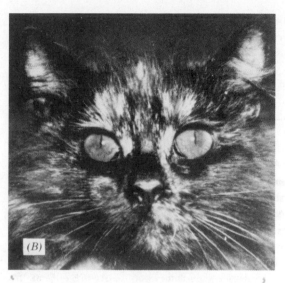

FIGURE 11.8.   The pupils of the cat in dilation (*a*), and in constriction (*b*) showing the extremely narrow vertical slits. (From S. Duke-Elder, *System of Ophthalmology*.

Volume 1, *The Eye in Evolution*, C. V. Mosby, St. Louis, 1958, p. 613. Reprinted by permission of the publisher.)

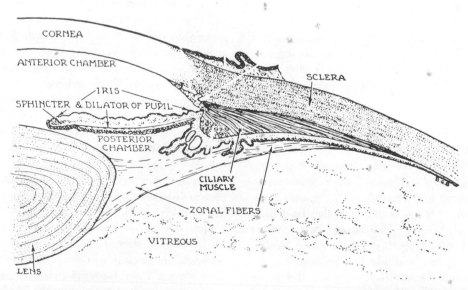

FIGURE 11.9.   Detail of anterior segment of human eye, showing anatomy of structures affecting the pupillary response and curvature of the lens. (Based on J. L.

Brown, in *Vision and Visual Perception*, edited by C. H. Graham, John Wiley, New York, 1965, p. 44. Reprinted by permission of the publisher.)

than smaller ones, nocturnal animals have evolved larger lenses relative to the size of their eyeballs than have day-active animals.

THE RETINA

Light passes through the lens to the retina at the back of the eyeball. The retina, which covers nearly 200° of the inside of the eyeball, is composed of a coating of interconnected nerve cells and photoreceptors that are responsive to light energy. Two distinct types of photoreceptors have been identified: **rods** and **cones,** named for their cylindrical and conic shapes, respectively (see Figure 11.10). Rods, which in the primate retina number about 120 to 130 million, are heavily concentrated in the peripheral region of the retina. Cones, which number about 6 to 8 million, are primarily concentrated in a small pit or indentation less than 1 mm across called the **fovea.** The central region of the retina that includes the fovea is marked by a yellow pigment, the **macula lutea,** over an area 2 to 3 mm in diameter.

The approximate distribution of rods and cones over the retina is illustrated in Figure 11.11. The gap in the curve corresponds to that part of the retina where the optic nerve fibers leave the eye (see Figure 11.5). There are no photoreceptors in this area, and accordingly there is no vision when light strikes this region of the retina. It is appropriately termed the **blind spot** (also called the **optic disk;** see Figure 11.12).

As illustrated in Figure 11.10, there is an apparently illogical relation between the location of the photoreceptors and incoming light in that the receptors do not face the light. In most vertebrates, the photoreceptors are located in the back of the retina and nerve fibers connected to them are gathered together in front. This means that light must travel through the network of nerve fibers, blood vessels, and other supporting cells before it reaches the photoreceptors: the retina thus appears anatomically inside out. However, functionally this poses little problem, for the blood cells are quite small and the nerve fibers and related cells are more or less transparent. Furthermore, as Figure 11.13 points

out, the nerve cells of the fovea are arranged in a spokelike fashion so that they do not interfere with the incoming light rays.

Two major kinds of connections, as illustrated in Figure 11.10, exist between photoreceptors and the nerve fibers leading to the brain. Groups of rods (sometimes with cones) and cones (sometimes singly) connect with intermediate neurons, **bipolar cells** (not labeled in the figure but are in the *inner nuclear layer*), which in turn connect to **ganglion cells,** whose connections are the optic nerve fibers. The total number of bipolar and ganglion cells that is present in the periphery of the retina is much less than the number of rods. It follows that each bipolar and ganglion cell receives the input from a large number of rods. In the extreme peripheral regions of the retina, as many as several hundred rods may be connected to one bipolar cell. In contrast, in the cone-rich area of the retina, the fovea, the number of cones more or less matches the number of intermediate neurons. Thus, the most direct transmission between the retina and the brain is with cones at the fovea. However, it would be an oversimplification to assume that foveal cones are independently or directly linked to cortical cells. There are many lateral connections between foveal cones at the level of the ganglia. In general, though, cones have fewer intermediate connections than do rods.

There is some functional significance of the neural connections of rods and cones to the intermediate ganglion cells. The fact that a number of rods share a common ganglion cell means that there is a convergence or *pooling* of receptor information from an appreciable part of the retina at a single ganglion cell. This pooling or spatial summation of stimulation results in an increase in the likelihood of the common ganglion cell reaching the energy level necessary to fire (see Figure 11.14; note also that single rods require slightly less energy for activation than do single cones). This is an aid to **sensitivity,** to perceiving in low levels of illumination. Of course, the pooling of stimulus information from a number of rods at the ganglia detracts from the discrete information given by any single rod; hence, image resolution or **acuity** is correspondingly coarse. In contrast

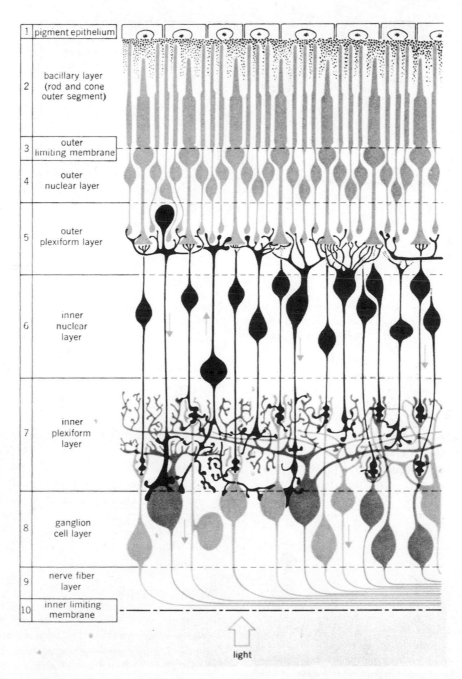

1	pigment epithelium
2	bacillary layer (rod and cone outer segment)
3	outer limiting membrane
4	outer nuclear layer
5	outer plexiform layer
6	inner nuclear layer
7	inner plexiform layer
8	ganglion cell layer
9	nerve fiber layer
10	inner limiting membrane

light

FIGURE 11.10.   Schematic diagram of the neural structures and interconnections of the vertebrate retina. Notice that the photoreceptors do not face the light but point toward the choroid layer (not shown). (From J.R. Mc-Clintic, *Basic Anatomy and Physiology of the Human Body*, John Wiley, New York, 1975, p. 303. Reprinted by permission of the publisher.)

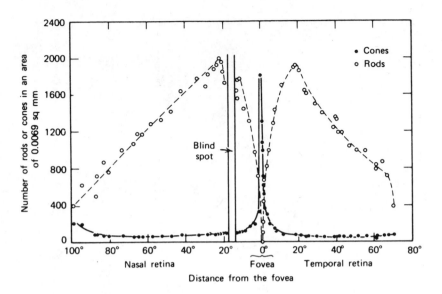

FIGURE 11.11.   Approximate distribution of rods and cones throughout the retina. The number of receptors per unit area from the fovea to the extreme periphery has been plotted. Cones are represented by solid, rods by open, circles. (From Chapanis, 1949, p. 7.)

to the neural connections of rods, if only one or a very few receptors are connected to a single ganglion cell, which is the case for foveal cones, the photoreceptors are then capable of contributing more independent information, such as that required for resolving stimulus patterns. Accordingly, a foveal cone, owing to its neural connection, is capable of relaying more information about its location of stimulation than is a rod. In short, at the fovea there is a heavy concentration of cones, hence a greater number of independently stimulated ganglia and nerve fibers and a greater capacity for differentiating an image. Indeed, when we look directly at a target we position our eyes so that the target image falls on the foveal cones. The result, of course, is increased acuity but at a sacrifice to sensitivity. Figure 11.14 points this out schematically. (We will return to the topic of acuity in the next chapter.)

EYEBALL MOBILITY

Human eyes are set in orbits and are capable of rotating within the skull. The eyes are moved about by three pairs of oculomotor muscles, as illustrated in Figure 11.15. Eyeball mobility is a useful mechanism for it allows a person to track moving objects by moving the eyes smoothly without turning the head or body. The eyes of many lower organisms are more rigidly attached to neighboring tissue. For example,

FIGURE 11.12.   The blind spot. Close the left eye and fixate the right eye on the cross. Slowly move the page back and forth from the eye between 5 and 15 in. (12.6 to 38 cm) until the position is reached at which the spot disappears. The spot is then falling on the region of the retina where the nerve fibers group together and leave the eye. There are no rods or cones at this region.

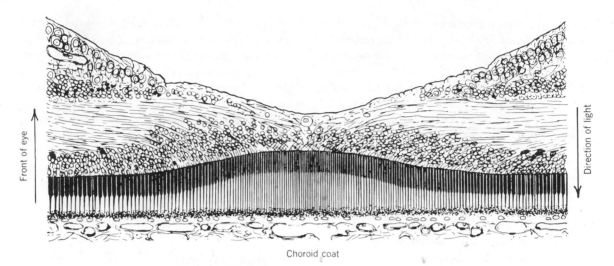

FIGURE 11.13.   Cross section of the central fovea of the human retina. The centermost region contains only cones, which are thin, long, and tightly grouped. Notice the spoke-like arrangement of the blood vessels and nerve fibers at the center region. This reduces the inter-ference and distortion of the incoming light rays. (From S. Polyak, *The Vertebrate Visual System*, University of Chicago Press, 1957, p. 276. Reprinted by permission of the publisher.)

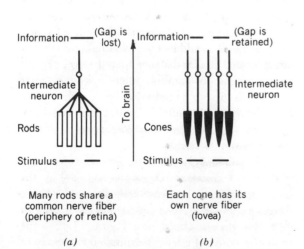

FIGURE 11.14.   Highly simplified schematic diagram of neural connections of rods and cones to intermediate neurons. In (*a*) the stimulation from a number of rods converge on a single neuron. Thus sensitivity is high but acuity is low and information of the gap in the stimulus line is lost. In (*b*) there is no convergence of cone stimulation, and acuity is high.

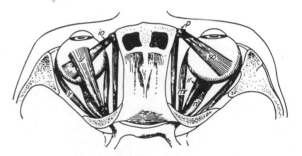

FIGURE 11.15.   Oculomotor muscles of human as seen from above in a dissected head. The eyeball is maintained in its orbit by six muscles that move it and enable it to direct the gaze smoothly to any position. The muscle labels are as follows: io—inferior oblique; ir—inferior rectus; lr—lateral rectus; mr—medial rectus; so—superior oblique; sr—superior rectus. On the left, a portion of the superior oblique has been cut away to reveal the inferior oblique; on the right, the superior rectus has been removed to permit a view of the inferior rectus under the optic nerve (n). Note that each oblique muscle operates by means of a tendon passing through a pulley hole (p) in the side of the bony orbit. (From G.L. Walls, *The Vertebrate Eye and Its Adaptive Radiations*, Hafner, New York, 1963, p. 37.)

the eyes of certain crustacea are rigid parts of the head, fixed and immobile. Ocular movements of these organisms must necessarily involve movement of the head or the entire body, thereby restricting the ability to track moving targets. Eye movement will be the topic of a separate section in the next chapter.

PLACEMENT OF THE EYES AND THE VISUAL FIELD

Vertebrates have either two laterally directed eyes at the sides of the head or two frontally directed eyes (see Figure 11.16). Laterally directed eyes have two relatively separate fields of vision, a small degree of binocular overlap (the area seen by both eyes), and a relatively large total view. Laterally directed eyes are an obvious anatomical adaptation, especially for prey animals that must maintain continual vigilance against predators. The panoramic vision of the rabbit, one of the most defenseless of mammals, is an example of this. In contrast, with frontally directed eyes, typical of predators, both foveae register essentially the same pattern of visual information. This

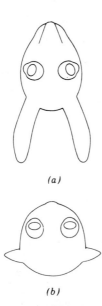

(a)

(b)

FIGURE 11.16. (*a*) Laterally directed eyes of the rabbit, typical of prey animals. Each eye looks in a different direction. (*b*) Frontally directed eyes of the cat, typical of predatory animals. Both eyes look in the same direction.

creates a relatively narrow total visual field, but it also produces a greater degree of binocular overlap. Binocular overlap enhances the perception of depth and distance and provides for an accurate means of locating objects in space, two factors that are especially important to predatory animals and animals like primates, that require acute depth perception to perform manipulative skills with their hands such as holding and grasping, and enabling leaping. Thus, there is a trade-off between frontal and lateral viewing, the style adopted depending on the survival needs of the species.

ACCOMMODATION

As light enters the eyeball, it is initially refracted or bent by the cornea. It is further refracted by the lens in a dynamic automatic process termed **accommodation.** Accommodation refers to the variable refractive capacity of the lens, that is, the change in the shape of the lens necessary to bring an image into sharp focus on the retina. When fixating on a near target, the lens refracts differently than when fixating on a far one. It should be noted that light rays from a target located at a far distance from the eye, say, 20 ft, are essentially parallel, whereas as the target approaches the eye its light rays become divergent. Accordingly in the latter condition the lens must converge or refract the divergent light rays in order to focus them on the retina.

The refractive power of the eye is expressed in units called **diopters** (D) which is based on the lens's focal length: the **focal length** of a lens is the distance between the lens and a sharp image it forms of a very distant object (see Figure 11.17). The refractive power of a lens is expressed as the reciprocal of its focal length (in meters). Thus, lenses whose focal lengths are $1/10$ meter, $1/4$ meter, or 5 meters have the refractive or dioptric power of $10\,D$, $4\,D$, and $0.2\,D$, respectively. Relatedly, the higher the dioptric power of the lens, the closer an object can be to the eye and produce a clear image. The total refractive power of the normal adult eye is approxi-

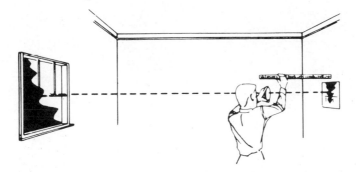

FIGURE 11.17.   Measuring focal length. The focal length of a lens is the distance between the lens and the sharp image it forms of a distant object. In the figure, the lens has been moved back and forth until the image of the tree is in sharp focus on the wall. The distance between the lens and the wall is the focal length of the lens. (From Cornsweet, 1970, p. 38. Reprinted by permission of the author and publisher.)

mately 66 *D* with the cornea contributing about twice as much refractive power as the lens.

Accommodation is not found in all levels of vertebrates, and it may differ somewhat for different animals. In general, there are two different accommodative techniques used by vertebrates for achieving a focused image—moving the lens in relation to the retina, or changing the curvature of the lens. The former technique is similar to the focusing mechanisms employed in the camera. The camera lens moves forward for focusing on a nearby target and moves backward for focusing on a distant target. This accommodative technique involving movement of the lens is used by fish, for example. The second technique of accommodation, used by higher species, is to change the curvature of the lens—flattening the lens for focusing on distant targets and thickening it when focusing on nearby ones. This change in lens shape is related to relaxing or contracting the ciliary muscle, which is attached to the zonal fibers or ligaments that suspend the lens in place (see Figures 11.9 and 11.18).

For the human the accommodative ability changes during infancy. The newborn human infant, less than one month of age, can focus only on targets at one distance, whose median value is 19 cm (about 7.5 in.; Haynes, White, & Held, 1965). Images of targets nearer or farther away are proportionately blurred. However, during the second month of in-fancy the accommodative system begins to respond adaptively to changes in target distance and approximates adult performance at nine weeks (Banks, 1980).

Accommodation has limits. As an object is brought toward the face, the ciliary muscle undergoes contraction, and the curvature of the lens increases, but when it cannot contract further, the object goes out of focus. If we are forced to maintain continued focus on near objects, say, 6 in. (15.2 cm) or less, the ciliary muscle soon fatigues and eye strain sets in. Generally, we must resort to optical devices to enable prolonged examination of objects that are located quite close to the eye.

As a target is gradually brought close to the eye, a distance is reached at which even the strongest contraction of the ciliary muscle will not produce a distinct image of the target. This is because the resultant light rays are so divergent that, even with full acommodation, the lens system cannot bring them to a focus on the retina. The nearest distance at which a target can be seen clearly, with full accommodation, is called the **near point.**

REFRACTIVE ERRORS

Accommodation of the human eye deteriorates with age and a form of **refractive error** called **presbyo-**

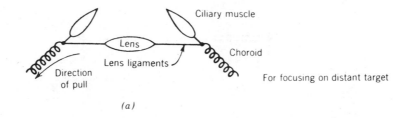

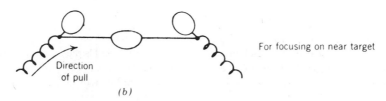

FIGURE 11.18.   Changes occurring during accommodation. (*a*) Ciliary muscle is relaxed for focusing on distant target. Elastic pull of choroid places tension on lens ligaments, flattening lens. (*b*) Ciliary muscle contracted

for focusing on close target. Tension is removed from lens ligaments, choroid is stretched, and the lens rounds up of its own elasticity. (From Crouch & McClintic, 1971, p. 584.)

pia occurs. With increasing age the elasticity of the lens progressively diminishes so that it becomes more difficult for the ciliary muscle to change the

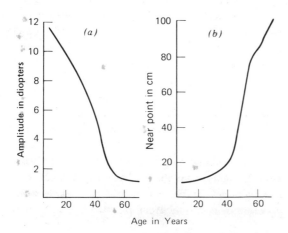

FIGURE 11.19.   Decrease in dioptric power (*a*) and increase in distance to near point of vision with age (*b*). (From T. C. Ruch, et al., *Neurophysiology*, W. B. Saunders Company, Philadelphia, 1965, p. 406. Reprinted by permission of the publisher.)

lens's curvature to accommodate or converge the divergent light rays from near objects. One result of presbyopia is that the dioptric power decreases and the near point increases with the aging process (see Figure 11.19). Hence, older persons with uncorrected lenses must often hold reading material abnormally far from their face in order to focus adequately.

When the ciliary muscle is relaxed an optically normal or **emmetropic eye** forms an image of a distant target on the retina (Figure 11.20*a*). As the distance between target and eye is reduced, the light rays diverge; hence the lens must accommodate or bulge, otherwise the focal plane of the image will be behind the retina, resulting in a blurred retinal image. In this instance, the lack of proper convergence is called **hypermetropia,** or **hyperopia** or farsightedness (see Figure 11.20*b*). This occurs because the lens is too weak or the eyeball is too short for the refractive capacity of the lens. Though the eye can focus the parallel light rays of a distant target, it cannot focus accurately on the divergent light rays of nearby targets. To correct for hypermetropia a converging (convex) lens must be worn to increase the refraction of the lens.

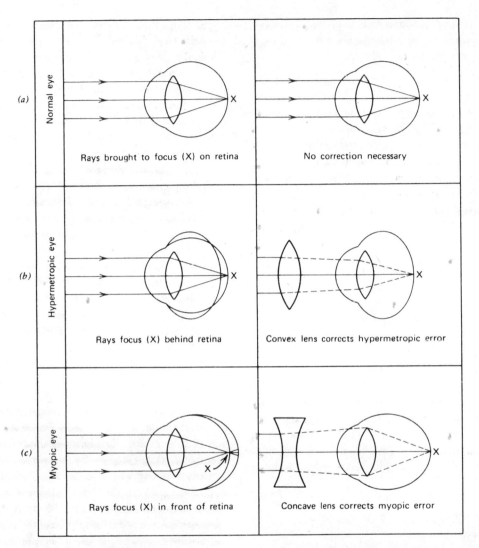

FIGURE 11.20. Diagram of the three refractive states of the eye. (*a*) Emmetropic (normal); (*b*) Hypermetropic (farsighted); (*c*) myopic (nearsighted). The diagram indicates the kind of lens required to bring the light rays to a focus on the retina. (From J.R. McClintic, *Basic Anatomy and Physiology of the Human Body*, John Wiley, New York, 1975, p. 302. Reprinted by permission of the publisher.)

MYOPIA

Another refractive error, shown in Figure 11.20c, is called **myopia** or nearsightedness. Myopia is a highly prevalent refractive disorder of the lens, affecting approximately 15 to 20% of the adult population. In myopia the parallel light rays of a distant object are brought to a focus in front of the retina because the eyeball is too long for the refractive capability of the lens. (Alternatively, the cornea and lens may provide an abnormal degree of refraction.) Thus, the myopic eye can focus on near targets well because their light rays are divergent but cannot focus accurately the parallel light rays of distant ones. To correct for myopia a diverging (concave) lens is required to diminish the refraction and focus the image on the retina.

Development of Myopia A note of interest concerns research bearing on the origin of myopia. Although generally recognized to be due primarily to heredity, Young (1970) has indicated that myopia may be partly due to a substantial amount of near viewing during childhood, the kind that requires continuous accommodation (e.g., as in learning to read). That is, a causal relationship may exist between excessive near vision and myopia (see Curtin, 1970; Wiesel & Raviola, 1986). This notion is sometimes referred to as the **near-work** or **use-abuse theory** (e.g., Angle & Wissman, 1980; Owens & Wolf-Kelly, 1987). Evidence for an experiential or environmental origin of myopia comes from research with animals. In one study almost 70% of a group of kittens deprived of distance vision (i.e., restricted to near vision), developed myopia, whereas about 90% of a comparison group that had ample experience with distance vision were hypermetropic (Rose, Yinon, & Belkin, 1974). Similar evidence is found with birds. Chicks whose vision was restricted to the frontal field of view (by means of special occluders, see Figure 11.21) from hatching until 4 to 7 weeks, became extremely myopic, whereas the vision of chicks restricted to a lateral

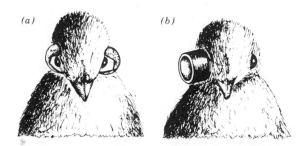

(a)   *(b)*

FIGURE 11.21. Occluding devices used to restrict the visual fields (fitted upon hatching). (*a*) Restriction to frontal vision. (*b*) Restriction to lateral vision. It was assumed that animals restricted to frontal vision experienced more close viewing than animals restricted to lateral vision. (Photo courtesy of J. Wallman.)

visual field did not differ from the vision of normal animals (see Wallman et al., 1987; Schaeffel, Glasser & Howland, 1988). Similar myopic effects were observed with primates (Macaque monkeys); refractive errors were produced experimentally by restricting and degrading form vision from birth to one year (by suturing the eyes shut; Raviola & Wiesel, 1985; Wiesel & Raviola, 1986). While no clear statement yet emerges as to the etiology of myopia, research does demonstrate that specific visual exposure, especially restricted form vision, blurred vision, and excessive near viewing as in long periods of reading, may contribute to or effect refractive errors and perhaps the structure of the eye (Wiesel & Raviola, 1986; Wallman et al., 1987). Relatedly, there are some proposals and preliminary evidence with humans suggesting that specific and controlled visual experience (i.e., by way of behavior modification) may reduce certain forms of myopia (Rosen, Schiffman, & Cohen, 1984; Rosen, Schiffman, & Myers, 1984).

LENS ABERRATIONS

Other forms of refractive errors, though not related to accommodation, are called *lens aberrations*. As Figure 11.22*a* shows, light rays passing through the peripheral parts of a spherical lens are refracted more strongly and brought to a focus at a closer plane than those rays passing through the central regions, a phenomenon called **spherical aberration.** That is, the rays from the marginal portion of the lens meet at a point nearer the lens than do the inner rays. Uncorrected, this can result in a blurred image. However, there are a number of corneal and lens mechanisms that serve in part to compensate for spherical aberration. Furthermore, under moderately good lighting conditions, the pupil constricts to limit the rays of light to the central part of the lens. A second form of lens aberration, called **chromatic aberration,** shown in Figure 11.22*b*, is due to the fact that lenses made of a single material refract rays of short wavelengths more strongly than those of longer wavelengths. Thus blue, for example, is brought to a shorter focus than red. However, this is

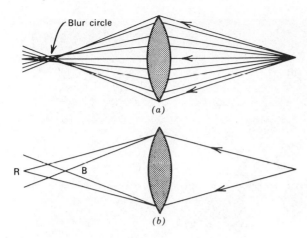

FIGURE 11.22. (*a*) Schematic of spherical aberration. The light rays that pass through the edge of a spherical lens are brought to a shorter focus than those that pass through the center. The result is that the image formed of a point is a blur circle. (*b*) Schematic of chromatic aberration. When light of various wavelengths is refracted by a lens made of a single material the light of shorter wavelengths is refracted more than that of longer wavelengths, for example, blue (B) is brought to a shorter focus than red (R). The result is that the image formed of a white point is a chromatic blur circle.

rarely a problem, since some of the very short wavelengths, where the chromatic error is greatest, are filtered out by the lens's yellow pigmentation acting as a color filter. (Short wavelengths are also filtered out or absorbed by the yellow pigment of the macula lutea.) About 8% of the visible spectrum is also absorbed by the lens.

ASTIGMATISM

Ideally the refractive surfaces of the cornea and the lens are spherical and symmetrical with the vertical and horizontal curvatures equalized. When the corneal surface is not spherical and symmetrical, an error of refraction called **astigmatism** occurs (see Figures 11.23*a,b*). Almost all eyes have some degree of astigmatism since it is unlikely that the cornea is perfectly shaped. Basically the astigmatic surface produces different degrees of curvature for the verti-

cal and horizontal orientations. In most instances of astigmatism the corneal surface is flatter from side to side than it is vertically, resulting in the blurring and distortion of parts of images. The correction for astigmatism is to employ a lens that equalizes the refraction in the orientations of least and greatest curvature.

PUPIL MOBILITY

The variable pupil, controlled by the iris, is ordinarily recognized as having two reflexive functions. It maintains an optimal intensity of light entering the eye. Too little light will not sufficiently excite the photoreceptors in the retina, and too much light will render them inefficient or perhaps injure them. When there is little available light, the pupil opens wide—dilates. When there is much light, the pupil closes down or constricts. A second function of the pupil's mobility is to restrict the incoming light mainly to the central part of the lens, the part that provides the best focus. As we noted with spherical aberration, the constriction of the pupil tends to keep out light that strikes the periphery of the lens, such light as would be focused at a different plane from

FIGURE 11.23*a*. Astigmatism chart. To an astigmatic viewer, some sets of lines will appear blurred relative to others.

FIGURE 11.23*b*.   Astigmatism and OP Art. Among the many striking perceptual effects in the painting reproduced here, for example, pulsating "squares," is the obvious one that the clarity of different groups of lines significantly vary. Wade's (1979) survey of the perceptual effects in geometric art suggests that such effects may derive from common forms of astigmatism. It has been observed that during fixation, lens curvature undergoes continual, small fluctuations which are not uniform over the lens surface. It follows that the effects may reduce in part to small, transient astigmatic variations. Since some slight astigmatism, associated with vertical and horizontal orientations, is quite common, some of the effects are more pronounced when the figure's contours are also vertical and horizontal, rather than oblique (i.e., tilt the figure 45°). (Source: Square of Three, by Reginald Neal; reproduction courtesy of the State Museum of New Jersey, Trenton, New Jersey.)

that coming through the center of the lens. A small pupil also enhances acuity by keeping out extraneous light. We perform this function when squinting in the presence of glare, thereby cutting down the light that enters the eye. The same effect may be achieved by viewing through a long tube, a procedure that yields somewhat sharper images than can be obtained with the naked eye. Of course, the restriction of peripheral light cannot occur when lighting is poor and a maximum opening or dilation is required. Thus, acuity or image resolution is greatest when the available light is bright and the pupil is appropriately constricted.

PUPILLOMETRY

The amount of available light is not the only determiner of pupillary variation. Heinrich in 1896 (see Bakan, 1967) and more recently Hess (e.g., 1965) have noted that the size of the pupil varies in response to strong emotional states, certain forms of ongoing mental activity and, in general, serves as a measure of arousal. The study of such psychological factors affecting the pupillary response is called **pupillometry** (see Hess, 1975a; Janisse, 1977). Hess (1965; Hess & Polt, 1960, 1966) demonstrated that while a subject is viewing visual stimuli, pupil size may serve as an indication of the interest value of the content of the stimuli. For example, the pupils of males dilated in reaction to viewing pictures of female pinups, and they constricted slightly to male pinups. In contrast, the pupils of female subjects constricted to the pictures of female pinups but dilated to the male pinups. Correlated attitude and emotional factors with pupillary reactions have also been observed for such diverse stimuli as foods (Hess & Polt, 1966) and political figures (Barlow, 1969).

Mental activity also produces changes in pupil size. Hess and Polt (1964) had subjects solve a graded series of verbally presented multiplication problems. Typically, the size of the pupils of each subject showed a gradual increase beginning with the presentation of the problem and reaching maximum diameter immediately before the subject's verbal answer was given. In addition the more difficult the problem, the greater was the increase in pupil size. The notion that pupil size reflects mental effort has generally been supported (e.g., Beatty & Wagoner, 1978).

Also Hess (1975a, b) has proposed that pupil size plays a major role in nonverbal communication. For example, in social interactions large (dilated) pupils tend to be associated with and communicate positive attributes such as friendliness and attractiveness.

EYEBLINKS

Eyeblinks, under normal conditions of vision, occur every few seconds. During the blink duration (300–400 msec), virtually all visual information to the eye is interrupted. However, despite this break in the flow of light stimuli for the visual process, perception is relatively unaffected: generally, the effect of the blink is scarcely noticed. This is all the more surprising in that if, say, room lighting were interrupted momentarily for even a briefer interval than produced by a typical eyeblink, the visual environment would appear dark.

An explanation of why the perceptual effect of an eye blink is so small when compared with the actual change it produces on the retina is based on the finding that a neural mechanism in the brain generates an inhibitory signal that accompanies the eyeblink. This inhibitory signal acts as a visual suppressor and produces a decrease in sensitivity for visual stimuli during the duration of the blink (Riggs, Volkmann, & Moore, 1981). Thus, a neural inhibitory mechanism accompanying the eyeblink diminishes its effects and thereby contributes to the stability and "continuity of vision."

EYE AND BRAIN

The optical and neural structures mediating vision have evolved together; hence, it is important to our understanding of vision to describe some of the salient characteristics and mechanisms linking the eye to the brain. There is a series of complex connections in the pathway between the retina and the visual area of the brain—the **occipital lobe.** A schematic diagram of the human visual system is shown in Figure 11.24. The optic nerves leave the

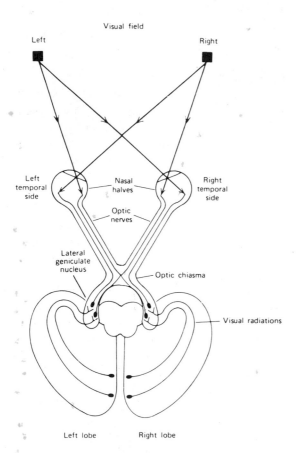

FIGURE 11.24. Highly simplified schematic diagram of the human visual system showing the projection of the visual fields through the system. Observe that fibers originating in the inner or nasal halves of the retinae intercross at the optic chiasma, whereas fibers originating in the outer or temporal halves of the retinae do not cross. Observe also that the right half of the visual field projects on the left half of each retina (and to the left lobe of the brain). Similarly, the left half of the visual field projects on the right half of each retina (and to the right lobe).

eye and converge at the **optic chiasma.** At the chiasma, fibers from the inner or *nasal* half of each retina cross whereas those from the outside or *temporal* half of each retina do not. After this partial crossing, the nerve fibers, or tracts, make connections at several relay stations. The most important is the **lateral geniculate nucleus (lgn),** a cluster of neurons that is the relay center for vision in the thalamus. **Visual radiations** from the lateral geniculate nucleus extend to the occipital lobes of the cerebral cortex; some fibers also connect to vision areas in the midbrain that are involved with ocular reflexes.

As shown in Figure 11.24, light from the right visual field stimulates the left half of each retina (i.e., the temporal and nasal halves of the left and right eyes, respectively) and light from the left visual field stimulates the right half of each retina (the nasal and temporal halves of the left and right eyes, respectively). It follows that stimulation of the left half of each retina activates the left occipital lobe. Similarly, stimulation of the right half of each retina activates the right visual occipital lobe. This means the right visual field is represented on the left side of the brain and the left visual field on the right side of the brain. Thus, only half of the total visual field is projected on each occipital lobe.

Our discussion of the partial crossing of optic fibers at the chiasma holds only for mammals. According to Walls (1963), for most vertebrates below mammals (e.g., fish and birds) all the optic nerve fibers from each eye cross over at the chiasma to form optic tracts on the opposite side. Thus, each eye is connected only with the opposite half of the brain. For mammals the relative amount of uncrossed fibers is closely proportional to the degree of frontal direction to the eyes. Walls (1963) writes that about 12 to 16% of the fibers remain uncrossed in the horse, 20% in the rat and opossum, 25% in the dog, one-third in the cat, and it reaches a maximum of one-half in higher primates.

RECEPTIVE FIELDS

As we have noted, there are numerous complex interconnections between the photoreceptors of the retina and the cortical cells of the visual area of the brain. A direct means of studying the relationship between the retina and various loci of the visual system is by recording the electrical responses of single nerve cells to light patterns. Basically a microelectrode is implanted, ideally, in a single cell of the ganglia, some relay station, or in the visual area of the cortex of an experimental animal. The animal is then shown an assortment of stimuli varying in size, orientation, pattern, etc., each projecting over a different region of the retina, until one of the stimuli produces a change in electrical activity in the cell or neuron (see Figure 11.25). The result is that an area of the retina called a **receptive field** is mapped out for which the presentation of a stimulus of sufficient intensity or quality will alter the firing activity of a sensory cell (recall that we encountered the notion of receptive fields for the skin in Chapter 7). In short, the receptive field for a given receptor cell is that region of the retina upon which appropriate stimulation excites or inhibits the cell's firing pattern. Employing such a technique it has been possible to map the receptive fields for various locations of the visual system.

Consider the receptive fields for ganglion cells. Typically ganglion cells fire at fairly steady rates in the absence of any light stimulation (20 to 30 times

per second). In one pioneering investigation a microelectrode was inserted in a ganglion cell of a cat (Kuffler, 1953). When a tiny spot of light was then projected into the cat's eye and was moved over various regions of the retina, the steady state was observed to vary. That the ganglion cell's rate of discharge was maximally altered by shining a small spot of light on a small circular retinal area indicates that the cell's receptive field is small and approximately circular.

It is important to note that as Figure 11.26 illustrates, the light stimulus alters the ganglion cell's discharge rate in different ways, depending on the part of the receptive field that is stimulated. In one type of ganglion cell, the receptive field consists of a small circular "on" area, in which the impulse rate of the cell increases at the onset of the light. Light stimulation to a surrounding peripheral "off" zone inhibits the ganglion cell's neural activity, and the cell shows a burst of impulses when the light stimulus is removed. Thus, these cells have concentric, **center-surround receptive fields.**

Another type of ganglion cell, also with a center-surround, antagonistic organization, has a reversed form of receptive field, consisting of an inhibitory "off" center and an excitatory "on" periphery. When the center of this cell's receptive field is illuminated,

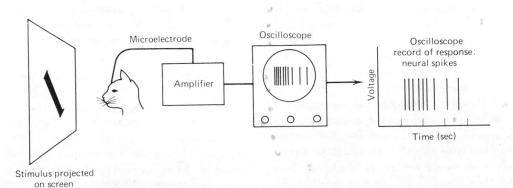

FIGURE 11.25.   Experimental arrangement for mapping and recording receptive fields. An electrode is inserted into a cell at some point in the visual system of the experimental animal. Various light stimuli are projected on a screen in front of the animal's eyes. The eyes are generally paralyzed so that particular locations on the screen project to particular locations on the animal's retina. The impulse activity of an individual cell in response to the stimuli (shown in the oscilloscope record) indicates the characteristics of that cell's receptive field.

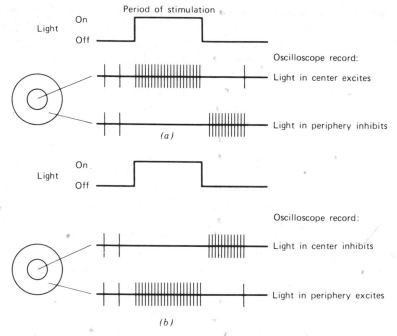

FIGURE 11.26. (*a*) Oscilloscope record shows strong firing by an "on" center type of ganglion cell when a circular spot of light strikes the field's center. If the spot hits an "off" (or surround) area, the firing is suppressed until the light goes off. This cell has a center-surround receptive field. (*b*) Oscilloscope record for ganglion cell with an "off" center and excitatory "on" periphery. If the light strikes the field's center, the discharge rate is suppressed, but there is a strong discharge when the light is terminated.

the background discharge rate of the ganglion cell is suppressed. However, when the illumination of the "off" center is terminated, there is a vigorous rebound discharge. Light striking only an "on" region produces a strong excitatory response. The more "on" area thus stimulated, the more vigorous the response. However, "on" and "off" regions are mutually antagonistic: if one spot of light is shone on an "on" area and a second spot on its adjacent "off" area, the two effects tend to neutralize each other, resulting in very weak "on" or "off" responses. Thus, diffusely lighting up the whole retina, thereby simultaneously affecting receptors throughout the retina, does not affect a single ganglion cell as much as does a small spot of light precisely covering its receptive field center. In summary, ganglion cells of the cat's retina have antagonistic center-surround receptive fields, and their primary function is reacting to a comparison between the illumination of a small concentric region and its immediate surround.

RECEPTIVE FIELDS FOR THE VISUAL CORTEX

The receptive fields for the lateral geniculate nucleus, the major relay center for vision in the thalamus introduced earlier, are similar to those of the retina and its ganglion cells, that is, such cells have an on-center and off-surround, or the reverse. However, as receptive fields are plotted for cells lying closer to the visual cortex, the optic array necessary for excitation becomes finer and more precise. Indeed, paralleling the increase in anatomical complexity upon ascending from the retinal to the cortical cells, there appears to be an increase in the complexity of requirements needed for cells to respond. The impressive research of David Hubel and Torsten Wiesel (Nobel laureates for physiology, 1981) on the functioning of the mammalian visual brain is relevant here (e.g., Hubel & Wiesel, 1959, 1962, 1979; Hubel, 1982). Much of their research concerns plotting the receptive fields of the primary visual cortex (also termed the striate cortex or Brodmann's area 17, located in the occipital lobe of the brain) that receives the primary connections from the lateral geniculate nucleus. They have reported that instead of having circular receptive fields with concentric "on" and "off" regions, as in the case of retinal ganglion cells, the neurons of the visual cortex of the cat's brain (and probably most mammals including humans) possess receptive fields of a very different character.

Effective stimuli for the receptive fields for neurons of the visual cortex have linear properties; that is, they are comprised of lines, bars, and various rectangular segments with definite edges. Some cortical neurons possess extremely small receptive fields and some possess relatively large receptive fields, especially for the peripheral parts of the retina (Hubel & Wiesel, 1962). Some cells have comparatively simple receptive fields, in that an optimum cortical response will occur from a linear light stimulus, such as a narrow slit or a bar of light (e.g., a dark bar against a light background or the reverse) or an edge. The receptive fields of these cortical cells also require that the stimulus be in certain orientation or particular location (see Figure 11.27). Hubel and Wiesel called the cells that respond to such simple but selective environmental features, **simple cells.**

In addition, there are cortical cells called **complex cells.** Like simple cells, complex cells are orientation-specific, that is, they react maximally to stimuli that are in a particular orientation. A complex cell also reacts to a precise and distinct stimulus feature, but it may occur within a relatively large region of the visual field. That is, the exact location of the particular feature within the visual field is not critical. Accordingly, the retinal regions to which a complex cell responds may be considerably larger

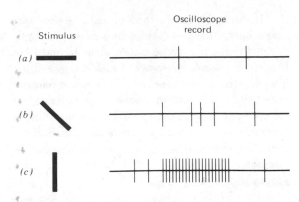

FIGURE 11.27.   Oscilloscope record of a simple cell whose maximal response is to a vertically oriented bar of light. Horizontal bar (*a*) produces no response; oblique bar (*b*) produces a weak response; vertical bar (*c*) produces a strong response.

than those for a simple cell. Also, a complex cell responds to movement of its particular feature within its receptive field area (see Figure 11.28), responding best to movement of the feature in a specific direction.

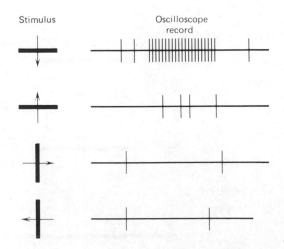

FIGURE 11.28.   Oscilloscope record of a complex cell sensitive to the direction of motion. This cell responds strongly only to downward stimulus motion. It responds weakly to upward motion, and does not respond at all to sideways motion.

Hubel and Wiesel also identified a third class of cortical cells that they labeled **hypercomplex** cells (located in the peristriate cortex, areas 18 and 19 of Brodmann, which receive and elaborate the input from the striate cortex, or area 17). These are similar to complex cells in that they have receptive fields that are optimally responsive to moving and specifically oriented stimuli including corners and angles. However, the distinguishing characteristic of a hypercomplex cell is that it responds best to stimuli of a particular length (see Figure 11.29). Thus, a hypercomplex cortical cell has a receptive field that will produce maximal cortical activity if the light stimulus is properly oriented, moves in a certain direction across the retina, and is of a limited length. Deviations from these requirements may yield weak responses or none at all in the cortical cell whose activity is being recorded.

Overall there appears to be a complex transformation of neural information at various levels in the visual system with apparently greater abstraction as information ascends into higher centers. Kandel (1981) summarizes it as follows:

At the lowest level of the system, at the level of the retinal ganglion and the lateral geniculate cells,

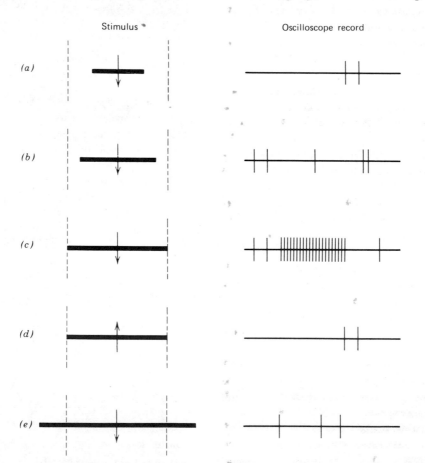

Stimulus   Oscilloscope record

FIGURE 11.29.   Oscilloscope record of a hypercomplex cell sensitive to direction and length of stimulus. Only a stimulus of a certain length and moving downward (c) yields a strong response. (The length of the receptive field is indicated by the distance bounded by the dashed vertical lines.)

neurons respond primarily to brightness contrast. As we move up the hierarchy to the simple and complex cells of the cortex, cells begin to respond to line segments and boundaries. The hypercomplex cells respond to changes in boundaries. Thus, as we progress up the system the stimulus requirements necessary to activate the cell become more complex. . . . At each level, each cell sees a greater perspective than at an earlier level, and its ability to abstract is increased. (p. 245)

There is much evidence that the complex cortical organization just described for the cat's visual system is similar to that of many higher species, for instance, primates (Hubel & Wiesel, 1968; Bridgeman, 1972), including the human (Thomas, 1970). For example, cortical cells (of the inferotemporal cortex, an area important for visual discrimination) of the Macaque monkey have been identified that are differentially sensitive to the size, shape, orientation, direction of movement, and color characteristics of the receptive field (Gross, Rocha-Miranda, & Bender, 1972). Moreover, there were some rather startling specific response characteristics. Gross et al. (1972) found one cell whose activity was triggered by the outline shape of a monkey's hand. Interestingly, fingers pointing downward elicited very little response compared to the outline hand with its fingers pointing upward or laterally; these latter orientations, of course, are the ones in which the monkey would ordinarily see its own hand. In addition neurons of the monkey's cortex have been identified that change their activity pattern more to profiles of monkey faces than to other stimuli (Desimone et al., 1984). As Figure 11.30 shows such neurons responded best to the monkey profiles and not to rear or front views or to stimuli such as a bottle brush. Additionally, altering or removing some of the elements of the profiles eliminated the response.

The possession of facial recognition neurons are not restricted to primates. Kendrick and Baldwin (1987) have observed neurons from the temporal cortex of a horned breed of sheep (while the sheep were conscious) that responded preferentially to life-size projections of various faces, ranging from

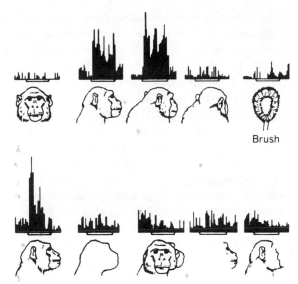

Brush

FIGURE 11.30. Activity of neurons of monkey inferotemporal cortex to profiles. Shown are some of the stimulus figures presented and a graphic rendering of the activity pattern of certain neurons of the monkeys' cortex. The graphs above each figure give the number of action potentials or pulselike electrical signals discharged by the neurons (vertical axis) over time (horizontal axis). The time during which each stimulus was presented is represented by the line under each graph. The figure shows that the neurons responded best to the monkey profiles and not to rear or front views or to a stimulus such as a brush. Moreover altering or removing some of the components of the profiles eliminated the response. (From R. Desimone et al., *Journal of Neuroscience*, 4, 1984, p. 2159. Reprinted by permission of the Society for Neuroscience.)

those of other sheep to other animals, including human faces. They report that neurons selectively responsive to facial stimuli could be linked to factors relevant to social interaction. For example, they found groups of neurons selectively responsive to the presence and size of horns on sheep faces, "possibly allowing for a rapid estimation of the perceived animal's sex or position in the dominance hierarchy" (p. 450).

We note here that the cortical organization we have outlined is not typical of the visual systems of many lower species. Animals possessing a comparatively primitive visual cortex (e.g., the rabbit and ground squirrel) or lacking it completely (e.g., the pigeon and frog) usually have highly integrative mechanisms in the retina (Michael, 1969).

Lettvin and his colleagues (1959) have published an important, now classic neurophysiological analysis of the frog's vision that identifies several distinct kinds of pattern or form detectors in the retina of the frog. By recording the neural activity of single fibers in the frog's optic nerve in response to different visual stimuli, several distinct types of fibers have been identified, each type concerned with a different sort of pattern or visual event. There were fibers that reacted to sharp edges and borders, movement of edges, and general dimming or darkening of illumination. Most interesting were the "bug perceivers," so called by the authors because these were nerve fibers that responded best to small dark objects intermittently moving across the visual field. In the authors' words:

> Such a fiber responds best when a dark object, smaller than a receptive field, enters that field, stops, and moves about intermittently thereafter. The response is not affected if the lighting changes or if the background (say a picture of grass and flowers) is moving, and is not there if only the background, moving or still, is in the field. Could one better describe a system for detecting an accessible bug? (p. 1951).

The functional value of bug perceivers to the frog, primarily an insect eater, is obvious. Thus the frog, possessing a primitive brain, has a highly complex retina that enables much of the processing, organizing, and interpretation of visual stimuli to occur peripherally. It appears that whether visual information is processed at the retina or in the brain depends on the evolutionary development of the species.

SUMMARY

This chapter served as the introduction to the nature of the visual stimulus, light or radiant electromag-

netic energy. Color or hue is the psychological correlate to the wavelength of light, and brightness is the psychological correlate to the physical intensity or the amount of radiant energy. The specification and measurement of the intensity dimension of light was examined in terms of the radiant energy falling on a surface—incident light or illuminance, and the intensity of a light reaching the eye from a surface —reflected light or luminance.

The basic anatomical structures of the eye were outlined and the functioning of certain parts were elaborated. The major parts given were the cornea, the iris and pupil, the lens, and their supporting structures. The retina and its neural connections and photoreceptors, the rods and cones, were identified and described. The functional significance of the neural connections of rods and cones for effecting sensitivity and acuity, respectively, was examined.

Some evolutionary trends in the placement of the eyes and binocular overlap were given. It was noted that there is a tendency for prey animals to possess laterally directed eyes resulting in a larger total visual field and less binocular overlap than is found in predatory animals or animals with a high degree of manipulative skill, such as primates.

The dynamic processes of pupil mobility, accommodation, and eyeblinks were described. Some errors of lens refraction were specified: presbyopia, hypermetropia, myopia, spherical and chromatic aberration, and astigmatism. A discussion of the development of myopia concluded that specific forms of visual exposure, especially excessive near viewing in the young of the species, may contribute significantly to the promotion of myopia. This notion is referred to as the use-abuse or near-work theory.

Finally, the complex connections in the neural pathways between the retina and the visual projection area of the brain were examined, and the notion of receptive fields for various loci of the visual system, including the occipital lobe, were discussed. In brief, a receptive field for a given receptor cell or neuron is that region of the retina, which when appropriately stimulated, excites or inhibits the cell's firing pattern. A number of different kinds of receptive fields and cells were identified. For ganglion cells and those of the lateral geniculate nucleus, there are antagonistic center-surround receptive fields (i.e., on-center and off-surround, or the reverse). For cells lying closer to the visual cortex, more complex optic arrays are necessary for activation. In the visual cortex simple, complex, and hypercomplex cells have been identified; the stimulus requirements necessary to excite each type of cell becomes more complex.

KEY TERMS

Accommodation

Acuity

Astigmatism

Bipolar cells

Blind spot

Brightness

Center-surround receptive fields

Choroid

Chromatic aberration

Ciliary muscle

Complex cells

Compound eye

Cones

Cornea

Diopter

Emmetropic eye

Focal length

Fovea

Ganglion cells

Hypercomplex cells

Hypermetropia (hyperopia)

Illuminance

Intensity

Iris

Lateral geniculate nucleus (lgn)

Lens

Luminance

Macula lutea

Myopia

Nanometer (nm)

Near point

Near-work (use-abuse) theory

Occipital lobe

Ommatidia

Optic chiasma

Optic disk

Presbyopia

Pupil

Pupillometry

Radiant electromagnetic energy

Receptive fields

Refraction

Refractive errors

Retina

Rods

Sclera

Sensitivity

Simple cells

Spherical aberration

Tapetum

Visual capture

Visual radiations

Wavelength

Whytt's reflex

STUDY QUESTIONS

1. Discuss the importance of vision for gaining spatial information. Indicate the kinds of information that are received by the visual system.

2. Distinguish between intensity and brightness and between illuminance and luminance.

3. What structural components are common to various kinds of image-forming eyes? Consider in what way the eye is like a camera.

4. Describe the functioning of each major component of the anterior of the eye, including the cornea, iris (or pupil), and the lens. Explain how the change in pupil size is due to changes in light conditions.

5. Identify the retina and its major elements (rods and cones), describing the functional mechanisms served by the rods and cones. Distinguish between rods and cones with respect to location relative to the fovea and their relative distribution in the retina. Define visual sensitivity and acuity and explain how the different neural connections of the rods and cones may account for sensitivity and acuity, respectively.

6. What is the functional significance of frontal and lateral placement of the eyes in the head for different species? Indicate the benefit of each for meeting the survival needs of a given species.

7. Outline the mechanism of accommodation and indicate how it is measured. Indicate its limits and describe the accommodative or refractive errors of presbyopia, hypermetropia, and myopia. Consider the origin of myopia. Outline evidence that supports the notion that myopia may be caused in part by experiential factors.

8. Describe lens aberrations and astigmatism. What limiting or distortion effects do these conditions have on the refractive capacity of the lens to form a true or useful image?

9. Outline the sorts of lighting conditions and cognitive processing tasks that affect pupil mobility. What stimulus features appear to cause pupil constriction and dilation?

10. Why don't we momentarily "see" darkness every time we blink?

11. Outline the major connections between the eye and brain, indicating points of neural tract crossing, relay stages, and the optical projections to the brain. Explain how the right visual field is represented on the left side of the brain and the left visual field is represented on the right side of the brain. Indicate these connections by tracing the visual field projections to the retina and the retinal projections to the brain.

12. What are receptive fields for vision? How do these compare to the receptive fields for the skin, introduced in Chapter 7? Describe the mutually antagonistic activity of receptive fields. Identify and describe the different kinds of receptive fields.

13. How do receptive fields in the visual cortex differ from those of the retina and lateral geniculate nucleus?

14. Discuss the various sorts of effective stimuli for the receptive fields of the visual cortex and identify and describe the different kinds of cortical cells defined by receptive field excitation (e.g., simple, complex, hypercomplex). Indicate what kinds of environmental or retinal stimuli are necessary for their excitation.

12

FUNDAMENTAL VISUAL FUNCTIONS AND PHENOMENA

227

The emphasis in the previous chapter was on light and its relationship to the anatomy, structures, and basic mechanisms of the visual system. In this chapter we continue with these topics, but with a greater functional emphasis focusing on those variables, phenomena, and processes that contribute to the efficiency of the visual system. In particular we will discuss how the optic array is transformed from patterns of light intensities to detectable target stimuli on the retina and how processes of the retina and the eye mediate the perception of these patterns.

SCOTOPIC AND PHOTOPIC VISION

The distinctions between rods and cones with respect to anatomy, relative distribution, and neural connections were described in the preceding chapter. These distinctions are also reflected in their functional properties. Vision accomplished with cones has been termed **photopic** vision and that with rods **scotopic** vision. A summary of the anatomical and functional properties of photopic and scotopic vision is given in Table 12.1. The relative number of rods and cones found in many species shows certain ecological trends. Nocturnal animals have primarily rod retinae. Accordingly, nocturnal animals possess retinae that are best suited for night vision—a high degree of light sensitivity rather than acuity. In contrast, diurnal or day-active animals have either relatively rod-free retinae (e.g., birds) or, as in the case of some species such as primates, possess retinae with both rods and cones.

In general, photopic vision is poor in a dimly lit environment and scotopic vision dominates. Thus, when looking at a faint star at night, we are more successful when we do not fixate directly on the star. By doing this we ensure that the image falls on the sensitive rods in the peripheral regions of the retina rather than the cone-concentrated fovea.

ADAPTATION

One of the functional differences between rods and cones occurs in response to the general conditions of lighting. When moving abruptly from a well-lighted to a poorly lit or dark environment, we initially experience a condition of temporary blindness. However, gradually some of the visual features in the dim surroundings become perceptible and we are able to resolve details. The process of adjustment to a dimly illuminated environment is called **dark adaptation.**

Table 12.1

Properties of Photopic (Cone) and Scotopic (Rod) Vision of Human

	Photopic	Scotopic
Receptor	Cones (ca. 7 million)	Rods (ca. 125 million)
Retinal location	Concentration in fovea	Peripheral retina
Functional luminance level	Daylight	Night light
Peak wavelength	555 nm	505 nm
Color vision	Trichromatic	Achromatic
Dark adaptation	Rapid (ca. 5 min)	Slow (ca. 30 min)
Temporal resolution	Fast reacting	Slow reacting
Spatial resolution	High acuity, low sensitivity	Low acuity, high sensitivity

One means of measuring the course of dark adaptation is as follows: the subject is first exposed to a brightly illuminated surface for a short period of time. This reduces the subject's sensitivity and also provides a well-defined starting level from which the temporal course of dark adaptation can be traced. The subject is then exposed to a dark environment, and at various intervals over the course of time, measurements are made of the absolute threshold for a light stimulus. The stimulus is of a specific wavelength, duration, and energy level and strikes a precise area on the retina. The result is a curve relating the minimum energy required to reach threshold as a function of time in the dark. Figure 12.1 presents a typical dark adaptation curve. The figure shows the decrease in the threshold (or increase in sensitivity, plotted on the ordinate) with continued exposure to the darkened environment (shown on the abscissa).

The dark adaptation curve of Figure 12.1 is composed of two segments, reflecting the two different rates of adaptive change taking place. The upper branch is for cones and the lower one for rods. During the early stages of adaptation there is an initial rapid fall in threshold that quickly reaches a stable plateau; this reflects the increase in sensitivity for cones. The total gain in the sensitivity of cones is much less extensive than that of the rods and it occurs in about 5 minutes of dark exposure. The lower segment of the curve of Figure 12.1 represents the dark adaptation of rods. The increase in sensitivity over time for rods requires from 20 to 30 minutes of continual exposure to the dark. Thus, after about a half-hour of dark adaptation the sensitivity of the eye is many times greater than what it was at the onset of the dark adaptation process. A speculation on the temporal course of dark adaptation is offered by Buss (1973):

> *At first glance the half hour required to adapt fully to the dark of night would appear to be maladaptive. A visually deficient animal would surely fall prey to other animals under these conditions, but . . . rapid changes from light to dark occur mainly in man's technological advanced civilization. In nature a rapid change from light to dark would occur only when an animal entered a cave, and most animals tend to avoid caves. The natural transition from light to dark requires approximately 20 minutes—the period of twilight between the sun's setting and darkness of night—and this period matches the time it takes for dark adaptation to be completed.* (pp. 196–197)

THE PHOTOCHEMICAL BASIS OF DARK ADAPTATION

Adaptation to the dark involves a complex chemical change within the rods. The rods of most vertebrates contain a light-absorbing pigment called **rhodopsin;** stimulation of this pigment marks the first stage in a response to light energy. A form of rhodopsin was originally discovered in the rods of the frog by Franz Boll of the University of Rome in 1876. It was a brilliant red pigment, which was subsequently named visual purple or rhodopsin (Wald, 1950; LeGrand, 1968). Rhodopsin is an unstable chemical readily altered by light energy; it is bleached and broken down by exposure to light and regenerates in darkness. Although there are important neural changes relevant to dark adaptation, it is recognized that rhodopsin regeneration is the basic

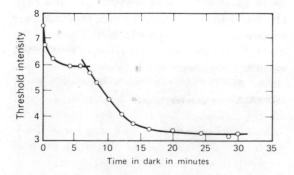

FIGURE 12.1.   Change in the visual threshold during the course of dark adaptation. The top branch of the curve is for cones, the bottom one for the rods. (After Hecht & Shlaer, 1938.)

photochemical process underlying dark adaptation. The multistate cycle of bleaching and the synthesis of rhodopsin as a function of the light environment of the eye is diagramed in Figure 12.2. Rhodopsin is bleached by light to form **retinal,** a yellow plant pigment found in all photoreceptors, and **opsin,** a colorless protein. With continued bleaching retinal is converted to a form of **vitamin A** (also called retinol). In the regenerative portion of the cycle, when the eye is kept in the dark, vitamin A joins with opsin to reconstitute rhodopsin. Thus, an equilibrium is established between the composition of rhodopsin and its subsequent synthesis from its constituent elements.

This photodynamic process is consistent with the fact that a critical deficiency of vitamin A can produce a condition of pathological insensitivity to dim lighting called **nyctalopia** (sometimes **hemeralopia** or merely **night blindness**). There is evidence of extensive retinal damage due to continued vitamin A deficiency. Dowling and Wald (1960) deprived rats (who have mainly rod retinae) of vitamin A and found that after 8 weeks of deprivation the rats' sensitivity decreased radically, requiring up to 1000 times more light to produce a retinal neural response. With continued vitamin A depletion the poor cell nutrition became irrevocable, the rods degenerated, and the rats became permanently blind (see also Dowling, 1966).

As exposure to the dark increases the sensitivity of the retina, exposure to the light decreases it in a process called **light adaptation.** The exposure of the dark-adapted eye to light results in an initial rapid elevation of the threshold that continues to rise briefly but at a slower rate and then levels off to completion in several minutes. When the dark-adapted retina is suddenly confronted with intense light, as when entering bright daylight from the interior of a dark auditorium, the experience from the intense stimulation of this phase of light adaptation is disagreeable and may even be painful.

It must be pointed out that factors other than changes in the concentration of rhodopsin are involved in adaptation (Schnapf & Baylor, 1987). In fact, visual sensitivity may vary significantly without correspondingly large changes in the concentration of rhodopsin Moreover, the cycle of rhodopsin bleaching and regeneration occurs more slowly than does an actual change in threshold or sensitivity (Baker, 1953).

SPECTRAL SENSITIVITY AND THE PURKINJE SHIFT

A fundamental distinction between photopic and scotopic vision is that cones and rods are not equally sensitive to the entire visible spectrum. Different wavelengths of light differ markedly in the extent to which they stimulate the eye. In Figure 12.3 the threshold values are plotted against wavelengths to obtain **spectral threshold curves.** This is a complex functional relationship because threshold level is dependent on the adaptive state of the eye and the kinds of receptors under stimulation. The threshold function for photopic vision, shown in the upper curve, results when the eye is light adapted to moderately high intensities. It is quite elevated relative to the function for scotopic vision of the dark-adapted eye, shown in the bottom curve. Reading from the figure, the wavelength of maximal sensitivity (lowest threshold) for photopic vision is in the region of 550 nm (appearing as a yellow-green color) whereas the threshold curve for scotopic vision indicates that maximum sensitivity lies within the region of 500 nm (green). In other words, the peak

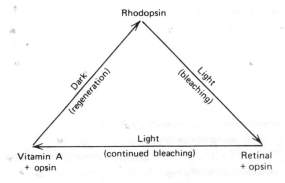

FIGURE 12.2. Photochemical cycle underlying dark adaptation. Rhodopsin also undergoes several intermediate chemical stages of decomposition before its molecule splits into retinal and opsin.

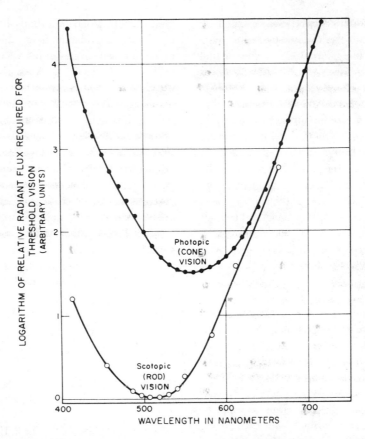

FIGURE 12.3.   Relative amounts of light energy required to reach threshold as a function of wavelength. The top spectral threshold curve is for photopic vision, the bottom one for scotopic vision. Observe that the rods require less radiant energy than the cones for threshold visibility at all wavelengths except for the very long ones where the photopic and scotopic thresholds are about the same. Also, the photopic curve is shifted about 50 nm to the right with respect to the scotopic curve, indicating that the rods are maximally sensitive to wavelengths of about 500 nm, the cones to wavelengths of about 550 nm. The vertical distance between the two curves represents the colorless photochromatic interval. (From Chapanis, 1949, p. 12.)

sensitivity for the rods is for shorter wavelengths when compared to the peak sensitivity for cones, and in general, the relative brightness of different wavelengths is related to the adaptive state of the eye.

It should be noted that it is only when light levels are sufficient to activate photopic vision that the perception of colors or hues occurs. When visual stimulation reaches only scotopic levels, stimulating only rods, weak lights are visible but not as colors; that is, all wavelengths are seen as a series of grays.

The colorless interval in radiant energy for a given wavelength—the interval between seeing only a light and seeing a color—is given as the vertical difference between the scotopic and photopic threshold curves in Figure 12.3, and it is called the **photochromatic interval.** The photochromatic interval is largest at the short wavelength end and is smallest at the long wavelength end of the spectrum, where rods and cones are about equally sensitive to radiant energy. This latter point means that a light whose wavelength is 650 nm or above, if it is of sufficient radiant energy to be seen at all, is also chromatically seen (as red).

These facts help to explain the phenomenon that when light energy is decreased so that visual function changes from photopic to scotopic levels, different colors may change in their relative brightness. For example, two equally bright surfaces matched in daylight, one red and one green, differ in brightness when viewed in dim lighting; the formerly red surface appears to be darker than the green. This is called the **Purkinje shift** after J. E. Purkinje, the physiologist who described it in 1825. In fact the shift is based upon Purkinje's own real-world observation: according to LeGrand (1968), Purkinje noticed that sign posts painted in blue and red looked somewhat different at different times of the day. Although the two colors appeared equally bright during the day, at dawn the blue appeared brighter than the red. Of course, what was occurring was a change in the brightness of various wavelengths coincident with the shift from photopic to scotopic vision. It follows that under conditions of reduced illumination utilizing scotopic vision, the light composed of shorter wavelengths appears to be relatively brighter than when it is observed in high illumination. Thus, during the approach of twilight, reds initially appear relatively bright compared to greens, but as twilight progresses the reddish colors appear darker. Since scotopic vision is colorless, within a certain illumination interval daylight greens change to moonlight grays and daylight reds change to moonlight blacks. It is then, as the English dramatist, John Heywood, wrote in 1546, "When all candles be out, all cats be gray."

An aspect of spectral sensitivity that warrants comment owing to its practical consequence concerns the wavelength of the preadapting light in dark adaptation. If the lighting just prior to adaptation consists of only a single long wavelength of light (monochromatic red), dark adaptation proceeds much more rapidly after the preadapting light is turned off than if other wavelengths are used. This is because the rods are relatively insensitive to the long wavelength end of the spectrum; hence, they show little light adaptation effects. There is an interesting practical application to this. If one must go rapidly

from a well-lighted to a dimly-lit environment, the process of dark adaptation may be begun in the light by wearing red goggles prior to entering the darkened environment. That is, if restricted only to long wavelengths, the eyes become fairly dark adapted while exposed to ordinary levels of illumination. Indeed, it is held that preadaptation with monochromatic red light is nearly as effective preparation for night vision as being in complete darkness. The red goggles serve several related functions: as with any light filter they reduce the overall amount of light reaching the eyes so that the eyes are light adapted to a lower energy level. More importantly, however, red goggles allow in only red light, to which the rods are relatively insensitive. Thus, it is mostly the cones that must subsequently undergo dark adaptation when the goggles are removed in the dark, and, as indicated in the top branch of Figure 12.1, dark adaptation proceeds most rapidly for photopic vision.

LIMITS OF BASIC VISUAL FUNCTION

ABSOLUTE THRESHOLD FOR INTENSITY

Under optimal conditions of testing, the least amount of radiant energy necessary to produce a visual sensation—the absolute threshold—is a remarkably small amount. The definitive, classic experiment on threshold determination was performed by Hecht, Shlaer, and Pirenne (1941, 1942). They derived some striking threshold measures when they were obtained under conditions that were conducive to assessing maximum sensitivity—such as testing the most sensitive part of the dark-adapted retina with the wavelength of light to which it is most sensitive. They found that the absolute threshold was in the range of 5 to 14 quanta (in luminance terms, the absolute threshold was of the order of 0.000001 mL). They also estimated that under optimal conditions a single quantum of radiant energy may be sufficient to activate a single rod. Although these values are essentially derived ones and pertain only to the maximal sensitivity that is theoretically possible, they do stress the remarkable sensitivity of the human eye as a light detector.

The limiting capacity of threshold vision appears to be linked to the physical nature of light in that if the eye were much more sensitive, under certain conditions the discreteness of photon emission would be perceptible and light would not be perceived as continuous or steady.

FACTORS AFFECTING THE ABSOLUTE THRESHOLD

A number of variables affect threshold levels such as the area, duration and wavelength of the light stimulus, and the region of the retina on which the stimulus is presented.

Area of Retina Stimulated

For relatively small visual areas in the central part of the retina, the likelihood of stimulus detection or a threshold response can be increased by either increasing stimulus intensity or increasing the retinal area stimulated. The relationship known as **Ricco's law,** is as follows: $A \times I = C$, where the product of area (A) and intensity (I) produces a constant threshold value (C). In general the law states that a constant threshold value is maintained by increasing the area stimulated while decreasing stimulus intensity, or the reverse. This makes sense in that the same product of area and intensity contain identical amounts of total light energy. For peripheral areas of the retina, covering substantial regions, the threshold depends on intensity alone. That is, $I = C$. No one law appears to extend over the full range of retinal area.

Duration of the Stimulus

Within limits, a form of temporal summation also occurs. For durations of about 100 msec or less, stimulus intensity and time bear a reciprocal relationship for a constant threshold value. Thus, a less intense light acting for a relatively long time and a more intense light acting for a relatively short time may produce the same effect. This is known as **Bloch's law** or the **Bunsen—Roscoe law.** Thus, with I and C as earlier, and T as the stimulation duration, $T \times I = C$. This relationship holds best for peripheral retinal regions. The effective temporal range over which the law holds may be as long as 100 msec. Thereafter the threshold is determined by intensity. Obviously, the law cannot hold over an indefinite range for that would imply that we could detect a light stimulus of almost infinitesimal intensity provided it was exposed for a sufficient duration.

Retinal Locus

As we noted earlier with the spectral threshold curves (Figure 12.3), the absolute threshold is dependent on the part of the retina stimulated. Recall that areas primarily containing cones have a much higher threshold than do areas containing rods. In general, the sensitivity of the eye is the greatest where the density of rods is maximal.

Wavelength

Two additional points noted earlier must be reiterated: the absolute threshold is not equally affected by radiant energy from all portions of the spectrum, but it is dependent upon the wavelength of the light (see Figure 12.3). Furthermore, the absolute threshold also depends on the adaptive state of the eye immediately preceding threshold determination. Of course, light adaptation produces an elevated threshold, whereas adaptation to the dark produces the opposite effect.

PERCEIVING CONTINUITY FROM INTERMITTENT LIGHT: THE CFF

We noted that the intensity and duration of a stimulus interact, and with certain specifications may be interchanged in order to reach a threshold response. This interaction extends beyond unitary stimuli. Under certain conditions of intensity and duration, an intermittent or flashing light stimulus may be perceived as continuously lit. Indeed many commonplace light sources (e.g., fluorescent, television, motion pictures) appear to give off a steady constant illumination, while in fact, they produce light that varies relatively rapidly in time. In part, this is due to the fact that once initiated, a visual image persists for a brief period after the physical stimulus is terminated.

There is a certain minimum rate or frequency at which a light must be flashed for it to be perceived as continuous. The rate at which flicker alternates with fusion is known as the **critical flicker frequency (CFF).** (CFF is also applied to the rate at which flicker disappears and the interrupted light appears steady. In this case CFF refers to **critical fusion frequency.**) Aside from the obvious variable of frequency of alternation, values of CFF depend on a number of factors, chief among them being the intensity of the light. Weak flashes show greater persistency and fuse at comparatively slow rates. The rods, which function maximally at low levels of illumination, thus have a lower CFF than cones. Generally, the more intense the stimulus, the greater the frequency required for the threshold of fusion to be reached. Beyond a certain rate fusion occurs regardless of intensity. In addition to intensity, CFF varies with retinal location, stimulus size, contrast (see Figure 12.4), the adaptive state of the eye, and with various other variables.

FIGURE 12.4. When this figure is rotated at gradually increasing speed, the thin inner ring continues to flicker after the rest of the black and white field has fused to yield a uniform gray. Through contrast the difference between the white and black of the ring has been heightened by their respective backgrounds. Hence they are slower to fuse.

ACUITY

We discussed briefly some of the anatomical bases of visual acuity in the previous chapter; we deal here with its measurement. Visual acuity, in a broad sense, refers to the ability to resolve fine details and to distinguish different parts of the visual field from each other (Figure 12.5). Actually there are a number of acuities, each involving a different task —detection, localization, resolution, recognition, and dynamic acuity. **Detection acuity** refers to the task of detecting the presence of a target stimulus in the visual field. Often a small object of a specified size must be detected against a darker background. **Localization** or **vernier acuity** concerns the ability to detect whether two lines, laid end to end, are continuous or whether one line is offset relative to the other. The amount of displacement can be varied, and the level at which the viewer cannot perceive the misalignment of the two lines sets the level of acuity (see Figure 12.6). Whenever we must line up or match two points or lines, such as unlocking a combination lock or aligning a dial on a scale in precision equipment, we are using localization or vernier acuity.

Resolution acuity refers to the ability to perceive a separation between discrete elements of a pattern (see Figure 12.7). Thus one might determine whether a pattern of line gratings can be seen as distinct and lying in a certain orientation (Figure 12.7c). As the lines become thinner and closer together, the grating pattern appears to lack any discrete lines or orientation; that is, the pattern cannot be resolved. (Note that there is a more definitive measure of acuity involving grating patterns called *contrast sensitivity*. However, because its description requires assumptions of the visual system that have not yet been introduced, we defer discussing it until Chapter 14.) The **Landolt rings,** shown in Figure 12.8, are also used to assess resolution acuity. **Recognition acuity** is perhaps the most familiar of the acuities. The usual task of recognition acuity requires the viewer to name the target stimuli. The **Snellen letters** (Figure 12.9) of the familiar eye

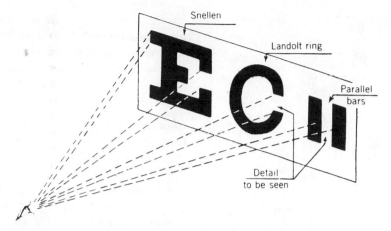

FIGURE 12.5.   Details of targets used in the measurement of visual acuity. The Snellen letters measure recognition acuity; the other two targets assess resolution acuity. The viewer must report the position of the break in the Landolt ring and the orientation of the parallel bars. (From Chapanis, 1949, p. 26.)

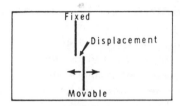

FIGURE 12.6.   Vernier acuity measurement with a movable line. (From R. G. Rubin and G. L. Walls, *Fundamentals of Visual Science*, Charles C Thomas, Springfield, Ill., 1969, p. 147. Reprinted by permission of the authors and publisher.)

(a)   (b)   (c)   (d)

FIGURE 12.7.   Targets for resolution acuity. (*a*) Parallel bars, (*b*) double dot target, (*c*) acuity grating, (*d*) checkerboard. Most commonly used is a grating pattern (*c*) in which the widths of the dark and bright lines are made equal. A series of gratings from coarse to fine is presented and visual acuity is specified in terms of the angular width of the line of the finest grating that can be resolved. (From L. A. Riggs, in *Vision and Visual Perception*, edited by C. H. Graham, John Wiley, New York, 1965, p. 325. Reprinted by permission of the publisher.)

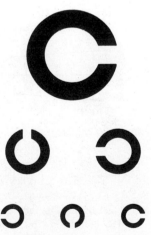

FIGURE 12.8.   Landolt rings used for assessing resolution acuity. The thickness of the ring is one-fifth the outer diameter. The gap width is also one-fifth the outer diameter. (From L. A. Riggs, in *Vision and Visual Perception*, edited by C. H. Graham, John Wiley, New York, 1965, p. 324. Reprinted by permission of the publisher.)

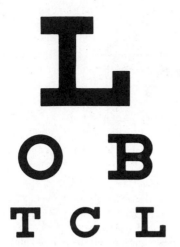

FIGURE 12.9. Snellen letters used for measuring recognition acuity. The Snellen letters are composed of lines and serifs having a thickness that is one-fifth the height or width of the whole letter. The Snellen eye chart was devised by the Dutch ophthalmologist, Herman Snellen, in 1862. (From L. A. Riggs, in *Vision and Visual Perception*, edited by C. H. Graham, John Wiley, New York, 1965, p. 324. Reprinted by permission of the publisher.)

chart are used to measure recognition acuity. **Dynamic acuity** refers to the task of detecting and locating areas in moving targets. Dynamic acuity is especially critical in such activities as driving.

VISUAL ANGLE

The degree of acuity differs for the different types. However, before discussing them further, we must introduce a general measure for specifying acuity that applies to all types. There is a good reason for this. It would not be very useful to always specify the size a target must be in order to be detected, because if it was of sufficient intensity and located close enough to the viewer's eyes, even a very small target would be visible. Conversely, an immense target might not be visible if it were located at a great distance from the viewer. Thus the visibility of a target varies with both size and viewer-distance. Accordingly, what is required is a measure whose specification is a product of both the target's absolute size and its distance from the viewer. Such a measure is the angular size of an image projected on the retina. The angular size of the just discriminable test target (or some critical detail of the target) is speci-

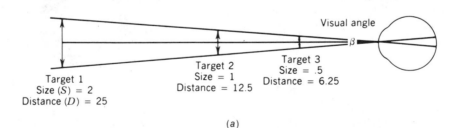

(a)

FIGURE 12.10. (a) The angle, β, is the visual angle of a target of size, S, that lies at a distance, D, from the retina along the line of regard. Note that other targets (e.g., Targets 2 and 3) of different sizes, lying at different distances have the same visual angle, β.
(b) Computation of the visual angle. Given the values of S and D for Target 1 above it is possible to compute the visual angle of a target using the equation:

$$\tan \frac{\beta}{2} = \frac{S}{2D}$$

where tan β/2 represents the trigonometric function for

half of the visual angle, S represents the size of the target, and D represents the distance of the target from the retina along the line of regard. The target distance is 25 units, and target size is 2 units, hence tangent β/2 is 1/25 or 0.04; that is, 1/2 of the target height divided by the distance of the target from the eye, or 1 divided by 25. The angle whose tangent is 0.04 is 2°18′. But this is only one-half of the target angle β, hence the full visual angle subtended by the target image at the retina is twice this value, or 4°36′. In many situations where the visual angle is relatively small, say 10° or less, the formula, tan β = S/D is applicable.

fied in terms of the **visual angle** its image projects onto the retina. In other words, the visual angle refers to the angle formed by the rays of light from the target and projected on the retina (see Figure 12.10a).

Visual angle is given in degrees (°), minutes ('), and seconds (″) of arc. In angular measure, 1° (degree) = 60' (minutes of arc), and 1' = 60″ (seconds of arc). An example showing the computation of the visual angle is provided in Figure 12.10b.

Observe from the figure that other targets of different sizes, located at different distances from the viewer, have the same visual angle as β. It should be noted, however, that even when expressed in terms of visual angle, the actual distance at which a target is located from the viewer may be an important consideration. Because of lens accommodation differences between viewers, acuity measurements are generally taken at a near distance, say, 13 or 16 in. (33 or 40.6 cm), and at a far distance, 20 ft (6.1 meters). For objects located at distances beyond about 20 ft accommodation remains fairly constant.

In terms of visual angle, the types of acuity have approximately the following optimal acuity values for human vision: detection acuity—0.5 sec of arc (Olzak & Thomas, 1986); localization or vernier acuity—2 sec of arc; for both resolution and recognition—30 sec of arc. Dynamic visual acuity is poorer than the static acuities. According to Schiff (1980), for stimuli moving at a rate of 60° per sec, dynamic acuity is about 1 to 2 min of arc. Some visual angle values associated with some typical objects and ocular structures are given in Table 12.2.

Because of its widespread use we have a bit more to say about recognition acuity. The most common form of acuity assessed in clinical practice is recognition acuity, and it is usually measured by means of the familiar eye chart. Typically, the chart contains lines of Snellen letters that vary in size. The viewer reads the line with the smallest letters that can be possibly read with accuracy. When this type of acuity is assessed, the resultant value is expressed as a ratio of the distance at which a line of letters can just be correctly seen to the distance at which the hypothetical average person with normal vision can read the same line. Accordingly, a ratio of 20/20 indicates that the viewer correctly sees at 20 feet letters what the average person can just read at 20 feet (20/20 = 1 min of arc). A ratio of 20/15 means that the viewer sees at 20 feet what the average person can just see at 15 feet—obviously better than average acuity. On

Table 12.2
Visual Angle Associated with Some Typical Objects and Ocular Structures

Alphanumeric character on CRT screen at 50 cm	17'
Diameter of sun and moon	30'
Lower case pica-type letter at reading distance of 40 cm (about 16 in.)	13'
Quarter at arm's length	2°
Quarter at 90 yards (about 82 meters)	1'
Quarter at 3 miles (about 5 km)	1″
Diameter of fovea	1°
Diameter of foveal receptor	30″
Position of inner edge of blind spot	12° from fovea
Size of blind spot	7.5° (vertical), 5° (horizontal)

Source: Based on T. N. Cornsweet, *Visual perception* (New York: Academic Press, 1970), and G. Westheimer, The eye as an optical instrument, in K. R. Boff, L. Kaufman, and J. P. Thomas (Eds.), *Handbook of perception and human performance*. Vol. 1. Sensory processes and perception (New York: John Wiley, 1986).

the other hand, a ratio of 20/30 means that the viewer can just read at 20 feet what the average person can read at 30 feet—poorer than average acuity.

We noted that many nocturnal animals have greater sensitivity in dim lighting than the human. In contrast many day-active animals, especially birds, possess a high degree of visual acuity. Indeed, it has been estimated that the resolution acuity of some diurnal animals such as the eagle may reach 3.6 times human visual acuity (Shlaer, 1972; Reymond, 1985). Similarly the vision of the falcon is estimated to be 2.6 times more acute than that of the human eye (Fox, Lehmkuhle, & Westendorf, 1976). In environmental terms these findings suggest that the falcon can just detect a target of 1 mm at 18 meters.

ACUITY AND RETINAL LOCUS

Visual acuity is best when the image falls on the fovea, where the cones are most densely packed, and acuity becomes increasingly poor as areas peripheral to the fovea are stimulated. The variation in visual acuity for different regions of the human retina is approximated by Figure 12.11. It is obvious that acuity is dependent on the distribution of cones when comparing this figure with a plot of the distribution of rods and cones in the retina (shown in the previous chapter, Figure 11.11). That is, acuity falls off rapidly as the image of a visual target moves from the fovea to the periphery.

The chart of Figure 12.12, devised by S. M. Anstis (1974), provides a pictorial impression of the variation in acuity as a function of increasing target distance from the fovea. According to Anstis's analysis, when the center of the chart is fixated, all letters in the figure should be equally legible at almost any viewing distance; this follows since any increase in viewing distance makes the retinal image of each letter smaller, but at the same time it also projects each letter closer toward the fovea, where acuity is higher. In brief, all letters appear equally legible since the size of the target letters decreases at the same rate as visual acuity increases.

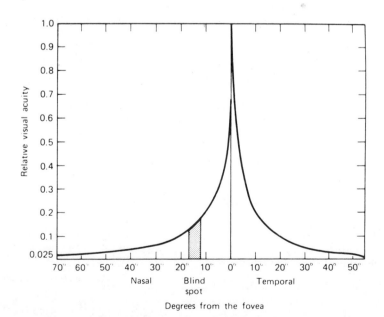

FIGURE 12.11.   Visual acuity at different retinal positions. These results were obtained from a grating target. All values are expressed as proportions of foveal acuity. (From Chapanis, 1949, p. 27; after Wertheim, 1894.)

FIGURE 12.12.   Demonstration that acuity decreases rapidly with target distance from the fovea. When the center of the chart is fixated at approximately normal viewing distance, all letters should be equally legible, since increasing target distance from the fovea (i.e., the fixation point) is accompanied by a corresponding increase in the size of the letter. (From S. M. Anstis, *Vision Research*, *14*, 1974, p. 591. Reprinted by permission of the author and Pergamon Press.)

ADDITIONAL FACTORS

Acuity is highest under photopic conditions and is dependent upon the level of illumination. In addition, the contrast between the target and its background is an important consideration, as is the amount of time spent viewing the target; generally the more time spent looking at a target the more visible it is (e.g., McKee & Westheimer, 1978). Furthermore, the viewer's eye movements, the size of the pupil, the wavelength of the target stimulus and background, the age and experience of the viewer, and other psychological factors may have an important effect on the level of acuity (see Olzak & Thomas, 1986). One of these factors, eye movements, is of sufficient importance not only to acuity but for a general understanding of the visual system to warrant some discussion.

EYE MOVEMENTS

As we noted in Chapter 11, the eyes are moved about by the action of the oculomotor muscles. We note here that eye movements are biologically adapted to orienting and searching in different directions and at different distances. This enables an observer to position the eyes so that they can fixate or focus on a target. In other words, the eyes move to a position so that the image of a target falls directly on the small central region of clearest, most acute vision—the fovea. A number of different types of eye movements have been identified.

SACCADES

The most common form of eye movement is called the **saccade**, which is a rapid and abrupt jump (of about 50 msec duration), made by the eye as it moves from one fixation to another. Saccades may be small (less than 3 min of visual angle) and large (20° of angle). Saccades are ballistic-type movements, in that they have a predetermined destination; that is, the direction and the distance of their excursions are preprogrammed or planned prior to their execution. Indeed Zingale and Kowler (1987) have reported that, as is the case with many voluntary motor tasks involving the limbs and fingers, saccadic eye movements are planned as patterned sequences prior to their execution.

Saccades are primarily used to search and explore in the visual field and place images of selected visual details onto the fovea where visual acuity is maximal; accordingly they are functional in such tasks as reading and the examination of stationary scenes. As Figure 12.13 shows, the pattern of eye movement may be partially determined by the kind of information to be extracted from a scene. It should be noted that saccades are but one component of a general planning mechanism that involves controlled movements of the head and certain body muscles in directing the eyes toward a target (Mack et al., 1985). In addition, saccadic movements are initiated to stabilize eye position when there is movement of the

head or body in space. In this case bodily movement is compensated for by eye movements.

Because vision is impaired during eye movements, it is not surprising that they are extremely rapid. Indeed, the muscles responsible for saccadic eye movements are among the fastest in the body. Typically, there are 1 to 3 saccades per second, but they occur so rapidly that they occupy only about 10% of the total viewing time. Saccades are generally voluntary for they can be made with the eyes closed or in total darkness, and they can be aimed or suppressed. However, they also show a reflexive nature. A suddenly appearing, flickering, or moving stimulus seen out of the corner of the eye can result in a saccade that moves the gaze directly on the stimulus. This is of adaptive significance "for in the primitive world, a slight movement glimpsed from the corner of the eye . . . might be the first warning of an attack" (Llewellyn Thomas, 1969, p. 406).

SACCADES AND READING

As we noted, saccadic eye movements are instrumental acts that contribute to the process of reading. It is well known that the pattern of eye movements during reading does not consist of smoothly executed tracking movements of successive rows of letters and words. Instead, in typical reading behavior, as indicated by Figure 12.14, the eyes execute a series of jumps or saccades interspersed with pauses or fixations and some refixations or regressive eye movements. It is, of course, during the fixation that reading is accomplished since functional vision is essentially blocked during the saccadic movement. The size and frequency of saccades in reading is affected by the reader's ability to resolve individual letters and by how well the letters form coherent, easily recognizable perceptual patterns (e.g., Kowler & Anton, 1987). Accordingly, the skilled reader requires fewer and briefer fixations and saccades and makes fewer regressions than the poorer one.

Moreover, the skilled reader may well be using some information from peripheral vision to organize and guide the pattern of saccades during the reading

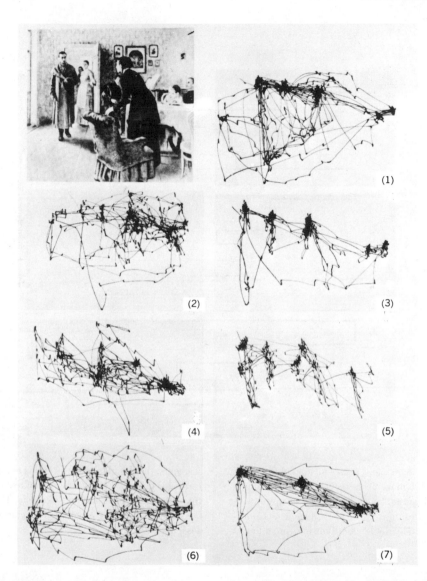

FIGURE 12.13. Seven records of eye movements by the same subject made to the same picture but viewed under different instructions. Each line represents a saccade. Each record lasted 3 min. The subject examined the picture with both eyes. (1) Free examination of the picture. Before the subsequent recording sessions, the subject was asked to (2) estimate the material circumstances of the family in the picture, (3) give the ages of the people, (4) surmise what the family had been doing before the arrival of the "unexpected vistor," (5) remember the clothes worn by the people, (6) remember the position of the people and objects in the room, (7) estimate how long the "unexpected visitor" had been away from the family. (From A. L. Yarbus, *Eye Movement and Vision*, Plenum Press, New York, 1967, p. 174. Reprinted with permission of Plenum Press.)

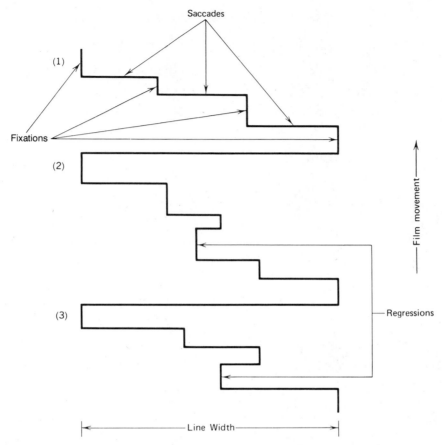

FIGURE 12.14. Schematic representation of film of lateral saccadic eye movements recorded during reading lines of text. Notice that since the film moves upward, the recording progresses downward. The extent of saccadic movements is given by the length of the horizontal line segments; the duration of the fixations is registered by the vertical segments. For the first line of text (1), the record shows three saccades and four fixations. The records for lines 2 and 3 show regressions (i.e., returns to previously passed text).

process (see Carr, 1986). Clearly, it would be more efficient for the reader to employ peripheral vision to search for and to fixate on nonredundant words carrying significant information than to pause on common words or on interword spaces (Balota & Raynor, 1983; Zola, 1984). Indeed, there is a tendency with static visual displays for fixations to fall on areas high in information, and for reading, the optimal location for a fixation is the center of the word (McConkie, et al., 1989). It follows then that when textual stimuli are typographically distorted or degraded, for example, by filling in the interword spaces so as to make physical features such as word shapes and word boundaries indiscriminable when viewed with peripheral vision (see Figure 12.15), the pattern of eye movements and reading behavior are severely affected. With such unusual text, peripheral vision is rendered useless and reading becomes almost totally a foveal activity (Schiffman, 1972; Carr, 1986).

thisisanexampleofreadingwithoutanyspacesbetweenthewords

REaDIngBecOMEseVEnmOReDifFICuLTwHEnUpPErAnDLoWErCaSEleTtERsARemIXeD

FIGURE 12.15.   Typographically altered text in which interword spaces are eliminated and upper and lowercase letters are randomly mixed. The difficulty experienced in reading this material suggests the importance of interword spaces in guiding saccadic eye movements. A reading of these sentences requires almost letter-by-letter fixations. The eye movement recordings obtained from readers of such sentences would be characterized by numerous regressions.

PURSUIT MOVEMENTS

Pursuit movements are almost completely automatic and generally require a physically moving stimulus. In contrast to saccades, pursuit movements are smoothly executed and are comparatively slow. Generally, they are used to track an object moving in a stationary environment; hence target velocity rather than target location is the appropriate stimulus. In this case, the velocity of the pursuit movement of the eye matches the velocity of the moving stimulus. This serves to more or less cast and preserve the image of a stationary target on the retina. Moving the eye in accordance with the movement of a stimulus may enhance the perception of the form of a stimulus. This follows because it is easier for the visual system to perceive the form of an image if it is relatively stationary on the retina rather than moving.

VERGENCE MOVEMENTS

The most recently evolved type of eye movements—called **vergence movements**—are those that involve the coordinated movements of both eyes. Vergence movements move the eyes in opposite directions in the horizontal plane, toward or away from each other, so that both eyes can focus on the same target. Such movements are found in animals like primates with frontal vision, for which the visual fields from both eyes overlap. A lack of proper vergence movements may result in *diplopia* or "double vision."

MINIATURE EYE MOVEMENTS

There are also a number of so-called **miniature eye movements** that may be identified and measured during maintained fixation. When a person maintains deliberate fixation on a target, a pattern of extremely small tremorlike eye movements is observable with proper recording techniques. Although in continual movement during fixation, the eye does not wander very far from its average focal position. It is recognized that if miniature eye movements were entirely eliminated, the image on the retina would fade and disappear. However, attempts to implicate miniature eye movements as necessary for the attainment of such perceptual capacities as acuity and form perception have been seriously questioned (Steinman et al., 1973; Steinman, 1986).

MIXED MODE EYE MOVEMENTS

Although we have identified and distinguished between several different types of eye movements, it should be stressed that most natural activities involving visual interaction with the environment employ a combination of the different forms of eye movements—a category of eye movements that Hallett (1986) labels **mixed mode eye movements.** For example, tracking a moving object in depth involves the execution of saccades, smooth pursuit, and vergence movements.

DEVELOPMENT OF EFFICIENT EYE MOVEMENTS

Finally we consider the role of experience on the development of efficient eye movements. As we have noted, eye movements are essential motor activities for the processing of the visual scene by an active organism. However necessary they may be, efficient eye movements involve skilled muscle movements that appear to improve with practice. Kowler and

Martins (1982) observed that the eye movements of preschool children, 4 and 5 years of age, differ from those of adults in a number of ways that affect efficient vision. For example, children could not easily maintain steady fixation. When instructed to fixate on a small bright stationary target in an otherwise darkened room, their line of sight was extremely unstable: their eyes darted about, scanning an area 100 times larger than would a typical adult in the same condition. In addition when tracking a moving target, children had difficulty controlling the timing of their saccades, and, unlike adults, they could not anticipate any change in the direction of the target's movement, even when the change was predictable; in fact, Kowler and Martins reported that about 200 msec elapsed before children would change the direction of their eye movements.

Quite clearly preschool children do not perform simple oculomotor tasks with the same degree of efficiency as do adults. Perhaps some of the difference in visual performance between the two groups may be attributed to the immature and incomplete oculomotor development of the children. Relatedly it is also possible that, as with the acquisition of skilled motor habits in general, preschool children have not yet learned efficient oculomotor control and, accordingly, have not acquired the specific motor skills necessary to perform effectively. It is reasonable to assume that the attainment of efficient eye movements is a skill that is acquired gradually with practice and experience, extending well beyond the preschool years.

SUMMARY

This chapter has focused on the phenomena and functioning of the visual system. The functional distinction between rods and cones introduced in the preceding chapter has been stressed throughout. Vision accomplished with only rods or only cones is termed scotopic or photopic vision, respectively.

One of the important functional differences between photopic and scotopic vision is in response to the general conditions of illumination, with photopic vision characteristic of higher luminance levels and scotopic vision applying under conditions of low luminance. Adjustment to a dimly illuminated environment is termed dark adaptation; it has a photochemical basis. Related phenomena, such as the Purkinje shift—the experiential effect owing to a shift from photopic to scotopic vision—and spectral sensitivity were discussed. Absolute threshold determinations for brightness were examined and the following relationships for the absolute threshold were described: intensity and the amount of area of the retina stimulated (Ricco's law), intensity and the duration of the stimulus (Bloch's law or Bunson–Roscoe law), and intensity and retinal locus. The perception of continuous stimulation from intermittent light (CFF) was also discussed.

The notion of visual acuity was introduced and five types were identified: detection, localization or vernier, resolution, recognition, and dynamic acuity. The measurement of visual acuity in terms of units of visual angle was presented as well as certain critical variables that affect acuity, such as the region of the retina upon which the target is imaged.

The last part of the chapter dealt with eye movements, and several were identified and discussed: saccadic (and their relevance to reading), pursuit, vergence, miniature and mixed mode eye movements. Finally, the development of efficient eye movements was considered. Evidence was introduced that the eye movements of preschool children are ineffective relative to those of adults. It was suggested that this may be due to the immature oculomotor development and the lack of skilled oculomotor habits of the children.

KEY TERMS

Bloch's (Bunsen-Roscoe) law
Critical flicker (fusion) frequency (CFF)
Dark adaptation
Detection acuity

Dynamic acuity

Landolt rings

Light adaptation

Localization (vernier) acuity

Miniature eye movements

Mixed mode eye movements

Night blindness (nyctalopia, hemeralopia)

Opsin

Photochromatic interval

Photopic

Purkinje shift

Pursuit movements

Recognition acuity

Resolution acuity

Retinal

Rhodopsin

Ricco's law

Saccade

Scotopic

Snellen letters

Spectral threshold curves

Vergence movements

Visual angle

Vitamin A

STUDY QUESTIONS

1. Compare the functional properties of scotopic and photopic vision, with special concern to the visual activities afforded by each. Compare the vision of nocturnal to day-active animals on the basis of their use of photopic and scotopic vision.

2. Explain dark adaptation. How is it demonstrated? What do the two segments of a typical dark adaptation curve illustrate about photopic and scotopic vision? Outline the photochemical basis of dark adaptation, indicating the changing state of rhodopsin relative to light exposure.

3. Identify and explain the Purkinje shift with respect to spectral threshold curves. What does the Purkinje shift signify concerning perception in bright and dim conditions of lighting?

4. Consider the minimal radiant energy requirements of the visual system to produce a sensation.

5. Identify the main factors that affect the absolute thresholds for vision: consider the role of stimulus intensity, area, duration, the region of the retina stimulated, and the wavelength of the stimulus applied. Examine these factors with respect to the Purkinje shift.

6. Describe CFF. What effect does stimulus intensity have on the CFF?

7. Identify and distinguish between the various kinds of acuities and consider the ways in which they are measured. What is visual angle and why is it a useful general measure for describing acuity?

8. What are some of the factors that affect visual acuity? Consider the effect on acuity of stimulus intensity and the area of the retina stimulated.

9. Identify the major forms of eye movements and indicate the role played by each toward the overall efficiency of the visual system. In particular, consider the contribution made by saccadic eye movements for exploration of the visual field and for reading.

10. Examine the role of experience on the development of efficient eye movements. How do the eye movements of preschool children differ from those of adults?

13
THE PERCEPTION OF COLOR

By color perception or color vision we refer to the capacity to perceive and discriminate between lights on the basis of their spectral or wavelength composition.

Few issues in perception have had as persistent and controversial a history as has color perception. Artists, philosophers, poets, physicists, as well as physiologists and psychologists have contributed in one way or another to the present state of our knowledge. It is not difficult to see why so much interest has been devoted to the nature of color perception. Color is a pervasive characteristic of the environment that not only specifies a certain fundamental attribute or quality of surfaces and objects, but in the case of the human it also has profound aesthetic and emotional effects and it provides a highly personal experience affected by associations and preference.

We must note that color perception is not a capacity that is shared by all animals. Indeed, there are no clear overall phylogenetic trends in its possession. The color vision of primates is highly developed, matched only by that of birds. Among mammals, some degree of wavelength discrimination has been cited for certain squirrels (Crescitelli & Pollack, 1965; Michels & Schumaker, 1968), cats (Brown et al., 1973; Loop & Bruce, 1978), and prairie dogs (Jacobs & Pulliam, 1973). Although few other mammals except primates possess color vision, many birds, fish, amphibia, reptiles, and arthropods have highly developed color vision (Ingle, 1985). In fact hummingbirds (Goldsmith, 1980) and goldfish (Ingle, 1985) can see near-ultraviolet wavelengths.

It is likely that there has been some incentive or biological advantage for the evolution of color vision. Clearly, color adds additional contrast between objects in the visual field and, hence, promotes their visibility. As Walls (1963) comments: "To the first animals which developed a system of color vision, it meant the life-saving difference between being sometimes able to discriminate enemies and prey against their backgrounds, and being *usually* able to do so" (p. 463). Wright (1967) proposes that along with serving a role in object identification, "primitive man must have used colour . . . to tell him about his crops, to help him judge the fertility of the soil, to make his weather forecast from the colour of the sunset" (p. 21).

There are many instances where animals employ color vision or coloration to their advantage, enhancing their survival capabilities. Some birds, for example, utilize "flash coloration," the abrupt exposure of color to startle or confuse an attacking predator,

thereby enabling the prey bird time to escape (Baker & Parker, 1979). The role of color in the mating behavior of birds, in which the color of the male's plumage initiates sexual activity, is a further example.

Of course color also plays a role in the prey–predator relationship of many species of terrestrial animals. Many prey animals often possess some concealment coloration or camouflage, generally limited to nature colors—greens and browns. If the coloration is effective in protecting the prey animals, then this suggests that the predator possesses color vision. In this sense the use of color for concealment is an adaptation to the predator's color vision.

Clearly, color may be considered as a dimension of the spatial environment, hence the ability to differentiate lights of different spectral compositions is informative. Color vision is thus part of the more general capacity to perceive the composition of surfaces and objects in the environment.

THE NATURE OF COLOR

Although we noted that many species possess some sort of color vision, we are dealing with a subjective phenomenon that generally requires a clear and precise discriminative response on the part of the perceiver; hence, much of the following discussion will focus on human color perception.

It must be stressed that color sensations are subjective, psychological experiences. That is, objects and surfaces themselves possess no color; moreover the light reflected from them is not "colored" in any way. Or as Isaac Newton observed in his treatise "Optiks" in 1704, ". . . the rays are not colored" (1704/1952, p. 124). Rather color is a totally psychological experience produced by the effect that the reflected light from certain wavelengths of the visible spectrum has on the nervous system of certain species, including, of course the human. Thus when we refer to a "blue" or a "red" light, we mean the light from those short or long wavelengths that produce the sensations of blue or red, respectively. This important distinction between the physical dimension specified by the wavelengths of light and the psychological phenomenon of color vision is summarized well by Wright (in an essay entitled, "The Rays are not Coloured," 1963, 1967): "Our sensations of colour are within us and colour cannot exist unless there is an observer to perceive them. Colour does not exist even in the chain of events between the retinal receptors and the visual cortex, but only when the information is finally interpreted in the consciousness of the observer" (p. 20).

With this distinction in mind we may note that color sensations are related in consistent and measurable ways to the physical features of the light. In order to consider them, we must first identify the stimulus for color vision. One of the earliest recognized comprehensive treatments of color vision was developed by Isaac Newton. He demonstrated in the seventeenth century that when a pinpoint beam of light is passed through a prism it is refracted and split into a number of rays of light of different wavelengths forming the visible spectrum (see Figure 13.1).

Although the main physical component of a color is generally recognized as the wavelength of the light, for a given color sensation three subjective or psychological dimensions have been identified: a color has the attributes of *hue*, *brightness*, and *saturation*. **Hue** corresponds to the common meaning of color and generally varies with changes in wavelength (see Table 13.1). (For the sake of simplicity, we will generally use the terms hue and color interchangeably.)

A given color is also specified by its brightness, which varies with physical intensity. As we noted in earlier discussions, brightness is directly (but not simply) related to the intensity of the light. Generally, the more intense the light, the whiter it appears; decreasing intensity produces a darker appearance. However, for a given intensity, some colors such as yellow appear brighter than colors produced by shorter wavelengths, say blue. In addition, the perceived hue of a stimulus will change slightly depending on the stimulus intensity. Specifically, if the intensity of wavelengths that appear as yellow-reds and yellow-greens are increased, they will not only appear brighter but they tend to take on a more yellow hue. Similarly, blue-greens and violets begin to appear bluer when their intensity is increased. This change in hue as a function of intensity is called the **Bezold-Brücke shift.**

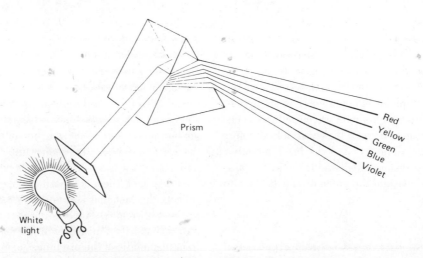

FIGURE 13.1.   Dispersion of white light by a prism. Due to refraction the white light is split into rays of light of different wavelengths, apparent as different colors.

Table 13.1
Typical Hue Names Associated with Spectral Energy Bands

Approximate Wavelength Region (in nm)	Associated Hue
380–470	Reddish blue
470–475	Blue
475–480	Greenish blue
480–485	Blue-green
485–495	Bluish green
495–535	Green
535–555	Yellowish green
555–565	Green-yellow
565–575	Greenish yellow
575–580	Yellow
580–585	Reddish yellow
585–595	Yellow-red
595–770	Yellowish red[a]

Source: *Color: A Guide to Basic Facts and Concepts,* by R. W. Burnham, R. M. Hanes, and C. J. Bartleson, John Wiley, New York, 1963, p. 56. Reprinted by permission of the publisher.

[a] A pure red with no tinge of yellow requires some blue (400 nm). Accordingly, a unique red is "extraspectral" in that no single wavelength produces it.

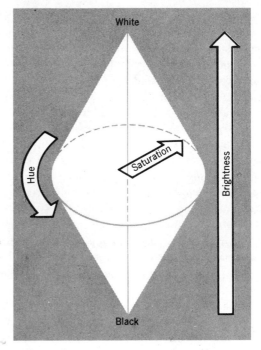

FIGURE 13.2. The color spindle. Hue is represented along the perimeter of the spindle, brightness along the vertical axis, and saturation as the distance from the center of the spindle to its perimeter.

Saturation corresponds to the spectral purity of the wavelength. The addition of other wavelengths, white light, or the addition of gray to a single wavelength reduces its purity and desaturates the color. As an example, a monochromatic green light of 510 nm, composed of a single wavelength, is spectrally pure and appears as a highly saturated color. However, if its intensity is held fixed as other wavelengths are systematically added to it, its saturation will decrease and the green color will begin to appear grayish.

COLOR SPINDLE

The relationship between the three psychological dimensions of hue, saturation, and brightness is simplified and represented visually in the **color spindle** or **solid** shown in Figure 13.2. Brightness is shown along the vertical axis, extending from white at the top to black at the base. The vertical line through the middle of the solid represents gray. Saturation is shown laterally with the most saturated colors located on the rim of the central circle and at the midpoint of the vertical distance between white and black. Finally, hue is expressed along the perimeter of the spindle. The conical or tapering shape of the spindle reflects the fact that saturation is maximal only at moderate brightness levels. In other words, saturation secondarily depends on brightness. The farther from the middle of the brightness axis, either lighter or darker, the less is the saturation of a hue.

COLOR MATCHING

There are numerous other ways of expressing and designating color quality. One of the most widely used descriptive systems is based on a *trichromatic* notion of color vision: that three lights of different wavelengths—producing so-called **primary colors** (colors that do not appear easily reducible into component colors)—may be combined in various proportions to match almost all spectral hues including white (with the possible exceptions of "metallic" colors, silver and gold). Many different sets of primaries are possible as long as no one primary can be matched by a mixture of the other two or can cancel out another's effects. In short, with certain restrictions and limitations, almost any spectral hue can be specified by the relative contribution of each of three primaries. Procedurally, this method of color specification consists of a quantitative expression of the relative amounts of each primary that must be added to produce a given color sensation. For example, spectral light of a given wavelength is shown on a test field, and the viewer adjusts the proportion of the three primaries that are mixed on an adjacent comparison field until a match is made. When this is done throughout the spectrum, a set of curves like those shown in Figure 13.3 results. Though many sets of tristimuli are possible, the primaries used in the example cited in Figure 13.3 are a 460-nm blue, a 530-nm green, and a 650-nm red. Based on a tristimulus specification of any color (C), a general color equation can be stated: $C = xR + yG + zB$, where x, y, and z are the coefficients or proportion of the three fixed wavelengths (plotted on the ordinate in Figure 13.3) whose sizes vary depending on the color to be matched. Thus, for example, equal amounts of red (650 nm) and green (530 nm) are required to match a yellow (roughly at 580 nm).

Of course, color specification is a highly technical matter, one that extends beyond our discussion. We note in passing, however, that color technologists have available standardized tristimulus spectral combinations whose mixtures are employed to match various parts of the spectrum. In particular an inter-

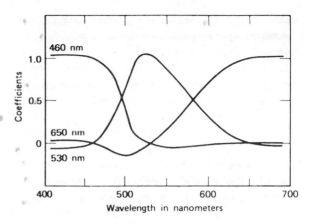

FIGURE 13.3.   Trichromatic stimuli for reproduction of spectral colors. The relative amounts of each primary—a 460 nm blue, a 530 nm green, and a 650 nm red needed to match any part of the visible spectrum are plotted for each spectral color. (A negative value indicates that some of that particular primary was added to the spectral color to be matched in order to reduce its saturation to a point where it could be matched by a mixture of the two remaining primaries.) (After Wright, 1928: From F. A. Geldard, *The Human Senses*, John Wiley, New York, 1972, p. 91. Reprinted by permission of the publisher.)

nationally adopted system specifying color stimuli in terms of their tristimulus values and colors was standardized by the Commission Internationale de L'Eclairage (CIE).

COLOR MIXTURE

Generally, pure colors of a single wavelength are perceived only under precise laboratory conditions. Most often the light that reaches the eye is composed of a mixture of various wavelengths, and the dominant wavelength determines the hue experienced. In the preceding section we noted that generally when lights of two or more different wavelengths are combined, a new color with a different hue is perceived from the mixture. Once the spectral lights are combined the eye cannot distinguish the components. In fact, to the human observer, the spectral composition of a chromatic surface cannot be determined from its appearance; that is, we cannot analyze a color mixture into its component colors by mere viewing. It follows that two chromatic surfaces may possess radically different spectral contents and yet appear identical to each other. As we stressed earlier, color experience is the subjective effect of nervous system excitation, not an inherent property of light energy. The lights themselves are unaffected by the mixture.

ADDITIVE COLOR MIXTURE

Additive color mixtures concern the addition of the excitations produced by each component color. A number of rules or principles governing the mixing of various wavelengths have been worked out, and the essential phenomena are summarized in the **color circle** of Figure 13.4. Every hue has its **complementary** that lies diametrically opposite it on the color circle, which when mixed together in the proper proportion, produces a mixture that appears neutral gray. The following are common pairs of complemen-

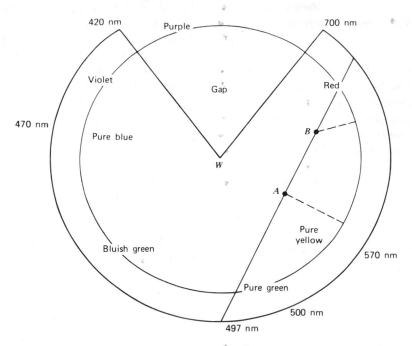

FIGURE 13.4. The color circle, corresponding to the central circle of the color spindle of Figure 13.2. Spectral stimuli from 420 nm to 700 nm are arranged in sequence about the circumference. The circle is arranged so that complementary pairs of colors lie at opposite ends of diagonals drawn through the center at W. Notice that the gap includes nonspectral hues, hues that have no single wavelength specification but result from the mixture of spectral hues.

The color circle can also be used to illustrate additive color mixture. The color of the mixture is indicated by the point lying on the line segment. (A) Equal proportions of red and green produce a yellow hue. (B) About two-thirds of the mixture is red, one-third green; hence, the resultant hue lies closer to the red. The hue of the mixture in both cases is indicated by the point at which the dotted line reaches the circumference. Notice that the saturation of the hue produced by the mixture lies closer to the center of the color circle; hence, it is less saturated than the saturations of the component hues.

taries: blue and yellow, red and blue-green, green and red-purple (note that purple lies within the gap of the color circle—an "extraspectral" region representing hues that have no unitary wavelength specification but can be produced only by mixtures of spectral lights). Mixtures of noncomplementary hues result in color sensations whose hue specifications lie intermediate on the color circle between the hues of the components. Two such physically different lights, whose spectral or wavelength compositions differ from a third light but whose mixture produces an apparent match with the third light, are called **metamers** or *metameric* pairs, and the color match is called a *metameric* match. If the colors are mixed in equal amounts, the new hue lies on the color circle halfway between the two component colors (*A* of Figure 13.4). If the colors are mixed in unequal amounts, we may gain an approximation of the resultant hue on the circle by drawing a line connecting the two component colors and placing a point on the line representing the proportion in which they are mixed. The location of the point designates the hue and saturation. As *B* of Figure 13.4 shows, the resultant hue of the mixture lies closer to the component that makes the greatest contribution.

The saturation of the mixture will be less than the saturation of one or both of the component colors. As an approximate rule, the farther away the constituent colors lie from each other, the less is the saturation of the resultant color. This is depicted graphically in Figure 13.4 in that any mixture falls nearer the center (the desaturated region) of the color circle than the components that comprise it. Finally, the brightness of the resultant color will appear as the average of the brightnesses of the two component colors. Notice that although we have described additive color mixture for only two hues, with certain modifications the preceding rules hold for any number.

The color circle, while providing a good qualitative summary of much of the basic phenomena of color mixture, is quite limited. For a precise quantitative designation of color mixtures, very sophisticated devices and methods must be employed.

There are a number of procedures for showing the additive nature of mixing colors. It is quite simply accomplished by projecting beams of light from three projectors onto a screen, each projector equipped with a different colored filter. The intersection of the beams, shown in Plate 1 (see color insert), illustrates the effect of the mixture.

Another simple means of observing additive color mixture is to employ a color wheel on which disks of colored paper are assembled (Figure 13.5). The colored disks can be overlapped and adjusted so that different sized angular sectors of each color are exposed, thereby varying the proportion of the component colors. When the wheel is rotated rapidly, a completely fused and uniform color is seen instead of the constituent colors. Although an additive method of color mixture is employed here, it is more an addition over time rather than over space.

Artists have also used an additive method of color mixture directly on their canvas. A technique called pointillism or divisionism was used by the French neo-impressionist painters (e.g., Seurat and Signac) in which they did little pallette mixing of the

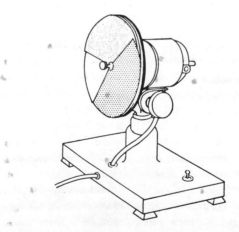

FIGURE 13.5.   A color wheel. Disks of colored paper are cut and assembled on the wheel, overlapping so that different sized sectors of each color are exposed. When the wheel is rotated rapidly, a completely mixed color is seen instead of the separate component colors. The proportions of mixtures can be varied by changing the size of angular sectors of two or more component colors.

paints; rather, they placed minute but discrete dots of different colored paint on the canvas. When viewed from a certain distance, the discrete dots are not visible as such, but apparently fuse to produce an additive color mixture. An example of this sort of color mixture is given in Plate 2.

Perhaps the most common example of additive color mixture occurs with color television. Generally, the screen of a color television set is composed of a mosaic of dots, usually red, green, and blue. Because the dots are very small, they cannot be resolved separately by the eye at the usual viewing distance; hence, they are apparently fused or blended together and their joint action—an additive color mixture —results in the perception of a distinct hue.

It may not be obvious to the casual viewer, but an apparent patch of yellow seen on a color television screen is composed of small red and green dots. To demonstrate this, place a magnifying glass against a "yellow" patch on the television screen. The discrete dots that appear will *not* look yellow. This is consistent with what we have said about additive color mixture.

SUBTRACTIVE COLOR MIXTURE

The principles of the color circle applies to the mixing of colored lights (as in Figure 13.6a) but not to mixing pigments, paints, or dyes or when two or more color filters are placed in series (that is, one in front of the other, as shown in Figure 13.6b). In the former case we are combining lights—colored lights *add* their dominant wavelengths to the mixture. It is an additive process in that the effects—receptor activation—of the wavelengths are added together in the nervous system. In contrast, colored pigments, for example, selectively absorb or *subtract* some wavelengths striking them and reflect the remaining wavelengths that give the pigment its unique hue.

The color of an object or surface depends on the wavelengths it reflects. A blue surface appears blue because the surface pigment absorbs or subtracts all but the wavelengths of light that appear as blue. Hence, when white light falls on the surface its "blue" wavelengths are predominantly reflected to

the eyes of the viewer whereas the other wavelengths are largely absorbed.

Similarly, the result of mixing two pigments involves a mutual absorption or subtraction, canceling the reflectance of all wavelengths but those that the two pigments jointly reflect. As an example of the difference between additive and subtractive mixtures, consider the combination of the complementaries blue and yellow (see Figure 13.6). As lights (Figure 13.6a), the additive mixture yields gray—a summation of the two spectral regions represented by blue and yellow—whereas as a **subtractive color mixture** of pigments (Figure 13.6b) their combined absorption produces the reflection of wavelengths that appear predominantly green. More specifically, the yellow pigment of the first filter absorbs (i.e., subtracts) mainly short wavelengths (e.g., blue, violet) and transmits longer ones. These strike the blue pigment of the second filter which absorbs primarily long wavelengths (i.e., yellow, orange, and red). This leaves the residual, middle band of wavelengths which are transmitted by both pigments, and which when reflected from the screen appear green. That is, all other wavelengths but those that appear green are absorbed in the combination. In practice it is quite a complex matter to predict accurately the resultant hue from a mixture of pigments because the hue of the combination is highly dependent on the physical and chemical properties of the constituent pigments as well as on the spectral composition of incident light.

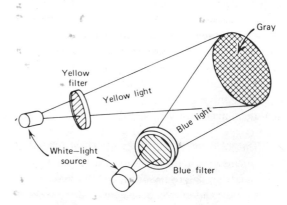

FIGURE 13.6a.   An additive mixture is illustrated. Blue and yellow appear gray.

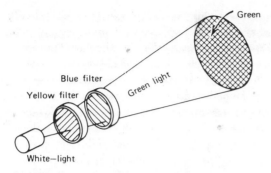

FIGURE 13.6*b*. A subtractive mixture of yellow and blue produces green. (Notice that the filters in series produce the same effect as do pigments.)

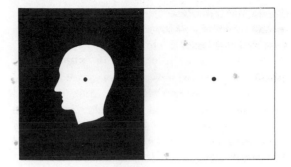

FIGURE 13.7 Demonstration of an achromatic negative afterimage. Stare at the dot in the white profile for about 30 seconds and then shift your gaze to the dot in the white square. You should see a negative afterimage in the white square; that is, a dark profile instead of a white one.

AFTERIMAGES

Effects of a visual stimulus may persist after its physical termination, in a form called **afterimages.** The usual means of demonstrating afterimages is to have a viewer stare at or fixate on a stimulus configuration or patch for about 30 to 60 seconds, after which the gaze is transferred to a different surface. There are two kinds of afterimages. One much less frequent and more fleeting is called a *positive afterimage,* in that the afterimage maintains the same black–white brightness relations and colors as the original stimulus. Positive afterimages most often occur after brief, intense stimulation of the dark-adapted eye. The more frequently occurring *negative afterimage* refers to the persistence of the image but in a reversed state. That is, the image occurs as an afterimage with the black and white and chromatic effects reversed, as in a photographic negative. Figure 13.7 presents an achromatic example of a negative afterimage.

SUCCESSIVE AND SIMULTANEOUS CONTRAST

If a chromatic stimulus is fixated on, the afterimage will be in the complementary color of the initial stimulus. This is called **successive contrast** and is in fact an example of a chromatic negative afterimage called a **complementary afterimage.** Plate 3 dem-

onstrates a complementary afterimage of a familiar object. Making use of a color's complementary color, unnatural color effects may be produced. If a blue patch is fixated on for a minute after which the gaze is transferred to a yellow surface, the surface will appear excessively saturated or "supersaturated." What has occurred is that the afterimage of the blue patch (yellow) has been projected onto a yellow surface. The explanation of this phenomenon is illustrated in Plates 4 and 5. If the instructions for Plate 4 are correctly followed, it will be clear that continual chromatic exposure of a particular region of the fovea produces a loss in saturation of that color. Interestingly, as Plate 4 demonstrates, the loss occurs without any clear or immediate perception of a change in saturation. Thus during fixation of the blue patch, the region of the retina that is stimulated becomes adapted, fatigued, or less sensitive to that particular color and it appears relatively desaturated. This is functionally equivalent to making the same retinal area more sensitive to its complementary, yellow. That is, prolonged exposure of a region of the retina to blue increases the sensitivity of that retinal region to yellow. Thus, when continued inspection of the blue patch fatigues the receptors normally mediating a blue sensation, a yellow afterimage results; if the gaze then shifts to a yellow surface, the additive mixture of the yellow afterimage and the yellow surface makes the yellow surface appear more saturated than is normal (Plate 5).

Similar effects are seen with **simultaneous contrast** or, as it is sometimes termed, spatial induction of the complementary. After continued fixation of a chromatic stimulus patch that appears against a neutral or gray background, the edge of the background bordering the patch appears to be tinged with its complementary. In part this is because with continued inspection the color patch loses in saturation (which coincides with the induction of its complementary). Since the eyes move slightly, even during fixation, the retinal image of the patch is not stationary, and the decreased saturation or slight appearance of the patch's complementary appears at its edges. If the color's complement is substituted for the neutral background, the usual complementary tinge of the patch sums with the chromatic background to produce a simultaneous "supersaturation" at the edges of the patch (see Plate 6). In many instances visually disturbing effects result from the simultaneous presentation of adjoining pairs of colors that are complementary to each other.

MEMORY COLOR

Within this context mention must be made of the influence of an object's familiarity on its apparent color. This is especially clear when stimuli whose colors are to be matched have distinctive shapes that are associated with objects that typically occur in a single color. The effects of past experience on apparent color are due to what Hering (1920) termed **memory color.**

A classic study by Duncker (1939) illustrates memory color. Cut-outs of a leaf and a donkey made from the same green felt material were successively shown bathed by hidden red illumination that was the complementary of the color of the cutouts; thus each stimulus cut-out reflected the same gray. According to the notion of memory color, past experience with objects associated with these shapes influences their

apparent color so that the cut-out of the leaf, typically green, should appear greener than the cut-out of the characteristically gray donkey. Matches of the apparent color of each stimulus made on a color wheel indicated that the amount of green required to match the color of the cut-out of the leaf was about twice as much as needed to match the color of the cut-out of the donkey. That is, although both stimuli reflected the same gray light, the cut-out of the leaf, presumably owing to the influence of memory color, appeared to be somewhat greener than the cut-out of the donkey. The obvious conclusion is that previous color and form associations—memory color—do exert an appreciable effect on perceived color. This experiment in a number of variations, has been repeated and its essential findings confirmed (e.g., see Delk & Fillenbaum, 1965; Epstein, 1967).

A variation of memory color using afterimages was reported by White and Montgomery (1976). In their demonstration, observers formed afterimages of either a flaglike pattern (i.e., an American flag printed in its complementary colors consisting of black stars, an orange field and blue-green stripes, like Plate 3) or a simple blue-green striped pattern (identical to the stripes in the flag pattern). Observers then adjusted a chromatic field to match the afterimage colors. The general result was that the observers perceived the complementary afterimages of the stripes in the flag pattern as more red than they did the afterimages of the same stripes in the simple striped pattern. These results indicate that memory color plays a role in afterimages, namely, that afterimages that represent familiar objects are affected by the colors in which the objects normally appear.

THEORIES OF COLOR PERCEPTION

There have been numerous theoretical accounts of the many diverse phenomena of color perception. However, two main theories emerge as most consistent with contemporary research and data. Accordingly, our discussion will be confined principally to them.

THE YOUNG–HELMHOLTZ THEORY
(TRICHROMATIC RECEPTOR THEORY)

The phenomena of color mixture suggest certain structural, functional, and neural mechanisms of the retina. Because three distinct and different wavelengths are sufficient to produce almost all the perceptible colors, it is possible that there are, correspondingly, three sets of receptors (cones) in the eye that respond differentially to different wavelengths; that is, the neural contribution of each set of receptors may vary appropriately for a given spectral light in the environment.

Thomas Young, an English scientist, in 1802 suggested just such a trichromatic receptor theory. Basing his theory on the assumption that there are three different kinds of receptors in the human retina, each sensitive to light of a specific spectral composition, he proposed that when they are stimulated by a given wavelength, their neural activity accounts for color experience. This proposal was revived in 1866 by Herman von Helmholtz, who extended Young's initial proposal by postulating a distinct spectral sensitivity curve for each of the three sets of receptors (Figure 13.8). Helmholtz modified Young's theory by questioning the idea that a given receptor for color can be activated by only one wavelength. His original proposal designated receptors not exclusively but *maximally* sensitive to wavelengths that correspond to the hues of blue, green, and red. In its simplest form the **trichromatic receptor theory** or the **Young–Helmholtz theory** maintains that only three types of receptors are required for the discrimination of hue. Stimulation by red, for example, produces a chromatic experience specifically due to a strong excitation of the "red" receptors (type 1, in Figure 13.8), together with weak stimulation of "green" and "blue" receptors (type 2 and 3 receptors of Figure 13.8). The result is a red sensation. "Yellow" light stimulates the "red" and "green" receptors to a moderate degree and the "blue" receptors very slightly with a resultant sensation of yellow. By this account, all the hues resulting from the distribution of spectral lights and their mixtures can be produced by the appropriate proportional contribution of a three-receptor system.

There is strong physiological evidence for the existence of a three-receptor system, thus supporting the notion of a retinal basis of color vision. Findings show the existence of three groups of distinct cones, each set maximally responsive to a different wavelength. Actually, it is three classes of photopigments that are segregated in three kinds of cones. Marks, Dobelle, and MacNichol (1964) directed a fine beam of light on isolated cone photoreceptors of the retinae of monkeys and humans and measured the absorption of light by the pigment of a single cone for different spectral wavelengths. The more a given wavelength is absorbed by the pigment of a cone, the more sensitive that cone is to light of that wavelength. The results, shown in Figure 13.9, indicate that for cones, peaks of absorption fall into three major groups, with maximum absorption at about 445 nm, 535 nm, and 570 nm. Following similar procedures, Brown and Wald (1964) reported similar maximal absorption at 450 nm, 525 nm, and 555 nm thus supporting the proposal that there are three distinct types of cone receptor pigments.

Further support for the existence of specific cone pigments has come from the research of Rushton (1962; Baker & Rushton, 1965) using different measuring techniques than just described. He reports the existence of a photosensitive pigment for

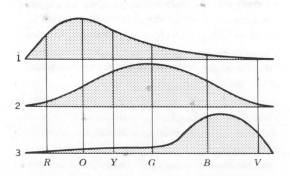

FIGURE 13.8.   Sensitivity functions of hypothetical red (1), green (2), and blue (3) receptors. (From L. A. Riggs, "The 'looks' of Helmholtz," *Perception & Psychophysics*, 2, 1967, p. 3; after Helmholtz, 1866. Reprinted by permission of Psychonomic Society, Inc.)

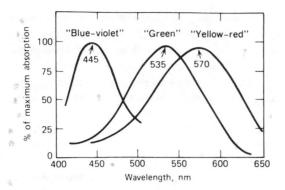

FIGURE 13.9.   Curves derived from the absorption spectra for cones of primates. Color vision appears mediated by three types of cone pigments with peaks at 445, 535, and 570 nm. The peak (570 nm) of the "red" curve is in the yellow region but extends far enough into the red region to account for the sensation of red.

green called **chlorolabe,** a red pigment, **erythrolabe** and possibly the existence of a third pigment for blue, **cyanolabe.** Thus, the collective evidence on pigment absorption indicates that three types of cone pigments are specialized to absorb portions of light over a limited range of wavelengths each with a maximum absorption at a particular region of the spectrum. Of interest, Nathans and his coworkers (Nathans, Thomas, & Hogness, 1986; Nathans, et al., 1986) not only verified the existence of the three different light-sensitive cone pigments but they have also identified their genetic coding.

These and numerous other studies, along with the facts of color mixture and matching lend considerable support to a trichromatic receptor theory of color vision, at least at the retinal level (see also Stroymeyer et al., 1980).

OPPONENT-PROCESS THEORY

A second major theory of color vision, the **opponent-process theory,** is traced to Ewald Hering, a German physiologist (1920). Like the Young–Helmholtz trichromatic receptor theory, Hering postulated three independent receptor types, but his theory differed in that the three classes of receptors were

each assumed to be composed of a pair of *opponent* color processes or neural systems: a blue-yellow, a green-red, and a white-black opponent process. The basic scheme held that each receptor is capable of two kinds of physiological and sensory responses that are mutually opposite or antagonistic to each other. That is, a receptor can respond in only one of two possible ways. It follows that either red *or* green, and yellow *or* blue is experienced, but not yellow *and* blue or red *and* green. Some interesting observations conform to this notion. Thus, if one member of a receptor pair is stimulated more than its opponent, the corresponding hue will be seen. If the stimulation of one member of a receptor pair is prolonged (and presumably fatigued), and the gaze is then shifted to an achromatic surface, a complementary afterimage may appear. If both members are equally stimulated, they cancel each other out (as is the case with mixtures of complementary colors) leaving only gray.

While retaining the general sense of trichromatic theory, Hurvich and Jameson (e.g., 1955, 1974) have elaborated on Hering's basic opponent notion and have proposed that three component photoreceptors (or cones), each sensitive to a different region of the visible spectrum, differentially affect three pairs of opponent-process neural mechanisms. In keeping with Hering's proposal, they postulate a blue-yellow and a green-red process and an achromatic white-black process. Within each pair of neural processes, one physiological response characteristic is opponent or antagonistic to the other.

According to the Hurvich and Jameson notion, it is not the photoreceptors themselves that provide the color coding but instead color coding occurs as a neurophysiological event—at a neural level of the opponent process. In addition, all three receptors affect the white-black opponent process. This opponent pair responds when any light affects any of the three types of photoreceptors. Its function is to transmit luminance rather than hue information and, accordingly, its activity contributes to the brightness and the degree of saturation of the chromatic response. Essentially what the Hurvich and Jameson model illustrates is that activity of neural processes with opponent properties can result from appropriate stimulation of receptors with trichromatic properties.

Based on an opponent process notion, it is possible to measure the perceived hue for any given wavelength of light. This has been done, basically as a quantification of the Hering theory, by Hurvich and Jameson (1955, 1957). Because the two members of a receptor process are mutually antagonistic, the magnitude of a given sensory response can be assessed by the amount of the opponent member needed to eliminate or cancel the color sensation. This **null** or **hue cancellation method** can be used to measure the spectral distribution of the chromatic response. Accordingly, the amount or relative strength of a blue response is determined by the amount of energy of a wavelength appearing yellow that must be added in order to *cancel* or *neutralize* the blue sensation. That is, the amount of the blue component is assumed to equal the amount of yellow that had to be added to cancel it. Similarly, the amount of the yellow response is determined by adding just sufficient blue light to cancel the yellow sensation. A similar statement can be made for the green and red response: the amount of red light added to wavelengths in the greenish region and the amount of green light added to wavelengths in the red region to cancel the appropriate chromatic responses are measures of the amount of green and red response, respectively. Clearly, the null method—as a direct measurement of opponent activity—enables the assessment of the chromatic response at all wavelengths across the visible spectrum.

COLOR CODING BEYOND THE RETINA

There is much neurophysiological evidence of an opponent-type process operating at neural levels beyond the retina. The general finding that emerges from the recordings of neural activity from the ganglion level or the lateral geniculate nucleus is that some cells increase their rates of firing (above a spontaneous or baseline level) for some wavelengths and decrease them for others. Wagner, MacNichol, and Wolbarsht (1960; see also Daw, 1967) found that the ganglion cells of the goldfish gave "on-off" responses to stimulation by white light. When lights of single wavelengths were presented, they found that for a given cell, an excitatory or "on" response to a

band of wavelengths turned into an "off" response to other wavelengths.

DeValois (1965*a*, *b*; DeValois, Abramov, & Jacobs, 1966) inserted microelectrodes into single cells in the lateral geniculate nucleus of the Macaque monkey and recorded the neural activity in response to the presentation of different wavelengths. Some cells directly increased or decreased their rates of firing in response to lights of any wavelength. However, evidence was also noted of opponent-type cells whose overall response rates varied with the wavelength of light; they were excited by some wavelengths and inhibited by others and generally showed differing firing rates to different wavelengths. Figure 13.10 provides an example of one such cell. If it is stimulated with long-wavelength red light (633 nm), it fires vigorously at the onset and throughout the duration of the light, whereas it is relatively inhibited at the offset of the light. In contrast, short wavelengths of blue or green light produce an inhibition of the cell during presentation of the light followed by activity at the offset of the light. This type of cell, showing excitation to red light and inhibition to green light, is categorized as a +R–G color opponent cell.

Such observations as these have been incorporated in a two-stage theory in which three types of receptors, like those proposed by the three cone, trichromatic receptor theory, feed into color-opponent units at further, postretinal stages in the visual system. A schematic depiction of such a two-stage color theory is illustrated in Figure 13.11. Although this is only an example of a model, it does suggest a process by which the color information in three types of cone receptors may feed into color opponent neural responses at stages beyond the retina in the visual system. The color information is thus encoded in terms of only excitation or inhibition of neural activity.

Blobs Further neural evidence supports a close correspondence between color coding and the postretinal neural response. Livingstone and Hubel (1984; Hubel & Livingstone, 1983; Livingstone, 1987) have reported the existence of a somewhat regular mosaic or polka-dotlike pattern of dark regions (each about 0.2 mm in diameter) that they call

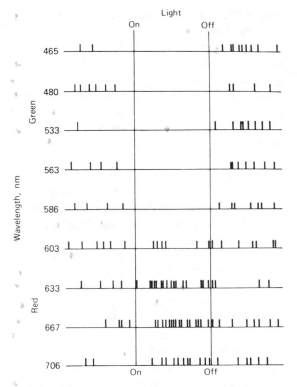

FIGURE 13.10. Responses recorded from a single microelectrode inserted in a cell of the lateral geniculate nucleus of a monkey. The cell that produced this record was classified as an opponent cell because of the opposite effects of the long and short wavelengths. Short wavelengths inhibited the cell, whereas long wavelengths excited it. This opponent cell turned out to be a red-excitatory, green-inhibitory cell (+R −G cell). [The firing before the stimulation (light onset) is due to the spontaneous firing of the cell.] (After DeValois, Abramov, & Jacobs, 1966, p. 970.)

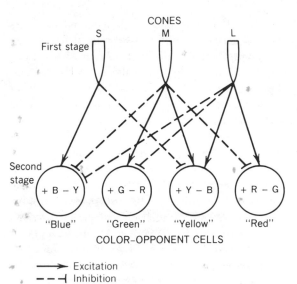

FIGURE 13.11. A schematic depiction of two-stage color theory. Three classes of cones with peak sensitivities at short (S), medium (M), and long (L) wavelengths feed into color-opponent cells of second stage. For example, a +B −Y opponent cell is excited by short wavelength cones and inhibited by both medium and long wavelength cones. That is, the cell is excited by blue and inhibited by yellow light. Similarly, a +R −G opponent cell is excited by long wavelength cones and inhibited by medium wavelength cones. Thus the cell is excited by red and inhibited by green light.

"blobs" that are distributed over the primary visual cortex (or striate cortex area 17). **Blobs** are composed of neurons that are not tuned or selective to orientation, shape, or movement, but react exclusively to color. Moreover, the activity of color-coded cortical neurons from these regions has been recorded that indicates that they possess concentric **double-opponent receptive fields** or processes (Michael, 1978a, b). The double-opponent process

cells have an antagonistic center-surround organization with each component having a dual effect. Thus the center increases its activity or firing rate to one color and decreases it to the complementary color; in contrast its surround has the exact opposite double-response pattern. Figure 13.12a shows the organization of a double-opponent cortical cell in which the center of its receptive field shows activation to red and inhibition to green, whereas the surround of the receptive field shows inhibition to red and increased activity to green.

Figures 13.12b and c suggests how a linear arrangement of the receptive fields of double-opponent color-coded neurons of the cortex may be organized to react to chromatic bars and rectangles.

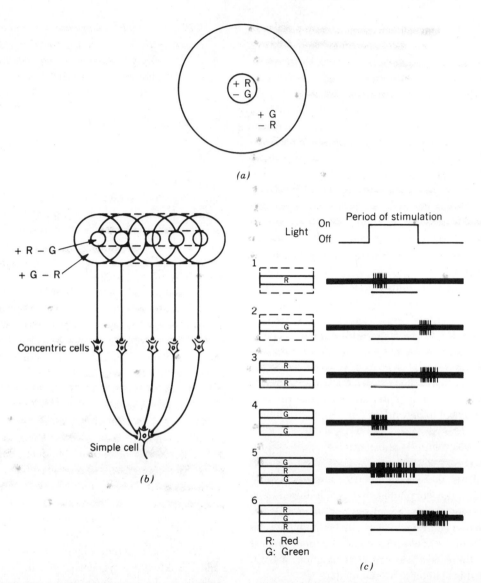

FIGURE 13.12.   Double-opponent color-coded cortical cells with concentric receptive fields. (*a*) Receptive field of a double-opponent color-coded cortical cell. The center is +R −G, and the surround is + G−R. (*b*) Linear arrangement of double-opponent receptive fields that are organized to respond to bars and rectangles of one opponent color system (center: +R −G; surround: +G −R). The output of the color-coded cells feed into a simple cortical cell. (*c*) Neural record of activity of simple cortical cell to bars of lights (red: 620 nm; green: 500 nm): (1) A red bar covering the central strip produced an "on" response. (2) A green bar covering the central strip produced an "off" response. (3) Two red bars covering the antagonistic surround elicited an "off" response. (4) Two green bars covering the surround evoked an "on" response. (5) A red bar covering the central strip and flanked by two green ones evoked a strong "on" response that extended for the duration of the stimulation. (6) A green bar covering the central strip and flanked by two red ones elicited a vigorous "off" response. (Based on Michael, 1978*b*, modified from Gouras, 1981.)

Shown are the cells of one opponent-color system (e.g., +R −G center) that have antagonistic flanking regions with a reverse double-opponent arrangement (+G −R surround). The neural activity of the concentric cells feed into a simple cortical cell. Figure 13.12c shows the response record to chromatic bars of light. Clearly, of the stimulus possibilities examined, the greatest neural effect to the presentation of the stimulus occurs when a red bar covers the central region and is flanked by two green bars (see row 5 of Figure 13.12c). The red bar stimulates the +R −G centers, whereas the adjacent green bars stimulate the +G −R surrounds. In short, the excitation from the red in the center is combined with the excitation of the green in the surround causing each cell to fire at its maximum. It seems reasonable to propose that the organization of double-opponent process cells plays some role in effecting the phenomenon of simultaneous contrast, such as shown in Plate 6. The activity of cells possessing double-opponent receptive fields is consistent with the heightened or exaggerated brightness that is apparent when fixation is on the border region of the two adjacent complementary colors (i.e., a red center and a green surround).

Much is yet to be worked out, but it is sufficient to say that the characteristics of a color stimulus are processed and neurally transmitted along the visual system by means of some opponent-type color coding process. Thus, there is evidence for an initial trichromatic retinal stage of photosensitivity, followed by an opponent system at a subsequent neural level. Rather than a controversy existing between the relative merits of the trichromatic and opponent-process theories, there is a sequential interaction of both. Consider this statement on the matter:

> All the evidence for the three-color, three-receptor cone system comes up against the earlier electrophysiological evidence for an opponent-color system farther along the visual pathway. Color vision is apparently at least a two-stage process, consistent with the Young-Helmholtz theory at the receptor level and with the Hering theory at the level of the optic nerve and beyond. Each receptor does not have its private route to the brain; three-color information is somehow processed in the retina and encoded into two-color on-off signals by each of the color-sensitive retinal ganglion cells for transmission to the higher visual centers. (MacNichol, 1964a, p. 56)

LADD-FRANKLIN THEORY

Before leaving our discussion of color theories we note in passing the early theory of Ladd-Franklin (1929) that stresses the possible evolutionary development of color vision based on the existence of distinct opponent-color zones on the retina. The **Ladd-Franklin Theory** is of interest to us because it draws upon some concepts from both the trichromatic receptor theory and the opponent process theory. Originally Christine Ladd-Franklin proposed that a primitive black-white achromatic sensitivity evolved into further differentiation; first into a sensitivity to blue and yellow, which at still later stages of evolution further differentiated into sensitivity to red and green. The theory also proposed that the central areas of the retina, where all hues are perceived, are the most evolutionarily developed and at the extremes of the retina are found the most primitive receptors responsive to only colorless light. In support of this notion, areas of the retina do manifest such color zones or regions. In fact, black-white sensitivity occurs first in the far periphery, blue and yellow zones occur next, and the more central region is required for seeing red and green. (A demonstration that approximates color-sensitive zones is given in Plate 7).

We must conclude, however, that while the Ladd-Franklin theory is consistent with the existence of distinct color-sensitive retinal zones, any conclusions concerning the evolutionary history of color vision in the mammal is quite speculative.

DEFECTIVE COLOR VISION

Although the vast majority of the human population possess normal color vision, a small proportion has some defect. Persons in this latter group match spectral colors with different amounts of primary colors than do persons with normal color vision. Except for those forms based on pathology (discussed shortly), defective color vision is inherited. Nathans and his colleagues (Nathans, Thomas & Hogness, 1986; Nathans et al., 1986; see also Botstein, 1986) have identified the genetic coding of the three retinal cone pigments that mediate color vision. Of interest, each cone contains a single pigment and each pigment has its own gene. Moreover the green and red genes are nearly identical and are localized on the X chromosome, which is critical in determining gender. Accordingly red and green defective color vision is usually a genetically transmitted sex-linked recessive characteristic and, as such, occurs primarily in males; about 8% of the male and less than 0.5% of the female population have some form of genetically transmitted color vision defect.

Color deficiencies may be divided into three major classes, depending on the number of primary colors required to match all spectral colors. The main forms are termed *anomalous trichromatism, dichromatism,* and *monochromatism.*

ANOMALOUS TRICHROMATISM

Normal color vision is trichromatic; however the defective or anomalous trichromat requires a different proportion of the three primary colors to match the colors of the spectrum when compared to a normal viewer. The more common form of **anomalous trichromatism** involves the perception of red and green. As we noted earlier, a yellow color can be matched by the suitable mixture of red and green. Anomalous trichromats, however, require more red or green in the mixture than do normals. The general device used to assess such defects in color matching is a special kind of color mixer that measures the proportions of monochromatic red that must be mixed with monochromatic green to match a monochromatic yellow. Appropriately, it is termed an **anomaloscope.**

Two kinds of anomalous trichromatism may be identified: **protoanomaly** and **deuteranomaly.**

The protoanomalous person requires much more red than normal in the mixture of red and green to match a yellow in an anomaloscope, and the deuteranomalous person needs a greater proportion of green than normal in the red-green mixture to match the yellow.

DICHROMATISM

In the case of **dichromatism,** dichromats match the spectrum with the appropriate combination of two colors rather than the three required by normal viewers. Dichromats may be divided into **deuteranopia** and **protanopia,** which refer to green and red deficiencies. For both deuteranopes and protanopes, the short-wavelength region of the spectrum appears blue and the long-wavelength region appears yellow. Moreover, both deuteranopes and protanopes confuse red and green, both colors appearing as desaturated yellow. However, persons who have deuteranopia, the most common form of dichromatism, are relatively insensitive to wavelengths in the green region, whereas protanopes are less sensitive than normal to the long wavelengths of light; that is, much higher than normal intensities of red light are required in order to be seen (see Plates 8 and 9) (Graham & Hsia,1954,1958; Hsia & Graham,1965).

A third form of dichromatism, which is quite rare, called **tritanopia,** is characterized by a deficiency in seeing blue and yellow; that is, tritanopes see only reds and greens and confuse yellows, grays and blues. In addition, tritanopes see only a neutral gray in the neighborhood of 570 nm (yellow); longer wavelengths appear reddish, and shorter wavelengths appear greenish (see Plate 9D) (Hsia & Graham, 1965; Geldard, 1972).

Although it is not possible to know how the colors that a dichromat sees compare with those seen by a normal person, some evidence bearing on this issue has been described. Graham and Hsia (1958) reported the case of a unilaterally color-blind subject, a woman who was a deuteranope in her left eye but normal in her right eye. By using color-matching procedures in which different hues could be shown to each eye independently, it was possible to measure the color vision in the defective left eye. The procedure was that for each color presented to her defective left eye she adjusted the color using the normal right eye so that it appeared as the same hue. The results of this color-matching procedure are shown in Figure 13.13. To her defective eye the colors extending the entire spectral range from green to red (502 nm to 700 nm) appeared identical to a single hue of yellow (about 570 nm) as seen by her normal right eye, and all the colors from green to violet looked blue (about 470 nm). The blue-green region (which occurred at about 502 nm) was seen as a neutral gray by the defective eye.

MONOCHROMATISM

Those who suffer from **monochromatism** match all wavelengths of the spectrum against any other wave-

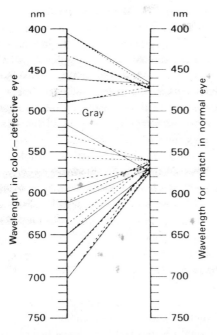

FIGURE 13.13. Results of the experiment with a unilateral color-defective subject. The wavelengths seen by the color-blind eye (left scale) are matched by the indicated wavelengths in the normal eye (right scale). (From C. H. Graham and Y. Hsia, "Color defect and color theory," *Science*, *127*, 1958, p. 679. Copyright © 1958 by the American Association for the Advancement of Science.)

length or a white light. This group could be termed "color-blind." Essentially, they have no chromatic response and usually suffer a reduction in other visual functions. It is likely that they have an abnormality in the number and kinds of cones in their retinae.

Color deficiencies have important theoretical implications for color vision. A reasonable explanation of color deficiencies is consistent with the notion that there are three classes of cones, each with a distinct pigment, and that one or more of the cones' photopigments is defective or totally lacking. That is, there is no absence of actual cones nor are the other functions of cones impeded—which is consistent with the fact that the acuity of most color-deficient persons, except for the monochromat, is at a normal level; however, there is an abnormal distribution of cone photopigments, or an abnormal set of cones that are less sensitive than normal cones to spectral lights (Frome, Piantanida, & Kelly, 1982). Accordingly the anatomical distinction between deuteranopes and protanopes is that each has a set of cones with a relative lack of the medium wavelength green pigment or the long wavelength red pigment, respectively.

CORTICAL COLOR BLINDNESS

As we noted earlier, regions of the visual cortex have specialized neurons for color coding. Accordingly localized damage to such regions from injury, strokes, multiple sclerosis, or tumors may seriously impair color perception. While this is a rare occurrence several clinical cases of total cortical color blindness (or, technically, cerebral **achromatopsia**) have been described and merit a brief discussion. The most unusual case (summarized by Sacks & Wasserman, 1987) is that of a 65-year-old successful abstract painter with normal vision, who suffered a concussion (and apparent damage to the visual association area of the cortex) as a direct result of an automobile accident. Immediately following the accident the patient discovered his total lack of color vision. Reds and greens appeared black, yellows and blues appeared almost white; moreover there was excessive contrast between visible objects and surfaces and a lack of brightness gradation that is typical of normal vision. Curiously, other aspects of vision were either unaffected, or as in the case of acuity, seemed heightened, due perhaps to the augmented contrast. In fact, the patient wrote, that, "Within days (following the accident), I could distinguish letters and my vision became that of an eagle—I can see a worm wriggling a block away. The sharpness of focus is incredible" (p. 25).

Not only did the patient totally lack the ability to see colors, but colored surfaces assumed an unnatural and unpleasant appearance. The authors write,

It was not just that colors were missing, but that what he did see had a distasteful, "dirty" look, the whites glaring, yet discolored and off-white, the blacks cavernous—everything wrong, unnatural, stained, and impure. . . . He saw people's flesh, his wife's flesh, his own flesh, as an abhorrent gray; "flesh-colored" now appeared "rat-colored" to him. This was so even when he closed his eyes. . . . The "wrongness" of everything was disturbing, even disgusting, and applied to every circumstance of daily life. Thus, unable to rectify even the inner image, the idea, of various foods, he turned increasingly to black and white foods—to black olives and white rice, black coffee, and yogurt. This at least appeared relatively normal, whereas most foods, normally colored, now appeared horribly abnormal. (p. 26)

Perhaps because he was an artist the patient's loss of color vision induced in him a profound sense of personal loss, at times bordering on extreme depression and despondency; it also provoked him to perform unusual, almost bizarre activities. The authors capture an instance of his unusual behavior as follows:

His despair of conveying what the world looked like, and the uselessness of the usual black-and-white analogies, finally drove him . . . to create an entire "gray room," a gray universe, in his studio, in which tables, chairs, and an elaborate dinner ready for serving were all painted in a range of grays. . . . The effect of this, in three dimensions and in a different tonal scale from the "black and white" we are all accustomed to, was indeed macabre, and wholly unlike that of a black-and-white photograph. (p. 27)

Finally after a depressed period of several months the patient resumed the representational and portrait painting of his youth, but now exclusively in black and white. He also turned to sculpture, perhaps making use of the visual modes that still remained—contour, form, depth, and texture. Almost two years after losing his color vision the patient appeared to have adjusted to the loss, or at least accepted it. He reported that the revulsions he initially felt toward certain objects and surfaces, like flesh, had passed.

The implications from this clinical study not only underscores the overwhelming personal significance that color has to the individual's environmental interactions, but at a physiological level, it further supports the notion that regions of the cortex contain specialized and distinct color analyzing mechanisms. Moreover, it makes clear that the nervous system uses separate parallel channels to transmit and process achromatic and chromatic information about the visual environment (see also Livingstone, 1987). Certainly the observation that green and red appeared to the patient as black, whereas blue and yellow were seen as white, is suggestive of the opponent processes implicated earlier in describing color vision (see Pearlman, Birch, & Meadows, 1979, for another example of this rare anomaly).

SUBJECTIVE COLORS

We end this chapter with a brief commentary on the production of chromatic sensations from colorless stimulation. We have noted repeatedly that color sensations result principally from the different wavelength compositions of light. However, it is possible to produce some chromatic sensations, called **subjective colors,** from only black and white stimuli. One of the configurations used to demonstrate subjective colors, called **Benham's top,** is shown in Figure 13.14. By rotating the disk in a clockwise direction at a rate of 5 to 10 Hz, very desaturated blues, greens, yellows, and reds may appear. When the direction of rotation is reversed, the order of the appearance of the colors also reverses. Clearly, neither wavelength variation of the physical stimulus nor differential bleaching of the cone pigments is likely to play a role in the resultant chromatic sensations. It is plausible that the patterns of black and white alternations bypass the contribution of the retina. That is, the step normally performed at the retina is eliminated, and patterns of excitation are set up beyond the retinal level. This implies that the intermittent stimulation created by rotation of the Benham disk produces a sequence of neural events that simulates or mimics the different temporal patterns of neural activity that normally result from viewing chromatic stimuli. Festinger, Allyn, and White (1971) showed that the sequence of intensity changes over time, produced by the rotation of a

figure like that in Benham's top, can also be produced by a stationary pattern of flickering lights. That is, by varying the amount of light emitted as a function of time, reliable color sensations resulted. According to this description, subjective colors are the result of neural stimulation in which the normal cone contribution has been bypassed (see Wade, 1977, 1978 for an analysis and history of this phenomenon). A demonstration of subjective colors from a black and white stationary stimulus is given in Figure 13.15.

SUMMARY

In order to describe the general nature of color vision, color was discussed in terms of its three psychologi-

FIGURE 13.15.   Subjective colors from an achromatic pattern. Examine the central region of the diagonal pattern of lines for about 15 sec. A faint shimmering stream of pale colors will appear, often zigzaging or moving perpendicular to the diagonal black lines. During inspection of the pattern, small voluntary and involuntary eye movements occur. These eye movements constantly displace the image of the diagonal lines over the retinal receptors, producing a temporal pattern of receptor activity. That is, the small eye movements create transient patterns of intermittent stimulation from a stationary pattern that simulate the neural activity that typically occurs from viewing colored stimuli (e.g., Piggins, Kingham, & Holmes, 1972; Young, 1977).

FIGURE 13.14.   Benham's top. When rotated, the figure produces various temporal sequences of black and white. However, subjective colors—desaturated blues, greens, yellows and reds—may appear.

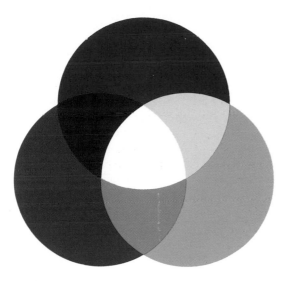

PLATE 1 Color mixture as additions of excitations. The partially superimposed projections of red, green, and blue result in: yellow (red and green), purple (red and blue), blue-green (blue and green). The mixture of all three (center) yields white. (Mednick, Higgins, and Kirschenbaum, *Psychology Explorations in Behavior and Experiences*. John Wiley & Sons, 1975.)

A

B

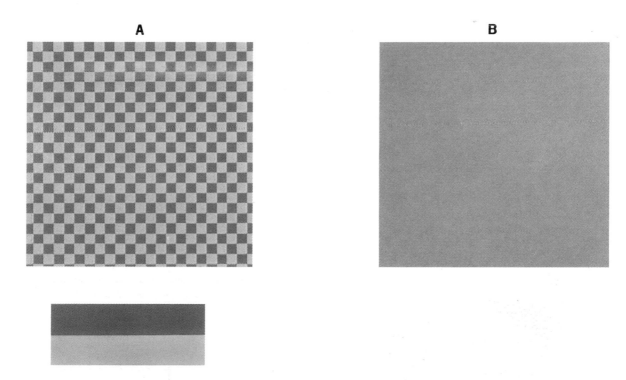

PLATE 2 Additive color mixture. The chromatic surface of square *A* is composed of a mosaic of red and green squares, each taken from the two stripes shown below square *A*. The chromatic surface of square *B* has a homogeneous yellow-orange appearance. In fact, squares *A* and *B* reflect very different sets of wavelengths and appear very different from each other. However, when the two squares are viewed from a distance between 10 and 12 feet (and lighted by incandescent light), the two surfaces appear almost identical. What has occurred is that, when viewed from a distance, the small red and green squares of *A* cannot be resolved individually and their combined (i.e., additive) effect on the visual system creates a chromatic match with square *B*.

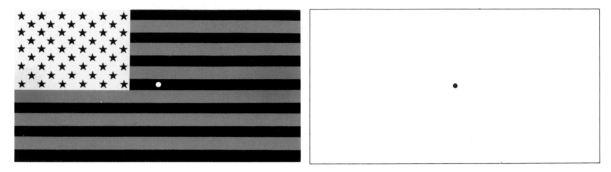

PLATE 3 Complementary or chromatic negative afterimages. Stare at the white dot at the middle of the flag for about 30 sec and then shift the gaze to the dot in the middle of the rectangle. Colors complementary to the green, yellow-orange, and black — the American flag in its normal colors — will appear as afterimages.

PLATE 4 Desaturation with continued exposure. Cover the right half of the rectangle with a piece of gray paper and stare at the fixation cross for 60 sec. Then remove the gray sheet while continuing to stare at the fixation mark. The left side will appear less saturated than the previously covered right side.

PLATE 5 Complementary afterimage and successive contrast. Stare at the fixation cross of the blue patch for 30 sec, then transfer the gaze to the cross of the yellow surface. A supersaturated yellow patch will appear.

PLATE 6 Simultaneous contrast. Stare at the cross for 20 sec. "Shimmering" effects may be seen at the border of the patch and its background because the two colors are complementaries.

7	**1**	**3**	**5**
3 4	6 4	8 5	7 9
2	9	2	6
x			
0°	10°	20°	30°

PLATE 7 Color zones of the retina. Cover the left eye and fixate on the x at 0° from about 5 to 6 in. (about 12 to 15 cm). With steady fixation you will see numerals printed in colored ink at 0° and probably at 10°, although numbers printed in red and green may not be distinguishable from each other. At 20° only the numbers printed in yellow and blue may be seen as colored. Further out, however, the numerals may be seen but not as colored. This shows that color discrimination varies with the retinal region stimulated. (Note that the angular measures given are only approximate.)

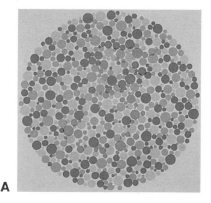
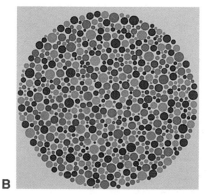

A **B**

PLATE 8 *A)* Individuals with normal color vision—trichromats—see the number 3, whereas red-green deficient dichromats see no number, only a random pattern of dots. *B)* Individuals with normal color vision see the number 42, dichromatic deuteranopes see only the digit 4, and protanopes see ony the digit 2. (Graham-Field Surgical Company.)

PLATE 9 Appearance of chromatic scene to individuals with normal color vision and to dichromats.

(A) Approximate appearance of chromatic scene to normal observer.

(B) Appearance to a protanope.

(C) Appearance to a deuteranope.

(D) Appearance to a tritanope.

(Burnham, Hanes, & Bartleson, *Color.* John Wiley & Sons, 1963.)

PLATE 10 "The Girl with a Red Hat" by Jan Vermeer (1632–1675). Depth and luminance quality is enhanced in the painting by the use of shading and diffused highlights. (The painting, c. 1665, was done on a wood panel. National Gallery of Art.)

PLATE 11 A reproduction of "Self-portrait as a Young Man" by Rembrandt van Rijn (1606–1669). When viewed directly, Rembrandt's self-portrait is an outstanding illustration of depth and distance in a picture. However, if viewed through a tube, reducing the cues of the picture's flatness, the depth effect is rendered more striking, approaching a real-world perception. (The picture was painted in oil on wood when Rembrandt was about 23 years old and represents the first of about 60 self-portraits painted by Rembrandt during his lifetime. The series itself is a dramatic study of the progression of physical age, rendered pictorially. Mauritshuis, The Hague.)

PLATE 12 A reproduction of "Self-Portrait" by Andy Warhol (1967). Compare Warhol's flat nonrepresentational self-portrait with the intensely realistic one by Rembrandt. In contrast to Rembrandt's rich and masterful use of shading, texture, and color — i.e., pictorial cues — Warhol's self-portrait intentionally lacks textural cues and makes little use of shading; instead it defines the facial features primarily by the use of adjacent contrasting light and dark areas of unusual colors. While it is a portrait of artistic interest, the Warhol work clearly lacks spatial depth and graphic realism. (Art Resource, © The Estate and Foundation of Andy Warhol, 1989. Courtesy Resource ARS, New York.)

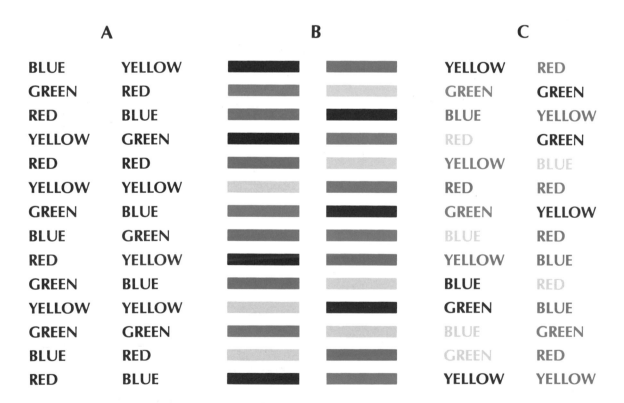

PLATE 13 The Stroop effect. The times required to read the list of color names in *(A)*, or to name the color of each patch in *(B)*, are significantly less than the time needed to name the colors of the list of color words in *(C)*.

cal attributes—hue, brightness, and saturation. These were related to the physical dimensions of wavelength, intensity, and purity, stressing the subjective nature of color vision. The facts of color matching and additive and subtractive color mixtures were outlined, and these were shown to be involved with many chromatic phenomena such as adaptation, color aftereffects and afterimages, successive and simultaneous contrast, and memory color.

Two major theories of color perception were outlined, the Young–Helmholtz or trichromatic receptor theory and the opponent-process theory. Evidence bearing on each was summarized, and it was concluded that aspects of both theories are consistent with contemporary research findings. Evidence of color coding beyond the retinal level was discussed. Neurophysiological evidence was presented of the existence of "blobs"—areas of the visual cortex that contain neurons whose activity are restricted and selective to color. Moreover it was noted that many color-coded cortical neurons from blobs have double-opponent receptive fields— that is, have an antagonistic center-surround organization with each component having a dual effect. A proposal was given as to how double-opponent color-coded cells may be organized to react to colored bars and rectangles. In addition, the Ladd-Franklin theory was noted. The topics of color deficiencies (anomalous trichromatism, dichromatism, monochromatism) and the striking anomaly of cortical color blindness—in which the total absence of color is due to localized damage of the visual cortex—were outlined. Finally, the perception of subjective colors was summarized. Subjective colors indicate that chromatic sensations can result without wavelength variation.

KEY TERMS

Achromatopsia
Additive color mixture
Afterimages
Anomaloscope

Anomalous trichromatism
Benham's top
Bezold-Brücke shift
Blobs
Chloralabe
Color circle
Color spindle (solid)
Complementary afterimage
Complementary colors
Cyanolabe
Deuteranomaly
Deuteranopia
Dichromatism
Double-opponent receptive field
Erythrolabe
Hue
Ladd-Franklin theory
Memory color
Metamers
Monochromatism
Null (hue cancellation) method
Opponent-process theory
Primary colors
Protoanomaly
Protanopia
Saturation
Simultaneous contrast
Subjective colors
Subtractive color mixture
Successive contrast
Tritanopia
Young–Helmholtz (trichromatic receptor) theory

STUDY QUESTIONS

1. Describe some of the functions served by color vision. Discuss the notion that color is a subjective experience. Distinguish between

the physical dimensions that produce color and the psychological phenomenon of color vision.

2. Indicate how the color spindle and color circle may represent and summarize the psychological dimensions of hue, saturation, and brightness. Outline some of the features illustrated by the color circle.

3. Describe trichromatic matching and indicate how three "primary" colors can be combined to match most color experiences.

4. What are complementary colors? How can they be demonstrated?

5. Distinguish between additive and subtractive color mixtures. Indicate what additive effects are demonstrated by metamers and colors that are complementary to each other. Describe how the color circle summarizes some of the effects of additive color mixtures.

6. Explain why the colors seen on color television and the artist's technique of pointillism are based on an additive color mixture. Explain why mixtures of blue and yellow paints produce a "green" color, whereas a mixture of blue and yellow light appears as an achromatic gray.

7. What is a negative afterimage? Explain successive and simultaneous contrast making use of negative afterimages.

8. What do negative afterimages indicate about the efficiency of cones after continual chromatic exposure? What role do involuntary eye movements play in producing simultaneous contrast?

9. Outline the contribution made by past experience and associations on the apparent color of familiar objects.

10. Outline the Young–Helmholtz (trichromatic receptor) theory, indicating supporting evidence based on cone activity.

11. Describe the opponent-process theory, drawing upon the neural response activity of regions beyond the retina.

12. Describe blobs and indicate how they enable an opponent-process type of color coding. Indicate what is meant by the concentric double-opponent receptive field that is characteristic of blobs.

13. Describe how the trichromatic and opponent-process theories account for the phenomena of chromatic afterimages such as in successive and simultaneous contrast.

14. Summarize the way in which the trichromatic and opponent-process theories may be integrated and may both be consistent with the phenomena of color perception.

15. Describe the Ladd-Franklin theory.

16. Indicate the main forms of color vision defects. In particular, distinguish between the two forms of dichromatism of protanopia and deuteranopia, and indicate, where applicable, possible causes.

17. Consider the implications of the clinical study of cortical color blindness concerning the opponent-process theory of color perception.

18. What are subjective colors and how can they be demonstrated? Note the contribution of sequences of colorless, intermittent stimulation in producing subjective colors. Consider how small transient involuntary eye movements may produce the neural activity that normally occurs when viewing colored stimuli.

THE PERCEPTION OF FORM AND SHAPE

Our concern up to this point has been with describing the retinal stimulus and the function of certain basic visual processes. We have not yet discussed much about the perception of spatial relations occurring within the visual field. Clearly, perception is quite different from the mere reception of the optic array emanating from the environment. The reflected light in the retinal image from objects and surfaces in the visual field is far too impoverished by itself to provide the visual characteristics that are experienced. Nor can the structures and known mechanisms of the eye or of the nervous system alone account for organized perception. Instead of a loose array of apparently discrete stimuli, one sees the visual field organized into related units with definite cohesive forms and shapes. Perception is thus a constructive achievement resulting from the operation of a set of unifying processes.

Our purpose in this chapter is to trace the development of the dynamics of form perception beginning with elementary aspects of the processes involved in perceptual organization. We consider how such processes are elaborated to produce the perception of form, and we also attempt to isolate some of the specific factors that account for, or contribute to, form perception.

CONTOUR AND CONTRAST PERCEPTION

An enormous number of interconnections exist among neighboring receptor cells within the eye and related structures; these interact to enable the perception of sharp visual contours. One of the contributions to the understanding of the perception of contour comes from investigation of the horseshoe crab (more a spider than a crab), **Limulus,** a form of marine life that has existed for millions of years in the same form as a kind of living fossil. The eye of the Limulus provides a simple model for analyzing higher visual systems. It is a compound eye consisting of about 1000 ommatidia (see Figure 11.4) that connect to intermediate cells to form the optic nerve. Because neighboring ommatidia react to partially

overlapping regions of the visual field, these cells interact when the ommatidia are stimulated by light and this interaction is inhibitory. That is, neighboring cells mutually suppress each other (Figure 14.1). The phenomenon is called **lateral inhibition.**

When two neighboring ommatidia are simultaneously activated, each discharges fewer impulses than when a single ommatidium receives the same amount of illumination by itself. The more widely separated the ommatidia, the smaller the mutual inhibitory effect. Thus, flooding the whole eye produces little activity because all cells inhibit each other. However, where there are light-intensity changes, such as at borders, interesting and significant visual effects occur.

Consider the following demonstration (Ratliff & Hartline, 1959): the Limulus eye was illuminated with a "step" pattern (a bright area adjacent to a dimmer one) (see Figure 14.2). Furthermore, the eye was masked so that only a single ommatidium was exposed to the pattern, which was moved to various loci. At each location the frequency of discharge was measured. The result, in terms of frequency of impulses, was a faithful representation of the pattern. That is, the frequency of response varied according to the position of the step pattern relative to the ommatidium. When the eye was unmasked so that all the ommatidia were exposed to the pattern, the response record from a single ommatidium indicated that the response frequency increased on the bright side of the step and decreased near the dim side. This increase in frequency on the bright side resulted because the stimulated cells nearest the border were inhibited only by excited cells on one side (since the other side was dim and contributed less inhibition). Similar logic explains the decrease in frequency on the dim side: a dimly illuminated area near the boundary is inhibited not only by its dimly illuminated neighbors but also by the nearby brightly illuminated ones. The total inhibition on this region will therefore be greater than that of dimly illuminated neighbors farther from the boundary and the frequency response is accordingly less. The net effect of this inhibition by lateral neural connections in the Limulus is to enhance the perception of

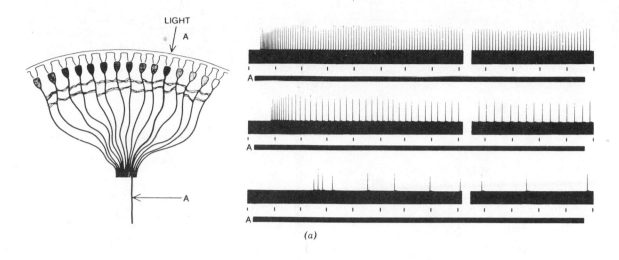

(a)

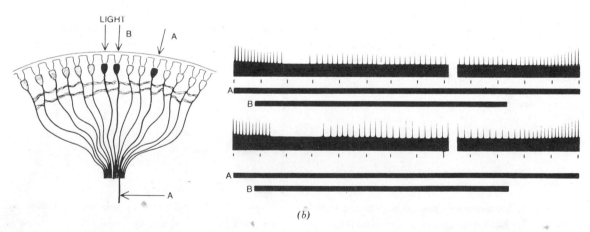

(b)

FIGURE 14.1.   Rate of discharge of nerve impulses (vertical lines) of single nerve fiber in the eye of the horseshoe crab Limulus. The nerve fiber is connected to an electrode from an amplifier and a recorder. (a) The record shows the response of the nerve fiber of a single ommatidium (A) to steady illumination. The top record shows the response of A to steady, high intensity light. The middle record shows the response to light of moderate intensity, and the lower record, the response to low intensity illumination. The duration of the light signal is indicated by the dark bar below the discharge record. Each mark above the bar indicates one-fifth of a second. (b) Inhibition of the steadily illuminated nerve fiber of single ommatidium (A) produced when neighboring ommatidia at B are also illuminated. This is shown in the record as a decrease in rate of discharge of nerve impulses on A. The upper record shows the effects on A of moderate intensity illumination of B. The lower record shows the effect on A of high intensity illumination of B. The stronger the illumination on neighboring receptors, the stronger the inhibitory effect. Notice the return to the earlier rate of nerve discharge when the illumination of neighboring ommatidia at B is terminated. (From F. Ratliff, "Contour and Contrast," *Scientific American, 226,* 1972, p. 93. Copyright © 1972 by Scientific American, Inc. All rights reserved.)

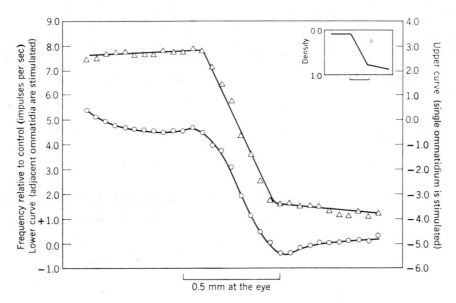

FIGURE 14.2. Contour enhancement is demonstrated by letting a "step" pattern of light move across the Limulus eye. Plotted is the discharge frequency of a single ommatidium relative to a control level as a function of the position of a luminance gradient (illustrated in insert). If the eye is masked so light strikes only one ommatidium (illustrated by triangles), a recording of its discharge frequency forms a simple step-shaped curve as the pattern moves along the eye. If the eye is unmasked so that adjacent receptors are also illuminated, the discharge frequency of the single ommatidium is inhibited in varying degrees, as illustrated by the circles. The net effect of the selective inhibition (lower curve) is to enhance the contrast at light-dark borders. Notice that the important point made by this figure is that the forms of the two curves differ; the difference in their absolute values is not relevant to our discussion. (From F. Ratliff and H. K. Hartline, "The responses of Limulus optic nerve fibers to patterns of illumination on the retinal mosaic," *Journal of General Physiology*, *42*, 1959, p. 1250. Reproduced by permission of the Rockefeller University Press.)

contours by heightening the contrast at light–dark borders. The basic features of an inhibitory interaction between neighboring retinal areas—lateral inhibition—apply to a wide variety of species including the human.

BORDER CONTRAST, LATERAL INHIBITION, AND MACH BANDS

Interaction between retinal areas—lateral inhibition—occurs with humans. For example, when looking at a step pattern consisting of a series of uniform bands graded from black to white, as shown in Figure 14.3*a* each vertical band appears to be lighter on the left than on the right side, producing a scalloping effect (Figures 14.3*b* and *c*). In fact, however, each band of the figure is of a uniform intensity from edge to edge. This is evident when the figure is covered so that only a single band is visible. This subjective contrast enhancement at the contours is called **border contrast.** The enhanced regions—which occur at the points of greatest change in luminance—are called **Mach bands,** after the Austrian physicist-philosopher, Ernst Mach. An explanation of border contrast in terms of lateral inhibition at the retinal ganglion cells is outlined in Figure 14.4.

The enhancement of stimulus differences—border contrast—is the result of the luminance from

FIGURE 14.3*a*.   A step pattern consisting of a series of uniform bands graded from black to white.

the different regions interacting with each other. One function of these interactions is obvious: it is an aid in the perception of borders, contours, and edges of an object even where there is not much physical difference in the light intensities between the object and its surroundings. The phenomenon of border contrast, by exaggerating the difference in the neural firing rates of receptors located at either side of the imaged boundary, enhances the perception of the contour and thereby provides a necessary step in the process of pattern recognition. Moreover, border contrast enhances the formation of discontinuities, which, as we will see in a following section, is necessary for the stable perception of form.

LIGHTNESS CONTRAST

Other spatial interactions, in which contrasting regions are adjacent, produce **lightness contrast** effects. The intensity of relatively large background regions can modify the lightness of smaller enclosed areas. Figure 14.5 illustrates this effect. The inner four gray squares are identical in the intensity of light they reflect, yet their perceived lightness differs. That the inner square on the far right appears to be lighter than the one on the far left indicates that the lightness of a region depends on the intensity of its background. (Note that the term **lightness** as used here refers to a surface quality and its perceived effects that are relatively unaffected by variations in the luminance or the intensity of the light reflected by a surface. As we noted in Chapters 11, 12 and 13 **brightness** refers to the subjective-perceptual effect that varies with light intensity, i.e., generally, changes in intensity produce changes in brightness. Note here that context and contrast effects promote lightness effects rather than brightness effects.)

It is worth noting that contrast phenomena are not restricted to the nervous system. A common occurrence is found with some xerographic processes, which reproduce only the edges of extended uniform areas. Homogeneous areas of black or gray are not copied adequately unless special precautions

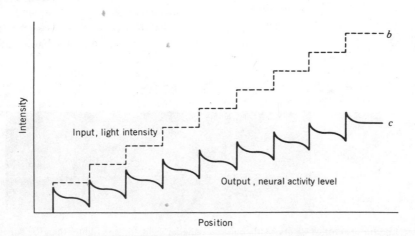

FIGURE 14.3*b*, *c*.   (b) The actual intensity distribution. (c) The lightness distribution. The scallops or furrows seen in Figure 14.3*a*—the Mach bands—are plotted here.

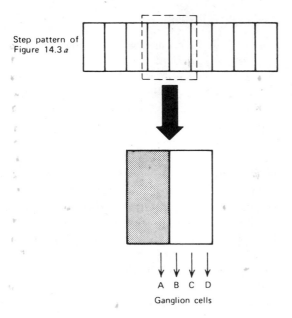

Step pattern of Figure 14.3*a*

A B C D
Ganglion cells

FIGURE 14.4. Schematic of lateral inhibition and border contrast. Assume that the lighter of the two uniform bands, shown in the bottom enlargement on the right, results in two units of inhibition to each adjacent ganglion cell, but the darker band results in one unit of inhibition. It follows that cell *C* receives four units of inhibition (two units from *B* and two units from *D*), whereas cell *B*, at the border of the dark and light bands, receives three units of inhibition (one from *A*, the darker band, and two from *C*). Thus cell *B*, stimulated by the border area, is less inhibited than cell *C*. This means that it will signal the presence of more light and thus accounts for the border's lighter appearance.

are taken. One technique is to cover the original image with a mesh (e.g., a halftone screen) that breaks up the image into a pattern of changes from light to dark. The xerographic copy produced in this way is much closer to the original pattern (Crovitz & Schiffman, 1968).

HERMANN GRID

Another example of contrast effects is given by the **Hermann grid** pattern of Figure 14.6. Although the luminance of the white stripes is uniform in all regions, faint gray spots are apparent at the intersections where there are four black corners. As with Mach bands, this phenomenon is a consequence of the luminance of different regions interacting with each other. Indeed, it has been suggested that the gray spots are a consequence of receptive field organization at the retinal ganglion level (Jung & Spillman, 1970). As illustrated, a receptor or unit of the visual system (whose presumed receptive field has an excitatory center and an inhibitory surround) activated by the region located at the intersection of the white stripes has a greater portion of its surround illuminated than a unit stimulated by a region located away from the intersection. Accordingly, there is more inhibition to units stimulated by the center of the intersection. The effect is that the lightness of the intersection is weakened relative to the lightness of neighboring regions.

That the gray spots do not appear at the points of fixation (i.e., for foveal stimulation) may be ex-

FIGURE 14.5. Lightness contrast effects. Although the physical intensities of the four inner squares are identical, they differ in lightness. That the square on the far right appears lighter than the square on the far left demonstrates that the lightness of a stimulus is affected by the intensity of its background.

FIGURE 14.6. The Hermann grid. Gray spots appear at the intersections of the white stripes. The concentric circles sketched within the four-rectangle section of the lower right insert suggest the way in which receptive fields of units with excitatory centers and inhibitory surrounds might be illuminated for two positions within the pattern. As illustrated, more of the inhibitory surround of the unit is illuminated at the intersection of the white stripes than at a region located to the right of the intersection. Accordingly, there is a greater inhibitory effect or weakened lightness response from stimulation at the intersection.

plained, in part, by evidence that the receptive fields for the fovea are much smaller than for the periphery (Jung & Spillman, 1970; Frisby, 1980).

THE GANZFELD: PERCEPTION IN A HOMOGENEOUS FIELD

Stimulation from the environment usually contains discontinuities of luminance and surface textures. However, when a completely textureless field of uniform brightness—an entirely homogeneous field called a **Ganzfeld**—is viewed, the resultant perception is of an unstructured ambiguous and disoriented environment. There are several means for producing a Ganzfeld; for example, having subjects look into a translucent globe (Gibson & Waddell, 1952) or by having subjects wear Ping-Pong ball halves over their eyes (Hochberg, Triebel, & Seaman, 1951). Under such conditions, viewers experience an undifferentiated space extending for an indefinite distance. "A diffuse fog" is a representative characterization (Cohen, 1957, p. 406). Such homogeneity—although quite unnatural—occurs from the simplest level of stimulation and produces the simplest possible perceptual experience. When the Ganzfeld surface is illuminated with colored light, subjects generally report that the color quality disappears within minutes (Hochberg, Triebel, & Seaman, 1951; Cohen, W., 1958). The most primitive level of form perception appears in the Ganzfeld with the introduction of a simple inhomogeneity such as a shadow or a gradient of intensity. With further stimulus changes, using definite contours, a segregation of portions of the Ganzfeld into a figure and a background occurs, and forms, figures, and surfaces may become perceptible. Not surprisingly, the greater the degree of stimulus change introduced, the greater is the perception of form qualities.

STABILIZED IMAGE

The Ganzfeld experience indicates that the visual system is incapable of functioning effectively with completely uniform stimulation. Normally this is not a problem. As we noted in Chapter 12, the eye is constantly in motion. Even when the eye is fixated on a stationary target, small involuntary eye movements persist. Accordingly, the target image on the retina of

the eye is kept in constant motion. However, it is possible to control or cancel the effects of eye movements on the retinal image. Several methods for stabilizing the retinal image exist but the general findings are similar so that we need consider only the following procedure. A contact lens on which is mounted a tiny self-contained optical projector is fitted directly over the cornea (see Figure 14.7). This device is set so that a focused image falls on the retina. Because the contact lens and projector move with the eye, the image projected onto the retina will not shift over the retina with movement of the eyeball. The result is that the effects of eye movements are eliminated. When a **stabilized image** is produced in this way or by another method, the image soon fades and disappears leaving an unstructured gray field.

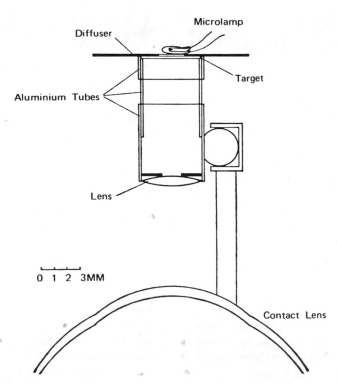

FIGURE 14.7. Stabilized-image device is a tiny projector mounted on a contact lens worn by the subject. The contact lens moves with every movement of the eyeball; so, therefore, does the projector, and as a result the tar-

get image is kept fixed at one point on the retina. The entire optical device weighs only 0.25 gram. (From Pritchard, Heron, & Hebb, 1960, p. 69.)

However, it can be quickly restored by the introduction of such stimulus changes as flickering of the image, changing its intensity level, and by movement of the image after its disappearance.

The significance of stimulus change on the perception of contour is illustrated by the demonstration of Figure 14.8. The two disks reflect the same amount of light; however, disk 1 has a blurry indistinct contour, and disk 2 has a sharp well-defined contour. Staring steadily with one eye on the center fixation of disk 1 will soon cause it to fade and disappear. However it will reappear if you blink or shift fixation to the X at the right. In contrast, even prolonged fixation of disk 2 will not produce its disappearance.

The explanation of this phenomenon is based upon the general principle raised in earlier discussions involving stimulus change and adaptation: all sensory channels require a certain level of stimulus change in order to maintain perception. When fixation is maintained on disk 2, patterns of very slight and abrupt involuntary eye movements occur. The result is that the eye movements produce strong intensity changes on the retina. In short, because of the involuntary eye movements the retinal region receiving the sharp contour stimulation is constantly changing, and accordingly, such changes contribute to the disk's continued visibility. However, consider the effect of eye movements when disk 1 is fixated. Due to its blurry contour, involuntary eye movements produce only a slight change in intensity on the retina; that is, with fixation the changes in stimulation due to the involuntary eye movements are not sufficient to maintain perception. Indeed in this condition no region of the retina undergoes even moderate changes in intensity. It follows that visibility of the blurred disk can be restored only after a significant change in illumination is produced such as from a large eye movement (e.g., shifting the gaze to the X) or opening and closing the eyes.

Stabilizing projections on the retina or rendering eye movements ineffective in promoting stimulus change, as in the demonstration of Figure 14.8, yield results similar to that produced by the Ganzfeld. In each case, eye movements are rendered incapable of bringing about a changing pattern of stimulation as

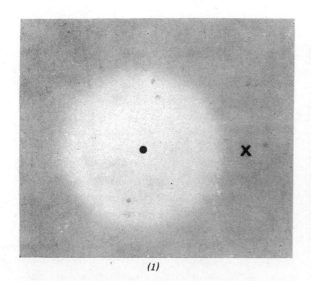

(1)

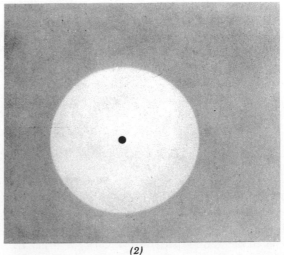

(2)

FIGURE 14.8.   Close one eye and steadily fixate on the dot in disk *1*. The disk will soon fade and disappear. However if you then blink or shift the gaze to the ✕ at the right of the disk, the disk will reappear. Fixation of disk *2* will not produce a fading effect. (Based on Cornsweet, 1969, p. 409.)

they normally do. In general, the results of this research demonstrate that variation and inhomogeneity of visual stimulation are a necessary condition for the formation and maintenance of a visual image.

SPATIAL FREQUENCIES

In a number of contexts, we have stressed that the ability to perceive the details of the visual environment is affected to a significant degree by contrast phenomena; that is, the perception of lightness differences due to the differences in the luminances of adjacent areas. In quite general terms, it is possible to analyze the composition of a visual display, consisting of contrasting areas—luminance variations —into its **spatial frequencies:** the number of changes in luminance over a given space. Spatial frequency is usually expressed in cycles (or the number of luminance changes) per degree of visual angle (which, will be recalled from the topic of visual angle in Chapter 12, varies jointly with the size of the contrasting areas and the distance from which they are viewed).

This analysis has much in common with an earlier discussion of auditory stimulation; whereas a pure tone is a regular periodic variation in air pressure over time, the visual stimulus is a periodic or cyclical variation in luminance across space. A simple example of this is shown in the grating patterns of Figures 14.9a and b. Their luminance profiles, or distributions of light, plotted below the patterns are of sine waves. That is, the luminance is modulated in a sinusoidal manner, producing peaks and troughs. Accordingly, the grating patterns are described as *sinusoidal* gratings. As a pure tone can be specified with respect to its amplitude and frequency, a grating pattern has the property of intensity (or contrast) accompanying its spatial frequency. Notice the grating pattern of Figure 14.9a has the same frequency as that of Figure 14.9b but differs in contrast. In general terms, the *contrast* refers to the difference in luminance between the light and dark areas. [More technically, contrast is defined as max-

imum or peak luminance minus the minimum or trough luminance divided by their sum, which yields a value varying from 1 (very high contrast) to 0 (no contrast).]

Just as complex sounds can be analyzed into combinations of pure tones, complex spatial patterns may be analyzed as combinations of simple spatial patterns or sinusoidal gratings. It is possible to take a complex spatial distribution of light, a pattern, and to perform a **Fourier analysis** or transform it into a set of Fourier components. That is, it is possible to decompose the pattern into a set of representative sine waves. Conversely, these Fourier components can be summed to produce the complex pattern. This recombination process, called **Fourier synthesis,** is suggested by Figure 14.9d for a square wave pattern like that illustrated in Figure 14.9c. Figure 14.9d outlines how pure sine wave grating patterns, labeled f, $3f$, $5f$, and $7f$, can be combined (transformed) to make a pattern that approximates a square wave ($f + 3f + 5f + 7f$). The resemblance of this pattern to the square wave pattern of Figure 14.9c increases as higher odd frequencies (e.g., $9f$, $11f$, $13f$, etc.), are added in proper phase.

CONTRAST SENSITIVITY FUNCTION

As we just noted, a pattern may be characterized by its spatial frequency (i.e., intensity or luminance variations) and its contrast (difference in intensity between pattern elements). There is a relation between spatial frequency and contrast such that certain spatial frequencies are seen more clearly than others, depending upon the contrast between the elements comprising the spatial frequency pattern. That is, less contrast is required to distinguish some spatial frequencies than others. Indeed the visual system appears more sensitive to certain spatial frequencies than to others in a manner similar to the ear's differential sensitivity to sound frequency. This is apparent when spatial frequency patterns of luminance variations are viewed such as the one illustrated in Figure 14.10a. The pattern consists of a varying sinusoidal grating whose frequency increases from left to right and whose contrast increases from

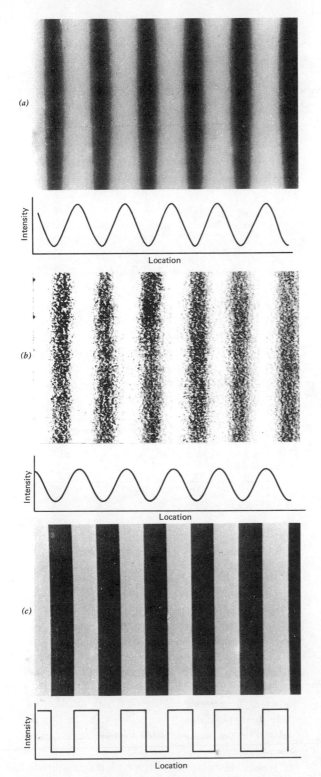

(a)

Intensity

Location

(b)

Intensity

Location

(c)

Intensity

Location

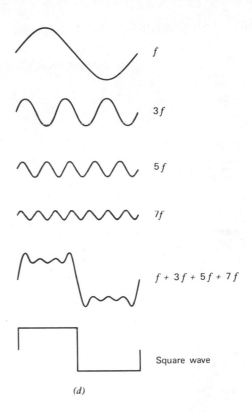

f

$3f$

$5f$

$7f$

$f + 3f + 5f + 7f$

Square wave

(d)

FIGURE 14.9. Grating patterns (below each is its luminance or intensity distribution). (a) Sinusoidal grating pattern. (b) Sinusoidal grating pattern with same frequency as (a) but lower in contrast. (c) Square wave grating pattern. (d) The Fourier synthesis of a square wave. The addition of Fourier components results in an approximation of a square wave (f refers to the frequency of the original sine wave).

top to bottom. Thus the further down on the pattern necessary to just distinguish the particular spatial frequencies, the greater is the degree of contrast required (i.e., the higher the threshold) and the less is the sensitivity of the visual system to those spatial frequencies. Similarly, the less contrast required to make certain spatial frequencies visible, the greater is the sensitivity to those frequencies.

It is possible to examine the functional relation of threshold levels of contrast to spatial frequency that describes the visual system's sensitivity for the range of spatial frequencies to which it responds. The relation between spatial frequency and threshold

279

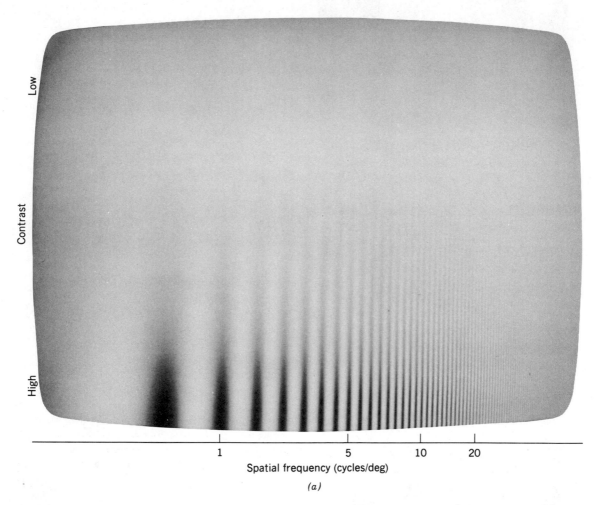

FIGURE 14.10a.   Stimulus pattern containing sinusoidal gratings that increase in frequency from left to right and in contrast from top to bottom. For most viewers the spatial frequencies in the middle appear most distinctly. Due to the printing process this rendering degrades or eliminates some of the original detail of the pattern and serves only as an approximation. (Photograph courtesy of F. W. Campbell.)

levels of contrast is called the **contrast sensitivity function.** A summary of the overall variation of contrast sensitivity with spatial frequency for the display of Figure 14.10a is illustrated in the contrast sensitivity function of Figure 14.10b. Generally for patterns having low spatial frequencies (i.e., comprised of broad gratings), the contrast threshold is high (left ordinate) and sensitivity is low (right ordinate); that is, high contrast is required to detect the pattern. As spatial frequency increases (e.g., moving from left to right on Figure 14.10a), less contrast is required for visibility and the contrast threshold decreases (and sensitivity increases). However, for patterns having *very* high spatial frequencies (approximated on the far right in Figure 14.10a), the contrast threshold increases and sensitivity falls again.

It should be clear that Figure 14.10b is a plot of

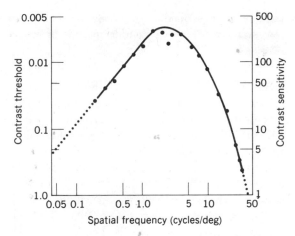

FIGURE 14.10*b*. Contrast sensitivity function. The curve relates threshold contrast and sensitivity to the range of spatial frequencies to which the visual system responds. The left ordinate specifies the contrast threshold values necessary to just distinguish each frequency. The less contrast required to make a spatial frequency visible, the greater the sensitivity. Thus, sensitivity, plotted on the right ordinate, is the reciprocal of the threshold value. The moderate spatial frequencies are visible with less contrast than either the low or high spatial frequencies. Hence of the range of frequencies examined, sensitivity is greatest for moderate spatial frequencies. (Based on Howard, 1982.)

the physical contrast necessary to detect a grating pattern relative to the pattern's intensity changes or spatial frequency. It shows that intensity changes are most effective in making a grating pattern visible when they occur at intermediate spatial frequencies (with a peak at about 3 cycles/deg.). When the intensity changes occur too frequently (i.e., very high spatial frequencies) or too infrequently (i.e., low frequencies), sensitivity to the changes is reduced. In short the visual system is less sensitive to very low and very high spatial frequencies than it is to intermediate ones.

One particular interest in spatial frequencies is based on the notion that a visual scene may be represented by a complex set of patterns specifiable in units of spatial frequencies. Thus, at a certain level, the visual system could be performing a Fou-

rier analysis on the spatial frequency content of the complex visual stimuli, that is, determining the Fourier components of the pattern. If this is the case, then the visual system may have a distinct signal or response for the sine wave components (i.e., Fourier components) of the complex patterns. In other words, there may be discrete and independent channels in the visual system, each tuned to a different but limited range of spatial frequencies to which it will maximally respond. One means of demonstrating independent **spatial frequency channels** is by employing the technique of selective adaptation.

SELECTIVE ADAPTATION

The existence of channels in the visual system specific to spatial frequencies can be demonstrated by making use of Figure 14.11. The top grating pattern at (*a*) is of a relatively low frequency, whereas the bottom grating pattern is of a high frequency. The spatial frequency of the two grating patterns on the right at (*b*) are identical and of an intermediate spatial frequency to those at (*a*). Cover the patterns at (*b*) and

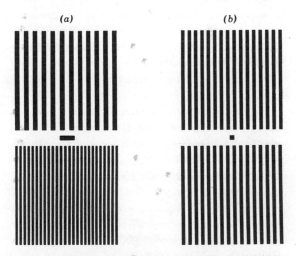

FIGURE 14.11. Inspection patterns (*a*) and test grating patterns (*b*) used to demonstrate the existence of spatial frequency channels in human vision. See text for explanation. (From C. Blakemore and P. Sutton, "Size adaptation: A new aftereffect," *Science*, *166*, 1969, p. 245. Copyright © 1969 by the American Association for the Advancement of Science.)

focus on the two patterns at (*a*) for at least 60 sec but with the gaze wandering back and forth along the horizontal fixation bar that separates the two patterns. After this period of adaptation, transfer the gaze to the fixation point between the two patterns of the right at (*b*). They will no longer appear identical in spatial frequency: the grating of a higher spatial frequency than the corresponding adapting grating will appear higher, and the grating with a lower spatial frequency than the appropriate adapting grating will appear lower in spatial frequency. What has occurred is an effect of **selective adaptation:** the fatiguing of channels (or neurons) that respond to low spatial frequencies (in the region of the upper grating of *a*) causes the appearance of the medium-frequency grating of the upper right at (*b*) to shift toward higher frequencies; similarly, adaptation of the channels that respond to high spatial frequencies, in the region of the bottom grating at (*a*), causes the medium-frequency grating on the bottom right at (*b*) to appear lower in frequency than that of the adapting grating. In other words if the visual system becomes adapted to a grating of a given spatial frequency, the apparent spatial frequencies of gratings with similar frequencies are shifted in just the way that one would predict from the existence of distinct and independent channels for spatial frequencies, namely, in a direction away from the spatial frequency of the adapting grating.

In general if an individual steadily views a grating pattern with a particular spatial frequency, the receptors or channels that respond to that frequency will selectively fatigue, reducing their sensitivity to that frequency, while leaving other frequencies relatively unaffected. The loss in sensitivity to a particular spatial frequency (or band of spatial frequencies) due to selective exposure of that frequency implies that there are different channels for detecting different spatial frequencies.

The analyses of spatial frequencies and selective adaptation are not restricted to simple sinusoidal-type grating patterns. The examples of Figures 14.12 emphasize this point. Indeed most optical patterns have a spatial frequency designation. Certainly a spatial frequency analysis applied to complex forms, described next, further indicates the potential role played by Fourier analysis in image processing.

IMAGE PROCESSING: BLOCK PORTRAITS

An example of the effect of spatial frequency specification on form perception is given in Figure 14.13*a*. The photograph—a **block portrait**—of an American president is the product of a picture that has undergone a form of computer processing; the original picture was divided into a pattern of small blocks, with each block assigned the same dark–light value as the average value of the original portion of the picture. That is, each block is uniform in luminance throughout its area or "block-averaged" (Harmon & Julesz, 1973; Harmon, 1973). This physically removes some of the sharpness and detail of the original picture because high spatial frequencies have been removed by the averaging process. At the same time a form of high-frequency "noise" has been introduced by the creation of sharp edges between the blocks.

When viewed directly and up close, the picture does not show an easily recognizable person. However, recognition of the block portrait is significantly improved by blurred viewing (for example, by viewing it at a distance or by squinting). The obvious explanation of what the blurring does is that it selectively filters out much of the high-frequency "noise" imposed by constructing a block portrait. That is, the perceptual effect of the sharp edges of the blocks produced by the computer is reduced (see Figure 14.13*b*). The back cover of the book also contains examples of block portraits.

SPATIAL FREQUENCY AND ACUITY

Analyzing visual performance in terms of contrast sensitivity provides a more informative measure of visual acuity than, say, the resolution acuity described in Chapter 12, which assesses acuity at only one spatial frequency. For example, it is possible for an individual to possess average sensitivity at one end of the spatial frequency spectrum and below

(a)

he second editor
estseller introduc
odern psycholog
udy of mental m
ms...concentrate
test research in n
tention and perc
demonstrates, w
rpts from curren
re, how recent de
ents in cognitive

(b)

odern psychology...the
udy of mental mechan-
ns...concentrates on the
est research in memory,
ention and perception.
demonstrates, with ex -
rpts from current litera-
re, how recent develop-
ents in cognitive
ychology explain human in
havior, everyday learning
oblems to stress perfor-
ance, skills memory,
ention. Ideal for courses
Memory, Information
cessing, Verbal Learning
d Cognitive Psychology

chapter as introduces the student to
influences aspects of the senses and
and emotion perception in an integral
students manner. Covers the main
The seconacts of psychophysics,
bestseller ructures and unctions
modern pshc orientations sense, au
study of mon, touch, taste, smell a
isms...conision. Extensively illustr
latest resead; inclnt cognitive theo
attention apper diding the place of
It demonstrates courses ness in moderi
cerpts from n on or emotional and
ture, how recent ational concepts
ments in cognitive ology of cognition
psychology explanation processing,
behavior, everyday of competing
problems to stresses, and a novel
mance, skills, men concept of arousal
attention. Ideal for the role of the aut
in Memory, Information nervous syste

odern psychology...the
udy of mental mechan-
ns...concentrates on the
est research in memory,
ention and perception.
demonstrates, with ex -
rpts from current litera-
re, how recent develop-
ents in cognitive
ychology explain human in
havior, everyday learning
oblems to stress perfor-
ance, skills memory,
ention. Ideal for courses
Memory, Information
cessing, Verbal Learning
d Cognitive Psychology

(a)

(b)

FIGURE 14.12.   Spatial frequency aftereffect for two examples of nongrating patterns (text and dots). Cover the patterns at (b) and gaze at the central horizontal bar at (a) for 40–50 sec. with the eyes moving back and forth along the bar. Then rapidly switch your gaze to the central spot at (b). For a brief time the material in the lower pattern of (b) will appear coarser (i.e., lower in frequency) and the upper material will appear denser (higher in frequency). Try this with both the text and the dots.

average at the other end. As an instance of this Owsley, Sekuler, and Siemsen (1983) found that contrast sensitivity for high spatial frequencies deteriorates more rapidly with age while sensitivity for low spatial frequencies remains relatively unchanged throughout adulthood. In addition, human infants are poorer than adults at distinguishing most spatial frequencies, but especially so for high frequencies (Dobson & Teller, 1978; Gwiazda, Brill, & Held, 1979; Norcia & Tyler, 1985). Relatedly Ginsburg (1981, 1986) reported evidence that the vision of individuals whose profession demands high levels of visual acuity, such as pilots, may be normal in terms of traditional acuity measures, but based on their contrast sensitivity functions show significant individual differences. In fact, Ginsburg (1981) found that some pilots showed higher contrast sensitivity to low spatial frequencies than did pilots who had greater visual acuity scores on the Snellen test (which is restricted to high frequencies). This heightened selective sensitivity may translate into an increased visibility of objects located at great distances or viewed in degraded conditions such as in fog. Ginsburg (Ginsburg et al., 1984; Ginsburg, 1986) proposes that about 10 to 15% of the population has good acuity as measured by Snellen testing but low contrast sensitivity to low and moderate spatial frequencies.

ROLE OF SPATIAL FREQUENCY ANALYSIS IN VISION

An important question to consider at this point is what direct role does spatial frequency analysis play

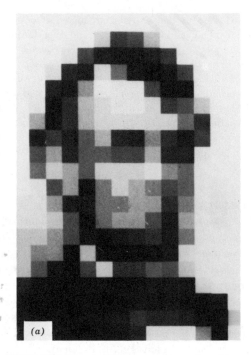

FIGURE 14.13*a*.   A block portrait produced by computer processing.

FIGURE 14.13*b*.   The same portrait after removal of the high-frequency "noise." (Photographs courtesy of Leon D. Harmon.)

in vision? Clearly such a scheme provides a powerful and elegant means of describing and summarizing a specifiable dimension of the physical stimulus. However the idea that an analysis of spatial frequencies by the visual system performs a *necessary* function in the processing of the visual input is not without question (e.g., Graham, 1980; Weisstein & Harris, 1980; Bruce & Green, 1985). Indeed it has been suggested that the encoding of spatial frequency information by the visual system is merely concomitant to, or even incidental to the processing of other more relevant features in the optic array.

However the notion that the visual system extracts spatial frequency components and performs a Fourier analysis does have strong conceptual appeal. Certainly it provides a a useful tool for describing the systematic manner in which the visual system analyzes, collates, and integrates the activity of an enormous number of receptors and links them in a

coherent way with a quite specifiable feature of the physical stimulus. Moreover, there is an impressive and growing body of psychophysical evidence supporting the view that form perception is fundamentally based on a kind of spatial image processing that may be best characterized in terms of an image's spatial frequency components (e.g., Gilden, MacDonald, & Lasaga, 1988; Bradley, Switkes, & DeValois, 1988). As we have seen, the description of the visual stimulus in terms of its spatial frequencies is quite useful in assessing acuity and is certainly far more informative than the traditional Snellen eye chart. At the least, spatial frequency analyses point out a way that the visual system could encode complex visual information for further processing. Hence it is probably unwise to assign less than a major role to such a system that appears so well suited to extracting spatial frequency components and performing a Fourier analysis on the patterned light reflected from the environment.

FIGURE–GROUND DIFFERENTIATION

Perhaps the first and most fundamental step in the complex dynamics of form perception is the almost effortless perceptual phenomenon that certain parts of any differentiated visual field stand out in a distinctive manner from other parts. As pointed out by the Danish psychologist Edgar Rubin in 1915, that part which appears as a sharply defined and distinct shape is known as the **figure,** and the remainder is called the **ground.** In the simplest case, where there is a total visual field consisting of two different portions, one portion is most likely to be seen as figure and the remaining part appears as the ground (see Figure 14.14). However, it is possible that *any* well-marked part of the visual field may appear as the figure, leaving the remainder as the ground. An unusual illustration of figure-ground organization appears in Figure 14.15. Here a central square is usually perceived, yet in fact the square is formed by components of the ground. According to Rubin, "The following principle is fundamental: if one of the two homogeneous, different-colored fields

FIGURE 14.15.   A central square is typically perceived, yet a design composed of diagonal lines at right angles may be seen as an alternative figure-ground organization (see Lawson et al. 1977, for an empirical analysis).

is larger than and encloses the other, there is a great likelihood that the small, surrounded field will be seen as figure" (Rubin, 1915/1958, p. 202).

A quantitative approach to the tendency to see a figure as a function of its relation to the total stimulus configuration was made by Oyama (1960). He presented the stimulus pattern shown in Figure 14.16 and instructed subjects to indicate whether the α or β crosses appeared as figure. When the angle of the sectors was varied, for either α or β crosses, the result was that the thinner the cross, the more likely it was seen as the figure regardless of whether it was dark gray or white.

AMBIGUOUS FIGURE–GROUND RELATIONSHIPS

The preceding example points to an interesting variation of figure-ground differentiation: the condition where there are two distinct homogeneous regions but neither is enclosed by the other. In addition, both parts share a common contour so that no tendency exists for either part to be seen as figure. Some examples of such configurations are shown in Figures 14.17a to e. One of the effects from these ambiguous

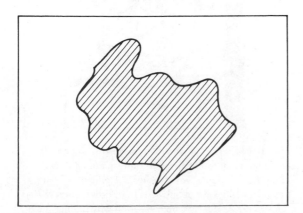

FIGURE 14.14.   A simple figure–ground relation.

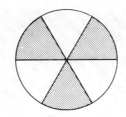

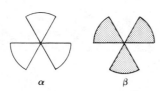

FIGURE 14.16. Stimuli used to examine the role of angle sector on figure-ground perception. (Based on Oyama, 1960.)

figures is that there is an initial perception of one portion as figure but this is followed by a reversal. In Figure 14.17a one sees alternately a radially marked or concentrically marked cross. If the concentric cross is seen as figure, the radial lines form the background. However, when the radial cross is seen as figure, the concentric lines, as part of the ground, do not appear interrupted. Thus, one has the impression that the concentric circles continue behind the figure. Clearly, the shift in figure and ground in such

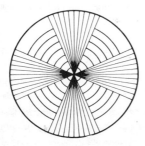

FIGURE 14.17a. Figure–ground reversal. Either a radially or concentrically marked cross is seen. (Source: Rubin, 1915/1958, p. 195.)

FIGURE 14.17b. The odd figural shape, seen in black against a white ground, may be reversed by turning the page around. The shape of a bird, in white against a black ground, should be perceived.

patterns can be produced by a shift in attention. After a brief period of exposure, the region seen as figure can be determined by the focus of attention. In ordinary commerce we have no difficulty resolving

FIGURE 14.17c. Reversible figure–ground pattern based on detail from Salvadore Dali's painting "The Three Ages." (From G. H. Fisher, "Ambiguous figure treatments in the art of Salvador Dali," *Perception & Psychophysics*, *2*, 1967, p. 329. Reprinted by permission of Psychonomic Society, Inc.)

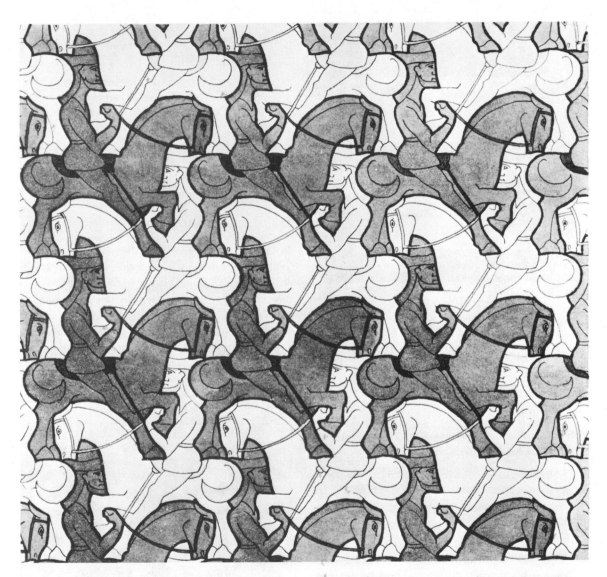

FIGURE 14.17*d*.   Reversible figure–ground pattern of procession of horsemen. (Based on woodcut of M. C. Escher, Beeldrect, Amsterdam/VAGA, New York, 1982, Collection Haags Gemeentemuseum.)

reversible figures. However in Figure 14.17*b*, a change in the orientation at which the form is viewed may be necessary to reverse its figure–ground organization. Ambiguous configurations such as Rubin's (Figure 14.17*a*) or Dali's (Figure 14.17*c*) or Escher's (Figure 14.17*d*) are rarely, if ever, confronted—certainly not as natural objects.

FIGURE 14.17e. Reversible figure–ground pattern. Either a goblet or a pair of silhouetted faces in profile is seen.

PERCEPTUAL DIFFERENCES BETWEEN FIGURE AND GROUND

Rubin (1915/1958) has identified the main differences between figure and ground as follows:

1. The figure has a "thing" quality and the contour appears at the edge of the figure's shape. In contrast, the ground has a characteristic more like a "substance" and appears relatively formless.

2. The figure appears closer to the viewer and in front of the ground, whereas the ground appears less clearly localized than the figure, extending continuously behind the figure. In fact Wong and Weisstein (1982) found an advantage to seeing a target stimulus on the part of the visual field seen as figure rather than when the same part of the visual field is seen as ground; thus when a subject viewed a target that was flashed on the "figure" of an ambiguous figure–ground pattern (a version of the goblet profiles of Figure 14.17e), the subject was at least three times as accurate in discrimi-

nating the orientation of the target as when the same region was seen as "ground" (see also Brown & Weisstein, 1988).

3. In relation to the ground, the figure appears more impressive, dominant, and better remembered. Also the figure suggests more associations of meaningful shapes than does the ground. As Figure 14.17e shows, the configuration appearing either as profiles or a goblet is easily assigned meaning, whereas the ground in either case is seen as shapeless.

FIGURE–GROUND AND LIGHTNESS

In addition to the perceived differences in figure and ground identified by Rubin there are also rather striking figure–ground effects on the perception of an area's lightness. As Figure 14.18 illustrates, a region perceived as figure appears lighter than when the same region is perceived as ground. In addition a region of the visual field with a constant luminance undergoes a greater contrast effect when it is perceived as figure than when it is perceived as ground.

FIGURE 14.18. Lightness of figure relative to ground. The central rectangle, seen as "figure," appears lighter than its background. In fact, the entire surface is covered with black squares on a homogeneous white surface. The "contours" creating the perception of the central rectangle are called subjective contours and are the subject of a discussion given later in this chapter. (Based on Kanizsa, 1979.)

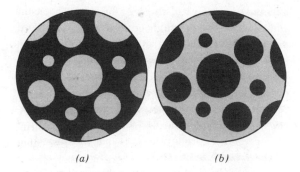

(a)   (b)

FIGURE 14.19.   The Wolff effect showing differential
lightness contrast effects of figure and ground. The light
and dark gray regions in both circles are equal in reflectance and area; however the light gray circles in (a), perceived as figure appear lighter than the identical light
gray region seen in (b) as ground. In like manner, the
dark gray circles in (b), as figure, appear darker than the
identical dark gray ground region in (a). (After Rock,
1986, p. 33-18; Kanizsa, 1979, p. 173.)

That is, "figures" show greater contrast effects than
do "grounds." A demonstration of this, reconstructed
by Kanizsa (1979) and by Rock (1986) and labeled
the **Wolff effect** (Wolff, 1935), is given in Figure
14.19. The light and dark grays of both (a) and (b) are
identical but the enclosed light gray circles seen at
(a) as *figure* appear lighter than the identical gray
region seen as *ground* in (b). Similarly the dark gray
circles in (b), seen as figure, appear darker than the
same dark gray seen as ground in (a). Notice that the
total areas of light and dark regions are equal in both
(a) and (b). This phenomenon indicates that a region
seen as figure is affected more by its contrast with its
surrounding ground than is the ground affected by its
contrast with the figure.

A demonstration, different from those just reviewed in that it apparently opposes contrast effects,
is the figure—of the classic **Koffka rings**—
shown in Figure 14.20a. (The phenomenon is gener-

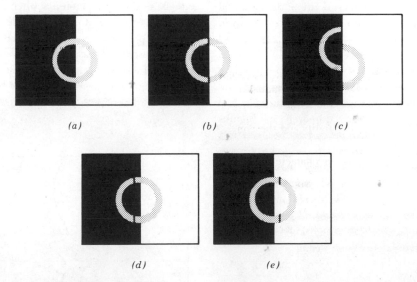

(a)   (b)   (c)

(d)   (e)

FIGURE 14.20.   The Koffka rings. The rings in all
figures are homogeneously gray. However each half
should be contrasted with its background and appear
different from each other: the part of the rings on the
left should appear lighter than the part of the rings on
the right. In (a) this is not the case, which suggests
that the dominant effect of perceiving the ring as a
unified configuration overrides the effect of

background contrast. However inserting vertical contours, which divide the ring into unified subparts, as
in (b) and (c), enables each part to be seen against its
background and introduces contrast. In (d) and (e) the
vertical contours enable the contrast effect to maintain
a uniform level of lightness within an entire unified
part of each ring, even when it extends into an opposing background.

ally attributed to Koffka, 1935, as well as to Wertheimer and Benussi; however Osgood, 1953, notes that much earlier, a form of it was used in lecture demonstrations by Wundt.) Clearly the display in Figure 14.20a contains all the elements for a contrast effect. The neutral gray ring is half against a black ground and half against a white ground, yet there is little or no lightness contrast. The portion of the ring on the left in a does not appear lighter than the portion on the right, although such an effect would be predicted based on the effects of contrast discussed earlier in this chapter (see Figure 14.5). Instead the ring appears a homogeneous neutral gray throughout.

What may be occurring during inspection of Figure 14.20a is the dominant effect of the unity or the total organization of a figure on perception: the coherence of a unified configuration overrides contrast effects. Thus being perceived as a single integrated unit, the entire ring is accordingly perceived as uniform gray. However, contrast effects immediately appear if vertical contours are introduced that separate the whole ring into two parts, as shown by b, or when the two halves of the rings are shifted vertically with respect to each other, shown by c. Thus when the ring is divided, it becomes two half rings, each seen against a different background, and the contrast effects occur appropriate to each half ring with its background. Moreover, as Figures 14.20d and e show, the imposed contour restricts apparent lightness to entire portions of the divided rings, even when part of a ring extends into an opposing background. That is, within limits, the contour prevents the lightness effect in one part of the ring from affecting the lightness in the other part, even when the parts of the ring, as defined by the contours, are seen against contrasting areas.

FIGURE–GROUND AND PERCEPTUAL ORGANIZATION

Figure-ground differentiation is recognized as the simplest step in the perception of a form. Evidence for the operation of a fundamental organizing tendency resulting in figure–ground differentiation comes from the reports by von Senden (1960) on patients who have had surgery (for removal of congenital cataracts) in adulthood, thus first given sight at maturity. He noted that such patients showed figure–ground differentiation before they could discriminate and recognize different figures. That the perception of figures is present in the first visual experience strongly suggests that figure–ground organization is independent of experience. Further evidence for its primitiveness is that figure–ground differentiation is among the first perceptual experiences to occur in the Ganzfeld when a slight inhomogeneity is introduced. Moreover, many lower forms of animal life demonstrate the capacity to distinguish figure from ground even with minimal visual experience.

Of related interest is that figure–ground differentiation occurs tactually as well as visually. When a raised-line version of a reversible drawing such as that depicted in Figure 14.21 was examined tactually by blind children, they experienced similar figural effects as those encountered when sighted viewers visually examine the figure (Kennedy, 1983; Kennedy & Domander, 1984). That is, on the basis of feeling the centrally located raised contour, the blind children interpreted, say, a profile as looking to the right as figure, immediately followed by the perception of a different profile as figure, this one looking to

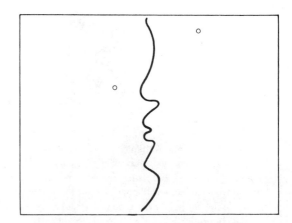

FIGURE 14.21. Reversible figure–ground drawing of profiles formed by the same contour.

the left. However, in perceiving the second profile (i.e., looking left), they did not recognize that they were making use of the same contour that they had felt only a moment before (a profile looking right). In short, without their awareness, the same contour was used in the perception of two different profile figures. This not only indicates that the reversal of figure–ground can occur tactually, but that "like the sighted, blind people have pictorial impressions that can modify their perception of unchanging forms. They seem to have something akin to a sighted person's perception of pictured foreground and background" (Kennedy, 1984, p. 23).

GESTALT GROUPING PRINCIPLES

Why do some elements of the visual field form the unified figure and others become ground? As we have seen this is a result of some organizing tendency based on certain features of the stimulus array. The study of what factors determine the formation of figure-like shapes was made by a group of German psychologists (in particular, Max Wertheimer, Kurt Koffka, and Wolfgang Köhler) at the beginning of this century. The school they founded is called *Gestalt* psychology. "Gestalt" is the German word for "form," "shape," or "whole configuration."

The Gestalt psychologists studied patterns of stimuli and observed the manner in which some stimuli appeared to be grouped together with figure-like qualities. This approach questioned the prevailing analytic or *Structuralist* view that was influenced strongly by the *elementism* which dominated the physical and biological sciences in the latter part of the nineteenth century. In chemistry, for example, significant scientific advancements were made as complex compounds were analyzed into their constituent elements of molecules and atoms. Taking its cue from the striking analytic achievements of chemistry, the emerging scientific psychology stressed the structural character of the mind. Thus the psychology of structuralism assumed a form of "mental chemistry" and by using a form of mental analysis called

analytic introspection (involving a highly disciplined technique of self-observation) attempted to determine the fundamental, irreducible units—the "mental molecules"—of form perception. It followed that the Structuralist view assumed that perceptions are composed of the linear sum of basic, elemental units—raw sensations.

In marked contrast, the Gestalt view was that a perception cannot be decomposed into elementary components. Rather the Gestalt psychologists argued, largely with compelling demonstrations, that the basic units of perception are themselves the perceptions—the "Gestalts" are the fundamental units. Indeed they argued that to perform an analysis on the perception, that is, to attempt to break down and reduce a perception into presumed elementary units, would be to lose sight of the perception. Consider as a Gestalt phenomenon the perception of a tune or melody. As we noted in Chapter 6 it is possible to hear a melody played in one key, yet when it is played again, in another key but with none of the original notes replayed, it can still be recognized as the same melody. Clearly something besides the mere reception and linear summation of discrete notes is involved when we hear and recognize a tune. Indeed we probably cannot learn very much about a tune by merely examining its notes in isolation. What is important in our example, then, is not the notes per se, but the context or the relationship that exists between them. Accordingly it is the perceived *relation* between the notes that gives rise to a tonal configuration—to a Gestalt.

Gestalt psychology emphasizes the unique role of the overall structure and the relationship between components in producing perceptual organization. Indeed the basic Gestalt theme is embodied in the often applied summary phase: *the whole is different than the sum of its parts*.

One of the most significant and enduring contributions of Gestalt psychology is the identification of the figural properties that enable the perception of form to emerge. According to the early Gestalt psychologists there appear to be fundamental, unlearned organizing tendencies to perceive the visual field on the basis of the arrangement and relative location of elements. A set of **Gestalt grouping principles,** supported by numerous illustrations, has been described by Wertheimer (1923; based on 1958 translation).

NEARNESS OR PROXIMITY

Grouping may occur according to the distance separating elements. Elements that are closer together tend to be organized or grouped together (see Figure 14.22). This is the principle of **proximity** or **nearness.** The proximity may be of a spatial or temporal nature.

SIMILARITY

With the proximity of elements equated, elements that are similar in physical attributes tend to be grouped together. Figure 14.23 provides an example of grouping by **similarity.**

GOOD CONFIGURATION

The principle of **good configuration** was stated as a very general organizing tendency, intended to encompass a number of figural characteristics such as good continuation, common fate, closure, and symmetry.

Good Continuation   Elements that appear to follow in the same direction such as along a straight line or a simple curve, are readily perceived as forming a group. Figure 14.24 presents an example of **good continuation.** All such elements appear to follow in a uniform direction so as to permit the continuation of an aspect of a figure (e.g., a line or curve) whose movement or direction has been established. (An arresting example of good continuation coupled with other organizing relations, is shown later in Figure 14.27.)

FIGURE 14.22.   Due to proximity a row of dots is spontaneously seen as a row of elements in the arrangement *ab/cd/ef . . .*, not *a/bc/de.*

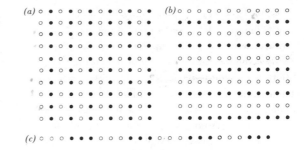

FIGURE 14.23.   One sees groups of elements that are determined by the principle of similarity. Thus, in the figure, one sees columns of elements in (*a*), rows in (*b*), and groups of o's and ●'s in (*c*).

Common Fate   Elements that move in the same direction are grouped together according to **common fate.** This is basically grouping on the basis of similarity but applied to moving elements. Thus, if a number of elements are seen in movement, those that appear to be moving in parallel paths tend to be grouped together to form a coherent pattern.

Closure   In **closure** grouping occurs in a way that favors the perception of the more enclosed or complete figure (see Figure 14.25).

As is true for all the Gestalt principles of organization, good continuation and closure enhance the perception of a stable environment. The line drawing in Figure 14.26 can be perceived as three discrete shapes, yet the most likely result is that it is seen as two bars, one standing in front of the other, the partially covered bar appearing continuous.

Another quite provocative example of the organizing effect of good continuation and closure is given in Figure 14.27. In (*a*) an apparent random scattering of irregular fragments shows no tendency to group into any meaningful pattern or configuration. However, in (*b*) the same shapes, left intact, but apparently covered by a "school of fish," produce a striking reorganization of the fragments: an irregular arrangement of five "heart" shapes is perceived. That is, one sees a group of hearts covered by a school of fish. It should be noted, however, that as with Figure 14.26,

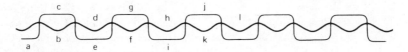

FIGURE 14.24.   The natural organization, due to good continuation, is to see *acegij* and *bdfhkl*, not *abefik* or *cdghjl*. That is, one tends to see two repeatedly intere-

secting curves, a sinusoidal curve overlapping a square wave, rather than the complex alternative. (After Wertheimer, 1958.)

other spatial–figural relationships are involved in promoting a meaningful grouping in this figure.

Symmetry   In **symmetry** priority in grouping is given the more natural, balanced, and symmetrical figure over the asymmetrical ones (see Figure 14.28).

MEASURES OF GROUPING EFFECTS

Clearly observers are sensitive to the structure of Gestalt patterns. In one experiment on the characteristics that affect perceptual organization, Beck (1966, 1982) showed that perceptual segregation or

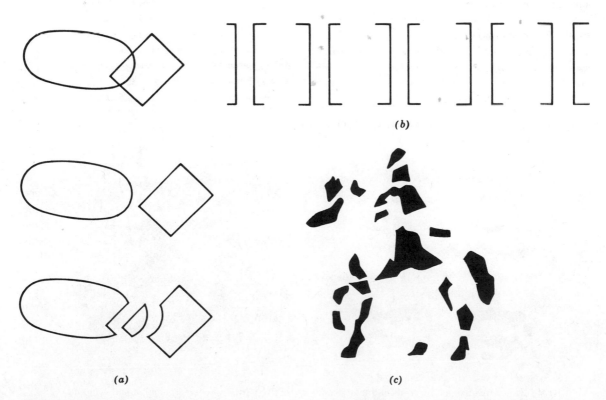

(b)

(a)

(c)

FIGURE 14.25.   (*a*) Due to the operation of closure, one sees two distinct and intersecting shapes, an ellipse and a rectangle, rather than three discrete enclosed areas. (After Wertheimer, 1958.) (*b*) One tends to see rect-

angles. In this example, the principle of closure predominates. (*c*) One tends to perceive a completed figure although only fragmentary stimuli are present.

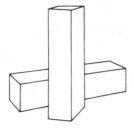

FIGURE 14.26.   At least three discrete shapes is a possible perception of the line drawing. Good continuation and closure tend to favor the perception of two bars, one lying in front of the other.

grouping of two-line figures may be influenced by the orientation of the lines comprising the figure. When subjects were instructed to divide the pattern shown in Figure 14.29 into two parts, the division was based primarily on the *orientation* of the figures; that is, figures with lines orientated in the same direction were grouped together. In the example given, the physical similarity of figures was not an important factor of perceptual grouping.

In a different kind of grouping experiment Girgus and her colleagues (Coren & Girgus, 1980; Enns & Girgus, 1985) demonstrated that Gestalt factors that promote perceptual grouping tendencies and enhance perceptual organization have direct and measurable consequences. They had subjects estimate the apparent distance between elements embedded in patterns that illustrated the Gestalt grouping principles of proximity, similarity, closure, and good continuation (see Figure 14.30). The findings were that subjects appeared sensitive to the structural relations in the Gestalt patterns and reflected this in a spatial distortion of their distance judgments. Thus subjects judged the distance between elements that were apparently embedded within the same perceptual pattern as smaller—that is, the elements appeared closer together—than they judged the same physical distance between elements that were in different perceptual groups, not related to each other in a Gestalt sense. In other words, elements that were subject to various grouping tendencies appeared to lie closer to each other than elements at identical distances from each other but

(a)

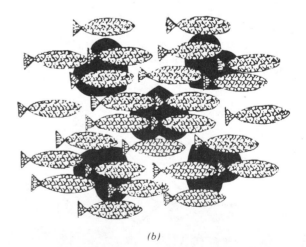

(b)

FIGURE 14.27.   Organization by good continuation and closure. The scattered irregular fragments seen in (a) appear unorganized and unrelated to any meaningful pattern or configuration. However if the fragments appear to be covered by a "school of fish" as in (b), the perception of five partially covered but apparently continuous "hearts" result. Note that occlusion or interposition also plays a role in the perception of the heart shapes. (Courtesy of Jan and Sue. Based on Bregman, 1981.)

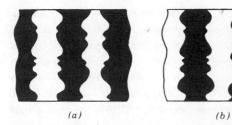

(a)   (b)

FIGURE 14.28.   The contours of the vertical shapes are identical but in (a), one sees the white "columns," and in (b), the black ones. In both cases organization follows the symmetrical pattern. (After Zusne, 1970, p. 116.)

not linked together in any Gestalt relation. (However, Enns and Girgus, 1985, report that the magnitude of these distance distortions decreases with age.)

SUBJECTIVE CONTOURS

A phenomenon, resembling a completion or closure-type process, may occur across a blank portion of the visual field to produce the appearance of contours called **subjective contours** (also referred to as illusory contours and apparent contours; note that in some cases not only contours but an overall figure

seems to emerge). Several examples of subjective contours are given in Figure 14.31.

A number of explanations has been proposed to account for subjective contours, but overall, none has been complete or fully accepted. For example, it has been proposed that a subjective contour is the edge of an apparent plane in depth (Coren, 1972); thus the contour serves to simplify a complex two-dimensional array of elements into an easily coded three-dimensional array of meaningful elements. However, the depth effect generally arises *after* the perception of a figure with subjective contours (Rock, 1986).

It has been argued that subjective contours derive from the differences in the lightnesses of adjacent regions due to lightness contrast effects (e.g., Frisby & Clatworthy, 1975; Jory & Day, 1979; Frisby, 1980). That is, the subjective contour is the perceived edge of a region that appears lighter than its background due to significant luminance differences. However, well-articulated subjective contours are apparent in conditions where the conditions for producing contrast effects are minimal (e.g., Figure 14.32).

A form of Gestalt–cognitive explanation to ac-

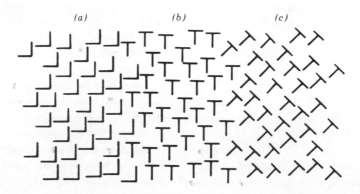

(a)   (b)   (c)

FIGURE 14.29.   Stimulus pattern used by Beck. When subjects were instructed to divide the pattern into two parts, the division was based on the orientation of the elements: elements with lines oriented in the same direction were grouped together. In the figure above the elements of (a) and (b) appeared to form a group distinct

from the elements of (c) although the elements of (b) had greater physical similarity to those of (c) than to those of (a). (From J. Beck, "Effect of orientation and of shape similarity on perceptual grouping," *Perception & Psychophysics*, 1, 1966, p. 300. Reprinted by permission of Psychonomic Society, Inc.)

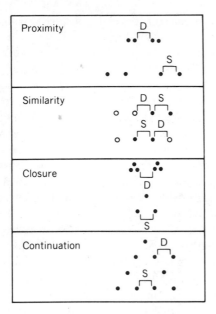

FIGURE 14.30. The effects of Gestalt grouping principles on the apparent distance between pattern elements. Subjects judged the linear distance between the extent markers, shown above selected dot pairs, by choosing from a graded series of horizontal distances (note that the extent markers did not appear on the patterns shown to subjects). The distance between the elements that appeared to be part of the same Gestalt pattern or group (labeled "S") was distorted, that is, judged less than the physically identical distance between elements appearing in different perceptual groups (labeled "D"). Thus, elements linked by Gestalt grouping principles appear closer together than elements that do not. (Based on Coren & Girgus, 1980; Enns & Girgus, 1985.)

count for the lightness difference between the apparent shape formed by the subjective contour and the background has been proposed by Bradley and Dumais (1975; Dumais & Bradley, 1976; Bradley & Petry, 1977). It is based on an effect of figure–ground organization noted earlier; the figure generally appears lighter or more intense than the background of equal reflectance. Thus, for example, since the central areas in Figures 14.18 and 14.31a appear as figures (i.e., circles, triangles, rectangles), it follows that they will be perceived as lighter than their

backgrounds. Thus the lightness effect is secondary to the perception of a figure. A provocative example of a cognitive approach to subjective contours is demonstrated by Figure 14.33, which shows a variation, with subjective contours, of a Necker cube (a variation of this was described in Chapter 1, Figure 1.1). The initial and most prominent perception is of a three-dimensional cubelike form, such that each corner of the cube appears to lie in front of a black disk, and "bars" connecting the corners of the cube appear between the disks. Although the cube is seen in its entirety, those portions of the cube apparent between the disks are illusory. An alternative perceptual organization for this figure is also possible whereby subjective contours are *not* apparent. The perceptual alternative is aided by assuming that the eight disks are eight apertures or holes on an interposing white surface. Thus, a cube appears to lie against a dark background behind the white surface, such that each corner of the cube is visible through one of the holes while the remainder of the cube is occluded by the interposing white surface. With this "cube-in-back" perceptual organization, the subjective contours previously seen extending between the disks do not appear.

Clearly, the formation of subjective contours is not due to a simple process, and it is likely a product of a number of stimulus variations. However, one feature that appears to be primary in the formation of subjective contours is the perception that a central figure is present. A salient feature of the configuration that appears to enhance this perception is that the contour-inducing elements—the "cut-out" gaps and wedges—that enclose the edges and corners of the "figure," appear interrupted and incomplete; that is, the shape of the elements suggest that some form or surface—the figure—is partially overlapping or occluding them in a consistent manner. Indeed the more that this overlapping feature is apparent within the configuration, the more immediate and compelling is the formation of the subjective contours (see Fig. 14.34). On the other hand when the contour-inducing elements are themselves identifiable as complete and coherent figures, subjective contour formation is tenuous or does not occur. In the latter

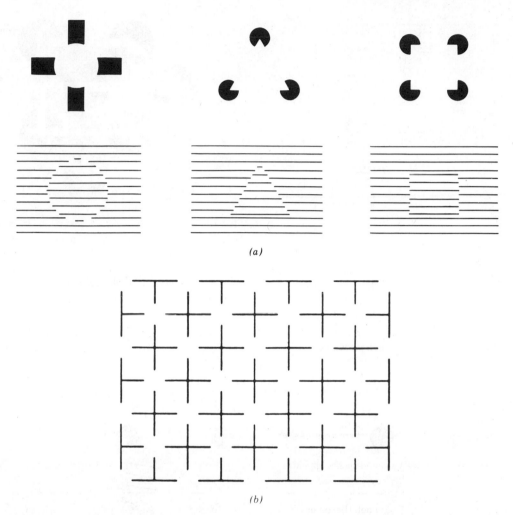

FIGURE 14.31.   (*a*) Subjective contours produce apparent shapes (i.e., circles, triangles, and rectangles). (*b*) Diagonal contours connected by circles are apparent at the missing intersections of the grid lines (Based on Ehrenstein, 1941).

instance the apparently *un*interrupted shape of the contour-inducing elements is inconsistent with the perception of a central occluding figure. This is illustrated in Figure 14.35. The central figures at (*a*) (a rectangle and a triangle) appear to cover a part of each corner inducing element. Indeed the shapes of the apparently fragmented elements help define the shape of the central figure and the nature of its subjective contours. However at (*b*) the corner elements are complete, self-contained figural shapes that are not consistent with an occlusion by a central shape. That is, they do not appear overlapped by part of any figure, and accordingly, neither figure nor subjective contours emerge. What is suggested here is that the formation of subjective contours is a cognitive achievement based on the inference that a central figure is present in the configuration. Rock (1986) refers to the resultant lightness effect produc-

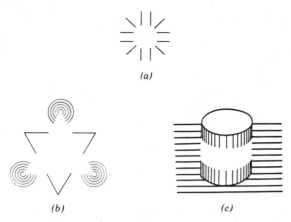

FIGURE 14.32. Low-contrast subjective contours. In (a), a central circle is apparent although only radiating lines are used. In (b), a triangle is apparent between the gaps of the three elements composed of concentric circles. In (c), the central portion of a cylinder, seen with a depthlike quality, is created by a series of linear segments. (Note that the bottom row of Figure 14.31(a) as well as (b) also demonstrates subjective contour formation from low-contrast linear elements.)

FIGURE 14.33.   A subjective Necker cube from which two perceptual alternatives are possible: an apparently complete cube whose corners are seen to lie against black disks (the dominant perception); and eight holes in an interposing white surface, through which the corners of a partially covered cube are seen. (Based on Bradley, Dumais, & Petry, 1976.)

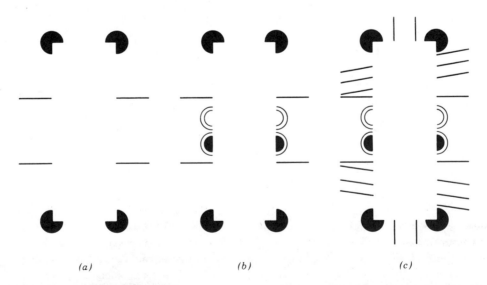

FIGURE 14.34.   The subjective contour effect is heightened as more cues are added to suggest that a central figure overlaps the background. Although moderate subjective contours may be observable in (a), when additional cues are added that enhance the perception of an overlapping rectangle, as in (b) and (c), the contours appear stronger.

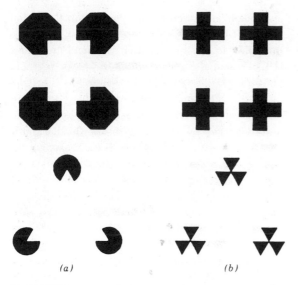

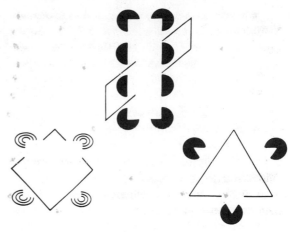

FIGURE 14.36. When lines and subjective contours intersect, the contours appear to pass through the plane formed by the lines. (Based on Kanizsa, 1979.)

FIGURE 14.35. In (a) central figures are seen with subjective contours. The figures appear to overlay or occlude part of the fragments at the corners or vertices. In (b) the elements at the corners and vertices are figural, self-contained units that do not contribute to the perception of a central shape.

ing the subjective contours as a **cognitive invention** that serves to rationalize the perception of a figure. Clearly some form of cognitive invention mediates a meaningful perception of Figure 14.36 in which the subjective contours define shapes that appear to pass through planes formed by line segments.

Certainly many other variables enter in the formation of subjective contours (see Parks, 1984, for a review). For example, Coren, Porac and Theodor (1986) observe a role of priming and instructions (or "set," described later in this chapter), whereas Wallach and Slaughter (1988) note the significance of familiarity with specific shapes on the formation of subjective contours. There is even evidence of neural activity in the cortex of alert monkeys that is associated with subjective contours (Heydt, Peterhans, & Baumgartner, 1984) and direct behavioral evidence that cats see subjective contours (Bravo, Blake, & Morrison, 1988). Clearly many issues remain to be clarified before the nature of subjective contours is

well understood. However, the conclusion is warranted that some form of cognitive processing plays a dominant role in their formation.

LAW OF PRÄGNANZ

Many of the Gestalt principles stated earlier along with several corollaries have been codified under the general label of the **law of Prägnanz,** or the law of the *good figure*, which refers to the tendency to perceive the simplest and most stable figure of all possible alternatives. However, as used by the Gestaltists, the descriptive term "good," although possessing some intuitive appeal, demands further elaboration. One attempt at a quantitative index of the structural properties of figural "goodness" was made by Hochberg and McAlister (1953). They suggested that figural goodness is inversely proportional to the amount of information necessary to specify a figure. That is, the less the amount of information needed to define a given organization as compared to other alternatives, the more likely is the perception of that organization and the greater is its figural goodness. Stated in another way, the good figure in the Gestalt sense is the simpler one.

Grouping or organizing the visual pattern on the basis of Gestalt principles leads to efficient, simpler perceptions. For example, a closed figure can be more easily defined than an open one—not requiring specification of the gap size and location—and a symmetrical figure can be succinctly described by indicating half of its features because the remaining half is its mirror image. Look at Figure 14.37. Its description is generally of two overlapping rectangles. Alternatively, however, it can be construed as five irregular shapes. In the latter instance more angles, lines, and points of intersections are required to specify the general configuration. Hence, according to the analysis of Hochberg and McAlister, this is the least likely perception. In contrast, because less information is necessary to specify the configuration as two rectangles, it is the figure most likely seen and it possesses greater figural goodness than alternatives (see also Palmer & Hemenway, 1978; Butler, 1982).

It should be noted here that, in general, well-organized, "good" figures in the Gestalt sense are remembered better than are disorganized ones (Howe & Brandau, 1983; Howe & Jung, 1986). Perhaps this is so because they are easier to encode and, accordingly, draw less upon the available cognitive resources (Hatfield & Epstein, 1985). Mermelstein, Banks, and Prinzmetal (1979) have demonstrated that when a visual configuration such as a picture of a face is organized and remembered as a "good" or unitary Gestalt figure, performance in subsequent detection of its component parts is facilitated (see also Purcell & Stewart, 1988). In fact there is a significant amount of evidence to support the notion that wholes are perceived better than their constituent parts. In one investigation Schendel and Shaw (1976) essentially compared the perception of whole letters to that of specific letter fragments (i.e., the interior linear segments from which the letters were constructed). For example, when subjects had to decide whether a flashed fragment was a short horizontal line (—) or a negatively-sloped diagonal (\) line, their performance was superior when the target fragments were part of the letters H or N (which, of course, contain the critical linear segments that just distinguish H from N) than when the fragments were presented in isolation. That is, the subjects' responses were more rapid and accurate when the task required processing entire letters than when processing the fragments alone (for a similar facilitative relation of words to letters, see Johnston & McClelland, 1973, 1974). There are also reports that target identification is facilitated when the target is part of a configuration that appears to be a three-dimensional drawing (Enns & Prinzmetal, 1984) or when the target appears to be part of some basic configuration compared to when the target is presented in isolation (Lanze, Maguire, & Weisstein, 1985).

We now turn to a consideration of some of the factors that affect the perception of form.

MASKING

Under certain conditions the perception of a stimulus is affected by stimuli that occur simultaneously with it and by those that immediately precede and follow it. The impairment to the perception of a target stimulus by the presentation of a closely following second *masking* stimulus is called **backward masking.** If the masking stimulus precedes and is close in time to the presentation of the target stimulus, the impairment to the presentation of the target stimulus is called **forward masking.** Although there are a number of further distinctions that can be made, in general, visual **masking** refers to the phenomenon in

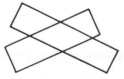

FIGURE 14.37.   Less information is required to specify this figure as two overlapping rectangles (8 line segments and 8 angles) than the alternative construction of five irregular shapes (16 lines segments and 16 angles).

which the perception of the target stimulus is obscured by presenting a masking stimulus close in time to a target stimulus. If, for example, a circular disk and a masking ring just circumscribing it are presented in sequence for a brief duration, when the pause between them, called the **interstimulus interval (ISI),** is of a certain duration, the presence of the disk may not be perceived, or it may appear dimmer or less structured than if shown without the ring. Masking of this sort is maximal when the borders of the masking stimulus are adjacent with the borders of the target stimulus; with increasing spatial separation between the masking and target stimulus, the masking effect falls off. Other variables that affect masking are the duration and intensity of the target and the masking stimulus.

Although a fully acceptable explanation of masking remains elusive, it is generally held that it involves some form of **visual persistence**. That is, the temporal course of sensory and perceptual events exceeds the course of stimulus events—in short sensation, or its effects, continues beyond the termination of the physical stimulus (e.g., Long, 1982; Long & Wurst, 1984). One consequence of this within the context of masking is that brief stimulus events that do not physically overlap in space or in time may be perceived as contemporaneous. Thus, if the pause between the target stimulus and the masking stimulus is of sufficient brevity, say, 100 msec or less, the two stimuli may be processed at the same time—the image of the target stimulus sums with the image of the masking stimulus—and the perception of the target stimulus is impaired. Accordingly, masking may be considered to be the result of the temporal summation of physically successive components that appear to be simultaneous.

MASKING AND SACCADIC OMISSION

As we noted in Chapter 12, typically vision is interrupted several times each second by rapid saccadic eye movements. During these rapid ocular excursions, the visual scene sweeps across the retina and, accordingly, should produce a brief period of retinal smearing or blurring. However, there is no blurred vision generated by the saccades, nor are we even aware of saccadic eye movements. The lack of perception during saccadic eye movements is often referred to as **saccadic omission.** Indeed, even when using a mirror we cannot see our eyes move. In contrast, if one looks at another person's eyes, their eye movements are readily perceived.

Masking effects may explain why, in the course of normal perception involving saccadic eye movements, we are not aware of our eye movement, and why we do not experience blurred vision during the movements. In an experiment on this problem, Campbell and Wurtz (1978; see also Cornfield, Frosdick, & Campbell, 1978) recorded the electrical response made during controlled eye movements, called the electrooculogram (EOG). The typical subject sat in a darkened room and was instructed to move his or her eyes from one red fixation light to another. When the eyes moved to change fixation, the EOG served as a signal to trigger a light flash which thus illuminated the room only during the duration of the saccade (50–70 msec). During the flash, the subject reported that the fixtures of the room, although visible, appeared blurred. Of course, this follows from the fact that room illumination occurred only during the 50–70 msec duration of the saccade. However, when the duration of the light was extended for an additional 40 msec, so as to illuminate the room, not only during the saccade but during the fixation period preceding or following the saccade, or both, the subject reported that the room and its furnishings (e.g., recording equipment) appeared clear and unblurred. This indicates that the normal visual image that a viewer forms during a fixation preceding or following a saccade *masks* the perception of the blurred image formed during the saccadic movement.

The functional significance of masking for saccadic eye movements is clear: as the eyes move about changing visual fixations abruptly and rapidly, the stimulus information from the preceding saccade is masked so that the next view is a clear one. Thus masking enables our eyes to move freely without producing visual smears or blurs of superimposed images (Breitmeyer, 1980, 1984).

FACILITATIVE INTERACTION

As we noted, the interaction of successive but different visual stimuli may, under the proper conditions, result in impaired perception, that is, produce masking effects. Given that some of the information in a briefly flashed stimulus momentarily lingers after the removal or termination of the initiating physical stimulus, we may ask whether a similar integrative mechanism will promote a facilitative effect on the perception of a stimulus if the two successive stimuli are identical. That is, if the sequential presentation of two *different* stimuli—the target and masking stimulus—interact to produce a reduction in recognition, then we can assume that if two stimuli are *identical* their effects on the visual system will summate to produce a **facilitative interaction** effect. A study by Eriksen and Collins (1967) illustrates this phenomenon. They presented briefly (6 msec) the dot pattern *a* and dot pattern *b* of Figure 14.38, simultaneously and sequentially with a brief pause (from 25 to 100 msec) between them. Notice that each pattern by itself appears to be meaningless. However, when they are properly aligned and exposed simultaneously, the resulting perception is of the nonsense syllable "VOH" of Figure 14.38*c*. With sequential presentation of the stimuli the identification of the nonsense syllable increased as the pause time between the presentation of the two dot patterns decreased.

Interestingly, summation of a similar kind has been reported even when the interval between stimuli was considerably longer than those used by Eriksen and Collins (1967). However, more than two presentations of the same stimulus were employed so that in relation to the study by Eriksen and Collins there was a trade-off between the duration of the interstimulus interval and the number of stimulus presentations. Haber and Hershenson (1965) flashed seven-letter, three-syllable words at a duration below recognition threshold (from 5 to 35 msec). This was repeated with the same word for a number of times with the result that successive flashes produced increasingly correct recognitions. With a constant but very brief exposure duration, the likelihood of correctly perceiving a word increased with the number of repetitions; the

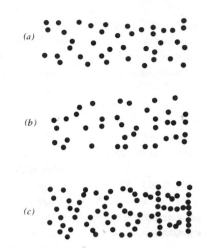

FIGURE 14.38. Stimuli used by Eriksen and Collins. When the upper two dot patterns, (*a*) and (*b*), are superimposed or when the temporal interval separating their sequential presentation is 100 msec or less, the likely perceptual result is the bottom stimulus pattern, (*c*), in which the nonsense syllable "VOH" can be read. Notice that to minimize the possibility that the nonsense syllable could be guessed from the dots on only one dot pattern, camouflaging dots were distributed over each pattern. (From C. W. Eriksen and J. F. Collins, "Some temporal characteristics of visual pattern recognition," *Journal of Experimental Psychology*, 74, 1967, p. 477. Reprinted by permission of the American Psychological Association.)

word appeared clear and distinct after a number of flashes even though on the first flash it appeared to be blank. The subjects' reports of the stimuli when the stimulus duration was extremely brief are summed up by the authors as follows. The subject

> was usually unaware of letters or parts of letters on the first flash . . . On the second or third flash, with no change in duration, beginnings of letters and sometimes whole letters would appear. After several more flashes, a number of letters would be present—often the whole word. (p. 41)

This positive cumulative effect of repeated exposure has been labeled by Haber and Hershenson (1965) as the *growth of a percept*. It should be pointed out that the presentation interval between the stimuli (ISI) was considerably longer in this study (at least 8 sec) than those employed in the study by Eriksen and Collins (1967). Accordingly, the increase in recognition due to the repetition of presentations in the Haber and Hershenson study and due to a reduction in the interstimulus interval in the Eriksen and Collins study reflects the operation of fundamentally different integrative processes. Overall, these studies show the integrative capacity of the visual system over time and the influence of stimulus repetition on form perception.

Visual persistence may play a role in facilitating the perception of successively presented stimuli (e.g., Long & Wurst, 1984). Indeed there are conceptual approaches to visual persistence that assign it a central role in such tasks. In one view, the "trace" amount that remains as a sort of fading image after termination of a stimulus is called an **icon** (Neisser, 1967), and special significance is ascribed to **iconic memory** as an initial and essential information extraction stage of visual pattern perception. Ordinarily, the fleeting trace or icon is not perceptible, but under the proper experimental conditions a surprising amount of the contents in the icon may be recovered (e.g., Sperling, 1960; Neisser, 1967; see Chapter 21 for a further discussion of this general issue).

AFTEREFFECTS

Having shown that even quite brief viewing of an image has an effect (i.e., masking) on subsequent perception, we now turn to the general topic of **aftereffects.** As we noted in the preceding chapter, if one stares at a colored shape for, say, 30 sec and the gaze shifts to a neutral achromatic surface, the shape is still perceived but in a reversed or complementary color. Perhaps the most common and pervasive aftereffect results from inadvertently viewing the very brief but intense light of a flash bulb. In other instances prolonged inspection of a stimulus configuration causes not only a form of stimulus persistence

but also creates a measureable distortion in the perception of other figures. Several main classes of aftereffects have been distinguished, in particular, *figural, shape,* and *contingent* aftereffects. In addition, there are a number of additional variations of these categories.

FIGURAL AFTEREFFECTS

An example of **figural aftereffects** is an often cited demonstration by Köhler and Wallach (1944), wherein the contours of shapes are apparently "displaced" from the region adjacent to the site of previously fixated contours. The typical arrangement is shown in Figure 14.39. If the X in Figure 14.39a is fixated for 40 sec and then the gaze is transferred to the X in Figure 14.39b, the distance between the two left squares in b will appear greater than that between the two right squares, whereas, in fact, the distances are equal. Although it is clear that this distortion is caused by the prior inspection of Figure 14.39a, there is no fully acceptable explanation of the general phenomenon. One hypothesized effect proposed by Köhler and Wallach (1944) to account for displacement effects has been termed "satiation." They contend that when a figure has been exposed for a period of time to a given region of the retina, the receptors of the region and of the areas immediately adjacent to the retinal site of exposure become fatigued, resistant to stimulation, or *satiated*. This causes new figures projected near the satiated retinal area to be apparently displaced from it. Accordingly, the distortion—the shift in apparent location—of the squares in b is due to their displacement from the retinal region to which the inspection figures had been previously exposed. Figure 14.39c is a schematic of the relation, indicating the appearance of components a and b of Figure 14.39 if they were combined. It follows that due to satiation the two left squares are pushed apart and the two right squares are pushed together. Figure 14.40 demonstrates a related aftereffect called the **tilt aftereffect**.

SHAPE AFTEREFFECTS

A second example of aftereffects occurs with changes in the apparent shape of figures. An experiment by

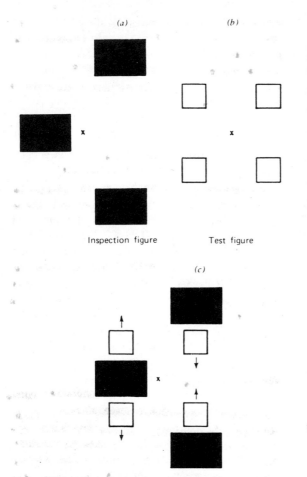

Inspection figure   Test figure

FIGURE 14.39.   Inspection or inducing figure (a) and test figure (b) used to demonstrate figural aftereffects. Following the inspection of the fixation × in (a) for about 40 sec, fixation of the × in (b) results in the two left squares of (b) appearing farther apart than the two on the right. This displacement is schematized in (c). The arrows indicate the apparent displacement. (After Köhler & Wallach, 1944.)

J. J. Gibson in 1933 with simple lines illustrates the phenomenon of **shape** (or curvature) **aftereffects**. Subjects wore special distorting prism glasses that displaced the incoming light rays so that straight vertical lines appeared curved. During the course of the exposure, the subjects reported that the extent of

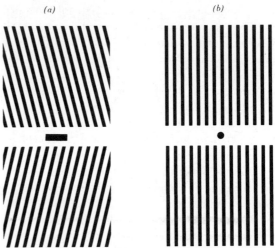

FIGURE 14.40.   The tilt aftereffect. Cover the vertical gratings of (b) and gaze at the tilted gratings of (a) for 30–40 sec with your gaze wandering back and forth along the central horizontal bar. Then rapidly transfer your gaze to the fixation circle of (b) that lies between the two vertical gratings. The vertical bars of (b) will briefly appear tilted in directions opposite to those of the gratings in (a).

the apparent curvature diminished. That is, the straight line curved by the prism glasses began to appear more straight. When the prism glasses were removed, an aftereffect of wearing them occurred: straight lines appeared curved in the direction opposite to the direction of apparent curvature produced by the glasses (see Figure 14.41). Gibson and Radner (1937) found that after a period of continuous visual inspection of tilted or curved lines the same aftereffect resulted: physically vertical straight lines appeared off-vertical (tilted or curved) in the direction opposite to that of the initial inspection. A demonstration of a similar shape aftereffect is illustrated in Figure 14.42.

The shape aftereffect is not restricted to the visual modality. In his original study Gibson (1933) reported that if a blindfolded subject feels along a curved edge for a duration, then a straight edge feels curved the other way; in other words, a kinesthetic-cutaneous aftereffect results (see Howard, 1982).

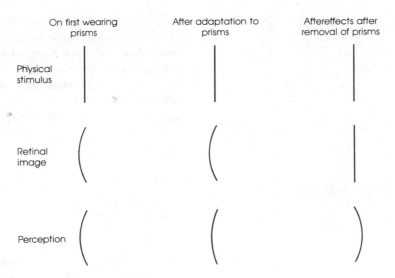

FIGURE 14.41.   Schematic description of the relations between physical stimulus, retinal image, and perception in the experiment on curvature aftereffects by Gibson (1933).

CONTINGENT AFTEREFFECTS

In the previous classes of aftereffects relatively prolonged exposure produces a distance or shape distortion in subsequent perception. In addition, there are numerous aftereffect phenomena that seem to show that it is possible to adapt selectively to *combinations* of stimulus properties such as color with orientation, or color with shape. Typically one of the properties is color and the resultant color aftereffect is *contingent* upon the presence of the other stimulus feature. Perhaps the first direct report of **contingent aftereffects** linked to a combination of stimulus properties is that of McCollough in 1965. She presented a grating of vertical black stripes on an orange ground for a few seconds, alternated with an identical grating of horizontal black stripes on a blue background for a total presentation time of between 2 to 4 min. After this exposure she found that a typical observer reported a faint orange aftereffect on the horizontally oriented grating of the black and white test pattern shown in Figure 14.43 and a faint blue-green aftereffect on the vertically oriented grating pattern. Thus, some units or channels of the visual system respond with decreased sensitivity to those wavelengths by which they have recently been most strongly stimulated, and, accordingly, this results in the antagonistic response (blue-green is approximately the complementary color of the orange used). What is interesting is that this color adaptation is specific to the orientation of the edges or contours of

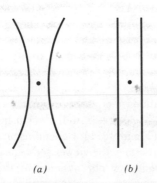

(a)   (b)

FIGURE 14.42.   Shape aftereffects. Stare at the central dot in (a) for 20 to 30 sec, then transfer your gaze to the central dot in (b). The physically vertical lines in (b) will appear to be bowed in the opposite direction to those of (a).

FIGURE 14.43.   Black and white test pattern used by McCollough. After adaptation to orange-vertical and blue-horizontal grating patterns, the left half appears blue-green (approximate complement of orange) and the right half appears orange.

the pattern. The result that the aftereffects are color sensitive *and* specific to the orientation of the stripes in the test pattern hints at the existence of units or channels of the human visual system that are selectively tuned to *both* color *and* orientation.

Contingent aftereffects that are movement-specific have also been found. For example, Hepler (1968) reported that after subjects alternately viewed green stripes (across a black background) moving up and red stripes against a similar ground moving down, they saw a pink aftereffect when white stripes moved up and a green aftereffect when white stripes moved down. That is, the paired-stimulus attributes of color and motion produced color aftereffects that were motion contingent. Numerous other studies have shown related variations on the theme of adaptation producing color- and motion-contingent aftereffects (e.g., Favreau, Emerson, & Corballis, 1972) and related phenomena such as curvature-contingent colored aftereffects.

In fact contingent aftereffects have been demonstrated in combinations of almost every stimulus

property that is subject to adaptation. Wyatt (1974) has even demonstrated contingent aftereffects for a combination of three stimulus properties, color, spatial frequency, and orientation. Contingent aftereffects argue that the visual system may be differentially sensitive to (and thereby adapted by) combinations of specific stimulus features. However, the precise nature of the channels remains to be clarified (Treisman, 1986).

PERCEPTUAL SET

As we noted at the beginning of this chapter, perception involves more than the reception of stimulation at the retina. Indeed, the optical array reflected from the environment—that is, patterns of discrete stimuli composed of lines, dots, and various luminance discontinuities—is insufficient to account for the meaningful structured visual world we experience. The perception of many aspects of the environment is due not only to the incoming stimulation and the functioning of sensory mechanisms, but it is also due to certain dispositions and existing intentions within the perceiver. There are psychological processes, more specific and modifiable than the Gestalt principles described earlier, that play a role in organizing the incoming stimulation toward a meaningful percept. Perception is directed in a particular manner by existing influences such as expectations and anticipations, resulting in a readiness to organize the visual input in a certain way. In other words, the perceiver expects to perceive or is *set* to perceive a particular thing.

The influence of **perceptual set**—as a kind of perceptual priming—is well demonstrated by the drawings of Figure 14.44. Depending on whether *a* or *b* is seen prior to *c*, the viewer sees *c* as a drawing of either a young or old woman. In this instance, perception occurs as a consequence of a set, which is caused by the prior inspection of either *a* or *b*. In general, the stimuli first presented establishes the context that determines the perception of an ambiguous figure. Figure 14.45 demonstrates how set may

(a)

(b)

(c)

FIGURE 14.44.   Whether a young woman or an old woman is seen in (*c*) can be due to the viewer's set. If (*a*) is seen first, the drawing in (*c*) is seen as a young woman; if (*b*) is seen first, (*c*) appears as an old woman. (Adapted from Boring, 1930.)

enable the perceptual organization of seemingly formless stimuli.

That perceptual set enables a meaningful perception of fragmentary or ambiguous stimulation is important, for it is typical for the visual input from the environment to be less than complete. An expectation owing to prior experience as to what "should be there" enables a meaningful interpretation and per-

11 12 13 14

A B C D

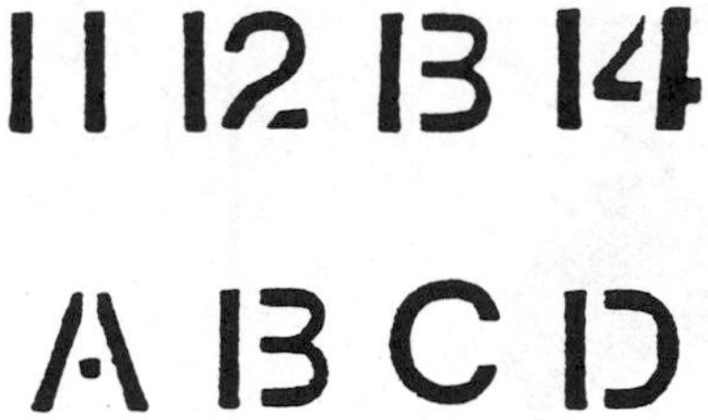

FIGURE 14.46.   The top line appears composed exclusively of numerals, whereas the bottom line is made up of letters. However, one ambiguous symbol is common to both lines.

FIGURE 14.45.   Concealed figure. Examine the apparently unstructured configuration. Among its details is a familiar shape. The solution is given in Figure 14.50 on page 313. (From K. M. Dallenbach, "A puzzle-picture with a new principle of concealment," *American Journal of Psychology, 54,* 1951, p. 432. Reprinted with permission of University of Illinois Press.)

ception as to what "is there" (Coren, Porac, & Theodor, 1986).

Set can be demonstrated easily. Read the two lines of Figure 14.46. Most individuals read the top line as the numerals from 11 to 14, whereas the bottom line is read as the first four letters of the alphabet. Notice however that the numeral read as "13" and the letter read as "B" are identical. The tendency to perceive an ambiguous stimulus in accordance with expectation is clear: perceptual organization may be powerfully determined by expectations built on past and concurrent commerce with the environment.

FIGURAL ORIENTATION AND FORM PERCEPTION

It has been proposed that the perceived shape of a stimulus figure involves a level of cognitive processing that requires decisions and corrections on the part of the viewer (e.g., Rock, 1983; Greene, Plastow, & Braine, 1985). For example, a major factor of form perception is the figure's orientation, in particular, the perceptual assignment by the observer of the location of the top, bottom, and sides of a figure. If these are altered in certain ways, perception accordingly changes. The unfamiliar shapes in Figure 14.47a, look different from those in 14.47b, yet the shapes in each row are geometrically equal but shown in different orientations. Clearly, to the naïve viewer each shape would be described quite differently.

In addition, for figures with a recognizable shape, it is not the orientation of the shape on the retina that is crucial to its perception but, rather, how the shape appears to be oriented with respect to gravity and to the viewer's visual frame of reference —what Rock (1973) calls **environmental orientation.** That is, generally a figure will not appear different in shape if its orientation is changed only with respect to its retinal coordinates. Thus once seen as upright, with an assigned "top," the ambiguous shape in Figure 14.48a, viewed with the head tilted 90° to the right side continues to be perceived as a bearded profile; similarly, the viewing of Figure 14.48b, with the head tilted 90° in the opposite direction still results in the perception of an outline map of the United States. However, in each case the orientation of the image of the shape on the retina is for the reversed perception. Thus, the environmen-

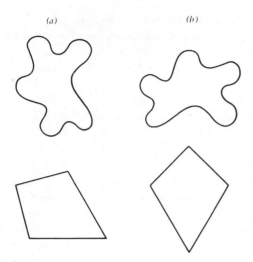

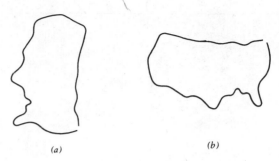

FIGURE 14.48.   The ambiguous figure above can be perceived as a different shape depending on its orientation. The drawing at (a) looks like a bearded profile in one orientation and as an outline map of the United States in another orientation. When viewed with the head tilted 90° to the right, (a) still appears as a profile; when the head is tilted 90° to the left, (b) still appears as a map. The viewer sees the shape that is upright in the environment rather than the shape that is upright on the retina. (Modified from Rock, 1973, p. 13.)

FIGURE 14.47.   The shapes in (a) appear different from those in (b). However, the shapes within each row are geometrically equivalent except that they have been rotated to the right. The upper left shape has been rotated 90° and the bottom left shape, 45°. (Modified from Rock, 1974, p. 81.)

tally upright as opposed to the retinally upright version of the figure is the one recognized.

That shapes are perceived on the basis of their environmental orientation rather than retinal orientation is due to the tendency of the perceptual system to correct or compensate for head or body tilt. Of course, the priority of perceiving things against a perceptually (though not necessarily retinally) stable background or environment has obvious adaptive significance. It makes more sense for a biological system to be able to compensate for its own physical displacements with regard to a stable environment than to perceive the environment tilted with every tilt of the body.

There are, however, interesting exceptions to the general rule that retinal orientation does not affect an object's perception: the perception of complex figures, characteristically seen in only one orientation, and composed of several meaningfully related parts, may be reduced by alterations in their retinal orientation. Thus printed or written words

seen upside down, that is, rotated 180°, or inverted photographs of faces, are not easily recognized. As Figure 14.49 shows we readily perceive that an inverted face is depicted, yet distorted details of its individual parts go unnoticed until the photograph is seen upright.

SUMMARY

In this chapter we have traced the dynamics of form perception, and perceptual organization in general, beginning with presumed basic visual processes and mechanisms; it was noted that processes such as lateral inhibition and border contrast contribute in significant ways to the perception of luminance discontinuities, contrast, and contours. Examples of the importance of stimulus inhomogeneity, discontinuities, and stimulus change for form perception were illustrated by the phenomena of the Ganzfeld and stabilized imagery.

The utility of analyzing the composition of a

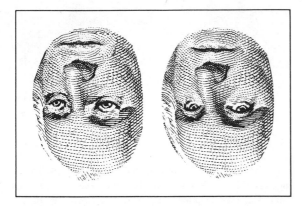

FIGURE 14.49.   The altered features in the left face are not evident as contributing to an extreme distortion in its expression until the face is viewed upright. The face on the right is the original photograph which was altered by inverting only the eyes and mouth.

visual display in terms of its contrasting areas—that is, a distribution of luminance variations—into its spatial frequencies and the resultant contrast sensitivity function for various spatial frequencies was discussed. The notion of a Fourier analysis and synthesis, introduced earlier in Chapter 4, was applied to spatial frequencies in an attempt to examine the possibility that a complex spatial scene can be represented by patterns specified in units of spatial frequencies; additionally we considered the related possibility that the visual system may be performing a Fourier analysis on the spatial frequency content of the visual input. Phenomena and research bearing on this possibility such as selective adaptation to spatial frequencies and block portraits were discussed. The role played by spatial frequencies on acuity was also outlined.

Gestalt psychology was introduced, beginning with the related notion of figure–ground; the general and specific stimulus effects that promote figure–ground and the special effect that the figure has on lightness was discussed and illustrated with a number of demonstrations such as the Wolff and Koffka figures. Gestalt grouping principles were outlined, and some contemporary research yielding measures of grouping effects was presented. Some covariant principles, such as closure associated with figure–

ground, were examined in a discussion of the striking phenomena of subjective contours. The general Gestalt notion of the "good figure" or the law of Prägnanz was discussed in the light of several contemporary studies.

Various forms of masking and their disruptive and facilitive effect on perception were outlined, including the related notion of figural persistence and the icon. Three main classes of aftereffects were identified and discussed: figural, shape, and contingent aftereffects. It was noted that, in general, aftereffects are the product of selective adaptation or the desensitization of channels or units specific to stimulus features such as color, orientation, shape, direction, and movement, and they may even extend to combinations of these features. The role of priming or perceptual set on form perception was briefly noted. It was pointed out that, to an extent, we tend to organize the sensory input on the basis of anticipations, expectations, and past experience.

Finally, we noted that a figure's apparent orientation may have an effect on the perception of its shape. Some shapes may tolerate extensive variations relative to their retinal coordinates without apparent distortions, whereas stimuli such as written or printed text or faces, which are characteristically seen in one orientation, are subject to significant distortion.

In general, this chapter has served to outline some organizational schemes for the perception of form. However, no single class of explanation emerges that is entirely sufficient to account for the visual ability to perceive form. Nor is there a general principle that unifies the many experiences of form perception. Form perception may be best understood as a constructive achievement resulting from the product of peripheral, neural–structural mechanisms interacting with central, cognitive, learning-based processes.

KEY TERMS

Aftereffects

Backward masking

Block portrait

Border contrast

Brightness

Closure

Cognitive invention

Common fate

Contingent aftereffects

Contrast sensitivity function

Environmental orientation

Facilitative interaction

Figural aftereffects

Figure–ground

Forward masking

Fourier analysis

Fourier synthesis

Ganzfeld

Gestalt grouping principles

Good configuration

Good continuation

Hermann grid

Icon

Iconic memory

Interstimulus interval (ISI)

Koffka rings

Lateral inhibition

Law of Prägnanz

Lightness

Lightness contrast

Limulus

Mach bands

Masking

Perceptual set

Proximity (nearness)

Saccadic omission

Selective adaptation

Shape aftereffects

Similarity

Spatial frequency

Spatial frequency channels

Stabilized image

Subjective contours

Symmetry

Tilt aftereffects

Visual persistence

Wolff effect

STUDY QUESTIONS

1. What is lateral inhibition? Discuss how it enhances contrast and the detection of contours based upon an analysis of the recorded activity of the Limulus eye. Indicate how the inhibition of receptor cells varies with the lightness distribution.

2. What is the relation of border contrast and Mach bands to lateral inhibition?

3. Identify the ocular mechanisms and phenomena that stress the significance and necessity of stimulus change for the perception of form.

4. Characterize spatial frequencies and support the notion that the visual system performs a spatial frequency analysis of the optic array.

5. What does a spatial frequency analysis indicate about the variable sensitivity of the visual system with respect to luminance changes and contrast? How does a Fourier analysis enable a complex spatial pattern to be decomposed or analyzed into components of simple spatial patterns?

6. Describe the computation of a contrast sensitivity function. What is the general trend in human contrast sensitivity as a function of spatial frequency?

7. Indicate how various forms of selective adaptation lends support to the notion that there are independent channels in the visual system for detecting different spatial frequencies.

8. What does the perception of block portraits indicate concerning a spatial frequency analysis of complex images?

9. In what ways does a spatial frequency analysis add to the traditional measures of visual acuity?

10. What is figure–ground differentiation and what fundamental principle does it indicate about the organized perception of the visual field?

11. What are some of the stimulus features that affect figure–ground differentiation? What factors determine whether a given region will be perceived as figure or ground?

12. What are the perceptual differences between figure and ground? Analyze the tendency of the figure to appear lighter than the ground, drawing on the phenomena illustrated by the Wolff figure and by the Koffka rings.

13. Discuss the ways in which figure–ground differentiation contribute to perceptual organization and enhance object identification. Describe the importance of the contour to figure–ground differentiation.

14. What is Gestalt psychology? How does it treat the notion of "fundamental" units of perception? What does it propose concerning the relational character of stimuli for perceptual organization?

15. Identify the main Gestalt organizing principles and present examples of proximity, similarity, good continuation, and closure.

16. Indicate how grouping effects may be measured.

17. What are subjective contours? What kinds of stimulus factors are critical in their formation? To what extent is an apparent partial overlap of the background by the subjective contour a necessary condition for their formation?

18. How does Rock's notion of a "cognitive invention" explain the emergence of subjective contours?

19. What is a "good figure" in the Gestalt sense? How can the characteristics of a good figure be assessed? What general features are typical of good figures. To what extent is the recognition of parts embedded in wholes better recognized than when they appear in isolation?

20. Describe masking, indicating its main forms (backward and forward). Indicate what variables affect masking.

21. What does masking indicate about the interaction effect of processing simultaneously and successively presented stimuli? Consider the question of why we don't experience blurred vision from the changing visual fixations created by saccadic eye movements.

22. Describe facilitative interaction due to the integration of successive visual stimulation. What does facilitative interaction indicate about the integration of stimuli over time and space by the visual system? Explain this phenomenon making use of the notion of an icon and of visual persistence at the receptor level.

23. Indicate how aftereffects can be demonstrated. Describe the main forms, indicating figural, tilt, shape, and contingent aftereffects. To what extent do aftereffects support the existence of selective neural channels for specific stimulus features?

24. What is perceptual set? What does set stress about the role of expectation and anticipation on perceptual processing? Discuss the contribution of past experience on perceptual set.

25. To what extent does the perceptual system compensate for head tilt on the position of the upright? How does the perception of an object's shape differ when it is tilted 90° to the right of a stationary observer, from when the the object is kept stationary but the observer shifts his or her head 90° to the right? In examining this question consider Rock's notion of environmental orientation.

FIGURE 14.50.   Solution to Figure 14.45. The head
of a cow facing forward at the left is outlined from the
detail of Figure 14.45. Once you see the cow's head,
it is easy to see it in Figure 14.45. (From J. Hochberg, "Visual perception," in *Stevens' Handbook of
Experimental Psychology*, 2nd ed., Volume 1, John
Wiley, New York, 1988, p. 258. Reprinted by permission of the publisher.)

15

THE PERCEPTION OF MOVEMENT

For the most part, our discussion of visual processes thus far has been confined to the perception of static or immobile stimuli by a stationary viewer. However, we confront many dynamic events; that is, we perceive *movement* in the environment. Most organisms are comparatively mobile and move about in an environment containing a variety of moving objects, objects to be pursued or potentially dangerous objects to be avoided. Clearly, the perception of movement has an important biological utility. To locomote effectively animals must be capable of detecting the relative location, direction, and often even the rate of movement of objects. Perhaps for all species the reception of information about movement is essential for survival.

Indeed, Gregory (1977) speculates that movement perception may have evolutionary priority over shape perception:

> *Something of the evolutionary development of the eye, from movement to shape perception, can be seen embalmed in the human retina. The edge of the retina is sensitive only to movement. This may be seen by getting someone to wave an object around the side of the visual field, where only the edge of the retina is stimulated. It will be found that movement is seen but it is impossible to identify the object. When the movement stops, the object becomes invisible. This is as close as we can come to experiencing primitive perception. The very extreme edge of the retina is even more primitive: when stimulated by movement we experience nothing, but a reflex is initiated which rotates the eye to bring the moving object into central vision, so that the highly developed foveal region with its associated central neural network is brought into play for identifying the object. The edge of the retina is thus an early-warning device, used to rotate the eyes to aim the sophisticated object-recognition part of the system on to objects likely to be friend or foe or food rather than neutral. (p. 93)*

The capacity to perceive movement is quite basic, in that movement perception has been observed in the very young of many species and in animals low on the evolutionary scale. In addition, investigations with amphibia, birds (Frost & Nakayama, 1983) and mammals (e.g., Cremieux, Orban & Duysens, 1984) give evidence that the perception of movement has a neural basis, that is, there is

evidence of directionally sensitive movement-detecting channels in the nervous system.

A dramatic clinical report also supports the notion that the perception of movement has a specific cortical locus. Zihl, von Cramon, and Mai (1983) reported the case of a patient who suffered from cortical lesions. Although she retained other visual functions such as visual acuity, binocular vision, and form and color perception, she lost the ability to perceive most movement in all three dimensions. Clinical assessments showed that while she had some movement perception along the vertical and horizontal axes, her perception was restricted to a small region of the inner visual field. In addition she showed a complete inability to see motion in depth. "She had difficulty, for example, in pouring tea or coffee into a cup because the fluid appeared to be frozen, like a glacier. In addition she could not stop pouring at the right time since she was unable to perceive the movement in the cup (or a pot) when the fluid rose" (p. 315). She also complained of difficulties following a conversation because she could not see the movements of the face and especially the speaker's mouth. If she found herself in a room where more than two other people were moving about, she felt extremely uncomfortable and usually left the room immediately, because "people were suddenly here or there, but I have not seen them moving" (p. 315). The patient experienced this problem to a greater extent in crowded places and where there was considerable movement, like the outdoors, which she avoided as much as possible. Thus she could not cross the street because of her inability to estimate the speed of the cars, although she could easily identify the car. "When I'm looking at the car first, it seems far away. But then, when I want to cross the road, suddenly the car is very near" (p. 315). Eventually, however, she learned to "judge" the distance of moving vehicles by means of their increase in loudness as they approached. It is of interest that her lack of movement perception was highly specific and limited to the visual modality. She was able to perceive motion given by tactual means (e.g., a stimulus moving over her skin surface) and by auditory cues (a moving sound source) with ease.

MOVEMENT SYSTEMS OF THE EYE

The most general condition for the perception of movement is the stimulation of a succession of neighboring retinal loci by an image. However, retinal displacement does not include all instances where the perception of movement occurs. The movement of a stimulus may be perceived when its image is held relatively stationary on the retina as in the case where the eyes follow or track a moving object.

Here movements of the eye match the target's movement, resulting in a more or less motionless retinal image.

Gregory (1977) has identified and proposed these as two interdependent movement systems: they are called the **image–retina movement system** and the **eye–head movement system** (see Figure 15.1).

THE IMAGE–RETINA MOVEMENT SYSTEM

The effective stimulation for the perception of movement of a physically moving stimulus, for the image–retina system, is successive stimulation of adjacent retinal loci. Generally, when the eye is held relatively stationary, as during fixation, a succession of

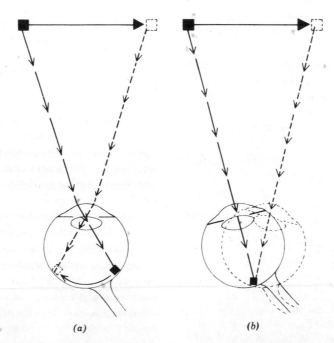

(a)   *(b)*

FIGURE 15.1.   Movement systems of the eye. (a) Image –retina movement system. The succession of images of a moving target stimulus across the retina provides information of movement to a stationary eye. (b) Eye–head movement system. A moving-target stimulus is tracked by a moving eye so that the image remains stationary on the retina, yet movement of the target stimulus is still perceived. Images that move across the retina are perceived as stationary background stimuli, and images that remain stationary on the retina while the eye moves are perceived as moving. (Adapted from Gregory, 1973, p. 93.)

images produced by a moving target stimulus shifts across the retina. The movement thus registered is due to the sequential activity of the receptors in the path of the image of the moving stimulus. This sort of movement detection system is well suited to the mosaic of ommatidia found in the compound eye of the arthropod. A neural model of a movement detector coincident with the image–retina movement system is suggested in Figure 15.2 (Schouten, 1967).

EYE–HEAD MOVEMENT SYSTEM

Of course, when we follow a moving target with our eyes, the image of the target remains more or less fixed on the same retinal region. In this case, eye movement compensates for target movement, yet the perception of the target's movement still occurs. If the moving target stimulus is tracked against a stationary textured background, the target's background moves across the retina. However, the perception of movement still results even when there is no background stimulation. A moving dot of light in an otherwise darkened environment provides sufficient information for movement perception, yet as the

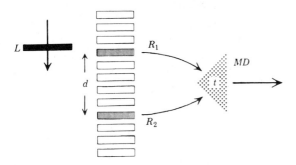

FIGURE 15.2. Neural model of a movement detector. Two retinal receptors, R_1 and R_2, spaced d apart, feed into the movement detector, MD. The movement detector reacts if the light, L, strikes receptor R_1 first and then, after or within a given period of time, t, strikes receptor R_2. (From J.F. Schouten, "Subjective stroboscopy and a model of visual movement detectors," in W. Wathen-Dunn (Ed.), *Modes for the Perception of Visual Form*, M.I.T. Press, Cambridge, Massachusetts, 1967. By permission of the M.I.T. Press.)

eye follows the dot, no background imagery shifts across the retina. This means that in the absence of successive stimulation of neighboring retinal elements (i.e., the lack of stimulation of the image–retina system), self-initiated neural signals that produce the rotation of the eyes in their sockets provide information for the perception of movement. That is, some neural mechanism takes account of command signals that move the eyes and relates them to the image on the retina. These neural signals to the ocular muscles commanding the execution of eye movements occur only when the eyes are voluntarily moved.

COROLLARY DISCHARGE AND OUTFLOW SIGNALS

The question arises why the visual environment appears stationary as we voluntarily move our eyes. Clearly, as we intentionally move our eyes a continuous flow of retinal imagery occurs, yet the visual world continues to be seen as stationary. The answer seems to be that when the eyes voluntarily move, **efferent signals** or motor command signals from the brain to the eye muscles are compared with the corresponding flow of images on the retina. To explain this, it has been proposed that when the brain sends an efferent or outgoing message to the eye muscles to initiate an eye movement, a related or **corollary discharge signal** (sometimes called **an outflow signal**) of this message is also sent to a hypothetical **comparator** center of the nervous system. The corollary discharge signal is compared with the **afferent signal** or incoming message of movement stimulation imaged on the retina as the eyes move (see Figure 15.3; see Matin, 1986). The outcome is a perceptual cancellation of the sequential flow of background imagery, that is, a cancellation of the image–retina system. We are thus able to differentiate between movements of the retinal image produced by voluntary eye movements and movements of the retinal image produced by the actual physical movement of objects. Hence, when the eyes voluntarily move, as during object tracking, the visual field of the target's background remains apparently stable, and only physically moving stimuli

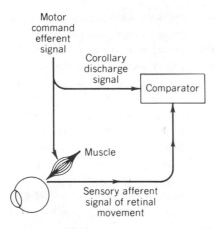

Motor
command
efferent
signal

Corollary
discharge
signal

Comparator

Muscle

Sensory afferent
signal of retinal
movement

FIGURE 15.3.   Schematic representation of function of corollary discharge signals. A voluntary motor command signal is sent to the eye muscle to move the eyeball. A related or corollary discharge signal of the command is sent to a hypothetical comparator. The incoming sensory signal of movement of the retinal image is compared with the motor command signal to move the eyeball. The result of the comparison of the outgoing and incoming signals is a cancellation of the incoming sensory signal; thus no movement in the visual field is perceived.

appear to move. In short, the perception of a stationary environment in spite of a changing retinal image is due to *intentional* outgoing or efferent motor command signals to execute the eye movements.

This explanation of the operation of the eye–head system accounts for the fact that when the movement of the eyeball is initiated passively, the total visual environment is erroneously seen as in movement because the eye–head system is not properly stimulated . If you close one eye and gently move a finger under the bottom lid of the open eye, moving the eye upward, the visual field appears to move in a direction opposite to the movement of the eye. This occurs because when the action is passively executed, impulses voluntarily directing eye movements and their related corollary discharge signals are lacking. Thus passive movements of the eyeball produce image–retina signals without corresponding corollary discharge signals, and the visual field does not appear stable (Bridgeman & Delgardo, 1984). It

is only with voluntary eye movements that cancellation of image–retina movement signals occurs and the visual field appears stationary .

It should be noted that the visual world does not appear to move very much as we move our head or body independent of eye movements, indicating that the central nervous system is also capable of taking into account an interplay of visual and vestibular or orientational information in a similar manner.

THE PATTERN OF OPTICAL STIMULATION FOR MOVEMENT PERCEPTION

In the visual world things move, and they move in different ways, in different directions, at different velocities, and with different accelerations. In addition as an observer moves through the visual world, the location from which the world is viewed continuously changes. All these dynamic events produce corresponding changes in the light array imaged on the retina. Thus the perception of movement is mediated by the complex pattern of changing stimulation in the retinal projection. Several specific variables, indexed by these changes, are especially informative in perceiving movement and are identified here.

KINETIC OPTICAL OCCLUSION

As an object moves in space, it also systematically covers and uncovers the physical texture of the surface that lies behind it. This changing flow of stimulation across the retinal surface is termed **kinetic optical occlusion** by J. J. Gibson (1966). As described by Gibson, there is a *wiping-out* or a deletion of texture at the leading borders, an *unwiping-out* or an uncovering of texture at the trailing borders, and a *shearing* of texture at the lateral borders of the moving object. That is, the retinal projection of an object moving across a textured background involves "a rupture of the continuity of texture" (p. 203).

OPTIC FLOW PATTERNS

The moving organism also generates an informative pattern of optical changes. The optic array of most surfaces (e.g., floors, walls, ceilings, roads, fields) registers a pattern of continuous changes (i.e., **optic flow patterns**) with the viewer's movement, that is, from a moving point of observation. When moving parallel to or directly approaching a surface, there is a continuous flow of retinal projections relative to the point of the viewer's fixation. For example, as outlined in Figure 15.4, with a point of focus *(F)*, toward which an observer is moving, contours appear to flow radially away from the focal point. The vectors in the figure suggest the changing optic patterns of the array. The information in this optic flow pattern is promoted by the movement of the observer and constitutes a reliable source for gauging the relative velocity and the direction of movement.

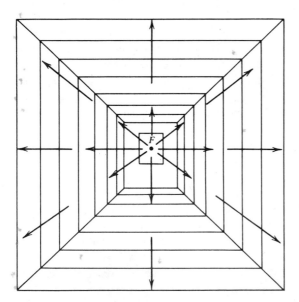

FIGURE 15.4.   Optic flow pattern. Movement toward (and away from) surfaces creates patterns that provide information about direction and relative velocity. The vectors indicate the direction of the optic flow pattern generated when movement is toward the fixation point (*F*) on the frontal surface.

Moreover, with movement toward a stationary surface, the retinal image of the surface expands; that is, as the observer moves toward a surface, the rate of expansion of the retinal image of the surface reflects the rate of the approach. In fact, the part of the optical array where the rate of the retinal expansion is highest corresponds to the image of the destination or "collision" point (Regan & Beverley, 1982). Indeed the rapid expansion of the retinal image is a potent signal in judging impending collision. A similar analysis can be made for the condition where objects appear to move toward the observer. The perception of the movement of an object in the frontal (near–far) plane may occur when the approach of the object is signaled by its increasing projected size. That is, the orderly increase in the projected size of an object on the retina of the stationary observer is perceived as movement toward the observer. (This phenomenon is called "looming," and it is discussed in some detail in Chapter 18.)

We should note here that at the neural level, there is evidence that the human visual system contains channels that are sensitive to the changes in the size of objects, suggesting the existence of a neural mechanism for optic flow patterns (Regan & Beverley, 1979; Beverley & Regan, 1979).

Of course, changes in the image size of an object could also signal the relatively unlikely occurrence of a size change in a stationary object. Thus an expanding retinal image may mean that an object is enlarging or growing *or* that it is moving closer. Reflecting upon the neural basis of perceiving size changes in an object as signals of environmental movement rather than as cues of an object's expansion, Regan, Beverley, and Cynader (1979) speculate that

> as long as an object's shape remains constant the visual system (possibly by means of some neural biasing system) responds as though changing size were caused by motion in depth. This might be described as a "best guess" solution. For an animal (including the human one) there would be little survival advantage conferred by a visual system that submitted for leisurely intellectual judgment the question of whether a predator was

approaching rapidly or swelling rapidly! (p. 142)

VISUAL FIELD

Perhaps one of the most influential variables for movement perception is the field on which a target is perceived. J. F. Brown in 1931 examined the role of the size of the target relative to the size of the field on which it appeared to move. In one experiment observers had to equalize the apparent movement of two sequences of squares that each moved behind a separate aperture. The squares, their spacings, and the size of the aperture of one display were twice the linear size of the other (see Figure 15.5 for an example of the display using dots instead of squares). The subjects adjusted the movement of the squares of the two displays until they appeared to move at the same speed. An equality match occurred when the

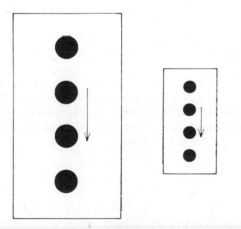

FIGURE 15.5.   An endless paper tape moving downward is observed behind each of the two apertures. A row of dots is printed on each tape. The size of the larger aperture is twice that of the smaller one; in addition its dots are twice as large and are twice as far apart from each other. The observer must adjust the speeds of the tapes until the dots in the two apertures appear to move at the same speed. The result is that the physical speed of movement of the tape behind the large aperture must be about twice the speed of the smaller for an equality match. (Based on Brown, 1931a; reprinted in 1965.)

physical speed of movement of the large squares moving behind the large aperture was set at almost twice the speed of the movement of the small squares. This general effect of target size and its background on perceived velocity has been recently confirmed and elaborated by Raymond (1988). Thus, perceived movement of an object is dependent on the relation of the object to the general structure of the visual field as well as on its physical velocity.

THRESHOLDS FOR MOVEMENT

Threshold values for the perception of movement vary with many physical and psychophysiological factors other than the actual velocity of a moving stimulus. The threshold varies with such factors as target size, target distance, luminance levels, the region of the retina stimulated, and the adaptive state of the eye. For example, thresholds for movement are lowest for well-illuminated moving stimuli. Under certain conditions, when stimulating the fovea, the movement of a well-illuminated target of 0.8 cm square seen at a viewing distance of 2 meters is just detected when it moves at a velocity of about 0.2 cm per second (Brown, 1931b; see Spigel, 1965). In contrast, when the velocity of a moving target at 2 meters from the viewer exceeds about 150 cm per second, the object appears as a blur rather than as a target in transit. Specific values aside, there is both a lower threshold—a minimum velocity, below which motion is not perceived (Bonnett, 1982)—and an upper threshold—a maximum velocity value, above which motion is not perceived (Burr & Ross, 1982; see Mack, 1986, for an analysis and summary of threshold measures for motion).

BIOLOGICAL MOTION

Our discussion thus far has dealt with the perception of movement per se, but one kind of environmental movement warrants specific consideration: the perception of the class of movements made by locomoting humans. We quickly recognize whether a person is walking or running, skipping or dancing, and so on. Moreover, we can detect slight deviations from the general norms of these motions. For example, we easily note a slight limp in one's walk, the slower gait of the aged, and we may even recognize (and mimic) a person on the basis of characteristic posture, style of walk, and pattern of gestures. The complex pattern of movements determining the perception of these Gestalt-like locomotor acts are constructed from combinations of pendulum-type motions that are specific for each type of activity. These complex patterns of motion have been studied and labeled **biological motion** by Johansson (1973, 1975).

Johansson has devised a method for directly studying the visual information for perceiving pure biological motion without any interference by the shape of the moving form. In one experiment an actor's movement was recorded on videotape. However, the movement was accomplished in complete darkness and only points or dots of light placed at 10 main body joints were visible. This effectively eliminated any traces of the visual field background or the actor's body contours (see Figure 15.6). When viewing the kinetic dot configuration shown at b of Figure 15.6, the spontaneous perception of a person's activity resulted even after the actor had taken only one or two steps. Indeed, the effect of the patterns of movement made by the joints was so compelling that subjects could neither combine the moving dots to establish alternative impressions of movement nor could they see the dots merely as a series of unrelated points of light in motion. When the motion ceased, the light configurations did not appear to represent a human form, indicating that it was the *pattern of movement* that determined the perception of the particular kind of locomotor activity.

Further studies of gait perception using point–light kinetic displays as stimuli have established that it is possible to recognize one's own walk as well as those of friends (Cutting & Kozlowski, 1977). Moreover, there are distinctive and identifiable patterns of movement belonging to male and female walkers (Cutting, Proffitt, & Kozlowski, 1978; Cutting & Proffitt, 1981). Point-light sequences were identified as male when the perception of shoulder movement

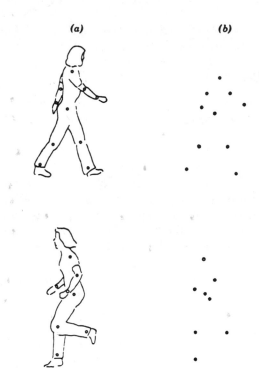

FIGURE 15.6. Outline contours of a walking and a running subject (a) and the corresponding dot configurations (b). After the first one or two steps, subjects viewing the dots of light perceive a walking (top dot configuration) or a running (bottom configuration) person. (Source: G. Johansson, "Visual perception of biological motion and a model for its analysis," *Perception & Psychophysics, 14,* 1973, p. 202. Reprinted by permission of the Psychonomic Society, Inc.)

was greater than of hip movement, and as female for the reverse light configuration (Barclay, Cutting, & Kozlowski, 1978; Cutting, 1978; Runeson & Frykholm, 1983).

The pickup of biological motion is immediate, suggesting it may be as fundamental an event as any basic feature of environmental motion. For example, short segments containing instances of biological motion flashed for only 100 msec are sufficient for viewers to identify aspects of familiar movements (Johansson, von Hofsten, & Jansson, 1980).

It is noteworthy that the perception of biological motion, even when defined by patterns of moving points of light on a television screen, is not restricted to adult humans. Research by Fox and McDaniel (1982) indicates that human infants can not only discriminate between simulations of biological and nonbiological forms of motion, but also show a distinct preference for viewing the former. The finding that it is perceived without significant experience and at very brief durations suggests that the stimuli that signal biological motion are easily organized and may provide a basic source of environmental information.

In summary, general body movements, even when represented by lights set at select joints of the body, produce visual combinations of joint interactions that are sufficiently informative to evoke strong and quite identifiable impressions of complex human locomotor activity. Moreover, it is possible to identify gender and even a familiar person from a dynamic point–light display.

DISTORTIONS IN THE PERCEPTION OF MOVEMENT

A number of dynamic events share in common a distortion of movement, promoted by either a reinterpretation or a misperception of the physical movement occurring in the visual field.

MOTION-PRODUCED DEPTH: KINETIC DEPTH EFFECT

If a pattern of two-dimensional shadows, such as those created by rotation of a cube wire form, are cast on a translucent screen, as shown in Figure 15.7, the impression is of a rotating rigid object in three dimensions. This phenomenon has been termed the **kinetic depth effect** by Wallach and O'Connell (1953). When the figure is stationary, the shadow of the wire form appears flat, in two dimensions. However, when set in rotation around its vertical axis, the changing shadow pattern is perceived as emanating

from a solid rotating cube, even though all the movement is imaged on a flat plane. What is occurring is that a sequence of visual images is projected that corresponds to the continuous imagery that normally results from the rotation of an actual three-dimensional object. As a consequence, the visual system interprets the changes in the pattern of shadows in accordance with the occurrence of a rotating three-dimensional object rather than a succession of changing flat patterns.

In fact viewing a totally unfamiliar object, such as a randomly bent wire, would also provide the same effect. As a stationary stimulus it would appear as a flat curve, and its shape would not be detectable; however, when rotated using the arrangement of Figure 15.7, its shape in three dimensions would be immediately perceived. Thus the phenomenon of the kinetic depth effect demonstrates an extremely important point: the perception of an object's motion may contribute to the perception of the object's form or shape.

ANORTHOSCOPIC PERCEPTION

The framework in which the pattern of movement is seen exerts considerable influence on the character of the perceived movement. Parks (1965) demonstrated that when a picture of a figure is moved horizontally behind an opaque cover with a stationary slit that is smaller than the figure, a viewer observing the pattern of stimulation at the slit will perceive the figure as a whole in the general vicinity of the slit (see Figures 15.8 and 15.9). This unusual effect, attributed to Zöllner in 1862 is called **anorthoscopic perception** (see Rock, 1986, for a brief history). Interestingly, with an anorthoscopic display, the entire figure may be recognized although only a narrow strip of it is visible at any instant. This suggests that the visual system can assemble a set of successive parts that fall on the same retinal region over time into a single unitary form. Along with the shape of the slit, the figure's perceived shape is dependent on the speed at which the figure travels behind the slit. At relatively slow speeds, the figure appears slightly elongated; when moved at relatively

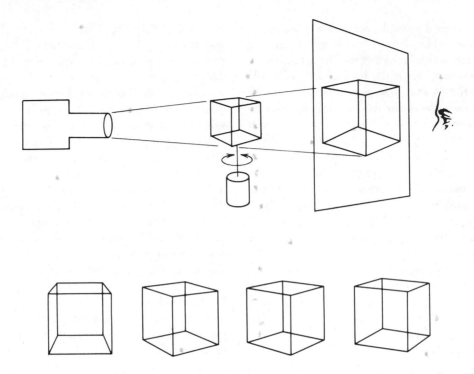

FIGURE 15.7.   Arrangement for demonstrating the kinetic depth effect. When stationary, the shadow of a cube
wire form looks flat. However, when it is rotated, the
changing shadow pattern reflected on the screen is perceived as a rotating rigid cube in three dimensions. Four
different orientations of the wire cube are shown at the
bottom.

high speeds, it appears compressed or condensed
(Anstis & Atkinson, 1967; Haber & Nathanson,
1968). In addition, the figure appears displaced in
the direction of its movement.

INDUCED MOVEMENT

What an observer perceives to be in motion is not
always in accordance with what is actually in motion.
As noted, the perception of movement is strongly
influenced by the spatial context or framework in
which the moving stimuli are seen. If two lighted
figures of different sizes are seen against an otherwise
darkened field and only the larger figure is in
physical motion, only the smaller one appears to
move. The larger moving stimulus is said to *induce*
the movement of the smaller one. If a stationary

luminous dot is enclosed by a luminous rectangle in
the dark and the rectangle is slowly moved to the
right, the enclosed dot appears to move to the left.
That is, the apparent movement of the dot is induced
by the physical displacement of the rectangle. This is
outlined in Figure 15.10. In a more familiar example, sometimes the moon appears to race behind
apparently stationary clouds, yet clearly it is the
clouds that are in physical transit and cover a
stationary moon. Thus **induced movement** is a form
of visual illusion in which movement in attributed to the wrong part of the stimulus array. In
general, the smaller and more enclosed stimulus
appears to move relative to the larger and enclosing
stimulus. Perhaps this is so because of our extensive
experience that it is usually small objects that move

FIGURE 15.8. A sample stimulus and outline of the arrangement for the demonstration of Park's effect. A simple outline figure (dashed line) is passed behind a stationary slit aperture in an opaque screen. At the appropriate speed the figure will be briefly seen in the region of the slit as moving slightly and being compressed (solid line drawing). The compression of the figure increases with the speed of its passage until only a blur is seen. The author termed this example, "Passing a camel through the eye of a needle." (From T. E. Parks, "Post-retinal visual storage," *American Journal of Psychology*, 78, 1965, p. 148. Reprinted with permission of the publisher, University of Illinois Press.)

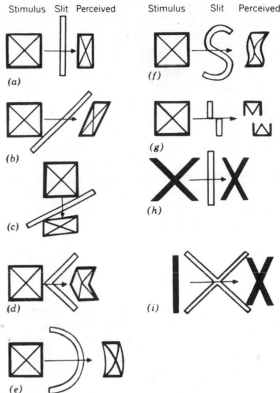

FIGURE 15.9. Examples of the distorted perception of figures moving behind a stationary slit. (*a*) The perceived figure appears displaced and compressed in the direction of its movement. (*b–g*) Slits that are tilted, curved or multiple make moving figures appear tilted, curved or multiple, respectively. (*h, i*) The shape of the figure and the slit can be interchanged. An "X"-shape figure seen through a vertical-line slit appears the same as a vertical-line figure seen through an "X"-shape slit. (From S. M. Anstis and J. Atkinson, "Distortions in moving figures viewed through a stationary slit," *American Journal of Psychology*, 80, 1967, p. 573. Reprinted with permission of the publisher, University of Illinois Press.)

whereas the larger objects in our environment are stable.

Interestingly, instances of induced movement are not restricted to apparent linear paths. Duncker (1929), in his classic treatise on induced movement, reported that movement of a patterned stationary disk can be induced by the rotation of a surrounding concentric patterned annulus (see Figure 15.11*a*; see also Figure 15.11*b* for a demonstration of a related effect. See Anstis & Reinhardt-Rutland, 1976, and Day, 1981).

A number of stimulus factors can be identified that reduce or promote induced movement. For example, induced movement diminishes when the motion of the inducing pattern increases in speed (Becklen & Wallach, 1985; Mack, 1986). A further variable affecting induced movement is the spatial relation between the background (e.g., surrounding frame) and the apparently enclosed stimulus. A

necessary condition for induced movement is that the frame that defines the background and the enclosed stimulus should appear to lie at the same distance from the viewer in the frontoparallel plane (i.e., that they appear to be spatially adjacent to each other). If

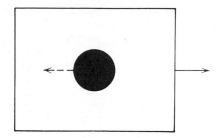

FIGURE 15.10. Induced movement. A luminous stationary dot enclosed by a luminous rectangle is seen in the dark. If the rectangle is physically displaced to the right (solid arrow), the enclosed dot appears to move to the left (dashed arrow). The apparent movement of the stationary dot is induced by the physical displacement of the rectangle.

the surrounding frame lies too far in front of or behind the enclosed stimulus, induced movement falls off appreciably (Gogel & Koslow, 1972). This result points out the complex interrelationship that exists between the perception of movement and apparent depth. A further example of this relationship follows.

PULFRICH EFFECT

An interesting perceptual distortion of physical movement, known as the **Pulfrich pendulum effect,** may occur when the two eyes are stimulated by different intensities of light. This effect is schematized in Figure 15.12. The pendulum bob is swung back and forth in a straight path in a plane perpendicular to the viewer's line of sight. However, when both eyes are open but one eye is covered with a dark glass or light filter (e.g., one lens of a pair of sunglasses), the pendulum bob appears to swing in an elliptical path arching toward and away from the viewer. According to Gregory (1973) and Enright (1970), this distortion is due in large measure to the fact that the reaction time of the visual system varies with stimulus intensity. The filter reduces the amount of light reaching one eye, which in turn results in a slight but significant delay in the signals from that eye reaching the brain. That is, at any instant the apparent position of the pendulum bob coded by the filtered eye lags slightly behind the position of the pendulum bob coded by the unfiltered

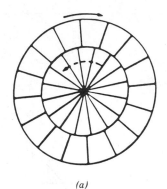

(a)

(b)

FIGURE 15.11. *(a)* Rotary-induced movement. If the inner disk is stationary and the surrounding annulus rotates, the motion of the disk is induced in a direction opposite to the movement of the annulus. (The continuous line indicates the direction of the physical movement of the annulus; the dashed line signifies the direction of the apparent movement of the disk.) *(b)* A related rotary-induced movement effect. Focus on the center cogwheel from about 12 in. When the page is oscillated back and forth at a rate of about once per second, the outside wheels will appear to move in one direction and the center cogwheel in the opposite direction. (Based on Le Grand, 1967.)

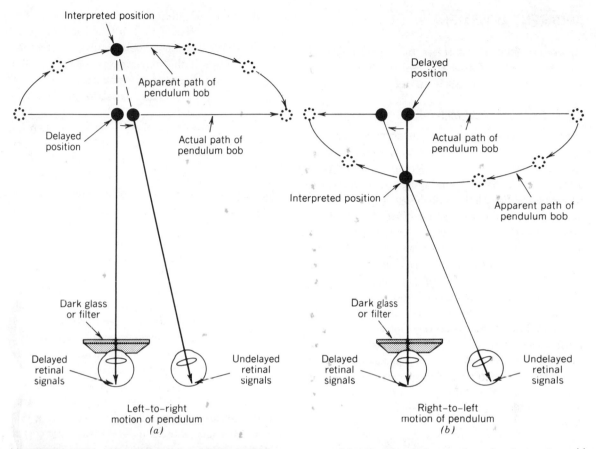

FIGURE 15.12.   Schematic diagram of the Pulfrich pendulum effect. When a pendulum swinging in a straight arc in a plane perpendicular to the line of sight is viewed with a filter over one eye, it appears to swing in an elliptical path. This is due to the signals being delayed from the eye covered by the filter. That is, because of the greater latency of the visual information induced by the filter, the apparent position of the pendulum bob as seen by the filtered eye lags behind the position seen by the unfiltered eye. The perceptual effect is that there is an apparent displace-

ment of the pendulum bob *away* from the viewer when it moves left to right, that is, from the filtered to the unfiltered side of the visual field (*a*), and a displacement *toward* the viewer when the pendulum bob moves in the opposite direction (*b*).

In both (*a*) and (*b*) the apparent paths created by the series of interpreted positions of the pendulum bob conform to the set of visual signals that would reach each eye if the bob actually moved away from and toward the viewer, that is, moved in depth.

eye. The fact that for the filtered eye the pendulum bob is seen slightly later in space means that at any given moment the pendulum bob appears at slightly different locations for each eye. The reconciliation of the disparity between the information arriving at the cortex from both retinae is an apparent displacement of the pendulum bob in an elliptical path in depth.

Ironically this phenomenon was explained in 1922 by the German physicist Carl Pulfrich who was blind in one eye and thus never able to experience the distortion effect. (A detailed account of the procedures, and presumed processes, involved in achieving the Pulfrich pendulum effect may be found in Walker, 1978, and Fineman, 1981.)

APPARENT MOVEMENT

Apparent movement refers to the perception of movement when there is no corresponding physical displacement of an object in space.

STROBOSCOPIC MOVEMENT

One of the most convincing instances of apparent movement occurs when two stationary lights, set a short distance apart, are alternately lighted at a certain rate (schematized in Figure 15.13). As light A flashes on and off, light B flashes off and on; that is, one light is onset just as the other offsets. If the pattern of stimulation is correct, the perception is of simple movement across the intervening space between A and B in the direction of light A to light B; that is, a single light is seen moving through the empty space between lights A and B. This type of movement, in its various forms, is termed **stroboscopic** or **beta** (β) **movement** or sometimes **phi** (φ). If the rate of alternation is too slow, only succession will be perceived—two lights alternately flashing. If the rate of alternation is too fast, the perception of apparent movement changes to one of simultaneity—two lights are perceived flashing, each at a different location.

A number of different kinds of apparent movement can be produced by two flashing lights (see Boring, 1942). The most crucial variables determining the nature of the apparent movement are the intensities of the lights, the time intervening between flashes of the lights, and the spatial distance between the lights.

In the classic stroboscopic effect, motion is perceived extending over the shortest path between two flashing lights. However, Shepard and Zare (1983) have reported a variation of this effect in which stroboscopic motion may be perceived over a curved path. Figure 15.14 shows the three main stimulus configurations employed by Shepard and Zare. First, they presented alternations of two black dots so that a single dot appeared to move back and forth in a linear path between them. In addition, they found that a connecting gray band flashed during the brief interval between the alternation of the black dots made the linear stroboscopic movement effect more compelling. However, most striking was the experience when a *curved* gray path was briefly flashed between alternations of the black dots: a single dot was observed moving back and forth over the curved path. The authors termed this **path-guided apparent motion** and, by extending this procedure, were able to induce the experience of apparent motion around paths of varying degrees of curvature, including a completely closed circle.

Clearly the perception of stroboscopic movement is an unusual as well as a meaningful and

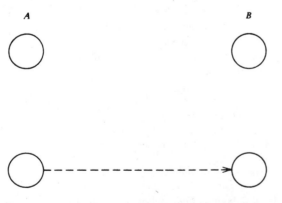

A   B

FIGURE 15.13.   Stroboscopic movement from two alternately flashing stationary lights, A and B. Depending on the intensity of the light flashes, the physical distance separating them, and the time interval between light flashes, the illusion of one light moving from A to B, schematized in the bottom figure with the dashed line, can be created with two lights flashing sequentially.

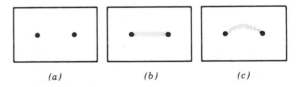

(a)   *(b)*   *(c)*

FIGURE 15.14.   Stimulus conditions for producing path-guided apparent motion. In all conditions the black dots were alternately flashed to produce an effect of apparent motion. In (b) and (c) a gray homogeneous path was flashed between alternations of the black dots. (a) Classic stroboscopic motion. (b) Enhanced stroboscopic effect through path-guided apparent motion. (c) Curved path-guided apparent motion. (Based on Shepard and Zare, 1983.)

reasonable attainment. On this point, Shepard (1981) comments:

> As we have evolved in a three-dimensional world populated with enduring, movable, and often animated semirigid objects, it is perhaps remarkable but not entirely uncomprehensible that the brain should have acquired the tendency to interpret the superficially different figural units in two successive glimpses as representing the same enduring object . . . (p. 312)

MOTION PICTURES

As shown in Figure 15.15, apparent movement from sequentially presented stationary stimuli is not limited to the stimulation from only simple lights or dots. The principles involved in perceiving apparent movement from stationary but intermittently presented stimuli lie at the basis of one of the most familiar and compelling examples of apparent movement—**motion pictures.** In motion pictures a series of still frames of slightly different photographs are projected on a screen in rapid succession. Each frame is a view of a slightly different spatial position of a moving object. When this succession of static frames is projected at the proper rate (usually at least 24 different frames per second), movement is perceived. As with stroboscopic movement, the quality of the movement varies with the rate of projection. If the rate is too slow, a succession of flickers, or at even slower rates, frames of discrete photographs, are seen, whereas, if the rate is too fast, a blur of images is seen. (Wead and Lellis, 1981, offer a concise history and technology of motion pictures, as well as an analysis of its perception; also see Hoch-

berg, 1986, for an extensive and provocative analysis of this topic.)

As noted in earlier contexts, once begun a visual response persists for a brief period even though the physical stimulus has terminated. In the case of motion pictures when the frames of photographs are shown at the proper rate, the image of each frame apparently fuses with the image of the preceding and following frame, thereby producing the perception of steady movement. Thus the visual system can integrate a series of successive but discrete images producing an apparently continuous visual environment or event.

It should be stressed however that while persistence of the visual response is a major factor in producing the perception of smooth, continuous movement from a succession of discrete images—especially enabling the darkness between images to go unnoticed—another significant factor is also involved. The perceptually smooth integration of the discrete frames is faciliated by a close correspondence between the features that are contained within each frame and the context that they share. The greater their relationship and the more structurally similar the adjoining frames are to each other—the greater their "phenomenal identity"—the more easily the visual system combines the sequentially presented information to enable the perception of fluid movement from physically discrete stimuli. When we view a segment of a movie, say, for example of a person running, and the changes in the separate units (e.g., arms, legs, body) are *consistent* from frame to frame, the apparent cohesiveness and the structural integrity of the units within the sequence is retained. That is, the visual system identifies the successive images as new positions of the same units—in short, it interprets these consistent changes as *movement*. On the other hand, the presentation of a succession of dissimilar, seemingly incompatible frames may pose unusual problems to the visual system; while there may be fleeting experiences of one form becoming another, overall there a reduction in the perception of smooth apparent movement. The conditions for producing this, of course, would probably occur only in a perception laboratory.

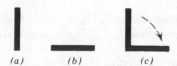

(a)   (b)   (c)

FIGURE 15.15.   Apparent movement with two successive stationary stimuli. When the vertical line (a) is succeeded by the horizontal line (b) after an interval of 60 msec, the vertical line will appear to rotate 90° clockwise, as shown by (c).

In actual practice, the light projected from each frame to the screen by most professional motion picture projectors is interrupted several times prior to the advancement to the next frame. This is necessary because at only 24 frames per second, we would still see flicker. To avoid this each frame is usually shown three times. This is accomplished by a shutter arrangement, so that each frame is projected on the screen as three flashes resulting in a frequency of 72 flashes per second. Old home movies run at 16 frames per second (48 flashes or projections per second), but because they are shown at a lower intensity level, the more readily they fuse and there is less of a tendency to see flicker. The image produced on the television screen results from a similar fusion principle, although it is technically quite different.

In this context we might offer an explanation to the puzzling phenomenon that the movement of the spokes of the wheels of vehicles obviously moving forward, as depicted in motion pictures, sometimes appear to move backward. The explanation outlined by Christman (1979) and Fineman (1981) is not that there is any illusion of movement (other than the apparent movement induced by the succession of frames themselves), but that there is a mismatch between the number of wheel revolutions per second and the number of frames photographed per second. If the camera takes 24 frames per second and the wheel is rotating at 23 revolutions per second, each successive frame of film will capture the wheel slightly before it completes a full revolution. Accordingly, when the film is projected, the wheel will appear to be moving in reverse or backward at the rate of 1 revolution per second. If the wheel revolves at 24 revolutions per second, it will appear stationary, and if it turns at 25 revolutions per second, it will appear to move in a forward direction at the rate of 1 revolution per second.

In summary, the perception of motion pictures from a succession of discrete intermittent images is a product of the persistence of vision and the recognition of related features and consistent changes from frame to frame. However, a full explanation of this unusual phenomenon is not available. As Wead and Lellis (1981) conclude, "Science has not explained the cause of the illusion. We know that under the right conditions we tend to perceive discrete objects as continuous units, but no one yet knows why this trickery occurs" (p. 41).

AUTOKINETIC MOVEMENT

An experience of movement may occur when fixating on a stationary point of light in an otherwise completely darkened environment. In this condition a spatial context or background is lacking, and there is no fixed visual framework to which the point of light may be referred. The result is that a single stationary point of light appears to drift or wander irregularly about, a phenomenon termed **autokinetic movement.** Typically, the point of light appears to make small excursions, but considerable movement is often noted. There are wide individual differences in the extent and direction of the apparent movement and autokinetic movement has been shown to be significantly affected by social influences (Sherif, 1936).

Several explanations for autokinetic movement, based primarily on the role of eye movements, have been proposed (see Post & Leibowitz, 1985; Mack, 1986). One appealing explanation offered by Gregory (1973) is based on the fact that there is a variation in the efficiency of the eye muscles to maintain fixation on the point of light. During continued fixation slight tremors of the eyes cause some fluctuation in fixation. Moreover, during prolonged fixation the eye muscles fatigue. To compensate for the lack of maintained fixation as well as for fatigue, the eye muscles require abnormal command signals to hold the gaze on the point of light. These abnormal signals are the same sort of signals that normally move the eyes when tracking moving stimuli. Thus, according to Gregory (1973) it is not the eyes moving, but the correcting signals applied to *prevent* them from moving that "cause" the spot of light to wander in the dark.

MOVEMENT AFTEREFFECTS

A passenger on a stopped train who has gazed at the imagery of a moving landscape for a while sees the landscape appear to move forward so persuasively that he or she may actually perceive the train as slowly moving backward. This is an example of a **movement aftereffect**. Similarly, if you stare at a region of a waterfall for a short period of time and then look at a stationary scene the scene will appear to move upward (this is called the **waterfall illusion,** described by Addams, 1834, and by Bowditch & Hall, 1882; see Fineman, 1981, for illustrated detail). An early device used to create the effect is shown in Figure 15.16. A similar movement aftereffect, owing in part to the pattern of involuntary eye movements made during fixation, is shown in the geometric pattern of Figure 15.17.

In general, movement aftereffects provide evidence that the perception of movement may result not only from a pattern of changing visual stimulation but may also persist after the moving pattern is removed.

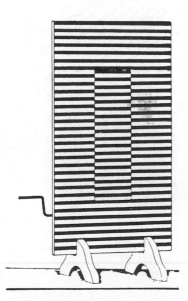

FIGURE 15.16.   Early device used to produce the waterfall illusion. A crank moves a striped band, seen through the central aperture, down (or up). When movement of the band ceases, the subject sees a reverse movement if he or she looks at the background or upon another surface. (Generally attributed to Bowditch and Hall, 1882, although Boring, 1942, speculates that a version of this device may be traced to William James.)

THE PREDICTION OF MOTION PATHS

As we have stressed in a number of earlier discussions most individuals constantly observe and interact with dynamic events in the environment, particularly those involving objects in motion. It is reasonable to assume that based upon this extensive experience, most individuals would develop a fundamental understanding of some of the basic principles and "laws" of physics and recognize that objects in motion move in predictable ways. However, despite considerable experience, certain systematic misconceptions and erroneous beliefs are maintained concerning the motion of objects in seemingly simple conditions. McCloskey, Carramazza, and Green (1980; see also Kaiser, Proffitt, & McCloskey, 1985) have assessed the ability of individuals to make accurate predictions about the trajectory or path of objects in motion based on the responses to a series of simple physical problems, exemplified by the first two presented in Figure 15.18. When asked to indicate the **motion path** that a moving object would follow upon emerging from the tube, a surprising number of subjects (college students, of whom almost 70 percent had at least a high school physics course) evidenced a somewhat naïve notion concerning a fundamental property of motion that is at variance with formal physical principles and laws. Their response to the problems was that when a moving object is passed through a curved tube, it will continue in a curved path even without any external force applied. Moreover, the increase in errors from Problem 1 to Problem 2 suggests that many subjects thought that the longer the moving object is in the curved tube, the more curved its motion will be upon its emergence. The correct answer applicable to both problems follows directly from the law of *inertia* or Newton's first law of motion: *There is no change in the motion of a body unless a resultant force acts upon it. If the body is at rest, it will continue at rest. If it is in motion, it will continue in motion at a constant speed in a straight line unless there is an externally applied force.*

Based on postexperimental interviews with the

FIGURE 15.17.   An example of a geometric pattern that produces afterimages in which motion can be perceived. If the center of the pattern is fixated for approximately 20 sec and then the afterimage is projected on a plain white surface, rotary motion is usually perceived. (From D.M. MacKay, "Ways of looking at perception," in W. Wather-Dunn (Ed.), *Models for the Perception of Visual Form*, M.I.T. Press, Cambridge, Massachusetts, 1967. By permission of the M.I.T. Press.)

subjects it appears that the erroneous prediction was not a matter of a visual distortion or a perceptual bias, but due to the nature of their naïve notions about motion. The general misconception was based on the belief that an object forced to travel in a curved path in a tube acquired a "momentum" or impetus that causes it to continue in curvilinear motion for a time even after it emerges from the tube and is uninfluenced by the original force; according to this erroneous conception, only after the impetus gradually dissipates does the object's trajectory become linear. McCloskey (1983a) traces these naïve notions of motion—clearly at odds with classical physics—to the pre-Newtonian *impetus* theory of motion prevalent during the Middle Ages. This early conception of physical mechanics claimed that an object set in motion acquires a force or impetus that serves to maintain the motion; the impetus gradually dissipates, causing the deceleration and eventual cessation of the object's motion.

Problem 1   Problem 2

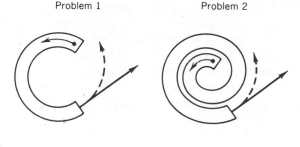

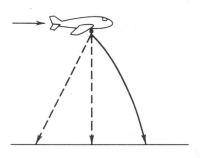

Problem 3

FIGURE 15.18.   Motion problems with correct solutions (solid lines) and common incorrect responses (dashed lines). For Problems 1 and 2 subjects were instructed that they are looking down on the tube. A metal ball is put into the end of the tube indicated by the arrow. The ball is then shot out of the other end of the tube at high speed. The subject's task is to draw the path the ball will follow after it comes out of the tube, ignoring air resistance. For Problem 1 an erroneous curved path was drawn by 33% of the subjects; for Problem 2, 51% drew a curved path.

In Problem 3 subjects were informed that the depicted aircraft is flying at a constant speed, parallel to the ground, in the direction indicated by the arrow. When the aircraft is in the position shown, it drops a metal ball. The aircraft continues flying at the same speed and altitude. The subject's task is to draw the path the ball will follow from the time it is dropped until it makes impact with the ground, ignoring wind or air resistance. For Problem 3, 51% drew an erroneous vertical path and 11% drew a backward path. (Based on McCloskey, Caramazza, and Green, 1980; McCloskey, 1983a; Kaiser, Proffitt, and McCloskey, 1985.)

Further evidence that it is the application of naïve notions concerning physical mechanics rather than any erroneous perceptual processes at play is based on the finding that subjects do *recognize* the correct trajectory of objects when they are observed in conditions of motion like those posed in Problems 1 and 2 of Figure 15.18 (Kaiser, Proffitt, & Anderson, 1985). When shown simulated sequences on a video screen of balls rolling through curved tubes and following a variety of straight and curved paths upon exit, almost all subjects selected the correct path. That is, when viewing a depiction of the ongoing event, subjects perceived the correct straight path as the most natural path and not the erroneous trajectory that was often predicted in stationary representational contexts.

There are also erroneous predictions about falling objects that may have a basis in perceptual processing. Problem 3 of Figure 15.18 depicts the problem of an aircraft traveling at a constant altitude and velocity that drops an object; the task is to indicate the trajectory that the object makes from the moment it is dropped to the moment of its impact with the ground. The correct, as well as common incorrect trajectories are given in the figure. The correct answer is that the object will continue to move forward while falling in a parabolic arc. However, McCloskey (1983a, 1983b) and his colleagues (McCloskey, Washburn, & Felch, 1983; Kaiser, Proffitt, & McCloskey, 1985) suggest that the common misconceptions are due to a visual illusion that is based upon extensive experience that objects which are dropped from a moving carrier often appear as falling straight down. When a person drops something while walking or running, the person in motion acts as a frame of reference against which the falling object is viewed. (This is closely linked to the earlier discussion of *induced* movement and refers to a phenomenon related to the effect in Figure 15.10.) That is, the perception of the object's falling motion is viewed against a moving frame of reference—the moving person. Accordingly, the perception of the object's motion *relative* to the moving background reference may be mistakenly perceived as motion relative to a stationary environment and thus be misinterpreted as the object's absolute motion. In short, an object dropped from a moving carrier falls straight down *relative to its carrier*, and so it may be perceived as falling in a straight vertical path. Generally speaking, misconceptions concerning the trajectories of carried objects develop from extensive experience with perceiving the motion against a moving reference frame (see also Kaiser, Proffitt, & McCloskey, 1985).

Finally, a section was devoted to the prediction of the paths of motion followed by physically moving objects. It was concluded that certain forms of motion paths are erroneously predicted because of misconceptions held concerning physical movement, whereas other forms of motion paths are erroneously predicted due to a bias in perceptual processing—a visual illusion based on induced movement.

SUMMARY

In this chapter we have described the perception of various forms of real and apparent movement. For the perception of real movement two main interdependent movement systems were identified: the image –retina and the eye–head movement system. In addition, the contribution made by outflow or corollary discharge signals initiated during voluntary eye movements to the eye–head system was noted.

Several categories of optical stimulation for movement perception were described: kinetic optical occlusion, optic flow patterns, and the background visual field. Also described was the unique perception of biological activity and the kinds of information obtained from biological motion.

Distortions in the perception of physical movement were discussed: kinetic depth effect, anorthoscopic perception, induced movement, and the Pulfrich pendulum effect.

Apparent movement—the perception of movement without any corresponding physical movement —was examined. Focus was especially placed on stroboscopic movement and its variations such as path-guided apparent motion. The relation of stroboscopic motion to motion pictures was noted, and an explanation of the latter was attempted in terms of visual persistence and the recognition of the consistency and correspondence of elements from frame to frame. Another form of apparent movement, the autokinetic effect, involving perception in a totally ambiguous spatial context, was introduced. A brief section was included on the aftereffects of perceiving certain kinds of motion.

KEY TERMS

Afferent signal

Anorthoscopic perception

Apparent movement

Autokinetic movement

Biological motion

Comparator

Corollary discharge signal

Efferent signal

Eye—head movement system

Image—retina movement system

Induced movement

Kinetic depth effect

Kinetic optical occlusion

Motion paths

Motion pictures

Movement aftereffect

Optic flow pattern

Outflow signal

Path-guided apparent motion

Pulfrich pendulum effect

Stroboscopic (phi, beta) movement

Waterfall illusion

STUDY QUESTIONS

1. Discuss the significance of movement perception for an animal's survival. Examine the

kinds of environmental information received by viewing objects and events in motion.

2. Compare the image–retina system with the eye–head movement system. Indicate the conditions in which each plays a dominant role.

3. Explain why the visual environment appears stationary when the eyes are voluntarily moved. Explain why passive movements of the eyeball cause apparent movement of the visual environment. Consider the role of corollary discharge and outflow signals in your answer.

4. Identify the main patterns of changes in the retinal projection as an object or an observer moves through the visual environment. Examine kinetic optical occlusion, optic flow patterns, and the effect of the relative size of moving objects to their backgound.

5. What is biological motion? What kinds of information does it convey? What stimulus factors are critical and most informative?

6. Identify the kinetic depth effect. Consider how the perception of an object's motion may contribute to the perception of the object's shape.

7. What is anorthoscopic perception?

8. Explain induced movement and describe how it can be demonstrated. What are some of the relational factors between an object and its background that may promote induced movement?

9. Explain the Pulfrich pendulum effect, taking into account delay of the retinal signals. Indicate how the effect simulates a pattern of visual signals that correspond to environmental depth.

10. What are apparent movement and stroboscopic movement? How does apparent movement differ from induced movement? What factors are crucial in producing apparent movement.

11. Explain the experience of motion pictures as an elaboration of stroboscopic motion. What factors explain the apparent integration and fusion of the discrete frames of motion pictures film?

12. Explain why the movement of the spoked wheels of vehicles that are apparently moving forward sometimes appear to move backward when they are seen in movies and television.

13. Distinguish autokinetic movement from induced movement. Explain autokinetic movement with respect to prolonged eye fixations and eye muscle fatigue.

14. How can movement aftereffects be demonstrated? What are some common examples?

15. What are some misconceptions about the predicted paths of objects set in motion that are based on the shape of the structures that emit them? To what extent do they fail to take into account the law of inertia? What kinds of errors are made concerning the predicted trajectories made by falling objects from moving vehicles? How may the effects of induced movement contribute to these errors?

16

THE PERCEPTION OF SPACE I: SPATIAL CUES AND CONSTANCY

The primary role of vision is to register the spatial arrangement of objects and surfaces in the environment. Indeed, objects are generally seen as solid forms lying at some distance in the terrain. The perception of space in depth and distance presents a most challenging problem: how is it possible that visual space is normally experienced as three dimensional, yet the retina and the corresponding retinal images are essentially flat two-dimensional surfaces? Part of the answer lies in the nature of the stimulation that arrives at the retina. For example, one sees differences in the brightness of different surfaces; objects take up different amounts of visual angle and are seen with varying degrees of clarity; some objects appear to partially cover other objects. Clearly, the pattern of stimulation contained in the optic array conveys information or "cues" that enable the perception of a three-dimensional space.

In this chapter we describe and discuss the relevant stimulus features or cues and mechanisms which are employed for perceiving depth and distance.

MONOCULAR CUES FOR SPATIAL PERCEPTION

A number of spatial cues require only a single eye for their reception and are labeled **monocular cues.** Graphics artists employ some of the *static* monocular cues (i.e., where the viewer and the scene are stationary), called **pictorial cues**, to represent depth pictorially, that is, to produce the impression of three-dimensional space on a two-dimensional surface.

INTERPOSITION

Interposition refers to the appearance of one object partially concealing or overlapping another. If one object is partially covered by another, the fully exposed one is perceived as nearer. Examples of interposition are shown by the simple line drawings of Figure 16.1. When the images are of familiar

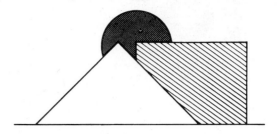

FIGURE 16.1a.   The circle appears to lie behind the rectangle, which appears to lie behind the triangle.

objects, the effectiveness of interposition for showing relative distance is increased. As a static pictorial cue it is quite effective, but it can provide only relative depth information—whether one object is nearer or farther than another from the viewer—not absolute depth or distance information. Figure 16.2 illustrates some curious effects of interposition. Shown are some ambiguous figures in which interposition provides conflicting information. Relative position is difficult to resolve since both parts of a given figure appear to possess mutually interposing segments.

AERIAL PERSPECTIVE OR CLEARNESS

When viewing the terrain outdoors, objects in the far distance are generally seen less clearly than objects located close by. This effect is called **aerial per-**

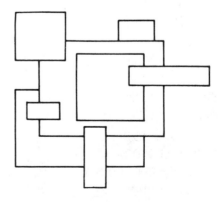

FIGURE 16.1b.   The appearance of overlapping planes suggests relative depth.

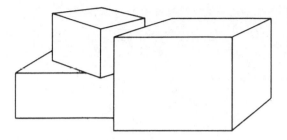

FIGURE 16.1c. Interposition contributes to the perception of the relative positions of line drawings of three-dimensional shapes.

spective (or **clearness**) and is due to the effect of very small particles in the atmosphere on light. Light rays traveling through suspended particles of dust, water vapor, and other atmospheric chemicals are scattered somewhat, decreasing the clarity of the details and the overall lightness of the images of objects reflected to the eye. Since light reflected from distant objects passes through more of the atmosphere than the light rays from nearby objects, the more distant objects appear hazy, dim, and even blurry. Thus, relatively large structures such as buildings appear closer when viewed on a clear day than on a hazy one. Aerial perspective may play a role in spatial perception, particularly when one is viewing over extensive distances. A depiction of aerial perspective is given later in Figure 16.14a.

It is of interest to note that because of the small size of the suspended atmospheric particles relative to the short wavelengths of light, they scatter the short wavelengths (which appear "blue") more than

they do the long wavelengths: the perceptual effect of this is that the sky appears blue.

SHADING AND LIGHTING

Generally, the surface of an object nearest the light source is the brightest. As the surface recedes from the light, it appears less bright and more darkly shadowed. The pattern of **lighting** and **shading** also contributes to the perception of apparent depth on a discontinuous surface. Observe the bumps and irregular indentations of Figure 16.3; then turn the page around. A convexity–concavity change has taken place. We are accustomed to the source of light coming from above (e.g., sunlight, ceiling lighting). Thus, when the picture is inverted, the bumps and indentations reverse because we continue to presume an overhead light source. In fact Berbaum and his colleagues (Berbaum, Bever, & Chung, 1983, 1984; Berbaum, Tharp, & Mroczek, 1983) have shown that areas of highlights and shading in a two-dimensional picture provide a potent source of depth information. Moreover, the impression of depth increases as the contrast between highlights and shadows increases. It is of interest that children as young as 3 years of age can discriminate concavities from convexities on the basis of shading (Benson & Yonas, 1973; Yonas, Kuskowski, & Sternfels, 1979). Interestingly, chickens, like humans, react to stimuli as if the stimuli were lighted by an overhead source of illumination (Hershberger, 1970).

The appropriate use of gradients of surface shading may also provide cues as to the shape of objects (Berbaum, Bever, & Chung, 1984). Generally illumination from a single light source will fall on a three-dimensional object in a consistent pattern. Since those surfaces closest to the light source receive the most illumination, the shape of the object has an effect on the pattern of light and dark areas produced: surfaces that face the light source appear lighter, while opposing surfaces are darker or shaded (see Figure 16.4). In addition, the distribution of lightness and darkness across an object aids in the perception of its surface characteristics. Thus the perception of a curved surface may result from a

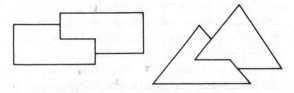

FIGURE 16.2. Interposition provides conflicting cues as to relative position.

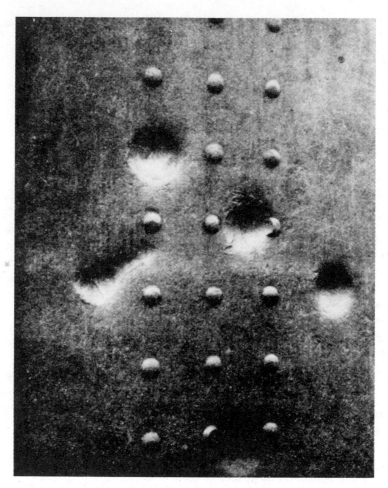

FIGURE 16.3.   Light and shade used as depth cues. When the figure is inverted, bumps and pits reverse.

gradual transition from light to dark, whereas an abrupt, sudden change from light to dark may be perceived as a change in planes such as a sharp corner.

The successful use of shading in a painting as a means of suggesting depth is given in Plate 10, which is a reproduction of one of Vermeer's works. Vermeer's art is known for its creative use of shading and lighting to produce compelling depth and luminance qualities on a flat surface.

ELEVATION

The horizon is higher in the vertical dimension of the visual field than is the foreground. Accordingly, objects appearing higher in the visual field are generally perceived as being located at a greater distance from the viewer than are objects that appear lower in the visual field. **Elevation** (sometimes called **height in the visual field**) may play a role in the perception of both relative and absolute distance

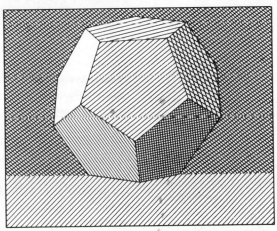

FIGURE 16.4.   A photograph of solid objects and an artist's rendering, indicating that the pattern of light and dark areas aids in the perception of familiar and unfamiliar shapes.

(Wallach & O'Leary, 1982). Elevation also contributes as a spatial cue when viewing two-dimensional pictures that attempt to depict a depth relationship (Berbaum, Tharp, & Mroczek, 1983).

LINEAR PERSPECTIVE

The perception of depth on a flat surface can be aided by the use of the geometric system of **linear perspective.** This involves systematically decreasing the size of more distant elements and the space separating them (see Figure 16.5). The image of a three-dimensional object undergoes such a transformation as it is projected onto the retina. A typical example is railroad tracks, as shown in Figure 16.6. The parallel tracks appear to converge at a point in the distance called the "vanishing point." Another illustration of perspective utilizing converging lines

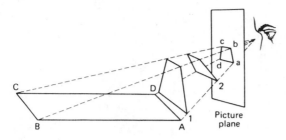

FIGURE 16.5.   The image of the rectangle is shown in perspective on the picture plane. The two dimensional projection of the rectangle ABCD is shown as trapezoid abcd on the picture plane. Clearly, the distances separating the more distant elements of the rectangle (segment BC) are decreased in their projection on the picture plane (bc). Notice also that since the stimulus pattern for the eye is in two dimensions, an infinite number of arrangements in three dimensions (shapes 1, 2, etc.) will produce the same pattern at the eye. (Modified from Hochberg, 1964, p. 37.)

is given in Figure 16.7. Observe that the edges that appear farther away are smaller than are those that appear closer. Artistic examples of the bizzare use of linear perspective are given in Figure 16.8.

The exact lineage of linear perspective as a precise graphic technique is somewhat controversial. However, it is generally agreed that the technique of linear perspective was discovered early in the fifteenth century by the Italian architect and sculptor Brunelleschi (Janson, 1962; Lynes, 1980) and soon after formalized by Alberti (Fineman, 1981; Kubovy, 1986).

TEXTURE GRADIENTS

A form of microstructure, generally seen as a grain or texture, is characteristic of most surfaces. This is obvious in many naturally occurring surfaces such as fields of grass, foliage, and trees, as well as in man-made surfaces such as roads, floors, and fabrics. As described by J. J. Gibson (1950), the texture of these surfaces possesses a density change or gradient that structures the light in the optic array in a way that is consistent with the arrangement of objects and surfaces in the environment. More specifically, when we look at any textured surface, the elements comprising the texture become denser as distance increases. As in linear perspective, the size of the elements and the distance separating elements decrease with distance.

Textural information is also available in flat surfaces, such as photographs (e.g., Gibson & Bridgeman, 1987). This is shown in Figure 16.9, which illustrates some examples of **texture gradients.** The gradient, or gradual refinement of the size, shape, and spacing of elements comprising the pattern of the texture, provides a source of information as to distance. In Figure 16.10a the longitudinal surface XY projects a retinal image, xy; the latter possesses a gradient of texture from coarse to dense, the coarser elements closer to x, the denser elements closer to y. The gradient of texture, transmitted in the optic array of xy, provides the observer with information that he or she is viewing a receding surface. Notice that with respect to the eye the change in texture reflected from the surface XY is at a constant rate. The frontal surface YZ, which is perpendicular to the line of sight, projects a different sort of image: there is no gradient since all the elements are equidistant from the eye. Thus, the pattern YZ (which projects a retinal image yz in Figure 16.10a) is perceived as a "wall," forming a 90° angle with the "floor" of pattern XY as shown in Figure 16.10b. Curvatures, edges, as well as information as to shape and inclination of a surface, are detected from discontinuities in the texture and from texture changes that are not a constant rate (see Figure 16.11).

Texture gradients, along with interposition and linear perspective, may be useful in the determination of perceived size. Neisser (1968) has noted that the increase in texture density on the retina, corresponding to an increase in the distance from the observer, provides a "scale" for object sizes. In the ideal case when all texture units are identical, figures of the same real size but different retinal sizes owing to their different distances from the observer will occlude the same number of texture units (see Figure 16.12). In other words, the relation between the

FIGURE 16.6.   Perhaps the most common and most striking instance of linear perspective is the apparent convergence in the distance of parallel railroad tracks. Of course, the actual space between the tracks is constant, but the corresponding retinal images and, accordingly, the size of the apparent separation of the tracks decreases with the distance of the tracks.

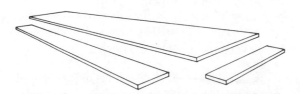

FIGURE 16.7.   Planks drawn in perspective. Parts of apparently rectangular planks that are diminished in size appear farther away.

retinal texture size and the object's retinal image is constant, in spite of changes in distance.

RELATIVE SIZE

The cue to distance called **relative size** applies when two similar or identical shapes of different sizes are viewed simultaneously or in close succession; in such cases the larger stimulus generally will appear closer to the viewer than the smaller one (e.g.,

FIGURE 16.8*a*. An artist's bizarre use of perspective. The sixteenth-century portrait shown in (*1*) was drawn in distorted perspective. When viewed obliquely through a notch in the frame, the distortion is corrected, as seen in (*2*). This also can be accomplished by holding the edge of the page to your eye and looking at the picture in (*1*). (Edward VI, by William Scrots. Reprinted by permission of The National Portrait Gallery, London.)

Hochberg, 1964). Thus, relative size is a cue to distance; it is illustrated in Figure 16.13. This cue to distance does not necessarily require any previous experience with the objects; rather, in certain situations images of the same shapes but of different sizes are sufficient stimuli for a depth relationship.

PICTORIAL PERCEPTION

The cues of linear perspective, texture gradients, and relative size express a common principle: the size of an object's image on the retina is proportional to the distance between the observer and the object. That is, these static monocular cues directly take into account the geometric fact that the size of the retinal image decreases with increasing distance. Of interest to us here is that this principle can enable the representation of depth and distance on a flat two dimensional surface. In fact the use of all the static monocular cues that we have described (e.g., interposition, shading and lighting, linear perspective, and so on) within a photograph or picture enables **pictorial perception**—the impression of depth from a two-dimensional surface (see Figure 16.14). The picture shown in Figure 16.15 contains an interesting mixture of spatial cues. Although some cues to distance are used appropriately, other conflicting cues create some "impossible" spatial relationships.

In viewing the real world less detail is perceived as elements recede in the distance. Accordingly, pictorial perception also may be promoted by varying the *detail* of elements that appear to lie upon a flat surface. Leonardo da Vinci termed the gradient of

FIGURE 16.8b.   A sense of apparent depth is created in a collage of building facades in linear perspective. (Collage courtesy of Jacob and Jenny Speil.)

detail in a picture the "perspective of disappearance" and observed that objects in a picture "ought to be less finished as they are remote" (cited in Bloomer, 1976, p. 83). Thus since greater detail is characteristic of nearness, an artist can manipulate apparent distance on the flat picture plane by varying the degree of detail. Note that Vermeer's painting in Plate 10 also exploits this principle in enhancing the depth effect.

Pictorial perception can be increased by reducing the information that indicates that the image is really of a flat surface. For example, looking at a

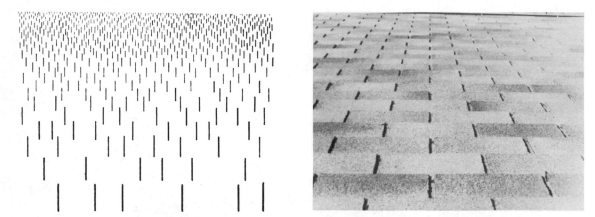

FIGURE 16.9. Examples of gradients of textures. The gradients of texture produce an impression of depth or distance on a flat surface.

two-dimensional picture through a rolled-up paper tube not only eliminates the frame effect of the picture, but also reduces the cue that the picture is a flat surface. This considerably enhances the depth effect (Schlosberg, 1941). Thus, viewing Plate 11 through a paper tube makes the depth effects of the Rembrandt more striking. In contrast, a similar viewing of the self-portrait by Warhol (Plate 12), in which pictorial perspective is relatively lacking, does not enhance any depth effect. In general, of course, *any* manipulation that reduces the perception of the static, flat quality of the picture plane will enhance the detection of its depth information.

Finally, we note that pictorial perception ap-

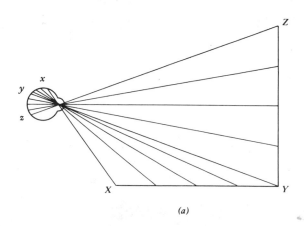

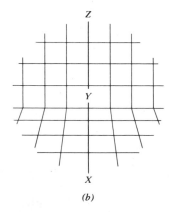

(a)   *(b)*

FIGURE 16.10. Two views of the optical projection of a longitudinal and a frontal surface. (*a*) A retinal projection from coarse to dense, *xy*, is produced by the longitudinal surface *XY*. A frontal surface, *YZ*, projects a uniform texture to the retina at *yz*. (*b*) Another view of the optical projections of the surfaces *XY* and *YZ*. The longitudinal projection from the surface *XY* is perceived as a "floor;" the frontal projection from the uniform texture of surface *YZ* is seen as a "wall." (Based on Gibson, 1950.)

pears early in the human. In fact pictorial perception from a television image has been demonstrated with humans as young as 14 months of age (Meltzoff, 1988; note that, on average, babies 2 years of age and younger generally are exposed to about 2 hours of television viewing each day). In one experiment babies watched a black and white television screen on which they saw a man solve a toy puzzle. Babies with this experience were then able to solve the same puzzle, indicating that they can pick up and absorb information that is depicted in two-dimensional imagery. In short, babies, with limited experience, can relate two-dimensional pictorial representations to their own actions on real objects in three-dimensional space.

MOTION PARALLAX

When the observer or the objects in the visual scene move, a source of monocular information concerning depth and distance is produced. As the observer moves, objects located at different distances in the visual field appear to move at different velocities. The relative apparent motion of objects as the observer moves the head is called **motion parallax**. Generally, when the head moves, elements of the visual field that lie close to the viewer appear to move faster than do distantly located elements; additionally, the apparent direction of movement differs for near and far objects. Both the relative velocities and the direction of the apparent movement depend on the location of the observer's fixation point.

The way in which motion parallax occurs in one set of conditions is illustrated in the schematic diagram of Figure 16.16. What is indicated by the diagram is how the terrain appears to move as an observer gazes out of a vehicle moving to the left. While maintaining fixation at point F, the nearer objects seem to move to the right, in a direction *opposite* to the observer's motion, whereas objects located beyond the fixation point appear to move to the left in the *same* direction as the movement of the

(a) Two receding surfaces meet to form a corner.

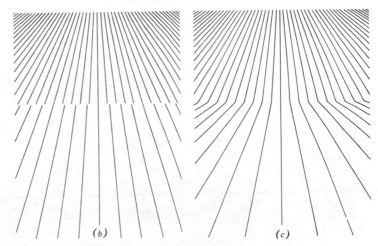

(b)   (c)

Discontinuities in textures: an edge is seen in *(b)*, a corner in *(c)*.

FIGURE 16.11.   Examples of apparent depth given by texture gradients with discontinuities and examples of texture changes that are not a constant rate. In (*d*) and (*e*), interposition also plays a role in the depth effect. In (*d*), the discontinuities in the surfaces increase the apparent depth of a "mesh" or "wire" room. In (*e*), a pattern of texture gradients on uniform surfaces provides information about the ceiling, floor, walls, and objects of an interior environment. (Source: *d*, courtesy of the Carpenter Center for the Visual Arts, Harvard University, Cambridge, Mass.)

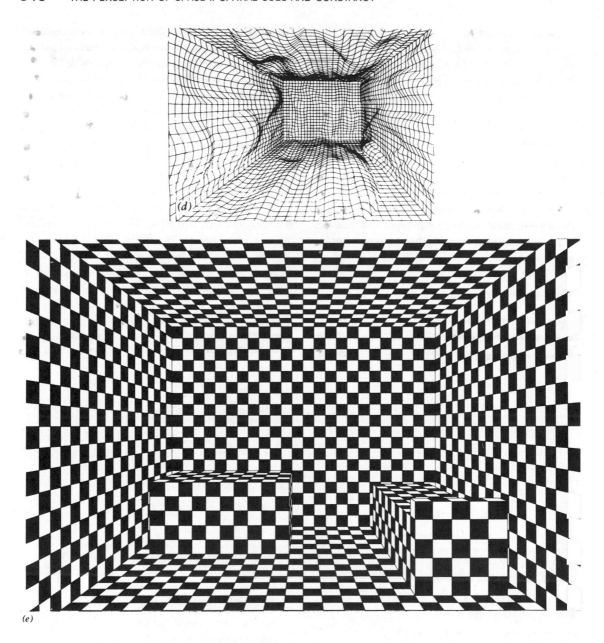

(d)

(e)

observer. In addition, objects located at different distances appear to move at different velocities. Specifically, the perceived velocity of an object diminishes the closer it lies to the fixation point, F.

The phenomenon of motion parallax can be simply demonstrated as follows: close one eye and hold up two objects, such as your fingers, in the direct line of sight, one about 25 cm (10 in.) in front of

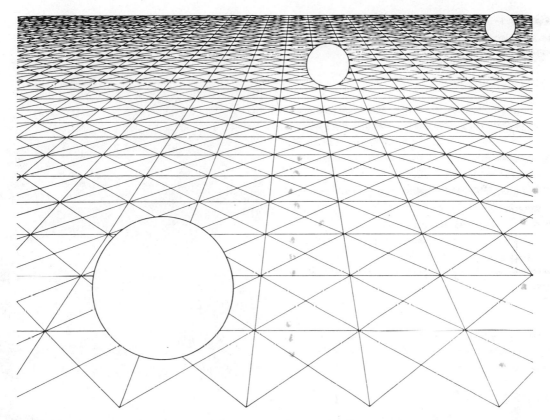

FIGURE 16.12.   The disks appear to lie at different frontal planes. Because each disk covers about the same amount of texture surface, they appear to be equal in size but located at different distances. As stated by Gibson (1979), this follows from "The rule of equal amounts of texture for equal amounts of terrain" (p. 162). (From U. Neisser, "Processes of vision," *Scientific American, 219,* 1968, pp. 204–205. Copyright © 1968 by Scientific American, Inc. All rights reserved.)

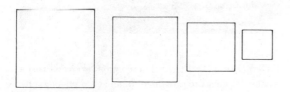

FIGURE 16.13.   Relative size. Images of the same shapes but of different sizes may furnish a depth cue. In this figure the larger squares give the appearance of lying closer to the viewer than do the smaller ones.

the other. If you move your head from side to side while maintaining fixation of the far finger, the image of the near finger will appear to move in the direction opposite to movements of the head. If fixation is on the near finger, the far finger will appear to move in the same direction as the movements of the head.

This form of differential visual information resulting from movement of the observer is an especially potent source of depth and distance information. Thus, by noting the direction and velocity of objects moving in the visual field, an observer may gauge their relative distances.

MOTION PERSPECTIVE

We should note here that the optic flow patterns created by movement toward or parallel to surfaces described in the preceding chapter (see Figure 15.4), may provide information about relative distance as well as relative velocity and the direction of movement. Thus, **motion perspective** provides cues to the relative distance of objects in the optic flow pattern. When movement is toward a surface, for example, it is possible to gauge the location of objects relative to oneself based on the continuous change in the perspective or position from which the objects are viewed (e.g., Clocksin, 1980; McCleod & Ross, 1983). Indeed it is a familiar experience that as you move through the terrain, objects that are close appear to flow by more rapidly than do distant objects, producing a pattern of streaming of the retinal image.

FAMILIAR SIZE

When viewing familiar objects there is not only visual information, but also nonvisual information as to the objects' spatial characteristics, such as size and shape, as a result of past experience. Although not, strictly speaking, a cue to depth or distance, **familiar size** may contribute to spatial perception. In other words, we "know" the sizes of many objects in our immediate surroundings and can give reasonably accurate size estimations of them from memory. However, to what extent we utilize this size information is not clear.

A number of studies suggest that the role of familiarity as a determinant of apparent size is a function of the conditions of viewing. In judging the sizes of familiar objects under ordinary conditions of viewing, it appears that judgments are based on the current visual stimulation (Fillenbaum, Schiffman, & Butcher, 1965). On the other hand, under viewing conditions such as when lighting and distance cues are impoverished, familiarity or knowledge of the objects' size plays a role in size judgments (Schiff-

(a)

(b)

FIGURE 16.14.   Pictorial perception. (a) Various static monocular cues are prominent in an aerial photograph. In particular, owing to aerial perspective, the perception of details of nearby buildings, depicted in the foreground, appear clearer and sharper than do the buildings and scenery of the receding background. (b) A photograph of an urban college scene contains many static monocular spatial cues. (Figure 16.14a is courtesy of Jan.)

FRONTISPIECE TO KERBY.

FIGURE 16.15. An artist's intentional misuse of some static depth cues is illustrated in this 1754 engraving by William Hogarth, entitled "False Perspective." The print was used originally as an illustration for the frontispiece or the title page of a book, and its accompanying description on the role of perspective is worth repeating: "Whosoever maketh a print without the knowledge of perspective will be liable to such absurdities as are shown on the frontispiece."

Clearly other cues besides perspective are misapplied in Hogarth's print, notably interposition and relative size. (Reproduced by permission of the Bettmann Archives.)

man, 1967). Furthermore, realistic representations of familiar objects can, under appropriate circumstances, affect the apparent location of them. For example, pictures of familiar coins, identical in projected size, but representing coins that differ in familiar size (photographs of a dime, quarter, and half dollar) were observed under cue-reduced, monocular conditions of viewing. Photographs of the

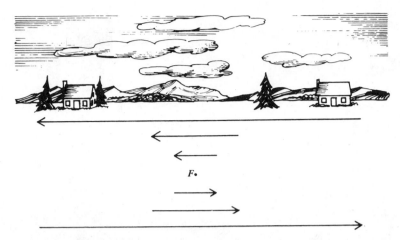

FIGURE 16.16. Schematic diagram of motion parallax. If an object located at *F* is fixated while the observer moves to the left, the images of the nearer objects appear to move to the right whereas farther objects seem to move to the left. The length of the arrows indicates that the apparent velocity of objects in the field of view increases in direct relation to their distance from the fixation point. (Based on Gibson, 1950.)

coins that represented larger sizes (e.g., a quarter), but that were of the same retinal size, were judged as more distant (Epstein, 1963, 1967; Fitzpatrick, Pasnak, & Tyler, 1982; Gogel & DaSilva, 1987).

ACCOMMODATION

We described earlier accommodation as a mechanism for focusing the lens to form a sharp retinal image. Because different accommodating responses are made for focusing on near and far objects, it is possible that oculomotor adjusting signals from the ciliary muscles (i.e., the degree of contraction) furnish information of a target's spatial location. Thus, **accommodation** may provide depth and distance information. However, accommodation is probably limited as an effective source of spatial information. For the human it would be of use only for distances up to about 2 meters; for targets located beyond this, accommodation is ineffective in furnishing accurate information about distance.

SCENE PERCEPTION

Thus far we have focused on the individual monocular visual cues that contribute to space perception, and we have indicated in a number of instances how they may be applied to perceiving objects. However, the typical spatial view that confronts an observer is a visual "scene" of the environment, composed of an array of objects against a background. Clearly **scene perception** differs from the perception of an individual object or a display of isolated objects: objects in a scene possess spatial and contextual relationships to one another and to the background which contribute to an overall cohesive and meaningful perception. Drawing, in part, from the monocular cues to space, Biederman (1981) has studied the role played by the normal relationships that exist among objects and between objects and their environment in the perception of an organized, well-formed rational scene. For example, certain objects characteristically occur in specific positions in a scene and not in others. To use one of Biederman's examples, fire hydrants characteristically appear on the sidewalk, not on mailboxes or counters. Biederman also stresses the role of the visual cue of familiar size. As described earlier, many objects have familiar, expected sizes; accordingly in real-world scenes the relative sizes of objects are meaningfully incorporated into the scene. Thus in a typical kitchen scene, the cup will not be bigger than the stove.

In one experiment in which several of these

relationships were studied Biederman, Mezzanotte, and Rabinowitz (1982) had observers decide whether a specified target object was located at a particular location in a scene. Immediately before each trial, the observer was given the name of the target, for example, a fire hydrant. A fixation point was presented, followed by a brief (150-msec) presentation of the scene, which was, in turn followed by a cue marking some position in the scene that had just been presented. The observer had to report whether the target had appeared in the location marked by the cue. However sometimes the target object was in its typical, normal position, and sometimes it violated one or more natural scene relations. Figure 16.17a shows a normal scene in which the target is the fire hydrant. In contrast, the location of the hydrant in Figures 16.17b and c is inappropriate and violates the natural relations among objects. Observers viewing scenes where the target object was incongruously located made many more errors in detecting the object than when the target object was located in a natural, appropriate location. Clearly, a scene that contains objects that share a coherent relationship to each other and to their background can facilitate the detection of a single object, even when the viewer is allowed only a single "glance" of less than a fifth of a second of the scene.

GIBSON'S DIRECT APPROACH TO THE PERCEPTION OF DEPTH AND DISTANCE

When we introduced some of the notions of J. J. Gibson in the introductory chapter, we stressed principally his organization of the perceptual systems and his adaptive "ecological" approach to perception. However, few psychologists have developed as influential an approach to the perception of space as has J. J. Gibson (1950, 1966, 1979). His theory is somewhat unorthodox in that he takes as his starting point the view that the information for perception is contained fully within the spatial and temporal pattern of the optic array. That is, the light that is reflected from surfaces and objects in the environment possesses a structure that specifies the spatial characteristics of the visual world. According to Gibson, sufficient information is carried by this

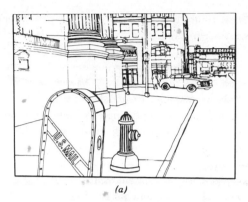

(a)

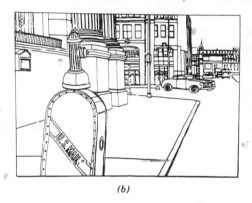

(b)

(c)

FIGURE 16.17.   Scenes used by Biederman, Mezzanotte, and Rabinowitz (1982). (a) The target (hydrant) is appropriately positioned in a normal location. In (b) and (c) the hydrant target is in an abnormal location and violates normal scene relations. (From I. Biederman, R. J. Mezzanotte, and J. C. Rabinowitz, *Cognitive Psychology,* *14*, 1982, p. 153. Reprinted by permission of the author and Academic Press.)

reflected light to account fully for the perception of the visual world.

His notion stresses that in spite of a moving observer, a changing environment and a changing retinal image, certain information remains constant —such information Gibson labels **invariants.** As an example, consider optic flow patterns and motion perspective: as an observer moves within the environment, contours sweep across the retina—with elements successively passing out of the bounded visual field as new elements enter—but the *pattern* of the optic flow does not change. The flow of the array remains invariant as the observer moves through the environment. Texture gradients also offer invariant information; that is, texture elements always appear finer or denser as distance increases, and they appear coarser with decreasing distance. A similar case exists with the information for motion parallax. The apparent velocity differences of different regions of the visual field resulting from movement of the observer directly reveal relative distance information.

Perhaps most controversial is that Gibson proposed a theory of **direct perception** that holds that invariant information about the spatial layout of the environment is picked up *directly*, rather than the result of the processing and analysis of depth and distance cues. According to Gibson, there is no need for judgment or mediation by cognitive processes. In short, the information contained within the optic array is "picked up" rather than "processed."

Most psychologists find much to agree and disagree with in Gibson's theory. Clearly the kinds of spatial variables stressed by Gibson, such as texture gradients and the optic flow pattern streaming past the moving observer, do provide potent sources of "invariant" information concerning depth and distance. However, his notion that space perception is in all cases directly registered in the optic array, unmediated by any inferential or cognitive processing, may be too restrictive for some psychologists (e.g., see Ullman, 1980; Hochberg, 1981; Bruce & Green, 1985). As we noted earlier in this chapter there are numerous informative cues to space that draw upon past experience and require some sort of processing. It seems reasonable to assume that, at

least in part, "We do not 'just see' the world but actively construct it from fragmentary perceptual data" (Bruce & Green, 1985, p. 203). It is clear, however, that Gibson's theory is significant, both as inspiration and in its identification and focus on the "invariant" variables.

BINOCULAR CUES

Monocular cues furnish a good deal of spatial information, and on the basis of monocular vision many visually guided skilled tasks can be performed. However, there are highly informative sources of information that require the joint activity of both eyes. We introduced some of the structural and functional aspects of binocular vision in an earlier chapter. We now turn to the kinds of spatial information provided by perception with two eyes: the **binocular cues.**

CONVERGENCE

Convergence refers to the tendency of the eyes to turn toward each other in a coordinated action to fixate on targets located nearby. Targets located at some far distance from the viewer, on the other hand, are fixated with the lines of sight of the eyes essentially parallel to each other. Because the degree of convergence is controlled by muscles attached to the eyeballs, it is possible that different states of muscular tension for viewing near and far objects may furnish a cue to depth or distance. However, like accommodation, convergent eye movements as a source of depth or distance information would be useful only for nearby objects.

BINOCULAR DISPARITY

We noted in Chapter 11 that in some animals, particularly primates, the two frontally directed eyes receive two slightly disparate or different images of the same three-dimensional scene (see Figures 16.18a and b). In the human this is due to the fact that the eyes are set about 2 to 3 in. (5 to 7.6 cm) apart. The slightly different relative views can be

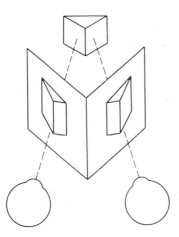

FIGURE 16.18*a*.   The different views of a wedge seen by the two eyes.

easily observed by sighting on nearby objects with each eye individually. Hence depending on location of the fixation point, the visual field seen by one eye is somewhat different from the visual field seen by the

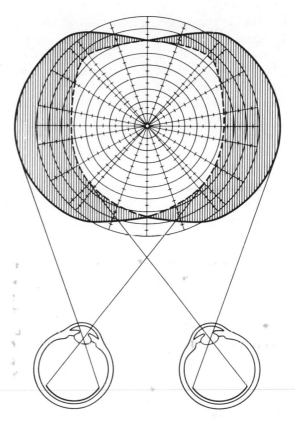

FIGURE 16.19.   The approximate visual fields of each eye and the binocular visual field. Note that the area seen by one eye does not fully coincide with the area seen by the other. The central area seen by both eyes is the binocular visual field.

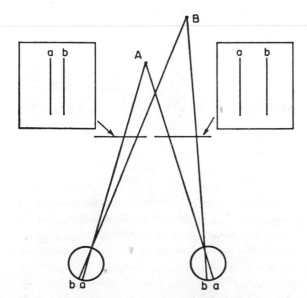

FIGURE 16.18*b*.   The perception of relative distance of two objects with binocular disparity information. The perception of the relative distance between two lines is due to the slight disparity (difference in separation) of the images projected on each eye, as indicated by the projections in the two boxes. (From Ogle, 1962, p. 275.)

other (see Figure 16.19). This difference in the two retinal images is called **binocular disparity** or sometimes *binocular parallax*.

The ability of the visual system to utilize binocular disparity information to detect the difference in depth between two objects is indeed impressive. According to Yellot (1981), a depth difference between two objects that corresponds to 1 micrometer (0.001 mm) in retinal disparity can be detected. That is, a difference of only 1 micrometer in the position of the images of objects reflected on the retinae is detectable. Thus, the visual system can reliably detect disparities that are substantially smaller than the diameter of the majority of photoreceptors.

Consider this practical illustration of the keen depth judgment made possible with binocular disparity. If you hold two vertically oriented objects such as pencils, one in each hand, at arm's length, it is possible for you to detect whether one of the pencils is as little as 1 millimeter (about 0.04 inches) closer to you than the other. The role of binocular disparity in this task is made evident when you close one eye: you will then observe that the available monocular cues are insufficient for the detection of the difference in depth.

CORRESPONDING RETINAL POINTS AND THE HOROPTER

When a small target is fixated, it forms images on the foveae of both eyes. The fixated target will appear single, since the eyes are converged to project the target image on corresponding foveal points of the two eyes. Such retinal locations are termed **corresponding retinal points.** That is, if the left retina and its image were superimposed on the right retina and its image, and the foveae were made to coincide, the images would also coincide. A small target imaged on corresponding retinal points is fused by the visual system and so appears as a single point. In fact, for a given degree of ocular convergence (which depends on fixation distance), there exists a set of spatial locations that project onto corresponding retinal points. A small target at any one of these locations is seen as a single target. The locus of all points in space that project onto corresponding retinal points and yield single images for a given degree of convergence produces an imaginary curved plane or zone called the **horopter** (see Figure 16.20).

For example, if a small target located at a 3 meter distance is fixated, it will appear as one object since the eyes converge to project its image on corresponding retinal points of the foveae. However, targets not lying on the horopter of the fixated target, located either nearer or farther than about 3 meters, will produce double images because they stimulate **noncorresponding retinal points.** That is, targets located nearer or farther than the fixated target form images in *different* positions on each retina, giving

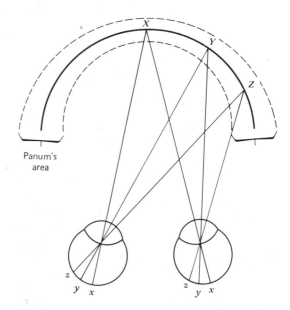

FIGURE 16.20.   A version of a horopter. The actual shape of the horopter varies with fixation distance and ocular convergence. Images of the points, X, Y, and Z will fall on corresponding retinal points in the two retinae and will be seen as single points. Points not lying on the horopter will appear as double images (with the exception of those points that lie in a narrow horizontal zone about the horopter known as Panum's fusion area).

rise to disparity. Thus, there exists a spatial plane of fused, single images flanked by areas of double images (note the exception of **Panum's fusion area,** the narrow region around the curved spatial plane, indicated in Figure 16.20).

The demonstration of Figure 16.21 summarizes the points just made. When fixation is on the near object, the image falls on the foveae of both eyes. However, images of the far, nonfixated object fall on noncorresponding retinal points, and two disparate images of the far object are observed. Although not depicted in this figure, when fixation is on the far object, the image of the near, nonfixated object will appear double. In general, the double images of nonfixated objects are usually suppressed and go unnoticed except under special conditions (such as those depicted in Figure 16.22).

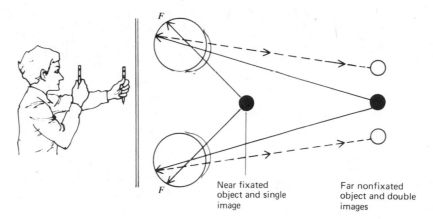

Near fixated
object and single
image

Far nonfixated
object and double
images

FIGURE 16.21.   Double images and binocular disparity. Holding a relatively near and far object as indicated and fixating on the near object will produce a single image of the near object and double images of the far nonfixated object. The image of the near object falls on corresponding retinal points of the fovea (F) of both eyes whereas the images of the nonfixated, far object fall on noncorresponding retinal points of each retina. The solid lines represent the light reflected from the two objects; the dashed lines indicate the apparent paths of the projected images from the far, nonfixated object.

STEREOPSIS

As a consequence of the disparity of the images projected on each eye, the unique appearance of depth with solidity, called **stereopsis** (from the Greek, *stereos*, for "solid," and *opsis*, for "vision"), results. An example of stereopsis is the entertaining depth effect experienced when viewing through a common stereo-viewer. The original stereo-viewer, called a **stereoscope** (see Figures 16.23a and b) was devised in 1838 by the English physicist Charles Wheatstone who reasoned that it should be possible to produce a synthetic impression of depth by casting on each eye similar but slightly disparate pictures called **stereograms** (Figure 16.23b), representing those views of a single object when observed by the separate eyes. When the pictures of the single object are properly paired and shown in a stereoscope, stereopsis results; that is, the object appears in depth or as three dimensional. In general, the stereoscope permits two different but lawfully related images to be projected independently on the two retinae resulting in stereopsis: a vivid and compelling experience of a single three-dimensional scene. Within limits the greater the disparity of the two pictures shown in the stereoscope, the greater the impression of solidity or depth.

The common stereo-viewer essentially performs the same function as the stereoscope, in that the viewer is presented with two different pictures of the same scene taken with a stereo camera—a camera that has a double lens, each lens separated by about the same distance as the separation of the two eyes. Thus, two pictures are taken simultaneously. When these are processed, mounted, and each presented by means of a stereo-viewer to the appropriate eye, the images fuse and the striking effect of stereopsis —depth and solidity of objects—occurs.

In some cases of binocular viewing, rivalry between images may occur. This is produced when each eye is presented with quite different stimuli. When binocular rivalry occurs, at one moment the stimuli from one eye may be dominant with a corresponding suppression of the stimuli from the other eye (e.g., see Engel, 1958). Dominance may fluctuate from eye to eye.

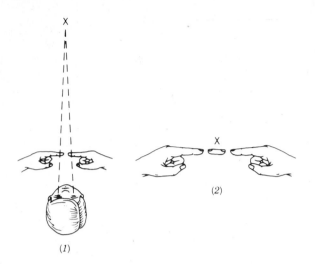

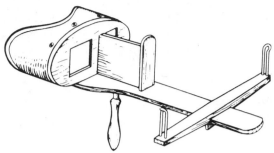

FIGURE 16.23a. A typical hand-held stereoscope devised to present disparate images to each eye. This type of stereoscope was designed by Oliver Wendell Holmes in 1861.

FIGURE 16.22. Binocular disparity may be used to create amusing effects. Bring the index fingers about 12 inches in front of the face at eye level so that the fingers are pointing at each other but are separated by about 1 inch. (*1*) Focus straight ahead, past the fingers on a wall or distant surface, shown in the figure by the fixation X. A phantom floating finger-joint or sausagelike shape will appear between the fingers (*2*). With a little practice you will be able to focus on the "sausage," and by moving the fingers up and down slightly, you may experience some unusual effects. In addition as you slowly move toward the surface upon which you focus, the size of the sausage will shrink.

The "sausage" is actually the result of the fused images of the tips of each finger as seen by the left and right eye. This can be easily verified by alternately blinking: monocular imagery prevails, and the sausage disappears. However, when both eyes are opened, the two monocular images are fused, and the sausage soon reappears. (Demonstration described by Sharp, 1928.)

CYCLOPEAN PERCEPTION

A particularly interesting form of stereo-viewing has been devised by Bela Julesz (1964, 1965, 1971, 1978). He has termed it **cyclopean perception** because the image on each eye is combined in a central visual area of the brain to produce the impression of depth. Julesz used a computer to print out two nearly identical displays of random dot patterns. An example of a pair of patterns is given in Figure 16.24a. The two patterns possess identical random dot textures except for certain areas that are also identical but shifted or displaced relative to each other in the horizontal direction. Although it is impossible to see any depth or shape by looking at either half of the pair of patterns, when the two patterns are stereoscopically fused, a central square corresponding to the horizontally shifted areas is vividly seen in its own depth plane, floating above the surround (see Figure 16.24b). As indicated in Figure 16.25, the regions that are shifted differ for the left and right squares of the stereogram. In the left square the shift is to the right, and in the right square the shift is to the left. As a result, there is binocular disparity between elements of texture for this central region, and it is perceived as being closer to the viewer than the remainder of the pattern. If the disparity relationship between the left and right squares were reversed, the shifted region would appear as lying farther away from the observer than the random surround. According to Julesz (1964, 1971), stereopsis is produced by a process of searching for and evaluating disparities. Indeed, it appears that disparity alone is a sufficient stimulus for achieving stereopsis since there is nothing in the pattern of the random-dot stereogram, such as the presence of pictorial depth cues, to suggest that one region is displaced relative to another.

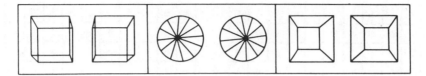

FIGURE 16.23*b*. Stereograms. When appropriately viewed through a stereoscope, each pair of figures is perceived as unitary and in three dimensions.

Another means of experiencing cyclopean perception is to view an **anaglyph** of this stereogram. An anaglyph of Figure 16.24*a* is produced by printing the two patterns on top of each other in different inks (usually red and green) to produce a composite picture. When the anaglyph is normally viewed, it yields the impression of a random texture without any clear global shape or contours or obvious cues to depth. However, when viewed through specially tinted filters that allow each eye to sort out a single

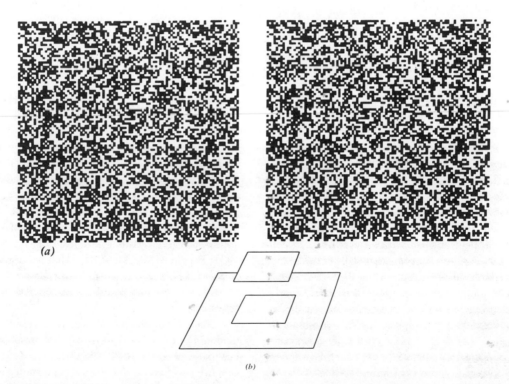

(a)

(b)

FIGURE 16.24. Random-dot stereogram. When the images are monocularly inspected in (*a*), they appear uniformly random with no depth characteristics, but when stereoscopically fused a center square is seen floating above the background in vivid depth (as depicted in *b*). Similarly, when an anaglyph of this stereogram is viewed with appropriately tinted glasses, a center square is seen above the surround. (From B. Julesz, *Foundations of Cyclopean Perception*, 1971, p. 21. Reprinted by permission of the author and publisher.)

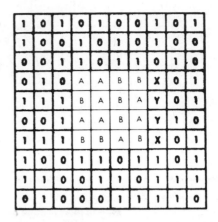

FIGURE 16.25. A schematic diagram indicating the process by which the random-dot stereogram of Figure 16.24a was generated. The left and right images are identical random dot textures except for certain areas that are shifted relative to each other in the horizontal direction as though they were solid sheets. The shifted areas, indicated by A and B cells, cover certain areas of the background, indicated by 1 and 0 cells; owing to the shift, areas become uncovered (X and Y cells) which are filled in by additional random elements. (From B. Julesz, *Foundation of Cyclopean Perception*, 1971, p. 21. Reprinted by permission of the author and publisher.)

pattern, the stereo depth effect is perceived. (Many of the "3-D" movies use a two-color composite printing process.)

Random-dot stereograms present a unique problem of ambiguity. When viewing simple stereograms such as those illustrated in Figure 16.23b, there is no ambiguity as to which of the line segments in the left and right retinal projections correspond to each other. Such a condition of unambiguous depth localization has been termed **local stereopsis.** In contrast, the random-dot stereograms are ambiguous with regard to which elements in the left and right retinal projections correspond to each other. Clearly, any dot projected on one eye could conceivably be matched to any other neighboring dot imaged on the other eye. Instead, however, the visual system matches up the patterns of disparity in the two eyes. Here a global process is required to search for the relatively numerous disparities necessary to perceive a three-dimensional surface. Since there must be an overall or global matching of disparate elements common to both halves of the random-dot stereograms rather than a point-for-point or local matching, the process yielding stereoscopic perception from random-dot stereograms is termed **global stereopsis.**

A physiological correlate of stereopsis with random-dot stereograms is indicated by the evidence that there are binocular depth processing and disparity-selective cells in various mammalian species, including the human, that are activated when neighboring clusters of stimuli of similar disparities reach each retina (e.g., Hubel & Wiesel, 1970; Ferster, 1981; Poggio & Poggio, 1984). That is, random-dot stereograms selectively stimulate various pools of binocular disparity cells, which are tuned to different disparities.

Some of the findings of cyclopean research with random dot pattern displays are that stereopsis occurs in the absence of monocular depth cues, convergent eye movements, and even recognizable or familiar shapes. Indeed, the perception of objects and patterns in the two retinal projections occurs without actual monocular recognition of contours, patterns, and objects. Hence, the perception of contour and shape is not a prerequisite for achieving stereopsis.

As Gulick and Lawson (1976) have stated ". . . instead of contours giving rise to depth, it is rather depth that gives rise to contours" (p. 272).

Stereopsis, using random-dot stereograms, is not limited to the adult human. It emerges in the human at between 3½ to 6 months of age (Fox et al., 1980; Petrig et al., 1981). Moreover this form of stereopsis occurs for other species. Falcons (Fox, Lehmkuhl, & Bush, 1977), cats (Fox & Blake, 1970), and monkeys (Bough, 1970) appear capable of perceiving depth with random-dot stereograms.

It should be noted that cyclopean stimulation occurs within a unique set of laboratory conditions in which the monocular and binocular information are separated. Most spatial events are viewed without such restriction. Typically space perception is accomplished within an environment containing a number of cues, and effective space perception depends on their integration.

However, the attainment of stereopsis does confer some special advantage to the spatial perception of the environment. It not only enables the extraction of information about the relative depth of objects and surfaces, but it also contributes to the *unitary* perception of those features in the visual environment that lie at a similar depth; that is, grouping together those features that lie at a similar depth from the viewer promotes object recognition. In line with this, Frisby (1980) speculates

perhaps the initial evolutionary advantage of having two eyes was as a solution to the problem of decoding camouflage. Perhaps two-eyed vision really came into its own when it provided a means of grouping together stripe features belonging to the tiger (or other predator, or desirable but hidden prey), and separating them from stripe features produced by the branches, twigs and leaves of the tree in which he was hiding, ready to pounce. This speculation is certainly in keeping with the discovery of random-dot stereograms, because they show just how superb a camouflage-breaking system stereopsis is: only after their binocular fusion can any object whatsoever be seen. . . . perhaps with the special kind

of depth perception which is stereopsis in its armoury, the visual system is very much better able to break up a scene into its constituent regions, and thereby to get on with the job of seeing what is present. (p. 155)

THE VISUAL CLIFF

An important experimental analysis of the cues used for the depth perception of a number of animal species has been made by Walk and Gibson (1961). The apparatus used in these experiments is called the **visual cliff**; it is shown in Figure 16.26. A centrally located start platform divides the floor of the apparatus into two sides, each side furnishing different kinds of stimulation. The "shallow" side lies directly over a patterned surface; on the "deep" side the same patterned surface is placed some distance below. Actually, a sheet of glass extends over both the deep and shallow sides for safety and to equate sources of thermal, olfactory, and echolocating stimulation for both sides. Thus with lighting equalized for both sides, only intentional visual information is allowed. In the usual situation, an animal is placed on the start platform separating the shallow and deep surfaces (see Figure 16.26). From this position the animal can see the shallow or "safe" side and the deep or "dangerous" side, an edge with a drop-off beyond it that is similar to what it would see if looking over the side of a cliff. A basic assumption of the visual cliff technique is, of course, that a tendency exists for animals to avoid a fall. As an adaptive mechanism preserving the species, it is reasonable to expect that most animals should be capable of depth perception; furthermore, this ability should be effective by the time the organism can locomote independently. The existence of this capacity is demonstrated by a preference for the shallow side. Indeed, based on research with turtles, birds, many species of small and some large mammals, primates, and human infants, there is a strong tendency to avoid the deep side.

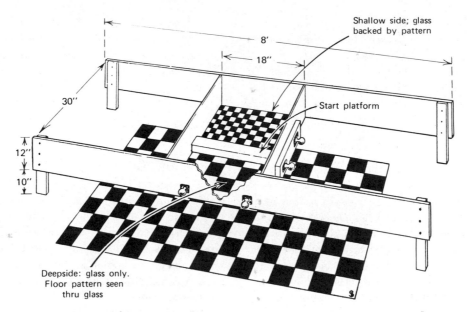

FIGURE 16.26.   A schematic diagram of a model of the visual cliff used for small animals. (From R. D. Walk, "The study of visual depth and distance perception in animals," in D. S. Lehrman, R. A. Hinde, and E. Shaw (Eds.), *Advances in the study of behavior*, Academic Press, 1965, p. 103. Reprinted by permission of the author and the publisher.)

A relevant question is: what are the cues used by the animals in making their depth discriminations? The evidence from a large number of studies indicates rather clearly that use of only one eye has little effect on the depth perception of a wide range of animal species on the visual cliff. That is, adequate depth perception is achieved with monocular viewing. Moreover, motion parallax appears to be the dominant cue for the depth perception of most animals.

CONSTANCY

The pattern of light reaching the visual system from an object undergoes continual changes as the spatial orientation of the object relative to the viewer changes. This can occur both by spatial displacements of the object and by movements of the observer. Accompanying the spatial changes are changes in the distribution of light striking the viewer's retinae; these are seen as variations in the object's projected size, shape, and intensity. However, in spite of these changes in stimulation, the stable and enduring qualities of the object are perceived.

The page before you does not look rectangular when viewed from one angle and trapezoidal when viewed from another angle of observation: normally the book is perceived as rectangular from every angle of observation. Neither does a person's size appear to contract or expand very much as the person moves away or advances. Yet the laws of spatial geometry dictate certain size changes in the retinal image corresponding to the relative displacement of the physical stimulus. Clearly, perception in this instance is based on more than the shape and size of the retinal image. This stability of perception in the presence of variation in physical stimulation is termed **perceptual constancy**.

The fact that perception is linked to the *invariant* properties of objects—for example, the actual size and shape—rather than the enormously changing light patterns reaching the visual system has clear adaptive significance: we perceive a world composed of reasonably stable objects with relatively permanent physical properties. Clearly, without the mechanism of constancy, the moment-to-moment variations in stimulation would appear as such—a series of chaotic sense experiences.

LIGHTNESS CONSTANCY

Although sometimes used interchangeably, a distinction must be made between lightness and brightness (Jacobsen & Gilchrist, 1988). Technically, *lightness* refers to the surface quality—the degree of gray of an object or surface, ranging from black to white—that is independent of illumination. The *brightness* of a surface refers to the perceptual effects of the intensity of the light reflected by a surface, that is, luminance. Thus, for example, a sheet of white paper will not change in its lightness dimension when viewed in intense or dim light (i.e., with luminance changes, it will continue to appear "white"), whereas its brightness will vary. In short, brightness changes with illumination whereas lightness generally does not.

Lightness constancy refers to the fact that the lightness (and usually the color) of an object tends to remain relatively constant or stable in spite of changes in the amount of illumination striking it. Thus, for example, we perceive a patch of snow in dark shadow as white and a chunk of coal in sunlight as black, yet the physical intensity of the light reflected from the surface of the coal may be greater than that from the snow! In some manner we are taking into account information about the general conditions of illumination. In searching for an explanation of this phenomenon, it is necessary to consider the surface property called **albedo** or **reflectance.** The albedo is the proportion of incident light that is reflected (i.e., the ratio of reflected/incident light) from an object or surface. Hence, it is independent of the degree of illumination. A sheet of white bond paper may have an albedo of, say, 0.80; this means it reflects approximately 80% of the light it receives. If, under ordinary conditions, a part of the paper is placed under dim illumination so that the sheet is not homogeneously illuminated, one still perceives the entire sheet as more or less uniformly light. The stability of the sheet's lightness occurs because the entire surface of the sheet reflects a constant portion of the light received, even though the amount of incident light may differ for different parts of the sheet's surface.

Relational Properties Of Lightness Constancy
To utilize albedo, there must be indications of the general conditions of lighting. Accordingly, constancy is poor in conditions where the sources of the incident lighting and the background illumination are obscured or lacking. If illumination is restricted to the object alone (e.g., by special means of projection so that no light falls on the background) then the perceived lightness of the object will depend entirely on its illumination, and constancy is absent.

We noted in an earlier discussion on lightness contrast that the lightness of an object is affected by the intensity of its surround. Specifically, in Figure 16.27 the lightness of the disk is a function of the ratio of its light intensity to the intensity of its surrounding ring (Wallach, 1948, 1963). However, as demonstrated in Figure 16.27, if both the intensities of the ring and disk are changed by the same proportion, lightness is unaffected. When an observer is required to adjust the intensity of the test disk (at *b*) to match the lightness of the standard disk (at *a*), rather than setting it at a level for a physically equal match, i.e., 180 millilamberts or mL, the adjustment is to 90 mL. That is, the intensity *ratio* of ring to disk of *a* (2:1) is maintained in *b* to produce an equal-lightness match. It is as if the overall level of illumination of *a* is halved in *b*. This sort of a fixed proportional change is what occurs in natural settings when the overall illumination changes (Figure 16.28). Normally objects do not appear in complete isolation in the visual field. Thus, since the light that is illuminating an object also falls on regions surrounding it, the ratios of the intensities of light of

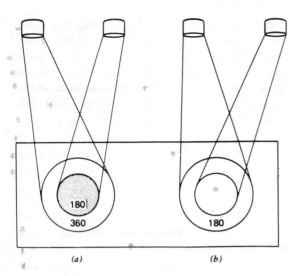

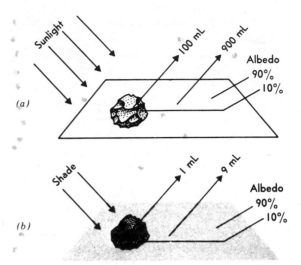

FIGURE 16.27. Sample arrangement for demonstrating lightness constancy as a function of the relative illumination of an area to its background. Each disk and its surrounding ring of light in (a) and (b) is projected on a screen in an otherwise darkened room by a pair of projectors. The intensities of the disks and rings are separately controlled. In (a), the ratio of ring intensity to disk intensity is set at 2:1 (360 mL:180 mL). In order for the disk at (b), with the intensity level of its ring set at 180 mL, to appear as light as the disk in (a), a setting of 90 mL is required. This shows that the perceived lightness of a disk is affected by the ratio of its intensity to the intensity of its background. Hence, decreasing the incident light of both the disk and ring by the same proportion does not affect its lightness. Thus, so long as the ratios of the intensities between the disks and their backgrounds remain constant, the two disks appear equally light in spite of the changes in overall illumination. (Based on Wallach, 1963.)

FIGURE 16.28. The objects of the scene in (b) are uniformly illuminated by one-hundredth of the amount of incident light in (a). However, since the objects reflect a constant proportion of the incident light (indicated by the albedos or reflectances), the intensity ratios of the chunk of coal to the sheet of paper in the scenes at (a) and in (b) are constant (1:9). Accordingly, the objects appear equally light in both scenes. (Modified from Hochberg, 1964, p. 50.)

adjacent objects are constant in spite of the changes in the absolute intensity of the overall illumination. As a consequence, the lightness of an object seen against a background does not appear to change.

We must conclude that one of the important variables for lightness constancy when viewing under ordinary conditions is the ratio of the intensity of light reflected from objects relative to the intensity of light reflected from the background (with the proviso that the light that is illuminating an object also falls on regions surrounding it). Accordingly, what is extracted is information about *relative* rather than absolute intensities. When the illumination on a scene is uniformly increased or decreased, the absolute intensities of the images of adjacent objects in the scene may change by different amounts (due to different albedos for different objects), but the ratios of the intensities of their images remain constant. In other words, the *proportion* of incident light that is reflected by the stimuli in the scene remains constant. The result is that the lightnesses of the objects does not change when there are changes in the overall level of illumination. Lightness constancy enables the perception of the lightness characteristic of an object or surface to remain constant even when the lighting changes (see Gilchrist, 1977; Jacobsen &

Gilchrist, 1988, for further discussion of the relational basis of lightness constancy).

SIZE CONSTANCY

The diagram in Figure 16.29 illustrates some relevant geometrical relations in image formation, such as that the size of the retinal image varies inversely with the distance from which an object is viewed. The size of an object's image on the retina may undergo considerable changes with variation in the object's distance from the viewer, but the size changes go relatively unnoticed in conditions of normal viewing. A man standing 7 meters away looks about as tall as when he stands at 14 meters away although the first image projected on the retina is twice the size of the second. An important fact about the perceived size of an object in normal viewing conditions is that it does not depend soley on the size of the image it casts on the retina. In short, perceived size does not regularly follow retinal size. Indeed, over a considerable range of distances, perceived size is somewhat independent of retinal size. The failure of perceived size to vary with retinal size is owing to the operation of **size constancy.**

Although a number of factors affect size constancy, the most important are apparent distance cues and background stimuli. As shown in Figure 16.30, when used properly, they help to effect size constancy in a picture.

Holway and Boring Experiment The classic **Holway and Boring experiment** (1941) on size constancy provides an examination of several of its influences. In the experiment the observer was stationed at the intersection of two long darkened corridors, as illustrated in Figure 16.31a. An adjustable, lighted comparison disk was placed 10 ft (about 3 meters) from the observer in one corridor; standard disks were placed one at a time at a number of distances varying from 10 to 120 ft (about 3 to 36 meters) in the other corridor. The sizes of the standard disks were graduated so as to cast the same size retinal image at every distance from the viewer's eye. The viewer's task was to adjust the comparison disk so it would look the same size as the standard disk. There were four experimental conditions: condition 1 provided binocular observation; condition 2 allowed monocular viewing; condition 3 allowed monocular viewing through a small hole, called an artificial pupil, which removed some of the sources of information normally used in distance perception, such as head movements; condition 4 provided an even further reduction of distance cues by surrounding the standard disks with black cloth creating a tunnel of black cloth, thereby severely limiting the distance cues originally provided by the floor, walls, and ceiling.

The amount of constancy exhibited in each condition is shown in Figure 16.31b. Notice that the top dashed line shows what the judgments would

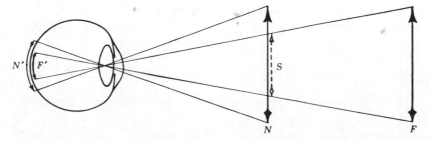

FIGURE 16.29.   A schematic diagram showing the relative size of two retinal images, N' and F', from the same-sized objects, N and F, but located at different distances. Object F is twice as far from the eye as object N; hence, its image on the retina is half as large. This is in accordance with the fact that the size of the retinal image is inversely proportional to the distance of the object from the eye. Notice that the smaller retinal image cast by object F could also be produced by the smaller object, S (smaller by one-half), located at the position of object N.

FIGURE 16.30. Size constancy in a picture. In (a), the near woman was 9 ft from the camera and the far woman 27 ft. The relative distances, and thus the relative retinal heights, are in the ratio 1:3. Size constancy is not complete; the distant woman appears somewhat smaller, but clearly not in the ratio 1:3, which is correct for the two women in the photograph. Compare this with (b). The far woman of (a) was cut out of the picture, brought forward next to the other woman, and pasted there with the apparent distance from the viewer equal for the two. The size ratio 1:3 is now apparent. The right-hand woman looks smaller in (b) than she did in (a), although physically unchanged in size on the page. This is an example of size constancy in a picture with perspective and elevation cues for distance. [Notice that the size constancy of (a) is diminished when the picture is inverted.] (From E. G. Boring, "Size constancy in a picture," *American Journal of Psychology*, 77, 1964, p. 497. Reprinted with permission of the publisher, University of Illinois Press.)

ideally be for perfect constancy: the adjusted size of the comparison disk would be exactly the same size as the standard disks that increased in size with distance. The bottom dashed line indicates the complete lack of constancy: the adjusted size of the comparison disk would be set to the size of the standard disk at 10 ft, regardless of the distance at which the standard disk was viewed—in short, a *retinal* match.

With binocular and monocular viewing (condi-

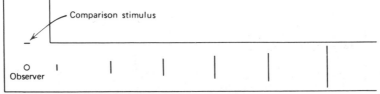

FIGURE 16.31a. Schematic diagram of experimental arrangement used by Holway and Boring for testing size constancy. The comparison stimulus was located 10 ft from the observer. The standard stimuli, located at various positions from 10 to 120 ft, always projected a visual angle of 1°. (After Holway and Boring, 1941.)

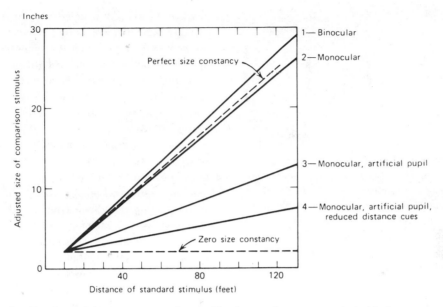

FIGURE 16.31b.   Results of size constancy experiment. The degree of constancy varied with the amount of visual information. (After Holway and Boring, 1941.)

tions 1 and 2) the achievement of size constancy was excellent, indicating that it makes little difference whether one eye or both eyes are used in the task. Both sets of adjustments conform closely to what would be predicted if size constancy were perfect. Artificial restrictions on observation, as in condition 3 in which viewing was through a tiny hole, caused a considerable drop in constancy. Condition 4 presented an even greater loss of distance cues, and the results indicate a greater decrement in constancy. Judgments in the latter two conditions, intentionally less influenced by distance cues, are principally determined by the size of the image projected on the retina. Hence, when the observer could see only the disks surrounded by darkness, their sizes were judged to be about the same at all distances. Constancy had nearly disappeared with a complete lack of distance cues. Clearly, then, distance cues and a visual framework are critical factors for the operation of size constancy.

Emmert's Law   The retinal size of an object and cues to its distance operate together as a system to determine the perceived size and/or the location of an object. Under certain conditions, the apparent size of an object when viewed as an *afterimage* (an image that persists after the termination of the original stimulus) is determined by the distance between the eye and the surface on which the image appears to be projected (see Figure 16.32). That the perceived size of the afterimage is directly proportional to the distance of the projection surface from the eye is known as **Emmert's law**. Thus an afterimage will appear larger as its projection surface increases in distance. This is because the area on the retina responsible for the afterimage is of a fixed or constant size. As the distance of the projection surface is increased, the size of an object necessary to reflect a constant retinal size must also be increased. In short, the size of the surface that the afterimage covers is a function of its distance.

The relationship between perceived size and distance for Emmert's law, outlined in Figure 16.32, can be easily demonstrated. Stare at a relatively small shape, such as the one shown in Figure 13.7 on page 255, for about 30 to 40 seconds so as to

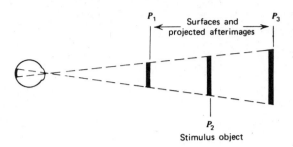

FIGURE 16.32.   Illustration of Emmert's law. A stimulus object (for example, a black square on a white background) is fixated and briefly inspected at P_2 to form an afterimage. Immediately afterward, the eyes fall upon a surface located nearer (P_1) or farther (P_3). The afterimage will appear to be projected on that surface, and its apparent size will be directly proportional to the distance of the surface from the eye.

produce an afterimage. Then hold a sheet of white paper about 12 inches in front of you, focus at a spot on its center and observe the afterimage. Next move the sheet of paper at about arm's length and focus in the same manner. The afterimage will now appear about twice as large. If you can still maintain the afterimage, focus at a more distant surface such as a blank far wall; the afterimage will appear even larger.

It is important to note that the apparent size of the afterimage is determined by the *apparent* as well as the actual distance of the projection surface. For example, if the afterimage is projected on a surface that is made to appear closer (or farther), then the size of the afterimage will appear smaller (or larger). The change in the apparent size of the afterimage in this case likely results from the same mechanisms that produce size constancy.

SHAPE CONSTANCY

We have seen that an object viewed under different conditions of illumination may appear equally light and an object viewed at different distances with different projected sizes may appear the same size. In addition, an object may appear to possess the same shape even when the angle from which it is viewed changes radically. The latter phenomenon is termed **shape constancy.** A typical window frame or a door appears to be more or less rectangular no matter at what angle it is viewed. Yet geometrically it casts a rectangular image *only* when it is viewed from a certain position directly in front of the viewer (see Figure 16.33).

Shape constancy is typically assessed when a subject judges the shape of objects such as a circular plate or disk tilted or slanted at an angle. It is found that the estimated shape (illustrated in Figure 16.34), obtained by having subjects draw the shape of a tilted disk or match it against a series of ellipses, is more circular than the elliptical shape projected on the observer's retinae (Thouless, 1931).

Shape constancy operates to maintain the perceptual integrity of the object's shape. As in the case of size constancy, it is a reasonable assumption that the degree of shape constancy varies with the availability of relevant spatial information as to orientation, such as the tilt or inclination of the object or the slant of the surface on which the object rests (Sedgwick, 1986). In general, shape constancy varies with indications of the distance and displacement of all spatial aspects of the object. It follows that when visual information as to the object's position relative to the viewer is lacking, shape constancy is impaired or breaks down completely.

Shape Constancy and Apparent Depth We should note that when viewing certain configurations, the processes underlying shape constancy may be automatic and may not be voluntarily suppressed (Shepard, 1981). As we noted in the depictions of Figure 16.33, when looking at certain two-dimensional drawings there is a tendency to interpret them as comprised of right angles representing shapes in three-dimensional space, that is, as two-dimensional drawings of three-dimensional objects. Thus doors, cubes, and even unfamiliar shapes appear rectilinear regardless of their actual retinal projections as trapezoids, parallelograms, and other unusual shapes. In fact, it is difficult to see these configurations as comprised of adjacent trapezoids and parallelo-

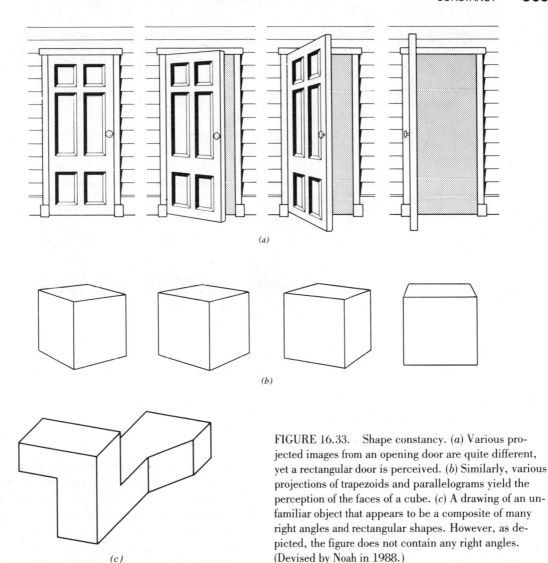

(a)

(b)

(c)

FIGURE 16.33.   Shape constancy. (a) Various projected images from an opening door are quite different, yet a rectangular door is perceived. (b) Similarly, various projections of trapezoids and parallelograms yield the perception of the faces of a cube. (c) A drawing of an unfamiliar object that appears to be a composite of many right angles and rectangular shapes. However, as depicted, the figure does not contain any right angles. (Devised by Noah in 1988.)

grams, all lying on the same flat plane. That we may have difficulty in seeing certain two-dimensional drawings as merely flat linear shapes, independent of any three-dimensional interpretation, is illustrated in the perception of the shapes depicted in Figure 16.35a and b. In Figure 16.35a two identical shaded parallelograms are presented, one with its long axis vertically oriented and the other with its long axis

horizontally oriented. For most observers there is only a small effect of apparent depth, and accordingly only a small difference in apparent size is noted between the two. However, as shown in Figure 16.35b, when these parallelograms appear as the top surfaces of two-dimensional drawings that strongly suggest the depiction of three-dimensional rectangular shapes in depth, a startling change in their

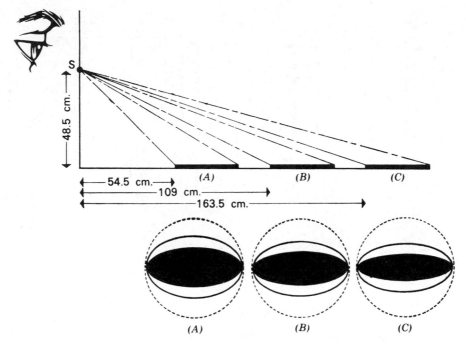

FIGURE 16.34. Shape constancy is shown in the reproduction of the tilted disks *A*, *B*, and *C* whose projected shapes are indicated by the black figures. The broken line shows the physical shape, and the continuous line gives the reproduced shape. The reproduced shape indicates that the perceived shape is more circular than the projected shape. (From Thouless, 1931, pp. 340, 343.)

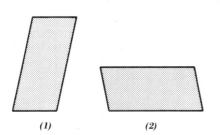

FIGURE 16.35*a*. The shaded parallelogram with its long axis vertically oriented (*1*) is identical to the shaded parallelogram with its long axis horizontally oriented (*2*). For most observers only a slight variation in size may be perceived and the physical identity of the figures is clear. However, a striking change in their appearance occurs when they are each seen as parts of more complex figures as shown in Figure 16.35*b*.

appearance occurs. This tendency toward three-dimensionality and depth biases the observer to perceive the parallelogram with the long vertical axis (*1*) as representing a foreshortened rectangle sloping back in depth. Certainly, in this context it looks much longer and more narrow than the rectangle portrayed by the physically identical parallelogram in (*2*).

In summary, we confront a dynamic environment whose retinal representation is comprised of continual changes in image luminance, size, and shape. However, our perceptual system takes account of these changes so that we perceive an environment that is essentially stable and unchanged, composed of *constant* properties—constant lightnesses, sizes, and shapes.

In closing we must emphasize that constancy effects result from the interplay of numerous factors.

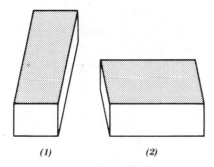

(1)   *(2)*

FIGURE 16.35*b*.   The parallelograms of Figure
16.35*a*, as surfaces of apparent rectangular shapes.
When imbedded in representations of three-dimensional shapes in depth, the two shaded identical parallelograms appear quite different from each other in
size and shape. (Based on Shepard, 1981.)

An obvious one, which likely plays some role in all
the constancies, is the familiarity of the objects in the
visual field. That is, past experience may serve to
influence the perception of the visual input in spite of
apparent distortions of objects and surrounding stimuli. However, as we have noted, constancy extends to
unfamiliar stimuli as well. Moreover, constancy appears very early in human perceptual development
(e.g., Day & McKenzie, 1981; Cook & Birch, 1984)
and it exists in animals far below the human (e.g.,
Ingle, 1985).

tion. In addition we discussed the contribution of
static monocular cues to perceiving depth on a flat
surface—called pictorial perception. The facilitative
role of monocular cues in the perception of a scene
was outlined, as well as the provocative "direct"
theory of J. J. Gibson.

The binocular cues of convergence and binocular disparity were described; related discussion also
included the topics of corresponding retinal points,
the horopter, random-dot stereograms, and local and
global stereopsis.

Research on depth perception using the visual
cliff apparatus was summarized briefly, and it was
concluded that information from the monocular cue
of motion parallax generally furnishes a sufficient
indication of depth in the visual cliff situation.

Finally, it was noted that objects in the environment are perceived as constant or invariant whereas
the conditions of stimulation, such as the physical
characteristics imaged on the retina (e.g., illumination, retinal size and shape) are quite variable. This
tendency to perceive the enduring characteristics of
objects is called perceptual constancy. The circumstances of occurrence of constancy were discussed
and three categories relating to the perceived stability of the lightness, size, and shape of objects were
identified. In all cases, constancy appears to depend
on the context of stimulus features and cues; that is,
constancy is relationally determined.

SUMMARY

In this chapter we have identified and described the
stimulus indicators and mechanisms that contribute
to the perception of three-dimensional space. The
relevant stimulus features were described under the
two main headings of binocular and monocular cues,
depending on whether or not the joint function of both
eyes is necessary. The monocular cues include such
stimulus features and visual processes as interposition, aerial perspective, shading, elevation, linear
and motion perspective, texture gradients, motion
parallax, familiar and relative size, and accommoda-

KEY TERMS

Accommodation

Aerial perspective (clearness)

Albedo (reflectance)

Anaglyph

Binocular cues

Binocular disparity

Constancy

Convergence

Corresponding retinal points

Cyclopean perception

Direct perception (Gibson)

Elevation (height in the visual field)

Emmert's law

Familiar size

Holway and Boring experiment

Horopter

Interposition

Invariants

Lightness constancy

Linear perspective

Local and global stereopsis

Monocular cues

Motion parallax

Motion perspective

Noncorresponding retinal points

Panum's area

Pictorial cues

Pictorial perception

Relative size

Scene perception

Shading and lighting

Shape constancy

Size constancy

Stereograms

Stereopsis

Stereoscope

Texture gradients

Visual cliff

STUDY QUESTIONS

1. Identify the monocular cues that contribute to the perception of a three-dimensional environment. Indicate the static monocular pictorial cues and distinguish them from physiological ones (e.g., accommodation) and dynamic monocular cues that require movement. In partic-

ular, describe the cues of linear perspective and motion parallax and indicate the ways in which they are utilized.

2. Explain why the scattering of the short wavelengths of light, involved in aerial perspective, causes the sky to appear "blue."

3. Making use of pictorial perception, examine how an artist may use pictorial cues to represent three dimensions on a two-dimensional surface. What cues are typically more prevalent and which are more useful in normal spatial perception?

4. Outline scene perception. According to the notion of scene perception, what contextual relations are important to the perception of an organized, rational scene?

5. Summarize J. J. Gibson's "direct" approach to the perception of space. In what ways is his notion unique? Why is it labeled a "direct theory"?

6. Examine the contribution made by "invariants" to Gibson's theory. What role does Gibson assign to past experience and cognitive processing in the perception of space?

7. What are the binocular cues and what information, in addition to that conveyed by monocular cues, do they furnish for spatial perception?

8. Describe the mechanism of binocular disparity, taking into account the horopter. In what ways does the information from binocular disparity provide information concerning the relative distance of objects to each other?

9. What is stereopsis? Analyze the process of stereopsis, indicating how it is produced and describe the stereoptic experience.

10. How does cyclopean perception differ from typical stereo viewing? How is it demonstrated? To what extent and in what forms is disparity information utilized in cyclopean perception?

11. What does the experience of cyclopean perception indicate about the necessity of monocular static cues, convergence, and the familiarity of objects for attaining stereopsis? To what extent

is the monocular perception of contours a prerequisite for stereopsis?

12. Examine the attainment of stereopsis with respect to the sorts of information it provides to the observer. Indicate in what ways and to what extent species with specific spatial needs profit by it.

13. To what extent is binocular vision a necessity for efficient spatial perception? What spatial tasks does it enable? Consider the possibility of performing precise spatial tasks exclusively on the basis of monocular information.

14. Describe the kinds of perceptual capacities that can be demonstrated and assessed on the visual cliff. Summarize the findings concerning the critical cues for depth perception on the visual cliff.

15. Describe the general notion of perceptual con-

stancy and indicate its significance as an adaptive mechanism.

16. Explain lightness constancy making use of the related notions of albedo and the relationship of the reflected light of an object to the light reflected by the background.

17. Outline the Holway-Boring experiment and summarize its significance to an explanation of size constancy. Describe Emmert's law and indicate in what ways it demonstrates size constancy processes.

18. Discuss shape constancy and indicate how it can be demonstrated, drawing upon familiar shapes such as circles, ellipses, squares, and trapezoids. Examine the contribution made by spatial cues to depth and distance in promoting shape constancy.

17

THE PERCEPTION OF SPACE II: ILLUSIONS

In the previous chapter we observed that the relative absence of a spatial context disturbs or reduces perceptual constancy. Similarly, we note here that when cues to space are lacking, are distorted, or are placed in apparent conflict with each other, not only may constancy be reduced but characteristic distortions in the perception of the physical environment —illusions—may result.

We have seen in a number of discussions that the stimulation received by the senses bears neither a simple nor an exact relation to the physical environment. Many transformations of the stimulation occur prior to perception. Moreover, numerous visual events contain a potential for perceptual ambiguity, and under certain circumstances they may furnish a distorted representation of the physical environment. It would be an oversimplification, however, to dismiss these illusory phenomena as curiosities, errors of perception, or rare exceptions to perceptual constancy. Not only do they pose many interesting and empirically fruitful problems, but the study of illusions may furnish clues to the more comprehensive and general mechanisms and principles of perception.

This chapter is devoted to a discussion of visual illusions, to presenting some of the attempts to explain them, and to showing how explaining them may help in the understanding of some of the general processes of "normal" perception. There are a vast number of visual illusions and many are included in this chapter. However we will focus on only a representative group that have clear relevance to the perception of space and have been the subject of recent research. In several cases provisional explanations are offered that embody comprehensive principles of perception; in almost all cases there is no single fully acceptable explanation.

TRANSACTIONALISM AND THE AMES ILLUSIONS

A provocative theory and a related set of illusions, with particular relevance to constancy and the cues to depth and distance, have been devised by Adelbert Ames (1946). They were an outgrowth of his examination of **aniseikonia,** an optical anomaly in which the image in one eye is larger than the other, resulting in a significant disparity between the images on each eye. This can be simulated with special lenses (see Figure 17.1). However, although optically there is a difference in the size of the two ocular images—with

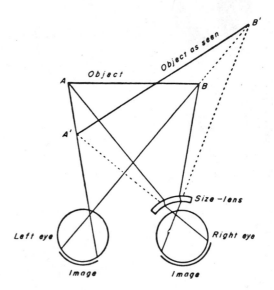

FIGURE 17.1   Simulation of aniseikonia. Special size lenses that produce images in one eye larger than in the other create incorrect and confusing depth cues. (From R. S. Woodworth and H. Schlosberg, *Experimental Psychology*, rev. ed., Holt, Rinehart and Winston, New York, 1954, p. 488.)

confusing depth cues—persons who are afflicted with aniseikonia perceive the environment in a relatively normal fashion. Objects and surfaces such as floors, walls, and so on appear to be rectilinear, although the images on the retina are sufficiently different to produce severe distortions. The seeming contradiction between the perception and the optical stimulation led Ames and his colleagues (see Kilpatrick, 1961) to the theoretical notion that experience with specific objects and surfaces plays a very important role in normal perception. This empirical theory, called **Transactionalism,** proposes that the perceptual world, in large measure, is constructed from experiences in dealing with the visual environment. Transactional theory is based on the observation that any stimulus pattern that impinges on a single retina could have been produced from an infinite number of objects (see Figure 17.2). Despite the possible perception that might arise from a given retinal pattern, the actual perception is usually quite

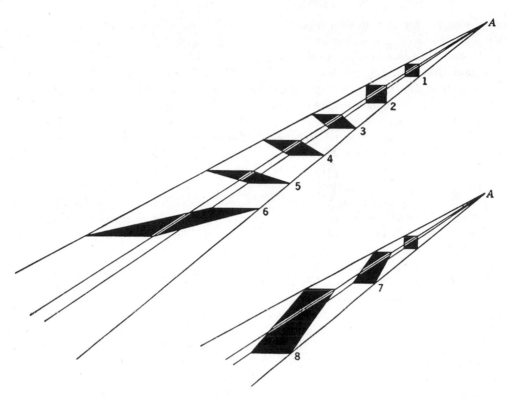

FIGURE 17.2.   An infinite number of surfaces, differently oriented with regard to the line of sight, may project the same visual angle at *A* as does the square at 1 and therefore may be perceived as a square when accompanying cues to space are lacking. (From S. H. Bartley, in *Handbook of Experimental Psychology*, edited by S. S. Stevens, John Wiley, New York, 1951, p. 924. Reprinted by permission of the publisher.)

restricted. Transactionalists attempt to account for this limitation by referring to the learning that takes place during the individual's active interactions with the environment. They argue that owing to a history of interactions or *transactions* with the environment, perceptual alternatives become limited in a way that corresponds closely to the world of real objects. Thus, according to the Transactionalists, we *assume* (and thereby perceive) the world to be stable and organized in a manner that conforms to our past commerce with it.

The **Ames illusions** are particularly effective in illustrating the role of learning and experience in perception. When observed, generally under quite restricted and contrived conditions (i.e., without information from binocular cues and motion parallax), they highlight the assumptions concerning spatial relations that the individual has developed in the course of environmental interactions. The illusions are most striking when the individual is forced to violate one set of assumptions about the spatial environment to preserve another. Although there are a number of demonstrations, our purpose is well served by considering the two most famous.

THE TRAPEZOIDAL WINDOW

The dramatic perceptual effects of the rotating trapezoid must be observed to be fully appreciated. The physical device consists of a trapezoidal surface with panes and shadows painted on both sides to give the appearance of a partially turned rectangular window (Figure 17.3), but is, in fact, a **trapezoidal window**. When viewed frontally, it appears to be rectangular in shape but turned at an angle (so long as there are not sufficient depth cues to indicate that it is not turned). It is mounted on a rod, connected to a motor, that can rotate at a slow constant speed about its vertical axis. When the rotating trapezoid is observed with one eye from about 3 meters (about 10 ft.) or with both eyes at 6 meters or more, it is perceived not as a rotating trapezoid but as an *oscillating* rectangular window reversing its direction once every 180°.

It must be emphasized that in terms of the available stimulus information, there are two mutually exclusive perceptual alternatives: an oscillating rectangle or a rotating trapezoid. However, based on prior experiences and the viewer's assumptions, the favored perception of the ambiguous stimulus figure is of a normal rectangular window turned slightly. It

follows that if it is seen as a rectangular window, then the character of its movement must be perceived as oscillation because the continuous array of images could occur only from a rectangular surface that oscillates.

The perception of the true motion of the surface—rotation—is inconsistent with the assumption that the figure is a rectangular window. In normal rotation of a rectangular surface, the retinal projection of only the farther edge is reduced. However, in the case of a rotating trapezoid, one of its sides is *always* longer than the other. Hence, the longer side continuously appears nearer the viewer. This sort of imagery could occur only from a moving rectangular surface when it undergoes oscillation. Hence, it follows that the projection of the apparently nearer long side appears to oscillate back and forth.

In an effort to assess the effect of past experience and assumptions about the environment on the illusory effect of the rotating trapezoid, Allport and Pettigrew (1957) performed a cross-cultural test of the illusion. The rotating trapezoid illusion was presented to subjects from cultures that differed in their experiences with rectangular environments. Specifically, some subjects came from cultures in which the environment was virtually devoid of windows and surfaces with right angles and straight lines, whereas other subjects came from typical urban environments. When the rotating trapezoid was presented under optimal conditions for producing the illusion, all subjects showed the illusion (i.e., perceived oscillation) despite presumed differences in the experiences of the cultures tested. However, under conditions that were marginal for perceiving the illusion, the subjects who had less experience with environmental cues of rectangularity were less susceptible to the illusion.

It should be noted that there are attempts to explain the rotating trapezoid illusion without recourse to the assumption that past experience produces a tendency to perceive rectangular shapes (e.g., Braunstein, 1976).

THE DISTORTED ROOM

The photograph of Figure 17.4*a* suggests a view into a specially built room. The interior of the room is

FIGURE 17.3.   The Ames trapezoid. A rendering of the frontal view (perpendicular to the line of sight) of the rotating trapezoid.

(a)

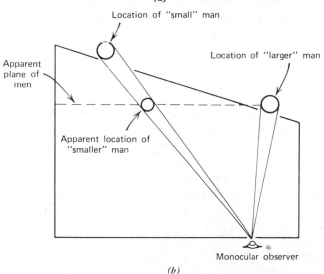

(b)

FIGURE 17.4.   Both men in (*a*) are the same size. The illusion is created by the design of the room as indicated by the floor plan in (*b*). (From H. C. Lindgren and D. Byrne, *Psychology*, John Wiley, New York, 1975, p. 231. Reprinted by permission of the publisher.)

usually seen through a small peephole that allows only a monocular view, thereby eliminating a number of depth and distance cues. Under these conditions of viewing, most observers see two men in the windows of an ordinary room, one unusually smaller than the other. It is an illusory perception in that both men are about the same size whereas the room is quite unusual. In fact, the apparently "smaller" man is really located farther away from the observer than the other person. That he does not appear so, according to the Transactionalists, indicates the compelling influence of assumptions about the shape of the environment formed by past experience. They contend that due to extensive experience with rectangular rooms, the viewer assumes the two men are standing against the usual background of a rectangular room. However, the floor, ceiling, some walls, and the far windows of the room are actually trapezoidal surfaces. As indicated by the outlined structure presented in Figure 17.4b, the room is carefully constructed so that the window with the "smaller" man is really farther from the observer than the window containing the apparently larger person. In brief, the more distant aspects of the room are correspondingly increased in size so that when seen in perspective the near and far parts appear to be at the same distance from the observer. As in the case of the rotating trapezoid, there are two perceptual alternatives in the **distorted room illusion**: two persons of similar size at different locations from the observer and standing against a trapezoidal surface, or two persons, quite different in size, standing against a rectangular background. The general observation is of a rectangular room with the size of the occupants distorted.

The rotating trapezoid and the distorted room are but two of a series of unusual demonstrations by Ames and his colleagues in support of Transactionalism. However, all point to the same conclusion: under the proper physical circumstances, past experience is an important factor in determining space perception.

THE HORIZONTAL—VERTICAL ILLUSION

A version of the **horizontal—vertical illusion**, introduced by Wundt in 1858, is presented in Figure 17.5a. The two intersecting lines are equal in length, although the vertical line appears to be appreciably longer. If required to adjust the extent of the horizontal line to appear equal in length to the vertical one, the extent of the horizontal line is over 30% longer

FIGURE 17.5a.   The horizontal-vertical illusion. The vertical and horizontal lines are the same length.

than the vertical (Figure 17.5b). The illusory relationship between vertical and horizontal extents is not confined to simple line drawings. Chapanis and Mankin (1967) demonstrated an overestimation in the perceived extent of the vertical dimension using such familiar objects as a building, a parking meter, a nail in a table, and a large tree, all viewed in a natural setting.

While there is no fully accepted explanation of the horizontal-vertical illusion, it is worth noting that both horizontal and the vertical segments individually contribute to the overall magnitude of the illusion. Masin and Vidotto (1983) have found that the vertical line in the illusory figure appears longer than the same vertical line presented in isolation; similarly the horizontal line appears shorter when it is embedded in the illusory figure than when it is

FIGURE 17.5b.   Apparently equal vertical and horizontal lines. To most observers the horizontal and vertical lines appear equal; however, the horizontal line is over 30% longer than the vertical line.

presented singly. That is, the horizontal–vertical illusion involves both an apparent lengthening of the vertical line *and* an apparent shortening of the horizontal line.

THE MOON ILLUSION

The **moon illusion** refers to the phenomenon that the moon appears larger (as much as 1.5 times) when it is viewed at the horizon than at the zenith, although the projected images in both cases are identical. In fact, the moon (as well as the sun) occupies a far smaller fraction of the visible sky than most individuals assume. The angle subtended by the moon is almost exactly 0.5 of a degree (Tolansky, 1964). An object as small as a quarter of an inch (about 6.4 mm) across, held 30 in. (76.2 cm) from the eye projects a visual angle of about 0.5 of a degree, yet when it is held in the correct position, it is large enough to blot out the image of the moon. The moon illusion has been subjected to numerous explanations. Several prominent attempts to explain it follow.

ANGLE-OF-REGARD HYPOTHESIS

Boring (Holway & Boring, 1940; Taylor & Boring, 1942; Boring, 1943) proposed that the apparent size of the moon is affected by the angle of the eyes relative to the head. That is, according to the **angle-of-regard hypothesis** the moon illusion is produced by changes in the position of the eyes in the head accompanying changes in the angle of elevation of the moon. In one task Holway and Boring (1940) had subjects match the moon, as they saw it, with one of a series of disks of light projected on a nearby screen. Viewing the horizon moon, with eyes level, most subjects selected a disk considerably larger than the disk chosen when their eyes were raised 30° to match the zenith moon. Similarly, when a subject lying on a flat table viewed the zenith moon from a supine position, with no raising or lowering of the eyes, or when a subject viewing from a supine position hung his or her head over the edge of a table to view the

horizon moon with the eyes elevated, the illusion was reversed: the horizon moon appeared smaller than the zenith moon. This latter effect can also be obtained by doubling over and looking at the horizon moon between one's legs.

Boring concluded that the moon illusion depends on raising or lowering the eyes with respect to the head. Mere movements of the neck, head, and body are not causal factors. However, there is no convincing psychological process to explain Boring's general findings in support of the notion that visual space is altered with eye movements in the vertical plane. As he stated in 1943,

> There is no satisfactory . . . theory for explaining this phenomenon. It is not due to physical causes outside the visual mechanism. . . . There remains only the suggestion that the effort of raising or lowering the eyes shrinks the perceived size of the moon. . . . Since we do not know why muscular effort in the visual mechanism should affect visually perceived size . . . we are forced to leave the problem there without ultimate solution. (pp. 59–60)

APPARENT DISTANCE HYPOTHESIS

An explanation of the moon illusion based on perceptual factors can be traced to Ptolemy (ca. 150 A.D.), the second-century astronomer and geometrician. He proposed that an object seen through filled space, such as the moon viewed across terrain at the horizon, is perceived as being farther away than an object located physically at the same distance but seen through empty space, as in the case of the moon at its zenith. In brief, the projected images of the moon in both cases are of identical size, but the horizon moon appears farther away. That it also appears larger follows from the linear relationship between apparent size and apparent distance. Thus if two objects project the same size retinal image but appear at different distances from the viewer, the object that appears farther from the viewer will typically be perceived as larger (see Figure 17.6). This relationship is called the **apparent distance hypothesis.**

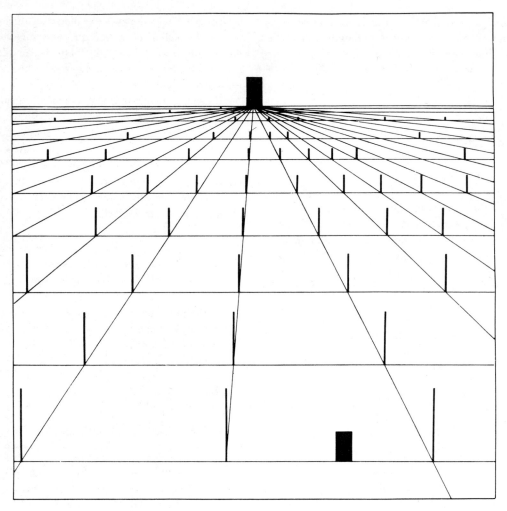

FIGURE 17.6.   The effect of apparent distance on apparent size. The black rectangle resting on the horizon appears larger than the one in the foreground, although they are identical in size. (From I. Rock and L. Kaufman, "The moon illusion. II." *Science, 136,* 1962, p. 1029. Copyright © 1962 by the American Association for the Advancement of Science.)

Applied here, the moon appears farther away at the horizon and, hence, appears larger.

Kaufman and Rock (1962*a,b*; Rock & Kaufman, 1962) examined the apparent distance hypothesis. They questioned the angle-of-regard hypothesis and in particular the method employed in determining the moon's apparent size. They argued that because the real moon is so far away from the observer it appears

as a large object but one of indeterminate size. To judge the size of a stimulus of indeterminate size with nearby comparison disks having a visibly specific size is to ask the viewer to compare things that are essentially incommensurable. Instead, Kaufman and Rock had subjects compare and match against each other two artificial "moons" seen against the sky. This, of course, is fundamentally the same sort of comparison as in the original illusion, though in the original case the two real moons are separated by both space and time. The technique used by Kaufman and Rock consisted of a projection device that permitted an observer to view an adjustable disk of light (artificial moon) on the sky. Using a pair of these devices, the observer was able to compare a standard disk set in one position (e.g., the horizon) with a variable disk set at another position (e.g., the zenith). The size of the variable disk that was chosen by the observer to match the size of the standard provided a measure of the magnitude of the illusion. The general result was that regardless of eye elevation, the horizon moon was perceived as being much larger than the zenith moon. From a series of studies these authors were able to conclude that the horizon moon appears farther away than the zenith moon and that this impression of distance is produced by the terrain considered as a plane extended outward from the observer. As we noted, if two objects have the same projected size but lie at different distances from the viewer, the one that appears to be farther away will look larger (Figure 17.7). It follows from the apparent distance theory of Kaufman and Rock that the apparently farther moon should appear larger. In short, perceived size is a function of perceived distance; with retinal size constant, the greater the apparent distance, the larger the perceived size.

It should be noted, however, that questions have been raised about the overall validity of the apparent distance notion, suggesting that a full explanation of the moon illusion involves additional factors. This is evidenced by additional theories.

RELATIVE SIZE HYPOTHESIS

Restle (1970) has offered an alternative explanation of the moon illusion that does not depend on apparent distance. The basic assumption of this **relative size hypothesis** is that the perceived size of an object depends not only on its retinal size but also on the size of its immediate visual surround. The smaller its boundary or frame of reference, the larger its apparent size. Accordingly, if the moon is judged relative to its immediate surround or bounding surface, then the horizon moon appears to be larger because it is compared with a small space (1° to the horizon). At the zenith the moon appears smaller because it is located in a large expanse of empty visual space (90° to the horizon). In this case, the moon illusion is considered to be an example of the relativity of perceived size, in that the same object may appear large in one context and small in another. Some role, perhaps subordinate to a version of the apparent distance hypothesis, is undoubtedly played by relative size (see Baird, 1982).

Finally, to underscore the diversity of factors and proposals in explaining the moon illusion, we note in passing that there is even an explanation of the moon illusion based on the fact that it is a *celestial* object whose movement creates different effects on the retinal image than do noncelestial objects (Reed, 1984, 1985). One of these is that typically the observer's retinal image of celestial objects, such as the sun and moon, does not change as these objects move across the sky, whereas the images of noncelestial objects, such as aircraft, do change in retinal size with variation in distance from the observer. According to this notion our experience and expectations from observing the motion of noncelestial objects is inappropriately applied to the movement of the moon and this produces a distortion effect.

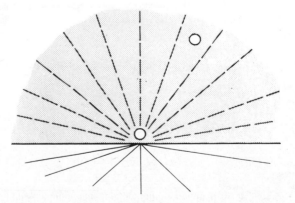

FIGURE 17.7.   The apparent distance hypothesis of the moon illusion. Presumably the horizon moon appears farther away due to the presence of the terrain. The viewer takes apparent distance into account and perceives the more distant horizon moon as larger.

In summary, explanations of the moon illusion attempt to account for the striking difference in the apparent size of the moon when seen at the horizon and zenith. The fact that the explanations are diverse and that the controversy continues suggests that a single, complete, and satisfactory explanation is yet to be found.

THE MÜLLER-LYER ILLUSION

The illusion shown in Figure 17.8, known as the **Müller-Lyer illusion** since it was devised by Franz Müller-Lyer in 1889, is perhaps the most familiar and studied geometric illusion. Clearly, the apparent length of a line is distorted when arrowheads are added to the ends. Although there are a variety of theories to account for this distortion, we will deal first with extensions of a **perspective-constancy theory** which holds that certain stimulus features

like the arrowheads of the Müller-Lyer figure are indicators of apparent distance. The perspective-constancy theory has been elaborated by Gregory (1963, 1966, 1968) and Day (1972) to encompass a number of size illusions. In the case of the Müller-Lyer figure, they contend that perspective features furnished by the arrowheads or wings of the figure provide false distance cues. As a consequence, size constancy is inappropriately induced to compensate for the apparent distance of the line segments. The result is a consistent error in the perceived length of the lines.

An example illustrating this is given in Figure 17.9. Drawings of corners and edges in perspective are shown with corresponding outline drawings of Müller-Lyer figures. According to a perspective-constancy explanation, the Müller-Lyer figures as well as the outline drawings are flat two-dimensional projections of three-dimensional shapes in depth, and due to the operation of a size-constancy mechanism, parts of the illustration that appear farther

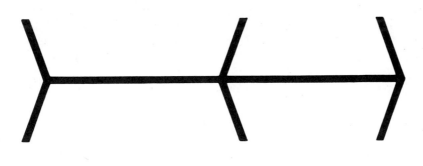

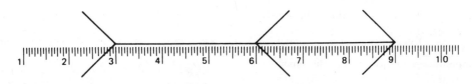

FIGURE 17.8.   The Müller-Lyer illusion. In both the top and bottom figures the segment on the left appears longer than the one on the right, although the left and right segments are the same length. The bottom figure indicates that the illusion persists in spite of the presence of a disconfirming measure.

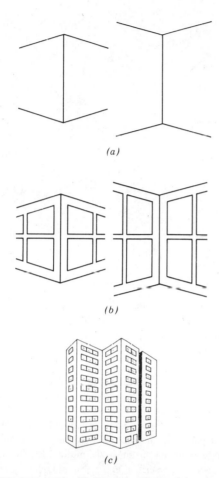

FIGURE 17.9.   The Müller-Lyer illusion (*a*) and perspective drawings of structures whose outlines match the illusion (*b*). The left drawing in (*b*) is characteristic of an outside corner of a building—the corner nearer to the viewer (also recall the collage of Figure 16.8*b*). The right drawing in (*b*) suggests the inside corner of a building—the corner farther away from the viewer. Perspective causes an apparent enlargement of the vertical projection of the farthest corner to compensate for its apparently greater distance from the viewer. How this perspective-constancy notion accounts for the Müller-Lyer illusion may be more readily seen in (*c*) which depicts a building in perspective. Since when actually viewing such a building we see all its vertical extents as about the same height, we are obviously compensating for apparent distance: the apparent length of the farthest inside corner is enlarged and the nearer outside corner is reduced in apparent length.

away are perceived as larger. In other words, the mechanism of size constancy compensates for the apparent distance of objects—a compensatory correction that normally occurs for a diminishing retinal image size when distance is increased.

The depth features inherent in the Müller-Lyer figure are largely confined to those of perspective, which is a potent indication of depth or distance. However, a more general statement has been made by Day (1972), termed the **general constancy theory,** in which he argues that if any of the traditional stimulus cues for distance that normally are utilized to preserve constancy (e.g., binocular disparity, motion parallax, linear perspective, interposition) are varied with the size of the retinal image of the object not correspondingly changed, variations in apparent size will result. In short, size constancy is brought into play inappropriately.

However appealing the perspective-constancy hypothesis is as an explanation of the Müller-Lyer illusion, it has been challenged. For the most part critics argue that the Müller-Lyer illusion can be understood without appealing to apparent depth features. For example, Fisher (1967*a*, 1968, 1970) contends that converging contours per se, not necessarily apparent distance inferences, induce distortions in perceived size. In addition, effects have been reported that are inappropriate to perspective-constancy predictions. For example, Waite and Massaro (1970) reasoned that if perspective features make the central shaft of an outward wings version of the Müller-Lyer figure appear more distant than an inward wings figure, then constancy should affect its length *and* its width in the same direction. That is, if perspective is responsible for the illusion, then both the apparent length and the apparent width of the central shaft should be enlarged for the outward wings figure. However, they reported that with modified Müller-Lyer figures, like those shown in Figure 17.10*a* and *b*, the distortion in the length of the shaft of *a* was in the opposite direction of the distortion of its width. That is, whereas the central shaft of *a* appeared longer than that of *b*, as predicted by perspective-constancy theory, the apparent width of the shaft of *a* was slightly *smaller* than for *b*, a finding

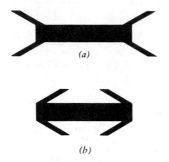

FIGURE 17.10. Modified Müller-Lyer figures with an enlarged width of the central shaft.

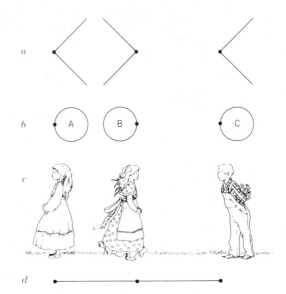

FIGURE 17.11. Müller-Lyer variations. (*a*) The distance between the dots on the arrowheads on the left and in the middle does not appear equal to the distance between the dots on the middle and right arrowheads. (*b*) The distance between the dots on the outer borders of circles *A* and *B* does not appear equal to the distance between the dots on the right side of *B* and the left side of *C*. (*c*) The distance between the eyes of the girl on the left and in the middle does not appear equal to the distance between the eyes of the boy on the right and the girl in the middle. (*d*) The actual distances described in (*a*), (*b*), and (*c*) are physically equal, as indicated by the equated line segments. (Part *c* is based on a demonstration by Edward Gorey, 1979.)

in opposition to that proposed by perspective-constancy theory.

Furthermore, the processes mediating the Müller-Lyer illusion are not restricted to the presence of line segments or regions apparently lying at different distances from the viewer, which are central to a perspective-constancy explanation. Figure 17.11 depicts such variations of the Müller-Lyer figure that produce significant distortion effects. The generality of perspective-constancy theory is also questioned by the reports that the Müller-Lyer illusion has been demonstrated with the pigeon (Malott & Malott, 1970; Malott, Malott & Pokrzywinski, 1967), the ringdove (Warden & Baar, 1929), the fish (cited in Gregory, 1966), and perhaps the fly (Geiger & Poggio, 1975). Understandably, it is not clear whether these animals are capable of interpreting the arrowheads as perspective cues.

The generality of a perspective-constancy explanation is further weakened by the finding that using tactual stimulation presumably devoid of depth cues, blind and normally sighted blindfolded persons are also susceptible to the Müller-Lyer illusion (Patterson & Deffenbacher, 1972; see also Rudel & Teuber, 1963; and Lucca, Dellantonio, & Riggio, 1986).

Finally, we should note that there is evidence suggesting that the standard Müller-Lyer illusion is actually a composite of two relatively distinct illusory processes, one acting on the wings-inward version

(causing an underestimation) and one affecting the wings-outward figure (producing overestimation) (Greist-Bousquet & Schiffman, 1981*a*, 1981*c*).

THE PONZO ILLUSION

An example of the **Ponzo illusion,** devised by Mario Ponzo in 1913, is given in Figure 17.12. Although the two horizontal lines are identical in length, the

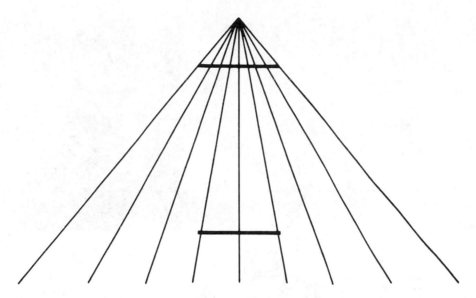

FIGURE 17.12.   A version of the Ponzo illusion. The two horizontal lines are equal. (Devised by M. Ponzo in 1913.)

line located closer to the point of convergence of the two bounding lines appears to be longer. The Ponzo illusion is so closely linked to an explanation based on perspective (or a perspective-constancy notion) that it is often referred to as the Ponzo perspective figure.

The perspective feature, as applied here, is produced by the bounding converging lines that are ordinarily associated with distance. Accordingly, the perspective cue falsely suggests depth—the line that appears farther away is perceived as larger—thereby producing a size illusion. In a study of the factors influencing this phenomenon, Leibowitz and his colleagues (1969) had subjects view, monocularly and binocularly, the actual scene illustrated in Figure 17.13b, from the point at which the photograph was taken. In a second phase, students were tested with the four two-dimensional pictorial stimuli shown in Figure 17.13. Procedurally, the upper line in the actual scene and in each subfigure of Figure 17.13 was constant while a series of lower lines were individually and randomly presented for an equality match with the upper line. The essential results are given in Figure 17.14. The findings, in general,

indicate that the magnitude of the Ponzo illusion is dependent on the presence of a context of cues to depth: the greater the context—the more the photographs simulate the real scene—the greater the magnitude of the illusion. Figure 17.14 indicates that the upper of two lines, when shown alone (d), is slightly overestimated. This is likely due to the cue of elevation. The addition of converging lines (a) produces an illusion value of approximately 10% (percentage overestimation of the upper line). When the two horizontal lines are shown against texture cues (c), a 20% illustory effect obtains, and the addition of perspective cues such as railroad tracks (b) results in about a 30% illusion. However, the greatest illusion resulted from the actual scene. This study is important in showing that the more the two-dimensional photograph approximates a representation of a three-dimensional scene—the more spatial cues to depth are available—the larger the magnitude of the illusion.

Leibowitz et al. also examined the role of experience on the magnitude of the Ponzo illusion depicted in Figure 17.13 by comparing the judgments described earlier (made by Pennsylvania college

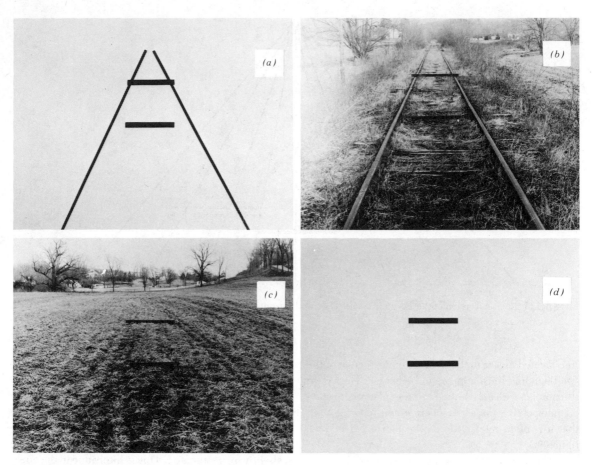

FIGURE 17.13. The stimuli used in the study by Leibowitz et al. (1969). The extent of the horizontal lines in
all figures is the same. (From H. W. Leibowitz, R. Brislin, L. Perlmutter, and R. Hennessy, "Ponzo perspective
illusion as a manifestation of space perception," *Science*,
166, 1969, p. 1175. Copyright © 1969 by the American
Association for the Advancement of Science. Reprinted
by permission of the authors and publisher.)

students) with those made by students native to Guam
who had less experience with perspective cues. The
results suggest that the magnitude of the illusion
depends upon previous experience with topographi-
cal features (as represented in Figures 17.13*b* and
17.13*c*). Other related findings (Leibowitz & Pick,
1972) indicate that previous exposure to pictorial
depth (as in two-dimensional printed material and
media sources such as photographs, movies, and
television) similarly affects the magnitude of the
Ponzo illusion.

Although a perspective-constancy explanation
of the Ponzo illusion appears reasonable, other research casts doubt on its completeness. For example,
when the interior lines are changed from their normal
horizontal orientation to a vertical orientation, the
illusion is eliminated (Schiffman & Thompson, 1978;
Gillam, 1980). Such a finding is inconsistent with a
perspective-constancy explanation since the line
closest to the converging contours should always
appear "farther" from the viewer and hence larger
than the "nearer" line no matter what the orientation.

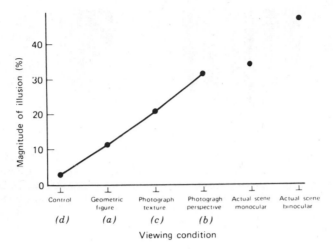

FIGURE 17.14.   The magnitude of the Ponzo illusion for the various conditions of the experiment by Leibowitz et al. (1969). The magnitude of the illusion represents the percentage overestimation of the upper member of the pairs of horizontal lines shown in the preceding figure. (After Leibowitz et al., 1969.)

Based on these results and other findings (e.g., Fisher, 1973; Jordan & Randall, 1987), we can conclude that a perspective-constancy explanation does not provide a complete account of the Ponzo illusion. However, in view of such findings as in the Leibowitz et al. study, it is clear that the illusion can be enhanced by providing additional depth cues.

Other explanations of the Ponzo illusion have been offered. An alternative approach is based on the effect of the differential framing of the two horizontal lines (e.g., Fisher, 1973). That is, the difference in the separation of the two horizontal lines from the surrounding oblique lines may determine or at least contribute to the magnitude of the distortion. In other words, the closer a line segment is to its border, the longer it appears. The horizontal line located near the apex of the surrounding oblique lines is closer to the borders than is the case for the line located near the diverging region. Accordingly, an effect based on the differences in framing for the two horizontal lines independent of any apparent distance cues, may account, in part, for the Ponzo illusion (see Jordan & Randall, 1987).

THE POGGENDORFF ILLUSION

The illusion presented in Figure 17.15a, the **Poggendorff illusion,** originated from the Zöllner illusion (see Figure 17.15b). It was J. C. Poggendorff, the editor of the journal to which Zöllner submitted his paper in 1860, who pointed out an additional effect contained in Zöllner's figure (Figure 17.15c); as a consequence, the Poggendorff illusion bears the name of the observant editor.

The two oblique lines in Figure 17.15a are actually aligned or collinear, yet to most observers an imaginary extension of the left line segment appears to be misaligned with the right line segment. That is, the segments of the diagonal line appear to be offset when intercepted by the vertical rectangle. Unlike the visual geometric illusions described earlier, the Poggendorff illusion is usually classified as an illusion of direction or misalignment. The Poggendorff effect occurs in real-life settings such as reading graphs (Poulton, 1985), viewing actual scenes (Lucas & Fisher, 1969) and viewing photographs (see Figure 17.16).

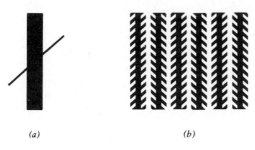  

(a)   (b)   (c)   (d)

FIGURE 17.15. The standard Poggendorff illusion (a) and the Zöllner illusion (b). In (a) the oblique lines are collinear, although they appear to be misaligned. In (b) the parallel lines appear to converge and diverge. An enlargement of a portion of (b) is shown in (c). Note in (c) that the oblique line segments forming the Zöllner illusion also appear misaligned. A variation of the Poggendorff illusion in (d) shows that when interrupted by two vertical rectangles, the segments of the continuous diagonal line appear to be even more offset than the version in (a).

THE POGGENDORFF ILLUSION AND PERSPECTIVE CONSTANCY

Although a number of explanations have been offered to account for the Poggendorff illusion we begin with an explanation based on the familiar perspective-constancy notion (Gillam, 1971, 1980). As applied to the Poggendorff illusion, the perspective-constancy theory holds that in the standard Poggendorff figure, the oblique lines are perceived as the outlines of apparently receding horizontal planes that lie on different planes (see Figure 17.17), whereas the rectangle is perceived as lying on the frontoparallel plane (i.e., all edges of the rectangle are perceived as equally distant from the observer). Figure 17.17

FIGURE 17.16. A photograph of a Poggendorff illusion. The diagonally growing tree in the background is nearly perfectly straight, yet the vertical tree in the foreground causes it to appear crooked. A straight-edge will verify this real-life Poggendorff illusion. (Photograph courtesy of S. Greist-Bousquet.)

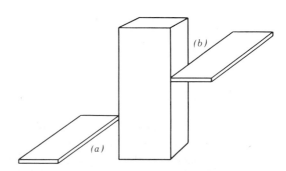

FIGURE 17.17. An elaboration of the Poggendorff figure that illustrates the perspective-constancy explanation of the illusory misalignment. In this case the obliques of the figure (a and b) are processed as belonging to different horizontal planes rather than as a single continuous receding plane. (Based on Rock, 1975.)

illustrates and elaborates these effects. It is clear that such perspective processing disrupts apparent collinearity in the Poggendorff figure.

A prediction from the perspective-constancy explanation is that when the rectangle of the figure is changed to depict a surface that appears to recede into the distance in the same apparent orientation of the oblique lines, the illusory misalignment effect should shrink. As illustrated in Figure 17.18, the illusion in this case is reduced (Gillam, 1971).

However, as we noted earlier, the perspective-constancy explanation alone is incomplete. For example as illustrated in Figure 17.19, there is a persistence of the misalignment for variations of the Poggendorff figure that do not appear to contain any perspective features. In Figure 17.19a, it is unclear how a single vertical line might be processed as a plane that differs in perspective from the presumably receding oblique lines, yet the misalignment illusion persists. The role of perspective as an explanation is equally tenuous in Figure 17.19b, in which the oblique lines are replaced by a circle.

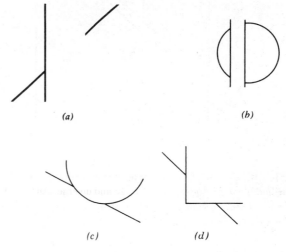

(a) (b)

(c) (d)

FIGURE 17.19. Variations of the Poggendorff figure that also produce misalignment effects. In (a) the oblique line segments would form a continuous line, but appear to be offset. In (b) the circle appears to be segments of two circles with different diameters when intercepted by the parallel lines. Misalignment effects also occur in (c) and (d). (See Greene, 1988.)

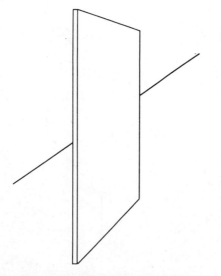

FIGURE 17.18. The Poggendorff illusion is reduced when perspective cues suggest a single receding plane.

THE POGGENDORFF AND THE MÜLLER-LYER ILLUSION

A recent explanation takes a somewhat different approach to the Poggendorff illusion. Greist-Bousquet and Schiffman (1981b, 1985, 1986, 1987) have proposed that the misalignment effect of the Poggendorff illusion may be understood, in part, by examining other, perhaps more primary, illusory effects that are embedded within it. It has been shown that there is an apparent foreshortening or decrease of the intercontour extent of the standard Poggendorff figure (i.e., the diagonal distance between the vertical parallel lines; Quina-Holland, 1977). Figure 17.20 illustrates how this apparent decrease could underlie the misalignment effect (see Zanuttini, 1976). Greist-Bousquet and Schiffman propose that the decrease in intercontour extent, and thus the misalignment effect of the Poggendorff illusion is attributable,

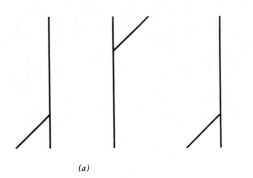 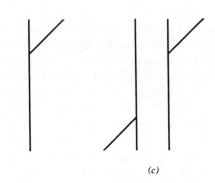

(a)   (b)   (c)

FIGURE 17.20.   The Poggendorff illusion may be attributable to an underestimation of the intercontour distance. In (a) the oblique lines are objectively collinear. By moving the right parallel horizontally in (b), an increase in the intercontour distance produces the impression of subjective collinearity although the oblique lines are actually misaligned. A decrease in the intercontour distance increases the misalignment effect (c).

at least in part, to the factors that produce the Müller-Lyer illusion. Figure 17.21 reveals that variations of the Müller-Lyer figure are contained within the Poggendorff figure. The incomplete variation of the wings-inward Müller-Lyer figure (Figure 17.21a) has been found to produce an underestimation of the intercontour extent. (Note that Figure 17.21b shows that there is also an embedded wings-outward Müller-Lyer component; however it has been shown that the magnitude of the overestimation owing to this component is very slight compared to the underestimation produced by the wings-inward component:

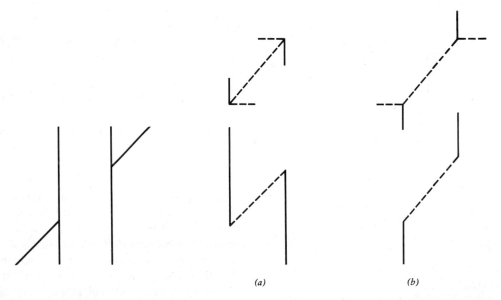

(a)   (b)

FIGURE 17.21.   The Poggendorff figure on the left contains incomplete wings-inward (a), and wings-outward (b), variations of the figures of the Müller-Lyer illusion (noted above each figure).

Warren & Bashford, 1977; Greist-Bousquet & Schiffman, 1981c).

Thus the standard Poggendorff figure may contain Müller-Lyer components within it that produce an apparent decrease in the intercontour extent (see also Greist-Bousquet & Schiffman, 1985). Accordingly, the illusory decrease in intercontour distance, due primarily to the wings-inward effect (Figure 17.21a), is held to be linked causally to the illusory misalignment (as suggested in Figure 17.20c). However, it should be noted that this explanation cannot be easily applied to the full range of misalignment effects attributed to the Poggendorff illusion. For example, the variations shown in Figure 17.19 do not appear to contain any Müller-Lyer components yet misalignment is obvious.

What is interesting about the foregoing explanation is that it stresses an approach to reduce the number of "different" illusions and their explanations. Indeed, other investigators have adopted similar economical approaches in the explanation of other geometric illusions. For example, the Sander parallelogram (Figure 17.22) contains Müller-Lyer components (Runyon & Cooper, 1970).

OTHER ILLUSIONS

We have focused attention on the visual illusions that have been the most widely studied. However, numerous other visual illusions have been cataloged. One set of these has often been categorized as **contrast illusions**. Contrast illusions consist of effects in which surrounding or contextual stimuli exert an opposing or *contrasting* effect on judgments of an embedded stimulus. The Ebbinghaus illusion depicted in Figure 17.23a is a prime example. The area of the surrounded circle in A appears inflated due to the smaller contextual circles; the identical center circle in B appears deflated due to the larger contextual circles. Other contrast illusions may be seen in Figures 17.23b and c. Contrast illusions are of particular interest since they suggest the importance of the role of context in making judgments of area, length, and orientation.

Other visual illusions of interest are shown in Figure 17.24. Distortions of apparent shape are contained in each of these illusion figures.

THEORETICAL CONSIDERATIONS

There is no single theory that accounts for the major geometric illusions nor is it likely that geometric illusions constitute a single class of effects. Although we noted that a form of perspective-constancy theory

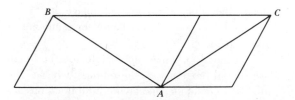

FIGURE 17.22. The Sander parallelogram. Diagonal line segment AB appears longer than segment AC although they are both the same length. Note that components of the wings-inward Müller-Lyer figure are embedded within the parallelogram. (Devised by F. Sander in 1926.)

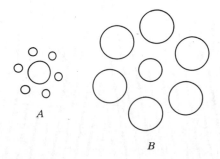

FIGURE 17.23a. The Ebbinghaus illusion and contrast effects. The center circle in A appears enlarged due to the smaller surrounding circles. The identical circle in the center of B appears diminished due the larger surrounding circles. (Described by Ebbinghaus in 1902.)

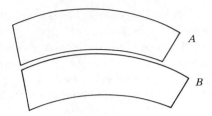

FIGURE 17.23*b*. An illusion attributed to Jastrow in 1891. Although the two figures are identical, *B* appears longer than *A*. The shorter side of *A* is viewed against the longer side of *B*; thus, *A* appears shorter and *B* appears longer.

has been implicated as an explanation for a number of geometric illusions, we must consider the viewpoint and the evidence that, in general, geometric illusions are multiply determined.

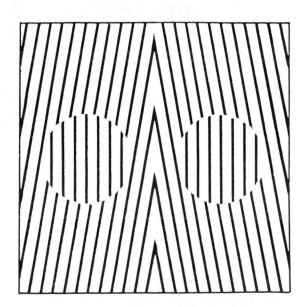

FIGURE 17.23*c*. The surrounded circular areas contain vertical lines, yet their apparent orientation is displaced in the direction opposite to the lines in the surrounding fields.

MULTIPLE DETERMINANTS OF ILLUSIONS

Since no single theory posing a single mechanism has been found entirely satisfactory, we can examine the notion that illusions may be the product of several different sources, such as the structure of the eye, peripheral and central neural interactions, and cognitive factors. Along these lines, Coren and Girgus (1978*a,b*) propose that there are two primary classes or levels of distortion mechanisms for illusory phenomena, which we may label optical-retinal (or structural) components and cognitive components.

Optical-retinal components are those that derive directly from the structural properties of the optical or neural system, that is, from anatomical or physiological mechanisms of the visual system. Structural factors would include the image-forming components of the eye such as the cornea and lens. An example of this kind of structural component is illustrated by the **subjective curvature** of Figure 17.25. Subjective curvature of straight lines occurs principally in indirect, peripheral vision and is due to the fact that the image is projected on a curved retinal surface. Perhaps because we seldom rely on peripheral vision for form or shape judgments, we are not usually aware of subjective curvatures; however, when they are isolated, they provide compelling examples of visual distortions.

Another kind of optical–retinal effect that could contribute to the perception of visual illusions, especially those illusory figures that contain converging lines and angles, is the smearing or blurring of the retinal image owing to imperfections of the eye. Indeed, the blur of the retinal image has been implicated as a contributing factor for a number of illusions (Chiang, 1968).

In general, when contours intersect or lie in close spatial proximity on the retina, there may be sufficient retinal blur, and lateral inhibitory interactions to produce distortions of apparent location. Furthermore, Ginsburg (1986) suggests that similar contour distortions may occur due to channels in the visual system that are differentially tuned to different spatial frequencies. According to this notion, elements of the spatial frequency components of a visual

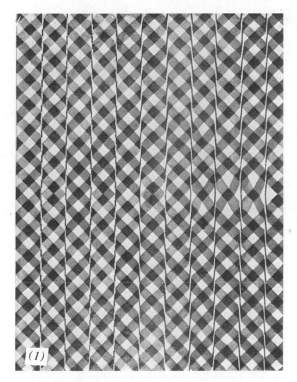

FIGURE 17.24a.   Twisted cord or Fraser illusion. (1) The straight lines seen against a checkerboardlike pattern appear curved. This illusion is called the twisted cord illusion because the effect can be obtained by view-

ing a twisted cord against a checkered background. (Devised by J. Fraser, 1908.) (2) The twisted cord effect as applied to circular forms. Spirals are perceived although the figure is composed of circles.

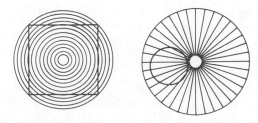

FIGURE 17.24b.   The concentric circles and spokes cause an apparent distortion in the inner square and circle, respectively. (After Orbison, 1939.)

image are extracted by specialized filters in the visual system. If the visual system filters information in this way, there is a loss of pattern detail or more precisely a loss of high spatial frequency informa-

tion. This loss introduces distortions much like the kind of errors that the visual illusions produce. To examine the general effect of these distortions in intersecting-line illusions such as the Müller-Lyer, investigators have eliminated the intersections by either removing various parts of the figure (Greist-Bousquet & Schiffman, 1981c) or by replacing the line ends and intersections of the figure with dots (e.g., Greist-Bousquet & Schiffman, 1981a). In most cases, a decrease in the magnitude of the illusion is observed with such manipulations, suggesting the involvement of structural components in intersecting-line illusions.

The point to be stressed is that structural factors of the eye, retina, and neural connections could contribute to the formation of visual illusions, and it is likely that these factors play some role. However,

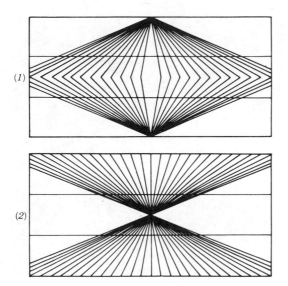

FIGURE 17.24c. (1) Wundt's illusion. The horizontal parallel lines appear to bend toward the middle. (Proposed by W. Wundt in 1896.) (2) Hering's illusion. The horizontal parallel lines appear to bow apart in the middle. (Proposed by E. Hering in 1861.)

their effects, in general, are somewhat limited and they cannot be extended to the full range of illusory figures. As we stated, optical–retinal factors are most applicable to figures or portions of figures that contain angles and intersecting lines, but it is unlikely that they can completely account for most geometric illusions. Although structural components

FIGURE 17.24d. The Münsterberg illusion. The edges of each row of the checkerboard pattern appear nonparallel. (Proposed by H. Münsterberg in 1897.)

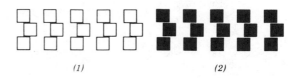

FIGURE 17.24e. The hollow squares or Taylor-Woodhouse illusion (1) and the café wall illusion (2). The figures produce illusory effects similar to the Münsterberg illusion (Figure 17.24d) in that the squares, in fact, lie on parallel lines (see Woodhouse & Taylor, 1987).

contribute some effects, a significant portion of illusory effects may be due to cognitive components.

Cognitive components that contribute to illusions include such previously described processes as those presumed to be involved in the perspective-constancy mechanism. The viewer's *attention* is another cognitive factor that has been proposed to be involved in judgments of visual illusions. For example, in an ambiguous Müller-Lyer figure (see Figure 17.26), the underestimation illusion can be created by focusing attention on the inner wings and overestimation is observed when attention is focused on the outer wings (Coren & Porac, 1983). Even in the absence of directly manipulating a viewer's attention, a reduced illusion is found when the wings of the Müller-Lyer figure are colored differently from the central segment (Sadza & de Weert, 1984), perhaps owing to an indirect manipulation of attention.

In addition to attention, *learning* seems to be another cognitive factor involved in visual illusion performance. It has long been observed that many visual illusions decline in magnitude with prolonged inspection. Feedback (or knowledge of the illusion) has been identified as playing a critical role in this decrement effect (Greist-Bousquet, Watson, & Schiffman, 1990). However, it should be noted that even if a decrease in the magnitude of many visual illusions occurs with continued inspection, the illusion does not decrease to zero. For example, no matter how long or often one inspects the Müller-Lyer figure shown in Figure 17.8, the illusion does not disappear.

FIGURE 17.25.   With one eye closed fixate on the center of the curved checkerboard design from about the distance specified by the vertical line segment on the right. The perception is of an ordinary checkerboard pattern comprised of black and white squares approximately equal in size and arranged in straight lines. Note that the curvatures of the lines used in the construction of this pattern were chosen to compensate for the subjective curvature of the lines that is seen in peripheral vision.

The viewpoint stressed here is that most visual illusions involve multiple causation. The illusory perception may owe some distortion effects to the structure of the eye, some to neural–retinal interactions, and some to cognitive processes. Accordingly, the search for a unitary mechanism is less reasonable than the acceptance of a general assumption that visual illusions are the product of several levels of visual processing mechanisms.

MULTIPLE ILLUSION FIGURES

The notion that visual illusions are the result of many contributing factors is consistent with the observation that many visual illusions probably contain several, more basic illusory effects. As previously noted with the Poggendorff illusion, many of these figures can be "dissected" into more elementary effects. The Müller-Lyer illusion is another example to consider. There is evidence that this illusion contains a minimal form of the **filled–unfilled space illusion.** Typically, the filled–unfilled space illusion refers to the phenomenon that a filled extent appears longer than an unfilled extent of equal length. However, in minimal form, even a simple line will appear longer

FIGURE 17.26.   An ambiguous Müller-Lyer illusion. An underestimation of the central space can be created by focusing attention on the interior wings. This effect can be reversed by focusing attention on the exterior wings. (Based on Coren & Porac, 1983.)

than an unfilled extent of equal length (Pressey & Moro, 1971). Accordingly, when the central line segment is removed in Müller-Lyer figures as in Figure 17.11a, judgments of the central extents decrease in both wings-inward and wings-outward figures (Greist-Bousquet & Schiffman, 1981c; Beagley, 1985). In other words, when the central space is unfilled in Müller-Lyer figures, it is judged shorter than when the central space is filled by a connecting line segment.

Of course, if we can dissect visual illusions into more elementary illusory effects, we can combine illusion effects to produce more dramatic visual illusions. For example, Figure 17.27 combines the Müller-Lyer illusion and the Ponzo illusion and is further enhanced by the additional perspective cues provided in the drawing.

AMBIGUOUS, REVERSIBLE, AND MULTISTABLE FIGURES

There are a number of figural organizations (quite similar to those of figure–ground, described earlier)

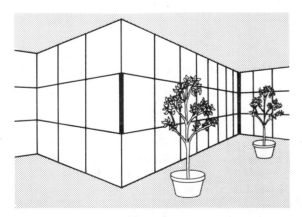

FIGURE 17.27.   A multiple illusion figure that contains the Müller-Lyer illusion, the Ponzo illusion, and further enhancement due to additional perspective cues. The heavy vertical line at the right appears longer than the one at the left; however, both are identical.

with inherent depth characteristics that may be ambiguously perceived with respect to their principal spatial orientation. After a brief period of inspection of any of the drawings shown in Figure 17.28, there is a spontaneous reversal in its spatial orientation. With continued inspection the reversal may occur periodically. The reversal occurs because there is insufficient stimulus information in a given configuration to assign to it a completely stable and unitary orientation in depth. Attneave (1971) has referred to the class of figures characterized by ambiguous and equivocal depth information as **multistable figures.** These figures are also referred to as **ambiguous** or **reversible.** For example, in the case of the standard Necker cube (Figure 17.28a) two simple three-dimensional organizations of a cube in depth are about equally possible: it can be seen as projecting upward *or* downward in depth but not both ways at the same time. In general, when the available depth information is of such a degree of ambiguity as to equally (or nearly equally) favor two or more different depth interpretations, alternative perceptions may be induced by the same figure.

In fact, after continued viewing of multistable figures such as the Necker cube, there is an increase in spontaneous reversals. An explanation of this is based upon a presumed selective-adaptation and fatigue-recovery mechanism. This account assumes that different visual cortical channels mediate each perceived variation of the reversible figure (Long,

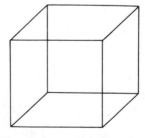

FIGURE 17.28a.   The Necker cube. After a brief period of inspection the cube spontaneously reverses in depth. (Based on a rhomboid figure devised by L. A. Necker in 1832.)

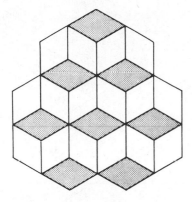

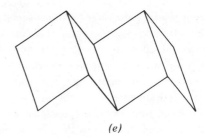

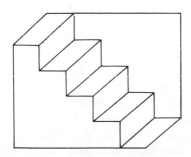

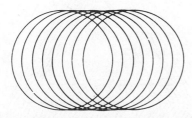

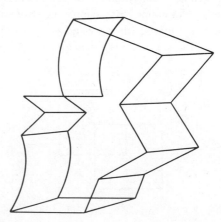

(e)

FIGURE 17.28*b*. The figure reverses so that either six or seven cubes are perceived.

FIGURE 17.28*e*. Mach illusion. With continued inspection the two-dimensional drawing of a folded sheet of paper will reverse in its orientation. (Devised by E. Mach in 1866.)

Toppino, & Kostenbauder, 1983; von Grünau, Wiggins, & Reed, 1984; Toppino & Long, 1987). Moreover, these channels involve mutually antagonistic processes enabling only one variation in orientation to be seen at a time (similar in nature to the presumed specific channels producing aftereffects of shape, color, tilt, and movement, discussed in earlier chapters). When one orientation of the multistable figure is perceived for a period of time, the perception of that orientation is selectively adapted and gradually fatigues, which is then supplanted by the figure's

FIGURE 17.28*c*. Schröder's staircase. The figure reverses from a staircase to an overhanging cornice. (Devised by H. Schröder in 1858.)

FIGURE 17.28*d*. Either end of the series of rings may be seen as the near or far end of a tube.

FIGURE 17.28*f*. An example of an ambiguous figure constructed without familiar shapes, right angles, or circles. (Devised by Noah in 1979.)

alternative orientation. Over time this second alternative also fatigues and is replaced by the original orientation, which meanwhile has "recovered" from fatigue. However, this recovery is incomplete, so that fatigue and reversal occur again but more rapidly. With extended viewing, this process continues but more and more rapidly until spontaneous reversals occur at a constant rate. Thus the fluctuation in the perceived orientation of configurations with ambiguous spatial characteristics is the result of a cyclical process of fatigue and recovery.

In contrast when depth cues, favoring a particular orientation, are added to an ambiguous figure, the perception appropriate to that orientation is significantly reported (see Figure 17.29). Spontaneous reversals decrease and there is an increase in the proportion of viewing time of the perception appropriate to the favored orientation.

IMPOSSIBLE FIGURES

So-called **impossible figures,** such as those shown in Figure 17.30, are disturbing as well as confusing to most observers who attempt to see them as depicting three-dimensional objects. This is because such displays contain inconsistent and contradictory sets of depth information that cannot individually be suppressed. Clearly, when viewed as a collection of individual linear segments and angles they appear as

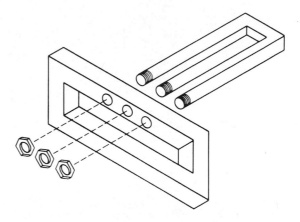

FIGURE 17.30*a*.   An "impossible" construction. The three-pronged figure is called a "trident." (From *North American Aviation's Skywriter*, February 18, 1966, Braun & Co., Inc.)

reasonable depictions of parts of a simple three-dimensional object in depth (see Figure 17.31); that is, the segments are "locally interpretable" (Simon, 1967). However, when globally seen as unitary objects, the depth characteristics of the individual features appear to be in conflict with each other and the figures appear spatially "impossible." Thus, the depth interpretation individually assigned to each part cannot be extended to the figure as a whole.

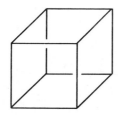

FIGURE 17.29.   Altered Necker cube. When the overlapping (or interposition) of line segments is made distinct, spatial ambiguity is reduced and the Necker cube is significantly less likely to reverse its apparent orientation.

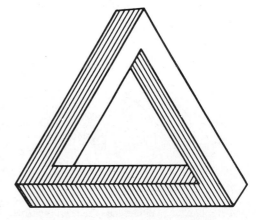

FIGURE 17.30*b*.   An "impossible" triangle.

FIGURE 17.30c.   A variation of the "impossible" triangle is portrayed on a Swedish postage stamp. Notice also that a change in figure–ground organization enables the perception of a centrally located "star."

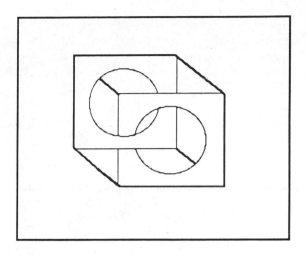

FIGURE 17.30d.   An "impossible" Necker cube. (Devised by Jan in 1989.)

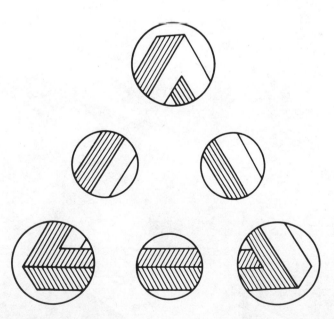

FIGURE 17.31.   When isolated parts of the "impossible" triangle are seen, they appear as simple drawings of angles and line lengths in depth. However, when the figure is viewed as a whole, apparently depicting a three-dimensional object, the depth interpretations assigned to the isolated features are in conflict with each other. (After Lindsay & Norman, 1977.)

FIGURE 17.32.   "Impossible" scene drawn by M. C. Escher (1971). According to Escher the figure incorporates the triangle of Figure 17.30b. (Beeldrect, Amsterdam/VAGA, New York, 1982, Collection Haags Gemeentemuseum.)

Some of the remarkable graphic drawings of the artist M. C. Escher (1971; see especially M. L. Teuber, 1974), utilizing contradictory depth cues, are fascinating examples of impossible three-dimensional scenes (see Figure 17.32).

SUMMARY

This chapter has introduced a variety of visual illusions and their explanations within the context of some of the general principles of space perception.

The Ames series of demonstrations was posed and explained by the Transactionalists, who contended that assumptions about the sizes and shapes of objects are created by past experience with similar objects. The horizontal–vertical illusion, although quite compelling, does not lend itself to a simple class of explanations. Several explanations of the moon illusion were discussed, including the angle-of-regard hypothesis, the apparent distance hypothesis, and the relative size hypothesis. A number of illusions, such as the Müller-Lyer and Ponzo, were explained in terms of a general perspective-constancy hypothesis, attributable to Gregory and Day. This notion contends that, owing to the spatial context, portions of certain illusion figures are seen as flat two-dimensional projections of three-dimensional shapes in depth. Accordingly, due to the compensatory operation of a size-constancy mechanism, parts of the illusion that are apparently farther away appear larger.

The Poggendorff misalignment illusion was discussed, and a number of explanations were outlined; an explanation based on mechanisms similar to those that produce the Müller-Lyer illusion was presented. Illusions involving contrast effects and shape distortions were also introduced.

The general theoretical emphasis was on the multiple determinants of illusions. This notion stresses that visual illusions may be the product of several different sources and two primary classes were proposed: optical–retinal components and cognitive components. Optical–retinal components refer to the structural factors that help account for the illusion effects and include subjective curvature, retinal blur, retinal interactions, and differential filtering of certain spatial frequencies. Cognitive components include the perspective-constancy mechanism, attention and learning. It was noted that many classic visual illusion figures contain several more basic illusion effects; thus if we can dissect visual illusion figures, we can also construct more striking illusions.

Finally, figures with ambiguous or contradictory depth information were discussed. It was concluded that the perceptual ambiguity in ambiguous, reversible, and multistable figures (e.g., the Necker cube) is due to the fact that their inherent depth indicators equally favor two or more perceptual organizations. So-called "impossible" figures were described as owing to the merging of incompatible depth cues within the same figure. When these depth features are viewed in isolation, they are easily interpretable, but when they are perceived together so as to appear as a unitary pictorial rendering of a three-dimensional object in depth, the total configuration appears to be spatially impossible.

KEY TERMS

Ames illusions

Angle-of-regard hypothesis

Aniseikonia

Apparent distance hypothesis

Cognitive components

Contrast illusions

Distorted room illusion

Filled–unfilled space illusion

General constancy theory

Horizontal–vertical illusion

Impossible figures

Moon illusion

Müller-Lyer illusion

Optical-retinal components

Perspective-constancy theory

Poggendorff illusion

Ponzo illusion

Relative size hypothesis

Reversible (multistable, ambiguous) figures

Subjective curvature

Structural components

Transactionalism

Trapezoidal window

STUDY QUESTIONS

1. Describe Transactionalism and the Transactional viewpoint concerning space perception. Explain the Ames illusions on the basis of perceptual assumptions about the spatial world developed through learning and experience. To what extent may size and shape constancy enter into the illusory effects produced by the trapezoidal window and the distorted room?

2. Consider how the horizontal-vertical illusion may be due to the combined perceptual effect of a lengthened vertical segment and a shortened horizontal segment.

3. How is the moon illusion demonstrated? What role do apparent distance cues play in producing the illusion? How may constancy mechanisms participate in producing the illusion? Outline additional theories proposed to explain the moon illusion.

4. How can the inappropriate elicitation of a perspective-constancy mechanism explain the Müller-Lyer illusion?

5. Examine the significance of two-dimensional pictorial cues in promoting visual illusions. Indicate how a "correction for apparent distance" may promote illusions. Which of the prominant illusions described appear most prone to the effects of pictorial cues?

6. In what ways does the perspective-constancy notion apply to the Ponzo illusion?

7. Outline and evaluate the explanations of the Poggendorff illusion. In particular, describe how structural aspects of the Müller-Lyer figure are imbedded within the Poggendorff figure.

8. Examine the general proposition that many illusions have multiple determinants. Identify possible structural and cognitive distortion components that may contribute to illusions.

9. Consider to what extent optical–retinal factors play a role in promoting illusions. Examine the effects of cognitive components such as attention and learning in observing the illusions.

10. Explain the perceptual effect of reversible or multistable figures. Describe the perceptual experience due to continued viewing, referring back to Chapter 1, Figure 1.1. Explain the effects of reversible figures on the basis of adaptation, fatigue, and recovery.

11. What are "impossible" figures and how can they be "explained?"

12. Discuss the contribution made to a general understanding of spatial perception by an analysis of visual illusions.

18

THE DEVELOPMENT OF PERCEPTION

The problem of whether the ability to perceive spatial features of the world is a totally acquired capacity, completely dependent on experience and learning, or whether it is based wholly on innate, genetic factors, predetermined by the way the sensory apparatus is constructed has long been a matter of philosophical inquiry and has had a great deal of influence on psychological research and theory. This issue—often

405

referred to as "**empiricism** versus **nativism**"—can be traced back to the writings of seventeenth- and eighteenth-century philosophers and nineteenth century scientists. Historically, the nativist approach, proposed by Descartes, Kant, Mueller, and others, asserts that perceptual abilities are inborn. More recently, the Gestalt school has also supported a form of nativist position claiming that the organization of the perceptual world is governed by tendencies and principles that are innately determined. On the other hand, the empiricists, who include Hobbes, Hume, Locke, Berkeley, and Helmholtz, and more recently the Transactionalists, maintain that perception occurs through a learning process—from commerce and experience with the environment. Although it has had a great effect on psychology, both as a philosophical and as an empirical disagreement, the empiricism–nativism issue has been impossible to resolve. Most contemporary psychologists hold that some forms of perceptual capacities and mechanisms are available soon enough after birth to preclude a strict empirical interpretation of the genesis of perception. Similarly, that experience plays some necessary or useful role for perception (for example, that it may modify some genetically endowed sensory mechanism) is not seriously questioned by most psychologists. As a contemporary controversy, the genesis of perception is largely one of emphasis with respect to the interaction of innate and learned factors. Moreover, the experiential and genetic factors are so intimately related that there are few experimental treatments that allow for independent manipulation of either variable. Finally, to a behavioral science, strict dichotomies and mutually exclusive alternatives such as empiricism *versus* nativism are to be avoided. It is possible to study and identify the variables that control and affect the *development of* perception without recourse to the learned–innate issue. As Fantz (1965a) puts it,

> *Perception is innate in the neonate but largely learned in the adult! This is presented partly as a resolution which is as good as can be found, and partly to point out that no real solution is possible. It is perhaps best to be content with determining the various developmental factors that influence various stages of . . . development, and to give up the attempt to prove either nativism or empiricism. (p. 400)*

It is of considerable interest to study the perceptually naïve organism to learn what it perceives of the normal world, as well as how and when these perceptual abilities develop. Psychologists investigating the occurrence of many forms of perceptual activities have gathered a fund of knowledge that tells something about the origin and the developmental course of perception. Indeed, we have already encountered a number of such instances in various contexts, but here it will be our primary focus. Specifically, what are the basic perceptual abilities of the individual? When and how do they develop? And what variables govern their operation?

DEVELOPMENT OF THE SENSORY SYSTEM

We begin by noting that the sensory system of the newborn human is surprisingly well developed (in fact, identifiable eye movements and blink–startle responses begin prior to birth, soon after 24 weeks of fetal life; Birnholz, 1981; Birnholtz & Benacerraf, 1983). The cornea and lens are capable of focusing an image on the retina, which is also quite functional. At higher levels of the visual system, structures, including the pathways between the lateral geniculate nucleus and the cortex, as well as parts of the cortex, are undergoing a rapid rate of development so that a reasonable level of maturity in anatomy occurs by about 6 to 8 weeks of age (e.g., Banks & Salapatek, 1983). In addition evidence with kittens and monkeys indicates that many of the features observed in the cortical cells of the adult of the species are present in the performance of cells of the infant. For example, like the receptive field activity of cortical cells of adult animals, the cells of the newborn are relatively unaffected by diffuse illumination, but show significant activity when bars of light, set at particular orientations, are shone onto a particular region of the retina.

On the other hand, the development of the visual system is quite sensitive to environmental influences. It is well accepted that during an animal's infancy, the development of sensory structures (such as the rods and cones) and perceptual processes (such as monocular and binocular vision) are quite susceptible to change and may even be irreversibly affected by restrictive or abnormal experience (Harwerth et al., 1986). This applies as well to cortical neurons and neural connections. Changes in the performance of components of the sensory nervous system as a consequence of visual deprivation or select visual experience suggest that the development and the maintenance of normal visual function may be due to an interplay of both genetic factors and experience.

We will first consider some of the provocative evidence that select forms of visual deprivation and biased stimulation may produce effects on the organization of the visual cortex.

CORTICAL EFFECTS OF RESTRICTION

Some of the research of Hubel and Wiesel (1963) points out the complex interactions of genetic and experiential factors. They have reported that the innate mechanism underlying the perception of visual movement, for example, requires appropriate stimulation to continue proper functioning. Kittens reared without patterned light for two months showed no activity in those cortical cells that normally react to visual movement. The indication, of course, is that the neural response was disrupted because of the extended duration of disuse due to **restricted visual stimulation**.

We should make note of the body of research that shows that selective monocular deprivation may cause defective growth or development of neurons in the visual pathways (e.g., the lateral geniculate nucleus, see Hubel, 1979) and the visual cortex (e.g., Freeman & Bonds, 1979; Rothblat & Schwartz, 1978). Moreover, if animals, such as kittens, are reared so that one eye receives much more experience than the other, the effective visual field of the less experienced eye becomes severely restricted. This suggests that an imbalance in the duration of stimulation may cause a subsequent selective suppression of a portion of the input from the less experienced eye (Tumosa, Tieman, & Hirsch, 1980). Similarly Stryker et al. (1978) reported that visual deprivation of specifically oriented contours during rearing can affect the development of cortical neurons in the cat. That is, many cortical neurons that are innately sensitive to those orientations that are absent during the rearing conditions become nonfunctional or unresponsive and, in general, lose their orientational selectivity. In short, exposure to a specific orientation is necessary to maintain and sharpen the innate response pattern for a given cortical neuron, whereas neurons deprived of activity become "silent" or nonfunctional.

In general, such studies indicate that visual experience is not necessary for the initial organization and functional connections of nerve cells subserving certain aspects of visual perception; however some patterning of light, depending on the specific nature of the visual response, is required to maintain those perceptual abilities that develop from innate structures.

CORTICAL EFFECTS OF BIASED AND SELECTIVE VISUAL STIMULATION

When the total visual stimulation is completely under experimental control, as with many sensory–physiological studies, specific aspects of the stimulus exposure may produce related changes in perception. Indeed, some of these studies, using **selective** or **biased visual stimulation,** indicate that changes in cortical organization may result from early and carefully controlled stimulus exposure (e.g., Hirsch & Spinelli, 1970; Shlaer, 1971). For example, kittens were raised from birth until 10 to 12 weeks of age with special mask devices that completely controlled their visual experiences; one eye was exposed only to three black horizontal lines and the other eye to three black vertical lines (Hirsch & Spinelli, 1970; see also Muir & Mitchell, 1973). The effect of this visual experience on the distribution of orientations of receptive fields (i.e., areas of the visual field in which stimulation produces changes in activity in specific neural cells) was striking; neurons with elongated receptive fields (i.e., neural cells activated by elongated stimuli) in the visual cortex were either horizontally or vertically oriented and lacking in oblique or diagonally oriented receptive fields (unlike normal kittens who possess manifold receptive field orientations). Cortical neurons with horizontal fields were activated only by the eye initially exposed to the horizontal lines; similarly, neurons with vertical fields were activated only by the eye exposed to the vertical lines. The authors' words best describe the study's relevance to our discussion:

> *The change in the distribution of orientations of cortical unit receptive fields that we found when kittens were raised with both eyes viewing different patterns demonstrates that functional neural connections can be selectively and predictably modified by environmental stimulation. (p. 871)*

Evidence suggests that the development of some cortical neurons requires exposure to specifically oriented environmental stimulation. Leventhal and Hirsch (1975) reported that cortical neurons in the cat which responded best to diagonal contours were found only in animals exposed to diagonal contours during rearing. However, they also report evidence of an innate response pattern for a group of neurons that appear to develop and maintain their specificity relatively free of the need for specific experience. They found that neurons which reacted selectively to horizontal or vertical contours did not require a specifically oriented visual input for maintenance or for development: exposure to diagonal contours was sufficient. That is, only neurons responding preferentially to diagonal contours required exposure to diagonal contours during rearing; the neurons sensitive to horizontal and vertical contours did not require specifically oriented contours for development.

Consider also an unusual experimental instance of the effect on the development of cortical neurons owing to the specific nature of environmental stimulation: cortical neurons of kittens, reared in a spherical, planetariumlike environment lacking straight-

line contours and having only point sources of light, were subsequently highly sensitive to spots of light but not to straight lines (Pettigrew & Freeman, 1973). This was in marked contrast to the cortical neural activity of normal animals in the presence of straight-line stimulation.

These findings led other researchers (e.g., Freeman, Mitchell, & Millodot, 1972; Freeman & Thibos, 1973) to propose that modification in the organization of neurons in the human visual system can be induced by early abnormal visual input. For example, it was suggested that uncorrected ocular astigmatism, if present during a critical period in the development of the visual system, can alter neural connections and permanently modify the brain (see also Annis & Frost, 1973; Mitchell, 1980). It has also been suggested that the early visual environment and experience play an important role in developing and modifying the optical characteristics of the eye and may influence the development of ocular abnormalities such as myopia (Young, 1970) and **amblyopia** (i.e., a sizable reduction in the acuity of one eye) (Eggers & Blakemore, 1978; Mitchell, 1978).

In summary, it appears that selective stimulation in infancy may produce developmental changes in cortical physiology and subsequent perception. In general the alteration in the organization of receptive fields resulting from exposure to biased stimulation in infancy is directly related to the character of the stimulation received.

RESTRICTION AND RESTORATION OF VISION WITH HUMANS

As we noted, the effects of light deprivation and biased stimulation stress the role of innate factors and sensitivity to environmental influences in the development of perception. But experimental manipulations such as restricted and biased stimulation are not possible with humans. However, a number of clinical observations have been reported in which otherwise normal individuals, functionally blind from birth because of congenital visual defects such as cataracts of the lens (a condition that eliminates pattern vision, allowing only clouded patches of light), have had their vision surgically restored (von Senden, 1960; Gregory & Wallace, 1963; Gregory, 1974).

Since 1728, when the first scientific citation on the effects of restored sight was made, a number of successful operations have been reported (see Pastore, 1971, for a history of restored vision). Although the reports are fragmentary, and for the most part have been unsystematically gathered and informally rendered, there is some concurrence on the effects of the **restoration of vision.** Generally, newly sighted persons do not "see" much at first. Basically, they perceive unitary shapes against a background—that is they perceive color and figure–ground organization—and they can fixate, scan, and follow moving figures. Although they may differentiate between objects, there is difficulty at first in identifying and recognizing an object as a member of a class of objects (von Senden, 1960; Hebb, 1949; London, 1960).

Some sense of the phenomenon of restored vision is given in a clinical report by Gregory and Wallace (1963; Gregory, 1974, 1977). The patient, named S.B. was a 52-year-old male, blind since the age of 10 months of age, who had a successful corneal transplant. When the surgical bandages were removed, he did not suddenly see a world of objects but only one of blurs. Yet within days he did attain some functional vision; he could walk the hospital corridors without recourse to touch; he was able to tell the time from a large wall clock; and presumably based upon his use of Braille, he could read uppercase letters. He made rapid progress in general visual abilities, and within months he could recognize the faces of friends and could name familiar objects with ease. However, he did experience pronounced difficulties with the perception of depth and distance. As Gregory (1977) writes, "We found that his perception of distance was peculiar. . . . He thought he would just be able to touch the ground below his window with his hands; but in fact the distance down was at least ten times his height" (p. 195). He also had difficulties with pictorial perception such as in making sense out of pictures in a magazine. Generally, S.B. appeared to lack perceptual constancy (Gre-

gory, 1974). Interestingly, he was relatively unsusceptible to certain geometric illusions that appear to have some apparent depth features. For example, he did not "reverse" ambiguous reversible figures such as the Necker cube and Schröder's staircase (illustrated in Chapter 17), nor did he experience the usual effect for the Poggendorff illusion. Moreover he was only minimally affected by a variation of the Ponzo illusion, and while he did show an illusory effect when viewing the Müller-Lyer figure, his errors were substantially less than that of the typical subject. Of course not all these illusions necessarily involve the scaling of apparent space, but it is interesting that figures that are typically seen "in depth" such as the Necker cube not only did not reverse to S.B. but, in fact, were not seen in depth by S.B. According to Gregory (1974), S.B.'s spatial skills were so arrested that he could not even grasp the concept of depth.

Several visual experiences were surprising and fascinating to S.B. One was first seeing the crescent-shaped "quarter" moon, and the other was seeing mirror reflections. In fact S.B. would spend hours sitting before a mirror in a local public house watching the reflections of people. On the other hand, he increasingly found the world drab and became upset by flaking paint and blemishes on things and often experienced depression when light faded. Over time his periods of depression deepened and became chronic, a not unusual effect when "restored vision" occurs in adulthood.

What meaning can we assign to this case study? The fact that reasonably effective figural identification and recognition occur only after a period of experience and training has been interpreted to indicate that these abilities are acquired rather than innately determined, and it has been incorporated into a decidedly empiricistic theory of perception (Hebb, 1949). However, we cannot directly compare the behavior of the visually naïve but otherwise sophisticated adult with that of the completely naïve infant. The blind adult with a store of knowledge accruing from the other senses is a very different organism than an inexperienced infant. In addition, as we noted earlier, there may be some neural reorganization in the adult due to disuse of the optical system so that abilities attributed only to the role of experience are unwarranted. Observations of the effects of vision restoration, although of some interest and suggestive of the role of learning a newly acquired sense, do not provide any straightforward conclusions (Wertheimer, 1951).

DEVELOPMENT OF THE PERCEPTION OF SPACE

DEPTH PERCEPTION

A number of studies concerned with the development of depth perception have been reported in which animals were reared from birth in a light-restricted environment. The assumption of such studies is that if an animal reared without light experience manifests efficient depth perception on emergence to the light, then this ability is likely unlearned. In general, the results of restriction studies are difficult to interpret precisely, but some findings, trends, and leads emerge in understanding the development of depth perception.

One of the earliest systematic studies on depth perception was reported by Lashley and Russell in 1934. They reared a group of rats in total darkness from birth to 100 days of age. On the day of the animals' first exposure to light, the experimenters accustomed the rats to orienting in visual space by placing each rat on a jumping stand and allowing it to jump a short gap to a target platform on which food was available (see Figure 18.1). The distance between the jumping stand and the target platform was systematically varied, and the animal's accuracy in perceiving distance was measured by the force of its leaps toward the target platform. The results were that the dark-reared animals exhibited a high correlation between the force of the jump and the distance of the target platform. In brief, the rats regulated their leaps in accordance with the actual distance. It would appear that little, if any, light experience is required for the rat to gauge depth accurately.

More recent research makes use of the *visual*

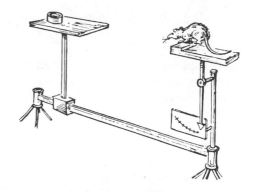

FIGURE 18.1. Jumping stand apparatus for the Lashley and Russell (1934) experiment. (From D. Krech and R.S. Crutchfield, *Elements of Psychology*, Knopf, New York, 1958, p. 139. Reprinted by permission of the authors.)

cliff apparatus, described in Chapter 16, which enables the testing of depth perception with no prior training or light experience: animals can be dark reared and tested immediately on emergence to the light.

Based on such research, rats discriminate depth on the visual cliff upon their first experience in a lighted environment (e.g., Carr & McGuigan, 1965; Walk, Trychin, & Karmal, 1965). It appears that depth perception is an ability requiring no training in the rat. In fact, infant rats have demonstrated depth perception shortly after their eyes opened (Lore & Sawatski, 1969; Bauer, 1973). Similar findings have been reported for monkeys (Rosenblum & Cross, 1963), hamsters (Schiffman, 1971), goats (Walk & Gibson, 1961), and chicks (Shinkman, 1963). The observation that the chick can locomote, accurately peck (e.g., Cruze, 1935) and manifests depth discrimination almost immediately after hatching indicates the overall innate origin of space perception for this animal. In general, the body of research with species capable of independent locomotion at or soon after birth and with species incapable of independent locomotion at birth suggests that visual depth perception is unlearned (see Walk, 1978).

However, some studies, in which animals were raised directly on the deep side of a visual cliff, have stressed an important role for experience in the development of depth perception. The general results for rats (Kaess & Wilson, 1964) and chicks (Tallarico & Farrell, 1964; Seitz, Seitz, & Kaufman, 1973), indicate that rearing conditions can influence descent behavior (see also Nyström & Hansson, 1974). That is, animals reared directly on the glass surface over the deep side do not avoid depth as do animals without this unusual perceptual experience. Thus, with certain experience an innate behavior pattern can be modified.

For obvious reasons light restriction with subsequent testing on the visual cliff cannot be performed with the human infant. However, human infants possess depth perception well before they can crawl (which is required for typical testing on the visual cliff). Interestingly, depth perception may develop before the onset of a fear of heights. In one study reported by Bertenthal and Campos (1989), locomotor (crawling) and prelocomotor infants about 7-months-old were placed directly on the glass over the deep side of a visual cliff. Fear of height was assessed in terms of accelerations in heart rate. The results were that only the infants with locomotor experience showed the accelerated heart rate indicative of fear of heights. A fear of heights appears to come about shortly after, and probably as a direct result of, locomotor experience (e.g., Campos et al., 1978; Bertenthal & Campos, 1989). As Campos et al. (1978) conclude, "the human infant perceives depth . . . before he can locomote but does not manifest fear of heights until some time after he can locomote" (p. 151).

DEVELOPMENT OF OBJECT AVOIDANCE: LOOMING

An object hurled at a person in the direct field of view will produce an automatic avoidance reaction. The perception of an approaching object—signaling an impending collision—is of obvious biological significance to an organism. The complex spatial information that specifies an imminent collision with an environmental object is called **looming** (Schiff, 1965). Basically this information occurs from an accelerated magnification—a change in size—of the

view of a shape or silhouette with a rate of expansion that causes it to loom up as it approaches, that is, to fill the visual field. One apparatus employed to study this phenomenon in the laboratory consists of a point source of light from a shadow-casting device that projects the silhouette of an object onto a projection screen (see Figure 18.2). By the appropriate placement of the object between the light and the screen, the projected shadow can be made to undergo continuous expansion or contraction. Expansion or magnification of the shadow results in the impression of an object approaching at a uniform speed. Contraction or minification yields the impression of an object receding into the distance. Notice that nothing actually approaches the observer; the physical information *simulates* something approaching or receding. Research with this arrangement has been performed with fiddler crabs, frogs, turtles, chicks, kittens,

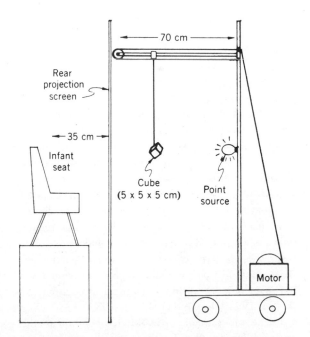

FIGURE 18.2. Shadow-casting apparatus. (From W. Ball and E. Tronick, "Infant responses to impending collision: Optical and real," *Science, 171,* 1971, p. 819. Copyright © 1971 by the American Association for the Advancement of Science.)

adult and infant monkeys, and adult and infant humans. Crabs responded particularly to magnification by running, flinching, or flattening out. Frogs reacted most often by jumping away from an expanding image. Chicks also responded to magnification with avoidance behavior: flinching, "back-pedaling," crouching or squatting, and hopping. Although their reaction was less consistent and conclusive, kittens also responded to image magnification (Schiff, 1965). Three species of turtles reacted to magnification of a circular image by withdrawal of their heads into the shell (Hayes & Saiff, 1967). Both adult and infant monkeys rapidly withdrew in response to the looming form, leaping to the rear of their cage (Schiff, Caviniss & Gibson, 1962). Alarm cries often accompanied the retreat of the younger animals. On the other hand, the optical projection simulating a receding form produced exploratory rather than avoidance or alarm reactions.

In a study by Ball and Tronick (1971) with 24 human infants ranging in age from 2 to 11 weeks, the responses to a symmetrically expanding shadow of a cube were various avoidance activities (e.g., blinking, moving the head back and away from the screen, bringing the arms toward the face, stiffening of the body, fear vocalizations). These responses did not occur for asymmetrical expanding shadows that produced the impression of an object approaching the infant on a *miss* path (in which case the infants showed tracking rather than avoidance responses) or for a contracting shadow. These results were observed in all infants regardless of age and were not different from the results obtained when real objects were used rather than silhouettes. Similar results have been reported with 6- to 20-day-old infants. The responses observed consisted of the eyes open wide, movement of the head back, and both hands moving between object and face (Bower, Broughton, & Moore, 1971; Dunkeld & Bower, 1980).

The function of an avoidance reaction to the optical information indicating a rapidly approaching object is clearly adaptive. Avoidance prevents collision. That the perception of imminent collision and its avoidance occurs in a number of animal species, and occurs in several species at very early ages,

indicates that it is unlearned. Moreover, it is further proposed that responses to looming may have a biological basis that is consistent with the view that the visual system contains functional subunits or channels for picking up and processing the rapid size changes that signal looming (e.g., Regan, Kaufman, & Lincoln, 1986).

PERCEPTION OF THE NEWBORN HUMAN

In this section we will deal primarily with some of the perceptual capacities and mechanisms of newborn infants that are functional with minimal visual experience. For the most part the focus will be on the newborn human, but where appropriate, comparative data will be included.

We have pointed out that the newborn of many species of animals meaningfully perceive a significant portion of their environment with little or no experience. Does this extend to the human infant? Empiricists have held that the newborn human sees merely an undifferentiated blur—that the newborn's visual world is, in the words of the nineteenth-century psychologist William James (1890) "one great blooming, buzzing confusion" (p. 488). However, the findings indicate otherwise.

That the very newly born can respond to the perceptual world is dramatically illustrated by a study in which an infant girl was tested for spatial localization three minutes after birth (Wertheimer, 1961). As the infant lay on her back, the click of a toy "cricket" was sounded next to her right or to her left ear. The response was whether her eyes moved to the right, left, or at all. On most of the trials on which eye movement occurred (18 of 22), her eyes moved in the direction of the click. Notice that when the experiment was over the subject was only 10 minutes old! The importance of this study is that it indicates that some spatial features of stimulation—spatially separated auditory signals—are picked up and are capable of guiding behavior, and that the perception of certain spatial features of direction (i.e., a rudimentary form of auditory localization) is likely innate. It also suggests a coordination between auditory space and visual space.

AUDITORY–VISUAL EVENTS

Direct evidence on the perception of correlated auditory and visual stimulation with somewhat older infants has also been reported. Infants 30 to 55 days of age showed distress on hearing their mothers speak to them while her voice was displaced in space (Aronson & Rosenbloom, 1971). In the experimental arrangement, the mother was located in a room with a window that directly faced the infant. The infant viewed its mother but by use of a stereo amplifier system heard her voice emanate from 90° to the right or left of its midplane. The results—that the infants perceived and reacted to this spatial discrepancy —indicate that the relationship between that auditory and visual information is perceived. It should be noted in this context that there is evidence that the newborn infant less than 3 days of age will also respond by sucking on a nonnutritive nipple in a specific manner to produce its mother's voice in preference to the voice of another female adult (DeCasper & Fifer, 1980). That is, with a specific experimental arrangement, newborn infants can learn to respond to produce their mothers' voices, and will appropriately respond to produce the maternal voice more often than another female voice. The newborn infant's preference for the maternal voice with only limited postnatal maternal experience suggests that a very brief period shortly after birth is significant for initiating infant bonding to the mother. Moreover, it is interesting to note that in addition to preferring their own mother's voice, newborn infants show a preference for a particular *Dr. Seuss* passage that was read aloud by the mother during her third trimester of pregnancy (DeCasper & Spence, 1986).

The perception of many spatial events concerning sound-emitting objects involve changes in sounds synchronized with changes in apparent distance. Thus as we see an object, such as an automobile, move toward or away from us, there is a corresponding change in its sound. Walker-Andrews and Lennon (1985; Walker-Andrews, 1989) assessed the ability of infants to process these two related sources of spatial information as specifying a single, unified event. They presented 5-month-old infants with two films side by side, one of an automobile approaching *and* another of an automobile driving away; simultaneously the infants heard a single soundtrack that either increased *or* decreased in acoustic amplitude, but was appropriate to only one of the films (i.e., appropriately, the soundtrack increased in loudness for the film showing an automobile approaching, and became softer for the film of an automobile driving away). Measures of the infants' looking behavior (i.e., fixation time) was significantly greater for the appropriate sound-matched film. That is, infants demonstrated a reliable visual preference for the film that was spatially synchronized with the sound, thus indicating that infants as young as 5 months of age can detect the relation between the sight and sound of a moving object.

Infants also appear capable of matching facial expressions with vocal expressions of emotions. Walker-Andrews (1986) studied this ability in 7-month-old infants using differences in looking behavior similar to the preceding experiment. Infants watched a pair of films, projected side by side, of an angry *and* a happy speaker while they heard a recording of either an angry *or* a happy voice. The lower third of the face of each film was covered so that infants could not simply match the voice to lip movements on the film. The results were that 7-month-old infants increased their fixations to a particular facial expression when it was matched by the appropriate vocalization. That is, infants who heard the happy voice tended to watch the happy face, whereas infants who heard the angry voice tended to watch the angry face. Interestingly, preference for a particular emotional expression was not found: infants did not look longer at the happy or the angry face, independent of the sound manipulation.

EYE FIXATIONS AND SCANNING

To make clear statements about the perceptual world of the human infant—particularly about which features of a stimulus attract the infant's attention—a series of studies was performed that focused on the relation between aspects of the visual display and **ocular fixations** of the infant. Salapatek and Kessen (1966; also see Kessen, 1967) exposed a black equilateral triangle on a white field to a group of newborn infants (see Figure 18.3*a*). In the experiment, the location of the infant's pupils was recorded relative to the triangle. A control group of 10 infants was similarly tested with a homogeneous black surface. The results were that the experimental group manifested more concentrated fixations than the control group, and the locus of their ocular fixations was particularly toward the vertices of the triangle (see Figure 18.3*b*). Most infants in the experimental group tended to fixate on a single vertex though not necessarily the same vertex on different trials. Infants, in general, did not scan the sides of the triangle. The general tendency by infants to direct their fixations toward a limited portion of a figure was supported by subsequent research with various geometric figures (Salapatek, 1969; Salapatek & Kessen, 1973).

As to the basis for scanning select parts of figures, Haith (1978, 1980) has suggested that more information lies at vertices (and edges, in general)

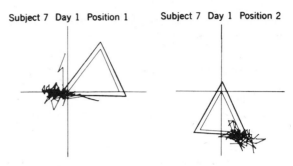

FIGURE 18.3*b*. Sample records of ocular fixations for a subject in the experimental group. The outer triangle represents the outline of the solid, black, equilateral triangle presented to the experimental subjects. (From W. Kessen, in *Early Behavior*, edited by H. W. Stevenson, E. H. Hess, and H. L. Rheingold, John Wiley, New York, 1967, p. 174. Reprinted by permission of the publisher.)

than at most other regions. Accordingly, by scanning those areas of a figure, the newborn also scans the most informative areas.

Scanning activity is subject to marked developmental changes. There appears to be a developmental change from fixation on a single element or limited set of features of the outer contour of a stimulus pattern (typical of the infant's scanning pattern exhibited within the first month of life) to a broader scanning pattern shown by an infant of 2 months of age. For example, Maurer and Salapatek (1976) reported that the 2-month-old is more likely than the 1-month-old to scan the internal elements of a display, such as the features of a face (see also Milewski, 1976). That is, the scanning of 1-month-old infants is more restricted to parts of the external contours with little fixation on internal elements. In contrast to both ages, 4-month-old infants scan both internal and external elements. Salapatek (1975) speculates that at about 2 months the infant begins to exhibit memory (e.g., Davis & Rovee-Collier, 1983; Rovee-Collier & Hayne, 1987) and perhaps accompanying general cortical maturation may enable more general scanning activity. Moreover, Maurer and Lewis (1979) report that 3-month-old infants can discriminate between grossly different figures lo-

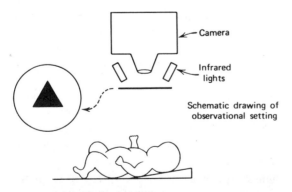

FIGURE 18.3*a*. Arrangement for measuring ocular fixations of the infant. The camera records the location of the infant's pupils that are marked by infrared lights. (From W. Kessen, in *Early Behavior*, edited by H. W. Stevenson, E. H. Hess, and H. L. Rheingold, John Wiley, New York, 1967, p. 153. Reprinted by permission of the publisher.)

cated as far out as 30° toward the periphery. That is, the 3-month-old infant can process stimuli with peripheral vision. It is reasonable to propose that there is a progression in infant perception from the focus on parts to the perception of wholes (see Aslin & Salapatek, 1975). That is, the increase in scanning with increasing age suggests that the infant may be integrating the individual fixated portions and features to perceive a form as a whole.

Although many questions of human infant perception remain, some of the important findings from these studies are that the newborn can select and maintain focus on a relatively circumscribed feature of a visual pattern and that the infant's attention to certain configural variations, such as contour and boundary, shows a developmental trend toward broader perception.

FORM PERCEPTION

Numerous laboratory experiments performed on the perception of the human infant newborn indicate that they possess form perception to a significant degree. A series of pioneer studies of early infant perception, particularly **preferential looking** and attention, has been made by R. L. Fantz (1961, 1963, 1966) based in part on the observation that infants show high attention and selectivity to their environment. An illustration of a form of the visual preference apparatus is shown in Figure 18.4. Generally, the infant is placed on its back in a small hammock crib inside a test chamber so that it must look up toward two panels, which contain pairs of contrasting stimuli. The experimenter records the movements of the infant's eyes to determine which of the two panels the infant looks at more often and for a longer duration. Such differences indicate not only the discriminative capacities of the infant, but they also suggest what sorts of stimuli attract the attention of the newborn. That is, preferential fixation of the infant shows both discrimination and selection on the basis of variations in form. Indeed, by the appropriate variation in the kinds of stimuli presented to the infant with this technique, it is possible to learn a considerable amount about early infant perception.

In one experiment, infants from 1 to 15 weeks of age were shown several pairs of test patterns (Fantz, 1961). The paired patterns, and results for the pairs yielding significant preference differences are shown in Figure 18.5. In terms of looking time, the more complex pairs drew the most attention. Furthermore, the relative attraction of the members of a pair depended on the presence of a pattern difference. Thus, there were strong preference differences between the stripes and bull's-eye and between the checkerboard and square, but not between the other pairs (i.e., a cross versus a circle and two identical triangles). Since these preferences were shown at all the ages tested, the role of learning appears to be minimal.

When pattern was compared to color and brightness, pattern appeared more attractive (Fantz, 1961, 1963, 1966). In one experiment, infants 10 hours to 5 days old and infants 2 to 6 months old were tested. Three objects had a pattern: a schematic face, a bull's-eye, and a patch of newsprint. Three were plain patches: red, yellow, and white. The response measure was the duration of the first fixation of each stimulus. The results are given in Figure 18.6. It is clear from the figure that infants in both age groups preferred the schematic face. Other findings with infants under 7 days of age indicate a significant preference, measured in terms of differential fixation times, for a curved member of a stimulus pair (Fantz & Miranda, 1975). Moreover, a trend in preferential looking for curved patterns in the newborn is evident throughout most of the first 6 months.

The preference for facial patterns was further examined with three patterns that were the size and shape of a head (Fantz, 1961, 1965b). One pattern had a schematic face, a second had the same features but in scrambled form, and the third pattern had the same amount of black and white area but in two solid sections (see Figure 18.7). The three objects were paired in all possible combinations and shown to infants, ranging in age from 4 days to 6 months. The results were that the schematic face was preferred over the other two patterns by almost all infants. Fantz's results are clear in that visual attention is controlled by some primitive distinguishing proper-

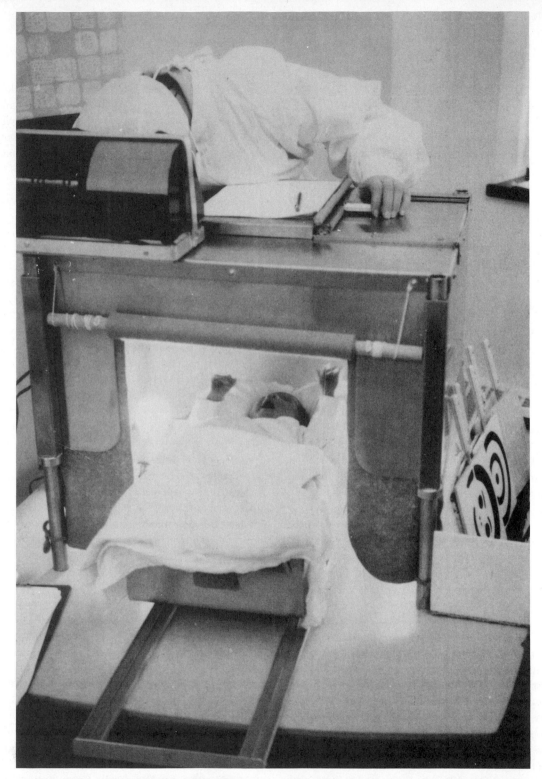

FIGURE 18.4. Chamber for measuring visual preferences in infants. The infant lies on a crib in the chamber,
looking at stimuli placed in panels at the ceiling. The
experimenter peers through a peephole and records the
attention given each object. (From R. L. Fantz, "Pattern
vision in newborn infants," *Science*, *140*, 1963, pp.
296–297. Copyright © 1963 by the American Association for the Advancement of Science.)

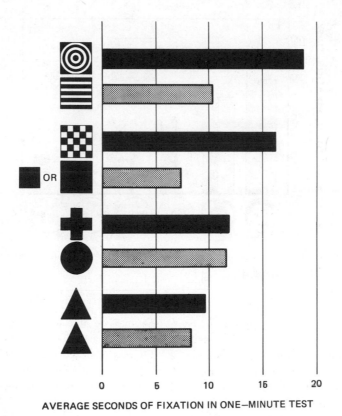

AVERAGE SECONDS OF FIXATION IN ONE−MINUTE TEST

FIGURE 18.5.   Pattern preference is shown by infants' reactions, measured by fixation time, to various pairs of patterns (shown on the left) presented together. The more complex pairs received the most attention, and within each of the pairs differential interest was based on pat- tern differences. (The small and large plain squares were used alternately.) (From R.L. Fantz, "Origin of form per- ception," *Scientific American, 204,* 1961, p. 70. Copy- right © 1961 by Scientific American, Inc. All rights reserved.)

ties such as pattern over color. Because the stimulus features of facelike patterns may have adaptive sig- nificance, it is tempting to consider the proposition that representations of the human face are innately recognized. Consider first, however, the stimulus complexity of a face. It contains figure–ground dif- ferences, contours, boundaries, edges, brightness contrast, shading, and so on, each of which may be an attractive or attention-demanding feature of the stimulus independent of its specific structural rela- tion. Furthermore, attention to facelike patterns over abstract forms has not been shown by all investigators

for all ages (Kagan, 1970). Although the evidence indicates a looking preference for facelike patterns in the infant, precisely what features of the pattern are critical for the preference is not clear. However, some empirical observations based on the visual fixation records of infants looking at real adult faces provide some age-dependent trends. Haith, Berg- man, and Moore (1977) recorded the eye fixations of 3- to 5-week-old, 7-week-old, and 9- to 11-week-old infants as the infants scanned an adult face. Their findings indicate that between 5 and 7 weeks of age there is a dramatic increase in face fixations, espe-

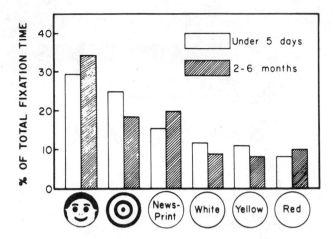

FIGURE 18.6.   Visual preferences of newborn and older infants for black-and-white patterned disks over plain and colored disks. (From Fantz, 1966.)

cially on the eyes of the adult face. Interestingly, when the adult was speaking, there was an intensification of fixations of the eye area by the two older groups; this suggests that the physical attributes of the face (such as lip and chin movement and lip–tooth contrast) are not sufficiently attractive by themselves to direct fixations away from the eye area. Perhaps as the authors propose the eyes become attractive to 7-week-olds partly because they convey socially relevant information and thus acquire significance for use in social interaction.

In any case, with increasing age, infants not only can recognize a person's face but by 4 to 6 months of

FIGURE 18.7.   Variations of facial patterns used by Fantz. Shown are a schematic face, a scrambled face, and a pattern containing the same amount of black and white as the faces but in only two sections.

age may be able to recognize a familiar face even when it is seen in a different pose or viewed from a different position (Fagin, 1976). Infants of this age can also discriminate between a happy and an angry facial expression (see review by Walker-Andrews, 1989).

COLOR PERCEPTION

It has been reported that infants as young as 3 weeks of age are capable of color discrimination (Clava-detscher et al., 1988). Infants also respond to differences in wavelengths as though they perceive the primary **hue categories** of blue, green, yellow, and red (where hue categorization is based on typical adult judgments). To demonstrate this, Bornstein, Kessen, and Weiskopf (1976) used a basic **habituation** technique. (In this case habituation refers to the phenomenon that an infant looks less at, i.e., habituates to, a stimulus that is repeatedly presented. A subsequent increase in looking time to a new or changed stimulus is termed *dishabituation* or recovery from habituation.)

Four-month-old infants were habituated to a "blue" 480-nanometer (nm) stimulus by fifteen 15-sec presentations. The infants' looking behavior (looking time) was then assessed on two physically different stimuli, one selected from the *same* adult hue category as the habituation stimulus (450 nm, also seen as "blue" by the adult) and one selected from a hue category adjacent to the habituation stimulus (510 nm, perceived by adults as mostly "green"). Thus, the blue habituation stimulus (480 nm), was the same physical distance in nanometers from a stimulus that to typical trichromatic adults appears blue (450 nm) as it was from a stimulus that to adults appears green (510 nm). The basic finding for this hue example was that infants looked more at the 510-nm stimulus (taken from a different hue category) than they did at the 450-nm stimulus (chosen from the same hue category); that is, they dishabituated to the 510-nm stimulus but not to the 450-nm stimulus. This indicates that 450- and 480-nm spectral wavelengths (both "blue" to adults) appear similar to infants and both wavelengths appear different from the 510-nm green stimulus. Similar results were reported when the primary hue boundaries of green, yellow, and red were subjected to the same habituation technique. These general findings support a claim that infants possess color vision and that the four primary hue categories of adults are matched by infants. As the authors state, "infants see the physically continuous spectrum as divided into the hue categories of blue, green, yellow, and red" (p. 201).

DEVELOPMENT OF VISUAL ACUITY

Visual acuity represents one of the most fundamental measures of the developing pattern vision in the human infant. Evidence indicates that it is a dynamic ability, displaying progressive developmental changes. Several electrophysiological and behavioral (or preference) techniques are used to assess acuity, each yielding somewhat different values (see Dobson & Teller, 1978). However, our purposes are well served by focusing on the method using preferential looking. The typical preferential technique for assessing infant acuity involves a modification of the forced choice preferential looking procedure of Fantz

(described earlier). However, the present procedures use grating patterns specified in terms of their spatial frequency (cycles per degree of visual angle, or c/deg). Typically, infants are placed before a uniform screen upon which the experimenter can flash a grating pattern on one side and a uniform field of equal size and luminance on the other side. The experimenter then records which side the infant preferentially fixates. A consistent preference for one of the two target fields indicates that the infant can discriminate between them. Typically, gratings are presented in order of increasing spatial frequency: when coarse grating patterns, of low spatial frequency, are paired with the uniform field, the grating is initially fixated; however, as the spatial frequency of the grating pattern increases, preference for the pattern decreases. The acuity threshold is reached when infants show no consistent or significant looking preference for either the blank field or a grating pattern, that is, where preference behavior of the infant for the pattern drops to about 50 percent. Thus, the highest spatial frequency that is preferentially fixated by the infant specifies the acuity threshold value. Results using this general procedure show that acuity increases rapidly in the first four months of life, from about 20/1200 (about 0.5 c/deg) at four weeks, to 20/200 (about 3.3 c/deg) at 17 weeks, to 20/60 (about 11 c/deg) at one year of age (Gwiazda, Brill, & Held, 1979; Dobson & Teller, 1978).

THE OBLIQUE EFFECT

The general acuity measures just described are based on grating patterns whose axes, with respect to the infant's retinal coordinates, are horizontally or vertically oriented. However, when the patterns are obliquely oriented, acuity measures are significantly lower. Moreover, when oblique grating patterns are paired with horizontal or vertical gratings, matched in spatial frequency, there is a marked preference for the vertical and horizontal grating patterns over the oblique ones. The reduction in acuity for oblique grating patterns as compared to either horizontal or vertical patterns is termed the **oblique effect.** It is an effect found in a number of species (Appelle,

1972), including the monkey (Bauer et al., 1979), most adult humans (Appelle, 1976; see Figure 18.8 for a demonstration), and human infants. Although there is some conflicting evidence as to its initial onset in human infancy, due in large measure to the various methods of assessment, a review of the evidence indicates that it emerges sometime between 6 weeks and 3 months of age (Leehey et al., 1975; Gwiazda et al., 1978; Sokol, Moskowitz, & Hansen, 1987; Braddick, Wattam-Bell, & Atkinson, 1986). In addition the oblique effect appears to increase with age (Mayer, 1977).

The basis of the effect is elusive. It has been

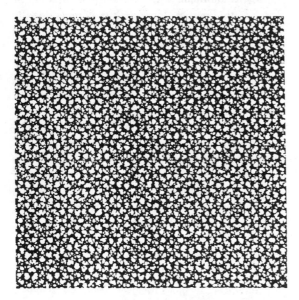

FIGURE 18.8.   Oblique effect in a modification of a painting by F. Morellet (in Davidoff, 1974). The linear segments comprising the painting are oriented about equally in a number of directions; however, the vertical and horizontal lines appear more visible than the oblique lines. The persistence of this effect can be demonstrated further by tilting the page in any direction: previously oblique lines, when made retinally horizontal or vertical, appear to stand out more clearly than do oblique lines that were previously horizontal or vertical. (From J. P. Davidoff; reproduced from *Perception*, 3, 1974, p. 47, by permission of Pion, London.)

attributed to experience with an urban environment (e.g., Annis & Frost, 1973; Mitchell, 1980), with its preponderance of vertical and horizontal contours over oblique ones. However, considering the infant's generally supine physical position and the visual environment it provides, it is unlikely that the typical infant's retina is exposed to more vertical and horizontal contours than oblique ones. Moreover, the findings of an oblique effect in early human infancy and with a wide range of lower species (Appelle, 1972) cast doubt upon a primary explanation based upon environmental biasing. Clearly, the weight of available evidence suggests that the oblique effect is not primarily a consequence of biased visual exposure during rearing but rather has an innate, genetic origin.

VISION AND AGING

Many of the just cited sensory and perceptual processes and functions that show a progressive, developmental trend appear to stabilize within the early part of the life span. However in adulthood, the efficiency of some visual capacities tends to show a decrease with aging, especially during the middle to latter part of the life span.

THE EYE AND AGING

A major source of age-related impairment in vision involves changes in the efficiency of some of the structures of the eye, namely, the cornea, pupil, lens, and the ocular muscles. Generally, these changes may make their first appearance between 35 and 45 years. As we noted in Chapter 11 in discussing *presbyopia*, with age the crystalline lens becomes sclerotic or hardens and loses its flexibility. Part of the reason for this is that the lens is composed of epithelial cells like those found in hair, nails, and skin that continue to grow throughout the life span. However, unlike the skin or nails, the lens cannot shed its excess cells and with age becomes densely packed and less flexible. The major effect of the loss of flexibility in the lens is a reduction in its ability to accommodate. That is, the lens loses its capacity to change its shape to focus upon nearby objects. With age the lens also becomes more yellow, which acts as a light filter reducing the amount of light reaching the retina; moreover, since yellow absorbs wavelengths from the blue-green end of the spectrum, there is a reduction in the sensitivity to surfaces that reflect short wavelengths.

The lens is the site of still another age-related condition, called **senile cataracts,** which is marked by an extreme reduction in its transparency. Cataracts are essentially a form of lens opacity or a clouding of the lens and are quite common in the aged population. It is estimated that well over half of the population over the age of 65 possess senile cataracts in one or both eyes. Although the exact cause is not known, there is evidence that excessive exposure to the ultraviolet radiation of the sun over the course of one's lifetime increases the risk of contracting senile cataracts (Taylor et al., 1988). Fortunately, in the majority of cases cataracts are treated effectively with surgery.

The effective size of the pupil also decreases with age so that in dim lighting the maximum degree of dilation becomes quite limited (e.g., Mayer et al., 1988). In fact in older adults the largest possible pupil opening may be less than half that of the young adult. This produces an appreciable reduction in the amount of light reaching the retina. A reduced pupil due to age is called **senile miosis.** In addition the pupil's response to changes in illumination—both for dilation and constriction—becomes sluggish with age. Accordingly visual function in both bright and dim lighting conditions may be affected.

VISUAL ACUITY AND AGING

Generally speaking there is degraded visual function and specifically a reduction in visual acuity with age (e.g., Pollack, 1978; Kline & Schieber, 1981). By about the seventh decade of life, the cumulative effects of an inflexible, yellowing lens, a diminished pupil, and a lifetime of eye use are sufficient so that poor acuity becomes a common occurrence (although

generally offset by corrective glasses). This is not surprising when we consider the estimate made by Sekuler and Blake (1987) that "by age 60 our eyes have been exposed to more light energy than would be unleashed by a nuclear blast" (p. 51).

There is also evidence that points to an age-related decrease in the efficiency of specific aspects of spatial vision. Using grating patterns (and controlling for visual acuity and ocular pathology), it has been observed that the sensitivity to grating patterns of high spatial frequencies decreases with age, while the sensitivity to patterns of low spatial frequencies remains relatively unaffected throughout adulthood (c.g., Owsley, Sekuler, & Siemsen, 1983; Crasini, Brown, & Bowman, 1988). Moreover, there is evidence that sensitivity to moving grating targets also decreases with age (Sekuler, Hutman, & Owsley, 1980; Owsley, Sekuler, & Siemsen, 1983). These sensory–perceptual reductions that accompany age may have serious implications for certain visually dependent abilities of the aging human. The performance of many routine, but critical, activities that require the detection of fine details and the perception of dynamic events, such as visually guided locomotion, and perhaps even postural stabilization, may be adversely affected by the diminished sensitivity to high spatial frequencies and moving targets. One obvious practical implication concerns traffic safety, in particular observing road signs from a moving vehicle: Evans and Ginsburg (1982) propose that young observers can discriminate a road sign at a distance 24% greater than can older individuals.

RETINAL EFFECTS OF AGING

Increasing age also brings with it the likelihood of damage to the photoreceptors at the retina due in large part to an overall reduction in circulation and blood supply along with an increasing possibility of disease. Such effects become noticeable between 55 and 65 years of age. A particularly serious retinal disease that afflicts the elderly is **senile macular degeneration (SMD).** The disease selectively produces a deterioration of the macula region of the retina where vision is acute, although generally sparing peripheral vision. The course of the disease builds slowly, progressing until visual acuity is severely affected, declining to between 20/50 and 20/100 or less. Within this range acuity is sufficiently reduced so that visual tasks such as reading are only possible with high-powered magnification.

A second visual disorder, **glaucoma,** is one of the most prevalent visual diseases and a leading cause of blindness in middle and late adulthood. Glaucoma is due to an abnormal intraocular pressure accompanied by irreparable retinal damage and eventual atrophy of the optic nerve. Among the major effects of glaucoma on visual function are a severe reduction in the size of the visual field and a marked reduction in acuity.

ties for effecting guided locomotion and detecting the information required for avoiding edges, drop-offs, obstacles and missiles are highly adaptive in the sense that for survival animals must "somehow discover where to go, what to seize, and what to avoid" (Gibson, 1970, p. 100).

In conclusion, we have outlined a number of perceptual capacities and mechanisms whose development, building upon their innate organization, provide the important foundation for the immense number of perceptual experiences that will subsequently confront the organism. It is the interaction of innate mechanisms and these experiences that is necessary for perceiving an orderly and meaningful environment.

CONCLUSIONS

Can we conclude that the development of perceptual abilities is due to biologically or innately driven processes, independent of experience, or that the development is principally the result of interactions and experiences in dealing with the environment? The discussion on the effects of biased stimulation on cortical cell organization suggests that many classes of cortical neurons develop independently of specific experience. On the other hand, for certain cortical neurons, at least in the cat's brain, experience with some broad forms of environmental stimulation (e.g., diagonal lines) is necessary for the subsequent perception of diagonality. Further research has indicated that the character of the environmental stimulation afforded to infant mammals in the first several months of life can affect the nature of cortical neurons and thereby exert a profound effect upon subsequent perception. With respect to the perceptual capacities so far described, infant animals of a number of species appear competent. The perception of form and pattern, features of space (e.g., depth) and events in space (e.g., looming) appear early, both in evolution and in age, suggesting that little if any learning may be required for their appearance. Clearly these are crucial attainments: the capabili-

SUMMARY

In this chapter we discussed the emergence and development of visual perception. In an effort to identify the origins and the developmental course of perceptual abilities, various experiential and genetic factors were discussed. Concerning the development of the sensory system, it was noted that visual restriction and biased stimulation in infancy may affect the organization of cortical neurons, receptive fields, and functional neural connections within the visual system: that is, these processes may be selectively and predictably modified by environmental stimulation. Thus if only certain forms of stimulation are available to an infant during a critical period in the development of its visual system, there may be disrupted and/or modified neural connections of its visual system and visual brain.

The possible contribution toward the understanding of perceptual development in the human by studies on restored vision with humans was proposed, and a detailed case study of an adult whose vision was restored was outlined.

Studies bearing on the capacity to perceive depth by perceptually naïve animals were outlined. It was concluded that the depth perception of a number of species of animals requires no direct experience or training. There is evidence that the human infant perceives depth before it can crawl but does not show a fear of heights until sometime after experience with crawling.

A number of studies were described in which the young of many species showed avoidance reactions to the optical information that specifies imminent collision with a rapidly approaching object—that is, to looming. It was concluded that learning does not play a significant role in reactions to looming. This same conclusion can be reasonably applied to the perception of certain features of space and form, and depth.

The perceptual capabilities of the newborn human infant were assessed. It was noted that the newborn human infant can respond in a number of meaningful ways to much of its perceptual world. It was noted that infants of about 6 months of age are capable of coordinating audio-visual events, that is, of relating auditory space to visual space. It was further observed that about by the age of 7 months, infants are capable of matching facial expressions with appropriate vocal expressions of emotion. The human infant also shows discriminative reactions to certain stimulus configurations and shows preferences for some stimuli over others. It was noted that the newborn can select and maintain focus on a relatively circumscribed portion of a visual display; in addition, certain features such as contours and boundaries affect the newborn human infant's attention. A brief section on the development of color vision indicated that 4-month-old infants possess color vision and perceive the adult hue categories of blue, green, yellow, and red.

In a section on the development of visual acuity, it was noted that whereas the visual acuity of the newborn is poor, it increases rapidly during the first year of life. Within this context, mention was made of the apparently unlearned preference and superior acuity in infants and adults for horizontal and vertical patterns over oblique ones.

A final section was presented on the effect of aging on vision. A number of age-related changes in the lens and pupil were noted that promote a reduction in visual function. It was also observed that with advancing age, there is a greater likelihood for the occurrence of certain disorders and diseases of the visual system. The effect of age particularly affects visual acuity. For example, human adults in the later part of their life span are much less sensitive to targets comprised of high spatial frequencies and to moving targets than are young adults.

KEY TERMS

Amblyopia

Biased and selective visual stimulation

Empiricism

Glaucoma

Habituation

Hue categories

Looming

Nativism

Oblique effect

Ocular fixations

Preferential looking

Restoration of vision

Restricted visual stimulation

Senile cataracts

Senile macular degeneration (SMD)

Senile miosis

STUDY QUESTIONS

1. What is the nativism–empiricism issue as applied to the study of sensation and perception?

2. What fundamental sensory–perceptual capacities appear prior to or within the first 2 months of life of the human? What structures and mechanisms in the newborn appear especially sensitive to the effects of experience?

3. Summarize the effects of sensory restriction on the developing nervous system. Consider the extent to which biased or selective visual stimulation modifies the nervous system and cortical organization (e.g., receptive fields) of the infant.

4. What is the relationship between the development of fear of heights and the perception of depth. What roles does locomotor experience play in the development of the fear reaction to height?

5. What is looming and how is it demonstrated? What general statement can be made concerning looming with respect to species and age? What is the functional significance of looming?

6. Examine the ability of the human infant to process and integrate concurrent and spatially related visual and auditory events. Consider the ability of the newborn to relate facial expression of emotion with appropriate vocal expressions.

7. What tendency do newborn humans show with respect to visual scanning and eye fixations on visual displays? What aspects of the visual display are most appealing or most likely to be fixated?

8. What is "preferential looking" and what sorts of sensory and perceptual abilities does it assess? What is the general trend in the development of preferences for and the recognition of human and humanlike faces?

9. Examine the capacity of infants to perceive the same hue categories as adults. Indicate how this may be assessed, using the selective habituation technique.

10. What acuity capabilities does the infant possess? Describe how acuity changes within the first year of life.

11. What is the oblique effect and what is its basis?

12. What are the general effects of aging on vision? How are the lens, cornea, and pupil affected? What are the functional consequences of aging on visual processes? Describe the age-related effects on acuity, taking into account the disorders of senile cataracts, presbyopia, senile macular degeneration, and glaucoma.

19

THE DEVELOPMENT OF PERCEPTUAL—MOTOR COORDINATION

In some of the research discussed in the preceding chapter, aspects of perceptual development were assessed by observing limb or body-part movement. In particular, an animal is seen to ward off a quickly approaching object (looming) or to move toward a shallow rather than a deep surface (depth perception). It is apparent that such behaviors involve the development of **perceptual—motor coordination.**

PERCEPTUAL-MOTOR COORDINATION

Normal **visually guided behavior** generally involves a motor response—such as intentional limb extension—to the pattern of optical stimulation. A question critical to the present discussion is: what is the functional relationship between self-initiated movement and normal perceptual development? An

425

important series of experiments utilizing a biased sensory input has been performed by Held and his colleagues to study the development of visually guided spatial behavior. Held and Hein (1963) raised kittens in the dark until they attained a level of motor maturity sufficient to perform the experimental task. At testing, the kittens were paired off and given three hours of daily light exposure in the "carousel" apparatus shown in Figure 19.1. The members of pairs of kittens were assigned to an **active** (A) and a **passive** (P) **movement** condition. Kitten A was placed in a neck harness and body clamp that allowed it to move in a circular path within a cylinder whose inside surface was painted in vertical stripes; kitten P was restricted to a gondola whose movements directly varied with those of kitten A. In the **carousel experiment,** the carousel was devised to provide identical optical and motion stimulation to each member of a pair. By means of the apparatus, the self-produced locomotor activity of kitten A controlled the activity of its mate, kitten P. In brief, the apparatus provided equivalent optical and movement stimulation to each member of a pair, but the movement was active and self-produced for kitten A and passively imposed for kitten P. Note also that kitten P was not immobilized. It was free to move its head about and could also move its paws along the floor of the gondola. However, the movements of kitten P, unlike those of kitten A, were not systematically associated with changes in the visual input.

The behavioral tests selected for assessing the effect of active versus passive movement experience included a test for **visual placing** (the automatic, visually mediated extension or reaching out of the paw as if to prevent collision when the animal is moved toward a surface), blinking to an approaching object, and depth perception on the visual cliff apparatus. Differences between active and passive kittens occurred on all tests. The onset of the visual-placing and blinking responses occurred earlier for the active than for the passive kittens. Tests on the visual cliff showed that the active kittens uniformly performed like normally reared animals, whereas the passive animals gave little evidence of depth dis-

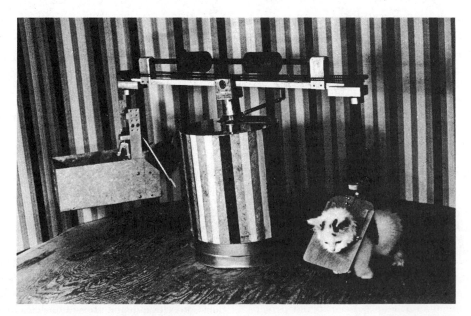

FIGURE 19.1.   Carousel apparatus for equating motion and consequent visual feedback for an actively moving kitten (on right) and a passively moved kitten (on left). (From Kimble, Garmezy, and Zigler, 1980, p. 94.)

crimination. That is, the active kittens did not descend to the deep side whereas the passive kittens descended to shallow and deep sides on a chance basis. The passive experience in the carousel must have interfered with the normal maturational process by which the responses develop. However, these perceptual–motor deficiencies of the passive kittens were readily remedied; after 48 hours of free movement in an illuminated room, the passive kittens performed normally on the tests. The major point raised by this experiment is that movement per se, in the presence of a stable optical input, is inadequate for normal perceptual–motor development; rather, variation in visual stimulation concurrent with and systematically dependent on self-produced movement is essential for the normal development of perceptual–motor coordination and visually guided spatial activity.

VISUALLY GUIDED BEHAVIOR: VISUAL PLACING

Hein and Held (1967) extended their research on perceptual–motor development, focusing on the accuracy of the visual-placing response. They contended that there are two aspects of the placing response: the mere extension of the forelimbs on approach to a surface and precise guidance of these limbs toward particular objects. From earlier research, they reasoned that although the visual-placing response will usually occur to the presence of an approaching surface, the *accuracy* of the animal's placing response requires prior experience with sight of the actively moving limbs. It follows that a kitten reared without sight of its limbs may show the placing response to an approaching surface but not with accuracy. To test this proposition Hein and Held reared six kittens in the dark until they were 4 weeks of age. They were then allowed six hours of free movement daily in an illuminated and patterned environment. However, during this time they wore lightweight opaque collars (see Figure 19.2) that prevented sight of their limbs and torso but that had little effect on their movement. For the remainder of the day, the collars were removed and the kittens

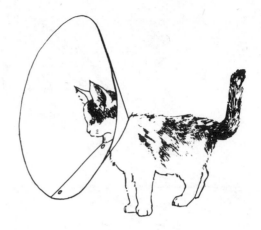

FIGURE 19.2.   Kitten wearing a collar that prevents sight of limbs and torso. (From A. Hein and R. Held, "Dissociation of the visual placing response into elicited and guided components," *Science, 158,* 1967, p. 391. Copyright © 1967 by the American Association for the Advancement of Science.)

were restricted to a lightless room. After 12 days of this treatment, all animals were tested for the visual-placing response with two different surfaces. One surface afforded a gross test for the visual-placing response. In this condition the kittens were carried toward a continuous surface. All kittens appropriately extended their paws—in short, they showed the visual-placing response. The second surface was a discontinuous surface interrupted by a series of cut-outs or prongs (see Figure 19.3). Use of this surface afforded a test of the accuracy of the visual-placing response in that it provided a measure of the animal's capacity to guide its limbs toward specific portions of a surface. Notice that if the animal's response is accurately guided by its vision, then its paws should fall on the solid prongs rather than the cut-out spaces. Of the limb extensions performed by the six experimental kittens, only half hit the prongs with their paws, whereas normally-reared kittens hit the prongs on 95% of the trials. The effects of the experimental restriction on the visual-placing response were eliminated after an average of 18 hours of free movement without the collar in a normally illuminated environment.

FIGURE 19.3. Kitten tested on discontinous surface. (From A. Hein and R. Held, "Dissociation of the visual placing response into elicited and guided components," *Science, 158*, 1967, p. 391. Copyright © 1967 by the American Association for the Advancement of Science.)

These findings suggest that visually guided forelimb extension in the kitten consists of two separate components: a visually triggered placing component that occurs when approaching a surface, which develops without any sight of the forelimbs, and a precise visually guided reaching component that requires experience with viewing of the limbs (Hein, 1980).

Generally perceptual–motor skills can be very specific to the conditions under which they are acquired. When the acquisition of visual guidance of movement is confined to one eye, accuracy in subsequent perceptual–motor activities is specific to the eye involved. That is, perceptual–motor skills acquired under the guidance of one eye do not necessary transfer to the other eye. Thus cats reared with one eye sutured shut for 10 months produce persistent defects in visually guided reaching, obstacle avoidance, and visual tracking when vision was subsequently limited to the deprived eye (e.g., Hein et al., 1979).

Some parallel results on visually guided reaching with monkeys essentially confirm what we observed with kittens (Held & Bauer, 1967; Bauer & Held, 1975). Monkeys were reared from birth, without sight of their limbs, in the apparatus shown in Figure 19.4. After 35 days, one hand was exposed to view. Visual fixation by the monkey of its newly exposed limb was extremely persistent and prolonged; and visually guided reaching was poor but improved with experience. It appears that early experience with viewing a moving limb provides the information necessary for the animal to match the location of its paw to target position. If movement and perception are not properly integrated, and if they do develop independently, as in some of the experimental arrangements just described, deficiencies in perceptual–motor development result. Extensions of this research to the human infant, particularly to perceptual–motor exploration applied to reaching and grasping, have similarly stressed the role of proper forms of experience (e.g., White, Castle, &

FIGURE 19.4. Apparatus for rearing an infant monkey without sight of its limbs. (From R. Held and J. A. Bauer, "Visually guided reaching in infant monkeys after restricted rearing," *Science, 155*, 1967, p. 719. Copyright © 1967 by the American Association for the Advancement of Science.)

Held, 1964; White, 1969; Zelazo, Zelazo, & Kolb, 1972).

We can reasonably conclude that the sight of actively moving parts of the body is important to the development of visually coordinated movements of those parts. Moreover, depending on species, such perceptual–motor experience must likely occur over a relatively extended period of time.

PERCEPTUAL ADAPTATION TO DISTORTED OPTICAL STIMULATION

A topic that is closely related to perceptual–motor development is the modifiability of perception to systematically distorted optical stimulation. The concern here is with the consistent rearrangement or alteration in the relationship between the external environment and an organism's normal optical stimulation. A familiar example of this occurs to the novice wearer of corrective lenses. The first day or two may be marked by visual distortion, perhaps motor disturbances such as inaccurately reaching or placing or, in general, poorly executed visually guided motor activities. However, these problems soon disappear. To the person wearing the lenses it seems that the total visual system adjusts, compensates, or adapts to the initial distortion, and the world as viewed through the lenses appears normal again (indeed, there should be an overall gain in that the lenses should aid the viewer's acuity). This general process of readjustment is referred to as **adaptation,** and it appears to involve a form of learning or relearning.

There are several important reasons for studying the modifiability of the perceptual system. It is of obvious importance to examine the manner in which rearranged directional information given to the senses serves to guide subsequent spatial responses. Moreover, studying the adaptability of the perceptual–motor system to consistent spatial displacement may contribute to an understanding of the origin and development of spatial perception. Clearly, the conditions that mediate adaptation may provide clues

and leads in search of the variables that control general developmental changes. Thus, there are factors common to adaptation in the adult and the development of spatial coordination in the newborn. It is possible that the manner in which the mature organism adapts to consistent spatial distortions basically re-creates the way in which perception normally develops in infancy. If this argument is acceptable, then the study of adaptation to visual distortion provides an empirical means for studying certain features of perceptual development. Although it is an appealing comparison, it must be qualified in view of the fact that the perceptual capabilities of the adult are far more rich and complex than those of the infant. Any number of compensatory mechanisms and preestablished relationships that normally are available to the adult may be used for the adaptation process. This suggests that with optical distortions in the mature organism, we may not be studying directly an original developmental process. However, with some reservations as to their generalizability, the findings that bear on perceptual adaptation do hint at the organization of the visual system and may suggest some developmental trends.

Generally, optical devices composed of prisms that produce precisely controlled transformations of optical stimulation are used to observe changes in the viewer's response over time on specific activities. Among the types of optical distortions are those achieved by the use of lens systems that optically induce inversion, reversal, lateral displacement, and curvature of the contours of the visual input. Howard (1982) has suggested a simple demonstration, using a wedge prism (see Figure 19.5) and a target-pointing task, in which the effects of lateral displacement can be easily experienced. As shown in Figure 19.6, several numbers are marked on the edge of a card that is placed horizontally under the viewer's chin. With the prism in front of one eye and the other eye closed or covered, the finger is directed toward a number on the edge of the card and then allowed to come into view. The arm is then returned to the side of the body, after which the aiming movement is repeated several times to each of the numbers in random order. The error in pointing may be very evident for the first few

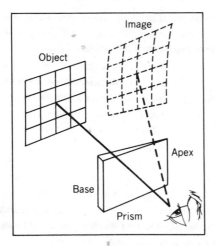

FIGURE 19.5. A wedge prism and its optical properties. The prism produces a lateral displacement of the visual field. As a result of the varying thickness of the prism and the angle of incidence of the light rays, the visual field appears expanded on the apex side and relatively compressed on the base side. In addition, vertical contours appear curved, particularly toward the apex side. Finally, up–down head movements performed while viewing through the prism induce an apparent seesaw motion of the visual field, whereas lateral head movements cause an alternating expansion and compression of the visual field. (After Welch, 1986.)

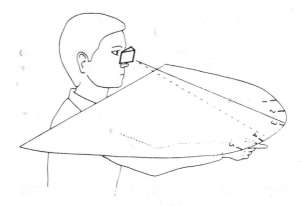

FIGURE 19.6. A simple arrangement, using a wedge prism, for demonstrating adaptation of pointing to displaced vision. (After Howard, 1982, p. 493.)

times, but accuracy is soon restored. Finally, when the prism is removed, it will be found that the first few aims will be off-target in the opposite direction of the error first experienced when the prism was in place.

In a classic experiment in 1896, George Stratton wore a specially designed optical system that produced an up–down inversion and a left–right reversal of the visual image. The subject, who in this case was Stratton, saw all objects reversed and upside down, as if the physical scene were rotated 180°. From a reading of his reports, there seems to have been marked disruption and disorientation of perceptual –motor coordination initially, but after several days he reported fleeting impressions of his visual world as normally oriented, and the tendency to correct deliberately and intentionally for movements decreased. With still longer experience with the displacing

optical system, a greater degree of normalcy was reported (Stratton, 1897a,b). In general, there was a strong suggestion that he was making some sort of adaptation or adjustment to his new visual world, although it is not clear from his account whether he began to "see" the world right side up or whether he only learned to adjust his behavior to a world that appeared reversed and upside down. The conclusion that some adjustment was made, despite the maintenance of a retinally distorted image, is strengthened by the fact that removal of the system produced an aftereffect, in that the world briefly appeared slightly distorted. Generally, these reports have been substantiated (Ewert, 1930; Snyder & Pronko, 1952).

Ivo Kohler (1962, 1964) reported an extensive investigation on adaptation to various forms of optical rearrangement. For example, after wearing spectacles that produced a reversal of left and right (i.e., mirror reversal) for 15 days, one subject reported the following: "It seems that everything in vision is the way it really is; the house, for instance, which I see through the right window, really appears to be on the right; and the parts of the car look just as they would feel if I were to touch them" (p. 154). Kohler writes that on the eighteenth day "very paradoxical impressions resulted. Approaching pedestrians were seen on the correct side, but their right shoulders were seen on the subject's right side. Inscriptions on buildings, or advertisements, were still seen in mirror writing, but the objects containing them were seen in the correct location. Vehicles . . . carried license numbers in mirror writing. A strange world indeed!" (p. 155). After 37 days, the subject

> *achieved almost completely correct impressions, even where letters and numbers were involved. In reading, for example, the first words to rectify themselves were the common ones, whereas those that had to be looked at attentively remained reversed. . . . After much practice, "mirror reading" became so well established and previous memories so secondary that even print looked all right, as long as attention was not too critical. (p. 160)*

It appears that individuals eventually achieve significant adjustment to optically reversed input. Moreover, Kohler reported that adaptation to spatial reversal was sufficient to enable the performance of complicated perceptual–motor activities such as skiing and bicycling.

Although it is not clear whether a real change in visual perception occurs—whether visual space appears unreversed or reinverted over time (depending on the nature of the optical distortion)—a reversing or inverting optical system does offer to the visual system a consistent and essentially intact source of information about the environment, although in an altered form. On the basis of the foregoing, human observers, with sufficient experience, appear to adapt. The important question here is: what are the necessary conditions and variables that produce the adaptation? We will consider first a brief and relevant theoretical account of perceptual–motor integration.

REAFFERENCE

Many researchers have stressed the importance of active movements for achieving adaptation to optical distortions. Among the first to formulate a clear

hypothesis was Holst (1954). Basically Holst argued, on the basis of experiments with animals, that a crucial component in gaining proper perceptual–motor coordination is the relation of *self-produced* movements of parts of the body to changes in the pattern of stimulation of the sense organs that these movements produce. He termed the sensory stimulation consequent to self-produced movement **reafference** (*afference* refers to sensory input). That is, the sensory feedback stimulation that is dependent on self-produced movements—in which the organism makes and observes the results of his or her movements—is reafference. In distinction, stimulation of the sense organs produced only by changes in the external world were termed **exafference**. For effective perceptual–motor activity, organisms must be capable of distinguishing between reafferent and exafferent stimulation. Exafferent and reafferent visual stimulation have different perceptual consequences even when they are optically equivalent. For an example of the distinction between reafference and exafference, consider the optically equivalent movements of the retinal image that result by voluntarily moving the eye versus having the eye moved involuntarily, as in the case of applying pressure to the eye with the finger. In the former case the world appears stationary; in the latter, the world appears to move. Distinguishing between reafferent and exafferent stimulation is accomplished by utilizing the information from the neural centers that control the movements of the parts of the body. (This distinction was also pointed out in Chapter 15.)

More to the point, to account for the organism's ability to distinguish an exafferent from a reafferent signal, Holst proposed that *efferent* impulses, which initiate movements, leave behind a centrally stored image or copy of the efferent signal (see Figure 19.7). The image, stored in the central nervous system, is called the **efference copy.** Thus, when the eye moves, an efference copy of the movement is available for comparison with a reafferent signal. Normally the reafferent signal returns to the central nervous system and matches the efference copy, with the result that the world does not appear to move as the eyes move. The critical distinction between the

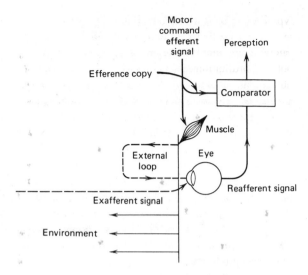

FIGURE 19.7.   Schematic diagram of the reafference process of Holst. An efferent motor command signal is sent to the muscle. An efference copy of this signal goes to the comparator, where it is compared with the reafferent signal. Note that the *exafferent signal* is externally imposed, uncorrelated with any motor command.

normal condition of reafference and the condition of exafference is that with exafference an efference copy is not available. That is, the exafferent signal is unmatched by an efference copy. Accordingly, it is this difference that enables an organism to distinguish between stationary and moving objects when both produce identical optical stimulation.

McBurney and Collings (1977) have called attention to the role that reafference may play in explaining why it is difficult if not impossible to tickle oneself. When, for example, you initiate the motor command signal to stroke the sole of your foot, an efference copy is generated that is matched or compared to the sensory feedback afferent signal induced by the stroking. According to the Holst proposal, this condition produces reafference and the experiential consequence of stroking oneself is to cancel the tickle sensation. However, when someone else strokes the sole of your foot (producing the same afferent signal), there is no efference copy for comparison with the afferent input signal of being

stroked: here the result is exafference. To tickle-sensitive individuals, the uncancelled exafferent signal produces the sensation of being tickled.

Weiskrantz, Elliott, and Darlington (1971), in fact, tested this application of reafference to tickling by employing a special device that enabled the tickling stroke to be controlled and administered to the sole of the bare foot in three ways: by the experimenter alone, by the subject alone, or by the experimenter, but with the subject's hand on the control so that the arm passively followed the movement of the tickling stimulus. The general results were that administration of the tickling strokes by the experimenter was most ticklish to the subjects, self-administered stroking the least, and the condition in which the subject was passive, intermediate between the two. Accordingly, these results indicate that a self-administered stroke is less effective in producing tickling than is an externally administered one and they are generally in line with the Holst position.

ACTIVE MOVEMENTS AND ADAPTATION

Held and his colleagues have extended Holst's notion on the importance of active movement to include any motor system that can be the source of reafferent stimulation. They have designed a series of experiments that compare the effectiveness of active, self-produced movements with that of passive movements to a displaced visual input in adult humans (Held & Hein, 1958; Held & Gottlieb, 1958; Held & Schlank, 1959). In one experiment, subjects watched their hands through a prism which produced an apparent lateral displacement of the hand and its movements. An *active* group watched their hands through the prism while they intentionally moved them from side to side. In contrast, a *passive* group watched their hands through the prism while they were moved passively by the experimenter. Immediately after several minutes of prism viewing, the subjects were required to perform a simple target marking task (essentially marking the corners of a square).

The results of the experimental manipulations indicate that only the group allowed active movement showed a compensating shift in the marking task and adapted to the displaced image produced by the prism viewing. Thus even though the subjects received the same visual input concerning body-part movement from active and passive conditions, passively imposed movement alone, without the connection between motor output and sensory input (i.e., lacking self-produced movement with contingent reafferent stimulation), appears insufficient to produce adaptation.

For movements of the entire body, a different experimental procedure was employed (Held & Bossom, 1961; see also Hay, 1981). Subjects wore prisms that displaced the retinal image 11° to the left. An active group walked for an hour along an outdoor path. Each subject in a passive group sat in a wheelchair and was moved along the same path for the same duration. The logic of the experiment was as follows: if prism adaptation is successful the subject should perceive the leftward displaced retinal location as being straight ahead. Thus when directed to point straight ahead immediately following prism adaptation, subjects should point 11° to the right side. The results coincide with the previous experiment: adaptation was significantly greater for the active group than the passive group.

An important aspect of active movement in these and related studies is that the displacement must be systematic. In other words, the causal link between actual movement and visual feedback, however perturbed or distorted, must not be broken. In brief, the necessary conditions for prism adaptation are that the rearrangement be stable and consistent (Welch, 1986). In contrast, if an arrangement is provided whereby signals from the motor system are wholly independent of visual feedback, that is, **decorrelated feedback,** adaptation does not occur (Held & Freedman, 1963). Generally these are signs of environmental instability—for example, where muscular movements do not produce corresponding bodily movement (the astronaut in free flight on zero-gravity maneuvers), or where passive bodily movements are produced entirely by external forces. Fortunately, under normal conditions of terrestrial life these events are rare.

COMPARATIVE STUDIES

Adaptation to the rearrangements produced by optical displacement techniques has been shown for animals other than the humans. Foley (1940) reported that monkeys can adjust some of their movements after wearing an inverting lens for eight days. Similarly, Bossom and Hamilton (1963) found that monkeys could adapt to a lateral displacement after two days. Cats (Howard & Templeton, 1966) and chickens have also been shown to adapt to optically displaced vision. Rossi (1968, 1969) reported that chicks, wearing laterally displacing prisms from the day of hatching, adapt after eight days of exposure to the displacement.

Of relevance to our discussion are studies that introduced spatial rearrangements by surgical modifications of the visual system. Sperry (1951), in one of a series of studies, inverted the eye of a frog. In one case, the eyeball was rotated through 180° and healed in this new position, producing a combined up–down inversion and front–back reversal. When tested for object localization, the frog reacted in the same manner as did humans with inverting lenses. As illustrated in Figure 19.8, object movement in one direction was responded to with a head movement in the diametrically opposite direction, showing displacement in both the up–down and front–back dimensions. In other cases, the eyes were removed, interchanged, and then grafted into position on the opposite side of the head, producing either an up–down inversion or a front–back reversal. The frog's responses to these anatomical displacements are shown in figures 19.8b and c. These inappropriate and obviously maladaptive responses (inappropriate to the physical environment, not to the visual image) persisted, uncorrected by experience.

These results suggest that there may be phylogenetic differences in adaptation in that not all species appear to benefit from systematic perceptual–motor feedback. Taub (1968) has argued that since a form of learning appears to be central to adaptation, then phylogenetic differences in the ability to adapt to optical displacements reflect phylogenetic differences in the ability to learn the necessary compo-

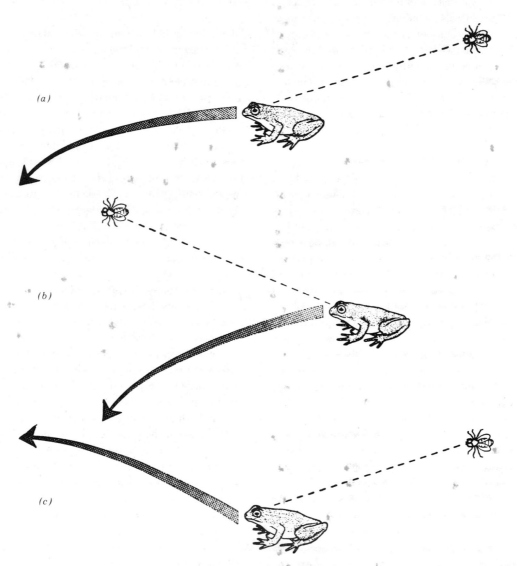

FIGURE 19.8.   Errors in spatial localization of small objects following rotation and inversion of the eye. (*a*) With eye rotated 180°, frog strikes at a point in the visual field diametrically opposite that at which the lure is actually located. (*b*) After up–down inversion of the visual field frog strikes correctly with reference to the front–back dimensions of the visual field but incorrectly with reference to the up–down dimensions. (*c*) After front–back inversion of the visual field, frog strikes correctly with reference to the up–down dimensions of the visual field, but incorrectly with reference to the front–back dimensions. (From R. W. Sperry, in *Handbook of Experimental Psychology*, edited by S. S. Stevens, John Wiley, New York, 1951, p. 244. Reprinted by permission of the publisher.)

nents for adaptation. In short, the capacity for adaptation and for learning are closely and causally linked. In light of the demonstration of adaptation in the chick, we conclude that the bird may represent the transitional stage of phylogenetic development for adaptation. That is, the phylogenetic level for the learning capacities required for the achievement of adaptation to a systematic optical rearrangement lies at or near the level of the bird.

ACTIVE VERSUS PASSIVE MOVEMENT

There remain many open questions and general reservations about the direct role of active movement and reafference for adaptation. For example, what is changed or learned when adaptation to optical distortions occurs? Is the site of adaptation visual or positional, cognitive, or peripheral? Harris (1965, 1980) suggests that the position sense is modified. For instance, in the case of image-reversing lenses, wearers feel their arms and legs to be where the lenses make them appear to be. That is, the felt position of the body becomes congruent with the visual input.

We must also note that there are studies in which passive subjects adapted to optical displacement (e.g., Pick & Hay, 1965; Singer & Day, 1966; Lackner, 1977; Welch, 1986). Indeed, based on the variety and number of studies that have demonstrated adaptation with passive movement, it cannot be concluded that self-produced movement in all cases is a prerequisite or necessary condition for perceptual–motor adaptation. Perhaps a statement more consistent with the research literature is that active, self-generated movement is considerably more effective than is passive movement in achieving adaptation, and it generally produces more rapid adaptation. It may be that the relative facility in achieving adaptation following active movement is due to the total increased stimulation afforded to the active over the passive viewer. Perhaps the passively moved viewer has less motivation to engage in visual exploration and, hence, samples less of the full range of stimulation available to the active viewer. Another explanation for the relative superiority of active over

passive movement for achieving adaptation is that the execution of active movements during exposure to optical displacement enables more effective pickup of the discrepancy between what is seen and what is felt than when passive movements are made (Lackner, 1977). For example, feedback from active movement provides information of the extent and the direction of the location placement errors, which in turn may provide a basis for correction or learning a new relation. Thus, according to this view, what appears to be crucial for adaptation is the availability of salient visual feedback regarding the mismatch between actual movement and its consequence.

In general, corrective feedback plays a critical role in motor learning and performance (e.g., Keele, 1986). It follows that the more information provided to viewers about the nature of their errors, the greater the perceptual adaptation to distortion.

SUMMARY

In this chapter we continued a discussion of perceptual development with a focus on the acquisition of perceptual–motor coordination and the development of accurate visually guided behavior. The studies reviewed employed a biased sensory input such as rearing animals lacking experience with visual stimulation concurrent with self-produced movement. It was noted that without such experience, there is a deficiency in the development of perceptual–motor coordination and precise visually guided activity. The findings from a number of studies suggest that if self-produced movement and visual stimulation are not properly integrated, deficiencies in perceptual–motor development may result.

Adaptation to systematically distorted optical stimulation was discussed. It was noted that the manner in which the adult organism adapts to consistent spatial distortions (e.g., as from viewing through distorting lens systems) may simulate the way in which perception normally develops in infancy. Research on this problem with humans indicates that self-initiated, active movement on the part of the subject, while not a necessary condition, is considerably more effective than passive movement in achieving adaptation to systematic optical distortion. One reason for this may be that active movement provides more salient information than does passive movement regarding the mismatch between what is seen and what is felt. A discussion of the role of self-produced movement and reafference in explaining why it is difficult to tickle onself was included in this section.

A brief outline of comparative studies concluded that animals below the level of the bird do not possess the necessary learning capacities to adapt to consistent optical displacements.

KEY TERMS

Active movement

Adaptation

Carousel experiment

Decorrelated feedback

Efference copy

Exafference

Passive movement

Perceptual–motor coordination

Reafference

Visual placing

Visually guided behavior

STUDY QUESTIONS

1. Summarize the studies that demonstrate the importance of sensory feedback from self-initiated, active movements for the development of visually guided behavior.

2. What conditions are necesary to produce adaptation to rearrangements and distortions of the incoming optical stimulation? Discuss the importance of systematic and consistent rearrangements and distortions.

3. Examine the possibility that an inversion of visual information of the visual field due to the wearing of a lens system will eventually appear upright and "normal." To what extent does such a possibility pertain to the acquisition of visually guided behavior in the infant?

4. Indicate how the use of a wedge prism can demonstrate adaptation. Discuss why the removal of the prism following adaptation briefly produces a distortion in a direction opposite to the "error" first experienced when the prism is used.

5. What is reafference and how does it help to explain the attainment and maintenance of perceptual–motor coordination? Indicate how reafference differs from exafference.

6. What is the perceptual difference between the changes in imagery of the visual field when the eyes are moved voluntarily and the identical changes produced when the eyes are moved by external means such as by someone's finger? Consider the role played by reafference in your discussion. How does this problem relate to the observation of not being able to tickle oneself?

7. By taking into account reafference, indicate how the tickling sensation can be reduced in a condition where someone must come in contact with a "ticklish" area.

8. Outline the experimental conditions for demonstrating adaptation to an image-displacing prism. Discuss the significance of self-produced, active movement for producing adaptation to the imagery of the prism.

9. To what extent is adaptation to optical displacement of the visual field restricted to certain species? What appears to be the transitional phylogenetic stage for adaptation?

10. How do active and passive movements differ with respect to the kinds of information they provide for promoting adaptation?

THE PERCEPTION OF TIME

The nature of time pervades many areas of intellectual thought, particularly literature, philosophy, physics, and biology. It follows that the perception of the duration of time as a subjective experience is of special interest to psychology. Of course, our main interest is not with the physical notion of time but, rather, with the duration of which one is aware. This subjective experience has been termed **protensity** (Woodrow, 1951) to distinguish it from physical duration. From the outset it should be clear that time perception is an oddity in that its variables are mental. There are no obvious sensory organs subserving it, nor any direct, observable source of cues that signify the subjective experience of time. Indeed, experienced time does not have the thinglike quality possessed by most physical stimuli. Although it is not fully clear whether the perception of time is a direct and immediate attribute of sensations emanating from the perception of temporal stimuli or whether time is judged indirectly by means of some mental process, a number of authorities on time perception have stressed the latter concept (e.g., Woodrow, 1951; Fraisse, 1963, 1984; Ornstein, 1969). That is, "Duration has no existence in and of itself but is the intrinsic characteristic of that which endures" (Fraisse, 1984, p. 2). If it is not an immediately given property then "time is a concept, somewhat like the value of pieces of money, that attaches to perception only through a judgmental process" (Woodrow, 1951, p. 1235).

Two main classes of explanations will be examined—the biological basis of time perception and time perception as a function of cognitive processing. Of course, these classes are neither mutually exclusive nor exhaustive.

BIOLOGICAL BASIS OF TIME PERCEPTION

The cyclical nature of many bodily functions is well known. A clear-cut example in the human is body temperature variation. There is about a 1.8° F difference in human temperature between the minimum at night and the maximum in the afternoon. In addition, for most animals many forms of behavior in some way reflect the cycle of day and night. The influence of the time of the day is obvious in many gross kinds of behavior such as general activity, the pattern of feeding and drinking, and in many other recurrent activities. Such activity patterns that regularly recur on a daily basis are termed **circadian rhythms** (from *circa*, "about," and *diem*, "day," because the cycles approximate 24 hours). Many biological cycles show a direct dependence on natural physical events,

especially daily and seasonal changes. The possession of a biological mechanism that varies bodily functions to certain temporally related environmental events offers a biological advantage to the organism, in that the internal rhythms react adaptively (e.g., bird roosting, hibernation) to periodic change (e.g., light, thermal) in the environment.

Understandably, a number of researchers have sought to find a chemical, neurological, or physiological mechanism in the nervous system that might serve as the workings of an internal **biological clock** or chronometer (Hoagland, 1933, 1935; Treisman, 1963; Holubář, 1969). According to this idea, biological time, as a matter of bodily functioning, determines experienced time. The concept of an internally directed time sense assumes that there exists some sort of automatic rhythm, occurring continuously in the body, and not easily or directly affected by environmental stimulation, with which the organism can compare the duration of stimuli or events. As noted, there is evidence of the existence of biological rhythms in a number of species of animals. These rhythms may serve as the candidates for a time-measuring mechanism. For example, periodic phenomena with measurable frequencies are found in the electrical activity of the brain, pulse and heart beat, respiration, metabolic and endocrine function, and general activity cycles (although many of these would not be good reference rhythms because they are markedly affected by external stimulation and hence can vary over wide ranges). Some of these internal processes have been the subject of research in time perception. In particular, the effect of temperature and metabolic processes have led to a theoretical account of time perception.

HOAGLAND'S HYPOTHESIS: THE BIOLOGICAL CLOCK

An attempt at a theory based on an internal biological clock or chronometer was made by Hoagland (1933, 1935). It is reported that he began his work when his wife became ill and developed a fever. After she made a temporal misjudgment, he explored the possibility that her high temperature had affected her sense of time. Hoagland had her count to 60 at what she felt was a rate of one count per second. Relating this measure of her subjective minute to her oral temperature, he found the relationship between speed of counting and temperature shown in Figure 20.1. Specifically, he found that a subjective or judged minute was shorter at the higher temperatures than at the lower ones. Thus, Hoagland's wife was experiencing **time overestimation;** that is, each real minute was perceived as longer than it ordinarily was perceived. This suggested the existence of an inner clock, a chemical chronometer, or pacemaker in the brain that controls the speed of the brain's metabolism and the rhythm of subjective time.

Hoagland's hypothesis was neither the only nor the first one to stress the effects of temperature on time perception. Earlier Pieron (see Cohen, 1964) suggested that if physiological processes are increased, subjective time will be lengthened. His pupil, M. Francois, put this to test by having some subjects tap a key at the rate of three times per second. When he raised their temperature, he found that they tapped faster. A number of studies have been performed since then in an attempt to explore the relationship between time perception and body temperature. Taken as a whole, the evidence is

mixed and the results are difficult to interpret. Some researchers reported no clear-cut relationship between time perception and body temperature (Bell & Provins, 1963; Bell, 1965; Lockhart, 1967; Wilson-croft & Griffith, 1985).

On the other hand, Thor (1962), Kleber, Lhamon, and Goldstone (1963), and Pfaff (1968), in basic agreement with Hoagland's notion that the internal clock accelerates when body temperature is raised, found that subjects overestimated the passage of physical time when body temperature was highest. As an interesting variation in the usual artificial employment of increased temperature (e.g., diathermy), Pfaff made use of the normal daily variations in body temperature during a 24-hour period.

Of course, it follows that time perception at reduced body temperature should have an opposite effect. That is, reduced body temperature should produce **time underestimation** and a real minute should be judged as shorter than normally perceived. Baddeley (1966) tested this with scuba divers in cold water (4°C or 39°F) off the coast of Wales during cold March weather. In the test the subjects were asked to count (to themselves) to 60 at what they felt was a rate of 1 per sec (as did Hoagland with his wife). The results pertinent to our discussion are shown in Table 20.1. Clearly, the subjects were colder after the dive and, in agreement with Hoagland's notion, counted more slowly. [It must be inserted here, however, that

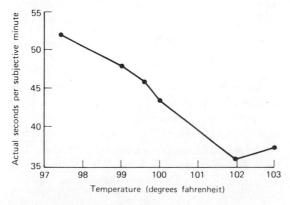

FIGURE 20.1. The relationship between body temperature and the estimated number of seconds in a timed minute. As temperature increases, fewer seconds are required for a subjective minute. (Based on data given in Hoagland, 1933.)

Table 20.1

Mean Temperature and Time Judgment in Very Cold Water

	Oral Temp. (°F)	Time Judged as 1 min (sec)
Before diving	97.39	64.48
After diving	95.03	70.44[a]
Difference	2.36	−5.96

Source: Based on Baddeley (1966).

[a] Notice that after diving, the subjects required 70.44 sec to count to 60; that is, they judged the passage of 70.44 sec to be equal to a minute. Thus, the lowered temperature produced an underestimation of time.

on the basis of an extensive analysis, Wilsoncroft and Griffiths (1985) have drawn attention to the rather weak and variable relation of body temperature to time perception and pose serious questions concerning any firm conclusions on this issue.]

TIME PERCEPTION AND THE EEG

A different attempt to establish the existence of an internal measuring mechanism based on a biological rhythm is given by Holubář (1969). He argued that the rhythmic activity of the brain, as measured by the electroencephalogram (or the **EEG,** which assesses the electrical activity of the brain), could serve as a time-measuring pacemaker or reference unit. In particular, Holubář concluded that the **alpha rhythm** (10 Hz) of the EEG serves as a fundamental reference unit for judging temporal intervals. It is of interest that the alpha rhythm, the most prominent human EEG rhythm, is a sort of personal constant, generally not under external influences, and unchanging with age in adulthood.

Other sources have also implicated the alpha rhythm of the EEG to serve in some form as the basic unit of time experience (Coffin & Ganz, 1977). An interval of 0.1 sec, which is the phase length of the alpha rhythm (i.e., one cycle of the alpha is 0.1 sec)—referred to as the **perceptual instant** or **moment**—has been hypothesized as the basic interval unit in which all input information is integrated and processed (Stroud, 1956; White, 1963). It must be noted, however, that the results from studies relating EEG activity to time perception are not conclusive (see Ornstein, 1969; Adam et al., 1971).

There are few hints as to what part of the brain may control the timing of events. According to Dimond (1964), the prefrontal area of the cortex is the site of the timing mechanism. That is, the comparison of temporally relevant information from the environment with the internal standard is performed in this area of the brain. In a related fashion Libet et al. (1979) propose that certain timing operations are localized in the somatosensory system (however, see Churchland, 1981*a,b*).

There are findings that suggest that the func-tional cerebral asymmetry outlined in Chapter 6 also pertains to time perception. Polzella, DaPolito, and Hinsman (1977) had subjects estimate the duration of dot patterns of varying numerosity which were flashed briefly to either the left or right visual field. Although the duration of all patterns was underestimated, the average of the estimated duration of dot patterns flashed to the left visual field was significantly less than the average estimated duration of patterns flashed to the right visual field. While it is inviting to attribute this perceptual asymmetry to functional differences between the two hemispheres, the role of cerebral activity in time perception, in general, remains far from clear.

DRUGS

There is evidence that a number of drugs influence the experience of time. Frankenhauser (1959) and Goldstone, Boardman, and Lhamon (1958) found that the administration of amphetamine lengthens time experience. In addition, Frankenhauser reported that caffeine was similarly effective in lengthening time experience whereas pentobarbital, a sedative, was not. The effect of the shortening of time experience has been observed with nitrous oxide (Steinberg, 1955) and other anesthetic gases (cyclopropane, ether, penthrane, and ethrane) (Adam et al., 1971). A general rule, according to Fraisse (1963), is that drugs that accelerate vital functions lead to an overestimation of time and those that slow them down have the reverse effect.

Among the most striking effects on time perception are those that occur with the administration of "psychedelic" drugs (marijuana, mescaline, psilocybin, LSD, etc.). Generally, these drugs produce a dramatic lengthening of perceived time duration relative to ordinary experience (e.g., Fisher, R., 1967; Weil, Zinberg, & Nelson, 1968). In the case of marijuana, this has also been demonstrated with the chimpanzee (Conrad, Elsmore, & Sodetz, 1972). However, whether the psychedelics produce their effect directly by influencing an endogenous biological clock or indirectly by altering various bodily processes is not clear. Moreover, these drugs are assumed to increase awareness and alertness, which could also influence temporal experience. We will consider the implications of this point shortly.

COGNITIVE THEORIES OF TIME PERCEPTION

A very different perspective of temporal experience is that it is the outcome of cognitive activity. Specifically, this view holds that the experience of the passage of time is based upon the nature and extent of the cognitive processing performed by a person during a given interval of time. Several such cognitive theories of temporal experience have been proposed (e.g., Gilliland, Hofeld, & Eckstrand, 1946; Michon, 1966; Kristofferson, 1967; Thomas & Weaver, 1975) but by far the most influential and studied one is that proposed by Ornstein (1969).

ORNSTEIN'S THEORY: INFORMATION STORAGE

Ornstein argues that the notion of an internal biological clock, whatever its location, is of limited utility in encompassing the very diverse findings that exist on time perception. His view is that it is more economical and integrative to assume that the reported effects of psychedelic drugs on time perception are due to their influence on cognitive rather than metabolic processes. Because they increase awareness and general mental activity, their administration could result in more information from the environment reaching consciousness. According to Ornstein, the reception of more information results in a greater perceived duration, which is in accord with the findings. However, Ornstein's notion extends well beyond explaining the effects of drugs on time perception. In general, his fundamental concern lies with cognitive manipulations as opposed to internal bodily ones (e.g., temperature, EEG activity). To Ornstein, duration is considered as a dimension of experience. Indeed, he argues that it is difficult to maintain that an increase in the number of elements that fill an interval—which lengthens time experi-

ence—also speeds up some vaguely defined internal mechanism. In contrast, an increase in temperature, which produces the same lengthening effect on time perception, can reasonably be viewed as affecting cognitive processes.

Ornstein's basic premise is that the amount of information registered in consciousness and stored in memory determines the duration experience of a particular interval. Conceptually, he adopts an information-storage or memory approach to time perception, assuming that the perceived duration is constructed from the contents of mental storage. Relating his central theme to a computer metaphor with regard to the storage space of information, Ornstein (1969) comments:

> *If information is input to a computer and instructions are given to store that information in a certain way, we can check the size of the array or the number of spaces or number of words necessary to store the input information. A more complex input would require a larger storage space than a simpler. An input composed of many varied items would similarly require more space than more homogeneous input. . . . In the storage of a given interval, either increasing the number of stored events or the complexity of those events will increase the size of storage, and as storage size increases the experience of duration lengthens. (p. 41)*

NUMBER OF EVENTS

Time perception described in this manner is quite amenable to empirical examination. According to Ornstein, one would expect that an increase in the number of events occurring within a given interval, or an increase in the complexity of these events, or a reduction in efficiency in the way events are coded and stored would each lengthen the experience of duration of that interval. Indeed, Ornstein has performed a series of experiments directed toward an examination of these expectations. He substantiated the findings that duration experience is a function of the *number* of occurrences in a given interval. He presented subjects with three tape recordings, each of the same physical time (9 min, 20 sec), that had sounds (500-Hz tones) that occurred at the rate of 40, 80, or 120 per minute. As expected, increasing the number of stimuli within an interval produced the perception of lengthened duration. The 40-tones-per-minute tape was judged shorter than the 80-tones-per-minute tape, and both were judged shorter than the 120-tones-per-minute tape. These results also have been confirmed within the visual (Mescavage et al., 1971; Mo, 1971; Schiffman & Bobko, 1977) and tactual modalities (Buffardi, 1971). That is, durations with more elements were judged longer than durations with fewer elements. (This also applies to children as young as 6 years of age: Arlin, 1989.)

Kowal (1987) reported an interesting finding based on the estimates of the durations of melodies. She found that sequences of musical notes that were judged to be more familiar, predictable, and organized were estimated as longer than their reverse melodic counterparts (i.e., the same melodies played backward). While on the face of it, the results appear inconsistent with Ornstein's storage–information-processing notion, Kowal also found that the familiar sequences were perceived to have significantly more notes than the perceptually unfamiliar sequences. Hence, Kowal's findings are consistent with Ornstein's notion that time perception varies positively with the number of events or elements *perceived* within an interval. Relatedly, Poynter and Homa (1983) report a positive relationship between duration estimations and the number of stimulus *changes* that occur within an interval of time.

Also congruous with this general notion is the well-documented observation that "filled" temporal intervals—time intervals containing simple stimuli such as sounds and lights—are typically judged longer than "empty" intervals—intervals consisting of only an intervening period of time between two bounding signals (e.g., Thomas & Brown, 1974; Thomas & Weaver, 1975; Gomez & Robertson, 1979; Long & Beaton, 1980). However, in an off-handed way the results of these experiments also apply to the "empty" situation where one is anxiously waiting for an event to occur, for example, the receipt of a letter, a person's arrival, or the results of one's test performance. The lengthening of time experience in such instances is attributed to the effects of anticipation or expectation. Expectancy reasonably leads to an increased vigilance with the effect that there is a greater amount of "awareness of input" and consequently a lengthening of perceived duration (Ornstein, 1969; Block, George, & Reed, 1980; Cahoon & Edmonds, 1980). This is summarized by the familiar maxim, "A watched pot never boils."

Interestingly, Ornstein's notion of duration experience is captured well by the words spoken by one of the characters in *Kinflicks*, a novel by Lisa Alther: "Perceived duration of time is directly proportional to the number of sensory impressions being received in the brain. If you're being flooded with sensations, more time will seem to have elapsed than if you're deprived of sensations. Big deal."

COMPLEXITY

To test the effects of varying the *complexity* of a stimulus on time perception, Ornstein graded a series of stimulus figures on a complexity scale based on the number of interior angles (see Figure 20.2). Each stimulus was shown for 30 seconds, and the task was to judge the duration of the exposure interval. A magnitude estimation task was used in which the standard stimulus (shown in bottom right of Figure 20.2) was always shown first and the subject judged the duration intervals of the other stimulus figures relative to the perceived duration of the standard. The results shown in Figure 20.2 give the ratio of the judged duration of each stimulus figure divided by the judged duration of the standard. In general, the less complex stimuli, stimuli 1 and 2, were judged shorter in duration than the standard, but stimuli 3, 4, and 5 were judged about equal in duration to the standard. It appears that as the complexity of a stimulus increased up to a limiting point, duration experience lengthened, and that further increases in complexity above that point no longer produced increases in perceived duration.

Further experiments examined the effect of

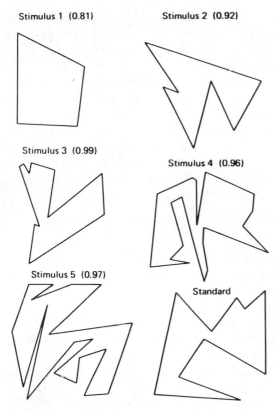

Stimulus 1 (0.81)

Stimulus 2 (0.92)

Stimulus 3 (0.99)

Stimulus 4 (0.96)

Stimulus 5 (0.97)

Standard

FIGURE 20.2.   Stimuli of various complexity used in the experiment by Ornstein. The values in parentheses are the ratios of the judged duration for the stimulus figure divided by the judged duration of the standard. (From R. E. Ornstein, *On the experience of time*, Penguin Books, Baltimore, Md., 1969, p. 60. Reprinted by permission of Penguin Books, Ltd.)

varying the complexity of a series of stimuli in order to manipulate the facility of coding the information. Two tapes, an "easily coded" and a "random" one, each of 5 minutes total duration were used. Each tape had the same total stimulus information, a series of 10 different sounds (e.g., a typewriter key striking the roller, tearing paper) presented 20 times each. On the easily coded tape the sounds were presented in an orderly fashion; each sound was played and repeated 20 times. In contrast, the different sounds were randomly distributed on the random tape. Each

subject heard the two tapes and then compared the perceived duration of one tape with the other. The overall result was that the duration of the random tape was judged on the average to be 1.33 times as long as the duration of the easily coded tape. Similar results were obtained, from essentially the same procedures, with visual stimuli (see Schiffman & Bobko, 1974). These results, according to Ornstein, suggest that an increase in complexity of the stimulus input produces an increase in perceived duration. Consistent with this is the report that time estimations are longer for more complex melodies than for simpler ones (Yeager, 1969).

TASK FAMILIARITY

Ornstein also explored the effect of some procedures that influence the processing and coding of information on duration experience. According to his notion, the perceived duration of an interval that involves the performance of a task will be shortened when the task is well practiced or familiar. In one experiment he had subjects work on a simple motor task, one on which a subject could easily achieve a high degree of proficiency. All subjects worked on the motor task for 2 minutes after which they judged its duration. In addition there were three conditions that manipulated the experience immediately prior to the 2-minute task. In one condition the 2-minute task was preceded by an additional 7 minutes of prior practice on the same task; a second condition allowed no prior practice; and in a third condition the 2-minute task was preceded by 7 minutes on an irrelevant motor task. As predicted, the interval of the well-practiced task was perceived as shorter than either the interval preceded by no practice or the one preceded by irrelevant practice.

ORGANIZATION AND MEMORY

According to Ornstein, perceived duration is also affected by how information presented within an interval is organized (i.e., coded and stored in memory), and the amount of stimulus information that is retained from the interval. It follows that the more information that is retained from a given interval, the longer its apparent duration. Relevant to this, Ornstein (1969) found that unpleasant stimuli are more poorly retained than neutral ones, and the perceived duration of unpleasant events are judged shorter. This can apply to the common experience that pleasant or interesting events are likely to be regarded in retrospect as longer than they were in passing. The reason may be that these sorts of events are better retained than uneventful, ordinary events; hence compared to ordinary events, they seem longer.

Mulligan and Schiffman (1979), in a direct approach to the role played by organization and memory in altering apparent duration, reported evidence in support of this aspect of Ornstein's theory. In one experiment they presented the ambiguous line drawing of Figure 20.3 for a given interval with instructions to the subjects to study and remember the figure. With regard to time perception, the duration of the interval was judged shorter if it was preceded or followed by a simplifying cue—a descriptive verbal label or caption—than if no cue was provided. In other words, the cue served to reduce the ambiguity of the figure and thus facilitated its memory. The results are in accord with the assumption that the cue, even when presented after the figure, should facilitate the organization of the figure's representation in memory: thus, intervals con-

taining stimuli that are well organized in memory are judged subjectively shorter than are intervals during which the same stimuli are represented in a less organized fashion.

Before turning from Ornstein's information-storage approach to time perception, we should note that his approach is neither the first to deal with temporal experience as a cognitive phenomenon (e.g., see Gilliland, Hofeld, & Eckstrand, 1946; Michon, 1966; Kristofferson, 1967), nor does it represent the sole cognitive view of time perception as evidenced in the next section.

COGNITIVE–ATTENTIONAL THEORY

An alternative notion to Ornstein's storage model of time perception holds that the focus of *attention* directly affects temporal experience. According to this **cognitive–attentional theory,** attention is divided between two processors: (1) a nontemporal **information processor** and (2) a **cognitive timer** that processes and encodes temporal information (see Thomas & Weaver, 1975; Underwood, 1975). Thus in a typical temporal task, observers divide their attention between the information-processing demands of the task and the processing of temporal information specific to the duration to be evaluated. It follows that the relative allocation of attentional resources to these two processes directly determines the nature of the time experience: the perception of time increases with the person's heightened temporal awareness and shortens with attention to nontemporal information processing. Based on this notion, temporal experience is a direct function of the amount of attention that is directed to the passage of time. As Fraisse (1984) observes: "The more one pays attention to time, the longer it seems. . . . Reciprocally, duration seems short when the task is difficult and/or interesting" (p. 31).

This idea lends itself to a number of laboratory and commonplace situations. Thus the perception of an "empty" time interval noted earlier (relatively lacking in sensory events or stimuli) may seem longer than a filled interval, that is, an interval filled with sensory stimuli in which a person is involved with the

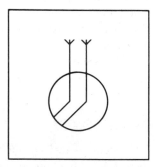

FIGURE 20.3. Ambiguous line drawing used by Mulligan and Schiffman (1979). The cue for reducing the figure's ambiguity is "an early bird who caught a very strong worm."

performance of some attention-demanding task (see Hogan, 1978). According to this notion, with a stimulus-filled interval of time, more attentional resources are directed toward meeting the cognitive demands of the task, and fewer attentional resources are allotted to the cognitive timer, thereby minimizing temporal awareness, with the result that time seems to pass quickly—duration experience becomes shortened. This is also supported by evidence that an increase in task difficulty results in a shortening of estimated time intervals (Zakay, Nitzan, & Glicksohn, 1983; Zakay & Fallach, 1984; Brown, 1985; Hogan, 1978).

Similarly with the performance of absorbing activities requiring concentrated effort (e.g., problem solving, test taking), there is an increase in information processing and a resultant decrease in temporal awareness; therefore time seems to pass rapidly. In contrast, when languishing in line, performing repetitive, boring tasks or experiencing the "watched pot" phenomenon (introduced earlier and explained in an alternative way by Ornstein's emphasis on the "awareness of input"), there is less information processing and a greater allocation of attention to the cognitive timer; the result is a greater temporal awareness—"time seems to weigh more heavily"—and temporal experience accordingly lengthens.

This analysis may also apply to the familiar temporal experience summarized by such phrases as "time flies when you're having fun." In such cases attention is more directed upon the activities with which one is engaged—that is, more directed toward nontemporal information processing—than upon the cognitive timer and temporal awareness; with less attention allotted to the passage of time, temporal experience is thus decreased. J. B. Priestly's (1968) somewhat impressionistic commentary summarizes this point:

> *as soon as we make full use of our faculties, commit ourselves heart and soul to anything, live richly and interestingly instead of merely existing, our inner time spends our ration of clock time as a drunken sailor his pay. What are hours*

outside seem minutes inside. (pp. 41–42, cited in Hogan, 1978, p. 419)

It must be noted that at present no conceptual scheme even closely encompasses the majority of the varied empirical findings. Moreover, the role played by select stimulus characteristics (e.g., numerosity, complexity, familiarity, organization and memory) and attentional-processing effort on experienced duration may vary with the absolute magnitude of the physical interval of time to be estimated. That is, using very brief intervals of time may induce a different relationship among the temporally sensitive variables than using moderate or relatively long intervals (see Poynter & Homa, 1983). In addition, with increases in duration, the role of memory and other less specifiable cognitive processes are more likely to be engaged (e.g., Ferguson & Martin, 1983). Clearly, firm conclusions concerning the relation between cognitive variables and temporal experience must be qualified in terms of the kinds of durations examined.

BIOLOGICAL VERSUS COGNITIVE BASIS OF TIME PERCEPTION

To review, there appears to be some kind of relationship between bodily activity and a time sense. Similarly, the time perception of complex events has been shown to be under select cognitive influences. How are we to resolve the obvious discrepancy between the two general classes of explanations? It should be pointed out that the sorts of temporal experiences and responses assessed by experiments that support an internal biological clock basis of time perception are of a very different nature from those employed in experiments supporting an explanation of time perception based on cognitive processes. The biological clock type of experiment often employs relatively brief intervals and utilizes response measures such as the rate of tapping. Perhaps the perception of very short intervals makes use of a very different psychological process from that employed in the perception of longer intervals of time. It may be that with very brief intervals attention can focus primarily on the interval itself and thus reflects the effect of physiological rhythms, whereas for longer durations judgments must rely on indirect cues such as the number and kind of activities. If this is the case, then two classes of explanations may be drawn upon: the internal biological explanation of time perception can most usefully be applied to the perception of very brief intervals, whereas longer intervals, necessarily perceived less directly and with greater reference to external events and nontemporal factors, fall under a cognitive explanation.

TIME PERCEPTION AND SPATIAL SCALE

A. J. DeLong (1981) has proposed an "experiential space-time relativity" where space and time are related to each other, each being psychological manifestations of the same phenomenon. According to this notion modification of spatial scale should affect the perception of duration. In a preliminary test DeLong (1981) examined the possibility that temporal experience is directly affected by the **scale size** of the environment that one confronts. According to DeLong, scale size refers to the size of an environment relative to the size of an observer. The method of production was used in which subjects were instructed to imagine they were engaged in some activity for 30 minutes while viewing three-dimensional architectural scale-model environments of one-sixth, one-twelfth, and one-twenty-fourth of full size. Each scale model consisted of partitioned rooms, with scaled-down furniture and scaled figures. Subjects were instructed

> to imagine themselves the scale figures in the space, to engage in . . . activities (such as waiting, relaxing and conversing) . . . and to inform the investigator when they subjectively felt the scale figure had been engaged in the activity in the scale-model environment for 30 min. (p. 681)

The results of this procedure were that subjects estimated duration in a manner that was proportional to the environmental scale: subjects who were asked to produce or "experience" a 30-minute interval while viewing a one-sixth scale-model environment actually produced an interval of about 5.4 min, a one-twelfth scale model yielded production estimates of about 2.7 min, and viewing a one-twenty-fourth scale-model environment resulted in producing intervals approximating 1.5 min. Although subjects obviously produced intervals that were shorter than 30 minutes, their subjective experience of time, in fact, was lengthened and directly proportional to the scale size of the environment viewed. Thus in the one-sixth scale model, each real elapsed minute was "experienced" as more than 5 minutes (i.e., 30/5.4); in the one-twelfth scale model, each elapsed minute was "experienced" as more than 10 minutes; and in the one-twenty-fourth scale model, each elapsed minute was "experienced" as approximately 20 minutes.

Employing more rigorous experimental procedures, Bobko, Bobko, and Davis (1986) essentially verified the general effect of scale size on perceived duration and extended the phenomenon to include two-dimensional visual displays that required viewers to process dynamic information continually within the display. Display scale was varied by use of three sizes of television screens, with diagonals of 0.13 meters, 0.28 meters, and 0.58 meters. Groups of subjects viewed each screen and engaged in a modified video game that was constant for all screens and fixed in duration at 55 seconds.

The results were that subjects' verbal estimates of the 55-second duration were a function of display size. This is shown in Figure 20.4, where time estimations are plotted against screen size. Note that the estimated time plotted on the ordinate is a derived score in which each estimation was converted to a ratio of the verbally estimated duration of the interval to its physical duration (i.e., 55 sec). Accordingly, ratios of 1.00 reveal perfect judgment, and ratios above 1.00 reflect an overestimation of the interval (i.e., a lengthening of perceived time and "time passes slowly"). The 55-second interval was overestimated for each screen size, and the magnitude of the overestimation *increased* as display size de-

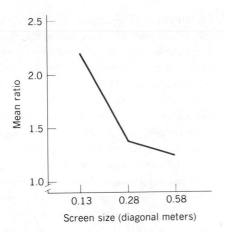

FIGURE 20.4. Mean ratios of verbally estimated time interval to actual interval (55 sec), plotted by viewing screen size. According to this conversion, ratios of 1.00 show perfect estimation, and ratios above 1.00 represent an overestimation of the interval ("time passes slowly"). (Based on Bobko, Bobko, and Davis, 1986.)

creased. Thus, the constant 55-second duration was experienced as *longest*—2.3—when viewing the *smallest* visual environment, the 0.13 meter video screen. Put in other words, clock time is experienced as longer when the observed environment is compressed: the smaller the scale of the visual environment, the greater the apparent duration.

Mitchell and Davis (1987) similarly found an inverse relation between scale size of model environments (consisting of model railways, living rooms, and abstract nonrepresentational interiors) and apparent duration: smaller environmental scale was related to a compression of experienced or subjective time relative to physical time. Overall, it appears that environmental scale size affects perceived duration. Although no compelling explanation for the phenomenon emerges, perhaps as Mitchell and Davis (1987) suggest, subjective time compression is related to differences in the *density* of the information to be processed in environments of different scale. Clearly experienced time and space have been shown to vary together in a consistent fashion. Two further manifestations of this interdependence are given next in the tau- and kappa-effects.

TIME PERCEPTION AND SPATIAL EVENTS: THE TAU- AND KAPPA-EFFECTS

A close interrelationship between experienced time and certain activities exists in that each can influence the other. Helson and King (1931) demonstrated that an observer's comparative perception of two tactually defined distances is influenced by the magnitudes of the temporal intervals associated with them: the greater the temporal intervals, the greater the experienced distance. This relationship between duration and distance is termed the **tau-effect** (see Figure 20.5). Consider the following as an example of the tau-effect: if three equidistant points on the forearm of a subject are stimulated (e.g., forming a tactual equilateral triangle) and the interval of time between stimulation of the first and the second point is greater than that between the first and third, the subject will perceive the distance between the first

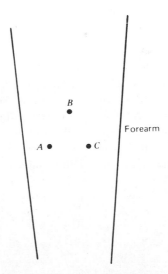

FIGURE 20.5. The tau-effect. Three equidistant points are stimulated on the forearm. If the interval of time between stimulating points *A* and *B* is greater than that between *A* and *C*, then the distance between *A* and *B* will be perceived as greater than between *A* and *C*. Thus, relative time differences can affect the perception of distance.

and second points as being greater than that between the first and third. In other words, if an observer is judging two equal distances, the distance that is defined by the longer interval of time will appear to be longer. A similar effect has been demonstrated in vision (Abbe, 1937) and in audition (Christensen & Huang, 1979).

A converse effect, in which time perception is influenced by the manipulation of distance, has also been identified and termed the **kappa-effect** (Cohen, Hansel, & Sylvester, 1953, 1955; Jones & Huang, 1982; Huang & Jones, 1982). Consider two equal temporal intervals defined by the onset of two successive stimuli (e.g., three lights arranged in a row as in Figure 20.6). If the distance between the first and second stimulus is greater than that between the second and third, the first interval will be perceived as being longer in duration. This also has been shown with audition (Cohen, Hansel & Sylvester, 1954) and with touch (Suto, 1955).

SUMMARY

In this chapter we have examined the perception of time or protensity. Two main classes of explanations were reviewed. A biological approach to time perception is founded on the cyclical nature of many bodily functions and processes, such as temperature variation, electrical activity of the brain, and general metabolic activities. The assumption made by its proponents is that there is some internal biological clock that controls the speed of metabolic processes and subjective time. It was noted that the findings bearing on this approach are equivocal.

A second class of explanation contends that time perception is a function of the kind and degree of cognitive processing and attentional focus. According to a major version (Ornstein's theory) of this notion, perceived duration is constructed from the contents of mental storage. Thus, the amount of information registered in consciousness and stored in memory determines the duration experience for a particular time interval. It was noted that for the present, a cognitive approach to explaining time perception serves as a useful scheme encompassing a broad range of findings.

An alternative approach to Ornstein's notion was also discussed that holds that attention is divided between two processors: an information processor and a temporal processor. According to this proposal, the less attention paid to the processing of information and the more attention directed to the passage of time (e.g., "endlessly" waiting in line), the greater is the temporal experience, whereas when attention is focused upon an absorbing task (e.g., solving problems, taking a test) temporal experience shortens.

It was also noted that temporal experience is affected by the scale size of the environment—the size of the environment relative to the size of the observer. Based on several studies it was concluded

FIGURE 20.6.   The kappa-effect. The three lights *A*, *B*, and *C* are successively flashed at equal temporal intervals. If the distance between lights *A* and *B* is greater than between *B* and *C*, then the interval of time between the flashing of lights *A* and *B* will be perceived as longer than the interval between *B* and *C*. Thus, the relative distance between stimuli can affect the perception of time.

that physical time is experienced as longer when the scale size of the environment decreases—in a form of experiential "space-time relativity." Finally, the relation of time perception to spatial events was outlined: the tau-effect refers to the effect of duration on perceived distance; the kappa-effect refers to the effect of physical distance on perceived duration.

KEY TERMS

Alpha rhythm

Biological clock

Circadian rhythms

Cognitive—attentional theory

Cognitive timer

EEG

Hoagland's hypothesis

Information processor

Kappa-effect

Perceptual instant (moment)

Protensity

Scale size

Tau-effect

Time overestimation

Time underestimation

STUDY QUESTIONS

1. Distinguish between physical time and protensity. What sensory structures and physical processes may mediate the subjective experience of time? Examine the possibility that the experience of time is an immediately given attribute derived from perception.

2. Identify periodic or cyclic variations in bodily processes, including circadian rhythms, that could serve as biological chronometers.

3. Outline Hoagland's biological clock theory of time perception and summarize the evidence in its support. How does variation in body temperature affect time perception? How does the EEG index time experience? Examine the role of the alpha rhythm of the EEG on the perceptual moment.

4. Summarize the effects of stimulant-type and depressant-type drugs on the experience of time.

5. Outline Ornstein's information-storage theory of time perception and indicate how it encorporates the effects of biological variations on time experience. Identify and examine the information-processing demands that influence time perception. Describe the effect of the number of events, stimulus complexity, task familiarity, and the role of memory on time experience.

6. How does the cognitive—attentional theory compare to Ornstein's storage model? Describe how the allocation of attention affects time experience. What is the "cognitive timer"?

7. Based on the cognitive—attentional theory, explain the experiences summarized in the phrases "A watched pot never boils" and "Time flies when you're having fun."

8. Describe the tau- and kappa-effects.

9. Discuss the effect of the spatial scale (or scale size) on time experience.

10. Relate over- and underestimation of time to the conditions when time passes quickly and slowly.

21

SENSATION, PERCEPTION, AND ATTENTION: SELECTED TOPICS

In this final chapter we examine some select issues and topics closely linked to sensation and perception, but ones that are often subsumed under such general headings as memory, cognition, information processing, and attention. However, because of their particular relevence to sensation and perception much of our discussion will focus on topics that typically fall under the heading of selective attention.

As we have encountered in a number of contexts and discussions, perception involves much more

451

than sense organ function. It is the case that adjustments of sensory organs are generally observable when attention is directed; for example, the eye scans the ambient scenery, the nose sniffs for odors, and the head turns toward the direction of a sound. However, the organism also attentively selects, evaluates, organizes, and transforms the incoming sensory input, making use of processes that are not readily observable. Some input is ignored, whereas a portion of the input becomes the focus of attention. For some species, the general selection, judging, and processing of the input information may be inflexibly automatic, whereas for others, such as the human, it is often heavily influenced by such factors as emotions, memories, and expectations. However, no matter what determines the allocation of attention, all organisms confront the same general problem: selectively apportioning attention to enhance the input of relevant information.

SELECTIVE ATTENTION

The individual's perceptual systems are continually fed with sensory information, but he or she does not and cannot attend to all the stimulation. Because of limitations in the amount of information that can be processed effectively (as well as limitations set by structural and biological factors), the individual must focus selectively on relevant stimuli and reject distracting and extraneous ones. Indeed, a basic aspect of **selective attention** is that of selective information reduction.

DIVIDED ATTENTION

The situations in which we confront multiple and competing inputs—where stimulation exceeds our processing capacity—are quite common. However, for the most part we deal with conflicting inputs—that is, the problem of **divided attention**—by focusing on a single input and apparently ignore the remaining ones.

Selective Listening: The Cocktail Party Phenomenon   One of the more common forms of coping with

the demands of divided attention occurs with audition and is sometimes referred to as the **cocktail party phenomenon** (Cherry, 1953; Cherry & Bowles, 1960). This particular problem is exemplified in the perceptual behavior that occurs in a crowded room with numerous and different conversations surrounding the listener. The problem, of course, is one of **selective listening,** the goal being to shut out all voices and noise except for a single focal conversation of interest. Clearly, on one level of analysis this is possible, but it is incorrect to assume that the nonfocal signals are totally ignored. Indeed, selective intrusions to the focal message may occur. Specifically, if the focal message does not require continuous monitoring, it is quite possible to switch attention from focal to nonfocal messages rather rapidly if something relevant is perceived in the nonfocal signals. It is as if we are continuously sampling the acoustic environment for meaningful signals. In short, the cocktail party phenomenon demonstrates not only the operation of selective attention, but it demonstrates the ongoing ability to monitor the complex sensory input to extract messages from the nonfocal input that may be relevant or important to the individual. Indeed, because of limited processing capacity this points out the functional, adaptive value of selective attention. It enables the selection of meaningful, interesting stimuli for direct processing while allowing the individual to monitor continuously the total input for relevance.

The cocktail party phenomenon, as a problem of selective attention, has been subject to laboratory study using a technique termed **shadowing** (Cherry, 1953). Basically, the subject simultaneously listens to two separate, recorded verbal messages, each presented to a different ear (i.e., a **dichotic listening** task); for example, one message is presented to the right ear and the other to the left. The subject is instructed to repeat aloud (i.e., to *shadow*) only one message as it occurs. This technique forces attention to one channel of incoming information.

Perception of Unattended Information   When we confront multiple messages, such as in a crowd, we generally attend or shadow one message, the primary one, and apparently ignore or filter out the secondary messages. We cannot, however, dismiss the perceptual relevance of the secondary messages.

In the laboratory example, the nonshadowed message is generally recognized as speech, although detailed aspects such as phrases, individual words, or semantic content (meaning) cannot be identified. However, some broad speaker characteristics are often perceived, such as a switch from a male to a female speaker or from speech to a pure tone. Thus, although focus is on the shadowed message, certain broad physical properties of the nonshadowed message are preceived (Cherry, 1953; Treisman & Riley, 1969).

There is evidence that the nonshadowed message, in fact, is processed and is briefly available, but because it is unattended, it remains only momentarily in an auditory or **echoic memory** and soon decays or fades. A direct assessment of this is revealed when both the competing input channels are terminated and immediately (within 5 sec or less after termination), a report of the material in the nonshadowed ear is obtained. The typical result is that subjects can report the last several words or digits (e.g., Norman, 1969; Glucksberg & Cowen, 1970; McKay, 1973).

Under certain conditions some meaningful information from the nonshadowed message may also be extracted by the listener. Moray (1959), for example, observed that portions of the nonshadowed message were perceived if the message was prefaced with the listener's own name. Along the same lines Treisman (1960) found that if the secondary message was semantically related to, or put in context with, information in the shadowed message, listeners would inadvertently switch attention and very briefly follow the nonshadowed secondary message. An outline of the experimental arrangement is schematized in Figure 21.1. The listener is instructed to shadow the message presented to the left ear (e.g., "I-saw-the-girl"), yet when the contextually consistent message ("jumping-in-the-street") continues on in the nonshadowed, presumably unattended ear, the listener occasionally shadows and repeats one or two words from that secondary message. The implication of this experiment is that context and meaning influence selective attention and that the nonshadowed material presented to the unattended ear is continually processed and analyzed for meaning (see also Forster & Govier, 1978).

Lewis (1970) also demonstrated with a dichotic task that if listeners shadowed a random list of words, the time necessary to repeat a given word delivered to the attended ear increased if a simultaneously presented word to the unattended ear was semantically

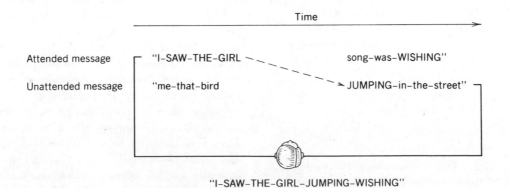

FIGURE 21.1. Schematic of Treisman's (1960) experiment on contextual influences of unattended information. The subject-listener is instructed to shadow the message presented to the left ear (i.e., "I-saw-the-girl-song-was-wishing"). The contextually sensible message spans both ears and causes the listener to switch inadvertently from the attended message to the unattended message (shown by the dashed arrow). The words spoken by the subject-listener are given in capital letters.

or meaningfully related to the shadowed word. Collectively these studies provide strong evidence that there is some semantic processing of the unattended input. Generally, it appears, then, that the secondary message is not ignored or only processed for physical–structural characteristics, but, at least in part, it is also analyzed for meaning.

Selective Looking   A visual analog to the selective listening involved in dichotic tasks, namely **selective looking,** was explored by Neisser and Becklen (1975). They videotaped two simple "games" (one involving hand touching and one involving ball throwing as shown in Figure 21.2*a* and *b*) and simultaneously presented them superimposed over each other as shown in Figure 21.2*c*. Viewers were instructed to attend to one of the games and to ignore the other. The results were that viewers were quite capable of attending to either one of the games while ignoring the other. Indeed it was nearly as easy

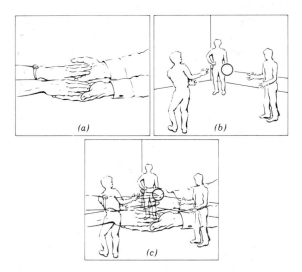

FIGURE 21.2.   Presentations used to assess selective looking. (*a*) Hand game; (*b*) ball throwing game; (*c*) simultaneous presentation of (*a*) and (*b*). (From U. Neisser and R. Becklen, "Selective looking: attending to visually specified events," *Cognitive Psychology*, 7, 1975, p. 485. Reprinted by permission of the first author and Academic Press.)

to follow one game when it was superimposed over another as when it was shown alone. In contrast when instructed to monitor *both* games, performance was very poor. Interestingly, as in the selective listening research, on occasion information from the unattended visual event may be perceived (Becklen & Cerone, 1983).

VISUAL SEARCH

Among the factors that affect selective attention in vision is the nature of the target and the background. One means of studying this aspect of attention is with a **visual search** or scanning task (Neisser, 1963, 1964). Typically, the subject is instructed to search through a list of background items (see Figure 21.3) for a particular target letter and to indicate the moment when it is found by stopping a timer.

In an extensive series of experiments, Neisser and his colleagues (1963, 1964; Neisser, Novick, & Lazar, 1963; Neisser & Stoper, 1965; Neisser & Beller, 1965) examined the role played by a number of stimulus factors in the visual search task. In one of the simpler conditions, subjects were instructed to search through a list for the presence of a specific target (e.g., the letter *K* in list *a* of Figure 21.3). This required less time than scanning a list for the *absence* of a letter in a line (e.g., searching for the line in list *b* that does not contain the letter *Q*). In the former task (list *a*, Figure 21.3), it is likely that little identification of the background material is needed, thus enabling a faster search time. However, for list *b*, the subject must scan each line in order to check for the *absence* of the critical target letter. A further finding indicates that the relation of the target's configuration or shape to that of the background context plays an important role in the search task. Thus, as illustrated in list *c* of Figure 21.3, the letter *Z* is seen more easily against a background of generally rounded letters than in a context of generally straight ones (see *d* of Figure 21.3). Neisser (1964) reports that subjects found the *Z* twice as quickly in the context of rounded letters as in the context of straight ones where more extensive and time-consuming processing is required. Thus,

(a)	(b)	(c)	(d)
QBVC	TZDFQB	DQRCGU	EXWMVI
VARP	QLHBMZ	QDOCGU	IXEMWV
LRPA	QMXBJD	CGUROQ	VXWEMI
SGHL	RVZHSQ	OCDURQ	MXVEWI
MVRJ	STFMQZ	UOCGQD	XVWMEI
GADB	RVXSQM	RGQCOU	MWXVIE
PCME	MQBJFT	GRUDQO	VIMEXW
ZODW	MVZXLQ	GODUCQ	EXVWIM
HDBR	RTBXQH	QCURDO	VWMIEX
BVDZ	BLQSZX	DUCOQG	VMWIEX
XSCQ	QSVFDJ	CGRDQU	XVWMEI
SDJU	FLDVZT	UDRCOQ	WXVEMI
PODC	BQHMDX	GQCORU	XMEWIV
ZVBP	BMFDQH	GOQUCD	MXIVEW
PEVZ	QHLJZT	GDQUOC	VEWMIX
SLRA	TQSHRL	URDCGO	EMVXWI
JCEN	BMQHZJ	GODRQC	IVWMEX
XLRD	RTBJZQ	GRUQDO	IEVMWX
XBOD	FQDLXH	DUZGRO	WVZMXE
PHMU	XJHSVQ	UCGROD	XEMIWV
ZHFK	MZRJDQ	ODUGQR	WXIMEV
PNJW	XVQRMB	QCDUGO	EMWIVX
CQXT	QMXLSD	CQOGRD	IVEMXW
GHNR	DSZHQR	QUGCDR	IVMXEW
IXYD	FJQSMV	URDGQO	EWVMIX
(a)	(b)	(c)	(d)

FIGURE 21.3.   Portions of sample lists used in various search tasks by Neisser (1963, 1964). (a) The target is the letter *K*. (b) The target line is the one that does *not* include a *Q*. For (c) and (d), the target is the letter *Z*. The target letter is seen more easily in list (c), a context of relatively rounded letters, than in (d), a list composed of letters containing straight lines.

search time is shorter if the features that distinguish targets from their backgrounds or nontarget elements are easy to differentiate. This means that it may not be necessary to identify each letter in the list to find the target letter. In short, the subjects do not search the list letter by letter, but instead focus on the distinctive feature of the target.

Generally speaking, visual search is enhanced as the difference between the target and its background is increased. Thus we can more easily select out the circle from the vertical bars in Figure 21.4a, and the white circle from the black shapes in Figure 21.4b. However when the target must be distin-

guished from its background on the basis of two dimensions, as in Figure 21.4c, both the shape and color of background elements must be analyzed in the search task. Of course other physical factors concerning the display, such as target luminance and contrast, may also play a role in the ease of visual search tasks (e.g., Long, 1985).

Other types of visual search tasks have also been studied. For example, Neisser (1963) examined the effect of searching for more than a single target at a time; for instance, rather than scanning the list for a *K*, the subject is required to search for a *K or* a *Q* and to indicate when either one is found. Neisser (1964)

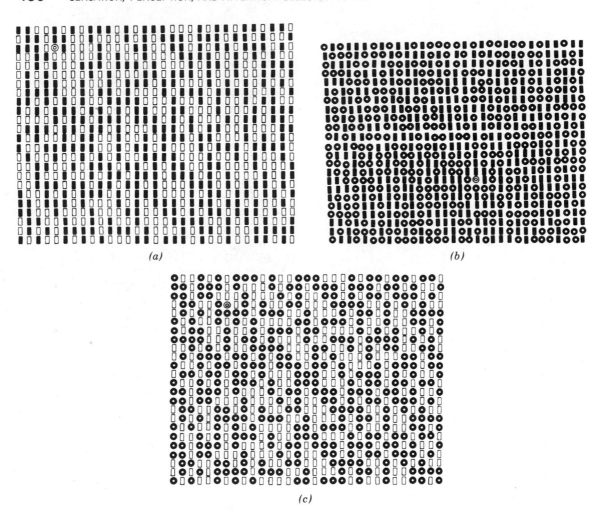

FIGURE 21.4. The target—a white circle—embedded in three background patterns that vary in their relation to the target. (a) Target can be easily detected on the basis of shape alone; (b) target can be easily detected on the basis of color alone; (c) target is not distinguishable from the background on the basis of a single dimension and detection is much more difficult than for (a) or (b). (From Glass and Holyoak, 1986, pp. 53–55; figure courtesy of Arnold Glass.)

reports that subjects searched as rapidly for either of two targets as for one alone. Moreover, with a multiple target search task, say, 4 or 10 targets in a list, after about two weeks of practice, subjects were scanning with about the same speed as they required for single targets. [We should note, however, that there are restrictions to this generality. Sperling and

Melchner (1976), using a somewhat different experimental arrangement, reported that subjects cannot simultaneously search for a large *and* a small target as well as they can search for two equal-sized targets.]

The finding that searching for up to 10 multiple targets does not, in general, require any more time than searching for single targets suggests that the search processes involved are carried out, at least partially, in parallel. That is, a number of decisions are made at once—a simultaneity of simple visual processing. [If the processes used in multiple search tasks were carried out serially or in sequence, each awaiting the outcome of earlier ones (e.g., in a given line, searching for Z, followed by searching for Q), then searching for two targets should require more time than searching for only one.]

Neisser (1964, 1967) points out a practical instance of the multiple search task: experienced readers for newspaper clipping agencies who daily search through newspapers and magazines for references to the agency's clients may search for hundreds of targets at once. According to Neisser (1964, 1967), it takes at least a year to train a clipping reader to scan newspaper and magazine text at a rate of well over 1000 words per minute for all references to the agency's clients. Moreover, as the agency loses old clients and acquires new clients, there is a gradual turnover of targets yet neither the error rate (about 10% for the best readers) nor the speed of scanning is affected by the agency gradually acquiring more clients (i.e., targets).

DUAL PROCESSING: SIMULTANEOUSLY RESPONDING TO MULTIPLE INPUTS

As we noted, the occasions in which we confront multiple sensory inputs are commonplace. Generally, we resolve the problem of competing inputs by selectively focusing attention on a single input (e.g., on the shadowed message), with some attentional sacrifice to those remaining. The outcome of such attentional restriction is generally a unitary experience—we hear one message, for example. However, the fact remains that we also frequently process more than one source of information and perform more than one activity; that is, we simultaneously and *intentionally* attend to multiple sources of information. This is called **dual processing.**

CONTROLLED AND AUTOMATIC PROCESSES

A general and obvious issue arises concerning the manner and extent to which attentional mechanisms concurrently receive, process, and react to two or more independent sources of information. In order to understand the capacity to deal with multiple sources we must recognize the distinction between **controlled** and **automatic processing**. That is, some cognitive and physical processes require intentional effort (under the control of the perceiver), whereas others occur automatically, independent of intentional or controlled processing (e.g., Shiffrin, 1988).

Research on performing multiple tasks and automatic processing has a history that stretches at least to the latter part of the nineteenth century. In 1896, Leon Solomons and Gertrude Stein (the writer, Gertrude Stein of "A rose is a rose is a rose is a rose" fame) reported their work on the gradual acquisition of the ability to perform the two distinct activities of reading and writing simultaneously. With extensive practice they progressed from reading while writing orally dictated words to reading one story while taking down another story from dictation; eventually one of the tasks (writing or reading) became "automatic." Since the researchers were themselves the subjects, their commentary on the acquisition of "automatic reading" bears mention:

> it is quite easy and the results are very satisfactory. The subject reads in a low voice, and preferably something comparatively uninteresting, while the operator reads to him an interesting story. If he does not go insane during the first few trials he will quickly learn to concentrate his attention fully on what is being read to him, yet go on reading just the same. (p. 503)

Clearly, many day-to-day activities, even complex ones, are seemingly performed simultaneously without any apparent extraordinary attentional expenditure or even any voluntary effort, and for the most part, these activities seem not part of conscious awareness. This is especially true for habitual mental processes and for well-practiced, learned activities such as driving an automobile. We may easily operate the auto and, apparently at the same time, hold a conversation or listen to the radio or perform mental operations. The performance of the activities required for driving in most situations has become so automatic that voluntary attentional focus can be, and usually is, diverted to other ongoing tasks with little or no loss in overall driving efficiency. Indeed, with numerous basic, well-practiced tasks that clearly require coordinated perceptual–motor skills —typing, driving, bicycling, walking, and perhaps reading—it is often difficult to focus intentionally on their performance; rather, skilled performance becomes *automatic*. We may thus question the possibility that we can, in all cases, exert control over the performance of certain processes. Are some processes so habitual, so well-practiced or overlearned that they lie outside of conscious control? In fact, there is evidence that for some tasks we cannot avoid automatically processing components that we may wish to ignore. A well-documented and easily demonstrated instance of this is the Stroop task, which requires a naming response *only*, yet another process appears to be automatically engaged.

THE STROOP EFFECT

The **Stroop effect** (1935, 1938; Jensen & Rohwer, 1966; Dyer, 1973) refers to a disruption and delay in naming the colors of words printed in colored ink when the letters of the words spell the names of incongruous or nonmatching colors.

In the typical procedure, subjects are presented with a list of names of colors, each printed in an ink that is a different color from the one spelled by the word: for example, the word *RED* printed in blue ink (see Plate 13 of the color insert). The subject's task is to go through the list as rapidly as possible, naming only the color of the ink of each word. The Stroop effect is a striking example of *automatic processing*. The response demands of the Stroop task require that the subject ignore the color words as stimuli to be read and attend only to the *colors* of the inks in which they are printed. That is, subjects must suppress the response of reading the color words, which competes

with the response of color naming. However, during performance of the color naming task, the interference caused by a tendency to read is obvious; indeed, subjects can even "feel" the effect and show signs of strain and increased effort. There may be an increase in the loudness of the voice, vocalization itself may falter, and occasionally the printed word rather than its color is mistakenly reported. In contrast, when the task is to ignore the color and read the word little interference occurs. The reason for this may be that reading a word is faster than naming a color; thus the response to a word may be emitted before there is an opportunity for any interference from its color to occur.

One explanation of the difficulty in ignoring or suppressing the reading response is that reading is such an overlearned, compulsive, involuntarily evoked skill that individuals cannot avoid reading the words despite the task instructions. Certainly most individuals have much more practice and experience in reading words than in naming colors. The interference in performing the Stroop task is due to the automatic activation of a reading process that is not under conscious control and hence is not consciously suppressed. Thus, in the Stroop task, the output of the automatic process of reading interferes with the output of the controlled process of identifying the color of ink.

We should stress, however, that the interference effect is not due solely to the fact that the colors print out *words* per se, but that it varies with the *type* of words used. Thus, if *non-color* words are printed in colored inks, the color naming task is subject to much less interference than if incongruous color words are used (Klein, 1964; Keele, 1972; Dalrymple-Alford, 1972). In both cases, the input contains divergent sources of information (i.e., words and colors), but by far the greatest degree of response conflict occurs with incongruous color words. That is, the ink color and the word itself each produce a different response, and the different responses compete with each other (Dalrymple-Alford & Azkoul, 1972; Duncan-Johnson & Kopell, 1981). [See Figure 21.5 for a related example on the problem of response selection (see also Warren & Lasher, 1974).] In

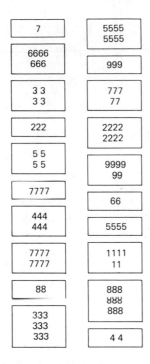

FIGURE 21.5.   An example of response competition. The task is to report the number of items in each box without "reading" the numerals. (Based on Lindsay and Norman, 1977.)

general, the efficiency of processing is affected by the number of simultaneous competing responses that can be made to the input (Flowers & Stroup, 1977; Neill, 1978).

DUAL ATTENTION

While many commonplace activities may be performed "automatically" in tandem with other more attention-demanding activities, we may consider the possibility of simultaneously attending to two or more independent sources of incoming stimulation and performing two unrelated activities, while consciously aware of each. An extension of the Solomons and Stein study, performed by Downey and Anderson in 1915, essentially verified this. After extensive practice with a task that required writing from dictation while reading stories, subjects attained signifi-

cant improvement in the performance of both tasks without reaching automaticity in either task; that is, they remained aware of the contents of each of the tasks performed, supporting the view that skilled cognitive activities can be concurrently performed without one of the tasks performed automatically.

More recently, several studies have reported that two activities could both be performed with a degree of awareness (Spelke, Hirst, & Neisser, 1976; Hirst et al., 1980). In one experiment subjects read stories silently while copying a different message (orally dictated words or sentences). The tasks were practiced extensively—one hour per day over the course of the semester. Upon subsequent testing, subjects showed a fair level of semantic comprehension both for the material read and for the material copied. While reading for comprehension at normal speeds, subjects were able to perceive relations among dictated words and to categorize words for meaning (Spelke, Hirst, & Neisser, 1976). In a task requiring copying dictated sentences while reading, subjects appear to be cognizant of much of the meaning of the sentences they had copied (Hirst et al., 1980). For example in one condition, subjects were able to integrate information from successively dictated sentences. The authors argue that such comprehension could not have been achieved had either task been performed at an automatic level. Accordingly, these findings suggest that the acquisition of a true skill in dual processing is possible where cognitive resources are successfully and intentionally shared. In short, dual processing is a controlled form of divided attention that is an acquired skill that improves with practice.

There is evidence, based on measures of cortical activity, indicating that attentional resources for performing concurrent tasks is limited and that tasks compete for a common and fixed supply of resources. For example, Wickens et al. (1983) had subjects perform a visual tracking (primary) task, along with an auditory counting (secondary) task. During the simultaneous performance of the two tasks, the experimenters recorded event-related brain potentials from the subjects' EEG (electroencephalogram). (Suffice it to say that these particular brain potentials are indices of the performance of perceptual–cognitive activities and can be used as measures of the resource demands of the tasks.) The investigators observed that as the demands of the primary tracking task were increased, brain potentials elicited by stimuli linked to that task increased in amplitude, whereas those elicited by stimuli related to the secondary auditory task decreased. This finding suggests that the allocation of resources to simultaneously performed tasks is reciprocal. That is, when tasks draw from common attentional resources, there is a trade-off in the availability of the common resources: minor task resources are less available as major task demands increase.

VISUAL MEMORY: THE ICON

We noted in our discussion of divided attention and the cocktail party phenomenon that auditory messages may remain briefly in a transient auditory memory called echoic memory. There is evidence of a transient visual memory, analogous to echoic memory, termed the **icon** or **iconic memory** (so named by Ulric Neisser in 1967). Iconic memory was briefly introduced in Chapter 14. It is generally held that iconic memory is a consequence of the visual persistence that typically follows any brief, moderately intense stimulus; the persistence effect is that of a rapidly fading visual image of the stimulus. Iconic (and echoic memory) may serve an important function in maintaining an intact representation of sensory input that can guide subsequent attention.

The seminal study of iconic memory was performed by Sperling (1960), who reported that immediately after visual presentation of a display containing letters or numbers, a significant amount of information remains for processing, but only for a very brief time. In his study, Sperling flashed grouped displays of alphanumeric symbols in three rows like that shown in Figure 21.6, for 50 msec (thereby precluding eye movements) and instructed subjects to recall as many of the symbols as possible

7 1 V F
X L 5 3
B 4 W 2

FIGURE 21.6. Typical form of the display used in one of the Sperling (1960) experiments.

in the total display. Subjects typically recalled between 4 and 5 of the 12 symbols correctly. However, in a second condition using a **partial-report procedure** the subject's attention was directed to only one row; immediately *after* the presentation of the display, subjects were given a tonal signal (high, medium, or low frequency) that designated which one of the three rows was to be "read" from the icon. A high-pitched tone was the cue for the top row, and tones of low or intermediate pitch indicated the bottom or the middle row, respectively. Note that the typical subject in this latter condition, cued by the tonal signal, was not aware of which signal to expect since the order was random and it was not sounded until *after* the stimulus display had terminated. That is, the information available to the subject was sampled immediately after the offset of the stimulus display.

Some of the general results for this experiment are summarized in Figure 21.7. Observe that with a tonal signal, using the partial-report procedure, the number of symbols correctly reported by the subject for the cued row is considered to represent only one-third of the total number of symbols available at the time the signal was given. This follows because as there are three rows in the total display, the subject could have presumably reported the same number of symbols from any of the rows. Put another way, if three out of four symbols in one row were recalled, it follows that an average of three symbols from any row was available. Thus, in a 3-row display with 4 symbols in each row, 9 of the 12 symbols of the total display were available for processing when the signal tone was sounded immediately after the termination of the display.

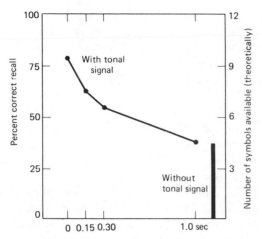

FIGURE 21.7.   Recall scores for 12-symbol display (Figure 21.6) as a function of the duration between the termination of the display and the tonal signal specifying the row to be reported. The bar at the right indicates the recall score for the condition that did not use a tonal signal. (Based on Sperling, 1960, p. 11.)

That the total display exists as a brief visual memory trace suggests why only four or five symbols were reported in the condition when no signal was used: the remaining display symbols had faded or decayed by the time the four or five symbols were reported. This is also shown in Figure 21.7, which plots several delays at which the tonal signal followed the display presentation. The relationship is clear: the shorter the delay, the greater the number of symbols reported, and the advantage of using the tonal signal disappears if the delay extends to more than a second. In brief, the accuracy, owing to the use of a tonal signal, is a sharply decreasing function of its delay.

In general, iconic (and echoic) memory enables the individual to briefly retain a representation of the sensory input; however, in that form, the information contained is quite susceptible to disturbance by subsequent stimulation.

VISUAL IMAGERY

Finally, we make note that humans are not limited to the processing of information from objects and events in the external environment, but we can process perceptionlike information from within, invoking **visual imagery** and a set of mental operations in "the mind's eye." For example, people can selectively manipulate a specific visual image or mental representation of an object and its possible transformations in space. In their pioneering study of this ability, which they termed **mental rotation,** Shepard and Metzler (1971; see also Cooper & Shepard, 1986; Finke & Shepard, 1986) had viewers decide whether pairs of relatively complex geometric figures, drawn in various perspective orientations relative to each other, depicted the same or different figures (see Figure 21.8). The task required subjects

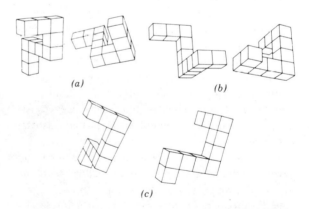

FIGURE 21.8.   Examples of perspective drawings of pairs of three-dimensional figures used for mental rotation task. Compare each pair of figures and decide whether they are identical objects that differ only in their orientation. (The pair in (*a*) are the same figure but differ by an 80° rotation in the picture plane; the pair in (*b*) are also of the same figure, but differ by an 80° rotation in depth; (*c*) contains a different pair.) (From R. Shephard and J. Metzler, "Mental rotation of three-dimensional objects," *Science, 171,* 1971, p. 702. Copyright © 1971 by the American Association for the Advancement of Science.)

to treat the figures as three-dimensional objects in space and to "rotate" the figures mentally, bringing them into alignment with each other to arrive at their decision. Of interest is that the decision time required to make a "same" judgment was directly proportional to the angular difference in the misalignment between the pairs of figures: the greater the misalignment between the two figures, the longer the time required to make a judgment, suggesting that subjects were performing mental rotations at a fixed rate of speed. In other words, we shift our "mental images" with direct regard to the degree of depicted misalignment.

SUMMARY

In this final chapter, we have examined several select, loosely related topics that bear on sensation and perception. We noted that attention serves a selective function, enabling the individual to focus on relevant signals and reject irrelevant ones. Several lines of research on this aspect of selective attention were discussed. It was noted that when an individual confronts competing messages, attention is directed primarily to one (e.g., the cocktail party phenomenon and selective looking); however, aspects from the nonattended message may also be perceived.

Research on visual search was examined and several findings were elaborated: it requires less time to search through a list of letters for the presence of a specific target than to search through a list for its absence; features that enable a target to be distinguished from its nontarget background enhance its detection; with practice, subjects can search for multiple targets about as well as they can for single targets.

The topic of dual processing or concurrently responding to multiple inputs was discussed, and it was noted that in some instances, this is accomplished by automatically processing some of the input. The Stroop interference effect was introduced in this context. It was concluded that the difficulty in naming the colors of the inks that print words that spell the names of incongruous colors is due primarily to the competition between the automatic response of reading a color word and the response of naming the color of the ink that prints the word.

Within the context of dual processing, it was also noted that there are conditions in which attention may be divided between multiple inputs without one being performed "automatically." It was suggested that such sharing of cognitive resources is a skill that is attained with practice.

The topic of visual memory—the icon—was discussed, and the evidence indicates that a significant amount of visual information (i.e., as an icon) exists immediately after the presentation of a visual display; however, it decays rapidly, much of it fading after about 1 second.

Finally a brief section on visual imagery and mental rotation indicated that it is possible to invoke and manipulate a mental image of a complex figure, taking into account such stimulus variables as the figure's displacement in depth.

KEY TERMS

Automatic and controlled processing

Cocktail party phenomenon

Dichotic listening

Divided attention

Dual processing

Echoic memory

Icon

Iconic memory

Mental rotation

Partial-report procedure

Selective attention

Selective listening

Selective looking

Shadowing

Stroop effect

Visual imagery

Visual search

STUDY QUESTIONS

1. Discuss the ways in which attentional processes have a direct effect upon determining what is perceived.

2. In what ways do we divide our attention when confronting competing sources of input information? Illustrate strategies of divided attention with respect to the cocktail party phenomenon, dichotic listening tasks, and selective looking.

3. Examine the stimulus factors that affect the overall efficiency of visual search.

4. Describe dual processing and distinguish between controlled and automatic processing.

Outline evidence that supports the claim that independent cognitive tasks, such as reading and writing, can be performed simultaneously.

5. Describe the Stroop task and indicate its relevance to automatic processing. Identify the sources of the interference in the typical Stroop task.

6. What evidence suggests that two independent and unrelated activities can be performed simultaneously, with conscious awareness of each?

7. What is iconic memory and how is it related to echoic memory? Outline Sperling's (1960) study of iconic memory.

8. Describe the mental rotation of visual images. Indicate to what extent the mental transformations of images are affected by their three-dimensional spatial representations.

GLOSSARY

Absolute Pitch
The rare ability to identify and reproduce isolated musical notes without any musical reference or standard. Also called *perfect pitch*.

Absolute Threshold
The least amount of physical intensity of a stimulus required for its detection.

Accommodation
The variable refractive capacity of the lens that brings an image into sharp focus on the retinal surface.

Achromatic
Lacking color.

Achromatism
Total color blindness.

Achromatopsia
A rare condition of total color blindness due to cortical pathology.

Acuity
The ability to detect, resolve, and perceive fine details of a visual display.

Acupuncture
An ancient Chinese medicinal practice of therapy for the general treatment of disease and control of pain. Acupuncture involves inserting needles into the body at precise loci.

Adaptation
(1) Relative loss in sensitivity or increase in threshold due to prolonged or repeated stimulation.
(2) The process of adjustment to the change in the conditions of lighting, that is, dark or light adaptation.
In general, adaptation refers to a reversible change in the state of an organism due to the effects of environmental events.

Adaptation-Produced Potentiation
The effect of imparting a particular taste to water because of adaptation to the taste of certain chemical substances.

Additive Color Mixture
Mixtures in which the addition of the excitations produced by different wavelengths produces a specific chromatic sensation.

Adjustment, Method of
A psychophysical procedure used to determine a threshold value in which the observer is required to adjust the intensity of the stimulus to a just-detectable level.

Aerial Perspective
A depth or distance cue in which objects whose retinal images are sharp or distinct appear closer

than those whose images are blurry or otherwise indistinct.

Afferent Impulses

Neural excitations toward the brain—sensory input.

Affordance

The adaptive relationship between an animal and its environment; specific environmental features *afford* animals opportunities and possibilities for adaptive action. Concept devised by J. J. Gibson.

Afterimage

Sensory effect following termination of a light stimulus. A negative afterimage is the visual sensation in which the hue and brightness of the original stimulus are reversed, for example, yellow is the apparent hue after staring at a blue hue. Positive afterimages are rarer and are sensations of the same apparent hue and brightness as the original stimulus.

Ageusia

Absence of taste.

Air-Righting Reflex

The tendency of some mammals to right themselves during a fall and land upright.

Albedo

A surface property that refers to the proportion of incident light that is reflected. Also known as *reflectance*.

Alpha Rhythm

Brain wave frequency of 8 to 12 Hz. Alpha rhythms predominate when the body is awake but relaxed, and the eyes are closed.

Amblyopia

Blurred vision owing to the disuse of one of the eyes.

Ames Illusion

A set of demonstrations devised by Adelbert Ames and used by Transactionalists to indicate the significance of experience in organized perception.

Amplitude

A general measure of stimulus magnitude.

Ampulla

Basal portion of the semicircular canal that contains the vestibular receptors.

Anaglyph

A form of stereo figure that is produced by printing two disparate patterns on top of each other in different inks to produce a composite picture. When viewed through the proper filters that enable each eye to sort out a single pattern, a stereo depth effect is perceived.

Analgesic

An agent, usually chemical, for reducing the sensation of pain.

Analytic Introspection

A highly disciplined technique of self-observation and mental analysis used by the nineteenth-century Structuralists to uncover the fundamental units of sensation.

Anechoic Chamber

A specially constructed acoustic environment that lacks sound-reflecting objects and hence is free of echoes.

Aniseikonia

An optical anomaly in which the image in one eye is larger than that in the other, resulting in a significant disparity between the images in each eye.

Anomaloscope

A special kind of color mixer that measures the proportions of two colors necessary to match a third color.

Anomalous Trichromatism

Defect in color vision in which a different proportion of the three primary colors than normal are needed in order to match the colors of the spectrum.

Anorthoscopic Perception

The perception of form resulting from viewing a figure in successive sections through a narrow slit. The term *anorthoscopic* ("abnormally viewed") was originally used by Zöllner and Helmholtz, in the nineteenth century, to refer to an arrangement of presenting stimuli in successive sections.

Anosmia

Insensitivity to odors.

Apparent Movement

The perception of movement from a stationary stimulus.

Aqueous Humor

Gelatinous fluid between the cornea and the lens.

Aristotle's Illusion

An illusory tactual experience attributed to Aristotle in which a single stimulus, if applied in a specific manner to two crossed adjacent fingers, produces the experience of two separate sensations. See Figure 7.7.

Astigmatism

Optic defect in which the corneal surface is not spherical.

Audiogram

A graph that shows hearing loss, in decibels, for pure tones as a function of frequency.

Audiometer

A device for assessing hearing loss.

Auditory Canal

The air-filled passage from the outer ear to the ear drum or tympanic membrane.

Auditory Fatigue

The elevation in the auditory thresholds after the termination of a masking tone. Also called sound-induced hearing loss and adaptation.

Auditory Masking

The rise in the threshold of one tone in the presence of a second, masking tone.

Auditory Nerve

The eighth cranial nerve. It contains the fibers from the cochlea and extends to the auditory cortex.

Autokinetic Movement

The phenomenon of apparent motion of a stationary point of light in an otherwise darkened environment.

Automatic Processing

The cognitive processing of input that occurs automatically, without controlled or intentional effort.

Average Error, Method of

A psychophysical technique for determining thresholds and constant errors, in which the observer adjusts a variable stimulus in relation to a standard. The average of a number of adjustments is generally taken as the threshold value.

Backward Masking

The impairment to the perception of a target stimulus by the presentation of a closely following second masking stimulus.

Basilar Membrane

A membrane upon which lies the organ of Corti.

Beats

The perception of a single throbbing tone of a single pitch, periodically varying in loudness. Beats can result from the simultaneous occurrence of two tones that are of similar intensity but slightly different in frequency.

Best Frequency

The frequency or frequency range of an auditory nerve fiber at which the intensity necessary to reach absolute threshold is at a minimum. Also called *characteristic* frequency.

Best Stimulus

The class of stimuli, specified with reference to one of the primary taste qualities, that is most effective in eliciting neural activity from a given taste fiber.

Bezold–Brücke Effect

The sensory effect in which the perception of long wavelength light apparently shifts toward yellow and short wavelength light shifts toward blue, with an increase in intensity.

Binaural

Involving both ears.

Binocular

Involving two eyes.

Binocular Depth Cues

Cues to the perception of depth and distance that require the use of both eyes.

Binocular Disparity

The difference in the two retinal images that provides a strong impression of depth and three-dimensionality of space. Also termed *retinal disparity*.

Binocular Fusion

The perceptual fusion of the images presented to each eye.

Binocular Rivalry

The phenomenon that occurs when each eye is presented with different stimuli. When binocular rivalry occurs, at one moment the stimuli from one eye may be dominant with a suppression of the stimuli from the other eye.

Biological Clock

A hypothesized internal clock or chronometer in the brain that controls the speed of metabolism and the rhythm of subjective time.

Biological Motion

The perception of the pattern of movement produced by locomoting humans. These forms of motion have been labeled *biological motion* by G. Johansson.

Biosonar

The term used to characterize the use of echoes by bats and other animals.

Bipolar Cell

Cells in the intermediate retinal layer that transmit impulses from the receptors to the ganglion cells.

Blind Spot

The region of the visual field that is reflected upon the optic nerve fibers (optic disk) exiting from the eyeball. No photoreceptors lie at this region, and accordingly, the viewer cannot perceive the corresponding part of the visual field.

Blobs

Distinctively patterned dark regions distributed over the visual or striate cortex that are selectively activated only by color and possess concentric double-opponent receptive fields.

Bloch's Law

Within certain limits, the threshold response to a visual stimulus is a product of stimulus intensity (I) and exposure time (I). Also known as the *Bunsen–Roscoe law*.

Block Portrait

An image that has been computer processed (or "block averaged") into a pattern of small blocks; each block is uniform in luminance throughout its area and is assigned the same dark-light value as the average value of the original portion of the picture.

Bone Conduction

Process by which sound is conducted to the cochlea of the inner ear through the cranial bones, rather than by the usual conduction structures.

Border Contrast

Subjective contrast enhancement that occurs at contours.

Braille

A tactual reading system composed of dots embossed on a surface that produces patterns of differential stimulation when contacted by the skin, usually the fingertip.

Brightness

One of the basic psychological dimensions of light. It varies primarily with physical intensity.

Caloriceptor

A presumed distinct sensory nerve ending whose activity varies only and directly as its temperature is increased or decreased. Evidence for a caloriceptor has little support.

Candela per Square Meter (cd/m^2)

Amount of light given off by a perfectly diffuse reflecting surface illuminated by one meter-candle. Also called *nit*.

Cataract

An opacity of the lens of the eye resulting in impaired vision.

Categorical Perception

A phenomenon in which the ability to discriminate among members of the *same* category is inferior to the ability to discriminate between members of *different* categories. As an example applied to speech perception, it is more difficult to discriminate between different forms of the consonant /p/ than it is to discriminate between the two consonants /p/ and /b/.

Causalgia

A severe and prolonged burning pain produced by a lesion in peripheral nerves.

Center-Surround Receptive Field

A receptive field of a ganglion cell which has a concentric organization. In one type of cell, stimulation to the central area will produce an excitatory response whereas stimulation to the surround will produce an inhibitory response. In another type of center-surround receptive field, the effects are reversed: stimulation to the center will produce an inhibitory response whereas stimulation to the surround will produce an excitatory response.

Cerebral Dominance

The relative dominance of one side of the brain over the other for certain perceptual processes. Also referred to as *brain asymmetry*.

Cerebral Hemispheres

The halves of the forebrain connected by the corpus callosum.

Chemonociceptor

Presumed receptor of the trigeminal nerve and the common chemical sense for the reception of chemical irritants.

Choroid Coat

The middle layer of the wall of the eye that is opaque, thus preventing stray light from activating the photoreceptors. It consists of blood vessels and provides a major source of nutrition for the eye.

Chromatic Aberration

Distortion of chromatic retinal images by the lens due to greater refraction of short wavelengths than of long ones.

Chromatic Scale

The 12 semitone notes spanning an octave interval. The 12 black and white keys within the octave interval on a piano keyboard sound the notes of the chromatic scale.

Chromesthesia

A form of synesthesia in which sounds produce vivid color sensations in addition to aural sensations.

Ciliary Muscle

Muscle that changes the shape or curvature of the lens and promotes accommodation.

Circadian Rhythms

Activity patterns that occur regularly on a daily (i.e., 24-hr) basis.

Closure

A Gestalt principle of perceptual organization; it is a tendency to "fill in" gaps in the structure of a figure or form so that it appears complete or closed.

Cochlea

Spiral-shaped portion of the inner ear containing the receptive elements (transducers) which convert sound to neural activity.

Cochlear Canal (or Duct)

Middle canal of cochlea of inner ear. It contains the organ of Corti. Also called the *scala media*.

Cocktail Party Phenomenon

The condition in which an individual is confronted with two or more simultaneously presented messages but apparently attends to only one. However, some of the unattended message(s) may be perceived.

Cognitive-Attentional Theory

A model of time perception which holds that the focus of attention directly affects temporal experience. Attention is divided between two processors: a nontemporal information processor and a cognitive timer that processes temporal information.

Cognitive Invention

A notion proposed by I. Rock to explain the resultant lightness effect that promotes subjective contours and shapes.

Cognitive Timer

A presumed mode of attention involved in time perception, which processes and encodes temporal information and heightens temporal awareness.

Cold Spot

Presumed region of the skin particularly sensitive to cold stimulation.

Color Circle

A circular arrangement used to specify the relation among hues and saturations. Hues are arranged around the perimeter of the circle, and saturation extends from the perimeter to the center of the circle.

Color Memory

The effect of past experience on apparent color or hue.

Color Spindle

A three-dimensional model used to show the relation among hue, brightness, and saturation. Hues are located around the perimeter, saturation from the center to the perimeter, and brightness is arranged from top to bottom. Also called the *color solid*.

Combination Tone

The auditory phenomenon produced when two tones of moderately differing frequencies are sounded together. The frequency of the resultant *combination* tone is a function of the frequency of the two tones.

Common Chemical Sense

A sensory system whose effective stimuli are typically chemical irritants. The sensory surface for the common chemical sense is the mucosa of the nose, mouth, eyes, respiratory tract, anus and genital apertures which is innervated by the trigeminal nerve.

Common Fate

A Gestalt grouping principle in which elements that move in the same direction are grouped together.

Comparator

A hypothetical center in the nervous system in which efferent signals from the brain to the eye muscles are compared with the flow of images on the retina, thereby canceling apparent movement due to the stimulation of the image-retina system.

Complementary Afterimage

After prolonged fixation of a color stimulus, the complementary color will appear if fixation is shifted to an achromatic surface.

Complementary Colors

The hues of two wavelengths that, when mixed in the correct proportions, yield achromatic gray or white. Complementary colors lie opposite each other on the color circle.

Complexity (Tonal)

The acoustic dimension of sound produced by vibrating bodies that do not vibrate at a single frequency. The psychological dimension of the resultant complex waveform is termed *timbre*.

Compound Eye

An image-forming eye (of arthropods) which consists of a mosaic of tubular units (ommatidia) that are clustered tightly together and arranged so that the outer surface forms a hemisphere.

Conditioned Taste Aversion

The behavioral effect of pairing a specific taste with an extremely unpleasant stimulus, such as a poison, that produces symptoms of illness. The effect of a conditioned taste aversion is that substances with the specific taste are subsequently avoided or rejected.

Conduction Hearing Loss

Deficiency in hearing due to a defect in the conduction mechanism of the auditory system. Hearing loss is distributed about equally over all frequencies. Also known as *transmission hearing loss*.

Cone of Confusion

The conical surface on the side of the median plane. Sounds originating on the conical surface that are parallel to the median plane provide the same interaural differences at the two ears and thus cannot be discriminated from each other in location.

Cones

Photoreceptor cells of retina that function in color vision and acuity. Such cells are most dense in the fovea and relatively absent in the periphery of the retina. There are approximately 6 to 8 million cones in the retina.

Congenital

Existing at or from birth.

Consonance

In audition, those combinations of tones that appear to blend well and sound pleasant together.

Constancy

The tendency of an object to be perceived as invariant regardless of changes in its retinal image produced by changes of orientation, distance, and intensity relative to a viewer.

Constant Error

A systematic error in judgment in which one stimulus tends to be either overestimated or underestimated relative to another.

Constant Stimuli, Method of

A psychophysical method employed for establishing thresholds. Each of a limited number of stimuli is presented repeatedly, and the degree to which each one elicits a sensation is used to determine the threshold value. Generally the stimulus value yielding a detection response 50 percent of the time is accepted as an approximation of the absolute threshold.

Contingent Aftereffects

The class of aftereffects that results from continued stimulation and selective adaptation or fatigue of combinations of specific stimulus features. Accordingly, the resultant aftereffect is linked to and contingent upon the presence of one of the adapted stimulus features. The McCollough effect is the classic example of contingent aftereffects.

Contralateral

Opposite side.

Contrast Sensitivity Function

A figure that represents the visual system's sensitivity for the range of perceived spatial frequencies. Specifically the figure plots the relation between spatial frequency and threshold levels of contrast.

Controlled Processing

The processing of input by an individual exercising controlled and intentional effort.

Convergence

The tendency of the eyes to turn toward each other in a coordinated action to fixate on targets located nearby.

Cornea

The transparent outer surface of the sclerotic coat lying in front of the iris and the lens.

Correct Rejection

A negative response given by an observer in a signal detection task when *no* signal is present.

Corresponding Retinal Points

Stimulation of identical areas in the left and right fovea by the same target. The resulting perception is of a single, fused target.

Corollary Discharge Signals

A presumed set of corollary signals sent to a hypothetical region of the central nervous system that matches the efferent motor command signals produced during self-initiated motor movements. Also referred to as *outflow signals*.

Cortex

Neural tissue covering most of the external surface of the brain.

Crista

The base of the cupula of the semicircular canal that registers rotary movement.

Criterion

The stimulus magnitude at and above which an observer will report a stimulus present in a signal detection experiment.

Critical Flicker Frequency (CFF)

The minimum frequency of intermittent light stimulation necessary for flicker to alternate with fusion.

Cross-Adaptation

The effect in which adaptation to one sapid substance (or odorant) affects the sensitivity or threshold to another sapid (or odorant) substance.

Cross-Fiber Patterning

Notion that each taste fiber has its own activity profile or pattern of firing; accordingly taste quality is due to the *pattern* developed across a number of fibers.

Cupula

Tongue-shaped protuberance lying within the ampulla of a semicircular canal.

Cutaneous Sensations

Sensations obtained by stimulation of the skin; such sensations are labeled pressure or touch, warmth, cold, and pain.

Cyclopean Perception

A form of stereo viewing devised by Bela Julesz based on the idea that the image on each eye is combined and synthesized in a central visual area of the brain to produce the perception of depth.

d'

A term derived in signal detection tasks that serves as a measure of the sensitivity of the observer to signal strength that is independent of response bias.

Dark Adaptation

Increase in sensitivity of the eye during the change from high to low levels of illumination.

Decibel (dB)

One-tenth of a bel. One bel is the common logarithm of the ratio between two intensities or energies. The bel is often expressed as the logarithm of the ratio of the square of two pressures:

$$\log_{10} \frac{p_1^2}{p_2^2}$$

It is the unit used to specify the amplitude or intensity of a sound wave.

Dendritic Knobs

The immediate connections for the olfactory cilia. With the olfactory cilia, dendritic knobs may be the receptor sites for odorants and are the structures involved in the initial stage of the transduction process in smell.

Density

A tonal quality that refers to the compactness or tightness of a sound. Generally greater density occurs with higher frequency tones.

Detection Acuity

The acuity task of detecting the presence of a target stimulus in the visual field.

Deuteranomaly

A kind of anomalous trichromatism in which the person requires much more green than normal in a mixture of red and green to match a yellow in an anomaloscope.

Deuteranopia

Color weakness characterized by the inability to distinguish between reds and greens and a relative insensitivity to those wavelengths that appear green to normal viewers.

Dichotic

The condition in which each ear hears a different sound or message at the same time.

Dichromat

Color-vision defective person who matches all wavelengths of the spectrum with two rather than three colors.

Difference Tone

A tone with the pitch that corresponds to the frequency difference of two primary tones simultaneously sounded.

Differential Threshold

The amount of change in stimulus magnitude of a given level of stimulation in order for a change to be detected. Also known as the *difference limen* or *just noticeable difference (jnd)*.

Diopter

The unit of refractive power of a lens. A lens with a focal length of one meter is designated as having the refractive power of one diopter. The refractive power of a lens is expressed as the reciprocal of its focal length, in meters.

Diotic

The condition in which the same tonal stimulation is presented to both ears simultaneously.

Direct Perception

The notion of J. J. Gibson that the information for perception is fully contained within the patterned input from the environment. It is a direct notion in that the spatial layout of the environment is picked up directly without processing and mediation by cognition.

Displacusis

An abnormality of hearing in which a simple tone is perceived as different in pitch by the two ears.

Dissonance

In audition, the result of combinations of tones that sound discordant or harsh when sounded together.

Doppler Shift

A change in the frequency and pitch of a moving sound source relative to a stationary listener.

Double-Opponent Receptive Fields

Receptive fields for "blob" neurons of the visual (striate) cortex. Double-opponent receptive fields have an antagonistic center-surround organization with each component possessing a dual effect. The center increases its activity to one color and decreases it to the complementary color; the surround has the exact opposite double-response pattern.

Dual Processing

When an individual simultaneously and intentionally attends to multiple sources of information.

Duplex Perception

The unique experience of hearing both speech and nonspeech from the same set of acoustic signals.

Dynamic Acuity

An acuity task involving the detection and location of moving targets.

Dyne per Square Centimeter (dynes/cm^2)

Equivalent to a microbar. They are both units of pressure. Ten dynes/cm^2 equals 1 N/m^2 (Newtons per square meter) and 10^{-5} dynes/cm^2 equals 1 μPa (microPascal).

Dysgeusia

A distortion in taste experience; most common forms of dysgeusia are persistent metallic, burning and sour tastes that are inappropriate to substances in the mouth.

Echoic Memory

The rapidly fading or decaying memory of auditory stimuli, analogous to iconic memory in vision.

Echolocation

The use of self-produced echoes to gain location information.

Efference Copy

A hypothetical copy or trace of efferent signals stored in the central nervous system.

Efferent Impulses

Neural excitation away from the brain. Such excitations as initiating movements are examples of efferent impulse activity.

Electroencephalogram (EEG)

A measure of the electrical activity of the brain.

Elementism

A view in nineteenth-century physical and biological sciences that stressed the analysis of compounds into their constituent elements. It was applied by the Structuralist school to the emerging science of psychology to uncover the fundamental units of sensations.

Elevation

A depth or distance cue in which objects appearing higher in the visual field are perceived as being farther away from the viewer than those lower in the visual field.

Emmert's Law

The apparent size of an afterimage is directly related to the apparent distance of the surface on which it is perceived.

Emmetropic Eye

Optically normal lens of the eye.

Empiricism

The view that perceptual organization is based primarily on past experience.

Endorphin

An endogenous analgesia. Opiatelike substance secreted by the pituitary that serves to inhibit pain.

Enkephalin

An endogenous analgesia. Opiatelike substance secreted by the body (especially brain and intestines) that serves to suppress pain.

Environmental Orientation

The orientation of a shape with respect to gravity and to the visual frame of reference.

Episodic Odors

Odors associated with real-life experiences.

Equal-Loudness Contours

Laboratory-derived contours or curves such that any sound whose frequency and intensity lies on a given equal-loudness curve appears equally as loud as any other sound on the curve although their frequencies and intensities may differ. The family of such curves indicates that loudness is secondarily affected by frequency. Also called *isophonic contours* or *Fletcher-Munson* curves.

Eustachian Tube

Tube that connects the middle ear chamber with the back of the mouth. The tube permits pressure from the outside to be equalized with air pressure in the middle ear. This is accomplished when the mouth is opened.

Exafference

Stimulation of the sense organs produced only by changes in the external world.

Exaltolide

A musklike synthetic odorant. For the human, the threshold for Exaltolide varies with gender.

Extraocular Muscles

The set of muscles that control the movement of the eyeball.

Eye—Head Movement System

The system of movement perception in which the eyes track a moving stimulus.

Facilitative Interaction

The summation of effects that occur with sequential presentation of stimuli.

False Alarm

Reporting the stimulus as present on a trial of a psychophysical or signal detection experiment when it is not actually present. Also called *false positive*.

Familiar Size

A possible memory-type cue for depth and distance based upon knowledge of the sizes of objects.

Fechner's Law

General law proposed by Gustav Fechner (1860) which states that the magnitude of a sensation is a logarithmic function of the stimulus.

Figural Aftereffect

Distortion effect after prolonged exposure to a given stimulus pattern or form that occurs when a new stimulus form falls on the same or nearby retinal region.

Figure—Ground

The tendency to perceive a portion of a stimulus configuration as a figure set apart from the background.

Filled-Unfilled Space Illusion

An illusion in which a filled extent appears longer than an unfilled extent of equal length.

Flavor

A combination of sensory effects that affect the overall palatability of a sapid substance, including its taste, smell, texture, temperature, color, irritability, and sound.

Focal Length

The distance between a lens and the sharp image it forms of a very distant object.

Foot-Candle (ft-c)

English unit of illuminance. One foot-candle is defined as the illumination received on a surface 1 foot square located 1 foot from a standard candle.

Foot-Lambert (ft-L)

English unit of luminance defined as the total amount of light emitted in all directions from a perfectly reflecting and diffusing surface receiving 1 foot-candle of light.

Formant

The concentration of acoustic energy that appears in spectrograms.

Forward Masking

The impairment to the perception of a target stimulus due to a preceding masking stimulus.

Fourier Analysis

The breakdown of a complex waveform into its component simple sine waves based on the mathematical theorem devised by the nineteenth century French scientist, Jean Baptiste Fourier.

Fovea

The central region of the retina. It is a small indentation about 0.3 mm across, subtending a visual angle of 1° to 2°. The fovea contains primarily cone photoreceptors.

Fractionation

A psychophysical procedure used to determine the relationship between pitch and frequency. An observer varies the frequency of one sound so that its pitch is perceived to be some fraction of the pitch of a fixed tone.

Free Nerve Endings

Unspecialized sensory neural receptors profusely distributed throughout the body.

Frequency (Audition)

A characterization of sound waves by the number of cycles or pressure changes completed in a second.

Frequency Cut-offs

A procedure involved in the study of speech perception in which there is a selective removal of bands of frequencies from a speech sequence.

Frequency Modulation

Changes in the frequency of a continuously vibrating body.

Frequency Theory

Theory that the basilar membrane vibrates as a whole to the frequency of the sound wave, thereby reproducing the vibrations of the sound. Pitch is thus determined by the frequency of impulses traveling up the auditory nerve, that is, it is directly determined by the frequency of the sound wave. Also known as the *telephone* or *periodicity theory*.

Frequency Tuning Curve

A curve for a given auditory nerve fiber that plots the frequency at which its absolute threshold is at a minimum.

Fundamental Tone

The lowest tone of the series of tones produced by a sound-emitting instrument. It is also called the *first harmonic*.

Ganglion Cells

Intermediate layer of neurons of the retina which forms the optic nerve.

Ganzfeld

A completely textureless and homogeneous field of uniform brightness.

General Constancy Theory

Theory proposed by R. H. Day that states that if any of the traditional stimulus cues for distance normally used to preserve constancy are independently manipulated with the size of the retinal image not correspondingly changed, variations in apparent size will result.

Gestalt Grouping Principles

A proposed set of fundamental organizing tendencies to perceive the visual field on the basis of the arrangement and relative location of elements.

Gestalt Psychology

A theoretical viewpoint of the organized nature of perception, begun by a group of German psychologists, especially Wertheimer, Köhler, and Koffka. The German word *Gestalt* means *form* or *configuration*.

Glaucoma

An age-related disorder due to abnormal intraocular pressure producing retinal damage and atrophy of the optic nerve. Glaucoma causes a marked reduction in visual acuity and the size of the visual field.

Glomerulus

A relay connection in the olfactory bulb where nerve fibers connect with the brain by olfactory tracts.

Good Configuration

The collective tendency, according to the Gestalt principles, of a certain pattern of stimuli to have the qualities of good continuation, closure, and symmetry.

Good Continuation

Gestalt tendency for stimulus elements to be perceptually grouped in a way so as to perceive the continuation of a line or curve in the direction that has been established.

Gravitoinertial Force

The combined force of gravity and acceleration.

Ground

The part of a total stimulus configuration that serves as the background for the apparent figure. It appears less well structured, extending behind the figure, and has less focus of attention.

Gust

An early unit of taste intensity expressed relative to the intensity of a 1 percent sucrose solution.

Gymnema Sylvestre

Tasting the leaves of the Indian plant Gymnema sylvestre can suppress the ability to taste sweetness without affecting the response to salty, acid, or bitter substances.

Habituation

A technique used to assess color perception in infants. An infant will look less at (or habituate to) a stimulus that is repeatedly presented.

Haptic

From the Greek "to lay hold of." A sensory-perceptual channel that refers to the combined input from the skin and joints.

Hertz (Hz)

The number of cycles completed within a second. Named for the nineteenth-century German physicist, Heinrich Hertz.

Hit

Correctly detecting the presence of a signal in a trial of a signal detection experiment.

Homunculus

A topographic representation of the relative amount of brain devoted to various parts of the body.

Horopter

The locus of all points in space whose images fall on corresponding retinal points and produce single images.

Hue

The chromatic sensation principally produced by the wavelength of a light.

Hypergeusia

Increased sensitivity to taste.

Hypermetropia

Refractive error of the lens of the eye in which the image formed of a nearby target falls on a focal plane behind the retina. Also known as *hyperopia* or *farsightedness*.

Hypogeusia

Diminished taste function.

Icilins

A class of synthetic compounds that produce sensations of cold by exerting selective stimulation on peripheral skin receptors.

Icon

Term coined by Neisser (1967) to refer to the brief trace or fading visual image remaining after the presentation of a stimulus.

Iconic Memory

A presumed memory process in which a "trace" visual stimulus or icon remains after the termination of a stimulus.

Illuminance

The amount of light falling on a surface.

Image—Retina Movement System

The system of movement perception in which there is a stimulation of a succession of neighboring retinal loci.

Impossible Figures

Displays containing inconsistent and contradictory sets of depth cues that cannot individually be suppressed. The graphic renderings of E. C. Escher are examples of such displays.

Incident Light

The radiant energy falling on a surface.

Incus

One of the chain of three small bones or ossicles of the middle ear. Also known as the *anvil*.

Induced Movement

Apparent movement of a stationary stimulus induced by movement of a nearby moving stimulus.

Inferotemporal Cortex

The lower part of the temporal lobe that is important in visual discrimination tasks.

Information Processor

A presumed mode of attention that concerns the nontemporal information processing demands of a task and shortens temporal awareness.

Inner Hair Cells

Specialized hair cells that lie on the organ of Corti and are the transducers for sound. Inner hair cells may register the frequency of sounds.

Intensity

A general term that refers to the magnitude of the physical energy stimulating a sense organ.

Interaural Intensity Difference

The intensity difference produced when the sound reaching one ear is of a different intensity than the sound reaching the other ear. This can serve as a cue to sound localization.

Interaural Masking

The phenomenon that an intense sound sent to one ear will mask a less intense sound delivered to the other ear.

Interaural Time Difference

The time difference produced when a sound reaches one ear before the other. This can serve as a cue to sound localization.

Interposition

A depth or distance cue in which the appearance of one object partially conceals or overlaps another.

Interstimulus Interval (ISI)

The duration between presentation of two stimuli.

Invariants

A presumed characteristic of the pattern of environmental energy for objects and event that is picked up by the observer which remains constant as other dimensions of the energy vary.

For example, the *rate of change* of the size of texture elements in the light reflected from a surface is invariant for different surfaces and for different distances.

Ipsilateral

Same side.

Iris

Circular diaphragm-type structure forming the colored portion of the eye that controls the size of the pupil opening.

Just Noticeable Difference (jnd)

The least change in the magnitude of a stimulus that is detectable.

Kappa-Effect

The effect in which time perception is influenced by the distance separating two stimuli.

Kinesthesis

The perception of body-part position and movement in space of the limbs and other mobile parts of the jointed skeleton.

Kinetic Depth Effect

Moving two-dimensional patterns perceived in three dimensions.

Kinetic Optical Occlusion

A dynamic cue of motion produced by the changes in the differentiated flow of stimulation across the retinal surface as an observer or object moves in space.

Koffka Rings

A contrast effect related to figure–ground segregation that illustrates that perceptual organization affects lightness contrast. See Figure 14.20.

Krause End Bulbs

Receptors in the skin presumed to account for the sensation of coldness.

Labeled Line

The label of a taste fiber that is assigned on the basis of the taste quality of the class of stimuli that elicits the greatest impulse discharge from that fiber.

Labyrinth

Bony cavities of the inner ears of mammals.

Ladd-Franklin Theory

An evolutionary theory of color vision that holds that primitive black-white achromatic sensitivity evolved into a sensitivity to blue and yellow, and at a later stage of evolution further differentiated into a sensitivity to red and green.

Lateral Geniculate Nucleus (lgn)

Relay center for vision located in the thalamus. Neural fibers from the lgn project to the visual area in the occipital lobe of the cortex.

Lateral Inhibition

The phenomenon in which adjacent or neighboring neural units mutually inhibit each other.

Lateral Line

A specialized sensory mechanism in fish consisting of a small fluid-filled tube that runs under the skin and appears as a line running along the side of the body from head to tail. It contains sensory cells (neuromasts) that respond to faint vibratory stimuli.

Lemniscal Neural System

A nerve pathway from the skin to the brain comprised of nerve fibers that are relatively large and fast conducting and that transmit precise positional information concerning touch and movement, and whose cortical (somatosensory) neurons possess receptive fields that are small and densely packed.

Lens

Structure of the eye that aids in focusing light rays on the retina.

Lightness

The surface quality—the degree of gray, ranging from white to black—that is relatively independent of illumination.

Lightness Constancy

The phenomenon that the lightness of an object or surface remains relatively constant despite changes in its illumination.

Lightness Contrast

An effect in which the intensity of large background regions can modify the lightness of smaller enclosed areas.

Limen

Latin term for threshold.

Limits, Method of

A psychophysical method employed for establishing thresholds. A series of stimuli of increasing or decreasing magnitude is presented until a stimulus value is reached at which the stimulus is just perceived or just fails to be perceived.

Limulus

Horseshoe crab, whose eye has been studied as a model for analyzing higher visual systems.

Line-Busy Hypothesis

An explanation of masking based on the activity of the masker and masked test tone on the basilar membrane. The notion assumes that the masker tone excites the same group of fibers as does the test tone, thus preventing the fibers from responding to the test tone.

Linear Perspective

The geometric technique that involves systematically decreasing the size of more distant elements and the space separating them. Linear perspective is a monocular spatial cue.

Linguistic Feature Detector

An assumed detector for speech perception that presumably is specialized to respond to very specific and distinctive characteristics and features of the speech signal.

Looming

The spatial and temporal information that specifies an imminent collision with an environmental object.

Loudness

The attribute of an auditory sensation in terms of which tones may be ordered from soft to loud. Loudness is primarily determined by the amplitude of a sound wave.

Luminance

The amount of light reflected from an illuminated surface.

Mach Bands

Perception of bands of brightness at borders where there are abrupt changes in luminance.

Macrosmatic

Possession of a keen sense of smell.

Macula Lutea

The yellowish retinal area that includes the fovea and adjacent regions.

Magnetic Sense

An orientation mechanism used by honeybees, in which navigation is aided by the reception of magnetic field information. Evidence of its use by other species is inconclusive.

Magnitude Estimation

A psychophysical method employed in scaling sensory magnitudes for Stevens' power law application.

Malleus

The first in the chain of three small bones or ossicles attached to the eardrum. Also known as the *hammer*.

Masking

The phenomenon in which the threshold for a stimulus is raised by the presence of a second stimulus.

McCollough Effect

A contingent aftereffect that suggests the existence of specific channels for certain classes of stimulation.

Mechanoreceptors

Receptors whose excitation is dependent on mechanical stimulation.

Meissner Corpuscle

Sensory receptor in touch-sensitive hairless skin regions, presumed to be a pressure receptor.

Mel

A dimension of pitch. By definition, the pitch of a 1000-Hz tone at 40 dB is assigned a value of 1000 mels.

Memory Color

The notion that familiarity with a chromatic stimulus influences its apparent color.

Ménière's Disease

A disorder due to abnormal pressure of the vestibular organ that produces a wide range of symptoms similar to motion sickness.

Mental Rotation

A form of mental imagery in which an individual mentally manipulates a specific visual memory or mental representation of an object and its possible transformations in space.

Metamers

Different lights whose mixture produces an apparent match with a third light.

Meter-Candle (m-c)

Metric unit of illuminance, defined as the illumination on a surface of 1 meter square located 1 meter from a standard candle. One meter candle equals 0.0929 foot-candles.

Microelectrode

Miniature electrode used to record neural activity from individual nerve cells.

Microsmatic

Relative lack of the sense of smell.

Middle Ear

It consists of a cavity containing the ossicles and the Eustachian tube.

Millilambert (mL)

Metric unit of luminance, equivalent to 0.929 foot-Lamberts. An often used alternative unit of luminance is candelas per square meter (cd/m^2), which is equal to 0.3142 mL.

Miniature Eye Movements

A pattern of extremely small, tremorlike eye movements that occur during fixation.

Miraculin

The fruit of a plant indigenous to tropical West Africa. Although the fruit is tasteless itself, exposure of the tongue to a thin layer of fruit pulp may cause any sour substance to taste sweet.

Miss

A negative response made by an observer in a signal detection task when the signal is actually present.

Mixed-Mode Eye Movements

A functional category of eye movements that involves several distinct eye movements. For example, tracking an object in depth requires the execution of saccadic, pursuit, and vergence eye movements.

Monaural

Stimulation of one ear.

Monochromatic Light

Light of a single wavelength.

Monochromatism

A color defect in which monochromats match all wavelengths of the spectrum against any other single wavelength or a white light.

Monocular

Involving one eye.

Monocular Depth Cues

Spatial cues requiring only one eye.

Monosodium Glutamate (MSG)

A chemical which enhances the palatability of food. It is a taste modifier and may also be a primary taste quality ("umami").

Moon Illusion

The illusory perception that the moon at the horizon appears significantly larger than when it is at the zenith.

Motion Parallax

The relative apparent motion of objects in the visual field as the viewer moves the head. Motion parallax is a monocular spatial cue.

Motion Paths

The predicted path or trajectory that a moving object will follow when set in motion.

Motion Perspective

A dynamic cue to depth and distance provided by the continuous change in the perspective or position from which objects are viewed; that is, the optic flow pattern that is created by movement toward or parallel to surfaces.

Motor Theory of Speech

A theory that proposes that the perception of spoken language is a result of knowledge of the articulatory gestures that are involved in the production of speech. That is, the sounds of speech are perceived by reference to the ways they are generated.

Myopia

Refractive error of the lens of the eye in which the image of a distant target is brought to a focus in front of the retina. Also known as *nearsightedness*.

Nanometer (nm)

A billionth of a meter.

Nativism

The notion that perceptual organization is inherent in the biological structure of the organism, and therefore experience and learning play a comparatively small role.

Nature–Nurture Controversy

The controversy as to the relative contribution of innate versus learned factors in perceptual organization.

Near Point

The closest distance to a viewer at which a target can be seen clearly.

Near-Work Theory

The theory that there is a causal relationship between excessive near vision and myopia. Also called the *use-abuse* theory.

Neonate

An infant that is considered an independent individual. The designation commences with the cutting of the umbilical cord.

Nerve Hearing Loss

Deficiency in hearing due to damage of the auditory nerves or to the basilar membrane or other neural connection of the cochlea. Hearing loss for nerve deafness is greatest for high-frequency sounds. Also called *sensorineural* hearing loss.

Neuron

The basic cellular unit of the nervous system that serves to conduct nerve impulses.

Newtons per Square Meter (N/m^2)

A measure of sound pressure. One N/m^2 equals 10 dynes/cm^2.

Night Blindness

Pathological insensitivity to dim lighting. Also called *nyctalopia* or *hemeralopia*.

Nociceptor

A receptor whose effective stimulation produces injury to the body and whose sensations are unpleasant.

Nocturnal

Pertaining to night activity.

Noncorresponding Retinal Points

Stimulation of slightly different areas in the left and right retina by the same target. The resulting perception is a double image.

Normal Curve

A theoretical curve having certain well-defined mathematical properties. It is a perfectly symmetrical, bell-shaped frequency curve. A distribution curve made up of many chance events approximates a normal curve.

Null Method

A method used to measure the spectral distribution of the chromatic response. The amount of a color response is determined by the amount of energy of a wavelength of the complementary color necessary to cancel or neutralize the color sensation. Also called the *hue cancellation method*.

Nystagmus

Series of reflexive, tremorlike eye movements of an oscillatory nature.

Oblique Effect

The reduction in acuity for oblique grating patterns as compared to either horizontal or vertical patterns.

Occipital Lobe

One of the main divisions of each cerebral hemisphere that is the primary sensory area for vision.

Octave

The interval between any two tones, one of which is exactly twice the frequency of the other.

Octave Equivalence

The perceptual similarity of tones that are exactly an octave apart.

Oculogyral Illusion

An illusory perception of stimulus movement produced when the observer experiences a period of rapid rotation in the dark while fixating on an illuminated light source (stimulus) that rotates with the movement.

Oculomotor System

The system of muscles that control the movements of the eyeballs in the skull sockets.

Ogive

A curve of a distribution of values whose frequencies are cumulative, that is, based on the sums of the frequencies. The cumulative frequency of any value is the sum of all frequencies of the values below plus the frequency of the value. The shape of such a distribution is sigmoidal or s-shaped.

Ohm's Acoustical Law

The finding that the ear can hear each tone separately when it is exposed to two tones simultaneously.

Olfactory Bulb

A mass of neural tissue into which the olfactory nerve fibers enter. Nerve tracts lead from the olfactory bulb into the brain.

Olfactory Cilia

Hairlike projections of the olfactory receptor cells that may provide the receptor sites for odorant molecules and are involved in the initial transduction stage of the olfactory process.

Olfactory Epithelium

Odor-sensitive tissue region located on both sides of the nasal cavity. Also called *olfactory mucosa*.

Ommatidium

Single element of a compound eye.

Opponent-Processes Theory

A theory of color perception that holds that there are three classes of neural receptors, each composed of a pair of opponent color processes: white-black, red-green, and blue-yellow.

Opsin

A colorless protein that is one of the chemical constituents of rhodopsin.

Optacon

An electronic reading aid that converts a visual image of a printed character directly into a tactual one, usually at the fingertip.

Optic Chiasma

The part of the visual system at which the optic nerve fibers from the nasal part of the retina cross over to the contralateral hemispheres.

Optic Disk

Region of the retina where the optic nerve fibers leave the eye. There are no photoreceptors in this area and thus no visual response when light strikes this region. The corresponding visual field is termed the *blind spot*.

Optic Flow Pattern

The pattern of apparent changes in the optic array of a surface, relative to a fixation point, occurring from an observer's movement parallel to or directly approaching the surface. The spatial information in optic flow patterns is termed *motion perspective*.

Optohapt

A system for converting printed material into touch stimulation.

Optokinetic Nystagmus

The pattern of reflexive eye movements that are induced by stimulation from the visual field.

Organ of Corti

Cochlear structure containing the auditory receptors. It lies between the basilar and tectorial membranes.

Osmics

The science of smell.

Ossicles

Three small bones of the middle ear that contribute to the conduction of sound to the inner ear.

Otocyst

Sensory organ in vertebrates that serves as a gravity detector.

Otoliths

Calcium carborate particles in vertebrates that lie within the otocyst cavity. They are generally free-moving and react to inertial forces and, accordingly, register gravity and linear movement.

Otology

The field of medicine that is concerned with the study of the ear.

Outer Hair Cells

Specialized hair cells that lie on the organ of Corti and are the transducers for sound. Outer hair cells register the presence of weak auditory signals and may be loudness detectors.

Overtones

Partial tones simultaneously occurring in a complex sound that have a higher frequency and pitch than the fundamental one. Also called *harmonics*.

Pacinian Corpuscle

Bulblike mechanoreceptor attached to nerve endings in various parts of the body, especially in the mobile portions of the jointed skeleton.

Panum's Fusion Area

A narrow region around the curved spatial plane of the horopter whose spatial points produce fused images.

Papillae

Clusters of taste buds seen as elevations on the tongue. Four have been distinguished on the basis of shape and location: fungiform, foliate, circumavallate, and filiform.

Paradoxical Cold

A cold sensation produced when a hot stimulus is applied to a cold spot on the skin.

Partial-Report Procedure

A technique used to assess iconic memory. A subject is cued by a signal to report the contents of one portion of a briefly presented visual display.

Path-Guided Apparent Motion

The apparent path or trajectory that results when two lights alternately blink on and off, and a connecting band is flashed during the brief interval between the alternation of the lights. If a curved band is flashed the apparent path will also be curved.

Pattern Theory (Pain)

A theory of pain which assumes that general stimulus intensity or the summation of neural impulses by a central mechanism are the critical determinants of pain.

Perceptual Instant

A presumed interval of time—0.1 sec, one cycle of the alpha rhythm—in which all input is integrated and processed. Also called the *perceptual moment*.

Permanent Threshold Shift (PTS)

The permanent effect on hearing due to chronic or extended exposure to intense noise.

Perspective-Constancy Theory

The theory that stimulus features that are indicative of distance invoke a size constancy mechanism and provoke a compensatory size correction; this perceptually "enlarges" apparently distant stimuli and promotes the correction that normally occurs for a diminishing retinal image size when distance is increased.

Phantom Limb Pain

The sensation of pain from an amputed limb. It is proposed that the pain arises in the stump tissue that possesses an abnormal amount of small-diameter, slow-conducting nerve fibers relative to large-diameter fibers.

Phase

The arrival of a sound wave specified with respect to the phase of its cycle. Two sound-waves that are at different phases within a cycle when they arrive at the two ears—for example, compressions occurring at different times relative to one another—change the quality of the sound and may serve as a cue for sound localization.

Pheromones

Chemical substances that serve as communicants or signals secreted to the external environment and exchanged among members of the same species.

Phon

A unit of loudness. It is a measure of the loudness level of a tone specified as the number of decibels of a standard 1000-Hz tone of equal loudness.

Phoneme

Smallest speech sound unit of a language that serves to distinguish one utterance from another.

Phonemic Restoration

The perceptual restoration or "filling in" of an omitted but contextually meaningful speech sound (phoneme).

Phonetic Boundary

A point at which a categorical change in a sound is heard when systematically and incrementally varying certain acoustic variables (i.e., the VOT).

Photochromatic Interval

The vertical distance between the photopic and scotopic threshold curves that specifies the "colorless" interval of radiant energy for a given wavelength; that is, the interval between seeing only a light and seeing a color or hue.

Photon

The quantum unit of light energy.

Photopic Vision

Vision accomplished with cones.

Physiological Zero

The temperature at which a sensation of neither warmth nor cold occurs.

Pictorial Cues

The set of static monocular cues for depth. Pictorial cues produce the impression of three-dimensional space on a two-dimensional surface.

Pictorial Perception

The impression of depth on a two-dimensional surface, such as a photograph or picture, promoted by the utilization of pictorial depth cues.

Pinna

Part of outer ear of mammals, an earflap. Also called the *auricle*.

Pitch (Auditory)

The psychological attribute of a tone that is described as high or low. Pitch is primarily mediated by the frequency of the tone.

Pitch (Orientation)

Rotation of the body about the y axis. The y axis runs side to side. Pitch rotation is thus forward or backward rotation. See Figure 3.4.

Place Theory of Hearing

A theory that maintains that different auditory nerve fibers lying on regions of the basilar membrane are activated by different frequencies.

Point Localization

The ability to localize pressure sensations on the region of the skin where the stimulation is applied.

Point of Subjective Equality

A psychophysical measure of the estimate that the magnitudes of two stimuli are perceptually equal.

Postrotary Nystagmus

The pattern of reflexive eye movements that occur after rotary movement.

Power Law

Psychophysical statement that holds that sensory magnitude grows in proportion to the physical intensity of the stimulus raised to a power.

Prägnanz, Law of

General Gestalt principle that refers to the tendency to perceive the simplest and most stable figure of all possible perceptual alternatives.

Precedence Effect

The phenomenon that the perception of the sound reaching the ears from the farther of two identical sound sources will be suppressed with regard to its localization.

Preferential Looking

A technique used to assess the characteristics of a stimulus to which an infant will preferentially attend.

Presbyacusis

A pathological condition of the auditory system in which there is a progressive loss of sensitivity to high frequency sounds with increasing age.

Presbyopia

A refractive error of the lens of the eye in which, with increasing age, the elasticity of the lens progressively diminishes so that it becomes more difficult for the ciliary muscle to change the lens' curvature to accommodate for near objects.

Pressure Phosphenes

The subjective lights and images resulting from pressure stimulation of the eye.

Proprioception

The class of sensory information arising from vestibular and kinesthetic stimulation.

Protanopia

Color weakness characterized by the inability to distinguish between red and green and a relative insensitivity to the long wavelength end of the spectrum.

Protensity

The subjective experience of time as distinguished from clock or physical time.

Protoanomaly

A kind of anomalous trichromatism in which the person requires much more red than normal in a mixture of red and green to match a yellow in an anomaloscope.

Proximity

A Gestalt principle of perception that separate elements making up a configuration will be perceptually organized into wholes according to their degree of physical closeness.

Psychophysics

The study of the relation between variation in specified characteristics of the physical stimulation and the attributes and magnitude of subjective experience.

Pulfrich Pendulum Effect

A perceptual distortion of physical movement produced when each of the two eyes is stimulated by different intensities of light.

Pupil

The opening formed by the iris of the eye through which light enters.

Pure Tone

A tone produced by sound energy emitted at a single frequency.

Purkinje Shift

The shift in relative brightness of lights from the two ends of the spectrum as illumination decreases owing to the shift from photopic (cone) to scotopic (rod) vision.

Pursuit Eye Movements

Involuntary eye movements executed in tracking moving targets.

Reafference

Neural excitation feedback that is dependent on voluntary movements.

Receptive Field

Precise region of the sensory system (such as the skin or retina) that when appropriately stimulated, alters the firing rate of specific neurons lying within or on route to the brain.

Recognition Acuity

The acuity task of recognizing target stimuli, such as naming the letters of an eye chart (Snellen letters).

Referred Pain

Condition in which pain originating from internal organs appears to occur from another region of the body, usually the surface of the skin.

Reflected Light

The light reaching the eye from an illuminated surface.

Relative Size

A depth or distance cue that occurs when two or more similar or identical shapes of different sizes are simultaneously viewed; the larger stimulus generally appears closer to the viewer than the smaller one.

Resolution Acuity

The acuity task of perceiving a separation between discrete elements of a pattern.

Resonance

The natural vibration frequency of an object. An external driving force matching the resonant frequency will set the object into sympathetic vibration.

Retina

A photosensitive layer at the back of the eyeball consisting of interconnected nerve cells and photoreceptors that are responsive to light energy.

Retinal

A pigment formed by the bleaching of rhodopsin (sometimes termed retinene).

Reversible Figures

Stimulus patterns that give rise to oscillation between two (or more) alternative perceptual organizations. The Necker cube is a common example. Also called *ambiguous* and *multistable figures*.

Rhodopsin

A light-absorbing pigment found in rods. Rhodopsin is sometimes called visual purple.

Ricco's Law

A law that states that a constant threshold response can be maintained by the reciprocal interaction of retinal area (A) and stimulus intensity (I). That is, $A \times I = $ a constant threshold value.

ROC Curve

Receiver operating characteristic curves that show the relationship between the proportion of hits and false alarms in a signal detection experiment.

Rods

Photoreceptors of retina found principally along the periphery of the retina.

Roll

Rotation of the body about the x axis. The x axis runs from front to back. Roll rotation is thus left–right or lateral rotation. See Figure 3.4.

Roughness Enhancement

A method of enhancing the perception of textural information of certain surfaces by rubbing a thin sheet of paper across a surface with the fingertip.

Ruffini Cylinders

Receptors of the skin presumed to mediate the sensation of warmth.

Saccade

A rapid and abrupt jump made by the eye as it moves from one fixation to another.

Saccadic Omission

The masking of the blurred image formed during saccadic eye movement.

Saccule

Fluid-filled sac that, along with the utricle, acts as an otocyst, registering the extent and direction of linear displacement and bodily position with respect to gravity.

Sapid

Capable of being tasted.

Satiation

Tendency for the prolonged viewing of a particular stimulus pattern to produce distortions in the perception of that pattern.

Saturation

The apparent degree of concentration of the hue of a spectral light. The corresponding physical dimension of saturation is chromatic purity. In general, the narrower the band of wavelengths comprising a light, the greater is its purity and saturation. Accordingly, white light, composed of radiant energy distributed among all wavelengths, lacks purity and appears desaturated.

Scale Size

A possible dimension that may affect temporal experience. It is defined as the size of an environment relative to the size of an observer.

Scene Perception

The perception of a scene containing objects that possess rational and coherent spatial and contextual relationships to one another and to the overall background.

Sclera

Outer coat of the eye continuous with the cornea. The sclerotic coat is seen as the "white" of the eye.

Scotopic Vision

Vision accomplished with rods.

Segmented Speech

The experimental procedure of segmenting the speech flow by inserting silent intervals in continuous speech.

Selective Adaptation

A procedure that selectively fatigues or adapts a specific linguistic or visual feature by a controlled form of overexposure.

Self-Adaptation

Prior exposure to an odorant increases the threshold for the identical odor.

Self-Vection

An illusion of apparent self-motion in which observers experience that they are in motion, when, in fact, they are stationary and the visual field is moving.

Semantic Priming

An experimental condition in which one stimulus, usually a word, facilitates or "primes" the perception of another word.

Semicircular Canals

Fluid-filled enclosures that lie above the inner ear at approximately right angles to each other and register motion of a rotary nature. The semicircular canals and the utricle and saccule comprise the vestibular organs which register gross bodily orientation.

Semitone

A division of the octave into 12 equal ratio intervals.

Senile Cataracts

An age-related reduction in the transparency of the lens.

Senile Macular Degeneration

An age-related deterioration of the macular region of the retina producing a severe reduction in acuity.

Senile Miosis

An age-related reduction in the pupil opening.

Sensitivity

Susceptibility to the perception of stimuli. In vision, sensitivity refers to perception in conditions of low level illumination.

Set, Perceptual

A readiness to make a particular perceptual response or class of responses to particular organizations of stimuli. Sets may be established by the prior conditions of exposure.

Shading and Lighting

A depth or distance cue in which the pattern of lighting and shading affects the apparent location of objects and surfaces relative to the viewer.

Shadowing

A technique employed for studying attention to auditory messages. Usually two messages are simultaneously presented, and the subject must attend to or "shadow" one of them.

Shape Aftereffects

After exposure to curved contours, subsequent exposure to straight lines appear curved in the opposite direction.

Shape Constancy

The tendency to perceive an object as relatively invariant in shape regardless of the orientation from which it is viewed or the shape of its image on the retina.

Signal Detection Theory

A psychophysical technique for estimating an observer's discriminative capacity or sensitivity to a signal independent of response bias. The measure of sensitivity is called d'.

Similarity

A Gestalt grouping principle in which elements that are similar in physical attributes tend to be grouped together.

Simultaneous Contrast

The tendency for the color of one region to affect the perception of the color of an immediately adjacent region. The adjacent region appears tinged with the complementary of the original region. Both hue and brightness are affected.

Sine Wave

A geometric function whose graphic depiction characterizes periodic phenomena such as air pressure changes over time as produced by a single frequency.

Size Constancy

The tendency to perceive the size of objects as relatively constant in spite of changes in viewing distance and changes in the size of the object's retinal images.

SL (Sensation Level)

Specification of the sound pressure for hearing in which the reference pressure for each frequency is given at its threshold value.

Somesthesis

Refers to kinesthetic and cutaneous sensation.

Sonar

A technique using sound for navigation in water (*SO*und *N*avigation *A*nd *R*anging).

Sone

A unit of loudness. One sone is defined as equivalent in loudness to a pure tone of 1000 Hz at 40 dB.

Sound-Induced Hearing Loss

A form of hearing loss attributed to exposure to intense sounds. The hearing loss effects may be temporary or permanent. Also called *noise-induced hearing loss*.

Spatial Frequency

The number of changes in luminance of a visual display over a given space. Spatial frequency is typically expressed in cycles per degree of visual angle.

Spatial Summation

The additive effect of separate stimuli spread over space.

Specific Receptor Theory

A theory which assumes that specific and distinct receptors exist for warmth and cold.

Spectral Threshold Curves

The set of curves that plots photopic and scotopic threshold levels of radiant energy by wavelength. Threshold vision is affected by wavelength: maximal sensitivity for photopic vision is at 555 nm and for scoptopic vision at 505 nm.

Spectrogram

A graphic reproduction of the frequency spectrum, intensity, and duration of a pattern of acoustic signals.

Speech Blanking

A procedure used in the study of speech involving the selective periodic removal of sections of the speech flow.

Speech Mode

A presumed unique form of specialized processing imposed on acoustic input recognized as speech.

Spherical Aberration

Distortion of the retinal image focused by a spherical lens. This is due to the fact that the light rays passing through the periphery of the lens are brought to a shorter focal plane than those passing through the center.

Spinal Gate Control Theory of Pain

Theory of pain that focuses on the afferent nerve impulse transmission from the skin to the spinal cord.

Spinothalamic Neural System

A nerve pathway from the skin to the brain comprised of nerve fibers that are small, relatively slow conducting, that carry input concerning nonlocalized touch, and whose cortical (somatosensory) neurons possess receptive fields that are large and less densely packed than those of the lemnisical system.

SPL (Sound Pressure Level)

Stimulus amplitude, utilizing the reference pressure of 0.0002 dynes/cm^2 or 0.00002 N/m^2, which approximates the least pressure necessary for the average human observer to hear a 1000 Hz tone.

Stabilized Images

A condition in which the effects of eye movements are eliminated, producing an invariant retinal image.

Stapes

The last in the chain of three small bones or ossicles that link the middle to the inner ear. The footplate of the stapes connects to the oval window of the inner ear. Also known as the *stirrup*.

Statocysts

Specialized sensory organs that serve as gravity detectors. Also known as *otocysts* in vertebrates.

Statoliths

Anatomical structures that lie within the statocyst cavity. They are generally free-moving and react to inertial forces and accordingly register gravity and linear movement. They are also known as *otoliths* in vertebrates.

Stereochemical Theory

A theory of olfaction that attempts to establish direct links between the chemical composition of substances and perceived odors. It assumes that the geometric properties (size and shape) of molecules of odorants "fit" into similar size and shape receptor sites. Also known as the *steric* or *lock-and-key theory*.

Stereognosis

The perception of three-dimensional shape information by palpation and manipulation of the hands.

Stereogram

Specially prepared pairs of pictures, each representing the view of a single object seen by a separate eye. When viewed in a stereoscope an impression of depth with stereopsis results.

Stereophonic Listening

A mild form of dichotic stimulation that produces an experience of aural space.

Stereopsis

A perceptual experience of depth occurring as a by-product of the disparity of the images projected on each eye.

Stereoscope

An optical instrument used for producing the fusion of two images, each from a slightly different view, so as to produce an impression of depth.

Stimulus

Physical energy that activates or excites a receptor.

Stroboscopic Movement

The phenomenon of apparent movement between two successive presentations of separate light sources. Also referred to as *beta* movement or *phi* movement.

Stroop Effect

The disruption and delay in naming the colors of words printed in colors when the letters of the words spell incongruous or nonmatching color words.

Subjective Colors

The chromatic sensations produced from black and white stimulation.

Subjective Contour

The perception of a contour across a blank portion of the visual field.

Subliminal Perception

A controversial form of perception in which stimuli are not detected or consciously perceived but exert some measurable influence on certain response outcomes.

Subliminal Stimuli

Stimuli whose magnitude is too weak to produce a detection response. Same as *subthreshold*.

Subtractive Color Mixture

The apparent result of mixing two chromatic substances, such as pigments, paints, or dyes, in which there is a mutual absorption or subtraction of wavelengths, canceling the reflectance of all wavelengths but those that the two substances jointly reflect.

Successive Contrast

A condition in which a chromatic stimulus is fixated, producing an afterimage in the complementary color of the initial stimulus.

Summation Tone

The pitch of a summation tone corresponds to the sum of the frequencies of two simultaneously sounded primary tones.

Symmetry

Gestalt tendency for the perceptual grouping of stimulus elements to form symmetrical patterns rather than asymmetrical ones.

Synesthesia

An experience in which stimulation of one sensory modality evokes an experience in a different sensory domain. Chromesthesia or color hearing, is an example.

Tadoma Method

A method used by the deaf-blind to receive some information from vocalized speech. The hand, placed in contact with specific regions of a speaker's lips, face, and neck, enables the pick up of spatiotemporal patterns of stimulation closely linked to the speaker's articulation.

Tapetum

A retinal layer (of the choroid) of some nocturnal animals that reflects back some of the light entering the eye. It accounts for the "eye shine" emanating from some animals at night.

Taste Bud

The basic receptor structure for taste, located in microscopically small pits and grooves of the mouth, soft palate, throat, pharynx, the inside of the cheeks and along the dorsal surface of the tongue.

Tau-Effect

The relationship between distance and perceived duration. The greater the temporal interval separating the presentation of two stimuli, the greater the experienced distance.

Tectorial Membrane

Membrane extending along the top of the organ of Corti.

Temporary Threshold Shift (TTS)

A measure of the temporary hearing loss or a change in threshold sensitivity due to exposure to intense sound stimulation.

Texture Gradient

The gradual refinement of the size, shape, and spacing of the form of microstructure, generally seen as a texture, that is characteristic of most surfaces. Elements of the texture appear denser as distance is increased.

Thalamus

A region of the forebrain concerned with relaying nerve impulses to the cerebral cortex.

Threshold

Smallest level of stimulation (or change in stimulation) that is detectable. Also called *limen*.

Timbre

An attribute of auditory sensation corresponding to the complexity of a tone.

Tinnitus

Auditory pathological condition manifested by a "ringing" in the ears of a relatively high pitch. It is a prominent symptom of a number of ear disturbances.

Tonal Gaps

Narrow ranges of frequencies which are inaudible. Audiometric techniques, such as Békésy's tracking procedure, may uncover the inaudible frequency range.

Tone Chroma

The position of a musical scale note within a given octave. See Figure 6.6.

Tone Height

A dimension assigned to musical notes that represents overall pitch. See Figure 6.6.

Tonotopic Organization

The spatial arrangement of neural elements of the auditory pathway so as to represent similar frequencies in adjacent neural areas.

Tracking Procedure (Békésy)

A clinical audiometric procedure in which the observer's response to the presence of a tonal signal that varies in intensity identifies narrow ranges of frequencies—tonal gaps—that are inaudible to the observer.

Transactionalism

An empiricist theory that holds that the perceptual world is, in large measure, constructed from experience. A class of demonstrations, Ames demonstrations, has been devised to illustrate the importance of the role of learning in perception.

Transducer

A process or structure that converts one form of energy to another.

Transduction

The conversion or translation of environmental, physical energy to neural activity.

Trapezoidal Window

One of the Ames demonstrations used to show the importance of experience for perception. The window is a trapezoidal shape that projects a retinal image of a rectangular window at a slant from the viewer's gaze line.

Traveling Wave

A waveform whose point of maximal displacement moves within an envelope. Proposed to occur within the cochlea of the inner ear.

Trigeminal Chemoreception

The reception of chemical irritants by stimulation of the common chemical sense. The sensory surface for the common chemical sense is the mucosa of the nose, mouth, eyes, and respiratory tract that is innervated by the trigeminal nerve.

Trigeminal Nerve

The Vth nerve, which provides innervation to much of the mucous membrane of the head, including the nasal, oral, and corneal regions. The trigeminal nerve is the major neural structure mediating the common chemical sense.

Tritanopia

A rare form of dichromatism characterized by a deficiency in seeing blue and yellow.

Trompe d'Oreille

An illusion of auditory space.

Tuned Fibers

A class of auditory nerve fibers that are maximally sensitive to a very narrow range of sound frequencies. Each such tuned fiber has a characteristic or *best* frequency to which it is most sensitive.

Two-Point Threshold

The minimal separation in distance of two simultaneous stimuli that gives rise to two distinct impressions of touch.

Ultrasonic

Sounds above the frequency limit of human hearing.

Umami

A possible basic taste employed in Japanese psychophysics. Umami translates loosely to "delicious taste" and is elicited by MSG (monosodium glutamate).

Utricle

A membranous fluid-filled sac that along with the saccule registers linear acceleration and gravity.

Vascular Theory

A theory of thermal sensation in which a single mechanism for both warm and cold sensations is proposed. It holds that thermal sensations occur from the stimulation of sensory endings that occur from constriction and dilation of the smooth muscle walls of the blood vessels of the skin.

Vergence Eye Movements

Eye movements that move the eyes in opposite directions in the horizontal plane in order that both eyes focus on the same target.

Vernier Acuity (Localization Acuity)

The acuity task of detecting whether two lines, laid end to end, are continuous or whether one line is offset relative to the other.

Vestibular

Refers to the sensory structure of the labyrinth of the inner ear that reacts to head and gross bodily movement.

Vibratese

A touch "language" devised by F. A. Geldard for use on the skin surface.

Vision Substition System

A system used for converting a visual image into a cutaneous pattern of stimulation.

Visual Angle

The angle formed by a target on the retina. Visual angle is given in degrees, minutes, and seconds of arc and specifies the retinal area subtended by a target as a joint function of the target's size and its distance from the viewer's eye.

Visual Capture

The dominance of vision over touch input. Thus an object "feels" as if it has the size or shape based on how it "looks."

Visual Cliff

An apparatus used for assessing depth perception. It consists of a glass surface extending over an apparent void (deep side) and an apparent near surface (shallow side).

Visual Masking

The reduction in the perception of a target stimulus when a second stimulus is present in close temporal proximity to the target stimulus.

Visual Persistence

The visual effect that the sensation persists briefly after the offset of the physical stimulus.

Visual Placing

The automatic elicitation of a visually mediated extension or reaching out of the paw as if to prevent collision when the animal is moved toward a surface.

Visual Search

An experimental procedure in which the subject must scan a complex pattern (e.g., list of words or letters) for the presence (or absence) or a target stimulus. Generally, the dependent variable is the amount of time required to locate the target stimulus.

Vitreous Humor

Gelatinous fluid filling the eyeball behind the lens.

Voice-Onset Time (VOT)

The short latency between the air release and vocal cord vibration when producing certain speech sounds. Thus the VOT for sounds such as /b/ are very brief relative to the VOT for sounds such as /p/.

Volatile

Characteristic of a substance to pass into a gaseous state—readily vaporizable.

Volley Principle

An assumption about neural transmission of the auditory stimulus that every nerve fiber does not fire at the same moment. Instead, the total neural activity is distributed over a series of auditory nerve fibers so that squads or volleys of fibers fire at different times. Accordingly, the neural pattern of firing corresponds to the frequency of the stimulus.

Volume

A tonal quality that refers to the size and expansiveness of a tone. Various combinations of frequency and intensity produce different volumes.

Vomeronasal System

A chemical communication system specialized for evaluating large, relatively nonvolatile molecules that typically require direct physical contact (such as licking) for their reception.

Waterfall Illusion

An example of movement aftereffects in which fixation of a waterfall for a short period will subsequently cause a stationary scene to apparently move upward.

Weber's Fraction or Ratio

Psychophysical principle that holds that the greater the magnitude of a stimulus (I), the greater the change required for a difference to be detected (ΔI). It is formulated as $\Delta I/I = k$, where k is a constant fraction that differs for different modalities.

White Noise

A complex mixture of tones of very many audible frequencies producing a "hissing" sound.

Whytt's Reflex

A reflexive constriction of the pupil of the eye in response to bright light.

Wolff Effect

An example of figure–ground perception that demonstrates that "figures" show greater contrast effects than do "grounds." See Figure 14.19.

Yaw

Rotation of the body around the z axis. The z axis passes down the length of the body. Yaw rotation is thus the rotation produced by spinning the upright person. See Figure 3.4.

Young–Helmholtz Theory

The color theory that maintains that there are three sets of receptors (cones) that respond differentially to different wavelengths. The theory is based on the fact that three different wavelengths, when mixed appropriately, are sufficient to produce almost all the perceptible colors. Also known as the *trichromatic receptor theory*.

REFERENCES

Abbe, M. The temporal effect upon the perception of space. *Japanese Journal of Experimental Psychology*, 1937, *4*, 83–93.

Adam, N., Rosner, B. S., Hosick, E. C. & Clark, D. L. Effect of anesthetic drugs on time production and alpha rhythm. *Perception & Psychophysics*, 1971, *10*, 133–136.

Addams, R. An account of a peculiar optical phenomenon seen after having looked at a moving body. *Philosophy Magazine*, 1834, *5*, 373.

Adler, K., & Pelke, C. Human homing orientation: Critique and alternative hypotheses. In D. S. Jones, B. J. MacFadden, & J. L. Kirschvink (Eds.), *Biomagnetism*. New York: Plenum, 1985.

Akil, H., Richardson, D. E., Hughes, J., & Barchas, J. D. Enkephalin-like material elevated in ventricular cerebrospinal fluid of pain patients after analgetic focal stimulation. *Science*, 1978, *201*, 463–465.

Alajouanine, T. Aphasia and artistic realization. *Brain*, 1948, *71*, 229–241.

Allport, G. W. & Pettigrew, T. F. Cultural influences on the perception of movement: The trapezoid illusion among Zulus. *Journal of Abnormal and Social Psychology*, 1957, *55*, 104–120.

Alpern, M., Lawrence, M., & Wolsk, D. *Sensory processes*. Belmont, Calif.: Wordsworth, Brooks/Cole, 1967.

Alther, L. *Kinflicks*. New York: Alfred A. Knopf, 1976.

Altman, J. *Organic foundations of animal behavior*. New York: Holt, Rinehart and Winston, 1966.

Ames, A. Binocular vision as affected by relations between uniocular stimulus-patterns in commonplace environments. *American Journal of Psychology*, 1946, *59*, 333–357.

Amoore, J. E. Current status of the steric theory of odor. *Annals of the New York Academy of Sciences*, 1964, *116*, 457–476.

Amoore, J. E. Psychophysics of odor. *Cold Spring Harbor Symposia in Quantitative Biology*, 1965, *30*, 623–637.

Amoore, J. E., Pelosi, P., & Forrester, L. J. Specific anosmias to 5 α-androst-16-en-3-one and ω-pentadecalactone: The urinous and musky primary odors. *Chemical Senses and Flavor*, 1977, *2*, 401–425.

Angle, J., & Wissman, D. The epidemiology of myopia. *American Journal of Epidemiology*, 1980, *111*, 220–228.

Annett, M. *Left, right, hand and brain: The right shift theory*. Hillsdale, N.J.: Lawrence Erlbaum, 1985.

Annis, R. C., & Frost, B. Human visual ecology and

orientation anisotropies in acuity. *Science*, 1973, *182*, 729–731.

Anstis, S. M. A chart demonstrating variations in acuity with retinal position. *Vision Research*, 1974, *14*, 589–592.

Anstis, S. M., & Atkinson, J. Distortions in moving figures viewed through a stationary slit. *American Journal of Psychology*, 1967, *80*, 572–586.

Anstis, S., & Reinhardt-Rutland, A. Interaction between motion aftereffects and induced movement. *Vision Research*, 1976, *16*, 1391–1394.

Appelle, S. Perception and discrimination as a function of stimulus orientation. *Psychological Bulletin*, 1972, *78*, 266–278.

Appelle, S. Figure embeddedness depends on contour orientation. *Perception & Psychophysics*, 1976, *19*, 109–112.

Arlin, M. The effects of physical work, mental work, and quantity on children's time perception. *Perception & Psychophysics*, 1989, *45*, 209–214.

Aronson, E., & Rosenbloom, S. Space perception in early infancy: Perception within a common auditory-visual space. *Science*, 1971, *172*, 1161–1163.

Arvidson, K., & Friberg, U. Human taste: Response and taste bud number in fungiform papillae. *Science*, 1980, *209*, 806–807.

Aslin, R. N. & Salapatek, P. Saccadic localization of visual targets by the very young human infant. *Perception & Psychophysics*, 1975, *17*, 293–302.

Attneave, F. Multistability in perception. *Scientific American*, 1971, *225*, 63–71.

Baddeley, A. D. Time-estimation at reduced body temperature. *American Journal of Psychology*, 1966, *79*, 475–479.

Bakan, P. Attention research in 1896 (note). *Science*, 1967, *143*, 171.

Baker, H. D. The instantaneous threshold and early dark adaptation. *Journal of the Optical Society of America*, 1953, *43*, 798–803.

Baker, H. D., & Rushton, W. A. H. The red-sensitive pigment in normal cones. *Journal of Physiology*, 1965, *176*, 56–72.

Baker R. R. Goal orientation by blindfolded humans after long-distance displacement: Possible involvement of a magnetic sense. *Science*, 1980, *210*, 555–557.

Baker, R. R., Mather, J. G., & Kennaugh, J. H. Magnetic bones in human sinuses. *Nature*, 1983, *301*, 78–80.

Baker, R. R., & Parker, G. A. The evolution of bird coloration. *Philosophical Transactions of the Royal Society of London*, 1979, *B287*, 63–120.

Ball, W., & Tronick, E. Infant responses to impending collision: Optical and real. *Science*, 1971, *171*, 818–820.

Balota, D. A. Automatic semantic activation and episodic memory encoding. *Journal of Verbal Learning & Verbal Behavior*, 1983, *22*, 88–104.

Balota, D. A., & Rayner, K. Parafoveal visual information and semantic contextual constraints. *Journal of Experimental Psychology: Human Perception and Performance*, 1983, *9*, 726–738.

Banks, M. S. Infant refraction and accommodations. In S. Sokol (Ed.), Electrophysiological and psychophysics: Their use in ophthalmic diagnosis. *International Ophthalmology Clinics*, 1980, *20*, 205–232.

Banks, M. S., & Salapatek, P. Infant visual perception. In P. H. Mussen (Ed.), *Handbook of child psychology*, Volume II. New York: John Wiley, 1983.

Barclay, C. D., Cutting, J. E., & Kozlowski, L. T. Temporal and spatial factors in gait perception that influence gender recognition. *Perception & Psychophysics*, 1978, *23*, 145–152.

Barlow, H. B., Blakemore, C., & Pettigrew, J. O. The neural mechanism of binocular depth discrimination. *Journal of Physiology*, 1967, *193*, 327–342.

Barlow, J. D. Pupillary size as an index of preference in political candidates. *Perceptual and Motor Skills*, 1969, *28*, 587–590.

Bartley, S. H. The psychophysiology of vision. In S. S. Stevens (Ed.), *Handbook of experimental psychology*. New York: John Wiley, 1951.

Bartoshuk, L. M. Water taste in man. *Perception & Psychophysics*, 1968, *3*, 69–72.

Bartoshuk, L. M. Bitter taste of saccharin related to the genetic ability to taste the bitter substance 6-*n*-propylthiouracil. *Science*, 1979, *205*, 934–935.

Bartoshuk, L. M., Lee, C-H., & Scarpellino, R. Sweet taste of water induced by artichoke (*Cynara Scolymus*). *Science*, 1972, *178*, 988–990.

Batteau, D. W. The role of pinna in human localization. *Proceeding of the Royal Society of London*, 1967, *168* (1011), Series B, 158–180.

Batteau, D. W. Listening with the naked ear. In S. J. Freedman (Ed.), *The neuropsychology of spatially oriented behavior*. Homewood, Ill.: Dorsey, 1968.

Bauer, J. A. Development of visual cliff discrimination by infant hooded rats. *Journal of Comparative and Physiological Psychology*, 1973, *84*, 380–385.

Bauer, J. A., & Held, R. Comparison of visually-guided reaching in normal and deprived infant monkeys. *Journal of Experimental Psychology: Animal Behavior Processes*, 1975, *1*, 298–308.

Bauer, J. A., Jr., Owens, D. A., Thomas, J., & Held, R. Monkeys show an oblique effect. *Perception*, 1979, *8*, 247–253.

Baxter, D. W., & Olszewski, J. Congenital universal insensitivity to pain. *Brain*, 1960, *83*, 381–393.

Beagley, W. K. Interaction of Müller-Lyer with filled-unfilled space illusion: An explanation of Müller-Lyer asymmetry. *Perception & Psychophysics*, 1985, *37*, 45–49.

Beatty, J., & Wagoner, B. L. Pupillometric signs of brain activation vary with level of cognitive processing. *Science*, 1978, *199*, 1216–1218.

Beauchamp, G. K. The human preference for excess salt. *American Scientist*, 1987, *75*, 27–33.

Beauchamp, G. K., & Moran, M. Dietary experience and sweet taste preference in human infants. *Appetite*, 1982, *3*, 139–152.

Beck, J. Effect of orientation and of shape similarity on perceptual grouping. *Perception & Psychophysics*, 1966, *1*, 300–302.

Beck, J. Textural segmentation. In J. Beck (Ed.), *Organization and representation in perception*. Hillsdale, N.J.: Lawrence Erlbaum, 1982.

Becklen, R., & Wallach, H. How does speed change affect induced motion? *Perception & Psychophysics*, 1985, *37*, 231–236.

Becklen, R., & Cerone, D. Selective looking and the noticing of unexpected events. *Memory & Cognition*, 1983, *11*, 601–608.

Beebe-Center, J. G., & Waddell, D. A general psychological scale of taste. *Journal of Psychology*, 1948, *26*, 517–524.

Beidler, L. M. Dynamics of taste cells. In Y. Zotterman (Ed.), *Olfaction and taste*, Volume I. New York: Macmillan, 1963.

Békésy, G. von. On the resonance curve and the decay period at various points on the cochlear partition. *Journal of the Acoustical Society of America*, 1949, *21*, 245–249.

Békésy, G. von. Description of some mechanical properties of the organ of Corti. *Journal of Acoustical Society of America*, 1953, *25*, 770–785.

Békésy, G. von. Human skin perception of traveling waves similar to those on the cochlea. *Journal of the Acoustical Society of America*, 1955, *27*, 830–841.

Békésy, G. von. The ear. *Scientific American*, 1957, *197*, 66–78.

Békésy, G. von. Frequency in the cochleas of various animals. In E. G. Wever (Trans., Ed.), *Experiments in hearing*. New York: McGraw-Hill, 1960, 500–534.

Békésy, G. von. Hearing theories and complex sounds. *Journal of the Acoustical Society of America*, 1963, *35*, 588–601.

Békésy, G. von. *Sensory inhibition*. Princeton, N.J.: Princeton University Press, 1967.

Békésy, G. von. Localization of visceral pain and other sensations before and after anesthesia. *Perception & Psychophysics*, 1971, *9*, 1–4.

Békésy, G. von. & Rosenblith, W. A. The mechanical properties of the ear. In S. S. Stevens (Ed.), *Handbook of experimental psychology*. New York: John Wiley, 1951, 1075–1115.

Bell, C. R., & Provins, K. A. Relation between

physiological responses to environmental heat and time judgments. *Journal of Experimental Psychology*, 1963, *66*, 572–579.

Bell, F. R. The variation in taste thresholds of ruminants associated with sodium depletion. In Y. Zotterman (Ed.), *Olfaction and taste*. New York: Macmillan, 1963.

Benedetti, F. Processing of tactile spatial information with crossed fingers. *Journal of Experimental Psychology: Human Perception and Performance*, 1985, *11*, 517–525.

Benedetti, F. Tactile diplopia (diplesthesia) on the human fingers. *Perception*, 1986, *15*, 83–91. (*a*).

Benedetti, F. Spatial organization of the diplesthetic and nondiplesthetic areas of the fingers. *Perception*, 1986, *15*, 285–301. (*b*).

Benedetti, F. Exploration of a rod with crossed fingers. *Perception & Psychophysics*, 1988, *44*, 281–284.

Benson, C., & Yonas, A. Development of sensitivity to static pictorial depth information. *Perception & Psychophysics*, 1973, *13*, 361–366.

Ben-Zeev, A. The passivity assumption of the sensation-perception distinction. *British Journal for the Philosophy of Science*, 1984, *35*, 327–343.

Berbaum, K., Bever, T., & Chung, C. S. Light source position in the perception of object shape. *Perception*, 1983, *12*, 411–416.

Berbaum, K., Bever, T., & Chung, C. S. Extending the perception of shape from known to unknown shading. *Perception*, 1984, *13*, 479–488.

Berbaum, K., Tharp, D., & Mroczek, K. Depth perception of surfaces in pictures: Looking for conventions of depiction in Pandora's box. *Perception*, 1983, *12*, 5–20.

Bergeijk, W. A. van, Pierce, J. R., & David E. E., Jr. *Waves and the ear*. Garden City, N.Y.: Anchor Books/Doubleday, 1960.

Bernstein, I. H., Bissonnette, V., Vyas, A., & Barclay, P. Semantic priming. Subliminal perception of context? *Perception & Psychophysics*, 1989, *45*, 153–161.

Bernstein, I. L. Learned taste aversion in children receiving chemotherapy. *Science*, 1978, *200*, 1302–1303.

Bernstein, I. L., & Webster, M. M. Learned taste aversions in humans, *Physiology and Behavior*, 1980, *25*, 363–366.

Berry, K. E., Sink, J. D., Patton, S., & Ziegler, J. H. Characterization of the swine sex odor (SSO) components in boar fat volatiles. *Journal of Food Science*, 1971, *36*, 1086–1090.

Bertenthal, B. I., & Campos, J. J. A systems approach to the organizing effects of self-produced locomotion during infancy. In C. Rovee-Collier & L. P. Lipsett (Eds.), *Advances in infancy research*, Volume 6. Norwood, N.J.: Ablex, 1989.

Best, C. T., Morrongiello, B., & Robson, R. Perceptual equivalence of acoustic cues in speech and nonspeech perception. *Perception & Psychophysics*, 1981, *29*, 191–211.

Bever, T. G., & Chiarello, R. J. Cerebral dominance in musicians and nonmusicians. *Science*, 1974, *185*, 537–539.

Beverley, K. I., & Regan, D. Separable after-effects of changing-size and motion-in-depth: Different neural mechanisms. *Vision Research*, 1979, *19*, 727–732.

Biederman, I. On the semantics of a glance at a scene. In M. Kubovy & J. R. Pomerantz (Eds.), *Perceptual Organization*. Hillsdale, N. J.: Lawrence Erlbaum, 1981.

Biederman, I., Mezzanotte, R. J., & Rabinowitz, J. C. Scene perception: Detecting and judging objects undergoing relational violations. *Cognitive Psychology*, 1982, *14*, 143–177.

Birnholz, J. C. The development of human fetal eye movement patterns. *Science*, 1981, *213*, 679–681.

Birnholz, J. C., & Benacerraf, B. R. The development of human fetal hearing. *Science*, 1983, *222*, 516–518.

Blakemore, C., & Sutton, P. Size adaptation: A new aftereffect. *Science*, 1969, *166*, 245–247.

Bliss, J. A reading machine with tactile display. In T. D. Sterling, E. A. Bering, S. V. Pollack, & H. G. Vaughan (Eds.), *Visual prosthesis*. New York: Academic Press, 1971.

Block, R. A., George, E. J., & Reed, M. A. A watched pot sometimes boils: A study of duration experience. *Acta Psychologica*, 1980, *46*, 81–94.

Bloomer, C. M. *Principles of visual perception*. New York: Van Nostrand Reinhold, 1976.

Bobko, D. J., Bobko, P., & Davis, M. A. Effect of visual display scale on duration estimates. *Human Factors*, 1986, *28*, 153–158.

Bonnet, C. Thresholds of motion perception. In A. Wertheim, W. Wagenaar, & H. W. Leibowitz (Eds.), *Tutorials in motion perception*. New York: Plenum, 1982.

Boring, E. G. A new ambiguous figure. *American Journal of Psychology*, 1930, *42*, 444–445.

Boring, E. G. *Sensation and perception in the history of experimental psychology*. New York: Appleton-Century-Crofts, 1942.

Boring, E. G. The moon illusion. *American Journal of Physics*, 1943, *11*, 55–60.

Boring, E. G. *A history of experimental psychology* (2nd ed.). New York: Appleton-Century-Crofts, 1950.

Boring, E. G. Size constancy in a picture. *American Journal of Psychology*, 1964, 77, 494–498.

Boring, E. G., Langfeld, H. S., & Weld, H. P. *Foundations of psychology*. New York: John Wiley, 1948.

Bornstein, M. H., Kessen, W., & Weiskopf, S. The categories of hue in infancy. *Science*, 1976, *191*, 201–202.

Bossom, J., & Hamilton, C. R. Interocular transfer of prism-altered coordinations in split-brain monkeys. *Journal of Comparative and Physiological Psychology*, 1963, *56*, 769–774.

Botstein, D. The molecular biology of color vision. *Science*, 1986, *232*, 142–143.

Bough, E. W. Stereoscopic vision in the macaque monkey: A behavioural demonstration. *Nature*, 1970, *225*, 42–44.

Bowditch, H. P., & Hall, G. S. Optical illusions of motion. *Journal of Physiology*, 1882, *3*, 297–307.

Bower, T. G. R., Broughton, J. M., & Moore, M. K. Infant responses to approaching objects: An indicator of response to distal variables. *Perception & Psychophysics*, 1971, *9*, 193–196.

Braddick, O. J., Wattam-Bell, J., & Atkinson, J. Orientation-specific cortical responses develop in early infancy. *Nature*, 1986, *320*, 617–619.

Bradley, A., Switkes, E., & DeValois, K. Orientation and spatial frequency selectivity of adaptation to color and luminance gratings. *Vision Research*, 1988, *28*, 841–856.

Bradley, D. R., & Dumais, S. T. Ambiguous cognitive contours. *Nature*, 1975, *257*, 582–584.

Bradley, D. R., Dumais, S. T., & Petry, H. M. Reply to Cavonius. *Nature*, 1976, *261*, 77–78.

Bradley, D. R., & Petry, H. M. Organizational determinants of subjective contour: the subjective necker cube. *American Journal of Psychology*, 1977, *90*, 253–262.

Bradshaw, J. L., & Nettleton, N. C. *Human cerebral asymmetry*. Englewood Cliffs, N.J.:Prentice Hall, 1983.

Branda, R. F., & Eaton, J. W. Skin color and nutrient photolysis: An evolutionary hypothesis. *Science*, 1978, *201*, 625–626.

Braunstein, M. L. *Depth perception through motion*. New York: Academic Press, 1976.

Bravo, M., Blake, R., & Morrison, S. Cats see subjective contours. *Vision Research*, 1988, *28*, 861–865.

Bregman, A. S. Asking the "what for" question in auditory perception. In M. Kubovy & J. R. Pomerantz (Eds.), *Perceptual organization*. Hillsdale, N.J.: Lawrence Erlbaum, 1981.

Breitmeyer, B. G. Unmasking visual masking: A look at the "why" behind the veil of the "how." *Psychological Review*, 1980, *87*, 52–69.

Breitmeyer, B. G. *Visual masking: An integrative approach*. New York: Oxford University Press, 1984.

Breitwisch, R., & Whitesides, G. H. Directionality of singing and non-singing behavior of mated and unmated northern mockingbirds. *Animal Behaviour*, 1987, *35*, 331–339.

Bridgeman, B. Visual receptive fields sensitive to absolute and relative motion during tracking. *Science*, 1972, *178*, 1106–1108.

Bridgeman, B., & Delgardo, D. Sensory effects of eye press are due to efference. *Perception & Psychophysics*, 1984, *36*, 482–484.

Brown, J. F. The visual perception of velocity.

Psychologische Forschung, 1931, *14*, 199–232. Reproduced in I. M. Spigel (Ed.), *Readings in the study of visually perceived movement*. New York: Harper & Row, 1965. (*a*)

Brown, J. F. The thresholds for visual movement. *Psychologische Forschung*, 1931, *14*, 249–268. Reproduced in I. M. Spigel (Ed.), *Readings in the study of visually perceived movement*. New York: Harper & Row, 1965. (*b*)

Brown, J. L. The structure of the visual system. In C. H. Graham (Ed.), *Vision and visual perception*. New York: John Wiley, 1965.

Brown, J. L., Shively, F. D., LaMotte, R. H., & Sechzer, J. A. Color discrimination in the cat. *Journal of Comparative and Physiological Psychology*, 1973, *84*, 534–544.

Brown, J. M., & Weisstein, N. A phantom context effect: Visual phantoms enhance target visibility. *Perception & Psychophysics*, 1988, *43*, 53–56.

Brown, P. K., & Wald, G. Visual pigments in single rods and cones in the human retina. *Science*, 1964, *144*, 45–52.

Brown, S. W. Time perception and attention: The effects of prospective versus retrospective paradigms and task demands on perceived duration. *Perceptions & Psychophysics*, 1985, *38*, 115–124.

Bruce, V., & Green, P. *Visual perception physiology, psychology and ecology*. Hillsdale, N.J.: Lawrence Erlbaum, 1985.

Buchsbaum, R. *Animals without backbones*. Chicago: University of Chicago Press, 1948.

Buffardi, L. Factors affecting the filled-duration illusion in the auditory, tactual, and visual modalities. *Perception & Psychophysics*, 1971, *10*, 292–294.

Burnham, R. W., Hanes, R. M., & Bartleson, C. J. *Color: A guide to basic facts and concepts*. New York: John Wiley, 1963.

Burr, D. C., & Ross, J. Contrast sensitivity at high velocities. *Vision Research*, 1982, *22*, 479–484.

Buss, A. H. *Psychology: Man in perspective*. New York: John Wiley, 1973.

Buss, A. H. *Psychology behavior in perspective* (2nd Ed.). New York: John Wiley, 1978.

Butler, D. L. Predicting the perception of three-dimensional objects from the geometrical information in drawings. *Journal of Experimental Psychology: Human Perception and Performance*, 1982, *8*, 674–692.

Butterworth, G., & Hicks, L. Visual proprioception and postural stability in infancy: A developmental study. *Perception*, 1977, *6*, 255–262.

Cagan, R. H. Chemostimulatory protein: A new type of taste stimulus. *Science*, 1973, *181*, 32–35.

Cahoon, D., & Edmonds, E. M. The watched pot still won't boil: Expectancy as a variable in estimating the passage of time. *Bulletin of the Psychonomic Society*, 1980, *16*, 115–116.

Cain, W. S. A history of research on smell. In E. C. Carterette & M. P. Friedman (Eds.), *Handbook of perception*, Volume VI, A: *Tasting and smelling*. New York: Academic Press, 1978.

Cain, W. S. To know with the nose: Keys to odor identification. *Science*, 1979, *203*, 467–470.

Campbell, F. W., & Wurtz, R. H. Saccadic omission: Why we do not see a grey-out during a saccadic eye movement. *Vision Research*, 1978, *18*, 1297–1303.

Campos, J. J., Hiatt, S., Ramsay, D., Henderson, C., & Svejda, M. The emergence of fear on the visual cliff. In M. Lewis & L. A. Rosenbaum (Eds.), *The development of affect*. New York: Plenum, 1978.

Cann, A., & Ross, D. A. Olfactory stimuli as context cues in human memory. *American Journal of Psychology*, 1989, *102*, 91–102.

Carmon, A., & Nashson, I. Ear asymmetry in perception of emotional non-verbal stimuli. *Acta Psychologica*, 1973, *37*, 351–357.

Carpenter, J. A. Species difference in taste preferences. *Journal of Comparative and Physiological Psychology*, 1956, *49*, 139–144.

Carr, T. H. Perceiving visual language. In K. R. Boff, L. Kaufman, & J. P. Thomas (Eds.), *Handbook of perception and human performance*. Volume II: *Cognitive processes and performance*. New York: John Wiley, 1986.

Carr, W. J., & McGuigan, D. I. The stimulus basis and modification of visual cliff performance in the rat. *Animal Behaviour*, 1965, *13*, 25–29.

Cazals, Y., Aran, J-M., Erre, J-P. & Guilhaume, A.

Acoustic responses after total destruction of the cochlear receptor: Brainstem and auditory cortex. *Science*, 1980, *210*, 83–85.

Chapanis, A. How we see: A summary of basic principles. In *Human factors in undersea warfare*. Washington, D.C.: National Research Council, 1949.

Chapanis, A., Garner, W. R., & Morgan, C. T. *Applied experimental psychology*. New York: John Wiley, 1949.

Chapanis, A., & Mankin, D. A. The vertical-horizontal illusion in a visually-rich environment. *Perception & Psychophysics*, 1967, *2*, 249–255.

Cheesman, J., & Merikle, P. M. Priming with and without awareness. *Perception & Psychophysics*, 1984, *36*, 387–395.

Cherry, E. C. Some experiments upon the recognition of speech, with one and with two ears. *Journal of the Acoustical Society of America*, 1953, *25*, 975–979.

Cherry, C., & Bowles, J. Contribution to the study of the cocktail party problem. *Journal of the Acoustical Society of America*, 1960, *32*, 884.

Chiang, C. A new theory to explain geometrical illusions produced by crossing lines. *Perception & Psychophysics*, 1968, *3*, 174–176.

Cholewiak, R.W., & Sherrick, C.E. A computer-controlled matrix system for presentation to the skin of complex spatiotemporal patterns. *Behavioral Research Methods and Instrumentation*, 1981, *13*, 667–673.

Christensen, J. P., & Huang, Y. L. The auditory tau effect and memory for pitch. *Perception & Psychophysics*, 1979, *26*, 489–494.

Christman, R. J. *Sensory experience* (2nd ed.). New York: Harper & Row, 1979.

Churchland, P. S. On the alleged backward referral of experiences and its relevance to the mind-body problem. *Philosophy of Science*, 1981, *48*, 165–181. (*a*)

Churchland, P. S. The timing of sensations: Reply to Libet. *Philosophy of Science*, 1981, *48*, 492–497. (*b*)

Clavadetscher, J. E., Brown, A. M., Ankrum, C., & Teller, D. Y. Spectral sensitivity and chromatic discriminations in 3- and 7-week-old human infants. *Journal of the Optical Society of America A*, 1988, *5*, 2093–2105.

Clocksin, W. F. Perception of surface slant and edge labels form optical flow: A computational approach. *Perception*, 1980, *9*, 253–271.

Coffin, S., & Ganz, L. Perceptual correlates of variability in the duration of the cortical excitability cycle. *Neuropsychologia*, 1977, *15*, 231–241.

Cohen, J. Psychological time. *Scientific American*, 1964, *211*, 116–124.

Cohen, J., Hansel, C. E. M., & Sylvester, J. D. A new phenomenon in time judgment. *Nature*, 1953, *172*, 901–903.

Cohen, J., Hansel, C. E. M., & Sylvester, J. D. Interdependence of temporal and auditory judgments. *Nature*, 1954, *174*, 642.

Cohen, J., Hansel, C. E. M., & Sylvester, J. D. Interdependence in judgments of space, time and movement. *Acta Psychologica*, 1955, *11*, 360–372.

Cohen, L. A. Analysis of position sense in human shoulder. *Journal of Neurophysiology*, 1958, *21*, 550–562.

Cohen, L. D., Kipnes, D., Kunkle, E. G., & Kubzansky, P. E. Observations of a person with congenital insensitivity to pain. *Journal of Abnormal and Social Psychology*, 1955, *51*, 333–338.

Cohen, W. Spatial and textural characteristics of the Ganzfeld. *American Journal of Psychology*, 1957, *70*, 403–410.

Cohen, W. Color-perception in the chromatic Ganzfeld. *American Journal of Psychology*, 1958, *71*, 390–394.

Cohn, R. Differential cerebral processing of noise and verbal stimuli. *Science*, 1971, *172*, 599–601.

Collings, V. B. Human taste response as a function of locus of stimulation on the tongue and soft palate. *Perception & Psychophysics*, 1974, *16*, 169–174.

Collins, C. C. Tactile vision synthesis. In T. D. Sterling, E. A., Bering, S. V. Pollack, & H. G. Vaughan (Eds.), *Visual prosthesis*. New York: Academic Press, 1971.

Conrad, D. G., Elsmore, T. F., & Sodetz, F. J. Δ^9-Tetrahydrocannabinol: Dose-related effects on timing behavior in chimpanzee. *Science*, 1972, *175*, 547–550.

Cook, M., & Birch, R. Infant perception of the shapes of tilted plane forms. *Infant Behavior and Development*, 1984, *7*, 389–402.

Cooper, L. A., & Shepard, R. N. Turning something over in the mind. In J. M. Wolfe (Ed.), *The mind's eye*. New York: W. H. Freeman, 1986.

Corbin, A. *The foul and the fragrant*. Cambridge, Mass.: Harvard University Press, 1986.

Coren, S. Subjective contours and apparent depth. *Psychological Review*, 1972, *79*, 359–367.

Coren, S., & Girgus, J. S. *Seeing is deceiving: The psychology of visual illusion*. Hillsdale, N.J.: Lawrence Erlbaum, 1978. (*a*)

Coren, S., & Girgus, J. S. Visual illusions. In R. Held, H. W. Leibowitz, & H.-L. Teuber (Eds.), *Handbook of sensory physiology*, Vol. VIII: *Perception*. New York: Springer-Verlag, 1978. (*b*)

Coren, S., & Girgus, J. S. Principles of perceptual organization: The Gestalt illusions. *Journal of Experimental Psychology: Human Perception and Performance*, 1980, *6*, 404–412.

Coren, S., & Porac, C. The creation and reversal of the Müller-Lyer illusion through attentional manipulation. *Perception*, 1983, *122*, 49–54.

Coren, S., Porac, C., & Theodor, L. H. The effects of perceptual set on the shape and apparent depth of subjective contours. *Perception & Psychophysics*, 1986, *39*, 327–333.

Coren, S., Porac, C., & Ward, L. M. *Sensation and perception* (2nd ed.). New York: Academic Press, 1984.

Cornfield, R., Frosdick, J. P., & Campbell, F. W. Grey-out elimination: The roles of spatial waveform, frequency and phase. *Vision Research*, 1978, *18*, 1305–1311.

Cornsweet, T. N. The staircase-method in psychophysics. *American Journal of Psychology*, 1962, *75*, 485–491.

Cornsweet, T. N. Information processing in human visual systems. *Stanford Research Institute Journal*, 1969, Feature issue 5 (Jan.).

Cornsweet, T. N. *Visual Perception*. New York: Academic Press, 1970.

Costanzo, R. M., & Gardner, E. P. A quantitative analysis of responses of direction-sensitive neurons in somatosensory cortex of awake monkeys. *Journal of Neurophysiology*, 1980, *43*, 1319–1341.

Costanzo, R. M., & Graziadei, P. P. C. Development and plasticity of the olfactory system. In T. E. Finger & W. L. Silver (Eds.), *Neurobiology of taste and smell*. New York: John Wiley, 1987.

Cotzin, M., & Dallenbach, K. M. "Facial vision:" The role of pitch and loudness in the perception of obstacles by the blind. *American Journal of Psychology*, 1950, *63*, 483–515.

Crassini, B., Brown, B., & Bowman, K. Age-related changes in contrast sensitivity in central and peripheral retina. *Perception*, 1988, *17*, 315–332.

Cremieux, J., Orban, G. A., & Duysens, J. Responses of cat visual cortical cells to continuously and stroboscopically illuminated moving light slits compared. *Vision Research*, 1984, *24*, 449–457.

Crescitelli, F., & Pollack, J. D. Color vision in the antelope ground squirrel. *Science*, 1965, *150*, 1336–1338.

Crook, C. K. Taste perception in the newborn infant. *Infant Behavior and Development*, 1978, *1*, 52–69.

Crouch, J. E., & McClintic, J. R. *Human anatomy and physiology*. New York: John Wiley, 1971.

Crovitz, H. F., & Schiffman, H. Visual perception and xerography. *Science*, 1968, *160*, 1251–1252.

Cruze, W. W. Maturation and learning in chicks. *Journal of Comparative Psychology*, 1935, *19*, 371–409.

Curry, F. K. A comparison of left-handed and right-handed subjects on verbal and nonverbal dichotic listening tasks. *Cortex*, 1967, *3*, 343–352.

Curtin, B. J. Myopia: A review of its etiology pathogenesis and treatment. *Survey of Opthalmology*, 1970, *15*, 1–17.

Cutietta, R. A., & Haggerty, K. J. A comparative study of color association with music at various age levels. *Journal of Research in Music Education*, 1987, *35*, 78–91.

Cutler, W. B., Preti, G., Krieger, A., Huggins, G. R., Garcia, C. R., & Lawley, H. J. Human axillary secretions influence women's menstrual cycles: The role of donor extract from men. *Hormones and Behavior*, 1986, *20*, 463–473.

Cutting, J. E. Generation of synthetic male and female walkers through manipulation of a bio-mechanical invariant. *Perception*, 1978, *7*, 393–405.

Cutting, J. E., & Kozlowski, L. T. Recognizing friends by their walk: Gait perception without familiarity cues. *Bulletin of the Psychonomic Society*, 1977, *9*, 353–356.

Cutting, J. E., & Proffitt, D. R. Gait perception as an example of how we may perceive events. In R. Walk & H. Pick (Eds.), *Intersensory perception and sensory integration*. New York: Plenum Press, 1981.

Cutting, J. E., Proffitt, D. R., & Kozlowski, L. T. A biomechanical invariant for gait perception. *Journal of Experimental Psychology: Human Perception and Performance*, 1978, *4*, 357–372.

Dallenbach, K. M. The temperature spots and end-organs. *American Journal of Psychology*, 1927, *39*, 402–427.

Dallenbach, K. M. A puzzle-picture with a new principle of concealment. *American Journal of Psychology*, 1951, *64*, 431–433.

Dalrymple-Alford, E. C. Associative facilitation and interference in the Stroop color-word task. *Perception & Psychophysics*, 1972, *11*, 274–276.

Darian-Smith, I., Sugitan, M., Heywood, J., Darita, K., & Goodwin, A. Touching textured surfaces: Cells in somatosensory cortex respond both to finger movement and to surface features. *Science*, 1982, *218*, 906–909.

Darwin, C. *The descent of man and selection in relation to sex*. 1871, New York: Modern Library Edition, 1948.

Daunton, N., & Thomsen, D. Visual modulation of otolith-dependent units in cat vestibular nuclei. *Experimental Brain Research*, 1979, *37*, 173–176.

Davidoff, J. B. An observation concerning the preferred perception of the visual horizontal and vertical. *Perception*, 1974, *3*, 47–48.

Davis, H. *Hearing and deafness: a guide for laymen*. New York: Murray Hill, 1947.

Davis, H., & Silverman, S. R. *Hearing and deafness* (4th ed.). New York: Holt, Rinehart and Winston, 1978.

Davis, J. M., & Rovee-Collier, C. Alleviated forgetting of a learned contingency in 8-week-old infants. *Developmental Psychology*, 1983, *19*, 353–365.

Daw, N. W. Goldfish retina: Organization for simultaneous color contrast. *Science*, 1967, *158*, 942–944.

Day, R. H. Visual spatial illusions: a general explanation. *Science*, 1972, *175*, 1335–1340.

Day, R. H. Induced rotation with concentric patterns. *Perception & Psychophysics*, 1981, *29*, 493–499.

Day, R. H., & McKenzie, B. E. Infant perception of the invariant size of approaching and receding objects. *Developmental Psychology*, 1981, *54*, 172–177.

DeCasper, A. J., & Fifer, W. P. Of human bonding: Newborns prefer their mother's voices. *Science*, 1980, *208*, 1174–1176.

DeCasper, A. J., & Spence, M. J. Prenatal maternal speech influences newborn's perception of speech sounds. *Infant Behavior and Development*, 1986, *9*, 133–150.

Deliege, I. Grouping conditions in listening to music: An approach to Lerdahl & Jackendoff's grouping preference rules. *Music Perception*, 1987, *4*, 325–359.

Delk, J. L., & Fillenbaum, S. Difference in perceived color as a function of characteristic color. *American Journal of Psychology*, 1965, *78*, 290–293.

DeLong, A. J. Phenomenological space-time: Toward an experiential relativity. *Science*, 1981, *213*, 681–683.

Denes, P. B. & Pinson, E. N. *The speech chain: the physics and biology of spoken language*. Garden City, N.Y.: Anchor Books/Doubleday, 1973.

Denton, D. A. *The hunger for salt*. New York: Springer-Verlag, 1982.

Denton, D. The most-craved crystal. *The Sciences*, 1986, *26*, 29–34.

Desimone, R., Albright, T. D., Gross, C. G., & Bruce, C. Stimulus-selective properties of inferior temporal neurons in the macaque. *Journal of Neuroscience*, 1984, *4*, 2051–2062.

Desor, J. A., & Beauchamp, G. K. The human capacity to transmit olfactory information. *Perception & Psychophysics*, 1974, *16*, 551–556.

Desor, J. A., Maller, O., & Turner, R. E. Taste acceptance of sugars by human infants. *Journal of Comparative and Physiological Psychology*, 1973, *84*, 496–501.

Dethier, V. G. The taste of salt. *American Scientist*, 1977, *65*, 744–751.

Deutsch, D. The psychology of music. In E. C. Carterette & M. P. Friedman (Eds.), *Handbook of perception*. Volume X: *Perceptual ecology*. New York: Academic Press, 1978.

Deutsch, D. Grouping mechanisms in music. In D. Deutsch (Ed.), *The psychology of music*. New York: Academic Press, 1982.

Deutsch, D. Auditory pattern recognition. In K. R. Boff, L. Kaufman, & J. P. Thomas (Eds.), *Handbook of perception and human performance*. Volume II: *Cognitive processes and performance*. New York: John Wiley, 1986.

DeValois, R. L. Analysis of coding of color vision in the primate visual system. *Cold Spring Harbor Symposia*, 1965, XXX. (*a*)

DeValois, R. L. Behavioral and electrophysiological studies of primate vision. In W. D. Neff (Ed.), *Contributions to sensory physiology*, Volume 1. New York: Academic Press, 1965. (*b*)

DeValois, R. L., Abramov, I., & Jacobs, G. H. Analysis of response patterns of LGN cells. *Journal of the Optical Society of America*, 1966, *56*, 966–977.

Dichgans, J., & Brandt, T. Visual-vestibular interaction: Effects on self-motion perception and postural control. In R. Held, H. W. Leibowitz, & H.-L. Teuber (Eds.), *Handbook of sensory physiology*. Volume VIII: *Perception*. New York: Springer-Verlag, 1978.

Dimond, S. J. The structural basis of timing. *Psychological Bulletin*, 1964, *62*, 348–350.

Dixon, F. *Subliminal perception: The nature of a controversy*. New York: McGraw-Hill, 1971.

Dobelle, W. H., Mladejovsky, M. G., & Girvin, J. P. Artificial vision for the blind: electrical stimulation of visual cortex offers a hope for functional prosthesis. *Science*, 1974, *183*, 440–444.

Dobson, V., & Teller, D. Y. Visual acuity in human infants: A review and comparison of behavioral and electrophysical studies. *Vision Research*, 1978, *18*, 1469–1483.

Dohlman, G. Some practical and theoretical points in labyrinthology. *Proceedings of the Royal Society of Medicine*, 1935, *28*, 1371–1380.

Doty, R. L., Brugger, W. E., Jurs, P. C., Orndorff, M. A., Snyder, P. J., & Lowry, L. D. Intranasal trigeminal stimulation from odorous volatiles: Psychometric responses from anosmic and normal humans. *Physiology and Behavior*, 1978, *20*, 175–187.

Doty, R. L., Green, P. A., Ram, C., & Yankell, S. L. Communication of gender from human breath odors: Relationship to perceived intensity and pleasantness. *Hormones and Behavior*, 1982, *16*, 13–22.

Doty, R. L., Shaman, P., Applebaum, S. L., Gilberson, R., Sikorski, L., & Rosenberg, L. Smell identification ability: Changes with age. *Science*, 1984, *226*, 1441–1442.

Doty, R. L., Snyder, P. J., Huggins, G. R., & Lowry, L. D. Endocrine, cardiovascular, and psychological correlates of olfactory sensitivity changes during the human menstrual cycle. *Journal of Comparative and Physiological Psychology*, 1981, *95*, 45–60.

Dowling, J. E. Night blindness. *Scientific American*, 1966, *215*, 78–84.

Dowling, J. E., & Wald, G. The biological function of vitamin A acid. *Proceedings of the National Society of Sciences*, 1960, *46*, 587–616.

Dowling, W. J. Scale and contour: Two components of a theory of memory for melodies. *Psychological Review*, 1978, *85*, 341–354.

Downey, J. E., & Anderson, J. E. Automatic writing. *The American Journal of Psychology*, 1915, 26, 161–195.

Dravnieks, A. Odor quality: Semantically generated multidimensional profiles are stable. *Science*, 1982, *218*, 799–801.

Duke-Elder, S. *System of ophthalmology*. (Vol 1), *The eye in evolution*. St. Louis: C. V. Mosby, 1958.

Dumais, S. T., & Bradley, D. R. The effects of illumination level and retinal size on the apparent strength of subjective contours. *Perception & Psychophysics*, 1976, *19*, 339–345.

Duncan, J. Two techniques for investigating perception without awareness. *Perception & Psychophysics*, 1985, *38*, 296–298.

Duncan-Johnson, C. C., & Kopell, B. S. The Stroop effect: Brain potentials localize the source of interference. *Science*, 1981, *214*, 938–940.

Duncker, K. Uber induzierte Bewegung. *Psychologisch Forschung*, 1929, *12*, 180–259. (Translated as "Induced motion," in W. D. Ellis (Ed.), *A source book of Gestalt psychology*. London: Paul, Trench & Trubner, 1938.)

Duncker, K. The influence of past experience upon perceptual properties. *American Journal of Psychology*, 1939, *52*, 255–265.

Dunkeld, J., & Bower, T. G. R. Infant response to impending optical collision. *Perception*, 1980, *9*, 549–554.

Dyer, F. N. The Stroop phenomenon and its use in the study of perceptual, cognitive, and response processes. *Memory & Cognition*, 1973, *1*, 106–120.

Dzendolet, E., & Meiselman, H. L. Gustatory quality changes as a function of solution concentration. *Perception & Psychophysics*, 1967, *2*, 29–33.

Edmister, J. A., & Vickers, Z. M. Instrumental acoustical measures of crispness in foods. *Journal of Texture Studies*, 1985, *16*, 153–167.

Eggers, H. M., & Blakemore, C. Physiological basis of anisometropic amblyopia. *Science*, 1978, *201*, 264–266.

Ehrenstein, W. Concerning variations on L. Hermann's brightness observations. *Zeitschrift fur Psychologie*, 1941, *150*, 83–91.

Eimas, P. D., & Corbit, J. D. Selective adaptation of linguistic feature detectors. *Cognitive Psychology*, 1973, *4*, 99–109.

Eimas, P. D., Siqueland, E. R., Jusczyk, P., & Vigorito, J. Speech perception in infants. *Science*, 1971, *171*, 303–306.

Engel, E. Binocular fusion of dissimilar figures. *Journal of Psychology*, 1958, *46*, 53–57.

Engen, T. Remembering odors and their names. *American Scientist*, 1987, *75*, 497–503.

Engen, T., & Ross, B. M. Long-term memory of odors with and without verbal descriptions. *Journal of Experimental Psychology*, 1973, *100*, 221–227.

Enns, J. T., & Girgus, J. S. Perceptual grouping and spatial distortion: A developmental study. *Developmental Psychology*, 1985, *21*, 241–246.

Enns, J. T., & Prinzmetal, W. The role of redundancy in the object-line effect. *Perception & Psychophysics*, 1984, *35*, 22–32.

Enright, J. T. Stereopsis, visual latency, and three-dimensional moving pictures. *American Scientist*, 1970, *58*, 536–545.

Epstein, W. The influence of assumed size on apparent distance. *American Journal of Psychology*, 1963, *76*, 257–265.

Epstein, W. *Varieties of perceptual learning*. New York: McGraw-Hill, 1967.

Erdelyi, M. A new look at the new look: Perceptual defense and vigilance. *Psychological Review*, 1974, *81*, 1–25.

Erickson, R. P. Sensory neural patterns and gustation. In Y. Zotterman (Ed.), *Olfaction and taste*. New York: Macmillan, 1963.

Erickson, R. P. Definitions: A matter of taste. In D. W. Pfaff (Ed.), *Taste, olfaction, and the central nervous system*, New York: The Rockefeller University Press, 1984.

Eriksen, C. W., & Collins, J. F. Some temporal characteristics of visual pattern recognition.

Journal of Experimental Psychology, 1967, *74*, 476–484.

Escher, M. C. *The graphic work of M.C. Escher*. New York: Ballantine, 1971.

Evans, D. W., & Ginsburg, A. P. Predicting age-related differences in discriminating road signs using contrast sensitivity. *Journal of the Optical Society of America*, 1982, *72*, 1785–1786.

Ewert, P. H. A study of the effect of inverted retinal stimulations upon spatially coordinated behavior. *Genetic Psychology Monographs*, 1930, 7, 177–363.

Fagan, J. F. Infant's recognition of invariant features of faces. *Child Development*, 1976, *47*, 627–638.

Fanselow, M. S. Odors released by stressed rats produce opioid analgesia in unstressed rats. *Behavioral Neuroscience*, 1985, *99*, 589–592.

Fantz, R. L. The origin of form perception. *Scientific American*, 1961, *204*, 66–72.

Fantz, R. L. Pattern vision in newborn infants. *Science*, 1963, *140*, 296–297.

Fantz, R. L. Ontogeny of perception. In A. M. Schrier, H. F. Harlow, & F. Stollnitz (Eds.), *Behavior of nonhuman primate*, Volume II. New York: Academic Press, 1965. (*a*)

Fantz, R. L. Visual perception from birth as shown by pattern selectivity. *Annals of the New York Academy of Sciences*, 1965, *118*, 793–814. (*b*)

Fantz, R. L. Pattern discrimination and selective attention. In A. H. Kidd & J. L. Rivoire (Eds.), *Perceptual development in children*. New York: International Universities Press, 1966.

Fantz, R. L., & Miranda, S. B. Newborn infant attention to form of contour. *Child Development*, 1975, *46*, 224–228.

Favreau, O. E., Emerson, V. F., & Corballis, M. C. Motion perception: A color contingent aftereffect. *Science*, 1972, *176*, 78–79.

Fay, R. R. Auditory frequency discrimination in the goldfish (*Carrassius auratus*). *Journal of Comparative and Physiological Psychology*, 1970, *73*, 175–180.

Ferguson, R. P., & Martin, P. Long-term temporal estimation in humans. *Perception & Psychophysics*, 1983, *33*, 585–592.

Ferster, D. A comparison of binocular depth mechanisms in areas 17 and 18 of the cat visual cortex. *Journal of Physiology*, 1981, *311*, 623–655.

Festinger, L., Allyn, M. R., & White, C. W. The perception of color with achromatic stimulation. *Vision Research*, 1971, *11*, 591–612.

Fillenbaum, S., Schiffman, H. R., & Butcher, J. Perception of off-size versions of a familiar object under conditions of rich information. *Journal of Experimental Psychology*, 1965, *69*, 298–303.

Fineman, M. B. *The inquisitive eye*. New York: Oxford University Press, 1981.

Finke, R. A., & Shepard, R. N. Visual functions of mental imagery. In K. R. Boff, L. Kaufman, & J. P. Thomas (Eds.), *Handbook of perception and human performance*. Volume II: *Cognitive processes and performance*. New York: John Wiley, 1986.

Fisher, G. H. A common principle relating to the Müller–Lyer and Ponzo illusions. *American Journal of Psychology*, 1967, *80*, 626–631. (*a*)

Fisher, G. H. Ambiguous figure treatments in the art of Salvador Dali. *Perception & Psychophysics*, 1967, *2*, 328–330. (*b*)

Fisher, G. H. Illusions and size-constancy. *American Journal of Psychology*, 1968, *81*, 2–20.

Fisher, G. H. An experimental and theoretical appraisal of the perspective and size-constancy theories of illusions. *Quarterly Journal of Experimental Psychology*, 1970, *22*, 631–652.

Fisher, G. H. Towards a new explanation for the geometrical illusions: II Apparent depth or contour proximity. *British Journal of Psychology*, 1973, *64*, 607–621.

Fisher, R. The biological fabric of time. In Interdisciplinary perspectives of time. *Annals of the New York Academy of Sciences*, 1967, *138*, 451–465.

Fitzpatrick, V., Pasnak, R., & Tyler, Z. E. The effect of familiar size at familiar distance. *Perception*, 1982, *11*, 85–91.

Flaherty, C. F. Incentive contrast: A review of behavioral changes following shifts in reward. *Animal Learning & Behavior*, 1982, *19*, 409–440.

Flaherty, C. F., & Grigson, P. S. From contrast to

reinforcement: Role of response contingency in anticipatory contrast. *Journal of Experimental Psychology: Animal Behavior Processes*, 1988, *14*, 165–176.

Flaherty, C. F., & Sepanek, S. J. Bidirectional contrast, matching, and power functions obtained in sucrose consumption. *Animal Learning & Behavior*, 1978, *6*, 313–319.

Fletcher, H. *Speech and hearing* (rev. ed.). New York: D. Van Nostrand Co., 1952.

Fletcher, H., & Munson, W. A. Loudness, its definition, measurement, and calculation. *Journal of the Acoustical Society of America*, 1933, *5*, 82–108.

Flock, A. Physiological properties of sensory hair cells in the ear. In E. F. Evans & J. P. Wilson (Eds.), *Psychophysics and physiology of hearing*. New York: Academic Press, 1977.

Flowers, J. H., & Stoup, C. M. Selective attention between words, shapes, and colors in speeded classification and vocalization tasks. *Memory & Cognition*, 1977, *5*, 299–307.

Foley, J. P. An experimental investigation of the effect of prolonged inversion of the visual field in the rhesus monkey (*Macaca mulatta*). *Journal of Genetic Psychology*, 1940, *56*, 21–51.

Foster, P. M., & Govier, E. Discrimination without awareness? *Quarterly Journal of Experimental Psychology*, 1978, *30*, 289–295.

Foulke, E., & Berlá, E. P. Visual impairment and the development of perceptual ability. In R. D. Walk & H. L. Pick, Jr. (Eds.), *Perception and experience*. New York: Plenum, 1978.

Fowler, C. A., Wolford, G., Slade, R., & Tassinary, L. Lexical access with and without awareness. *Journal of Experimental Psychology: General*, 1981, *110*, 341–362.

Fox, R., Aslin, R. N., Shea, S. L., & Dumais, S. T., Stereopsis in human infants. *Science*, 1980, *207*, 323–324.

Fox, R., & Blake, R. R. Stereopsis in the cat. Paper presented at the tenth meeting of the Psychonomic Society, San Antonio, Tex. November 1970.

Fox, R., Lehmkuhle, S. W., & Bush, R. C. Stereopsis in the falcon. *Science*, 1977, *197*, 79–81.

Fox, R., Lehmkuhle, S. W., & Westendorf, D. H. Falcon visual acuity. *Science*, 1976, *192*, 263–265.

Fox, R., & McDaniel, C. The perception of biological motion by human infants. *Science*, 1982, *218*, 486–487.

Fraisse, P. *The psychology of time*. New York: Harper & Row, 1963.

Fraisse, P. Perception and the estimation of time. *Annual Review of Psychology*, 1984, *35*, 1–36.

Frank, M. An analysis of hamster afferent taste nerve response function. *Journal of General Physiology*, 1973, *61*, 588–618.

Frank, M. The distinctiveness of responses to sweet in the *Chorda tympani* nerve. In J. W. Weiffenbach (Ed.), *Taste and development*. Bethesda, Md.: U.S. Department of Health, Education, and Welfare, Public Health Service, 1977. DHEW Publication No. (NIH) 77–1068.

Frankenhauser, M. *Estimation of time*. Stockholm: Almqvist & Wiksell, 1959.

Freedman, S. J., & Fisher, H. G. The role of the pinna in auditory localization. In S. J. Freedman (Ed.), *The neuropsychology of spatially oriented behavior*. Homewood, Ill.: Dorsey, 1968.

Freeman, R. D., & Bonds, A. B. Cortical plasticity in monocularly deprived immobilized kittens depends on eye movement. *Science*, 1979, *206*, 1093–1095.

Freeman, R. D., Mitchell, D. E., & Millodot, M. A neural effect of partial visual deprivation in humans. *Science*, 1972, *175*, 1384–1386.

Freeman, R. D., & Thibos, L. N. Electrophysiological evidence that abnormal early visual experience can modify the human brain. *Science*, 1973, *180*, 876–878.

French, N. R., & Steinberg, J. C. Factors governing the intelligibility of speech-sounds. *Journal of the Acoustical Society of America*, 1947, *19*, 90–119.

Frisby, J. P. *Seeing*. New York: Oxford University Press, 1980.

Frisby, J. P., & Clatworthy, J. L. Illusory contours: Curious cases of simultaneous brightness contrast? *Perception*, 1975, *4*, 349–357.

Frome, F. S., Piantanida, T. P., & Kelly, D. H.

Psychophysical evidence for more than two kinds of cone in dichromatic color blindness. *Science*, 1982, *215*, 417–419.

Frost, B. J., & Nakayama, K. Single visual neurons code opposing motion independent of direction. *Science*, 1983, *220*, 744–745.

Galambos, R., & Davis, H. The response of single auditory-nerve fibers to acoustic stimulation. *Journal of Neurophysiology*, 1943, *6*, 39–57.

Galanter, E. Contemporary psychophysics. In R. Brown, E. Galanter, E. H. Hess, & G. Mandler (Eds.), *New Directions in Psychology*, New York: Holt, Rinehart and Winston, 1962.

Galanter, E. *Textbook of elementary psychology*. San Francisco: Holden-Day, 1966.

Gambert, S. R., Garthwaite, T. L., Pontzer, C. H., & Hagen, T. C. Fasting associated with decrease in hypothalamic β-endorphin. *Science*, 1980, *210*, 1271–1272.

Gandelman, R., Zarrow, M. X., Denenberg, V. H., & Myers, M. Olfactory bulb removal eliminates maternal behavior in the mouse. *Science*, 1971, *171*, 210–211.

Garcia, J., Hankins, W. G., & Rusiniak, K. W. Behavioral regulation of the milieu interne in man and rat. *Science*, 1974, *185*, 824–831.

Gardner, E. *Fundamentals of neurology*. Philadelphia: W. B. Saunders, 1947.

Gardner, M. B., & Gardner, R. S. Problem of localization in the median plane: Effect of pinnae cavity occlusion. *Journal of the Acoustical Society of America*, 1973, *53*, 400–408.

Garrett, M. F. Production of speech: Observations from normal and pathological language use. In A. W. Willis (Ed.), *Normality and pathology in cognitive functions*. New York: Academic Press, 1982.

Gazzaniga, M. S., & Hillyard, S. A. Language and speech capacity of the right hemisphere. *Neuropsychologia*, 1971, *9*, 273–280.

Geiger, G., & Poggio, T. The Müller-Lyer figure and the fly. *Science*, 1975, *190*, 479–480.

Geldard, F. A. Some neglected possibilities of communication. *Science*, 1960, *131*, 1583–1588.

Geldard, F. A. *Fundamentals of psychology*. New York: John Wiley, 1962.

Geldard, F. A. Body English. *Psychology Today*, December 2, 1968, 42–47. (*a*)

Geldard, F. A. Pattern perception by the skin. Chapter 13 in D. R. Kenshalo (Ed.), *The skin senses*. Springfield, Ill.: Charles C Thomas, 1968. (*b*)

Geldard, F. A. *The human senses* (2nd ed.). New York:John Wiley, 1972.

Gesteland, R. C. Neurophysiology and psychology of smell. In E. C. Carterette & M. P. Friedman (Eds.), *Handbook of perception*. Volume VI, A: *Tasting and smelling*. New York: Academic Press, 1978.

Gesteland, R. C., Lettvin, J. Y., & Pitts, W. H. Chemical transmission in the nose of the frog. *Journal of Physiology*, 1965, *181*, 525–559.

Gesteland, R. C., Lettvin, J. Y., Pitts, W. H., & Rojas, A. Odor specificities of the frog's olfactory receptors. In Y. Zotterman (Ed.), *Olfaction and taste*. New York: Pergamon, 1963.

Getchell, T. V., & Getchell, M. L. Peripheral mechanisms of olfaction: Biochemistry and neurophysiology. In T. E. Finger & W. L. Silver (Eds.), *Neurobiology of taste and smell*. New York: John Wiley, 1987.

Giampapa, V. C. Personal communication, 1989.

Gibbons, B. The intimate sense of smell. *National Geographic*, 1986, *170*, 324–361.

Gibson, E. J. The development of perception as an adaptive process. *American Scientist*, 1970, *58*, 98–107.

Gibson, J. J. Adaptation, after-effect, and contrast in the perception of curved lines. *Journal of Experimental Psychology*, 1933, *16*, 1–31.

Gibson, J. J. *The perception of the visual world*. New York: Houghton Mifflin, 1950.

Gibson, J. J. Observations on active touch. *Psychological Review*, 1962, *69*, 477–491.

Gibson, J. J. *The senses considered as perceptual systems*. New York: Houghton Mifflin, 1966.

Gibson, J. J. What gives rise to the perception of motion? *Psychological Review*, 1968, *75*, 335–346.

Gibson, J.J. The theory of affordances. In R. Shaw & J. Bransford (Eds.), *Perceiving, acting, and knowing*. Hillsdale, N.J.: Lawrence Erlbaum, 1977.

Gibson, J. J. *The ecological approach to visual perception*. Boston: Houghton Mifflin, 1979.

Gibson, J. J. Notes on affordances. In E. Reed & R. Jones (Eds.), *Reasons for realism*. Hillsdale, N. J.: Lawrence Erlbaum, 1983.

Gibson, J. J., & Bridgeman, B. The visual perception of surface texture in photographs. *Psychological Research*, 1987, *49*, 1–5.

Gibson, J. J., & Radner, M. Adaptation, aftereffect and contrast in the perception of tilted lines. I. Quantitative studies. *Journal of Experimental Psychology*, 1937, *20*, 453–467.

Gibson, J. J., & Waddell, D. Homogeneous retinal stimulation and visual perception. *American Journal of Psychology*, 1952, *65*, 263–270.

Gilbert, A. N., & Wysocki, C. J. The smell survey results. *National Geographic*, 1987, *172*, 514–525.

Gilchrist, A. L. Perceived lightness depends on perceived spatial arrangement. *Science*, 1977, *195*, 185–187.

Gilden, D. L., MacDonald, K. E., & Lasaga, M. I. Masking with minimal contours: Selective inhibition with low spatial frequencies. *Perception & Psychophysics*, 1988, *44*, 127–132.

Gillam, B. A depth processing theory of the Poggendorff illusion. *Perception & Psychophysics*, 1971, *10*, 211–216.

Gillam, B. Geometrical illusions. *Scientific American*, 1980, *242*, 102–111.

Gilliland, A. R., Hofeld, J., & Eckstrand, G. Studies in time perception. *Psychological Bulletin*, 1946, *43*, 162–176.

Ginsburg, A. P. Spatial filtering and vision: Implications for normal and abnormal vision. In L. Proenza, J. Enoch, & A. Jampolski (Eds.), *Clinical applications of psychophysics*. New York: Cambridge University Press, 1981.

Ginsburg, A. P. Spatial filtering and visual form perception. In K. R. Boff, L. Kaufman, & J. P. Thomas (Eds.), *Handbook of perception and human performance*. Volume II: *Cognitive processes and performance*. New York: John Wiley, 1986.

Ginsburg, A. P., Cannon, M. W., Evans, D. W., Owsley, C., & Mulvaney, P. Large sample norms for contrast sensitivity. *American Journal of Optometry and Physiological Optics*, 1984, *61*, 80–84.

Glaser, E. M., & Haven, M. Bandpass noise stimulation of the simulated basilar membrane. *Journal of the Acoustical Society of America*, 1972, *52*, 1131–1136.

Glass, A. L., & Holyoak, K. J. *Cognition* (2nd ed.). New York: Random House, 1986.

Glass, B. Foreword to M. P. Kare, & O. Haller (Eds.). *The chemical senses and nutrition*. Baltimore, Md.: John Hopkins Press, 1967.

Glucksburg, S., & Cowen, G. N. Memory for nonattended auditory material. *Cognitive Psychology*, 1970, *1*, 149–156.

Gogel, W. C., & DaSilva, J. A. Familiar size and the theory of off-sized perceptions. *Perception & Psychophysics*, 1987, *41*, 318–328.

Gogel, W. C., & Koslow, M. The adjacency principle and induced movement. *Perception & Psychophysics*, 1972, *11*, 309–314.

Goldfoot, D. A., Essock-Vitale, S. M., Asa, C. S., Thornton, J. E., & Lechner, A. I. Anosmia in male rhesus monkeys does not alter copulatory activity with cycling females. *Science*, 1978, *199*, 1095–1096.

Goldsmith, T. H. Hummingbirds see near ultraviolet light. *Science*, 1980, *207*, 786–788.

Goldstone, S., Boardman, W. K., & Lhamon, W. T. Effect of quinal barbitone, dextroamphetamine, and placebo on apparent time. *British Journal of Psychology*, 1958, *49*, 324–328.

Gomez, L. M., & Robertson, L. C. The filled-duration-illusion: The function of temporal and nontemporal set. *Perception & Psychophysics*, 1979, *25*, 432–438.

Gonzalez-Cruzzi, F. *The five senses*. San Diego: Harcourt Brace Jovanovich, 1989.

Good, P. A sculpture is created with the blind in mind. *The New York Times*, October 23, 1988, p. 20 (New Jersey supplement).

Good, P. R., Geary, N., & Engen, T. The effect of

estrogen on odor detection. *Chemical Senses and Flavor*, 1976, *2*, 45–50.

Goodwin, M., Gooding, K. M., & Regnier, F. Sex pheromones in the dog. *Science*, 1979, *203*, 559–561.

Goolkasian, P. Cyclic changes in pain perception: An ROC analysis. *Perception & Psychophysics*, 1980, *27*, 499–504.

Gordon, I. E., & Cooper, C. Improving one's touch. *Nature*, 1975, *256*, 203–204.

Gould, J. L., & Able, K. P. Human homing: An elusive phenomenon. *Science*, 1981, *212*, 1061–1063.

Gould, J. L., Kirschvink, J. L., & Deffeyes, K. S. Bees have magnetic remanence. *Science*, 1978, *201*, 1226–1228.

Graham, C. A., & McGrew, W. C. Menstrual synchrony in female undergraduates living on a coeducational campus. *Psychoneuroendocrinology*, 1980, *5*, 245–252.

Graham, C. H., & Hsia, Y. Luminosity curves for normal and dichromatic subjects including a case of unilateral color blindness. *Science*, 1954, *120*, 780.

Graham, C. H., & Hsia, Y. Color defect and color theory. *Science*, 1958, *127*, 675–682.

Graham, N. Spatial-frequency channels in human vision: Detecting edges without edge detectors. In C. S. Harris (Ed.), *Visual coding and adaptability*. Hillsdale, N.J.: Lawrence Erlbaum, 1980.

Grau, J. W. Influence of naloxone on shock-induced freezing and analgesia. *Behavioral Neuroscience*, 1984, *98*, 278–292.

Graybiel, A., & Lackner, J. R. Treatment of severe motion sickness with antimotion sickness drug injections. *Aviation, Space, and Environmental Medicine*, 1987, *58*, 773–776.

Green, B. G. Localization of thermal sensation: An illusion and synthetic heat. *Perception & Psychophysics*, 1977, *22*, 331–337.

Green, B. G. Tactile roughness and the "paper effect." *Bulletin of the Psychonomic Society*, 1981, *18*, 155–158.

Green, D. M. *An introduction to hearing*. Hillsdale, N.J.: Lawrence Erlbaum, 1976.

Green, D. M., & Swets, J. A. *Signal detection theory and psychophysics*. New York: John Wiley, 1966.

Greene, E. The corner Poggendorff. *Perception*, 1988, *17*, 65–70.

Greene, S. L., Plastoe, E., & Braine, L. G. Judging the location of features of naturalistic and geometric shapes. *Perception & Psychophysics*, 1985, *37*, 148–154.

Gregory, R. L. Distortion of visual space as inappropriate constancy scaling. *Nature*, 1963, *199*, 678–680.

Gregory, R. L. *Eye and brain*. New York: World University Library, 1966.

Gregory, R. L. Visual illusions. *Scientific American*, 1968, *219*, 66–76.

Gregory, R. L. *Eye and brain* (2nd Ed.). New York: World University Library, 1973.

Gregory, R. L. *Concepts and mechanisms of perception*. New York: Scribners, 1974.

Gregory, R. L. *Eye and brain: The psychology of seeing* (3rd ed.). New York: World University Library, 1977.

Gregory, R. L., & Wallace, J. G. Recovery from early blindness: A case study. *Experimental Psychology Society Monographs* (No. 2). Cambridge: Heffner, 1963.

Greist-Bousquet, S., & Schiffman, H. R. The many illusions of the Müller–Lyer: Comparisons of the wings-in and wings-out illusion and manipulations of standard and dot forms. *Perception*, 1981, *10*, 147–154. (*a*)

Greist-Bousquet, S., & Schiffman, H. R. The Poggendorff illusion: An illusion of linear extent? *Perception*, 1981, *10*, 155–164. (*b*)

Greist-Bousquet, S., & Schiffman, H. R. The role of structural components in the Müller–Lyer illusion. *Perception & Psychophysics*, 1981, *30*, 505–511. (*c*)

Greist-Bousquet, S., & Schiffman, H. R. Poggendorff and Müller-Lyer illusions: common effects. *Perception*, 1985, *14*, 427–447.

Greist-Bousquet, S., & Schiffman, H. R. The basis of the Poggendorff effect: An additional clue for Day and Kasperczyk. *Perception & Psychophysics*, 1986, *39*, 447–448.

Greist-Bousquet, S., & Schiffman, H. R. A note on enhancing the Poggendorff illusion. *Perception & Psychophysics*, 1987, *42*, 202–203.

Greist-Bousquet, S., Watson, M., & Schiffman, H. R. An examination of illusion decrement with inspection of wings-in and wings-out Mueller-Lyer figures: The role of corrective and contextual information. In press, 1990.

Griffin, D. R. *Listening in the dark*. New Haven, Conn.: Yale University Press, 1958.

Griffin, D. R. *Echoes of bats and men*. Garden City, N. Y.: Anchor Books/Doubleday, 1959.

Griffin, D. R. Foreward to papers on magnetic sensitivity in birds. *Animal Learning & Behavior*, 1987, *15*, 108–109.

Gross, C. G., Rocha-Miranda, C. E., & Bender, D. B. Visual properties of neurons in inferotemporal cortex of the Macaque. *Journal of Neurophysiology*, 1972, *35*, 96–111.

Grünau, v. M. W., Wiggins, S., & Reed, M. The local character of perspective organization. *Perception & Psychophysics*, 1984, *35*, 319–324.

Grzegorczyk, P. B., Jones, S. W., & Mistretta, C. M. Age-related differences in salt taste acuity. *Journal of Gerontology*, 1979, *34*, 834–840.

Guilford, J. P. *Psychometric methods*. New York: McGraw-Hill, 1954.

Guirao, M., & Stevens, S. S. The measurement of auditory density. *Journal of the Acoustical Society of America*, 1964, *36*, 1176–1182.

Gulick, W. L. *Hearing: Physiology and psychophysics*. New York: Oxford University Press, 1971.

Gulick, W. L., & Lawson, R. B. *Human stereopsis: A psychophysical analysis*. New York: Oxford University Press, 1976.

Gustavson, C. F., & Garcia, J. Aversive conditioning: Pulling a gag on the wily coyote. *Psychology Today*, 1974, *8*, 68–72.

Gwei-Djen, Lu, & Needham, J. A scientific basis for acupuncture. *The Sciences*, 1979, *19*, 6–10.

Gwiazda, J., Brill, S., & Held, R. New methods for testing infant vision. *The Sightsaving Review*, 1979, *49*, 61–69.

Gwiazda, J., Brill, S., Mohindra, I., & Held, R. Infant visual acuity and its meridional variation. *Vision Research*, 1978, *18*, 1557–1564.

Haber, R. N., & Hershenson, M. Effects of repeated brief exposure on the growth of a percept. *Journal of Experimental Psychology*, 1965, *69*, 40–46.

Haber, R. N., & Nathanson, L. S. Post-retinal storage? Some further observations of Parks' camel as seen through the eye of a needle. *Perception & Psychophysics*, 1968, *3*, 349–355.

Haith, M. M. Visual competence in early infancy. In R. Held, H. W. Leibowitz, & H.-L. Teuber (Eds.), *Handbook of sensory physiology*. Volume VIII: *Perception*. New York: Springer-Verlag, 1978.

Haith, M. M. *Rules that babies look by*. Hillsdale, N.J.: Lawrence Erlbaum, 1980.

Haith, M. M., Bergman, T., & Moore, M. J. Eye contact and face scanning in early infancy. *Science*, 1977, *198*, 853–855.

Hall, J. L. Two-tone distortion products in a nonlinear model of the basilar membrane. *Journal of the Acoustical Society of America*. 1974, *56*, 1818–1828.

Hallett, P. Eye movements. In K. R. Boff, L. Kaufman, & J. P. Thomas (Eds.), *Handbook of perception and human performance*. Volume I: *Sensory processes and perception*. New York: John Wiley, 1986.

Hanson, D. R., & Fearn, R. W. Hearing acuity in young people exposed to pop music and other noise. *Lancet*, Aug. 2, 1975, no. 7927, Vol II, 203–205.

Hardy, J. D., Stolwijk, J. A. J., & Hoffman, D. Pain following step increase in skin temperature. Chapter 21. In D. R. Kenshalo (Ed.), *The skin senses*. Springfield, Ill.: Charles C Thomas, 1968.

Hardy, J. D., Wolff, H. G., & Goodell, H. *Pain sensations and reactions*. Baltimore, Md.: Williams & Wilkins, 1952.

Harmon, L. D. The recognition of faces. *Scientific American*, 1973, *229*, 70–82.

Harmon, L. D., & Julesz, B. Masking in visual recognition: Effects of two-dimensional filtered noise. *Science*, 1973, *180*, 1194–1197.

Harris, C. S. Perceptual adaptations to inverted,

reversed and displaced vision. *Psychological Review*, 1965, *72*, 419–444.

Harris, C. S. Insight or out of sight? Two examples of perceptual plasticity in the human adult. In C. S. Harris (Ed.), *Visual coding and adaptability*. Hillsdale, N.J.: Lawrence Erlbaum, 1980.

Harris, J. D. Pitch discrimination. USN Bureau of Medicine and Surgery Research Report, Project NM 033 041.22.04, No. 205, June 20, 1952.

Harwerth, R. S., Smith III, E. L., Duncan, G. C., Crawford, M. L. J., & von Noorden, G. K. Multiple sensitive periods in the development of the primate visual system. *Science*, 1986, *232*, 235–238.

Hatfield, G., & Epstein, W. The status of minimum principle in the theoretical analysis of visual perception. *Psychological Bulletin*, 1985, *97*, 155–186.

Hay, J. C. Reafference learning in the presence of exafference. *Perception & Psychophysics*, 1981, *30*, 277–282.

Hayes, W. N., & Saiff, E. I. Visual alarm reactions in turtles. *Animal Behavior*, 1967, *15*, 102–106.

Haynes, H., White, B. L., & Held, R. Visual accommodation in human infants. *Science*, 1965, *148*, 528–530.

Hebb, D. O. *The organization of behavior*. New York: John Wiley, 1949.

Hecht, S., & Shlaer, S. An adaptometer for measuring human dark adaptation. *Journal of the Optical Society of America*, 1938, *28*, 269–275.

Hecht, S., Shlaer, S., & Pirenne, M. H. Energy at the threshold of vision. *Science*, 1941, *93*, 585.

Hecht, S., Shlaer, S., & Pirenne, M. H. Energy, quanta, and vision. *Journal of General Physiology*, 1942, *25*, 819–840.

Heffner, R., & Heffner, H. Hearing in the elephant (*Elephas maximus*). *Science*, 1980, *208*, 518–520.

Heffner, R. S., & Heffner, H. E. Hearing in larger mammals: Horses (*equus caballus*) and cattle (*Bos taurus*). *Behavioral Neuroscience*, 1983, *97*, 299–309. (*a*)

Heffner, R. S., & Heffner, H. E. Hearing in large

and small dogs: Absolute thresholds and size of the tympanic membrane. *Behavioral Neuroscience*, 1983, *97*, 310–318. (*b*)

Hein, A. The development of visually guided behavior. In C. S. Harris (Ed.), *Visual coding and adaptability*. Hillsdale, N.J.: Lawrence Erlbaum, 1980.

Hein, A., & Held, R. Dissociation of the visual placing response into elicited and guided components. *Science*, 1967, *158*, 390–392.

Hein, A., Vital-Durand, F., Salinger, W., & Diamond, R. Eye movements initiate visual-motor development in the cat. *Science*, 1979, *204*, 1321–1322.

Held, R., & Bauer, J. A. Visually guided reaching in infant monkeys after restricted rearing. *Science*, 1967, *155*, 718–720.

Held, R., & Bossom, J. Neonatal deprivation and adult rearrangement: Complementary techniques for analyzing plastic sensory-motor coordinations. *Journal of Comparative and Physiological Psychology*, 1961, *54*, 33–37.

Held, R., & Freedman, S. J. Plasticity in human sensorimotor control. *Science*, 1963, *142*, 455–462.

Held, R., & Gottlieb, N. Techniques for studying adaptation to disarranged hand-eye coordination. *Perceptual and Motor Skills*, 1958, *8*, 83–86.

Held, R., & Hein, A. Adaptation of disarranged hand-eye coordination contingent upon reafferent stimulation. *Perceptual and Motor Skills*, 1958, *8*, 87–90.

Held, R., & Hein, A. Movement-produced stimulation in the development of visually guided behavior. *Journal of Comparative and Physiological Psychology*, 1963, *56*, 872–876.

Held, R., & Schlank, M. Adaptation to disarranged eye-hand coordination in the distance dimension. *American Journal of Psychology*, 1959, *72*, 603–605.

Heller, M. A. Tactile retention: Reading with the skin. *Perception & Psychophysics*, 1980, *27*, 125–130.

Heller, M. A. Haptic dominance in form perception

with blurred vision. *Perception*, 1983, *12*, 607–613.

Heller, M. A. Tactile memory in sighted and blind observers: The influence of orientation and rate of presentation. *Perception*, 1989, *18*, 121–133.

Helson, H. *Adaptation-level theory*. New York: Harper & Row, 1964.

Helson, H., & King, S. M. The *tau*-effect. An example of psychological relativity. *Journal of Experimental Psychology*, 1931, *14*, 202–218.

Henning, G. J., Brouwer, J. N., Van Der Wel, H., & Francke, A. Miraculin, the sweet- inducing principle from miracle fruit. In C. Pfaffmann (Ed.), *Olfaction and taste*. New York: Rockefeller University Press, 1969.

Hepler, N. Color: A motion-contingent aftereffect. *Science*, 1968, *162*, 376–377.

Hering, E. *Outlines of a theory of the light sense*. Cambridge, Mass.: Harvard University Press, 1964. (Translated from the original 1920 publication by L. M. Hurvich & D. Jameson.)

Herman, B. H., & Panksepp, J. Ascending endorphin inhibition of distress vocalization. *Science*, 1981, *211*, 1060–1062.

Hershberger, W. Attached-shadow orientation perceived as depth by chickens reared in an environment illuminated from below. *Journal of Comparative and Physiological Psychology*, 1970, *73*, 407–411.

Hess, E. H. Attitude and pupil size. *Scientific American*, 1965, *212*, 46–54.

Hess, E. H. *The tell-tale eye*. New York: Van Nostrand 1975. (*a*)

Hess, E. H. The role of pupil size in communication. *Scientific American*, 1975, *233*, 110–119. (*b*)

Hess, E. H., & Polt, J. M. Pupil size as related to interest value of visual stimuli. *Science*, 1960, *132*, 349–350.

Hess, E. H., & Polt, J. M. Pupil size in relation to mental activity during simple problem-solving. *Science*, 1964, *140*, 1190–1192.

Hess, E. H., & Polt, J. M. Changes in pupil size as a measure of taste difference. *Perceptual and Motor Skills*, 1966, *23*, 451–455.

Heydt, von der, R., Peterhans, E., & Baumgartner, G. Illusory contours and cortical neuron responses, *Science*, 1984, *224*, 1260–1262.

Hill, D. L. Development and plasticity of the gustatory system. In T. E. Finger & W. L. Silver (Eds.), *Neurobiology of taste and smell*. New York: John Wiley, 1987.

Hirsh, H. V. B., & Spinelli, D. N. Visual experience modifies distribution of horizontally and vertically oriented receptive fields in cats. *Science*, 1970, *168*, 869–871.

Hirst, W., Spelke, E. S., Reaves, C. C., Caharack, G., & Neisser, U. Dividing attention without alternation or automaticity. *Journal of Experimental Psychology: General*, 1980, *109*, 98–117.

Hoagland, H. The physiological control of judgments of duration: Evidence for a chemical clock. *Journal of General Psychology*, 1933, *9*, 267–287.

Hoagland, H. *Pacemakers in relation to aspects of behavior*. New York: Macmillan, 1935.

Hochberg, J. F. *Perception*. Englewood-Cliffs, N.J.: Prentice Hall, 1964.

Hochberg, J. Perceptual organization. In M. Kubovy & J. R. Pomerantz (Eds.), *Perceptual organization*. Hillsdale, N.J.: Lawrence Erlbaum, 1981.

Hochberg, J. Representation of motion and space in video and cinematic displays. In K. R. Boff, L. Kaufman, & J. P. Thomas (Eds.), *Handbook of perception and human performance*. Volume I: *Sensory processes and perception*. New York: John Wiley, 1986.

Hochberg, J. Visual perception. In R.C. Atkinson, R.J. Hermnstein, G. Lindzey & R.D. Luce (Eds.), *Stevens' Handbook of Experimental Psychology* (2nd ed.), Volume 1. New York: John Wiley, 1988.

Hochberg, J. E., & McAlister, E. A quantitative approach to figural goodness. *Journal of Experimental Psychology*, 1953, *46*, 361–364.

Hochberg, J. E., Triebel, W., & Seaman, G. Color adaptation under conditions of homogeneous visual stimulation (Ganzfeld). *Journal of Experimental Psychology*, 1951, *41*, 153–159.

Hogan, H. W. A theoretical reconciliation of competing views of time perception. *American Journal of Psychology*, 1978, *91*, 417–428.

Hollins, M., & Kelley, E. K. Spatial updating in blind and sighted people. *Perception & Psychophysics*, 1988, *43*, 380–388.

Holst, E. von. Relations between the central nervous system and the peripheral organs. *British Journal of Animal Behavior*, 1954, *2*, 89–94.

Holubář, J. *The sense of time: an electrophysiological study of its mechanism in man*. Cambridge, Mass.: M.I.T. Press, 1969.

Holway, A. H., & Boring, E. G. The moon illusion and the angle of regard. *American Journal of Psychology*, 1940, *53*, 109–116.

Holway, A. H., & Boring, E. G. Determinants of apparent visual size with distance variant. *American Journal of Psychology*, 1941, *54*, 21–37.

Houpt, K. A. & Houpt, T. R. The neonatal pig: A biological model for the development of taste preferences and controls of ingestive behavior. In J. M. Weiffenbach (Ed.), *The genesis of sweet preference*. Bethesda, Md.: U.S. Department of Health, Education, and Welfare, Public Health Service, National Institutes of Health, 1977. DHEW Publication No. (NIH) 77-1068.

Howard, I. P. *Human visual orientation*. New York: John Wiley, 1982.

Howard, I. P. The perception of posture, self motion, and the visual vertical. In K. R. Boff, L. Kaufman, & J. P. Thomas (Eds.), *Handbook of perception and human performance*. Volume I: *Sensory processes and perception*. New York: John Wiley, 1986.

Howard, I. P., & Templeton, W. B. *Human spatial orientation*. New York: John Wiley, 1966.

Howe, E. S., & Brandau, C. J. The temporal course of visual pattern encoding: Effects of pattern goodness. *Quarterly Journal of Experimental Psychology*, 1983, *35*, 607–633.

Howe, E. S., & Jung, K. Immediate memory span for two-dimensional spatial arrays: Effects of pattern symmetry and goodness. *Acta Psychologica*, 1986, *61*, 37–51.

Hsia, Y., & Graham, C. H. Color blindness. In C. H. Graham (Ed.), *Vision and visual perception*. New York: John Wiley, 1965.

Huang, Y. L., & Jones, B. On the interdependence of temporal and spatial judgments. *Perception & Psychophysics*, 1982, *32*, 7–14.

Hubel, D. H., The visual cortex of normal and deprived monkeys. *American Scientist*, 1979, *67*, 532–543.

Hubel, D. H. Evolution of ideas on the primary visual cortex, 1955–1978: A biased historical account. *Bioscience Reports*, 1982, *2*, 435–469.

Hubel, D. H., & Livingstone, M. S. The 11th J. A. F. Stevenson Memorial Lecture: Blobs and color vision. *Canadian Journal of Physiology and Pharmacology*, 1983, *61*, 1433–1441.

Hubel, D. H., & Wiesel, T. N. Receptive fields of single neurons in the cat's striate cortex. *Journal of Physiology*, 1959, *148*, 574–591.

Hubel, D. H., & Wiesel, T. N. Receptive fields, binocular interaction and functional architecture in the cat's visual cortex. *Journal of Physiology*, 1962, *160*, 106–154.

Hubel, D. H., & Wiesel, T. N. Receptive fields of cells in striate cortex of very young, visually inexperienced kittens. *Journal of Neurophysiology*, 1963, *26*, 994–1002.

Hubel, D. H., & Wiesel, T. N. Receptive fields and functional architecture of monkey striate cortex. *Journal of Physiology*, 1968, *195*, 215–243.

Hubel, D. H., & Wiesel, T. N. Stereoscopic vision in macaque monkey. *Nature*, 1970, *225*, 41–42.

Huggins, A. W. Distortion of the temporal pattern of speech: Interruption and alternation. *Journal of Acoustical Society of America*, 1964, *36*, 1055–1064.

Hurvich, L. M., & Jameson, D. A quantitative theoretical account of color vision. *Transactions of the New York Academy of Sciences*, 1955, *18*, 33–38.

Hurvich, L. M., & Jameson, D. An opponent-process theory of color vision. *Psychological Review*, 1957, *64*, 384–404.

Hurvich, L. M., & Jameson, D. Opponent processes

as a model of neural organization. *American Psychologist*, 1974, *29*, 88–102.

Ingle, D. J. The goldfish as a retinex animal. *Science*, 1985, *227*, 651–654.

Jacobs, G. H., & Pulliam, K. A. Vision in the prairie dog. *Journal of Comparative and Physiological Psychology*, 1973, *84*, 240–245.

Jacobs, H. L. Observations on the ontogeny of saccharine preference in the neonate rat. *Psychonomic Science*, 1964, *1*, 105–106.

Jacobs, H. L. Taste and the role of experience in the regulation of food intake. In M. R. Kare & O. Maller (Eds.), *The chemical senses and nutrition*. Baltimore, Md.: Johns Hopkins Press, 1967.

Jacobsen, A., & Gilchrist, A. The ratio principle holds over a million-to-one range of illumination. *Perception & Psychophysics*, 1988, *43*, 1–6.

James, W. *The principles of psychology*. New York: Henry Holt, 1890.

Janisse, M. P. *Pupillometry*. Washington, D.C.: Hemisphere, 1977.

Janson, H. W. *History of art*. Englewood Cliffs, N.J.: Prentice Hall, 1962.

Jensen, A. R., & Rohwer, W. D. The Stroop colour-word test: A review. *Acta Psychologica*, 1966, *25*, 36–93.

Jerome, N. W. Taste experience and the development of a dietary preference for sweet in humans: Ethnic and cultural variations in early taste experience. In J. W. Weiffenbach (Ed.), *Taste and Development*. Bethesda, Md.: U.S. Department of Health, Education, and Welfare, Public Health Service, National Institutes of Health, 1977. DHEW Publication No. (NIH) 77–1068.

Jewesbury, E. C. O. Insensitivity to pain. *Brain*, 1951, *74*, 336–353.

Johansson, G. Visual perception of biological motion and a model for its analysis. *Perception & Psychophysics*, 1973, *14*, 201–211.

Johansson, G. Visual motion perception. *Scientific American*, 1975, *232*, 76–88.

Johansson, G., von Hofsten, C., & Jansson, G. Event perception. *Annual Review of Psychology*, 1980, *31*, 27–64.

Johnson, O., & Kozma, A. Effects of concurrent verbal and musical tasks on a unimanual skill. *Cortex*, 1977, *13*, 11–16.

Johnsson, L. G., & Hawkins, J. E. Sensory and neural degeneration with aging, as seen in microdissections of the human inner ear. *Annals of Otology, Rhinology and Laryngology*, 1972, *81*, 179–193.

Johnston, J. C., & McClelland, J. L. Visual factors in word perception. *Perception & Psychophysics*, 1973, *14*, 365–370.

Johnston, J. C., & McClelland, J. L. Perception of letters in words: Seek not and ye shall find. *Science*, 1974, *184*, 1192–1194.

Jones, B., & Gwynn, M. Functional measurement scale of painful electric shocks. *Perception & Psychophysics*, 1984, *35*, 193–200.

Jones, B., & Huang, Y. L. Space-time dependencies in psychophysical judgment of extent and duration: Algebraic models of the tau and kappa effects. *Psychological Bulletin*, 1982, *91*, 128–142.

Jones, M. R. Dynamic pattern structure in music: Recent theory and research. *Perception & Psychophysics*, 1987, *41*, 621–634.

Jordan, K., & Randall, J. The effects of framing ratio and oblique length on Ponzo illusion magnitude. *Perception & Psychophysics*, 1987, *41*, 435–439.

Jory, M. K., & Day, R. H. The relationship between brightness contrast and illusory contours. *Perception*, 1979, *8*, 3–9.

Julesz, B. Binocular depth perception without familiarity cues. *Science*, 1964, *145*, 356–362.

Julesz, B. Texture and visual perception. *Scientific American*, 1965, *212*, 38–48.

Julesz, B. *Foundations of cyclopean perception*. Chicago: University of Chicago Press, 1971.

Julesz, B. Global stereopsis: Cooperative phenomena in stereoscopic depth perception. In R. Held. H. W. Leibowitz, & H.-L. Teuber (Eds.)

Handbook of sensory physiology. Volume VIII: *Perception*. Berlin: Springer-Verlag, 1978.

Jung, R., & Spillman, L. Receptive-field estimation and perceptual integration in human vision. In F. A. Young & D. B. Lindsley (Eds.), *Early experience and visual information processing in perceptual and reading disorders*. Washington, D.C.: National Academy of Sciences, 1970.

Jusczyk, P. Speech perception. In K. R. Boff, L. Kaufman, & J. P. Thomas (Eds.), *Handbook of perception and human performance*. Volume II: *Cognitive processes and performance*. New York: John Wiley, 1986.

Kaess, D. W., & Wilson, J. P. Modification of the rat's avoidance of visual depth. *Journal of Comparative and Physiological Psychology*, 1964, *58*, 151–152.

Kagan, J. The determinants of attention in the infant. *American Scientist*, 1970, *58*, 298–306.

Kaiser, M. K., Proffitt, D. R., & Anderson, K. Judgments of natural and anomalous trajectories in the presence and absence of motion. *Journal of Experimental Psychology: Learning, Memory, and Cognition*, 1985, *11*, 795–803.

Kaiser, M. K., Proffitt, D. R., & McCloskey, M. The development of beliefs about falling objects. *Perception & Psychophysics*, 1985, *38*, 533–539.

Kallman, H. J., & Corballis, M. C. Ear asymmetry in reaction time to musical sounds. *Perception & Psychophysics*, 1975, *17*, 368–370.

Kandel, E. R. Visual system III: Physiology of the central visual pathways. In E. R. Kandel & J. H. Schwartz (Eds.), *Principles of neural science*. New York: Elsevier, 1981.

Kanizsa, G. *Organization in vision: Essays on Gestalt psychology*. New York: Praeger, 1979.

Kare, M. R., & Ficken, M. S. Comparative studies on the sense of taste. In Y. Zotterman (Ed.), *Olfaction and taste*. New York: Macmillan, 1963.

Katsuki, Y. Neural mechanism of auditory sensation in cats. In W. A. Rosenblith (Ed.), *Sensory communication*. Cambridge, Mass.: M.I.T. Press, 1961.

Katsuki, Y., Watanabe, T., & Suga, N. Interactions of auditory neurons in response to two sound stimuli in cat. *Journal of Neurophysiology*, 1959, *22*, 603–623.

Kauer, J. S. Coding in the olfactory system. In T. E. Finger & W. L. Silver (Eds.), *Neurobiology of taste and smell*. New York: John Wiley, 1987.

Kaufman, L., & Rock, I. The moon illusion, I. *Science*, 1962, *136*, 953–961. (*a*)

Kaufman, L., & Rock, I. The moon illusion. *Scientific American*, 1962, *207*, 120–132. (*b*)

Keele, S. W. Attention demands of memory retrieval. *Journal of Experimental Psychology*, 1972, *93*, 245–248.

Keele, S. W. Motor control. In K. R. Boff, L. Kaufman, & J. P. Thomas (Eds.), *Handbook of perception and human performance*. Volume II: *Cognitive processes and performance*. New York: John Wiley, 1986.

Keim, H. A. *How to care for your back*. Englewood Cliffs, N.J.: Prentice-Hall, 1981.

Kellar, L. A., & Bever, T. G. Hemispheric asymmetries in the perception of musical intervals as a function of musical experience and family handedness background. *Brain and Language*, 1980, *10*, 24–38.

Kellogg, W. N. Sonar system of the blind. *Science*, 1962, *137*, 399–404.

Kelly, D. D. Somatic sensory system IV: Central representations of pain and analgesia. Chapter 18. In E. R. Kandel & J. H. Schwartz (Eds.), *Principles of neural science*. New York: Elsevier, 1984.

Kendrick, K. M., & Baldwin, B. A. Cells in temporal cortex of conscious sheep can respond preferentially to the sight of faces. *Science*, 1987, *236*, 448–450.

Kennedy, J. M. What can we learn about pictures from the blind? *American Scientist*, 1983, *71*, 19–26.

Kennedy, J. M. The tangible world of the blind. *Encyclopaedia Britannica Medical and Health Annual*. Chicago, 1984.

Kennedy, J. M., & Campbell, J. Convergence principle in blind people's pointing. *International*

Journal of Rehabilitation Research, 1985, *8*, 189–210.

Kennedy, J. M., & Domander, R. Pictorial foreground-background reversal reduces tactual recognition by blind subjects. *Journal of Visual Impairment and Blindness*, 1984, *78*, 215–216.

Kenshalo, D. R. Psychophysical studies of temperature sensitivity. In W. D. Neff (Ed.), *Contributions to sensory physiology*, Volume 4. New York: Academic Press, 1970.

Kenshalo, D. R. The cutaneous senses. In J. R. Kling & L. A. Riggs (Eds.), *Experimental psychology* (3rd ed.). New York: Holt, Rinehart and Winston, 1971.

Kenshalo, D. R. Biophysics and psychophysics of feeling. In E. L. Carterette & M. P. Friedman (Eds.), *Handbook of perception*, Volume VI, B. New York: Academic Press, 1978.

Kenshalo, D. R., & Gallegos, E. S. Multiple temperature-sensitive spots innervated by single nerve fibers. *Science*, 1967, *158*, 1064–1065.

Kenshalo, D. R., & Nafe, D. R. A quantitative theory of feeling: 1960. *Psychological Review*, 1962, *69*, 17–33.

Kenshalo, D. R., & Scott, H. A. Temporal course of thermal adaptation. *Science*, 1966, *151*, 1095–1096.

Kessen, W. Sucking and looking: Two organized congenital patterns of behavior in the human newborn. In H. W. Stevenson, E. H. Hess, & H. L. Rheingold (Eds.), *Early behavior: Comparative and developmental approaches*. New York: John Wiley, 1967.

Khanna, S. M., & Leonard, D. G. B. Basilar membrane tuning in the cat cochlea. *Science*, 1982, *215*, 305–306.

Kiang, N.Y.S. Peripheral neural processing of auditory information. In I. Darian-Smith (Ed.), *Handbook of physiology*. Bethesda, Md.: American Physiological Society, 1984.

Kilpatrick, F. P. *Explorations in transactional psychology*. New York: New York University Press, 1961.

Kimble, G. A., Garmezy, N., & Zigler, E. *Principles of General Psychology* (5th ed.). New York: John Wiley, 1980.

Kimbrell, G. M., & Furchgott, E. The effect of aging on olfactory threshold. *Journal of Gerontology*, 1968, *18*, 364–365.

Kimura, D. Cerebral dominance and the perception of verbal stimuli. *Canadian Journal of Psychology*, 1961, *15*, 166–171.

Kimura, D. Left-right differences in the perception of melodies. *Quarterly Journal of Experimental Psychology*, 1964, *16*, 355–358.

Kimura, D. Functional asymmetry of the brain in dichotic listening. *Cortex*, 1967, *3*, 163–178.

Kimura, D., & Folb, S. Neural processing of backwards-speech sounds. *Science*, 1968, *161*, 395–396.

Kirk-Smith, M. D., Van Toller, C., & Dodd, G. H. Unconscious odour conditioning in human subjects. *Journal of Biological Psychology*, 1983, *17*, 221–231.

Kirschvink, J. L., Jones, D. S., & MacFadden, F. J. (Eds.) *Magnetite biomineralization and magnetoreception in organisms, a new biomagnetism*. New York: Plenum Press, 1985.

Klatzky, R. L., Lederman, S. J., & Metzger, V. A. Identifying objects by touch: An "expert system." *Perception & Psychophysics*, 1985, *37*, 299–302.

Kleber, R. J., Lhamon, W. T., & Goldstone, S. Hyperthermia, hyperthyroidism, and time judgment. *Journal of Comparative and Physiological Psychology*, 1963, *56*, 362–365.

Klein, G. S. Semantic power of words measured through the interference with color naming. *American Journal of Psychology*, 1964, *77*, 576–588.

Kline, D. W., & Schieber, F. Visual aging: A transient/sustained shift? *Perception & Psychophysics*, 1981, *29*, 181–182.

Knouse, K. Citation in *Rutgers Magazine*, 1988, *67* (Sept.–Oct.), 8.

Knox, C., & Kimura, D. Cerebral processing of nonverbal sounds in boys and girls. *Neuropsychologia*, 1970, *8*, 227–237.

Knudsen, E. I., & Konishi, M. A neural map of

auditory space in the owl. *Science*, 1978, *200*, 795–797.

Koffka, K. *Principles of Gestalt psychology*. New York: Harcourt Brace, 1935.

Kohler, I. Experiments with goggles. *Scientific American*, 1962, *206*, 62–86.

Kohler, I. The formation and transformation of the perceptual world. *Psychological Issues*, 1964, *3* (Whole No. 4).

Köhler, W., & Wallach, H. Figural aftereffects: an investigation of visual processes. *Proceedings of the American Philosophical Society*, 1944, *88*, 269–357.

Kowal, K. H. Apparent duration and numerosity as a function of melodic familiarity. *Perception & Psychophysics*, 1987, *42*, 122–131.

Kowler, E., & Anton, S. Reading twisted text: Implications for the role of saccades. *Vision Research*, 1987, *27*, 45–60.

Kowler, E., & Martins, A. J. Eye movements of preschool children. *Science*, 1982, *215*, 997–999.

Krech, D., & Crutchfield, R. S. *Elements of psychology*. New York: Alfred A. Knopf, 1958.

Kristofferson, A. B. Attention and psychophysical time. *Acta Psychologica*, 1967, *27*, 93–100.

Krueger, L. E. David Katz's der Aufbau der Tastwelt (the world of touch): A synopsis. *Perception & Psychophysics*, 1970, *7*, 337–341.

Krueger, L. E. Tactual perception in historical perspective: David Katz's world of touch. In W. Schiff & E. Foulke (Eds.), *Tactual perception: A sourcebook*. New York: Cambridge University Press, 1982. (*a*)

Krueger, L. E. A word-superiority effect with print and Braille characters. *Perception & Psychophysics*, 1982, *31*, 345–352. (*b*)

Krueger, L. E., & Ward, M. E. Letter search by Braille readers: Implications for instruction. *Journal of Visual Impairment and Blindness*, 1983, *77*, 166–169.

Krumhansl, C. L., & Kessler, E. J. Tracing the dynamic changes in perceived tonal organization in a spatial representation of musical keys. *Psychological Review*, 1982, *89*, 334–368.

Kubovy, M. Overview. In K. R. Boff, L. Kaufman, &

J. P. Thomas (Eds.), *Handbook of perception and human performance*. Volume II: *Cognitive processes and performance*. New York: John Wiley, 1986.

Kuffler, S. W. Discharge patterns and functional organization of mammalian retina. *Journal of Neurophysiology*, 1953, *16*, 37–68.

Kuhl, P. K. Perception of auditory equivalence classes for speech by infants. *Infant Behavior and Development*, 1983, *6*, 263–285.

Lackner, J. R. Adaptation to visual and proprioceptive rearrangement: Origin of the differential effectiveness of active and passive movement. *Perception & Psychophysics*, 1977, *21*, 55–59.

Lackner, J. R., & Graybiel, A. Head movements elicit motion sickness during exposure to microgravity and macrogravity acceleration levels. In M. Igarashi & F. O. Black (Eds.), *Vestibular and Visual Control on Posture and Locomotor Equilibrium*, pp. 170–176. Proceedings of the VII International Symposium of the International Society of Posturography, Houston, Tex., 1983, Basel, Switzerland: S. Krager, 1985.

Lackner, J. R., & Graybiel, A. Head movements in non-terrestrial force environments elicit motion sickness: Implications for the etiology of space motion sickness. *Aviation, Space, and Environmental Medicine*, 1986, *57*, 443–448.

Lackner, J. R., & Graybiel, A. Head movements in low and high gravitoinertial force environments elicit motion sickness: Implications for space motion sickness. *Aviation, Space, and Environmental Medicine*, 1987, *58*, A212–A217.

Ladd-Franklin, C. *Colour and colour theories*. New York: Harcourt Brace, 1929.

Laing, D. G. Natural sniffing gives optimum odour perception for humans. *Perception*, 1983, *12*, 99–118.

Lancet. Noise-induced hearing loss (Editorial Summary). *Lancet*, Aug. 2, 1975, no. 7927, Vol. II, 215–216.

Langfeld, H. S. Note on a case of chromaesthesia. *Psychological Bulletin*, 1914, *11*, 113–114.

Lanze, M., Macguire, W., & Weisstein, N. Emergent features: A new factor in the object-superiority effect? *Perception & Psychophysics*, 1985, *38*, 438–442.

Lashley, K. S., & Russell, J. T. The mechanism of vision: XI. A preliminary test of innate organization. *Journal of Genetic Psychology*, 1934, *45*, 136–144.

Lawless, H. T. Recognition of common odors, pictures, and simple shapes. *Perception & Psychophysics*, 1978, *24*, 493–495.

Lawless, H. T. Sensory interactions in mixtures. *Journal of Sensory Studies*, 1986, *1*, 259–274.

Lawless, H. T. Gustatory psychophysics. In T. E. Finger and W. L. Silver (Eds.), *Neurobiology of taste and smell*. New York: John Wiley, 1987.

Lawless, H., & Engen, T. Associations to odors: Interference, mnemonics, and verbal labels. *Journal of Experimental Psychology: Human Learning and Memory*, 1977, *3*, 52–59.

Lawless, H. T., Rozin, P., & Shenker, J. Effects of oral capsaicin on gustatory, olfactory and irritant sensation on flavor identification in humans who regularly or rarely consume chili pepper. *Chemical Senses*, 1985, *10*, 579–589.

Lawless, H. T., & Stevens, D. A. Responses by humans to oral chemical irritants as a function of locus of stimulation. *Perception & Psychophysics*, 1988, *43*, 72–78.

Lederman, S. J. "Improving one's touch". . . and more. *Perception & Psychophysics*, 1978, *24*, 154–160.

Lee, D. N., & Aronson, E. Visual proprioceptive control of standing in human infants. *Perception & Psychophysics*, 1974, *15*, 529–532.

Leehey, S. C., Moskowitz-Cook, A., Brill, S., & Held, R. Orientational anisotropy in infant vision. *Science*, 1975, *190*, 900–902.

Le Grand, Y. *Form and space vision*. Bloomington: Indiana University Press, 1967.

Le Grand, Y. *Light, colour and vision*. London: Chapman and Hall, 1968.

Le Grand, Y. History of research on seeing. In E.C. Carterette and M.P. Friedman (Eds.), *Handbook of perception*. Volume V: *Seeing*. New York: Academic Press, 1975.

Leibowitz, H. W., Brislin, R., Perlmutter, L., &

Hennessy, R. Ponzo perspective illusion as a manifestation of space perception. *Science*, 1969, *166*, 1174–1176.

Leibowitz, H. W., & Pick, H. A. Cross-cultural and educational aspects of the Ponzo perspective illusion. *Perception & Psychophysics*, 1972, *12*, 430–432.

Lele, P. P., & Weddell, G. The relationship between neurohistology and corneal sensibility. *Brain*, 1956, *79*, 119–154.

Lenneberg, E. H. Understanding language without ability to speak: A case report. *Journal of Abnormal and Social Psychology*, 1962, *65*, 419–425.

Lettvin, J. Y., Maturana, H. R., McCulloch, W. S., & Pitts, W. H. What the frog's eye tells the frog's brain. *Proceedings of the Institute of Radio Engineers*, 1959, *47*, 1940–1951.

Leukel, F. *Introduction to physiological psychology*. St. Louis: C. V. Mosby, 1972.

Leventhal, A. G., & Hirsch, H. V. B. Cortical effect of early selective exposure to diagonal lines. *Science*, 1975, *190*, 902–904.

Levy, C. M., Fischler, I. S., & Griggs, R. A. *Laboratory in cognition and perception*. Iowa City, Iowa: Conduit, 1979.

Lewin, R. Mockingbird song aimed at mates, not rivals. *Science*, 1987, *236*, 1521–1522.

Lewis, J. L. Semantic processing of unattended messages using dichotic listening. *Journal of Experimental Psychology*, 1970, *85*, 225–228.

Lewis, J. W., Cannon, J. T., & Liebeskind, J. C. Opioid and nonopiod mechanisms of stress analgesia. *Science*, 1980, *208*, 623–625.

Lewis, M. E., Mishkin, M., Bragin, E., Brown, R. M., Pert, C. B., & Pert, A. Opiate receptor gradients in monkey cerebral cortex: Correspondence with sensory processing hierarchies. *Science*, 1981, *211*, 1166–1169.

Liberman, A. M., Cooper, F. S., Harris, K. S., MacNeilage, P. F., & Studdert-Kennedy, M. Some observations on a model for speech perception. In W. Wathen-Dunn (Ed.), *Models for the perception of speech and visual form*. Cambridge, Mass.: M.I.T. Press, 1967. (*a*)

Liberman, A. M., Cooper, F. S., Shankweiler, D.

P., & Studdert-Kennedy, M. Perception of the speech code. *Psychological Review*, 1967, *74*, 431–461. (*b*)

Liberman, A. M., & Studdert-Kennedy, M. Phonetic perception. In R. Held, H. W. Leibowitz, & H.-L. Teuber (Eds.), *Handbook of sensory physiology*. Volume VIII: *Perception*. Berlin: Springer-Verlag, 1978.

Libet, B., Wright, E. W., Jr., Feinstein, B., & Pearl, D. K. Subjective referral of the timing for a conscious sensory experience: A functional role of the somatosensory specific projection in man. *Brain*, 1979, *102*, 193–224.

Licklider, J. C. R., & Miller, G. A. The perception of speech. In S. S. Stevens (Ed.), *Handbook of experimental psychology*. New York: John Wiley, 1951.

Lieberman, P. *Information, perception, and language*. Research Monograph No. 38. Cambridge, Mass.: M.I.T. Press, 1968.

Lieberman, P., & Crelin, E. S. On the speech of Neanderthal man. *Linguistic Inquiry*, 1971, *2*, 203–222.

Lieberman, P., Crelin, E. S., & Klatt, D. H. Phonetic ability and related anatomy of the newborn and adult human, Neanderthal man, and the chimpanzee. *American Anthropologist*, 1972, *74*, 287–307.

Lindgren, H. C., & Byrne, D. *Psychology*. New York: John Wiley, 1975.

Lindsay, P. H., & Norman, D. A. *Human information processing: An introduction to psychology* (2nd ed.). New York: Academic Press, 1977.

Linn, C. E., Jr., Campbell, M. G., & Roelofs, W. L. Pheromone components and active spaces: What do moths smell and where do they smell it? *Science*, 1987, *237*, 650–652.

Lishman, J. R., & Lee, D. N. The autonomy of visual kinaesthesis. *Perception*, 1973, *2*, 287–294.

Livingstone, M. S. Art, illusion and the visual system. *Scientific American*, 1987, *258*, 78–85.

Livingstone, M. S., & Hubel, D. H. Anatomy and physiology of a color system in the primate visual cortex. *The Journal of Neuroscience*, 1984, *4*, 309–356.

Livingstone, M., & Hubel, D. Segregation of form, color, movement, and depth: Anatomy, physiology, and movement. *Science*, 1988, *240*, 740–749.

Llewellyn Thomas, E. Search behavior. *Radiological Clinics of North America*, 1969, *7*, 403–417.

Lockhart, J. M. Ambient temperature and time estimation. *Journal of Experimental Psychology*, 1967, *73*, 286–291.

London, I. D. A Russian report on the postoperative newly seeing. *American Journal of Psychology*, 1960, *73*, 478–482.

Long, G., & Beaton, R. J. The contribution of visual persistence to the perceived duration of brief targets. *Perception & Psychophysics*, 1980, *28*, 422–430.

Long, G., Toppino, T. C., & Kostenbauder, J. F. As the cube turns: Evidence for two processes in the perception of a dynamic reversible figure. *Perception & Psychophysics*, 1983, *34*, 29–38.

Long, G., & Wurst, S. A. Complexity effects on reaction-time measures of visual persistence: Evidence for peripheral and central contibutions. *American Journal of Psychology*, 1984, *97*, 537–561.

Loomis, J. M., & Lederman, S. J. Tactual perception. In K. R. Boff, L. Kaufman, & J. P. Thomas (Eds.), *Handbook of perception and human performance*. Volume II: *Cognitive processes and performance*. New York: John Wiley, 1986.

Loop, M. S., & Bruce, L. L. Cat color vision: The effect of stimulus size. *Science*, 1978, *199*, 1221–1222.

Lore, R., & Sawatski, D. Performance of binocular and monocular infant rats on the visual cliff. *Journal of Comparative and Physiological Psychology*, 1969, *67*, 177–181.

Lucas, A., & Fisher, G. H. Illusions in concrete situations: II Experimental studies of the Poggendorff illusion. *Ergonomics*, 1969, *12*, 395–402.

Lucca, A., Dellantonio, A., & Riggio, L. Some observations of the Poggendorff and Müller-Lyer illusions. *Perception & Psychophysics*, 1986, *39*, 374–380.

Lynes, J. A. Brunelleschi's perspective reconsidered. *Perception*, 1980, *9*, 87–99.

Mack, A. Perceptual aspects of motion in the frontal plane. In K. R. Boff, L. Kaufman, & J. P. Thomas (Eds.), *Handbook of perception and human performance*. Volume I: *Sensory processes and perception*. New York: John Wiley, 1986.

Mack, A., Fendrich, R., Chambers, D., & Heuer, F. Perceived position and saccadic eye movements. *Vision Research*, 1985, *25*, 501–505.

MacKain, K., Studdert-Kennedy, M., Spieker, S., & Stern, D. Infant intermodal speech perception is a left-hemisphere function. *Science*, 1983, *219*, 1347–1349.

MacKay, D. M. Ways of looking at perception. In W. Wathen-Dunn (Ed.), *Models for the perception of speech and visual form*. Cambridge, Mass.: M.I.T. Press, 1967.

MacNichol, E. F. Three-pigment color vision. *Scientific American*, 1964, *211*, 48–56. (*a*)

MacNichol, E. F. Retinal mechanisms of color vision. *Vision Research*, 1964, *4*, 119–133. (*b*)

Madden, R. C., & Phillips, J. B. An attempt to demonstrate magnetic compass orientation in two species of mammals. *Animal Learning & Behavior*, 1987, *15*, 130–134.

Mair, R. G., Bouffard, J. A., Engen, T., & Morton, T. H. Olfactory sensitivity during the menstrual cycle. *Sensory Processes*, 1978, *2*, 90–98.

Maller, O. Specific appetite. In M. R. Kare & O. Maller (Eds.), *The chemical senses and nutrition*. Baltimore, Md.: Johns Hopkins Press, 1967.

Malott, R. W., Malott, M. K., & Pokrzywinski, J. The effects of outward-pointing arrowheads on the Mueller–Lyer illusion in pigeons. *Psychonomic Science*, 1967, *9*, 55–56.

Mandenoff, A., Fumeron, F., Apfelbaum, M., & Margules, D. L. Endogenous opiates and energy balance. *Science*, 1982, *215*, 1536–1538.

Manley, G. A. Some aspects on the evolution of hearing in vertebrates. *Nature*, 1971, *230*, 506–509.

Marcel, A. J. Conscious and unconscious perception: Experiments on visual masking and word recognition. *Cognitive Psychology*, 1983, *15*, 197–237.

Marks, L. E. Synesthesia. *Psychology Today*, 1975, *9*, 48–52.

Marks, L. E. *The unity of the senses*. New York: Academic Press, 1978.

Marks, L. E., & Stevens, J. C. Perceived cold and skin temperature as functions of stimulation level and duration. *American Journal of Psychology*, 1972, *85*, 407–419.

Marks, W. B., Dobelle, W. H., & MacNichol, E. F. Visual pigments of single primate cones. *Science*, 1964, *143*, 1181–1183.

Marler, P. R. & Hamilton, W. J. *Mechanisms of animal behavior*. New York: John Wiley, 1966.

Marx, J. L. Brain peptides: Is substance P a transmitter of pain signals? *Science*, 1979, *205*, 886–889.

Masin, S. C., & Vidotto, G. A magnitude estimation study of the inverted-T illusion. *Perception & Psychophysics*, 1983, *33*, 582–584.

Mason, J. R., & Silver, W. L. Trigeminally mediated odor aversion in starlings. *Brain Research*, 1983, *269*, 196–199.

Masterton, B., & Diamond, I. T. Hearing: Central neural mechanisms. Chapter 18 in E. C. Carterette & M. P. Friedman (Eds.), *Handbook of perception*. Volume III: *Biology of perceptual systems*. New York: Academic Press, 1973.

Masterton, B., Heffner, H., & Ravizza, R. The evolution of human hearing. *Journal of the Acoustical Society of America*, 1968, *45*, 966–985.

Matin, L. Visual localization and eye movements. In K. R. Boff, L. Kaufman, & J. P. Thomas (Eds.), *Handbook of perception and human performance*. Volume I: *Sensory processes and perception*. New York: John Wiley, 1986.

Matthews, L. H., & Knight, M. *The senses of animals*. London: Museum Press, 1963.

Mattingly, I. G. Speech cues and sign stimuli. *American Scientist*, 1972, *60*, 327–337.

Maurer, D., & Lewis, T. L. Peripheral discrimination by three-month-old infants. *Child Development*, 1979, *50*, 276–279.

Maurer, D., & Salapatek, P. Developmental changes in the scanning of faces by young infants. *Child Development*, 1976, *47*, 523–527.

Mayer, M. Development of anisotropy in late child-hood. *Vision Research*, 1977, *17*, 703–710.

Mayer, M. *Sensory perception laboratory manual*. New York: John Wiley, 1982.

Mayer, M. J., Kim, C. B. Y., Svingos, A., & Glucs, A. Foveal flicker sensitivity in healthy aging eyes. I. Compensating for pupil variation. *Journal of the Optical Society of America A*, 1988, *5*, 2201–2209.

McBurney, D. H. Psychological dimensions and perceptual analyses of taste. In E. C. Carterette & M. P. Friedman (Eds.), *Handbook of perception*, Volume VI, A: *Tasting and smelling*. New York: Academic Press, 1978.

McBurney, D., & Collings, V. *Introduction to sensation and perception*. Englewood Cliffs, N.J.: Prentice Hall, 1977.

McBurney, D. H., Collings, V. B., & Glanz, L. M. Temperature dependence of human taste responses. *Physiology and Behavior*, 1973, *11*, 89–94.

McBurney, D. H., Levine, J. M., & Cavanaugh, P. H. Psychophysical and social ratings of human body odor. *Personality and Psychology Bulletin*, 1977, *3*, 135–138.

McBurney, D. H., & Pfaffmann, C. Gustatory adaptation to saliva and sodium chloride. *Journal of Experimental Psychology*, 1963, *65*, 523–529.

McBurney, D. H., & Shick, T. R. Taste and water taste of twenty-six compounds for man. *Perception & Psychophysics*, 1971, *10*, 249–252.

McBurney, D. H., Smith, D. V., & Shick, T. R. Gustatory cross-adaptation: Sourness and bitterness. *Perception & Psychophysics*, 1972, *11*, 228–232.

McCleod, R. W., & Ross, H. E. Optic-flow and cognitive factors in time-to-collision estimates. *Perception*, 1983, *12*, 417–423.

McClintic, J. R. *Basic anatomy and physiology of the human body*. New York: John Wiley, 1975.

McClintic, J. R. *Physiology of the human body* (2nd ed.). New York: John Wiley, 1978.

McClintock, M. K. Menstrual synchrony and suppression. *Nature*, 1971, *229*, 244–245.

McClintock, M. K. Estrous synchrony: Modulation of ovarian cycle length by female pheromones. *Physiology and Behavior*, 1984, *32*, 701–705.

McCloskey, M. Intuitive physics. *Scientific American*, 1983, *248*, 122–130. (*a*)

McCloskey, M. Naïve theories of motion. In D. Gentner & A. L. Stevens (Eds.), *Mental models*. Hillsdale, N.J.: Lawrence Erlbaum, 1983. (*b*)

McCloskey, M., Caramazza, A., & Green, B. Curvilinear motion in the absence of external forces: Naïve beliefs about the motions of objects. *Science*, 1980, *210*, 1139–1141.

McCloskey, M., Washburn, A., & Felch, L. Intuitive physics: The straight-down belief and its origin. *Journal of Experimental Psychology: Learning, Memory, and Cognition*, 1983, *9*, 636–649.

McCollough, C. Color adaptation of edge-detectors in the human visual system. *Science*, 1965, *149*, 1115–1116.

McConkie, G. W., Kerr, P. W., Reddix, M. D., Zola, D., & Jacobs, A. M. Eye movement control during reading: II. Frequency of refixating a word. *Perception & Psychophysics*, 1989, *46*, 245–253.

McFadden, D., & Plattsmier, H. S. Aspirin can potentiate the temporary hearing loss induced by intense sounds. *Hearing Research*, 1983, *9*, 295–316.

McGivern, R. F., & Berntson, G. G. Mediation of diurnal fluctuations in pain sensitivity in the rat by food intake patterns: Reversal by naloxone. *Science*, 1980, *210*, 210–211.

McKay, D. G. Aspects of the theory of comprehension, memory, and attention. *Quarterly Journal of Experimental Psychology*, 1973, *25*, 22–40.

McKee, S. P., & Westheimer, G. Improvement in vernier acuity with practice. *Perception & Psychophysics*, 1978, *24*, 258–262.

Meltzoff, A. N. Imitation of televised models by infants. *Child Development*, 1988, *59*, 1221–1229.

Melzack, R. Phantom limbs. *Psychology Today*, 1970, *4*, 63–68.

Melzack, R. *The puzzle of pain*. New York: Basic Books, 1973.

Melzack, R., & Wall, P. D. Pain mechanisms: A new theory. *Science*, 1965, *150*, 971–979.

Mermelstein, R., Banks, W., & Prinzmetal, W. Figural goodness effects in perception and memory. *Perception & Psychophysics*, 1979, *26*, 472–480.

Mescavage, A. A., Heimer, W. I., Tatz, S. J., & Runyon, R. P. Time estimation as a function of rate of stimulus change. Paper presented at the annual meeting of the Eastern Psychological Association, New York, April, 1971.

Messing, R. B., & Campbell, B. A. Summation of pain produced in different anatomical regions. *Perception & Psychophysics*, 1971, *10*, 225–228.

Michael, C. R. Retinal processing of visual images. *Scientific American*, 1969, *220*, 104–114.

Michael, C. R. Color vision mechanisms in monkey striate cortex: Dual-opponent cells with concentric receptive fields. *Journal of Neurophysiology*, 1978, *41*, 572–588. (a)

Michael, C. R. Color vision mechanisms in monkey striate cortex: Simple cells with dual opponent-color receptive fields. *Journal of Neurophysiology*, 1978, *41*, 1233–1249. (b)

Michael, R. P., Bonsall, R. W., & Warner, P. Human vaginal secretions: Volatile fatty acid content. *Science*, 1974, *186*, 1217–1219.

Michael, R. P., & Keverne, E. B. Pheromones in the communication of sexual status in primates. *Nature*, 1968, *218*, 746–749.

Michels, K. M., & Schumacher, A. W. Color vision in tree squirrels. *Psychonomic Science*, 1968, *10*, 7–8.

Michon, J. Tapping regularity as a measure of perceptual motor load. *Ergonomics*, 1966, *9*, 401–412.

Miczek, K. A., Thompson, M. L., & Shuster, L. Opioid-like analgesia in defeated mice. *Science*, 1982, *215*, 1520–1522.

Milewski, A. E. Infant's discrimination of internal and external pattern elements. *Journal of Experimental Child Psychology*, 1976, *22*, 229–246.

Miller, E. F., & Graybiel, A. Thresholds for the perception of angular acceleration as indicated by the oculogyral illusion. *Perception & Psychophysics*, 1975, *17*, 329–332.

Miller, G. A. The masking of speech. *Psychological Bulletin*, 1947, *44*, 105–129.

Milne, L. J., & Milne, M. *The senses of animals and men*. New York: Atheneum, 1967.

Mitchell, C. T., & Davis, R. The perception of time in scale model environments. *Perception*, 1987, *16*, 5–16.

Mitchell, D. E. Effect of early visual experience on the development of certain perceptual abilities in animals and man. In R. D. Walk & H. L. Pick (Eds.), *Perception and experience*. New York: Plenum, 1978.

Mitchell, D. E. The influence of early visual experience on visual perception. In C. S. Harris (Ed.), *Visual coding and adaptability*. Hillsdale, N.J.: Lawrence Erlbaum, 1980.

Miyazaki, K. Musical pitch identification by absolute pitch possessors. *Perception & Psychophysics*, 1988, *44*, 501–512.

Mo, S. S. Judgment of temporal duration as a function of numerosity. *Psychonomic Science*, 1971, *24*, 71–72.

Monahan, C. B., Kendall, R. A., & Carterette, E. C. The effect of melodic and temporal contour on recognition memory for pitch change. *Perception & Psychophysics*, 1987, *41*, 576–600.

Moncrieff, R. W. *The chemical senses*. London: Leonard Hill, 1951.

Moncrieff, R. W. *Odour preferences*. New York: John Wiley, 1966.

Money, K. E., & Cheung, B. S. Another function of the inner ear: Facilitation of the emetic response to poisons. *Aviation, Space, and Environmental Medicine*, 1983, *54*, 208–211.

Montagna, W. The skin. *Scientific American*, 1965, *212*, 56–66.

Montgomery, J. C., & MacDonald, J. A. Sensory tuning of lateral line receptors in antarctic fish to the movements of planktonic prey. *Science*, 1987, *235*, 195–196.

Moray, N. Attention in dichotic listening: Affective cues and the influence of instructions. *Quarterly*

Journal of Experimental Psychology, 1959, *11*, 56–60.

Mosel, J. N., & Kantrowitz, G. The effect of monosodium glutamate on acuity to the primary tastes. *American Journal of Psychology*, 1952, *65*, 573–579.

Mozell, M. M. Olfactory discrimination: Electrophysiological spatiotemporal basis. *Science*, 1964, *143*, 1336–1337.

Mozell, M. M. The spatiotemporal analysis of odorants at the level of the olfactory receptor sheet. *Journal of General Physiology*, 1966, *50*, 25–41.

Mozell, M. M. Olfaction. In J. W. Kling & L. A. Riggs (Eds.), *Experimental psychology* (3rd ed.). New York: Holt, Rinehart and Winston, 1971.

Mueller, C. G. *Sensory psychology*. Englewood Cliffs, N.J.: Prentice-Hall, 1965.

Muir, D. W., & Mitchell, D. E. Visual resolution and experience: Acuity deficits in cats following early selective visual deprivation. *Science*, 1973, *180*, 420–422.

Mulligan, R. M., & Schiffman, H. R. Temporal experiences as a function of organization in memory. *Bulletin of the Psychonomic Society*, 1979, *14*, 417–420.

Murphy, C. Olfactory psychophysics. In T. E. Finger & W. L. Silver (Eds.), *Neurobiology of taste and smell*. New York: John Wiley, 1987.

Murphy, C., & Gilmore, M. M. Quality-specific effects of aging on the human taste system, *Perception & Psychophysics*, 1989, *45*, 121–128.

Murphy, M. R., & Schneider, G. E. Olfactory bulb removal eliminates mating behavior in the male golden hamster. *Science*, 1969, *167*, 302–303.

Nachman, M. Taste preferences for sodium salts by adrenalectomized rats. *Journal of Comparative and Physiological Psychology*, 1962, *55*, 1124–1129.

Nafe, J. P. The pressure, pain, and temperature senses. In C. A. Murchison (Ed.), *A handbook of general experimental psychology* (Chap. 20). Worcester, Mass.: Clark University Press, 1934.

Nathans, J., Piantanida, T. P., Eddy, R. L., Shows, T. B. & Hogness, D. S. Molecular genetics of inherited variation in human color vision. *Science*, 1986, *232*, 203–210.

Nathans, J., Thomas, D. & Hogness, D. S. Molecular genetics of human color vision: The genes encoding blue, green, and red pigments. *Science*, 1986, *232*, 193–202.

Neale, J. H., Barker, J. L., Uhl, G. R., & Snyder, S. H. Enkephalin-containing neurons visualized in spinal cord cell cultures. *Science*, 1978, *201*, 467–469.

Neill, W. T. Decision processes in selective attention: Response priming in the Stroop color-word task. *Perception & Psychophysics*, 1978, *23*, 80–84.

Neisser, U. Decision-time without reaction-time: Experiments in visual scanning. *American Journal of Psychology*, 1963, *76*, 376–385.

Neisser, U. Visual search. *Scientific American*, 1964, *210*, 94–102.

Neisser, U. *Cognitive psychology*. New York: Appleton-Century-Crofts, 1967.

Neisser, U. The processes of vision. *Scientific American*, 1968, *219*, 204–214.

Neisser, U., & Becklen, R. Selective looking: Attending to visually specified events. *Cognitive Psychology*, 1975, *7*, 480–494.

Neisser, U., & Beller, H. K. Searching through word lists. *British Journal of Psychology*, 1965, *56*, 349–358.

Neisser, U., Novick, R., & Lazar, R. Searching for ten targets simultaneously. *Perceptual and Motor Skills*, 1963, *17*, 955–961.

Neisser, U., & Stoper, A. Redirecting the search process. *British Journal of Psychology*, 1965, *56*, 359–368.

Newton, I. *Optiks, or a treatise of the reflections, refractions, inflections & colours of light* (1704) (4th ed.). New York: Dover, 1952.

Nicolaus, L. K., Cassel, J. F., Carlson, R. B., & Gustavson, C. R. Taste-aversion conditioning of crows to control predation on eggs. *Science*, 1983, *220*, 212–214.

Nienhuys, T. G. W., & Clark, G. M. Frequency discrimination following the selective destruction of cochlear inner and outer hair cells. *Science*, 1978, *199*, 1356–1357.

Norcia, A. M., & Tyler, C. W. Spatial frequency sweep VEP: Visual acuity during the first year of life. *Vision Research*, 1985, *25*, 1399–1408.

Norman, D. A. Memory while shadowing. *Quarterly Journal of Experimental Psychology*, 1969, *21*, 85–93.

Novick, A. Echolocation in bats: Some aspects of pulse design. *American Scientist*, 1971, *59*, 198–209.

Nowlis, G. H., Frank, M. E., & Pfaffmann, C. Specificity of acquired aversions to taste qualities in hamsters and rats. *Journal of Comparative and Physiological Psychology*, 1980, *94*, 932–942.

Nyström, M., & Hansson, S. B. Interaction between early experience and depth avoidance in young eider ducks (*Somateria* molissima L.). *Behavior*, 1974, *48*, 303–314.

Ogle, K. N. The optical space sense. In H. Davson (Ed.), *The eye*. New York: Academic Press, 1962.

Oldfield, S. R., & Parker, S. P. A. Acuity of sound localisation: A topography of auditory space. III. Monaural hearing conditions. *Perception*, 1986, *15*, 67–81.

Olzak, L. A., & Thomas, J. P. Seeing spatial patterns. In K. R. Boff, L. Kaufman, & J. P. Thomas (Eds.), *Handbook of perception and human performance*. Volume I: *Sensory processes and perception*. New York: John Wiley, 1986.

O'Mahoney, M., Kingsley, L., Harji, A., & Davies, M. What sensation signals the salt taste threshold? *Chemical Senses and Flavor*, 1976, *2*, 177–188.

O'Mahoney, M., & Wingate, P. The effect of interstimulus procedures on salt taste intensity functions. *Perception & Psychophysics*, 1974, *16*, 494–502.

Orbison, W. D. Shape as a function of the vector field. *American Journal of Psychology*, 1939, *52*, 31–45.

Ornstein, R. E. *On the experience of time*. Baltimore, Md.: Penguin Books, 1969.

Osgood, C. E. *Method and theory in experimental psychology*. New York: Oxford University Press, 1953.

Oster, G. Phosphenes. *Scientific American*, 1970, *222*, 82–87.

Oster, G. Auditory beats in the brain. *Scientific American*, 1973, *229*, 94–102.

Owens, D. A., & Wolf-Kelly, K. Near work, visual fatigue, and variations of oculomotor tonus. *Investigative Ophthalmology and Visual Science*. 1987, *28*, 743–749.

Owsley, C., Sekuler, R., & Siemsen, D. Contrast sensitivity throughout adulthood. *Vision Research*, 1983, *23*, 689–699.

Oyama, T. Figure-ground dominance as a function of sector angle, brightness, hue, and orientation. *Journal of Experimental Psychology*, 1960, *60*, 299–305.

Palmer, E. E., & Hemenway, K. Orientation and symmetry: Effects of multiple, rotational, and near symmetries. *Journal of Experimental Psychology: Human Perception and Performance*, 1978, *4*, 691–702.

Palmerino, C. C., Rusiniak, K. W., & Garcia, J. Flavor-illness aversions: The peculiar roles of odor and taste in memory for poison. *Science*, 1980, *208*, 753–755.

Papanicolaou, A. C., Schmidt, A. C., Moore, B. D., & Eisenberg, H. M. Cerebral activation patterns in an arithmetic and a visuospatial processing task. *International Journal of Neuroscience*, 1983, *20*, 283–288.

Parker, D. E. The vestibular apparatus. *Scientific American*, 1980, *243*, 118–135.

Parks, T. E. Post-retinal visual storage. *American Journal of Psychology*, 1965, *78*, 145–147.

Parks, T. E. Illusory figures: A (mostly) atheoretical review. *Psychological Bulletin*, 1984, *95*, 282–300.

Pasternak, G. W., Childers, S. R., & Snyder, S. H. Opiate analgesia: Evidence for mediation by a subpopulation of opiate receptors. *Science*, 1980, *208*, 514–516.

Pastore, N. *Selective history of theories of visual perception*. New York: Oxford University Press, 1971.

Patterson, J., & Deffenbacher, K. Haptic perception of the Müller–Lyer illusion by the blind. *Perceptual and Motor Skills*, 1972, *35*, 819–824.

Patterson, R. L. S. Identification of 3α-hydroxy-

5α-androst-16-ene as the musk odour component of boar submaxillary salivary gland and its relationship to the sex odour taint in pork meat. *Journal of the Science of Food Agriculture*, 1968, *19*, 434–438.

Pearlman, A. L., Birch, J., & Meadows, J. C. Cerebral color blindness: An acquired defect in hue discrimination. *Annals of Neurology*, 1979, *5*, 253–261.

Petrig, B., Julesz, B., Kropfl, W., Baumgartner, G., & Ankliker, M. Development of stereopsis and cortical binocularity in human infants: Electrophysiological evidence. *Science*, 1981, *213*, 1402–1405.

Pettigrew, J. D., & Freeman, R. D. Visual experience without lines: Effect on developing cortical neurons. *Science*, 1973, *182*, 599–601.

Pfaff, D. Effects of temperature and time of day on time judgments. *Journal of Experimental Psychology*, 1968, *76*, 419–422.

Pfaffmann, C. The sense of taste. In J. Field, H. W. Magoun, & V. E. Hall (Eds.), *Handbook of physiology*, Volume I. Washington, D.C.: American Physiological Society, 1959.

Pfaffmann, C. Taste stimulation and preference behavior. In Y. Zotterman (Ed.), *Olfaction and taste*. New York: Macmillan, 1963.

Pfaffmann, C. Taste, its sensory and motivating properties. *American Scientist*, 1964, *52*, 187–206.

Pfaffmann, C. Specificity of the sweet receptors of the squirrel monkeys. In *Chemical senses and flavor*. Dordrecht-Holland: D. Reidel Co., 1974.

Pfaffmann, C. The vertebrate phylogeny, neural code, and integrative processes of taste. In E. C. Carterette & M. P. Friedman (Eds.), *Handbook of perception*, Volume VI, A: *Tasting and smelling*. New York: Academic Press, 1978.

Pfaffmann, C., Frank, M., Bartoshuk, L. M., & Snell, T. C. Coding gustatory information in the squirrel monkey chorda tympani. In J. M. Sprague & A. N. Epstein (Eds.), *Progress in psychobiology and physiological psychology*, Volume 6. New York: Academic Press, 1976.

Pick, H. L., & Hay, J. C. A passive test of the Held re-afference hypothesis. *Perceptual and Motor Skills*, 1965, *20*, 1070–1072.

Piggins, D. J., Kingham, J. R., & Holmes, S. M. Colour, colour saturation, and pattern induced by intermittent illumination: An initial study. *British Journal of Physiological Optics*, 1972, *27*, 120–125.

Poggio, G. F., & Poggio, T. The analysis of stereopsis. *Annual Review of Neuroscience*, 1984, *7*, 379–412.

Pollack, R. H. A theoretical note on the aging of the visual system. *Perception & Psychophysics*, 1978, *23*, 94–95.

Polyak, S. *The vertebrate visual system*. Chicago: University of Chicago Press, 1957.

Polzella, D. J., DaPolito, F., & Hinsman, M. C. Cerebral asymmetry in time perception. *Perception & Psychophysics*, 1977, *21*, 187–192.

Pons, T. P., Garraghty, P. E., Friedman, D. P., & Mishkin, M. Physiological evidence of serial processing in somatosensory cortex. *Science*, 1987, *237*, 417–420.

Post, R. B., & Leibowitz, H. W. A revised analysis of the role of efference in motion perception. *Perception*, 1985, *14*, 631–643.

Postman, L., & Egan, J. P. *Experimental psychology*. New York: Harper & Row, 1949.

Poulton, E. C. Geometric illusions in reading graphs. *Perception & Psychophysics*, 1985, *37*, 543–548.

Povel, D. J., & Essens, P. Perception of temporal patterns. *Music Perception*, 1985, *2*, 411–440.

Poynter, W. D., & Homa, D. Duration judgment and the experience of time. *Perception & Psychophysics*, 1983, *33*, 548–560.

Prah, J. D., & Benignus, V. A. Trigeminal sensitivity to contact chemical-stimulation—A new method and some results. *Perception & Psychophysics*, 1984, *35*, 65–68.

Pressey, A. W., & Moro, T. L. An explanation of Cooper and Runyan's results on the Mueller-Lyer illusion. *Perceptual and Motor Skills*, 1971, *32*, 564–566.

Preti, G., Cutler, W. B., Garcia, C. R., Huggins, G.

R., & Lawley, H. J. Human axillary secretions influence women's menstrual cycles: The role of donor extract of females. *Hormones and Behavior*, 1986, *20*, 474–482.

Priestly, J. B. *Man and time*. New York: Dell, 1968.

Pritchard, R. M., Heron, W., & Hebb, D. O. Visual perception approached by the method of stabilized images. *Canadian Journal of Psychology*, 1960, *14*, 67–77.

Prosen, C. A., Moody, D. B., Stebbins, W. C., & Hawkins, J. E., Jr. Auditory intensity discrimination after selective loss of cochlear outer hair cells. *Science*, 1981, *212*, 1286–1288.

Purcell, D. G., & Stewart, A. L. The face-detection effect: Configuration enhances detection. *Perception & Psychophysics*, 1988, *43*, 355–366.

Quadagno, D. M., Shubeita, H. E., Deck, J., & Francoeur, D. Influence of male social contacts, exercise and all female living conditions on the menstrual cycle. *Psychoneuroendochronology*, 1981, *6*, 239–244.

Quina-Holland, K. Spatial distortions within the Poggendorff figure and its variants: A parametric analysis. *Perception & Psychophysics*, 1977, *21*, 118–124.

Rabin, M. D. Experience facilitates olfactory quality discrimination. *Perception & Psychophysics*, 1988, *44*, 532–540.

Radinsky, L. Cerebral clues. *Natural History*, 1976, *55*, 54–59.

Rakerd, B. Vowels in consonantal context are perceived more linguistically than are isolated vowels: Evidence from an individual differences scaling study. *Perception & Psychophysics*, 1984, *35*, 123–136.

Ratliff, F. Contour and contrast. *Scientific American*, 1972, *226*, 90–101.

Ratliff, F., & Hartline, H. K. The responses of *Limulus* optic nerve fibers to patterns of illumination on the retinal mosaic. *Journal of General Physiology*, 1959, *42*, 1241–1255.

Raviola, E., & Wiesel, T. N. An animal model of myopia. *The New England Journal of Medicine*. 1985, *312*, 1609–1615.

Raymond, J. E. The interaction of target size and background pattern on perceived velocity during visual tracking. *Perception & Psychophysics*, 1988, *43*, 425–430.

Reason, J. T., & Brand, J. J. *Motion sickness*. New York: Academic Press, 1975.

Reed, C. F. Terrestrial passage theory of the moon illusion. *Journal of Experimental Psychology: General*, 1984, *113*, 489–516.

Reed, C. F. More things in heaven and earth: A reply to Loftus. *Journal of Experimental Psychology: General*, 1985, *114*, 122–124.

Reed, C. M., Doherty, M. J., Braida, L. D., & Durlach, N. I. Analytic study of the Tadoma method: Further experiments with inexperienced observers. *Journal of Speech and Hearing Research*, 1982, *25*, 216–223.

Regan, D., & Beverley, K. I. Visually guided locomotion: Psychophysical evidence for a neural mechanism sensitive to flow patterns. *Science*, 1979, *205*, 311–313.

Regan, D., & Beverley, K. I. How do we avoid confounding the direction we are looking and the direction we are moving. *Science*, 1982, *215*, 194–196.

Regan, D., Beverley, K. I., & Cynader, M. The visual perception of motion in depth. *Scientific American*, 1979, *241*, 136–151.

Regan, D. M., Kaufman, L., & Lincoln, J. Motion in depth and visual acceleration. In K. R. Boff, L. Kaufman, & J. P. Thomas (Eds.), *Handbook of perception and human performance*. Volume I: *Sensory processes and perception*. New York: John Wiley, 1986.

Remez, R. E., Rubin, P. E., Pisoni, D. B., Carrell, T. D. Speech perception without traditional speech cues. *Science*, 1981, *212*, 947–950.

Restle, F. Moon illusion explained on the basis of relative size. *Science*, 1970, *167*, 1092–1096.

Reymond, L. Spatial visual acuity of the eagle *Aquila audax*: A behavioural, optical and anatomical investigation. *Vision Research*, 1985, *25*, 1477–1491.

Reynolds, G. S., & Stevens, S. S. Binaural summation of loudness. *Journal of the Acoustical Society of America*, 1960, *32*, 1337–1344.

Rice, C. E. Human echo perception. *Science*, 1967, *155*, 656–664.

Richter, C. P. Salt taste thresholds of normal and adrenalectomized rats. *Endocrinology*, 1939, *24*, 367–371.

Richter, C. P. Total self-regulatory functions in animals and human beings. *Harvey Lectures*, 1942, *38*, 63–103.

Riggs, L. A. Visual acuity. In C. H. Graham (Ed.), *Vision and visual perception*. New York: John Wiley, 1965.

Riggs, L. A. The "looks" of Helmholtz. *Perception & Psychophysics*, 1967, *2*, 1–13.

Riggs, L. A., Volkmann, F. C., & Moore, R. K. Suppression of the blackout due to blinks. *Vision Research*, 1981, *21*, 1075–1079.

Rock, I. *Orientation and form*. New York: Academic Press, 1973.

Rock, I. The perception of disoriented figures. *Scientific American*, 1974, *230*, 78–85.

Rock, I. *An introduction to perception*. New York: Macmillan, 1975.

Rock, I. *The logic of perception*. Cambridge, Mass.: Bradford Books/M.I.T. Press, 1983.

Rock, I. *Perception*. New York: Scientific American Library, W.H. Freeman, 1984.

Rock, I. The description and analysis of object and event perception. In K. R. Boff, L. Kaufman, & J. P. Thomas (Eds.), *Handbook of perception and human performance*. Volume II: *Cognitive processes and performance*. New York: John Wiley, 1986.

Rock, I., & Harris, C. S. Vision and touch. *Scientific American*, 1967, *216*, 96–104.

Rock, I., & Kaufman, L. The moon illusion, II. *Science*, 1962, *136*, 1023–1031.

Rock, I., & Victor, J. Vision and touch: An experimentally created conflict between the senses. *Science*, 1964, *143*, 594–596.

Rodgers, W., & Rozin, P. Novel food preferences in thiamine-deficient rats. *Journal of Comparative and Physiological Psychology*, 1966, *61*, 1–4.

Roederer, J. G. *Introduction to the physics and psychophysics of music*. New York: Springer-Verlag, 1973.

Rogel, M. A critical evaluation of the possibility of higher primate reproductive and sexual pheromones. *Psychological Bulletin*, 1978, *85*, 810–830.

Rollman, G. B., & Harris, G. The detectability, discriminability, and perceived magnitude of painful electrical shock. *Perception & Psychophysics*, 1987, *42*, 257–268.

Rose, J. E., Brugge, J. F., Anderson, D. J., & Hind, J. E. Phase-locked response to low-frequency tones in single auditory nerve fibers of the squirrel monkey. *Journal of Neurophysiology*, 1967, *30*, 769–793.

Rose, L., Yinon, U., & Belkin, M. Myopia induced in cats deprived of distance vision during development. *Vision Research*, 1974, *14*, 1029–1032.

Rosen, R. C., Schiffman, H. R., & Cohen, A. S. Behavior modification and the treatment of myopia. *Behavior Modification*, 1984, *8*, 131–154.

Rosen, R. C., Schiffman, H. R., & Myers, H. Behavioral treatment of myopia: Refractive error and acuity changes in relation to axial length and intraocular pressure. *American Journal of Optometry and Physiological Optics*, 1984, *61*, 100–105.

Rosenblum, L. A., & Cross, H. A. Performance of neonatal monkeys in the visual-cliff situation. *American Journal of Psychology*, 1963, *76*, 318–320.

Rosenzweig, M. R. Representations of the two ears at the auditory cortex. *American Journal of Psychology*, 1951, *67*, 147–158.

Rosenzweig, M. R. Cortical correlates of auditory localization and of related perceptual phenomena. *Journal of Comparative and Physiological Psychology*, 1954, *47*, 269–276.

Rosenzweig, M. R. Auditory localization. *Scientific American*, 1961, *205*, 132–142.

Rosenzweig, M. R., & Leiman, A. L. *Physiological psychology*. Lexington, Mass.: D. C. Heath, 1982.

Rossi, P. J. Adaptation and negative aftereffect to lateral optical displacement in newly hatched chicks. *Science*, 1968, *160*, 430–432.

Rossi, P. J. Primacy of the negative aftereffect over positive adaptation in prism adaptation with newly hatched chicks. *Developmental Psychobiology*, 1969, *2*, 43–53.

Rothblat, L. A., & Schwartz, M. L. Altered early environment: Effects on the brain and visual behavior. In R. D. Walk & H. L. Pick (Eds.), *Perception and experience*. New York: Plenum, 1978.

Rovee-Collier, C., & Hayne, H. Reactivation of infant memory: Implications for cognitive development. *Advances in Child Development and Behavior*, 1987, *20*, 185–238.

Rowell, T. E. Agonistic noises of the rhesus monkeys (*Macaca mulatta*). *Symposium of the Zoological Society of London*, 1962, *8*, 91–96.

Rozin, P., Gruss, L., & Berk, G. Reversal of innate aversions: Attempts to induce a preference for chili peppers in rats. *Journal of Comparative and Physiological Psychology*, 1979, *93*, 1001–1014.

Rubin, D. S., Groth, E., & Goldsmith, D. J. Olfactory cuing of autobiographical memory. *American Journal of Psychology*, 1984, *97*, 493–507.

Rubin, E. Figure and ground. In D. C. Beardslee & M. Wertheimer (Eds.), *Readings in perception*. New York: D. Van Nostrand, 1958. Based on an abridged translation by Michael Wertheimer of pp. 35–101 of Rubin, E., *Visuell wahrgenommene Figuren* (translated by Peter Collett into German from the Danish *Synsoplevede Figurer*, Copenhagen: Gyldendalske, 1915). Copenhagen: Gyldendalske, 1921.

Rubin, M. L., & Walls, G. L. *Fundamentals of visual science*. Springfield, Ill.: Charles C Thomas, 1969.

Ruch, T. C., Patton, H. B., Woodbury, J. W., & Tawe, A. L. (Eds.), *Neurophysiology* (2nd Ed.). Philadelphia: W. B. Saunders, 1965.

Ruckmick, C. A. A new classification of tonal qualities. *Psychological Review*, 1929, *36*, 172–180.

Rudel, R. G., & Teuber, H. L. Decrement of visual and haptic Müller–Lyer illusion on repeated trials: A study of cross-modal transfer. *Quarterly Journal of Experimental Psychology*, 1963, *15*, 125–131.

Runeson, S., & Frykholm, G. Kinematic specifications of dynamics as an informational basis for person-and-action perception: Expectation, gender recognition, and deceptive intention. *Journal of Experimental Psychology: General*, 1983, *112*, 585–615.

Runyon, R. P., & Cooper, M. R. Enhancement of Sander illusion in minimal form. *Perception & Psychophysics*, 1970, *8*, 110–111.

Rushton, W. A. H. Visual pigments in man. *Scientific American*, 1962, *207*, 120–132.

Russell, M. J. Human olfactory communication. *Nature*, 1976, *260*, 520–522.

Russell, M. J., Switz, G. M., & Thompson, K. Olfactory influence on the human menstrual cycle. *Pharmacology, Biochemistry and Behavior*, 1980, *13*, 737–738.

Rymer, W. Z., & D'Almeida, A. Joint position sense: The effects of muscle contraction. *Brain*, 1980, *103*, 1–22.

Sacks, O., & Wasserman, R. The case of the color-blind painter. *The New York Review of Books*, 1987 (Nov. 19), 25–34.

Sadza, K. J., & de Weert, C. M. M. Influence of color and luminance on the Müller-Lycr illusion. *Perception & Psychophysics*, 1984, *35*, 214–220.

Safire, W. On language. *The New York Times Magazine*, May 27, 1979, pp. 9–10.

Salapatek, P. The visual investigation of geometric pattern by one- and two-month-old infants. Paper read at the annual meeting of the American Association for the Advancement of Science, Boston, December, 1969.

Salapatek, P. Pattern perception in early infancy. In L. B. Cohen & P. Salapatek (Eds.), *Infant perception: From sensation to cognition*, Volume I. New York: Academic Press, 1975.

Salapatek, P., & Kessen, W. Visual scanning of triangles by the human newborn. *Journal of Experimental Child Psychology*, 1966, *3*, 113–122.

Salapatek, P., & Kessen, W. Prolonged investigation of a plane geometric triangle by the human newborn. *Journal of Experimental Child Psychology*, 1973, *15*, 22–29.

Sawusch, J. R., & Jusczyk, P. W. Adaptation and contrast in the perception of voicing. *Journal of*

Experimental Psychology: Human Perception and Performance, 1981, *7*, 408–421.

Schaeffel, F., Glasser, A., & Howland, H. C. Accommodation, refractive error and eye growth in chickens. *Vision Research*, 1988, *28*, 639–657.

Scharf, B. *Experimental sensory psychology*. Glenview, Ill.: Scott, Foresman, 1975.

Scharf, B., & Buus, S. Audition I: Stimulus, physiology, thresholds. In K. R. Boff, L. Kaufman, & J. P. Thomas (Eds.), *Handbook of perception and human performance*. Volume I: *Sensory processes and perception*. New York: John Wiley, 1986.

Scharf, B., & Houtsma, A. J. M. Audition II: Loudness, pitch, localization, aural distortion, pathology. In K. R. Boff, L. Kaufman, & J. P. Thomas (Eds.), *Handbook of perception and human performance*. Volume I: *Sensory processes and perception*. New York: John Wiley, 1986.

Schendel, J. D., & Shaw, P. A test of the generality of the word-context effect. *Perception & Psychophysics*, 1976, *19*, 383–393.

Schiff, W. The perception of impending collision: A study of visually directed avoidant behavior. *Psychological Monographs*, 1965, *79* (Whole No. 604).

Schiff, W., Caviness, J. A., & Gibson, J. J. Persistent fear responses in rhesus monkeys to the optical stimulus of "looming." *Science*, 1962, *136*, 982–983.

Schiffman, H. R. Size-estimation of familiar objects under informative and reduced conditions of viewing. *American Journal of Psychology*, 1967, *80*, 229–235.

Schiffman, H. R. Depth perception of the Syrian hamster as a function of age and photic conditions of rearing. *Journal of Comparative and Physiological Psychology*, 1971, *76*, 491–495.

Schiffman, H. R. Some components of sensation and perception for the reading process. *Reading Research Quarterly*, 1972, *VII*, 588–612.

Schiffman, H. R., & Bobko, D. J. Effects of stimulus complexity on the perception of brief temporal intervals. *Journal of Experimental Psychology*, 1974, *103*, 156–159.

Schiffman, H. R., & Bobko, D. J. The role of number and familiarity of stimuli in the perception of brief temporal intervals. *American Journal of Psychology*, 1977, *90*, 85–93.

Schiffman, H. R., & Thompson, J. G. The role of apparent depth and context in the perception of the Ponzo illusion. *Perception*, 1978, *7*, 47–50.

Schiffman, S. S. The range of gustatory quality: Psychophysical and neural approaches. First Congress of the European Chemoreception Research Organization. Université de Paris. Sud, Campus d'Orsay, July 1974. (*a*)

Schiffman, S. S. Physiochemical correlates of olfactory quality. *Science*, 1974, *185*, 112–117. (*b*)

Schiffman, S. S. Personal communication, 1975.

Schiffman, S. S. Taste and smell in disease. *New England Journal of Medicine*, 1983, *308*, 1275–1279, 1337–1343.

Schiffman, S. S. The use of flavor to enhance efficacy of reducing diets. *Hospital Practice*, 1986, *21*, 44H–44R.

Schiffman, S. S. Recent developments in taste enhancement. *Flavor Trends & Technologies*, 1987, *41*, 72–73, 124.

Schiffman, S. S. Personal communication, 1988.

Schiffman, S. S., & Dackis, C. Taste of nutrients: Amino acids, vitamins, and fatty acids. *Perception & Psychophysics*, 1975, *17*, 140–146.

Schiffman, S. S., Diaz, C., & Beeker, T. G. Caffeine intensifies taste of certain sweeteners: Role of adenosine receptor. *Pharmacology, Biochemistry & Behavior*, 1986, *24*, 429–432.

Schiffman, S. S., & Erickson, R. P. A theoretical review: A psychophysical model for gustatory quality. *Physiology and Behavior*, 1971, *7*, 617–633.

Schiffman, S. S., Gill, J. M., & Diaz, C. Methyl xanthines enhances taste: Evidence for modulation of taste by adenosine receptor. *Pharmacology, Biochemistry & Behavior*, 1985, *22*, 195–203.

Schiffman, S. S., Hornack, K., & Reilly, D. Increased taste thresholds of amino acids with age.

American Journal of Clinical Nutrition, 1979, *32*, 1622–1627.

Schiffman, S. S., Mass, J., & Erickson, R. P. Thresholds of food odors in the elderly. *Experimental Aging Research*, 1976, *2*, 389–398.

Schlosberg, H. Stereoscopic depth from single pictures. *American Journal of Psychology*, 1941, *54*, 601–605.

Schouten, J. F. Subjective stroboscopy and a model of visual movement detectors. In W. Wathen-Dunn (Ed.), *Models for the perception of speech and visual form*. Cambridge, Mass.: M.I.T. Press, 1967.

Schwartz, J., & Tallal, P. Rate of acoustic change may underlie hemisphere specialization for speech perception. *Science*, 1980, *209*, 1320–1381.

Scott, T. R. & Chang, F.-C. T. The state of gustatory neural coding. *Chemical Senses*, 1984, *8*, 297–314.

Sedgwick, H. A. Space perception. In K. R. Boff, L. Kaufman, & J. P. Thomas (Eds.), *Handbook of perception and human performance*. Volume I: *Sensory processes and perception*. New York: John Wiley, 1986.

Seitz, V., Seitz, T., & Kaufman, L. Loss of depth avoidance in chicks as a function of early environmental influences. *Journal of Comparative and Physiological Psychology*, 1973, *85*, 139–143.

Sekuler, R., & Blake, R. Sensory underload. *Psychology Today*, 1987, *21*, 48–53.

Sekuler, R., Hutman, L. P., & Owsley, C. J. Human aging and spatial vision. *Science*, 1980, *209*, 1255–1256.

Senden, M., von. *Space and sight: The perception of space and shape in congenitally blind patients before and after operation*. London: Methuen, 1960.

Seyforth, R. M., Cheney, D. L., & Marler, P. Monkey responses to three different alarm calls: Evidence of predator classification and semantic communication. *Science*, 1980, *210*, 801–803.

Sharp, W. L. The floating-finger illusion. *Psychological Review*, 1928, *35*, 171–173.

Shepard, R. N. Recognition memory for words, sentences, and pictures. *Journal of Verbal Learning and Verbal Behavior*, 1967, *6*, 156–163.

Shepard, R. N. Psychophysical complementarity. In M. Kubovy & J. R. Pomeranz (Eds.), *Perceptual organization*. Hillsdale, N.J.: Lawrence Erlbaum, 1981.

Shepard, R. N., & Metzler, J. Mental rotation of three-dimensional objects. *Science*, 1971, *171*, 701–703.

Shepard, R. N., & Zare, S. L. Path-guided apparent motion. *Science*, 1983, *220*, 632–634.

Sherif, M. *The psychology of social norms*. New York: Harper & Row, 1936.

Sherrick, C. E., & Cholewiak, R. W. Cutaneous sensitivity. In K. R. Boff, L. Kaufman, & J. P. Thomas (Eds.), *Handbook of perception and human performance*. Volume I: *Sensory processes and perception*. New York: John Wiley, 1986.

Shiffrin, R. M. Attention. In R. C. Atkinson, R. J. Herrnstein, G. Lindzey, and R. D. Luce (Eds.), *Stevens' handbook of experimental psychology*. New York: John Wiley, 1988.

Shinkman, P. G. Visual depth discrimination in day-old chicks. *Journal of Comparative and Physiological Psychology*, 1963, *56*, 410–414.

Shlaer, R. Shift in binocular disparity causes compensatory change in the cortical structure of kittens. *Science*, 1971, *173*, 638–641.

Shlaer, R. An eagle's eye: Quality of the retinal image. *Science*, 1972, *176*, 920–922.

Sidtis, J. J., & Bryden, M. P. Asymmetrical perception of language and music: Evidence for independent processing strategies. *Neuropsychologia*, 1978, *16*, 627–632.

Silver, W. L. The common chemical sense. In T. E. Finger & W. L. Silver (Eds.), *Neurobiology of taste and smell*. New York: John Wiley, 1987.

Silver, W. L., & Maruniak, J. A. Trigeminal chemoreception in the nasal and oral cavities. *Chemical Senses*, 1981, *6*, 295–305.

Silverstein, R. M. Pheromones: Background and potential for use in insect pest control. *Science*, 1981, *213*, 1326–1332.

Simmons, F. B., Epley, J. M., Lummis, R. C., Guttman, N., Frishkopf, L. S., Harmon, L. D., & Zwicker, E. Auditory nerve: Electrical stimulation in man. *Science*, 1965, *148*, 104–106.

Simmons, J. A. The sonar receiver of the bat. *Annals of the New York Academy of Sciences*, 1971, *188*, 161–174.

Simmons, J. A., Fenton, M. B., & O'Farrell, J. Echolocation and pursuit of prey by bats. *Science*, 1979, *203*, 16–21.

Simon, H. A. An information-processing explanation of some perceptual phenomena. *British Journal of Psychology*, 1967, *58*, 1–12.

Singer, G., & Day, R. H. Spatial adaptation and aftereffect with optically transformed vision: Effects of active and passive responding and the relationship between test and exposure responses. *Journal of Experimental Psychology*, 1966, *71*, 725–731.

Sivian, L. J., & White, S. D. On minimum audible sound fields. *Journal of the Acoustical Society of America*, 1933, *4*, 288–321.

Sloboda, J. A. *The musical mind: The cognitive psychology of music*. (Oxford Psychology Series No. 5). Oxford: Oxford University Press, 1985.

Smith, D. V. Brainstem processing of gustatory information. In D. W. Pfaff (Ed.), *Taste, olfaction, and the central nervous system*. New York: Rockefeller University Press, 1984.

Smith, D. V., & McBurney, D. H. Gustatory cross-adaptation: Does a single mechanism code the salty taste? *Journal of Experimental Psychology*, 1969, *80*, 101–105.

Smith, J. D. Conflicting aesthetic ideals in a musical culture. *Music Perception*, 1987, *4*, 373–391.

Smith, K. U., Thompson, G. F., & Koster, H. Sweat in schizophrenic patients: Identification of the odorous substance. *Science*, 1969, *166*, 398–399.

Snyder, F. W., & Pronko, N. H. *Vision with spatial inversion*. Wichita, Kan.: University of Wichita Press, 1952.

Snyder, S. H. The brain's own opiates. *Chemical & Engineering News*, 1977, *55*, 26–35.

Sokol, S., Moskowitz, A., & Hansen, V. Electrophysiological evidence for the oblique effect in human infants. *Investigative Ophthalmology & Visual Science*, 1987, *28*, 731–735.

Solomons, L., & Stein, G. Normal motor automatism. *Psychological Review*, 1896, *3*, 492–512.

Sparks, D. W. The identification of the direction of electrocutaneous stimulation along lineal multistimulator arrays. *Perception & Psychophysics*, 1979, *25*, 80–87.

Spear, P. D., Penrod, S. D., & Baker, T. B. *Psychology: Perspectives on behavior*. New York: John Wiley, 1988.

Spelke, E., Hirst, W., & Neisser, U. Skills of divided attention. *Cognition*, 1976, *4*, 215–230.

Sperling, G. The information available in brief visual presentations. *Psychological Monographs*, 1960, *74* (No. 11).

Sperling, G., & Melchner, M. J. Information processing in visual system. In V. D. Glezer (Ed.), *Information processing in visual system*. Proceedings of the Fourth Symposium on Sensory System Physiology. Leningrad, U.S.S.R.: Academy of Sciences, Pavlov Institute of Physiology, 1976.

Sperry, R. W. Mechanisms of neural maturation. In S. S. Stevens (Ed.), *Handbook of experimental psychology*. New York: John Wiley, 1951.

Spigel, I. M. *Visually perceived movement*. New York: Harper & Row, 1965.

Spreen, O., Spellacy, F. J., & Reid, J. R. The effect of interstimulus interval and intensity on ear asymmetry for nonverbal stimuli in dichotic listening. *Neuropsychologia*, 1970, *8*, 245–250.

Springer, S. P., & Deutsch, G. *Left brain, right brain* (rev. ed.). New York: W. H. Freeman, 1985.

Steinberg, A. Changes in time perception induced by an anaesthetic drug. *British Journal of Psychology*, 1955, *46*, 273–279.

Steinman, R. M. Eye movement. *Vision Research*, 1986, *26*, 1389–1400.

Steinman, R. M., Haddad, G. M., Skavenski, A. A., & Wyman, D. Miniature eye movements. *Science*, 1973, *181*, 810–819.

Sternbach, R. A., & Tursky, B. Ethnic differences among housewives in psychophysical and skin potential responses to electric shock. *Psychophysiology*, 1965, *1*, 24–246.

Stevens, S. S. The relation of pitch to intensity. *Journal of the Acoustical Society of America*, 1935, *6*, 150–154.

Stevens, S. S. (Ed.) *Handbook of experimental psychology*. New York: John Wiley, 1951.

Stevens, S. S. The direct estimate of sensory magnitudes-loudness. *American Journal of Psychology*, 1956, *69*, 1–25.

Stevens, S. S. To honor Fechner and repeal his law. *Science*, 1961, *133*, 80–86. (*a*)

Stevens, S. S. Psychophysics of sensory function. In W. A. Rosenblith (Ed.), *Sensory Communication*. Cambridge, Mass.: M.I.T. Press, 1961. (*b*)

Stevens, S. S. Neural events and the psychophysical law. *Science*, 1970, *170*, 1043–1050.

Stevens, S. S. *Psychophysics, and social scaling*. Morristown, N.J.: General Learning Press, 1972.

Stevens, S. S. *Psychophysics: Introduction to its perceptual, neural and social prospects*. New York: John Wiley, 1975.

Stevens, S. S., & Davis, H. *Hearing*. New York: John Wiley, 1938.

Stevens, S. S., & Volkman, J. The relation of pitch to frequency. *American Journal of Psychology*, 1940, *53*, 329–356.

Stevens, S. S., & Warshofsky, F. *Sound and hearing*. New York: Life Science Library, 1965.

Strange, W., & Jenkins, J. J. Role of linquistic experience in the perception of speech. In R. D. Walk & H. L. Pick, Jr. (Eds.), *Perception and experience*. New York: Plenum, 1978.

Stratton, G. M. Some preliminary experiments on vision without inversion of the retinal image. *Psychological Review*, 1896, *3*, 611–617.

Stratton, G. M. Upright vision and the retinal image. *Psychological Review*, 1897, *4*, 182–187. (*a*)

Stratton, G. M. Vision without inversion of the retinal image. *Psychological Review*, 1897, *4*, 341–360. (*b*)

Stroop, J. R. Studies of interference in serial verbal reactions. *Journal of Experimental Psychology*, 1935, *18*, 643–662.

Stroop, J. R. Factors affecting speed in serial verbal reactions. *Psychological Monographs: General & Applied*, 1938, *50*, 38–48.

Stroud, J. M. The fine structure of psychological time. In H. Quastler (Ed.), *Information theory and psychology*, Glencoe, Ill.: Free Press, 1956.

Stroymeyer, C. F., Kronauer, R. E., Madsen, J. C., & Cohen, M. A. Spatial adaptation of short-wavelength pathways in humans. *Science*, 1980, *207*, 555–557.

Stryker, M. P., Sherk, H., Leventhal, H. G., & Hirsch, H. B. Physiological consequences for the cat's visual cortex of effectively restricting early visual experience with oriented contours. *Journal of Neurophysiology*, 1978, *41*, 896–909.

Supra, M., Cotzin, M. E., & Dallenbach, K. M. "Facial vision": The perception of obstacles by the blind. *American Journal of Psychology*, 1944, *57*, 133–183.

Suto, Y. The effect of space on time estimation (*S* effect) in tactual space. II: The role of vision in the *S* effect upon the skin. *Japanese Journal of Psychology*, 1955, *26*, 94–99.

Swets, J. A. The relative operating characteristic in psychology. *Science*, 1973, *182*, 990–1000.

Tallarico, R. B., & Farrell, W. M. Studies of visual depth perception: An effect of early experience on chicks on a visual cliff. *Journal of Comparative and Physiological Psychology*, 1964, *57*, 94–96.

Taub, E. Prism compensation as a learning phenomenon: A phylogenetic perspective. In S. J. Freedman (Ed.), *The neuropsychology of spatially oriented behavior*. Homewood, Ill.: Dorsey, 1968.

Taylor, D. W., & Boring, E. G. The moon illusion as a function of binocular regard. *American Journal of Psychology*, 1942, *55*, 189–201.

Taylor, H. R., West, S. K., Rosenthal, F. S., Muñoz, B., Newland, H. S., Abbey, H., & Emmett, E. A. Effect of ultraviolet radiation on cataract formation. *New England Journal of Medicine*, 1988, *319*, 1429–1440.

Teghtsoonian, R., & Teghtsoonian, M. Two varieties of perceived length. *Perception & Psychophysics*, 1970, *8*, 389–392.

Terhardt, E. The two-component theory of musical consonance. In E. F. Evans & J. P. Wilson (Eds.), *Psychophysics and physiology of hearing*. New York: Academic Press, 1977.

Terman, G. W., Shavit, Y., Lewis, J. W., Cannon, J. T., & Liebeskind, J. C. Intrinsic mechanisms of pain inhibition: Activation by stress. *Science*, 1984, *226*, 1270–1277.

Teuber, M. L. Sources of ambiguity in the parts of Maurits C. Escher. *Scientific American*, 1974, *231*, 90–104.

Theberge, J. B. Wolf music. *Natural History*, 1971, *80*, 37–42.

Thomas, E. A. C., & Brown, I. Time perception and the filled duration illusion. *Perception & Psychophysics*, 1974, *16*, 449–458.

Thomas, E. A. C., & Weaver, W. B. Cognitive processing and time perception. *Perception & Psychophysics*, 1975, *17*, 363–367.

Thomas, J. P. Model of the function of receptive fields in human vision. *Psychological Review*, 1970, *77*, 121–134.

Thor, D. H. Diurnal variability in time estimation. *Perceptual and Motor Skills*, 1962, *15*, 451–454.

Thouless, R. H. Phenomenal regression to the real object. *British Journal of Psychology*, 1931, *21*, 338–359.

Tolansky, S. *Optical illusions*. Oxford: Pergamon, 1964.

Toppino, T. S., & Long, G. Selective adaptation with reversible figures: Don't change that channel. *Perception & Psychophysics*, 1987, *42*, 37–48.

Treisman, A. Properties, parts, and objects. In K. R. Boff, L. Kaufman, & J. P. Thomas (Eds.), *Handbook of perception and human performance*. Volume II: *Cognitive processes and performance*. New York: John Wiley, 1986.

Treisman, A. M. Contextual cues in selective listening. *Quarterly Journal of Experimental Psychology*, 1960, *112*, 242–248.

Treisman, A. M., & Riley, J. G. A. Is selective attention selective perception or selective response? A further test. *Journal of Experimental Psychology*, 1969, *79*, 27–34.

Treisman, M. Temporal discrimination and the indifference interval: Implications for a model of the "internal clock." *Psychological Monographs*, 1963, *77* (Whole No. 576).

Treisman, M. Motion sickness: An evolutionary hypothesis. *Science*, 1977, *197*, 493–495.

Tumosa, N., Tieman, S. B., & Hirsch, H. B. Unequal alternating monocular deprivation causes asymmetric visual fields in cats. *Science*, 1980, *208*, 421–423.

Ullman, S. Against direct perception. *The Behavioral and Brain Sciences*, 1980, *3*, 373–415.

Underwood, G. Attention and perception of duration during encoding and retrieval. *Perception*, 1975, *4*, 291–296.

Valenta, J. G., & Rigby, M. K. Discrimination of the odor of stressed rats. *Science*, 1968, *161*, 599–601.

Van Toller, C., Kirk-Smith, M. D., Wood, N., Lombard, J. & Dodd, G. H. Skin conductance and subjective assessments associated with the odour of 5-^{a}androstan-3-one. *Journal of Biological Psychology*, 1983, *16*, 85–107.

Veraart, C., & Wanet-Defalque, M.-C. Representation of locomotor space by the blind. *Perception & Psychophysics*, 1987, *42*, 132–139.

Verrillo, R. T. Cutaneous sensations. In B. Scharf (Ed.), *Experimental sensory psychology*. Glenview, Ill: Scott, Foresman, 1975.

Vickers, Z. M. Sensory, acoustical, and force-deformation measurements of potato chip crispness. *Journal of Food Science*, 1987, *52*, 138–140.

Vierling, J. S., & Rock, J. Variations of olfactory sensitivity to Exaltolide during the menstrual cycle. *Journal of Applied Physiology*, 1967, *22*, 311–315.

Vokey, J. R., & Read, J. D. Subliminal messages: Between the devil and the media. *American Psychologist*, 1985, *40*, 1231–1239.

Wade, N. J. A note on the discovery of subjective colours. *Vision Research*, 1977, *17*, 671–672.

Wade, N. Op art and visual perception. *Perception*, 1978, *7*, 47–50.

Wagner, H. G., MacNichol, E. F., & Wolbarsht, M. L. The response properties of single ganglion cells in the goldfish retina. *Journal of General Physiology*, 1960, *43*, 45–62.

Waite, H., & Massaro, D. W. A test of Gregory's constancy-scaling explanation of the Müller-Lyer illusion. *Nature*, 1970, *227*, 733–734.

Walcott, C., Gould, J. L., & Kirschvink, J. L. Pigeons have magnets. *Science*, 1979, *205*, 1027–1028.

Wald, G. Eye and camera. *Scientific American*, 1950, *183*, 32–41.

Wald, G. Life and light. *Scientific American*, 1959, *201*, 92–108.

Walk, R. D. The study of visual depth and distance perception in animals. In D. S. Lehrman, R. A. Hinde, & E. Shaw (Eds.), *Advances in the study of behavior*. New York: Academic Press, 1965.

Walk, R. D. Depth perception and experience. In R. D. Walk & H. L. Pick (Eds.), *Perception and experience*. New York: Plenum, 1978.

Walk, R. D., & Gibson, E. J. A comparative and analytical study of visual depth perception. *Psychological Monographs*, 1961, *75*, 15 (Whole No. 519).

Walk, R. D., Trychin, S., & Karmel, B. Z. Depth perception in the dark-reared rat as a function of time in the dark. *Psychonomic Science*, 1965, *3*, 9–10.

Walker, J. The amateur scientist (visual illusions that can be achieved by putting a dark filter over one eye). *Scientific American*, 1978, *238*, 142–153.

Walker-Andrews, A. S. Intermodal perception of expressive behaviors: Relation of eye and voice. *Developmental Psychology*, 1986, *22*, 373–377.

Walker-Andrews, A. S. Infant's perception of the affordances of expressive behaviors. In C. Rovee-Collier & L. P. Lipsett (Eds.), *Advances in infancy research*, Volume 6. Norwood, N.J.: Ablex, 1989.

Walker-Andrews, A. S., & Lennon, E. M. Auditory-visual perception of changing distance by human infants. *Child Development*, 1985, *56*, 544–548.

Wall, P. D., & Sweet, W. H. Temporary abolition of pain in man. *Science*, 1967, *155*, 108–109.

Wallace, P. Individual discrimination of humans by odor. *Physiology and Behavior*, 1977, *19*, 577–579.

Wallach, H. Brightness constancy and the nature of achromatic colors. *Journal of Experimental Psychology*, 1948, *38*, 310–324.

Wallach, H. The perception of neutral colors. *Scientific American*, 1963, *208*, 107–116.

Wallach, H., Newman, E. B., & Rosenzweig, M. R. The precedence effect in sound localization. *American Journal of Psychology*, 1949, *62*, 315–336.

Wallach, H., & O'Connell, D. N. The kinetic depth effect. *Journal of Experimental Psychology*, 1953, *45*, 205–217.

Wallach, H., O'Leary, A., & McMahon, M. L. Three stimuli for visual motion perception compared. *Perception & Psychophysics*, 1982, *32*, 1–6.

Wallach, H., & Slaughter, V. The role of memory in perceiving subjective contours. *Perception & Psychophysics*, 1988, *43*, 101–106.

Wallman, J., Gottlieb, M. D., Rajaram, V., & Fugate-Wentzek, L. A. Local retinal regions control local eye growth and myopia. *Science*, 1987, *237*, 73–77.

Walls, G. L. *The vertebrate eye and its adaptive radiation*. New York: Hafner, 1963.

Warden, C. J., & Baar, J. The Müller–Lyer illusion in the ring dove, *Turtur risorius*. *Journal of Comparative Psychology*, 1929, *9*, 275–292.

Warkentin, J., & Carmichael, L. A study of the development of the air-righting reflex in cats and rabbits. *Journal of Genetic Psychology*, 1939, *55*, 67–80.

Warren, R. E., & Lasher, M. D. Interference in a typeface variant of the Stroop test. *Perception & Psychophysics*, 1974, *15*, 128–130.

Warren, R. M. Perceptual restoration of missing speech sounds. *Science*, 1970, *167*, 392–393.

Warren, R. M., & Bashford, J. A. Müller–Lyer illusions: Their origin in processes facilitating object recognition. *Perception*, 1977, *6*, 615–626.

Warren, R. M., & Warren, R. P. A critique of S. S.

Stevens' "New Psychophysics." *Perceptual and Motor Skills*, 1963, *16*, 797–810.

Warren, R. M., & Warren, R. P. Auditory illusions and confusions. *Scientific American*, 1970, *223*, 30–36.

Warren, W. H. Perceiving affordances: Visual guidance of stair climbing. *Journal of Experimental Psychology: Human Perception and Performance*, 1984, *10*, 683–703.

Warrington, E. K. Neuropsychological studies of object recognition. *Philosophical Transactions of the Royal Society of London*, 1982, *B298*, 15–33.

Wasacz, J. Natural and synthetic narcotic drugs. *American Scientist*, 1981, *69*, 318–324.

Watt, D. G. Responses of cats to sudden falls: An otolith-originating reflex assisting landing. *Journal of Neurophysiology*, 1976, *39*, 257–265.

Wead, G., & Lellis, G. *Film: Form and function*. Boston: Houghton Mifflin, 1981.

Wegel, R. L., & Lane, C. E. The auditory masking of one pure tone by another and its probable relations to the dynamics of the inner ear. *Physiological Review*, 1924, *23*, 266–285.

Wei, E. T., & Seid, D. A. AG-3-5: A chemical producing sensations of cold. *Journal of Pharmacy and Pharmacology*, 1983, *35*, 110–111.

Weil, A. T., Zinberg, N. E., & Nelson, J. M. Clinical and psychological effects of marijuana in man. *Science*, 1968, *162*, 1234–1242.

Weinstein, S. Intensive and extensive aspects of tactile sensitivity as a function of body part, sex, and laterality. Chapter 10 in D. R. Kenshalo (Ed.), *The skin senses*. Springfield, Ill.: Charles C. Thomas, 1968.

Weiskrantz, L., Elliott, J., & Darlington, D. Preliminary observations on tickling oneself. *Nature*, 1971, *230*, 598–599.

Weiss, D. J. The impossible dream of Fechner and Stevens. *Perception*, 1981, *10*, 431–434.

Weisstein, N., & Harris, C. S. Masking and the unmasking of distributed representations in the visual system. In C. S. Harris (Ed.), *Visual coding and adaptability*. Hillsdale, N.J.: Lawrence Erlbaum, 1980.

Welch, R. B. *Perceptual modification: Adapting to altered sensory environments*. New York: Academic Press, 1978.

Welch, R. B. Adaptation of space perception. In K. R. Boff, L. Kaufman, & J. P. Thomas (Eds.), *Handbook of perception and human performance*. Volume I: *Sensory processes and perception*. New York: John Wiley & Sons, 1986

Welker, W. I., & Campos, G. B. Physiological significance of sulci in somatic sensory cerebral cortex in mammals of the family *procyonidae*. *Journal of Comparative Neurology*, 1963, *120*, 19–36.

Wendt, G. R. Vestibular functions. Chapter 31 in S. S. Stevens (Ed.), *Handbook of experimental psychology*. New York: John Wiley, 1951.

Wenger, M. A., Jones, F. N., & Jones, M. H. *Physiological psychology*. New York: Holt, Rinehart and Winston, 1956.

Wenzel, B. M. Chemoreception. In E. C. Carterette & M. P. Friedman (Eds.), *Handbook of perception*. Volume III: *Biology of perceptual systems*. New York: Academic Press, 1973.

Wertheimer, Max. Principles of perceptual organization. In D. C. Beardslee & M. Wertheimer (Eds.), *Readings in perception*. New York: D. Van Nostrand, 1958. An abridged translation by Michael Wertheimer of Untersuchungen zur Lehre von der Gestalt, II. *Psychologische Forschung*, 1923, *4*, 301–350.

Wertheimer, Michael. Hebb and Senden on the role of learning in perception. *American Journal of Psychology*, 1951, *64*, 133–137.

Wertheimer, Michael. Constant errors in the measurement of kinesthetic figural aftereffects. *American Journal of Psychology*, 1954, *67*, 543–546.

Wertheimer, Michael. Psychomotor coordination of auditory and visual space at birth. *Science*, 1961, *134*, 1692.

Westheimer, G. The eye as an optical instrument. In K. R. Boff, L. Kaufman, & J. P. Thomas (Eds.),

Handbook of perception and human performance. Volume I: *Sensory processes and perception*. New York: John Wiley, 1986.

Wever, E. G. *Theory of hearing*. New York: John Wiley, 1949.

Wever, E. G., & Bray, C. W. Present possibilities for auditory theory. *Psychological Review*, 1930, *37*, 365–380.

Whalen, D. H., & Liberman, A. M. Speech perception takes precedence over nonspeech perception. *Science*, 1987, *237*, 169–171.

White, B. L. Child development research: An edifice without a foundation. *Merrill-Palmer Quarterly of Behavior and Development*, 1969, *15*, 47–78.

White, B. L., Castle, P., & Held, R. Observations on the development of visually-directed reaching. *Child Development*, 1964, *35*, 349–364.

White, B. W., Saunders, F. A., Scadden, L., Bach-y-Rita, P., & Collins, C. C. Seeing with the skin. *Perception & Psychophysics*, 1970, *7*, 23–27.

White, C. T. Temporal numerosity and the psychological unit of duration. *Psychological Monographs*, 1963, *77*, 12 (Whole No. 575).

White, C. W., & Montgomery, D. A. Memory colors in afterimages: A bicentennial demonstration. *Perception & Psychophysics*, 1976, *19*, 371–374.

Wickens, C., Kramer, A., Vanasse, L., & Donchin, E. Performance of concurrent tasks: A psychophysiological analysis of the reciprocity of information-processing resources. *Science*, 1983, *221*, 1080–1082.

Wiesel, R. N., & Raviola, E. The mystery of myopia. *The Sciences*, 1986, *26*, 46–52.

Wightman, F. L., & Green D. M. The perception of pitch. *American Scientist*, 1974, *62*, 208–215.

Willer, J. C., Dehen, H., & Cambier, J. Stress-induced analgesia in humans: Endogenous opioids and naloxone-reversible depression of pain reflexes. *Science*, 1981, *212*, 689–691.

Wilsoncroft, W. E., & Griffiths, R. S. Time perception and body temperature: A review. *Psychological Documents*, 1985, *15*, 1–12.

Witelson, S. F. The brain connection: The corpus callosum is larger in left-handers. *Science*, 1985, *229*, 665–668.

Witkin, H. A. The perception of the upright. *Scientific American*, 1959, *200*, 50–70.

Wolf, G. Innate mechanisms for regulation of sodium intake. In C. Pfaffmann (Ed.), *Olfaction and taste*. New York: Rockefeller University Press, 1969.

Wolff, W. Induzierte helligkeitsveranderung. *Psychologische Forschung*, 1935, *20*, 159–194.

Wong, E., & Weisstein, N. A new perceptual context-superiority effect: Line segments are more visible against a figure than against a ground. *Science*, 1982, *218*, 587–589.

Wong, R., & Jones, W. Saline intake in hamsters. *Behavioral Biology*, 1978, *24*, 474–480.

Wood, H. Psychophysics of active kinesthesis. *Journal of Experimental Psychology*, 1969, *79*, 480–485.

Woodhouse, J. M., & Taylor, S. Further studies of the café wall and hollow squares illusions. *Perception*, 1987, *16*, 467–471.

Woodrow, H. Time perception. In S. S. Stevens (Ed.) *Handbook of experimental psychology*, New York: John Wiley, 1951.

Woodworth, R. S. *Experimental psychology*. New York: Henry Holt, 1938.

Woodworth, R. S. *Psychology (4th ed.)*. New York: Henry Holt, 1940.

Woodworth, R. S., & Schlosberg, H. *Experimental psychology*. New York: Henry Holt, 1954.

Worshel, P., & Dallenbach, K. M. "Facial vision": Perception of obstacles by the deaf-blind. *American Journal of Psychology*, 1947, *60*, 502–553.

Worshel, P., & Dallenbach, K. M. The vestibular sensitivity of deaf-blind subjects. *American Journal of Psychology*, 1948, *61*, 94–98.

Wright, W. D. A re-determination of trichromatic coefficients of the spectral colours. *Transactions of the Optical Society of London*, 1928-1929, *30*, 141–164.

Wright, W. D. The rays are not coloured. *Nature*, 1963, *198*, 1239–1244.

Wright, W. D. *The rays are not coloured*. New York: American Elsevier, 1967.

Wyatt, H. J. Singly and doubly contingent aftereffects involving color, orientation and spatial frequency. *Vision Research*, 1974, *14*, 1185–1193.

Wysocki, C. J., & Meredith, M. The vomeronasal system. In T. E. Finger & W. L. Silver (Eds.), *Neurobiology of taste and smell*. New York: John Wiley, 1987.

Yaksh, T. L. Opiate receptors for behavioral analgesia resemble those related to depression of spinal nociceptive neurons. *Science*, 1978, *199*, 1231–1233.

Yarbus, A. L. *Eye movement and vision*. New York: Plenum Press, 1967.

Yeager, J. Absolute time estimates as a function of complexity and interruptions of melodies. *Psychonomic Science*, 1969, *15*, 177–178.

Yellott, J. I. Binocular depth inversion. *Scientific American*, 1981, *245*, 148–159.

Yin, T. C. T., Kuwada, S., & Sujaku, Y. Interaural time sensitivity of high-frequency neurons in the inferior colliculus. *Journal of the Acoustical Society of America*, 1984, *76*, 1401–1410.

Yonas, A., Kuskowski, M., & Sternfels, S. The roles of frame of reference in the development of responsiveness to shading information. *Child Development*, 1979, *50*, 495–500.

Young, F. A. Development of optical characteristics for seeing. In F. A. Young & D. B. Lindsley (Eds.), *Early experience and visual information processing in perceptual and reading disorders*. Washington, D.C.: National Academy of Sciences, 1970.

Young, R. A. Some observations on temporal coding of color vision: Psychophysical results. *Vision Research*, 1977, *17*, 957–965.

Zahorik, D. M., & Maier, S. F. Appetitive conditioning with recovery from thiamine deficiency as the unconditional stimulus. *Psychonomic Science*, 1969, *17*, 309–310.

Zakay, D., & Fallach, E. Immediate and remote time estimation—A comparison. *Acta Psychologica*, 1984, *57*, 69–81.

Zakay, D., Nitzan, D., & Glicksohn, J. The influence of task difficulty and external tempo on subjective time estimation. *Perception & Psychophysics*, 1983, *34*, 451–456.

Zanuttini, L. A new explanation for the Poggendorff illusion. *Perception & Psychophysics*, 1976, *20*, 29–32.

Zelazo, P. R., Zelazo, N. A., & Kolb, S. "Walking" in the newborn. *Science*, 1972, *176*, 314–315.

Zelman, S. Correlation of smoking history with hearing loss. *Journal of the American Medical Association*, 1973, *223*, 920.

Zihl, J., von Cramon, D., & Mai, N. Selective disturbance of movement vision after bilateral brain damage. *Brain*, 1983, *106*, 313–340.

Zimbardo, P. G., Anderson, S. M., & Kabat, L. G. Induced hearing deficit generates experimental paranoia. *Science*, 1981, *212*, 1529–1531.

Zingale, C. M., & Kowler, E. Planning sequences of saccades. *Vision Research*, 1987, *27*, 1327–1341.

Zola, D. Redundancy and word perception during reading. *Perception & Psychophysics*, 1984, *36*, 280.

Zöllner, F. On a new way of pseudoscopy and its relation to the movement phenomena described by Plateau and Oppel. *Annalen der Physik und Chemie*, 1860, 110 (whole series 86), 500–522.

Zotterman, Y. Studies in the neural mechanism of taste. In W. A. Rosenblith (Ed.), *Sensory communication*. Cambridge, Mass.: M.I.T. Press, 1961.

Zurek, P. M., & Sachs, R. M. Combination tones at frequencies greater than the primary tones. *Science*, 1979, *205*, 600–602.

Zusne, L. *Visual perception of form*. New York: Academic Press, 1970.

Zwicker, E., & Scharf, B. Model of loudness summation. *Psychological Review*, 1965, *72*, 3–26.

Zwislocki, J. J. Sound analysis in the ear: A history of discoveries. *American Scientist*, 1981, *69*, 184–192.

SUBJECT INDEX